American Government

Eighth Edition

ALAN R. GITELSON
LOYOLA UNIVERSITY OF CHICAGO

ROBERT L. DUDLEY
GEORGE MASON UNIVERSITY

MELVIN J. DUBNICK
UNIVERSITY OF NEW HAMPSHIRE

Houghton Mifflin Company
Boston   New York

To Doug for all that he brings to our family, and to Bob, Mel, and Claudio, my kindred spirits in the academic world. A.R.G.

To Lawrence, Neva, and the memory of Phebe. They say you cannot choose your family, but even if you could, I could not have done better. R.L.D.

To my new friends in Belfast and Durham, who refreshed my enthusiasm for the academic life, and to Randi, who tolerates missteps on life's dance floor. M.L.D.

Executive Publisher: Patricia A. Coryell
Publisher: Suzanne Jeans
Senior Sponsoring Editor: Traci Mueller
Development Editor: Christina Lembo
Editorial Assistant: Tiffany Hill
Associate Project Editor: Kristen Truncellito
Art and Design Coordinator: Jill Haber
Senior Photo Editor: Jennifer Meyer Dare
Composition Buyer: Chuck Dutton
Senior Manufacturing Buyer: James Lonergan
Executive Marketing Manager: Nicola Poser
Marketing Associate: Karen E. Mulvey

Cover image: © Harold Burch, Harold Burch Design, NYC

Illustration and text credits appear on pages C-1–C-2, which constitute an extension of the copyright page.

Printed in the U.S.A.

Library of Congress Control Number: 2006925774

Instructor's examination copy
  ISBN-10: 0-618-73028-1
  ISBN-13: 978-0-618-73028-5
For orders, use student text ISBNs
  ISBN-10: 0-618-64367-2
  ISBN-13: 978-0-618-64367-7

123456789-DOC-10 09 08 07 06

Brief Contents

Contents

3 Federalism and Intergovernmental Relations 66

4 The Heritage of Rights and Liberties 95

7 Campaigns and Elections 184

10 Congress 266

11 The Presidency 296

14 Domestic Policy and Policymaking 402

15 Foreign and Defense Policy 444

Preface

As we wrote this eighth edition of *American Government*, it became clear that two events, more than any others in recent years, have had a significant impact on our nation and the way many of us view government and the political process. The first of these events, the September 11, 2001, terrorist attacks on New York City, the Pentagon in Washington, D.C., and an airplane flight over Pennsylvania, continues to affect our daily lives even now that several years have passed. We still feel the effects of 9/11 in the form of enhanced national security preparations and in our concern over future terrorist attacks that could take place in the United States. In addition, issues ranging from airport security to the impact of new laws affecting our civil liberties and the threat that other nations might pose to our health and safety continue to be discussed widely by many Americans.

The second recent event with enormous national impact, Hurricane Katrina, struck the Gulf Coast states (and, most severely, the greater New Orleans area) in August 2005, and now looms in the minds of many Americans as a failure by government to respond to a disaster affecting the lives of hundreds of thousands of citizens. Damages from Hurricane Katrina, one of the deadliest and most destructive hurricanes in U.S. history, eventually topped $80 billion with a loss of more than 1,800 lives, and left many American citizens, including public officials, with a bad taste in their mouths regarding the ineffective response of the federal, state, and local governments to the tragedy.

These events and concerns and many others have, in a number of ways, had an impact on the writing of the eighth edition. Our discussion of almost every topic has been shaped in both small and significant ways by the events of 9/11 and Hurricane Katrina. This will be apparent to the reader as he or she reads the eighth edition.

As always, in preparing every edition of *American Government*, including this new eighth edition, we have committed ourselves to two major goals: (1) to write a concise yet comprehensive textbook that (2) helps students think critically about the U.S. political system. To meet the first objective, we have organized the book into fifteen chapters that follow the coverage of the typical introductory American Government course. As important, we have kept each chapter to a reasonable length and have provided up-to-date illustrations and other pedagogical tools.

To achieve our second objective, we employ a distinctive approach that has worked well for each of us in the classroom—an exploration of the contrast between the myths that many Americans believe about their government and the realities of how our political system operates. A myth, as defined in Chapter 1, is a shorthand way of thinking about the role and activities of government and politics. Myths often take the form of stories, stereotypes, proverbial sayings, or pervasive and popular attitudes that help us to comprehend "the way things are"—or at least the way we believe them to be.

While often helping us make sense of American government and politics, many myths also reflect and promote some of the misunderstandings that ordinary citizens have about the political system and how it works. We believe that through understanding some of the myths of American politics and how they evolved, students will be able to think more critically and systematically about our complex political system. Therefore, we begin each chapter with a vignette and a short statement of one or two preconceptions commonly found in political discussions.

In this eighth edition, as in the previous seven, we have paid attention to both the changing realities and the changing myths of American government. Thus, in preparing the eighth edition, we have thoroughly reviewed and updated all chapters in terms of both research and current events. As a result, in this edition we have included not only discussion of the response of our government to the Hurricane Katrina disaster, but also thorough coverage of the 2006 elections, the reshaping of the Supreme Court as the result of two new appointments by President George W. Bush, and recent civil liberties decisions. We have also given additional emphasis to the media, public opinion, intergovernmental relations, and international policy, including the war in Iraq. We have also scrutinized every chapter to refine, clarify, and tighten the text.

The changing myths have been more difficult to pinpoint, but we have tracked them through attention to trends in America's ever-changing popular culture. If the popular culture reflected a trend during the 1990s, it was that of a strong and growing public distrust of government. The popular belief in government inefficiency and political conspiracies seemed pervasive for a time. The events of 9/11 and the aftermath of Hurricane Katrina refocused the attention of many Americans on just how vulnerable the nation is to attack and natural disasters, and suddenly our fears—imagined and real—have taken center stage in our political lives. They also focused our attention on the role of government at all levels and the responsibility of the federal government to protect us against both man-made disasters (9/11) and nature-made disasters (Katrina). Now, more than ever, we need to develop a critical appreciation of the myths that sustain and guide our civic life—and the realities that lie beneath them.

Highlights of the Eighth Edition

As part of the unique approach of this textbook, the discussion of myths and their role in our understanding of American government and politics are the focus of Chapter 1. We continue to examine, in the introductory chapter, the greater sense of vulnerability that now pervades our lives. Chapter 2 is focused on the "myth of the living Constitution" and the debate over the role of the Constitution in American government, especially in light of current controversies over executive power and judicial interpretation. Chapter 3 discusses the "myth of state sovereignty," and includes coverage of the Supreme Court's recent ruling on eminent domain. In all three chapters, the impact and challenges of the post-9/11 and Hurricane Katrina world are considered, especially the growing concern of the role of government in our everyday lives. In Chapter 4, "The Heritage of Rights and Liberties," we cover recent Supreme Court decisions on civil liberties, including decisions on affirmative action, police searches, and the death penalty, as well as other important cases.

Chapter 5, "Public Opinion and Political Participation," includes new polls on the changing attitudes of Americans to a variety of issues regarding the role of government. Chapter 6, "Political Parties," discusses the changing roles that the Republican and Democratic parties play in the electoral process, including in the 2006 congressional elections. Chapter 7, "Campaigns and Elections," includes timely coverage of the 2004 and 2006 elections and significant updates on campaign finance practices. Chapter 8, "Interest Groups," updates our coverage of interest groups, political action committees, and the newly emerging 527 committees. Chapter 9, "Media and Politics," has been revised and updated to include the political strategy behind "going public" and a discussion of the role of blogs in politics.

In Chapter 10, "Congress," we discuss several changes in both the House and the Senate as a result of partisan division, as well as the impact of the 2006 election. In Chapter 11, "The Presidency," we provide updated discussions of presidential power in the Bush administration and the president's attempt to reassert what he considers to be the lost power of the presidency, including his frequent use of signing statements. Chapter 12, "Bureaucracy," discusses the influence of Hurricane Katrina on both the organization and operations of the federal government, as well as the growing prevalence of government contracting, indecency standards enforced by the FCC, and the Bush White House's approach to performance assessment. In Chapter 13, "Courts, Judges, and the Law," we provide coverage of the two new appointments to the Supreme Court and the threat by Republican leaders of the Senate to use the "nuclear" option to stop filibusters of judicial nominees.

Chapter 14 includes discussions of education policy and "No Child Left Behind," plus coverage of the government's approaches to economic and social welfare issues, earmarking, and President Bush's recent efforts to reform Social Security. Chapter 15 retains the emphasis on the myth of vulnerability, giving special attention to the changes that have occurred in both foreign and defense policy since the end of the Cold War, and now includes a second myth, the myth of the American project, which explores America's vision of world order in these turbulent times. The chapter features expanded coverage of the war on terrorism, including the war in Iraq and domestic wiretapping, and an examination of power theory. Both Chapters 14 and 15 pay special attention to globalization and its impact on domestic and foreign policy.

Features in the Eighth Edition

The eighth edition includes two new boxed features, "Asked & Answered" and "Global Politics," which appear in many of the chapters. "Asked & Answered" uses an accessible question-and-answer format to take a closer look at political issues of interest to students, while "Global Politics" examines political institutions, orientations, and organizations from an international perspective. The "Politics & Popular Culture" (formerly titled "Myths in Popular Culture") boxes that worked so well in previous editions continue to be a staple of most of the chapters in *American Government*, examining how popular culture reflects and influences government and politics, as are the "Net Work" website sections at the end of each chapter and the marginal "Critical Thinking" questions, several of which appear in each chapter.

The eighth edition also features several new chapter-opening vignettes, which examine the following topics: the impact of Hurricane Katrina on the nation's sense of vulnerability (Chapter 1); creating the Iraqi Constitution (Chapter 2); K Street lobbyists and pork barrel spending (Chapter 8); Dan Rather, George W. Bush, and media bias (Chapter 9); the successes and failures of FEMA (Chapter 12); and the impact of illegal immigration on foreign and defense policy (Chapter 15).

In addition, we have retained the popular and helpful pedagogical aids of previous editions. For example, each chapter still opens with a preview outline, includes focus questions that correspond with the major sections of each chapter, and ends with a point-by-point summary (which now reviews each of the chapter's focus questions) and a conclusion that provides a retrospective glance at the highlighted myths in light of the whole chapter discussion.

Several useful appendixes are included at the end of the text, including the Declaration of Independence, the U.S. Constitution, and Federalist Papers Nos. 10 and 51. A list of presidents appears on the inside back cover.

Instructor Ancillary Package

The eighth edition of *American Government* offers an extensive package of supplementary materials for instructors:

- Each chapter of the **Instructor's Resource Manual**, written and revised by the authors, provides a chapter overview, teaching objectives, a lecture outline paralleling the text, critical thinking activities, questions for discussion, classroom activities, a list of multimedia resources, and a list of suggested readings. With the exception of Chapter 1, each chapter also includes a bonus lecture that explores a specific chapter theme or concept in greater detail. This manual is available on the text's ONLINE TEACHING CENTER at http://college.hmco.com/pic/gitelson8e. Please contact your Houghton Mifflin sales representative to obtain the user name and password for the site.

- The **Test Bank**, written by the authors and revised for this edition by P. S. Ruckman of Rock Valley College, is available electronically and as Word files on the **HM Testing CD-ROM**. The CD-ROM, available from your Houghton Mifflin sales representative, includes both multiple-choice test items and short essay questions.

- Text-specific **PowerPoint Slides**, which include chapter outlines and figures from the eighth edition, are available for download at the ONLINE TEACH-ING CENTER (http://college.hmco.com/pic/gitelson8e).

- **In-Class Clicker Quizzes**, PowerPoint slides for use with Personal (or Class-room) Response Systems, are available for download at the ONLINE TEACHING CENTER (http://college.hmco.com/pic/gitelson8e). Half of the questions in the slides are available to students as a pre-class quiz on the ONLINE STUDY CENTER (http://college.hmco.com/pic/gitelson8e), and you can use these questions in combination with questions that students have not seen to motivate students in studying before class.

- New to the eighth edition, the American Government course management cartridge (available in **Blackboard, WebCT, or Eduspace**, Houghton Mif-flin's publisher-hosted platform) contains online content correlated to American Government course topics. Resources include graded homework, primary source documents with quizzes, Associated Press Interactive ani-mations, simulations, writing assignments and tutorials, discussion assign-ments, a threaded message board, and video clips of election ads. Contact your sales representative to learn more about these platforms or to set up your own online course.

- *American Government* can be packaged for free with a number of reading and reference materials, including the Rand McNally Atlas of U.S. Politics and the 2006 Election Supplement. A new packaging option, Politics of Natural Disasters, written by William L. Waugh of Georgia State University, analyzes the natural disasters that occur most often in the United States, the government policy created to deal with them, and the future of emer-gency management. For those who cover Constitution Day, the Annotated Constitution option provides an annotated Constitution, history of the Constitution, and list of Supreme Court justices. The Primary Sources op-tion features more than thirty documents that have shaped American gov-ernment, from Marbury v. Madison to the Civil Rights Act and beyond. Please contact your Houghton Mifflin sales representative for more infor-mation on any of these packaging options.

Student Ancillary Package

The text's ONLINE STUDY CENTER website, accessible at http://college.hmco.com/pic/gitelson8e, contains a wealth of study aids and resources for students, including assets previously available via the Student Study Guide that are now online free of charge. These study resources, carefully revised and updated by Alec Thomson of Schoolcraft College, include chapter summaries, learning objectives, flashcards and key terms quizzes, pre-class quizzes to prepare students for class discussion, ACE practice tests, and sample essay questions. A number of these items can be printed off the site for students wishing to review material "on the go."

Acknowledgments

Many people contribute to the success of a textbook, and such is the case with the eighth edition of *American Government*. We gratefully acknowledge the many helpful comments of the following reviewers: Robert E. Botsch (University of South Carolina–Aiken), Christos Bourdouvalis (Augusta State University), Irasema Coronado (University of Texas–El Paso), Rick Donohoe (Napa Valley College), Casey Hubble (Midland College), Godwin Okafor (Georgia Southern University), and Alexander Thomson (Schoolcraft College).

We would also like to thank Alec Thomson for writing a first-rate revision of the Study Guide assets, and Kevin Fullam for his very able research assistance.

In a venture of this magnitude, authors realize that the success of a textbook is closely tied to the editors associated with the project. We have been fortunate enough to work with a dedicated, creative, and sensitive editorial staff at Houghton Mifflin. For the eighth edition, we are indebted to Traci Mueller, Christina Lembo, Jean Woy, Tiffany Hill, Kristen Truncellito, and Nancy Benjamin. Every textbook author also recognizes, with appreciation, the importance of individuals like Nicola Poser and Karen Mulvey in the Marketing Department and the many publisher's representatives across the country who represent our book to university and college faculty. We want to give an unqualified thanks, with love, to Idy, Laura, and Rachel Gitelson and Douglas Nilson; Judy, Pat, and Michael Dudley; and Randi, Heather, and P. D. Dubnick, for all of their support and patience during the writing of this book.

Finally, we would like to emphasize the equal role played by all three authors in the writing of this textbook. There was no junior partner in this project. Alan Gitelson's name appears first on the cover because he administered the project. A flip of the coin determined the order of the names for Bob Dudley and Mel Dubnick.

A. R. G.
R. L. D.
M. J. D.

About the Authors

Alan Gitelson is Professor of Political Science, Assistant Provost, and former Chair of the Department of Political Science at Loyola University of Chicago. He received his Ph.D. from the Maxwell School, Syracuse University. In addition to numerous scholarly articles, his books include *American Political Parties: Stability and Change* (with M. Margaret Conway and Frank Feigert), *Public Policy and Economic Institutions* (with Melvin Dubnick), and *American Elections: The Rules Matter* (with Robert L. Dudley). Dr. Gitelson is a former member of the American Political Science Association Standing Committee on Education and Professional Development. He is a frequent guest commentator on radio and television, speaking on topics including campaigns and elections, campaign financing, political parties, the media, and interest groups.

In 1996, Dr. Gitelson was designated a Master Teacher by the College of Arts and Sciences at Loyola University of Chicago. In 1998, he received the "Outstanding Faculty Member of the Year" award from Loyola University of Chicago. He was awarded the Edwin T. and Vivijeanne F. Sujack Award for Teaching Excellence in 1999. When not teaching, reading, or writing, Alan enjoys music,

Left to right: Melvin Dubnick, Robert Dudley, Alan Gitelson

travel, sailing with his wife, Idy, and visiting with his daughters, Laura and Rachel, and son-in-law, Doug.

Robert L. Dudley is Chair of the Department of Public and International Affairs at George Mason University. A native of Illinois, he received his Ph.D. from Northern Illinois University and has been on the faculty at Loyola University in Chicago and Colorado State University. A specialist in judicial politics, Dr. Dudley has contributed articles to several professional journals, including the *American Journal of Political Science, American Politics Quarterly, Journal of Politics,* and *Political Research Quarterly.*

Dr. Dudley has also served as a consultant to the U.S. Department of Transportation, the National Institutes of Health, the Center for Scientific Review, and the National Gambling Impact Study Commission.

When not working, he prefers to spend his time with his wife, Judy, and, when they are around, their sons, Patrick and Michael. He and Judy enjoy biking and hiking in the Virginia countryside.

Melvin Dubnick is Professor of Political Science and directs the Master of Public Administration program at the University of New Hampshire. He received his Ph.D. from the University of Colorado–Boulder in 1974, and he has held positions at Emporia State University, Loyola University of Chicago, the University of Kansas, Baruch College/City University of New York, and Rutgers University–Newark. He is also affiliated with the Institute of Governance at Queen's University, Belfast (Northern Ireland) where he was a Fulbright Distinguished Fellow and Senior Fellow from 2003–2005. He has taught courses in Japan, Korea, Panama, and Colombia for Oklahoma University and the School of International and Public Affairs at Columbia University. In addition to *American Government,* Dr. Dubnick has co-authored textbooks on public policy analysis and American public administration. He has served as managing editor of *Public Administration Review,* as well as coeditor-in-chief of *Policy Studies Journal.*

Dr. Dubnick has been actively engaged in efforts to improve and advance political science education. He was co-chair of the American Political Science Association's Task Force on Civic Education in the Next Century and managed APSA-CIVED, a listserv focused on issues related to civic education. He is currently experimenting with innovative grading methods, distance learning technologies, and the integration of the Internet in the political science classroom.

In his spare time, he is an active partner in Pencilneck Records, which promotes the music of his son's band, The Dubnicks (www.thedubnicks.com).

1

Myth and Reality in American Politics

MYTH & REALITY

What is the role of myths in American government?

FOCUS QUESTIONS

* How do myths help us to better understand American government? What are the functions of myths?

* How do we define government and politics? What has been the role of government in American history?

* How does the U.S. political system deal with the issues of who should govern, where authority should be vested, and how much government should do?

T he impact of the events of September 11, 2001, on the American public and its governments—federal, state, and local—cannot be overstated. The hijacking of four passenger aircraft and the devastation that followed heightened emotions beyond feelings of loss and sorrow for the thousands of individuals who lost loved ones that morning in New York, at the Pentagon, and in a field in rural Pennsylvania. This was a national tragedy, and it generated a wide range of emotional reactions from millions of Americans. Some described their feelings in terms of shock and disbelief, while others expressed sadness mixed with a vengeful anger. As time passed, many of those emotions gave way to the demands of everyday life, although they were rekindled intermittently on national holidays and at public events during which the tragedy was remembered and memorialized. But one emotion seemed to remain with Americans almost every minute of every day: a sense of the nation's vulnerability to attack from its enemies.[1]

Almost four years later, in late August 2005, another disaster of a different sort sent shock waves throughout the United States. Hurricane Katrina had formed over the Bahamas on August 23, but by the time it dissipated nine days later it had substantially altered the lives of thousands along the U.S. Gulf Coast and put the very future of one of America's major cities—New Orleans—in jeopardy. Of course, Americans in almost every part of the nation are subject to natural disasters, whether they are floods along the many rivers that wind

September 11, 2001

The shock and pain are evident in the faces of these witnesses to the September 11, 2001, World Trade Center terrorist attacks. Most Americans felt vulnerable, angry, and terrified about an uncertain future that might be filled with other incidents of violence and loss of life.

Hurricane Katrina, 2005

In the aftermath of Hurricane Katrina in New Orleans, Louisiana, a man awaits rescue from the top of a vehicle in his flooded neighborhood. Flooding engulfed much of New Orleans with tens of thousands of citizens evacuated to other parts of the state and nation. Many citizens wondered if the government could have done more for the victims of the hurricane.

Critical Thinking

How vulnerable do you think we are as individuals and as a nation in light of the events of September 11, 2001, and Hurricane Katrina in 2005?

through the country, tornadoes in the Midwest and Southeast, mudslides in rain-soaked California or West Virginia, or snowstorms in New England or the Upper Midwest. In that sense, the aftermath of a hurricane would not be exceptional. But this particular storm, Katrina, was different, not merely for the vast path it cut through Louisiana and Mississippi in a season already unusual for its many storms, but also because the response of government agencies to this storm was surprisingly inept at all levels. Watching the TV reports from New Orleans as the Ninth Ward flooded and thousands were stranded in the Louisiana Superdome and the city's Morial Convention Center, in every section of the nation Americans began to wonder if any of us might find ourselves abandoned by our own government in the face of natural disasters. Once again, the feeling of vulnerability was palpable nationwide.

After both of these disasters, the news media reported on the impact that this sense of vulnerability was having on individuals and families. In the wake of September 11, many of those living in or near tall buildings or near nuclear power plants or other facilities that might be subject to terrorist attacks dealt with the uncertainty and insecurity of feeling vulnerable by preparing for the worst-case scenario; many considered moving from their homes because of such concerns. Still others made sure that their wills and other personal affairs were in order.[2] Businesses, hospitals, public utilities, and computer network managers were taking steps to deal with the new world of vulnerability that few had even thought about before September 11. Vulnerability was clearly on the minds of top government officials, who immediately began to develop strategies and means for enhancing America's "homeland security." The White House created a special

Office of Homeland Security less than a month after the attacks, and nine months later it proposed the creation of a Department of Homeland Security (see Chapter 12, on bureaucracy). Similar actions were taken at the state and local levels of government as the feeling of vulnerability became even stronger over time.

After Katrina, issues were raised about the competence and preparations of the Federal Emergency Management Agency (FEMA), which is supposed to act as the overall coordinator of government response to such emergencies (see Chapter 12), the timeliness of government response, and the degree to which emergency management personnel were prepared to deal with especially vulnerable populations such as the aged, the infirm, and the poor. Looking at the devastation of the Gulf Coast and the response of various levels of government, Americans began to question whether public officials are able to meet the demands of such critical events.

Critical Thinking

How have the events of September 11 and Hurricane Katrina shaped your view of the role of government in our lives?

Americans are no strangers to the feeling of vulnerability. The first colonial settlers were often preoccupied with the threats posed by what they perceived to be the "savagery" of Native Americans, and English settlers were particularly anxious about their vulnerability to attack by French and Spanish colonists.[3] Their precarious situation on the edge of a never-ending frontier made the earliest settlers feel increasingly vulnerable,[4] and many historians believe that this frontier culture played a major role in shaping the American character.[5] A strong case can be made that the American Revolution had its roots in the colonists' feeling that they were too vulnerable to the whims of King George III and the British Parliament. Historian Richard Hofstadter has argued that there is a distinct "paranoid style" in American politics, and that the country's sense of vulnerability to conspiracies has played a substantial role in American political history.[6] More recently, feelings of vulnerability fostered by memories of economic hardship during the Great Depression have had a major effect on the way Americans think about government's role in the economy, and the potential for nuclear war with the Soviet Union during the Cold War shaped U.S. foreign policy for nearly a half century after World War II.

In short, Americans' sense of vulnerability has played an important role in shaping the way they view the political world. Whether the perceived threats to Americans' safety and security were real or imagined, the impact of those feelings has been significant. Vulnerability is one of many feelings and beliefs through which Americans see and understand the complex world of political and social life.

There is little doubt that after September 11 and Hurricane Katrina, Americans have every reason to feel vulnerable. And those feelings most assuredly can lead (and have led) to individual and collective actions designed to reduce our anxiety. But just how vulnerable are we, and how much should we alter our behavior to deal with our insecurities in light of the events of September 11 and the aftermath of Katrina? Should we completely close our borders to anyone from any country that is suspected of harboring potential terrorists? Should we pass laws and regulations that prohibit Americans from living on floodplains and other areas subject to catastrophic flooding? Should we detain all young

Islamic males and clerics residing in the United States and interrogate them about their beliefs and with whom they associate? Should we develop evacuation plans that force all residents to leave areas threatened by a potential hurricane, or suspend the basic rights of anyone who is arrested as a suspected terrorist? Does the level of our vulnerability warrant such steps?

To answer those questions about our responses to the events of September 11 and Katrina, we must understand and appreciate what is at stake when we engage in the practice of governing ourselves. Terrorism and natural disasters are just two of the many challenges we face as a nation and in our communities, and over time we have established institutions and procedures for developing and implementing responses. These institutions and procedures (both public and private) constitute what political scientists call **governance**, and it is through the structures and rules of governance that we exercise our collective power as a nation.[7] Like our sense of vulnerability, our views of governance are built on feelings and beliefs about those institutions and procedures—feelings that they are effective and fair, and beliefs that they are worthy of our support and commitment. These too must be put to the test of seeing whether they meet our expectations.

Governance Public and private institutions and procedures through which a society deals with its collective problems.

It is possible for each of us to rely on our feelings and beliefs alone in determining how we react and respond to the challenges of political life. We can go with our gut feelings and take the position that government officials should do whatever it takes to protect us from the many things that threaten our physical and economic security. But doing so without giving some thought to whether government is capable of dealing with those problems, or what potential dangers are posed by giving a government free rein in handling those threats, is very risky. What we as citizens need are the capacity, skills, and knowledge to reflect on the collective problems we face and our collective abilities to deal with them.

Our objective in this textbook is twofold. First, we intend to provide you with some basic information about the U.S. political system that will enable you to make sense of the issues we face as a nation and the governance mechanisms we have developed to deal with them.

Second, we will offer a relatively simple framework, based on the ideas of myths and realities, that will help you reflect on a wide range of questions about American government and politics. It is easy enough to say that we should increase our capacity and knowledge about governance, but we must also acknowledge that we come to this task with both explicit and implicit—often deep-seated—notions about American government and politics. These notions, which we will approach as widely held myths, need to be factored into our understanding of the complex subject of how we govern ourselves. For example, is that sense of vulnerability that has been part of the U.S. political scene for at least two centuries based on myth or reality? If that sense is based on myth (the "myth of vulnerability"), then what are the implications of how we view and approach our role as citizens in the U.S. system of governance? In short, our overall goal is to empower you to become a citizen who does more than merely react to the challenges of political life. For us, the ideal citizen is one who takes action based on informed reasoning.

Myths and American Government

FOCUS QUESTION   HOW DO MYTHS HELP US TO BETTER UNDERSTAND AMERICAN GOVERNMENT? WHAT ARE THE FUNCTIONS OF MYTHS?

How do we understand our world? That is a question that philosophers and other scholars have asked since ancient times. The ancient Greeks made a distinction between two types of human understanding: *mythos* and *logos*.[8] *Mythos* was the kind of understanding obtained through listening to stories and other forms of narrative that seem to reflect the world. If you wanted to understand the reason for a devastating drought or a major defeat on the battlefield, you would rely on a story about how the drought or defeat resulted from the actions of angry or vengeful gods. This was the way you might understand the world if knowledge relied on *mythos* alone.

In contrast, the Greeks regarded *logos* as understanding gained through reasoned analysis and rational argument. According to Karl Popper, one of the twentieth century's greatest philosophers, the major contribution of the ancient Greeks was to promote the value of *logos* as a means of enhancing the knowledge derived from *mythos*. For Popper, the roots of modern science are found in the efforts made by the Greek philosophers to question and scrutinize the mythical stories that they constantly encountered. Scientific study, in other words, emerged not by uncovering new truths, but by challenging the truths expressed in the mythical understanding of the world.[9] By applying logic and argumentation based on evidence, classical Greek thinkers began to test these mythical understandings against reality, and in the process they began either to modify the myths or to develop alternatives that seemed to offer a better fit with the world they observed.

In this and the chapters that follow, we will treat myths in the same way. For our purposes, **myths** are those stories, proverbial sayings, pervasive attitudes, and other narratives that we use to help us think about the world around us. Myths play an important role in the way Americans think about government and politics, and in each chapter we will address one or two major myths associated with a given topic. For example, in Chapter 2, on constitutional foundations, we will consider the myth of the living Constitution, and in Chapter 12, on bureaucracy, we focus on two widely held beliefs: the myth of bureaucratic incompetence and the myth of the unresponsive bureaucracy. In these and the other chapters, we are using the term *myth* the way the ancient Greeks applied the concept of *mythos*: as one way of comprehending the world.

In taking this approach to myth, we are expressly avoiding some of the other ways in which the term is commonly used.[10] Many students of ancient cultures use the term *myth* to refer to sacred stories about ancient gods and other supernatural beings and events such as the creation of the world.[11] Others apply the term *myth* as synonymous with false belief, as, for example, when someone attempts to argue that the world is flat. Still others use the term to refer to symbolic allegories, or stories designed to mask realities that we cannot deal with directly. For our purposes, myths are as much about daily life as they are about

Myths Those stories, proverbial sayings, pervasive attitudes, and other narratives that we use to help us think about the world around us.

The Cherry Tree Myth

In this painting, titled *Parson Weems' Fable*, Grant Wood makes fun of the famous patriotic myth that George Washington could tell no lies. Wood painted young Washington with an adult face to emphasize the myth-making of the adoring parson, who invented the story.

the life of gods, and, following in the footsteps of the ancient Greeks, we will approach our myths as important stories that are subject to reasoning and testing against reality (*logos*) rather than as outright lies or falsehoods.

Applying this approach, we will find that many myths are indeed outright lies, such as the long-held myth that women and African Americans are intellectually or morally incapable of exercising the political judgment necessary to vote. We will also find that many myths are oversimplifications rather than outrageous falsehoods. The myth that any boy or girl can grow up to be president of the United States is not precisely false, but it does offer a naive picture of the possibilities for most of America's children. Most often, however, we will find that popular myths have at least a kernel of truth in them that makes them attractive to people as a way of helping them make sense of a very complex and uncertain world.

In this book, we are interested in several types of modern myths. In some cases we will focus on myths that take the form of *stories* (fictional as well as historical) about national heroes. The story of George Washington saying to his father that he could not tell a lie and admitting that he had indeed chopped down the cherry tree is mythical in the classic sense,[12] as are the rags-to-riches stories of Horatio Alger, with their message that hard work leads to success. But today there are equally powerful stories told about our nation's leaders—about the lives and accomplishments of political families like the Roosevelts and the Kennedys, about individual presidents like Richard Nixon and Bill Clinton, and about institutions like the U.S. Senate and the Pentagon.

Such stories are powerful forces in shaping the public's views about government, as are stories about the actions of bureaucratic agencies and historical figures. For some people, a story about a government agency spending $10,000 for one toilet seat, for example, might confirm the widely held belief that government bureaucracy is inefficient and wasteful;[13] on a different level, the story of John Hancock signing the Declaration of Independence supports the popular images of the American Revolution, what it stood for, and the risks and sacrifices made by those who chose to break with England in 1776. In each case, the myth helps to shape our understanding of and attitudes toward our system of government.

But not all myths involve stories in the traditional sense. Instead, some of today's most important myths take the form of *stereotypes* (such as "All Democrats are big-spending liberals" and "The Republican party represents big business"), *proverbial sayings* (such as "You can't fight city hall"), and *pervasive attitudes* (such as "All politicians are crooks") that have an impact on the way we think about government and the American political system.

In our post–September 11, post–Hurricane Katrina world, the *myth of vulnerability* is an important one. As noted previously, it is a myth with deep historical roots in Americans' colonial and frontier experiences and the nation's memories of economic calamities (such as the Great Depression) and international tensions (for example, the Cold War). It represents a belief that, despite our hard work and good intentions as individuals and as a nation, we are always subject to threats and challenges from both natural and human sources. Like other myths that affect our political lives, it reflects a realistic understanding of our country's history. Just as important, this myth has had a special impact on how Americans perceive the international arena and how U.S. foreign and defense policies have been made over the two centuries of the country's existence (see Chapter 15, on foreign and defense policy). And like the other myths we will consider in this book, the myth of vulnerability needs to be tested against today's realities so that we can better understand our political system.

Critical Thinking

Do you agree with the myth of vulnerability?

Functions of Myths

Why should we engage in testing myths against reality? The importance of myths in our political lives cannot be underestimated. We rely on myths for a variety of reasons.[14] First, like the ancients, we sometimes use myths to *help us simplify the complex world in which we live.* Myths help us "to live in a world in which the causes" of our problems "are simple and neat and the remedies are apparent."[15] During the recession of the early 1990s, many Americans blamed the Japanese for the economic woes of the United States. Stories about unfair pricing strategies used by Japanese firms as well as widely publicized remarks by Japanese officials regarding poor American work habits helped to fuel a myth about an "economic war" with Japan.[16] The popularity of both Japan-bashing and "buy American" campaigns reflected a tendency on the part of too many

Americans to seek scapegoats. In the meantime, these same Americans ignored the more complex national and international economic transitions that were responsible for the problems.[17]

Second, myths often *help us define our place in the world and provide us with a common social and political identity.*[18] Many of us perceive the United States in mythical terms: "as a community of free and equal self-governing citizens pursuing their individual ends in a spirit of tolerance for their religious and other forms of diversity."[19] This and other myths held by Americans are supported by stories — of the first Thanksgiving, of Washington cutting down the cherry tree, of the deeds of young Abe Lincoln — that reinforce our national "belief in innocence, in honesty, in freedom, in the use of the wilderness, in adaptability, in the right of the individual to act freely without restraint. . . . Like all myths, their function is to say this is the way it was with Americans, this is the way it is, and this is the way it ought to be."[20] Without such myths, the political system might crumble, as that of the former Soviet Union and other parts of Eastern Europe did in the late 1980s and early 1990s.[21]

Third, we frequently depend on myths to *help guide and rationalize our behavior.* The myth of good citizenship tells us that we ought to vote because that is the only effective way to influence the behavior of government officials.[22] As already noted, myths also have an impact on how we conduct our foreign policy.[23] In addition to the myth of vulnerability, many critics of American foreign policy feel that our national behavior in international affairs is shaped by a national myth of progress — a vision of "America as the wave of the future."[24] "Americans see history as a straight line," comments essayist Frances FitzGerald, "and themselves standing at the cutting edge of it as representatives for all mankind."[25]

Fourth, myths often *help us make sense of the behavior of others.* In foreign affairs, and especially during wartime or periods of great tension, we often rely on images and stories of our enemies and allies that help guide our behavior. The negative image of our German and Japanese enemies found in movies and posters during both world wars helped to keep the war efforts going, as did the stereotypical pictures of the Soviets during the Cold War. President Ronald Reagan, for example, labeled the Soviet Union an "evil empire" during his terms in office, and after September 11 President George W. Bush spoke of the "evildoers" and the "axis of evil" when referring to those countries that he claimed supported terrorism. In contrast, positive images and stories of our allies took on mythical tones during the same periods.[26]

A fifth and final function of myths is that many of the most significant ones *reflect views of the past or the future.* Many of the myths surrounding our most important governmental institutions — the U.S. Constitution, the presidency, Congress, and the Supreme Court — reflect the judgments of history on those bodies and the people who served in them. For example, although Abraham Lincoln is regarded today as one of the nation's great presidents, he was highly criticized by other politicians and the media while he occupied the White House. His status as a great president — much of it reflected in stories and myths — is well established in our eyes, despite the low regard in which he was held by many of his contemporaries.

POLITICS & POPULAR CULTURE

Mirrors and Shapers of Images

Popular culture—the music and movies and stories that we hear and see in the mass media every day of our lives—plays an important role in American social life. The words and images generated and marketed by the "pop culture" industry reflect the realities of American life, and frequently help shape those realities. In some cases, images and sounds from pop culture are relevant to the way we see and think about government and politics.

For example, over the past fifty years, Hollywood has produced many films that use conspiracies as a central plot line. While initially the conspiracies took the form of alien invasions from outer space (e.g., the 1956 classic *Invasion of the Body Snatchers*), the focus soon turned to government conspiracies. The plot for *Seven Days in May* (1964) centered on a conspiracy by military leaders to take over the U.S. government, while the 1967 spy spoof *The President's Analyst* featured a similar plot undertaken by the telephone company. The conspiracy thriller took a more serious turn in the 1970s with the release of films like *All the President's Men* (1976), an examination of the real-life conspiracy behind Nixon's cover-up of the Watergate break-in.

In the 1990s Oliver Stone carried on the legacy of conspiracy films with his controversial *JFK* (1991) and the 1995 release *Nixon*, while formulaic action films like *Mission Impossible* (1996) and thrillers like *A Few Good Men* (1992) featured plot lines based on government conspiracies and cover-ups. More recently, the film *Syriana* (2005) explored the covert ties between the government and oil companies doing business in the Middle East.

Popular music has also mirrored the politics of the day—and at times actually taken the lead in trying to influence and shape political action. Starting in the early 1960s, folk singers gained a

significant audience for their songs that protested injustice and war. Woody Guthrie's tunes from the 1930s (e.g., "This Land Is Your Land") and songs by Pete Seeger (e.g., "Where Have All the Flowers Gone?") made it to the top of the Billboard charts in 1962, and Peter, Paul, and Mary's version of "Blowin' in the Wind" sold millions of copies. The music itself became a political force as these and other popular "hits" were heard again and again at civil rights and antiwar rallies over the next decade.

In the aftermath of September 11, popular music emerged as one of the major vehicles through which Americans were able to deal with the emotional scars left by the attacks. Some songs, like Toby Keith's "Courtesy of the Red, White, and Blue (The Angry American)," gave expression to the renewed sense of patriotism that came to the surface immediately after the tragic events. Other releases, like Neil Young's "Let's Roll," celebrated the heroism of some of those who lost their lives in the attacks, and Bruce Springsteen's 2002 song "Empty Sky" alluded to the personal feelings of loss and anger felt by many.

More recently, a number of political songs have been released in response to the controversial wars in Afghanistan and Iraq, and several of them—including Pearl Jam's "Worldwide Suicide" and Green Day's "Holiday"—have received considerable radio play.

As we will demonstrate in feature boxes like this one throughout this book, popular culture has always played a major role in reflecting and shaping public opinion, political activity, and even the development of governmental institutions in our nation. It is important that we recognize the role that popular culture plays in our political lives, for today the music and movies and words that we hear or read are major sources of the images and myths we have about government and politics.

We also adopt many future-oriented myths that often shape our expectations of what government officials can or will do. For example, among military professionals, the failure of America's military venture in Vietnam during the 1960s and early 1970s was often blamed on the civilian authorities' lack of commitment to the military's efforts. What emerged from that experience can be called the "Vietnam War myth," a widely held belief among our nation's top military leaders that American military forces will not be successful in the future unless enough forces are sent to do the job and military commanders are allowed to act without interference from the politicians back in Washington. This myth had a significant influence on President George H. W. Bush's decisions concerning the use of military force against Iraq in 1991: He committed more than 500,000 U.S. troops and gave military commanders considerable freedom to determine how to deal with the forces of Saddam Hussein that had invaded Kuwait.[27] Given the relative success of that mission, some would argue that the myth was proved correct. However, for our purposes, what is important is that the Vietnam War myth had a significant impact on the attitudes and decisions of key policymakers as well as those of the American public.

And, of course, many of our myths focus on the present to help us deal with what is taking place in Washington, Topeka, or Sacramento, for example, right at this moment. Many people believe in the myth of special-interest government, which, correctly or incorrectly, helps many of us understand why Congress or a state legislature passes a law providing a new tax break for some major or local industry, even though this will ultimately increase the general taxpayer's burden. According to this myth, such laws are passed because special interests are able to hire high-priced lobbyists in Washington or a state capital that are effective in influencing legislators, whereas the general public has no one representing its interests (see Chapter 8, on interest groups).

From these examples, it should also be obvious that myths focus on a wide range of subjects—from the nature of American society and our national Constitution to everyday political and governmental activities and our perception of world affairs. Individually, many of us have adopted myths about whether American society is racist or sexist, about the efficiency and effectiveness of local firefighters and law enforcement personnel, and about how important our participation in the political system is or can be. The wide range of topics covered by myths will become increasingly evident as you read through this textbook.

As a student of American government, it is essential that you understand the role that myths play in our governmental and political systems. By taking myths into account, you will be able to make sense of some features of the American system that might have puzzled you in the past. The fact that some myths are either outright lies or some distortion of the truth should put you on notice that we all must focus critical attention on what we hear and believe about government and politics. The fact that other myths help us to get things done or resolve complicated problems should also be factored into your approach. In any case, you must also have a clear picture of the institutional and political reality that underpins our national government. Before we learn to run, however, we must learn to walk. Therefore, let us turn to some fundamental questions.

The Nature of Government and Politics

HOW DO WE DEFINE GOVERNMENT AND POLITICS?
WHAT HAS BEEN THE ROLE OF GOVERNMENT IN AMERICAN HISTORY?

Government Those institutions and officials whose purpose it is to write and enact laws and to execute and enforce public policy.

What is government, and how does it carry out its varied responsibilities? In brief, **government** comprises those institutions and officials whose purpose it is to write and enact laws and to execute and enforce public policy. The goals of government in the United States are to maintain order through the rule of law, provide goods and services that benefit the lives of all citizens, and promote equality among members of society. The activities directed at achieving these goals are conducted by legislators, presidents, or other chief executive officers (such as governors and mayors), judges, bureaucrats, and other elected and appointed officials who work in the institutions that make up the executive, legislative, and judicial branches of federal, state, and local governmental systems. Ultimately, these officials carry out their responsibilities through their authority to enact and enforce laws that are crucial to the functioning of government.

Politics Those activities aimed at influencing or controlling government for the purpose of formulating or guiding public policy.

What is politics? In its most general sense, **politics** refers to activities aimed at influencing or controlling government for the purpose of formulating or guiding public policy. We will be discussing the politics of running for or being appointed to office; choosing policy alternatives; and bargaining, negotiating, and compromising to get policies enacted and executed. The politics of federal student loan programs, for example, involves presidents and legislators—influenced by students, parents, bankers, and college administrators—negotiating the issue of who receives loan benefits and who pays the bills.

Has government always been important in the lives of most Americans? Despite some popular feelings to the contrary, the answer is probably yes. Historian Arthur M. Schlesinger Jr. has pointed to a "cherished national myth" ascribing the economic development of the nation "to the operations of unfettered individual enterprise."[28] In fact, history shows that American government has always affected economic and social life. As early as colonial times, citizens expected government to perform such traditional functions as ensuring law and order and resisting foreign aggression. But even then government often did more than that.

Role of Government in American History

From the time the first European settlers established communities in America, colonial governments, under the general authority of the British government, played a major role in developing and regulating local economies. Colonial (and later state) governments helped finance new enterprises, build ports, and construct turnpikes and canals; they sometimes even controlled wages and prices in local markets.

Shortly after the United States gained its independence, a series of laws written by Congress during the 1780s, collectively called the Northwest Ordinance, established rules for selling land and organizing local governments in the large territory stretching from the Ohio River to the Mississippi and north to the Great Lakes (see Chapter 14, on domestic policy and policymaking). Land was even reserved to support public schools. One of the earliest examples of the national government's role as "an active promoter of the economy" was its 1803 purchase of the Louisiana Territory. That vast region was vital to the prosperity of farmers working the lands along the entire length of the Mississippi. Historians have also found other examples of early government efforts to plan, manage, and promote the new country's resources.[29]

The role of government continued to expand during the 1800s and early 1900s. Attempts to solve the economic and social problems that arose during the Great Depression of the 1930s, a depression that left millions of Americans jobless and homeless, led to an explosion of new programs. Soon an army of bureaucrats was managing the economy, promoting stable economic growth by helping to find jobs for the unemployed, and enforcing price controls designed to hold down the prices of goods and services.

As the United States became a more complex society, Americans demanded that the national government pay more attention to problems that had once been solved by families and communities — problems of the poor, the handicapped, and the elderly, among others. Ever since the New Deal, all Americans have been touched directly or indirectly by programs in such areas as early childhood nutrition, health care, unemployment benefits, food stamps, or social security.[30]

Moreover, the government has not limited its interest to the economy and social welfare programs. As destruction threatened the vast American forests

Critical Thinking

How important was government in the development of the American economy?

Signs for an Anxious Time

As part of the war on terror, the federal government established a five-level alert system through which national, state, and local governments can warn citizens of potential threats. Here, Homeland Security Chief Tom Ridge describes the system to the media in March 2002.

and pollution tainted air and water, Americans turned to government for environmental management, ranging from conservation programs to regulations affecting many polluting industries. In support of such goals as preventing environmental damage and ensuring a steady supply of energy, government has lowered speed limits on highways, pushed for the development of nuclear energy, and implemented a variety of other policies.[31]

In recent years, a growing number of Americans have concluded that perhaps we have been depending too much on government to solve our problems. The results of the 1994 congressional elections made it clear to many officials that the public wanted a change, if not a redirection, in government priorities. By 1996 the White House too was admitting that it was time for a change. "The era of big government is over," declared President Bill Clinton in his State of the Union address.

The events of September 11, however, may alter that conclusion. Talk about relying less on government and reducing government spending has been replaced by calls for more government programs aimed at strengthening "homeland security." Instead of focusing on shrinking the size of government, attention has turned toward reorganizing and enhancing local, state, and federal agencies that help guard the nation against the new vulnerabilities brought on by the threat of terrorism. Thus, government has played, and continues to play, an important role in the development of the modern American social and economic system.

Critical Thinking

Do you think, as President Clinton declared in 1996, that "the era of big government is over," or do you think that recent events affecting our national security will expand the role of government?

Fundamental Issues of Government and Politics

FOCUS QUESTION   HOW DOES THE U.S. POLITICAL SYSTEM DEAL WITH THE ISSUES OF WHO SHOULD GOVERN, WHERE AUTHORITY SHOULD BE VESTED, AND HOW MUCH GOVERNMENT SHOULD DO?

The fact that government has always played an important role in the lives of Americans does not mean that its activities have been uncontroversial. Several basic questions about government and politics have constantly emerged — questions about who should govern, where governmental authority should be located, and how much government should be doing.

Who Should Govern?

The fact that government plays a critical and pervasive role in everyone's life should automatically raise the question of who should control the use of this important social institution. In other words, who should govern? The answer to that question has taken two forms, one focused on governmental authority and the other on the wielding of governmental power.

Authority. For many students of government, the question "Who should govern?" refers to who should be officially authorized to control governmental institutions. In other words, who should exercise formal authority in government? **Authority** can be defined as the capacity to make and enforce public policies possessed by individuals who occupy formal governmental roles.[32]

As we have already noted, government comprises the institutions and officials who make and enforce public policies. The roles that those officials play in conducting the business of government are derived from a variety of sources. Some are defined in constitutions and other legal documents (see the discussion of constitutional foundations in Chapter 2), whereas others may be the result of long-standing traditions. In either case, when we are concerned with who should occupy those official roles, we are dealing with the issue of authority.

Among the first to try to answer the question of who should govern through the exercise of authority was the ancient Greek philosopher Aristotle. He classified governments into three types: government by one, government by the few, and government by the many. For each type, he believed, there is a good, or "right," form and a bad, or "wrong," form. A right form of government serves the common interests of the people, whereas a wrong form of government serves the personal interests of the ruler or rulers.

Aristotle called a government by the many that serves the common interests of the people a polity and a government by the many that serves their personal interests a democracy. Like many other political thinkers through the ages, Aristotle feared democracy, for he assumed that self-interest would rule if government were turned over to the "rabble in the streets." In fact, his other term for democracy was "mobocracy," or rule by the mob. Americans admire democracy as much as Aristotle feared it, and most believe that it is the most appropriate type of government for the United States. Americans' idea of **democracy** can best be summed up as a belief in *government where authority is based on the consent and will of the majority*. If asked the question "Who should govern?" a vast majority of Americans would state that the people should govern.

Nevertheless, the American concept of democracy does not mean a commitment to direct rule by the majority. As we will see, the framers of the Constitution did not believe that governmental authority should be directly in the hands of the people. They envisioned the United States as a **republic**, or **representative democracy**, in which the people *govern indirectly by electing certain individuals* — the president, members of Congress, governors, mayors, state legislators, and others — *to make decisions on their behalf.* Thus, the people do not vote on or directly make specific policy decisions; they do so indirectly, through those they elect to represent their interests.

Despite this general acceptance of representative democracy, controversies still arise over the need for greater or lesser citizen participation in government decision making. Some argue that much more should be done to increase public input into policy decisions through procedures called **initiative and referendum**. Both involve placing questions of public policy on the ballot for voters to

Authority The capacity to make and enforce public policies possessed by individuals who occupy formal governmental roles.

Democracy To Americans, a government where authority is based on the consent and will of the majority.

Republic A system in which people govern indirectly by electing certain individuals to make decisions on their behalf.

Representative democracy See Republic.

Initiative and referendum Methods of democratic decision making that place questions of public policy on the ballot for voters to consider directly. Initiatives are placed on the ballot by petition, whereas a referendum is generated by the legislature.

consider directly; however, the initiative process allows members of the general public to place such questions on the ballot, whereas it is the state or local legislative body that places a referendum on the ballot for public consideration.

Others believe that too much public input through direct participation can be damaging. David Broder, one of the most respected political journalists in America, has written in depth about the dangers that initiatives pose to our constitutional system of checks and balances (see Chapter 2) and how they have been subject to manipulation by special interests. Others have noted that state and local requirements that proposed tax increases and school budgets, which were put before the voters in a referendum, have created budgetary crises in recent years because local voters have constantly turned down requests to increase revenues.

Power. The question "Who should govern?" can also be approached from the perspective of politics. As defined previously, politics involves activities intended to influence or control what goes on in government. Those who have the ability to wield such influence are said to possess power. From this perspective, the question about who governs should really be, "Who should wield power over the operations of government?"

What does it take to possess power?[33] Reduced to its basics, **power** is a relationship between two parties, A and B. We say that A — let's call her Alice — has power relative to B — let's call him Bob — if Alice can influence Bob's choices or decisions. To do that, Alice should probably possess something that Bob finds desirable or irresistible. That something, called a *resource,* can be some special knowledge or expertise, a dynamic and winning personality, the promise of financial reward, or even an outright threat to do Bob harm if he does not cooperate. Just as important, Bob must find Alice's knowledge, reward, or threat credible. If Bob, for instance, does not believe that Alice is an expert, then Alice will not have that form of influence over him.

From the perspective of power, the answer to the question "Who should govern?" rests on how dispersed the resources for wielding power are in a society. Those who believe in democracy want to see such resources distributed as widely as possible. For them, the ideal situation would be for each and every citizen to be able to exercise the same degree of influence over governmental actions. Under such conditions, government would do what the majority of citizens wanted done. This is called the **majoritarian view of power**.

However, most students of government agree that politically influential resources are unequally distributed in society; consequently, some members of society will be able to influence governmental actions more than others. Thus, the question really becomes whether it is more desirable to have those resources concentrated in the hands of a few ("elitism") or dispersed as widely as possible ("pluralism").

Those who advocate the **elitist view of power** argue that the general public is best served when there is a basic consensus among a country's top leaders regarding fundamental issues. Although these leaders may disagree on minor

Power The capacity and ability to influence the behavior and choices of others through the use of politically relevant resources.

Majoritarian view of power The view that political power should be distributed as equally as possible in a political system in order to facilitate meaningful majority rule.

Elitist view of power The view that political power should be in the hands of a relatively small part of the general population that shares a common understanding about the fundamental issues facing society and government.

issues or even compete against one another for positions of authority in government, the fact that they share a common view on issues that might otherwise split the nation is regarded as an important foundation for governing.

Pluralist view of power The view that political power should be dispersed among many elites who share a common acceptance of the rules of the game.

In contrast, while not denying that power-relevant resources are unequally distributed in society, those who support the **pluralist view of power** advocate a political system in which many elites, not just one, influence government. For pluralists, it is not important that members of some small elite agree on fundamental issues. Rather, it is crucial that membership in the elite be open to all in society; members need only agree to abide by the rules of the game in government and politics. From the pluralist perspective, members of this open elite serve the public good by competing among themselves for the attention of government, as well as for control of public offices.

Whether it is focused on authority or on power, the issue of who should govern is an important one. It helped to shape the American political system, and it remains a critical question in today's hotly contested political environment.

Where Should Governmental Authority Be Vested?

Critical Thinking

Where should governmental power in the United States be vested — at the national, state, or local level — and on what issues?

Should governmental authority be vested in local communities, in governments close to the people? Should it be vested in the political center of the nation, Washington, D.C.? Or should it be vested in the fifty state capitals — in Harrisburg, Springfield, Austin, Sacramento, Columbus, Tallahassee, and all the others? These questions do not have simple answers because of the broad range of governmental activities.

To illustrate, would it make sense for the national government to run your town's fire department? Who should be responsible for collecting your town's garbage, running your town's parks, and hiring your school district's schoolteachers? Many people trust local government to deal with these important issues. There is no way, however, that towns and cities or even states can deal effectively with foreign policy, national defense, regional unemployment, and other major economic and social issues. Consequently, most Americans believe that the national government, with its vast economic resources and national perspective, should tackle these issues. Many also argue that national policies can better reflect the general will and values of the American people and are less likely to discriminate against racial, religious, and political minorities than local policies are.

Most complex societies have found that to ensure effective governance, they need intermediate levels of government as well. Different nations have solved this problem in different ways. The United States has developed a unique solution that allows national, state, and local governments to share power. But even this solution is incomplete, and the debate continues over the role of each level of government in delivering services to the American public. We discuss the struggles over the vesting of power in greater detail in Chapter 3, on federalism and intergovernmental relations.

How Much Should Government Do?

What should be the scope of governmental activity? The answers to this question vary from society to society and from era to era. We can find a partial answer by examining the dominant ideologies of our nation. If myths help orient us toward our government by shaping our attitudes and understanding about what government does, ideologies provide us with the tenets for assessing the world of politics and the work of government. **Ideologies** are the *conceptual tools we use to think about whether government is doing what it ought to be doing.* They offer us general priorities and principles about what government could or should do and suggest the means for doing it.[34] Whereas myths help us to understand and deal with the world, ideologies reflect our beliefs about the way we think the political world does or ought to operate.

Ideologies Conceptual tools used to help us think about whether government is doing what it ought to be doing.

Although some governments have attempted to establish an official ideology, in most democratic nations there is competition among two or more dominant ideologies. Until the middle 1980s, the leaders of the Soviet Union endorsed and enforced a Marxist-Leninist ideology that made opposition to the government a crime.[35] More common, however, is the situation in many Western European democracies, where competition among followers of different ideologies is at the heart of the representative system. In France, Italy, Belgium, Denmark, and even Great Britain, differences in ideology are often reflected in differences among the political parties.[36] Although the American approach has been less overtly ideological, ideology does play an important — and increasingly controversial — part in shaping our political life (see "Asked & Answered," p. 19).

Bridging the Ideological Gap

Ideological differences among politicians are sometimes bridged on specific issues. Senator John McCain of Arizona, a well-known Republican conservative, formed an alliance with Senator Russ Feingold, a Democratic liberal from Wisconsin, in pursuit of campaign finance reform legislation.

ASKED & ANSWERED

ASKED: How do I know what my political ideology is?

ANSWERED: While there is no "official" or dominant political ideology in the United States, most of us would probably fall into one of four major types of popular ideologies based on how we would respond to two central questions regarding how much government should do. The first question has to do with deciding to what extent government should intervene in economic affairs. Some Americans believe that government should not interfere in the marketplace unless absolutely necessary; others believe that government regulation and management of the economy are crucial for the nation's health. The second question focuses on the extent to which the government should meddle in the private affairs of Americans. At one extreme are those who believe that government has no right to intrude in their personal choices and that the areas of personal freedom must be extended as much as possible. At the other end of the spectrum are those who believe that government sometimes has a moral obligation to intercede in the private lives of people who might otherwise make unwise decisions. From that perspective, governments should be permitted to make and enforce laws related to smoking, abortion rights, same-sex marriage, and so on.

Taken together, the intersection of American beliefs on these two issues has generated four ideologies that seem to represent four general answers to the question of to what extent the government should intervene in the activities of private citizens and in economic life of the country (see Figure 1.1).[1] **Liberalism** is the label typically applied to the position of those who favor increased government intervention in the economy but oppose increased limits on personal freedom. In contrast, **conservatism** is the label usually given to the position of those who favor increased regulation of private lives for moral purposes but oppose government interference in the economy.

Traditionally, liberalism and conservatism have constituted the mainstream ideological positions of most Americans. But in recent years many Americans have found that their views do not fit neatly into either perspective: They are "liberal" on certain issues and "conservative" on others. As a result, two other popular ideological perspectives have emerged: Modern-day **populists** are inclined to favor government intervention in both economic and personal matters, whereas **libertarians** take a strong stand against intervention in both.

The growing popularity of the populist and libertarian ideologies reflects some fundamental problems and potential shifts in the American ideological landscape. Some observers of American government and politics have remarked that our dominant ideological perspectives, liberalism and conservatism, seem increasingly inconsequential to Americans. Some argue that there is a growing gap between the dominant ideologies and the realities of American political life. "The categories that have dominated our thinking for so long are irrelevant to the new world we face," contends E. J. Dionne Jr.[2] Others see our contemporary problems as being rooted in a widening "discrepancy" and tension between our dominant ideologies and the myths of American government that help define our expectations of how our political system should be operating.[3] In either case, ideological responses to questions about what government does are important to understanding American government.

1. William S. Maddox and Stuart A. Lilie, *Beyond Liberal and Conservative: Reassessing the Political Spectrum* (Washington, D.C.: The Cato Institute, 1984).
2. E. J. Dionne Jr., *Why Americans Hate Politics* (New York: Simon & Schuster, 1991), p. 11.
3. H. Mark Roelofs, *Ideology and Myth in American Politics: A Critique of a National Political Mind* (Boston: Little, Brown, 1976), pp. 4–5.

FIGURE 1.1

Issues and Ideologies

The four major ideologies of American politics have been shaped by debates over government's role in economic and personal matters.

Source: Adapted from William S. Maddox and Stuart A. Lilie, *Beyond Liberal and Conservative: Reassessing the Political Spectrum* (Washington, D.C.: The Cato Institute, 1984), p. 5. Reprinted by permission.

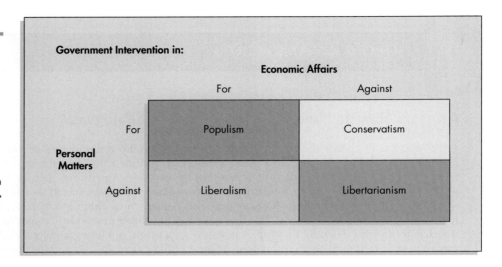

Liberalism A set of ideological beliefs usually favoring government intervention in the economy, but tending to oppose government interference in the private lives of individuals.
Conservatism A set of ideological beliefs tending to resist government interference in economic matters while favoring government action to regulate private affairs for moral purposes.
Populism A set of ideological beliefs that tends to favor government intervention in both economic and personal affairs.
Libertarianism The ideological belief that government should do no more than what is minimally necessary in the areas of both economic affairs and personal freedom.

Overview of This Book

American government and politics form a complex subject involving more than knowledge of the institutions and people who make our systems work. The choices made through the governmental and political systems are greater in number than the fundamental issues described above. Yet these institutions, people, and issues form the basics of what we must know in order to understand American government. As the political turmoil of recent years in Eastern Europe and the former Soviet Union has demonstrated, we must also understand and appreciate how myths operate in our own governmental and political systems. These are the objectives of the chapters that follow.

The first step in developing an understanding of American politics is to become informed about the major governance institutions and processes of government. Chapters 2 through 4 offer an overview of the historical and constitutional basis for the organization and functioning of the American governmental system. Chapter 2 focuses on the Constitution—its creation and its principal features. Chapter 3, on federalism and intergovernmental relations, considers the relationships among the various levels of government. Chapter 4 looks at some limits on governmental power: the civil liberties protected by the Constitution and the civil rights guaranteed to citizens by the Constitution and by law.

The next five chapters consider the activities and institutions that link citizens to their government. In Chapter 5, we discuss the opinions that people have about government and how these opinions affect their participation in politics. Chapter 6 deals with the role of political parties, and Chapter 7 examines the most widespread forms of participation: nominations, campaigns, and elections. That discussion is followed by an analysis of two important institutions that influence the political system: interest groups, in Chapter 8, and the media, in Chapter 9. Interest groups shape politics by making it possible for people with similar goals to band together to influence public policy. The media have an impact on the way people perceive politics.

Chapters 10 through 13 examine the four central institutions of government: Congress, the presidency, the bureaucracy, and the courts. Finally, in Chapters 14 and 15, we probe the relationship between politics and policymaking in domestic and foreign policy.

In each chapter, we point out one or more myths associated with each topic. In some instances, as in Chapter 2, we focus on a myth (the myth of the living Constitution) that distorts the truth but that has helped to generate popular and consistent support for our governmental institutions. In other instances, we consider myths that seem closer to the truth but that have misrepresented the reality of American government. For example, in Chapter 10, on Congress, we tell you about the myth of congressional ineffectiveness, quoting one political commentator who suggested that it would take Congress thirty days to make a cup of instant coffee. Then we ask whether this myth misrepresents not only what Congress does but also what it is supposed to do. As we consider that myth and others, we show you the nuggets of truth that have given rise to them, as well as the ways in which they often reflect and distort reality at the same time — sometimes for good, sometimes not. Only through an understanding of these and related myths can we comprehend the nature and work of our system of government.

We hope that you will find this approach stimulating and that it will provoke thought, discussion, and debate about your basic assumptions about government and politics. We also hope that our discussion will prompt you to ask additional questions about the dynamics of our exciting political process. Like the classic tales of the Greek gods, the myths of American politics reflect the rich imagination and the anxieties of those who created them.

Key Terms

Governance (5)
Myths (6)
Government (12)
Politics (12)
Authority (15)
Democracy (15)
Republic (15)
Representative democracy (15)
Initiative and referendum (15)

Power (16)
Majoritarian view of power (16)
Elitist view of power (16)
Pluralist view of power (17)
Ideologies (18)
Liberalism (20)
Conservatism (20)
Populism (20)
Libertarianism (20)

Net Work

The growing popularity of the Internet has given
students of American government access to information resources that used to be readily available
only to experts. As a result, learning to work the Net
in order to find that information is a critical part of
your education. We have included this section, "Net
Work," at the end of each chapter to guide you in
your use of this incredible resource.

The best way for you to learn about the vast resources that are available on the Internet is to engage in your own explorations. Our purpose in the
"Net Work" section is to give you some guidance to
help you launch those explorations. That guidance
takes several forms. In each chapter we highlight
some of the more significant websites relevant to
the topics covered in that chapter. We also pose
some questions and offer a challenging exercise that
can help you to see what the Internet has to offer.

For instance, do you want to learn more about
how the federal government is responding to terrorist threats? You can start by visiting the White
House website (**www.whitehouse.gov**) and selecting
links dealing with the war on terrorism and homeland security. But you might also want to find alternatives to that site; if so, you can turn to one of the
many fine search engines that are provided for free
on the Internet.

Search engines are online services that are capable
of finding information on those parts of the Internet that they are programmed to scan. Some search
engines cover as much of the Internet as they can
(universal engines), while others are more specialized. Perhaps the most popular and effective search
engine is Google (**www.google.com**). Among the oldest and most established universal search engines
is AltaVista, found at **www.altavista.com**. Other popular search engines are Yahoo! (**www.yahoo.com**),
Looksmart (**www.looksmart.com**), Excite (**www.excite
.com**), Lycos (**www.lycos.com**), and Northern Light

(**www.northernlight.com**). Universal search engines
are also provided by some of the most popular
Internet service providers (ISPs), such as America
Online (**http://search.aol.com**) and MSN (**http://
search.msn.com**).

There are also a number of more specialized
search engines that cover a range of topics or serve
specific communities (e.g., children). To find out
more about these search engines, visit "Search-
Ability" at **www.searchability.com**. One that should
prove especially helpful is FirstGov (**www.firstgov.gov**),
a site designed and operated for the federal government that is citizen-oriented and user-friendly. The
Political Information site (**www.politicalinformation
.com**) offers a search engine that focuses on more
than 5,000 political and policy-relevant websites.
Those with more general interests can explore the
Net through the Social Science Information Gateway search engine (**http://sosig.esrc.bris.ac.uk**).

Take some of these search engines for a spin. See
if you can find the reality behind some of Americans' most venerable political myths on the Internet. What is the real story behind the Washington
"cherry tree" myth? What about all those stories we
were told about young Abe Lincoln? While one
must always be cautious about giving too much
weight to information drawn from the Web, you are
likely to find some interesting history sites using
one of the better search engines. For a good example, see Plimoth Plantation at **www.plimoth.org**.

There are also several encyclopedias on the
Web that might prove useful. Some are free (see
www.encyclopedia.com), others charge for access to
premium service (**www.britannica.com**). Perhaps
the best known is Wikipedia, a unique, open collab-
orative site accessible in several languages that is
constantly updated by its users. As an ongoing work-
in-progress, the popular Wikipedia is a valuable resource that must be used cautiously.

2

Constitutional Foundations

Is the Constitution a living document?

FOCUS QUESTIONS

* What were the circumstances surrounding the framing of the Constitution?
* Who were the framers of the Constitution?
* What were the important traditions underlying the Constitution?
* What do the various provisions of the Constitution accomplish?
* What are the major principles of American constitutionalism?

T he U.S.-led invasion of Iraq in 2003 and the subsequent efforts to re-build that nation both politically and economically have proven to be a significant challenge to the administration of President George W. Bush. Among the most difficult tasks was the need to develop a new constitution for the war-ravaged country, made all the more complicated by the ongoing insurgency and the deep-rooted regional and religious divisions, that became very apparent once the repressive regime of Saddam Hussein had been replaced.[1] Nevertheless, the United States pressed that a draft of an Iraqi constitution be completed by August 15, 2005. The proposed constitution would then be put before the Iraqi voters in October of that year.

The drafting effort itself proved much more difficult than expected. As the mid-August deadline approached, it became evident that major issues had yet to be resolved, especially those related to the autonomy of the Kurdish regions under the new constitutional power sharing arrangements and the degree to which the new constitution would embrace Islamic principles. When the deadline for completing the draft passed without one, U.S. President George W. Bush offered the following observation on August 22 in response to concerns expressed about the delay:

> Producing a constitution is a difficult process that involves debate and compromise. We know this from our own history. Our Constitutional Convention was home to political rivalries and regional disagreements. The Constitution our founders produced has been amended many times over. So Americans understand the challenges facing the framers of Iraq's new constitution. We admire their thoughtful deliberations; we salute their determination to lay the foundation for lasting democracy amid the ruins of a brutal dictatorship.[2]

A week later, the final version of the proposed Iraq constitution was announced; in less than two months after that, it was approved by a vote of the people.

Was President Bush correct in his comparison of the Iraqi situation and the challenges facing the framers of the U.S. Constitution? Despite radically different circumstances between the two events, the process of creating a constitution that took place in Iraq was similar in some respects to what took place in Philadelphia more than two centuries earlier. Representatives from various factions that divided the nation gathered to develop a framework for governing that would prove to be filled with imperfections that many hoped would be worked out later.

How has our imperfect Constitution survived over the past two centuries? As we will see, in part it has done so through formal changes found in twenty-seven amendments that have been added to the document through an elaborate and difficult process set out in the Constitution itself (see "Asked & Answered," p. 46). But most often the necessary adjustments and changes have come about through a range of methods, from judicial interpretations to traditions and practices that have been adopted over time.

Central to the acceptance and success of these changes has been an important and power myth of American government — the *myth of the living constitution.* The myth of the living constitution has its roots in a comment made by

Chief Justice John Marshall in an 1819 decision in which he noted that the Constitution was "intended to endure for ages to come, and consequently to be adapted to the various crises of human affairs."[3] According to this myth, America's Constitution has been successful not because it is like some marvelously engineered machine, but because it is like an adaptable organism capable of evolving to meet the challenges thrown up by its environment. "[C]onstitutions are not mere legal documents," wrote then-professor Woodrow Wilson in 1892, "they are the skeleton frame of a living organism."[4] As that organism adapted to changing conditions, so did its skeletal structures. The conditions brought about by technological, economic, and social changes over the past two centuries raised issues that challenged the values and structures of an American government established in a very different era. According to this myth, the constitutional foundations of the American political system had proved themselves by allowing for the adjustments that had been needed for government to succeed in the more complex and challenging modern world order.

This view gained prominence among academics during the period from the 1880s to the 1920s, known as the Progressive Era, and it was reflected in the history and civics textbooks of the time.[5] By the 1920s and 1930s, it was playing a prominent role in the way lawyers and judges thought about the growth and development of the American legal system, and eventually this "living constitution" perspective was adopted as an approach for handling questions of constitutional law in the highest courts of the land.[6]

As we will see, the myth of the living constitution has helped to shape our understanding and appreciation of the role of the Constitution in our political system. But in recent years this myth has been subject to major challenges. There are those who question whether the myth really reflects the history of our constitutional system, and others who challenge its use as a standard for interpreting the Constitution. To appreciate both the value of the myth and the arguments of those who challenge it, we need to understand more about our constitutional system and how it emerged.

The Setting for Constitutional Change

FOCUS QUESTION WHAT WERE THE CIRCUMSTANCES SURROUNDING THE FRAMING OF THE CONSTITUTION?

Why do people develop constitutions? The obvious and simple answer is that when two or more people work together to resolve common problems, they eventually must organize and establish rules under which to operate. At a minimum, constitutional structures and procedures help sustain collective efforts and prevent the deterioration of social relationships into violent clashes over who is in charge and how things get done.

For the framers of the U.S. Constitution, that question is not so clearly or simply answered. For one thing, when they met in Philadelphia in May 1787, there was already a constitution in place.

Articles of Confederation The first constitution of the United States, ratified in 1781. They established a loose union of states and a congress with few powers.

The **Articles of Confederation** were written in 1777 and ratified in 1781 as America's first constitution. They established a loose union of states (a "firm league of friendship") and a relatively weak national congress. The national congress consisted of a single body in which each state had one vote. That body could exercise significant powers if it could muster the nine-thirteenths majority that was needed to pass any major legislation. For instance, under the Articles, the congress was empowered to make war and peace, send and receive foreign ambassadors, borrow money, and establish a monetary system, build a navy and develop an army in cooperation with the states, fix uniform standards of weights and measures, and even settle disputes among the states. However, it was powerless to levy and collect taxes or duties, and it could not regulate foreign or interstate commerce. There was no executive to enforce acts of the congress and no national court system. As for amending the Articles themselves, it took a unanimous vote of the member states to make such fundamental changes in the national government.

The meeting at Philadelphia was convened because many of the country's political leaders saw that the national government under the Articles lacked the strength to cope with the young republic's problems. For example, by 1787 it was clear to many officials that the national government under the Articles could not conduct an effective foreign policy. Despite the colonists' victory in the American Revolution, the British had not relinquished the Northwest Territories along the Great Lakes. Furthermore, the Spanish remained a hostile presence in Florida and what was then the Southwest. Encouraged by both Britain and Spain, Native American tribes harassed Americans all along the new nation's frontier.

The national government was just as ineffective within its borders. One group of North Carolinians declared an independent "State of Franklin" in 1784 and actively sought annexation by the Spanish; and while New York and New Hampshire argued over claims to the territory of Vermont, residents of that area attempted to have themselves annexed by the British as part of Canada.[7]

Even worse was the Confederation's inability to deal with the nation's financial problems. Lacking the power to tax, the national congress had to rely on funds provided by the states. However, its requests for funds from the states were increasingly ignored. The country had accumulated a large public debt during the Revolutionary War, and much of it remained unpaid. When some states began to print worthless paper money to pay off their debts, spiraling inflation hit the economy.

Economic conditions under the Articles were not good. Within the states, many small farmers faced bankruptcy and the loss of their farms. In western Massachusetts, where the situation was particularly bad, a group of farmers, led by a former Revolutionary War officer, Daniel Shays, disrupted court foreclosure proceedings in September 1786 and several months later tried unsuccessfully to seize a national government arsenal. That incident, known as *Shays's Rebellion*, convinced some of the country's most politically influential leaders that changes had to be made in America's system of government.[8] Several of those leaders were no doubt motivated by a genuine concern for the future of the young republic. Others, however, were stirred to action by fear and anxiety about their own economic future unless something was done—and sooner rather than later.

The Framers

FOCUS QUESTION WHO WERE THE FRAMERS OF THE CONSTITUTION?

There has been an ongoing debate among historians and students of American politics about those who wrote the Constitution and their motivations. Who were those leaders? What do we know about them? Some believe they were statesmen who had led the fight for independence from Britain and were now concerned about the future of their fledgling nation. Others believe they were members of the wealthy landholding and slave-owning classes, motivated by the need to protect and promote their personal economic interests. Still others see the framers as pragmatic politicians who were trying to do the best they could to resolve critical differences among themselves. What we know for certain is that the fifty-five people who came to Philadelphia in 1787 were all white males. Women and African Americans, as well as other racial minorities, were excluded from this momentous gathering. Although we frequently honor these men as the nation's "Founding Fathers," most of their names are unfamiliar to us. Among them were merchants, physicians, bankers, planters, and soldiers. Their average age was forty-three; the youngest, Jonathan Dayton of New Jersey, was twenty-six, and the oldest, Benjamin Franklin, was eighty-one. More than half of them were trained in the law, and more than two-thirds had served in the Continental Congress, which had governed the new nation during the Revolutionary War. At least twelve were receiving a major portion of their income from public office at the time the Philadelphia convention assembled. That summer they

Constitutional Convention

The Constitution was shaped by several compromises reached through the debates at the 1787 convention.

took part in a rare moment of "decisive political creation": They applied their knowledge and experience of government to the design of a new constitution.[9]

According to observers at the time, the delegates included some rather interesting personalities. Gouverneur Morris, a delegate from Pennsylvania, played a major role in drafting the Constitution. A member of a well-known family who had lost a leg in a childhood accident, Morris had been active in New York State politics before relocating to Philadelphia. A contemporary noted that he possessed "one of the best organized heads on the continent, but without manners, and, if his enemies are to be believed, without principles." Hugh Williamson, a delegate from North Carolina, was a Pennsylvania-born physician, preacher, mathematician, astronomer, and businessman. A "leading light" at the convention, Williamson was regarded as "extremely bizarre, loving to hold forth, but speaking with spirit." And Nicholas Gilman, a bachelor delegate from New Hampshire who played a relatively minor role in the proceedings, was characterized as a "pretentious young man; little loved by his colleagues."[10]

Mostly well educated and wealthy, the delegates included at least two men of international reputation: George Washington and Benjamin Franklin. Washington, a popular and imposing figure,[11] was unanimously elected to chair the meeting. A tight-lipped person, the fifty-five-year-old general contributed little to the convention's debates but could enforce its strict rules because the delegates feared his anger.

Benjamin Franklin[12] was well regarded by the other delegates, and many constantly sought his opinions. He was eighty-one years of age, however, and his physical powers were failing him. He was so ill at times that prisoners from the city jail were assigned the task of carrying him from his home to the nearby sessions in a specially designed sedan chair. Despite being well prepared for the meetings, he was not always attentive during the convention's debates and rarely spoke. Nevertheless, he was influential in the eventual adoption of the document. During the final days of the convention, he expressed his support by noting that whenever a group of men are gathered to write a constitution, "you inevitably assemble with those men all their prejudices, their passions, their errors of opinion, their local interests, and their selfish views." One can hardly expect, he argued, that any such gathering would produce a "perfect" government. "It therefore astonishes me," he continued, "to find this system approaching so near to perfection as it does. . . . Thus I consent . . . to this Constitution, because I expect no better, and because I am not sure that it is not the best."[13]

The Roots of the Constitution

FOCUS QUESTION WHAT WERE THE IMPORTANT TRADITIONS UNDERLYING THE CONSTITUTION?

From a historical perspective, Franklin's astonishment is itself surprising, for the framers of the Constitution were hardly as diverse in their "prejudices" and "passions" as he thought. Despite many disagreements and debates over specifics, the framers shared a common legal and intellectual heritage. In that sense, the roots of the Constitution run deep. To understand the unique circumstances that led to its creation, we must explore the traditions that guided its authors.[14]

The British Constitutional Heritage

With few exceptions, the leaders of the American Revolution respected the British constitutional system. Indeed, many of them saw the Revolution as a fight to secure the rights they had assumed to be theirs as Englishmen.[15] Therefore, when the time came for them to devise their own system of government, the framers relied heavily on the British constitutional tradition.[16]

What was that tradition? The question is not easy to answer. The British constitution was not then — and is not now — found in any single document. Rather, it is made up of three British legal institutions with deep historical roots: charters, common law, and several major statutes.

Charters. During the Middle Ages, **feudalism** dominated European society: This system included social, political, and economic arrangements through which landless families secured farmland and protection in exchange for providing services and resources to the land's owner. These arrangements were sometimes written down in agreements called **charters**. A charter described the rights and duties of both the landowner and those bound to him. It was usually drawn up to settle or avoid disputes in the feudal relationship.

In 1215 such a disagreement about the rights of those who served under the British Crown caused a major conflict between King John and the English nobility. After losing on the battlefield, John signed the **Magna Carta**, a document that reaffirmed long-standing rights and duties of the nobility and placed certain defined limits on the king. That charter stands for the principle that everyone, including the king, must obey the law. Over the centuries it became an almost sacred guarantee of law and justice for citizens of the United States as well as England.[17]

Common Law. During medieval times, monarchs, not legislatures, made laws. A king or queen would proclaim something to be the law of the land, sometimes (but not always) after seeking the advice of a legislative body. Legislatures did not become a major source of laws in England until the 1600s. However, there was often a large gap between the broad coverage of most royal proclamations and the details of legal disputes.

Into that legal breach stepped judges appointed by the British Crown to settle such disputes, and from their work came common law. **Common law**, also called judge-made law, represents the collection of legal doctrines that grew out of the many cases heard by those judges. Over an extended period of time, some of those doctrines developed into basic principles of law that were applied throughout England and its expanding colonial empire.

When the British Parliament eventually began to pass laws, conflicts arose between its statutes and the common law that was being applied by the British

---

Feudalism A medieval political and economic system in which landless families secured protection and the use of farmland in exchange for providing services and resources to the land's owner.

Charter A legal institution that originated during the Middle Ages and formed part of the British constitution. Specifically, a formal agreement describing the rights and duties of both the landowner and those bound to that person.

Magna Carta A document signed by King John in 1215 reaffirming the long-standing rights and duties of the English nobility and the limits placed on the king. It stands for the principle that government is limited and that everyone, including the king, must obey the law.

Common law The collection of legal doctrines that grew out of the many cases heard, beginning in medieval times, by judges appointed by the British Crown; also called judge-made law. It is part of the British constitution.

courts. These conflicts emerged, in part, because many English judges and lawyers believed that common-law principles represented a set of "immutable and eternal" rules against which Parliament's actions should be measured.[18] The conflicts came to a head in 1610, when an English court held that an act of Parliament could be overturned if a judge determined that the law violated the basic tenets of common law.

Even though legal reforms have reduced the high stature of common-law rules in both England and the United States, that tradition contributed two important constitutional principles. First, it established the idea that there was a higher law against which legislative actions should be measured. In the United States, the Constitution became that higher standard.[19] Second, this common-law tradition provided a basis for the power of courts to apply that higher-law standard and to nullify statutes and government actions that they judged to be in violation of it. That became the foundation of judicial review, which is a key ingredient in the operation of the American constitutional system.[20] (See the discussion of checks and balances later in this chapter.)

Major Statutes. Several major acts of Parliament also shaped the British constitutional tradition. The British Bill of Rights (1689), for instance, established some basic principles of constitutional government: Parliament's supremacy over the monarchy, the guarantee of a jury trial, and prohibitions against excessive bail and cruel and unusual punishment. Other laws asserted the independence of the judicial branch from the monarchy (Act of Settlement, 1701) and the right of representation in determining taxes (Petition of Right, 1629) — an issue that would be central to the complaints of the North American colonists.

The Colonial Heritage[21]

Mayflower Compact
A document written by the Pilgrims that set forth major principles for the Plymouth Colony's government.

Most British colonies were established under royal charters that allowed settlers to govern themselves in many matters. In several colonies, the settlers modified or supplemented these agreements. For example, the **Mayflower Compact**, written by the Pilgrims, set forth several major principles for the Plymouth Colony's government. That agreement and similar ones found throughout the colonies became part of the colonial heritage that helped shape the Constitution.

When we think about colonial rule, we often picture an oppressed people dominated by foreign rulers. We rarely think of colonial government as a breeding ground for self-government and openness. Yet from the 1630s until the American Revolution, England let its North American colonies govern themselves, making no major effort to establish a central administration for its growing empire.[22]

Each of the colonies remained primarily a self-governing entity, and by the early 1700s most of them had developed similar governmental structures. A typical colony had three branches of government: a governor appointed by the king, a legislature, and a relatively independent judiciary. Local government consisted of self-governing townships and counties. The future leaders of the American Revolution gained political experience and an understanding of how governments operate through participation in these colonial institutions.[23]

Intellectual Roots

The intellectual atmosphere of the time also influenced the framers of the Constitution.[24] Raised in a society that took its religion seriously, they grew up with such concepts as equality before God and the integrity of each human life — concepts rooted in their *Judeo-Christian religious traditions.* The idea of a covenant, or contract, among members of society developed from those traditions, as did the distrust of the monarchy and the perception of a need for a system of laws to protect individual rights.[25]

The framers were also children of the **Enlightenment**.[26] Usually dated from the 1600s through the 1700s, that period in European intellectual history was dominated by the idea that human reason, not religious tradition, was the primary source of knowledge and wisdom. On issues related to government and politics, a number of writers set the tone for the discussions among the framers and their peers in the colonies.

Among the most controversial Enlightenment writers was Thomas Hobbes. Writing in the middle 1600s, Hobbes argued that governments were not formed because God had conferred political authority on a specific ruling family. In his most famous work, *Leviathan* (1651), Hobbes contended that governments were formed by an agreement among rational individuals who, living without government in a brutish state of nature, realized that it was in their self-interest to subject themselves to an all-powerful ruler. Thus, Hobbes argued that government depended on the consent of the governed. Although he was no advocate of democracy (he wrote in defense of the British monarchy), his views proved helpful in establishing the rational basis of government.[27]

Another British political philosopher, John Locke, was perhaps the most influential of the Enlightenment authors among the colonists. He offered an explanation of political life that carried Hobbes's argument further by asserting that people possess an inherent right to revolution. In *Two Treatises on Government* (1690), Locke argued that individuals form governments as a matter of convenience to deal with the depraved behavior of some individuals. Thus, a government can continue to exist as long as it proves convenient to its citizens and does not interfere with their pursuit of life, liberty, and property. But if the government violates this arrangement, then the citizens have a right to emigrate or resist. Ultimately, this view sanctions the right of citizens to replace a government that does such things with another.[28]

The work of a French aristocrat, Charles de Montesquieu, clearly influenced the writers of the Constitution. The framers relied especially on his book *The Spirit of the Laws*, which was first published in Paris in 1748. In that work, Montesquieu argued that the best government is one that is designed in such a way that no person or group can oppress others. This end is best achieved, Montesquieu wrote, by separating the legislative, executive, and judicial functions into three distinct branches of government.[29]

Finally, just as the seeds of the American Revolution were being planted in the 1750s and 1760s, a Swiss-born philosopher, Jean-Jacques Rousseau, published several works arguing for a more extreme version of **popular sovereignty** than that offered by Locke. According to Rousseau, the best form of government is

Enlightenment The period from the 1600s through the 1700s in European intellectual history. It was dominated by the idea that human reason, not religious tradition, was the primary source of knowledge and wisdom.

Popular sovereignty The concept, first described by Jean-Jacques Rousseau around the time of the American Revolution, that the best form of government is one that reflects the general will of the people, which is the sum total of those interests that all citizens have in common.

one that reflects the general will of the people, or popular sovereignty, which is the sum total of the interests that all citizens have in common. Rousseau's major writings influenced the French Revolution of 1789 much more than the American Revolution, and most of the framers probably regarded him as too radical. Nevertheless, he was read widely and had many followers in the American colonies. Among them was Thomas Paine, a British-born American revolutionary whose pamphlets had a great influence during the American Revolution. His best-known work, *Common Sense* (1776), is among the most often cited of the writings that came out of the American Revolution.

The Onset of Revolution

In the 1760s, British policies toward the North American colonies changed. After nearly 150 years of relative freedom from direct interference from England, the colonists found themselves under increasing pressure from London. Britain needed men and resources to fight the French and so began to impose demands and commercial restrictions on the American colonists. Given their legal, political, and intellectual heritage, it is not surprising that some colonists responded with calls for revolutionary action.

In 1765 the British passed the *Stamp Act*—the first tax levied directly on the colonists by Parliament. Relying on their view of the rights granted to all British subjects under English law, colonial leaders protested against this "taxation without representation." The Stamp Act was repealed within a few months, but other controversies soon arose. For instance, the British granted a monopoly on the sale of tea to a British firm, thus interfering with the interests of many colonial merchants. In 1773 a group of Boston citizens responded by raiding a ship loaded with tea and dumping its contents overboard. That incident, now known as the *Boston Tea Party*, caused the British to close Boston Harbor and tighten control over the colonial government in Massachusetts. The events leading to rebellion soon escalated, and by 1774 even some of the moderate voices in colonial politics were calling for change.

Representatives from the colonies gathered as the First Continental Congress in Philadelphia in September 1774. After passing resolutions protesting the recent British actions, the delegates set a date for reconvening the next year and adjourned. By the time they met again as the Second Continental Congress in May 1775, colonists and British troops had exchanged gunfire at Concord and Lexington.

The Second Continental Congress took a number of steps that officially launched the American Revolution. It organized itself as a provisional government, and in June 1775 it created a continental army, to be headed by George Washington. In May 1776, the congress voted to take the final step of drawing up a statement declaring the colonies free and independent states. On July 2, 1776, it adopted the **Declaration of Independence**. Two days later, independence was formally declared.

The Declaration of Independence achieved several objectives. It denounced the British for abusing the rights given the colonists under the British constitu-

Critical Thinking

Was the American Revolution inevitable? What would have happened if the British had treated the North American colonies better?

Declaration of Independence The document declaring the colonies to be free and independent states and also articulating the fundamental principles under which the new nation would be governed that was adopted by the Second Continental Congress in July 1776.

tion and long-standing traditions of self-government. It proclaimed the intention of the colonial revolutionaries to sever their ties with England and explained the reasons for such drastic action. Most important, it articulated two fundamental principles under which the newly formed nation would be governed. First, the Declaration held that governments have one primary purpose: to secure the "unalienable rights" of their citizens, among which are "life, liberty, and the pursuit of happiness." Second, it stated that governments derive their powers and authority from the "consent of the governed." The signers of the Declaration asserted that when any government violates the rights it was established to secure, "it is the Right of the People to alter or to abolish it" and to create a new government in its place.[30]

What the Framers Did

FOCUS QUESTION **WHAT DO THE VARIOUS PROVISIONS OF THE CONSTITUTION ACCOMPLISH?**

As noted before, the new government created in the immediate aftermath of the American Revolution — the Articles of Confederation — had developed some significant flaws by 1787, leading to the Philadelphia meeting. Although originally charged with just recommending changes to the Articles, the delegates soon assumed the broader task of constructing an entirely new set of institutions and rules.

The framers designed a system of government that met several of the basic requirements of any constitution. To shape a viable national government, they needed to establish its legitimacy and work out its basic structures. Through the Constitution, they created the three branches of government and defined and limited their powers. They also devised formal procedures by which the Constitution itself could be amended.

Establishing Legitimacy

Critical Thinking

What are the alternatives to legitimacy? How does a government get people to obey the law without relying on legitimacy?

Legitimacy The belief of citizens in a government's right to pass and enforce laws.

A government cannot be effective unless it possesses power — that is, unless it has the ability to carry out its policies and enforce its laws. Even more important, its citizens must believe that the government has the ability to exercise authority and power (see the discussion in Chapter 1). How many Americans would voluntarily pay their federal income taxes by April 15 each year if they thought that the government could not collect those revenues? How many car manufacturers would include pollution-reducing devices in their vehicles if they believed that the government could not enforce its environmental protection laws?

The power and authority of any government are enhanced by the willingness of its citizens to obey government officials. A government is most effective when its citizens believe that those officials have a right to pass and enforce laws. That is why the establishment of government **legitimacy** is so important. It provides government with the effective authority that it needs if it is to govern.

GLOBAL POLITICS

Comparing Constitutions

There are many definitions of the political instrument we call a constitution, and there is no one set of features that can be considered common to all documents given that classification. In very general terms, what distinguishes a constitution from other legal documents is that it is a "law *of* government" that must exist in order for us to have a "government of laws."

Since constitutions can differ from one another, how does the U.S. Constitution compare to those adopted by other countries? Comparisons of constitutions depend on which constitutional feature you seek to focus on. As summarized in the text and Table 2.1, we can compare constitutions by how they deal with five different issues: establishing legitimacy, structuring authority, describing and distributing powers, setting limits on those powers, and arranging for constitutional change. Anyone of those functions can be used to help us compare how the U.S. Constitution compares with others.

In structuring authority, for example, the U.S. and other modern constitutions are typically categorized and compared on the basis of how they select their chief executive. In a parliamentary system such as that of the United Kingdom or Italy, the chief executive (usually called the prime minister or premier) is selected from among members of the legislative body—usually the leader of the majority party or a coalition of parties that controls the parliament. Some of these countries (such as Israel) will have a formal official called the president, but that role is typically ceremonial in parliamentary systems. In presidential systems like that of the United States, the chief executive is selected in a distinct election in which specific candidates from opposing parties face off against each other. Some countries, like France, have a

mixture of both presidential and parliamentary systems, in which a powerful president shares authority with a prime minister who may at times be a member of the opposition party.

Another major difference among constitutional systems is found in the way in which members of the legislative body are elected. In the United States, members of Congress are normally selected from single-member constituencies. That is, typically an election for a single seat in the legislature is held in a geographically distinct district. Two or more parties may compete for the seat, but only one goes to Congress. This is also the system used in England. Under other constitutions (for example, in most European countries), several members of the legislature are selected from a district through proportional representation, where the district seats are allocated to parties in proportion to the number of votes that a party or candidate receives in an election.

Every modern nation state operates under a constitution, and each is unique in how it deals with each of the functions we have highlighted here. During the twentieth century, however, certain global standards emerged that any constitution is expected to meet. It is assumed, for example, that a modern constitution will be found in a single written document rather than rely (as the British have successfully done for centuries) on an unwritten tradition for their law of government. Modern constitutions are also expected to be stable and "entrenched"—that is, they should be constructed for the long term and be relatively difficult (although not impossible) to change. Most constitutional scholars will also say that a national constitution should be the foundation for the country's legal system and be treated as the "supreme law of the land." At the same time, it should be open and flexible so it can be adapted to changing conditions through legislative clarification and judicial interpretation. You can make your own comparisons of national constitutions at a number of websites. For example, at the University of Richmond's Constitution Finder site (http://confinder .richmond.edu), you can find links to more than 500 modern constitutions.

The legitimacy of the U.S. government is rooted in the Preamble to the Constitution. In a few words at the beginning of the Preamble, the framers make clear the source of authority for the republic: "We the People." The choice of words is important. The government created under the Articles of Confederation in 1777 was called a "firm league of friendship" among the states. Ultimately, all authority was retained by the states. The Constitution, in contrast, leaves no doubt that the national government's right to exercise authority—its legitimacy—comes directly from the people and not from the states (see Table 2.1).[31]

TABLE 2.1

Comparing America's Two Constitutions		ARTICLES OF CONFEDERATION	CONSTITUTION OF THE UNITED STATES
	Establishing legitimacy	Through a "firm league of friendship" among the states	Through "We the People"—all citizens of the nation
	Structuring authority	Through a confederacy, with ultimate authority residing in the states Within the national government, in a single body—the congress	Through a federal arrangement, with national and state governments dividing and sharing authority In three distinct branches of government: legislative, executive, and judicial
	Describing and distributing powers	Number of foreign and domestic powers listed in Article IX, many limited so as not to interfere with state authority	Delegated and implied powers for national government in Article I Concurrent and reserved powers for states
	Limiting powers	Many limitations on national powers, with deference to states	Provision in Article I Bill of Rights
	Allowing for change	Amendments require unanimous vote of states No national courts to interpret meaning of Articles	Elaborate amendment process requiring significant majorities rather than unanimity Judicial review implied

Structuring Authority

In deciding how to structure the authority of the new government, the framers of the Constitution faced two challenges. First, they had to create a stronger national government while at the same time allowing the states to retain their authority. Second, they had to deal with the issue of how to allocate authority within the national government itself.

Balancing National and State Authority. The framers knew that they had to create a stronger national government in order to contend with the problems plaguing the country under the Articles of Confederation. At the same time, they needed to make certain that their new constitution did not threaten the traditional authority of the thirteen states.

Under the Articles, ultimate governmental authority rested with the states. Whatever power the national government had was the result of the states' willingness to give up some of their authority to a central government. Such an arrangement is called a **confederation**; hence the title of the Articles.

In considering alternatives, the framers could have proposed a constitution based on a **unitary system** of government. In a unitary government, the ultimate authority rests with the national government, and whatever powers state or local governments have are given to them by the central government. The framers would not have had to look far for examples, as each of the thirteen states was in fact a unitary government. Although each state contained towns, counties, and boroughs, those local governments exercised only such powers as were granted to them by a charter issued by the state government.

While they sought to move toward a stronger national government, the framers realized that their new constitution would not be ratified if it called for a unitary form of government. In the end, they created a hybrid—a mixture of confederation and unitary system that is now called a **federation**. In a federation, the authority of government is shared by both the national and the state governments. In its ideal form, a federal constitution gives the national government exclusive authority over some governmental tasks, while giving the states exclusive authority over other governmental matters.[32] There are also some areas where the two levels of government share authority. Which areas of government were given to the national government and which to the states is discussed later in this chapter.

Structuring Authority Within the National Government. Having established a national government with authority, the framers also had to develop structures of authority within the national government so that it could exercise its powers. Under the Articles of Confederation, whatever powers the national government possessed were exercised by a single body: the congress. In contrast, and following the model elaborated by Montesquieu in his *Spirit of the Laws*, the framers created three branches of government: Congress, the presidency, and the courts. The first three articles of the Constitution define these primary structures of government and outline the roles, powers, and responsibilities of the public officials in each one.

Confederation An arrangement in which ultimate governmental authority is vested in the states that make up the union, with whatever power the national government has being derived from the states' willingness to give up some of their authority to a central government.

Unitary system A form of government in which the ultimate authority rests with the national government, with whatever powers state or local governments have being given to them by the central government.

Federation (federal system) A system in which the authority of government is shared by both national and state governments. In its ideal form, a federal constitution gives the national government exclusive authority over some governmental tasks, while giving the states exclusive authority over other governmental matters; there are also some areas where the two levels of government share authority.

The basic structure of American government was the result of a series of compromises reached among the delegates to the Constitutional Convention. When the convention opened, the delegation from Virginia offered a series of resolutions for the meeting to consider. Under the *Virginia Plan*, there would be a **bicameral** (two-house) congress in which each state's representation would be based on its population relative to that of other states. Under the Articles of Confederation, a state could send several representatives to the congress, but each state had only a single vote. The Articles of Confederation also did not provide for a separate executive or judicial branch of government at the national level; the Virginia Plan called for both.

Delegates from states with larger populations welcomed the provisions of the Virginia Plan. However, after lengthy debate, some delegates from the smaller states put forward a counterproposal. Known as the *New Jersey Plan*, it called for strengthening the existing Articles by adding executive and judicial offices. It also increased the powers of the Articles' **unicameral** (one-house) congress, especially its ability to force reluctant states to cooperate with the national government.

The delegates voted to reject the New Jersey Plan. However, the discussions about it drew attention to the many delegates who remained uncomfortable with key provisions of the Virginia Plan, especially the question of representation. To avoid a stalemate, the delegates adopted what has become known as the **Great Compromise**. That proposal, offered by the Connecticut delegation (and therefore sometimes called the Connecticut Compromise), led to the structure of the American national government as we know it today. It called for the establishment of a bicameral congress consisting of a House of Representatives in which states would be represented according to their population size and a Senate in which each state would have an equal voice. Article I of the Constitution outlined the composition of Congress and described the rules and restrictions that apply to both legislative bodies.

Furthermore, the Great Compromise also contained provisions for executive and judicial branches of government. Article II of the Constitution established the executive offices of president and vice president and specified the qualifications for these offices, and later in the convention the methods for selecting those officials were worked out (see the discussion of the electoral college later in this chapter). Later sections of Article II described the president's general responsibilities and provided guidelines for relations with Congress. Article III created a judicial branch of government that is composed of "one supreme Court, and . . . such inferior Courts as the Congress may from time to time ordain and establish."

The Great Compromise was just one of many agreements among the framers to resolve the complex issues that they faced (see Table 2.2). Out of such compromises came major provisions of the Constitution. Most important, these compromises made it possible for the framers to complete their work and create a document that had some hope of ratification.

The Case of the Electoral College. Of all the compromises developed by the framers, perhaps none has proved more troublesome — for them as well as for many generations of Americans — than the decision to establish an **electoral college** as the means for selecting the president and vice president of the United

Bicameral Refers to a legislature that is divided into two separate houses, such as the U.S. Congress.

Unicameral Refers to a legislature that has only one house.

Great Compromise The proposal offered by the Connecticut delegation to the Constitutional Convention in 1787. It called for the establishment of a bicameral congress, consisting of a House in which states were represented according to their population size and a Senate in which each state had an equal voice.

Electoral college The constitutional body designed to select the president. Described in Article II of the Constitution.

TABLE 2.2

The Major Compromises

DEMANDS	COMPROMISES	DEMANDS
	GREAT COMPROMISE	
States to have equal representation in Congress (New Jersey Plan)	Bicameral Congress with equal representation in Senate and population-based representation in House	States to be represented in Congress on the basis of population (Virginia Plan)
	THREE-FIFTHS COMPROMISE	
Slaves to be counted for representation purposes, but not for taxation purposes	All slaves to be counted as three-fifths of a person for both representation and taxation purposes	Slaves not to be counted for representation purposes, but to be counted for taxation purposes
	COMMERCE/SLAVE TRADE COMPROMISE	
National government not to regulate slave trade or exports	Congress given power to regulate interstate and foreign commerce but not to impose a tax on exports from any state; Congress not to act on slave trade until 1808	National government to have authority over all interstate and foreign trade
	FEDERALISM	
States to retain their legitimate authority in the governmental system	Division of legitimate authority between states and national government	An effective national government to be established

Critical Thinking

Should the electoral college be abolished or modified to make it fit better with today's democratic norms?

States. Unlike most of the other issues faced by the framers, the presidential selection issue did not have two clear sides pitted against each other. It was not a matter of deciding between direct election and indirect election of the president and vice president, as many now believe. Instead, it was a question of how to design a selection system that would fit into the complex arrangements for balancing national and state interests that had already been agreed upon, while at the same time making certain that the presidency would not be beholden to either chamber of Congress. By August 6, 1787, the best the framers had been able to do was to have the president elected by a joint ballot of Congress—a solution that could not get enough support for inclusion.

In late August, with time running out and their frustrations running high, the framers established a special Committee of Eleven to deal with several "postponed matters," including how to select the president. Out of the committee came the basics of the electoral college proposal, and what followed was two days of debate that resulted in still more revisions designed to make this strange and unique mechanism as fair and accommodating as possible. As reasonable as the electoral college compromise seemed at the time, however, its flaws became evident in the elections of 1796 and 1800, when it was put through its first real tests and was found wanting. In 1804 a revised electoral college (as set forth in the Twelfth Amendment) was in place.

But that "fix" proved to be only a superficial one, for the electoral college system was soon modified through the development of national political parties and state-level decisions regarding how the electors would be selected (see Chapter 7, on campaigns and elections). In the presidential elections of 1824 and 1876, major problems with the party-dominated electoral college process resulted in election outcomes in which the candidate receiving the largest number of votes lost the election. But despite many efforts over the decades to change the system, nothing was done to modify its basic structure. Then came the presidential election of 2000, and once again the electoral college compromise of 1787 became a critical issue that drew the attention of Americans for six frantic weeks.[33]

Distributing and Describing Governmental Powers

Having established a two-level structure of authority in the federal system, and having created the three branches within the national government, the framers next faced the task of dividing up the powers among the various institutions.

Delegated powers The powers the Constitution gives to Congress that are specifically listed in the first seventeen clauses in Section 8 of Article I; sometimes referred to as "enumerated powers."

Concurrent powers Those powers that the Constitution grants to the national government but does not deny to the states, for example, the power to lay and collect taxes.

Necessary and proper clause The eighteenth clause of Article I, Section 8, of the Constitution, which establishes "implied powers" for Congress that go beyond those powers listed elsewhere in the Constitution.

Powers in the Federal System. The history and present-day operations of the federal system designed by the framers will be discussed in greater detail in Chapter 3, which focuses on federalism and intergovernmental relations. It is important at this juncture to understand how the framers allocated governmental authority between the national government and the states. The powers given to Congress in Article I are central to the operation of the national government. The article includes a detailed list of these powers, such as the authority to tax, borrow money, regulate interstate commerce, coin money, declare war, and raise and support an army and navy. These and other powers identified in Section 8 of Article I constitute the **delegated powers** of the American national government (see Figure 2.1). Many of these powers — such as the power to coin money, make treaties, and lay import duties — are granted exclusively to the national government; that is, they are denied to the states. Other delegated powers, however, are granted to the national government but not denied to the states — for example, the power to lay and collect taxes and the power to define criminal behavior and set punishments. These are called **concurrent powers**.

Article I, Section 8, of the Constitution also provides Congress with the authority "to make all Laws which shall be necessary and proper for carrying into Execution the foregoing Powers, and all other Powers vested by this Constitution in the Government of the United States." This **necessary and proper clause,**

Implied powers Those powers given to Congress by Article I, Section 8, clause 18, of the Constitution that are not specifically named but are provided for by the necessary and proper clause.

found in paragraph 18 of Section 8, establishes **implied powers** for Congress that go beyond those powers listed elsewhere in the Constitution. In *McCulloch v. Maryland* (1819), the U.S. Supreme Court resolved the issue of the constitutionality of implied powers.

In that case, the Court considered whether Congress had the right to charter a Bank of the United States. The national bank was a controversial institution from the moment it was created by the first Congress, especially in the South and West, where bank policies were blamed for the nation's economic woes. Several states decided to challenge the constitutionality of the bank by imposing a tax on its local branches. When Maryland officials assessed a tax of $15,000 on the bank's Baltimore branch, the head cashier took state officials to court, charging that they did not have the authority to tax an agency of the national government. Maryland countered that the Bank of the United States was not a legally constituted agency of the federal government because no provision in the Constitution explicitly gives Congress the power to establish a national bank. The bank's lawyers, however, insisted that the power to charter a bank was implied in the constitutional authority to collect taxes, borrow money, and regulate commerce.

The Supreme Court unanimously sided with the national government. "Let the end be legitimate," stated Chief Justice John Marshall, "let it be within the scope of the Constitution, and all means which are appropriate, which are plainly adapted to that end, which are not prohibited, but consistent with the letter and spirit of the Constitution, are constitutional." In that decision (in which he also laid the groundwork for what would later develop into the myth of the living constitution), Marshall was agreeing with the national government that by giving Congress the explicit power to regulate commerce, the framers of the Constitution implicitly granted Congress the right to charter a bank. This broad interpretation of the necessary and proper clause (also called the "elastic clause") altered the position of the states by greatly expanding the potential powers of the national government. The Bank of the United States survived until the 1830s, when President Andrew Jackson's opposition to it caused it to close. In 1913, Congress once again set up an agency for managing the banking system. That agency, the Federal Reserve System, still regulates the nation's major banks.[34] The right of Congress to establish such an agency is implied in the necessary and proper clause.

The Constitution does not provide a specific list of the powers left to the states. In fact, there is no evidence that the framers of the Constitution even considered doing so. Writing in defense of the Constitution, James Madison noted that the framers felt that there was no need for this because the only powers given to the newly formed national government were those "enumerated" in the body of the Constitution. This approach left to the states the power over "all other objects."[35] This position was made explicit in the Tenth Amendment, which was added to the Constitution in 1791 (see the discussion of the Tenth Amendment and the current controversies surrounding it in Chapter 3). That amendment declares that "powers not delegated to the United States by the

Powers Granted by the Constitution

To the national government ("delegated" or "enumerated" powers; "implied" powers)	To both national and state governments ("concurrent" powers)	To the state governments ("reserved" powers)
• To "lay and collect taxes, duties, imposts, and excises" • To regulate interstate and foreign commerce • To borrow and coin money • To declare war • To raise and support an army • To maintain a navy • To provide for a militia • To govern territories and national property • To define and punish piracies and other high sea felonies • To establish post offices and post roads • To grant patents and copyrights • To set standards of weights and measures • To "make all laws necessary and proper to carry out the foregoing powers" (the "elastic clause" that grants "implied powers")	• To levy and collect taxes • To borrow money • To charter banks and corporations • To make and enforce laws • To establish courts • To take property for public purposes	• To conduct elections • To establish local governments • To regulate commerce within the state • To protect public health, safety, and morals • To ratify amendments to the Constitution • And all other powers not delegated to the national government nor denied to the states

Powers Denied by the Constitution

To the national government	To both national and state governments ("prohibited" powers)	To the state governments
• To tax commerce within a state • To give preference to one state over another in matters of commerce • To change state boundaries without state permission • To violate the Bill of Rights	• To grant titles of nobility • To tax exports • To permit slavery (added through 13th Amendment) • To deny citizens the right to vote because of race, color, sex (added through Amendments 15 and 19)	• To tax imports and exports • To coin money • To make treaties • To wage war • To deny due process and equal protection of the laws (added through 14th Amendment)

FIGURE 2.1

Constitutional Basis of the Federal System

The top middle box lists powers shared by the two levels of government; the bottom middle box shows powers denied to both. Powers on the upper left belong to the national government exclusively; those on the upper right belong to the states.

Reserved powers The powers that the Constitution provides for the states, although it does not list them specifically; sometimes called "residual powers." As stated in the Tenth Amendment, these include all powers not expressly given to the national government or denied to the states.

Constitution, nor prohibited by it to the States, are reserved to the States respectively or to the people." Historically, these **reserved powers** have included such responsibilities as providing for public education, building local roads and highways, and regulating trade within a state's borders.

Powers Within the National Government. Following Montesquieu's prescriptions, the framers gave each of the three branches of the national government a distinct part of the functions that any government must perform. According to this model, any government must do three things: It must pass laws (legislate), enforce those laws (execute), and settle disputes or controversies arising from application of the laws (adjudicate).

In Article I of the Constitution, the framers established Congress as the legislative branch. It is notable and important that they also chose Article I as the place to locate the delegated powers of the national government. That placement reflects the framers' desire to make certain that the representative parts of the national government—the House of Representatives and the Senate—would be the primary fount of authority at the national level.

In contrast, the description of executive power in Article II takes the form of noting what roles the president will play and what duties he or she will carry out. Chapter 11, on the presidency, describes in greater detail how those roles and duties have expanded over the two centuries since the Constitution was written.

Finally, Article III says little more than that the "judicial power of the United States shall be vested in one Supreme Court" and in whatever lower courts Congress establishes. As we discuss later in this chapter and in more detail in Chapter 13, on the judiciary, the meaning of "judicial power" was articulated in the landmark case of *Marbury v. Madison* in 1803.

Critical Thinking

Is our elaborate constitutional system too complex and slow to deal with today's problems?

Limiting Governmental Powers

The Constitution also sets limits on the powers of both the national and the state governments. For example, Section 9 of Article I forbids Congress to suspend the privilege of a **writ of habeas corpus** except in time of rebellion or invasion. A writ of habeas corpus is a court order that individuals can seek in order to protect themselves against arbitrary arrest and detention. By issuing such a writ, a court can order public officials to bring a suspect or detainee before a judge to determine whether he or she is being held on legal grounds.

Writ of habeas corpus A court order that protects people against arbitrary arrest and detention by requiring officials to bring the "body" (i.e., the person) before the court.

The writ of habeas corpus privilege is taken for granted during peacetime, and in most instances it is used by lawyers to get their clients released when the criminal justice system seems to be acting too slowly in processing someone who has been arrested for a crime. But the fact that the Constitution permits its suspension in time of war ("rebellion or invasion") has made it the focus of debate since the events of September 11, 2001. While the privilege has not been suspended in the aftermath of September 11, the government has used a variety of means (e.g., declaring someone to be a "material witness" or an "enemy combatant") for detaining individuals it suspects of involvement in terrorism.

Critical Thinking

Under what circumstances should guarantees such as the writ of habeas corpus be suspended?

Habeas Corpus and the War on Terror

José Padilla (also known as Abdullah al-Muhajir) is a U.S. citizen who was at the center of legal controversy involving habeas corpus rights. Arrested and detained as an "enemy combat" in the war on terror in June 2002, he was finally charged with a crime in January 2006.

The most famous historical instance of the suspension of the writ of habeas corpus was an order to that effect issued by Abraham Lincoln to General Winfred Scott in April 1861, covering an area from south of Philadelphia to Baltimore. The public response to the suspension was so negative that Lincoln later asked for (and received) congressional approval (Habeas Corpus Act of 1863) for the suspension of the privilege in areas where there seemed to be threats of violence. Just as important, the Supreme Court (in *Ex Parte Milligan*, 71 U.S. 2 [1866]) later determined that what is suspended under such acts is the "privilege" rather than the writ itself. Thus, someone who is detained under conditions of martial law, but in an area where the civilian courts are still functioning, can seek a writ of habeas corpus in order to have a judge determine if the petitioner has been unconstitutionally deprived of the privilege. Until the recent terrorist attacks, questions related to the suspension of the writ have rarely been raised,[36] but such questions may become more relevant in the future.

Another provision prohibits the national government from passing a bill of attainder or an ex post facto law. A **bill of attainder** is a legislative act that declares a person guilty of a crime and sets punishment without the benefit of a formal trial. An **ex post facto law** makes an action criminal even though it was legal when it was performed.

Bill of attainder A legislative act declaring a person guilty of a crime and setting punishment without the benefit of a formal trial.

Ex post facto law A law declaring an action criminal even if it was performed before the law making it illegal was passed.

Bill of Rights In the
United States, the first
ten amendments to the
Constitution, which col-
lectively guarantee the
fundamental liberties of
citizens against abuse by
the national government.

Perhaps the best-known limits on the powers of the national government are
provided in the **Bill of Rights**, a term usually applied to the first ten amendments to the Constitution, which were added in 1791 (see Table 2.3). Most of
these amendments guarantee the fundamental liberties of citizens (see Chapter
4, on rights and liberties). They were added to the Constitution to satisfy the demands of critics who complained during the ratification process that the original document did not adequately protect individual rights.[37]

The First Amendment protects freedom of expression—speech, press, assembly, and religion. Other amendments prohibit national officials from in-
fringing on the right to bear arms (Second), from arbitrarily ordering families
to quarter soldiers (Third), from conducting unreasonable searches and seizures (Fourth), from forcing any person to testify against himself or herself in a
criminal trial (Fifth), and from requiring excessive bail or inflicting "cruel or
unusual punishment" (Eighth).

The Fifth Amendment also forbids the national government to take any action that might deprive a person "of life, liberty, or property" without "due
process of law" or "just compensation." The Sixth Amendment ensures a
"speedy trial, by an impartial jury" in criminal cases, and the Seventh Amendment extends the right of jury trial to civil cases.

The Constitution also places limits on the powers and actions of the states.
Section 10 of Article I, for instance, contains a list of powers denied to the
states. Other sections set limits on the power of the states in relation to one

TABLE 2.3

**The Bill of Rights
Adopted in 1791**

RIGHTS ADDRESSED	AMENDMENT
Freedom of expression	1. Freedom of religion, speech, press, assembly, and petition
Personal security	2. Right to bear arms 3. No quartering of troops without consent 4. Protection against unreasonable searches and seizures
Fair treatment under law	5. Right to presentation of indictment; guarantee against double jeopardy and self-incrimination; guarantee of due process of law and just compensation 6. Right to speedy and public trial 7. Right to jury trial in civil cases 8. Guarantees against excessive bail, fines, and punishments
Reserved rights and powers	9. Powers reserved to the people 10. Powers reserved to the states

another and to the national government. Article IV requires that each state give **full faith and credit** to the "Acts, Records, and judicial Proceedings of every other state." Thus, a divorce granted in Nevada must be honored in New York, and vice versa. There are exceptions, of course. In 1996, as several states began to consider revising their marriage laws to permit same-sex unions, Congress passed the Defense of Marriage Act that allowed each state to make its own laws related to that subject but also allowed other states to avoid honoring such legal unions. In 1999 Vermont passed a law to allow civil unions, and in 2004 Massachusetts decided to allow same-sex marriages for its citizens (see Asked and Answered, p. 46). In both cases, the 1996 Act precluded the recognition of those legal unions and marriages under the Full Faith and Credit provision of the Constitution.

The Constitution also mandates that the "Citizens of each State shall be entitled to all Privileges and Immunities of Citizens in the Several States." For example, before 1984 when the federal government passed legislation that required all states to limit the sale and public possession of alcohol to individuals age twenty-one and older, state laws differed on the minimum age for purchasing and consuming alcohol. Under this **privileges and immunities** guarantee, an eighteen-year-old resident of New Jersey who could not purchase alcohol under that state's laws could cross over to New York and buy alcoholic beverages without fear of violating the law. New York State could not apply the law differently just because that person was a resident of New Jersey. We take these provisions of the Constitution for granted today, but they were the source of considerable debate and compromise at the convention as the framers sought to create a strong national government while maintaining state autonomy.

Another problem the framers faced was how to ensure that the laws of the national government would take priority over the laws of the states. One proposal called for giving Congress the power to declare state laws illegal if they interfered with congressional policies. Another asked for a constitutional provision allowing national officials to use armed force if necessary to obtain state compliance. In the end, the delegates settled for a statement found in Article VI. It declares that the Constitution and all laws and treaties "made in Pursuance thereof" would be considered "the supreme Law of the Land." Commonly referred to as the **supremacy clause**, this provision was to be enforced through both national and state courts.

Allowing for Change

If constitutions are to endure, they need to include means and mechanisms that allow them to change. Students of constitutions focus on at least four ways in which constitutions can be changed: revolution, formal amendment, interpretation, and construction.

Revolution. *Change through revolutionary action* would involve tossing out the current system and replacing it with an entirely new one. Such a revolution does

ASKED & ANSWERED

ASKED: So, you want to change the Constitution?

ANSWERED: In November 2003, the Supreme Judicial Court of Massachusetts declared that, under that state's constitution, Massachusetts officials are required to offer marriage licenses for same-sex unions. On February 24, 2004, President Bush announced that he supported a constitutional amendment that would define marriage in the United States as a union only between a man and a woman. What would have to happen for such an amendment to become part of the U.S. Constitution?

Formally amending the U.S. Constitution is no easy task, as many advocates of such changes have learned over the years. In one form or another, literally thousands of amendments have been proposed in Congress, but only thirty-three have made it through the congressional part of the process and thus far only twenty-seven have actually been ratified and become part of the Constitution. Of

that number, twelve were sent out to the states by the first Congress in 1789, and ten of those made it into the Constitution as the Bill of Rights. In short, the odds against changing the Constitution through the amendment process are slim.

What is that process? Amendments can be formally proposed in two ways, either by members of Congress who submit resolutions to be considered in their respective chambers, or by two-thirds of the state legislatures who request that a constitutional convention be convened to consider their proposals (this process has never been used). In the case of a proposal made in Congress, a two-thirds vote of both houses of Congress is required for the proposed amendment to be sent to the states for ratification. Congress decides how the amendment will be ratified: by three-fourths of the legislatures or by ratifying conventions in three-fourths of the states (a method used for only one of the Constitution's

not necessarily have to involve violence, as demonstrated by the framers who met at Philadelphia in 1787. They were sent as delegates to a meeting that was to consider changes in the Articles of Confederation, but instead they took the revolutionary initiative of starting with a clean slate. There have been some — including Thomas Jefferson — who have advocated convening constitutional conventions every so often to take the "revolutionary" steps that the framers did and literally draw up a new constitutional document to reflect the issues and concerns of the era.[38] While Article V of the Constitution mentions the possibility of convening a constitutional convention "on the application of the legislatures of two thirds of the several states," such a meeting would be limited to considering proposed amendments to the current Constitution rather than writing an entirely new document.

Amendments. The framers included an elaborate *formal amendment process*, but they did not make it easy for those who wanted to change the Constitution. The procedures require action at both the state and the national levels (see Figure 2.2, p. 47, and "Asked & Answered," above).

twenty-seven amendments—the single exception was the Twenty-first Amendment, which repealed the Eighteenth) (see Figure 2.2).

Congress can also set a time limit for the amendment's ratification by the states, typically seven to ten years. For example, a proposed Equal Rights Amendment stated that "equality of rights under the law shall not be denied or abridged by the United States or by any State on account of sex." Beginning in 1923, the ERA was introduced in Congress at almost every session, but it remained tied up in the legislative process until 1972, when it finally received the approval of both the House and the Senate. As proposed, the ERA needed to be ratified by thirty-eight states by June 30, 1982,[1] to become an amendment to the Constitution. Thirty-five states had given their approval of the ERA by 1978, but supporters could not muster enough votes in three other state legislatures to pass the proposed amendment. Despite that defeat, the ERA has been reintroduced in Congress at each session since 1983.

But there are cases where no time limit is set. In the case of the Twenty-seventh Amendment, it took 203 years for it to receive the ratification of enough states to become part of the Constitution.

Originally proposed as part of the Bill of Rights in 1789, that amendment set limits on the power of sitting members of Congress to increase their own compensation. Unlike the ERA, the original proposal sent to the states had no set deadline for ratification. By the end of 1791, only six of the ten states needed for adoption at that time had voted to ratify the proposal. The proposal languished, until the effort to pass the amendment was revived in the 1980s, when it became the pet project of a political science graduate student at the University of Texas who had stumbled on the proposal. On May 7, 1992, the Michigan legislature formally ratified the amendment, giving it the support of the thirty-eight states required for adoption.

As for the role of the White House in all this, despite President Bush's announced support for the definition-of-marriage amendment, he actually would have no formal role in the process. Although some presidents in the past have added their signature to the thirty-three congressional resolutions proposing amendments for ratification, such an action was legally meaningless.

1. The deadline, originally set for 1979, was later extended for thirty-nine months by congressional action.

FIGURE 2.2

How the Constitution Can Be Amended

The framers created four methods for amending the Constitution. With the exception of the Twenty-first Amendment, all amendments so far have used the Congress/state legislature route (at top).

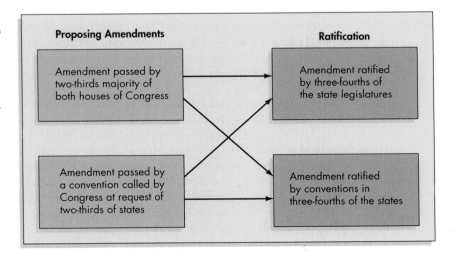

How difficult is this amendment process? Many proposed amendments are introduced in Congress but never come to a vote in either body. Some come to a vote in Congress but fail to get the required two-thirds majority in each chamber. In June 1992, for example, a constitutional amendment requiring a balanced federal budget received a majority of votes in the House but still fell nine votes short of the two-thirds required for passage. At that point, a pending vote on the amendment scheduled for the Senate was withdrawn, but supporters vowed to renew their efforts the next year. In 1993, another balanced-budget amendment was introduced in the Senate. It too went down to defeat and so was taken off the House agenda. The proposal met similar fates in 1995 and 1997. Eventually, the economic boom of the 1990s began to generate budget surpluses, and supporters found little support for considering the amendment again. Other proposals are not adopted because they fail to get the required number of states to ratify them (see "Asked & Answered," p. 46).

The Constitution has been successfully amended seventeen times since the Bill of Rights (see Table 2.4).[39] Four amendments extend voting rights to a variety of groups: to all men, regardless of race (Fifteenth); to women (Nineteenth); to residents of Washington, D.C. (Twenty-third); and to all citizens eighteen years of age or older (Twenty-sixth). In addition, the Twenty-fourth Amendment eliminated the practice of using poll taxes to stop a citizen from voting. Another group of amendments changed some of the rules for electing officials and the period of time and conditions under which they serve in office.

The Twelfth Amendment spells out the process for electing the president and vice president. The Seventeenth Amendment calls for the direct election of senators; before its adoption, senators were elected by state legislatures. The Twentieth Amendment changes the dates for the inauguration of the president and the convening of Congress, and the Twenty-fifth clarifies the procedures for presidential succession in case of the disability, death, or resignation of the president. The Twenty-second Amendment limits the tenure of elected presidents to two full four-year terms. The Twenty-seventh Amendment prohibits a sitting Congress from giving itself a raise.

Other amendments altered the constitutional powers of government institutions. For example, the Eleventh Amendment limits the power of federal courts to hear cases involving the states (see the discussion in Chapter 3, on federalism), and the Sixteenth Amendment gives Congress the power to establish a national income tax.

The Thirteenth and Fourteenth Amendments address the rights of citizens. The Thirteenth Amendment ended slavery. The Fourteenth forbids states to deny individuals the rights guaranteed under the Constitution; these rights include due process and equal protection of the law for all. In Chapter 4, on rights and liberties, we discuss the important role that the Fourteenth Amendment has played in the development of American civil liberties and civil rights. Only two amendments have actually addressed questions of public policy explicitly. In fact, both of these focused on the same issue: the production and consumption of alcoholic beverages in the United States. In 1919 the states formally ratified the Eighteenth Amendment, prohibiting the manufacture, sale, or

TABLE 2.4

Amendments 11–27
to the Constitution

Amendment	Year Proposed by Congress	Year Adopted	What It Does
11	1794	1798	Gives states immunity from certain legal actions
12	1803	1804	Changes the selection of president and vice president through the electoral college
13	1865	1865	Abolishes slavery
14	1866	1868	Defines citizenship and citizens' rights; provides due process and equal protection of the laws
15	1869	1870	Extends the right to vote to African American males
16	1909	1913	Gives Congress power to impose an income tax
17	1912	1913	Provides for direct election of U.S. senators
18	1917	1919	Outlaws alcoholic beverages
19	1919	1920	Extends the right to vote to women
20	1932	1933	Changes the dates for the start of congressional and presidential terms
21	1933	1933	Repeals the Eighteenth Amendment
22	1947	1951	Limits presidential tenure in office
23	1960	1961	Extends the right to vote in presidential elections to residents of the District of Columbia
24	1962	1964	Prohibits the use of tax payment (poll tax) as a basis for eligibility to vote
25	1965	1967	Establishes procedures for presidential succession, for determining presidential disability, and for filling vacancy in vice presidency
26	1971	1971	Lowers the voting age to eighteen
27	1989	1992	Limits Congress's ability to change its own compensation

transportation of alcoholic beverages in the United States. In 1933, however, the Twenty-first Amendment repealed that prohibition.

Interpretations and Constructions. While making the formal amendment process difficult, the framers left the door open to changes that might occur by other means.[40] As a document built through many compromises, the Constitution has provisions that leave a great deal of room for elaboration.[41] One of the framers, Alexander Hamilton, stated that a constitution "cannot possibly calculate" the effects of changing conditions and must therefore "consist only of general provisions."[42] Giving meaning to those general provisions can be accomplished in two ways other than through amending or replacing the document: through constitutional interpretation and constitutional construction.[43]

Constitutional interpretation involves attempts to discover the meaning of the words used in the different provisions. Consider the phrase "necessary and proper" found in Article I, Section 8. The meaning of that phrase was subject to controversy even among the framers once they took office. As George Washington's secretary of the treasury, Alexander Hamilton interpreted those words broadly (as an "elastic clause") and pushed for the establishment of the national bank that became so controversial during the early history of the United States. Clearly the words can be read differently—for example, they can be read as stating that the national government could do only what was absolutely necessary and proper to carry out its functions and no more. As it turned out, in the case of *McCulloch v. Maryland*, discussed earlier in this chapter, Hamilton's more liberal interpretation was upheld by the Supreme Court.

Or consider the various interpretations that can be given to the term *commerce*, which is also found in Article I, Section 8: "The Congress shall have the power . . . To regulate commerce with foreign nations, and among the several states, and with the Indian tribes." Early in our constitutional history, the term *commerce* was strictly defined to mean real goods and services crossing real borders. That narrow view limited the authority of Congress to pass laws regulating such things as the manufacture or quality of goods and services produced within states. Thus, even though there was growing public support during the late 1800s and early 1900s for federal laws regarding child labor or the quality of agricultural production, Congress could do nothing. However, as the courts began to define commerce more broadly, the arena for national government actions broadened considerably. This was most clearly demonstrated by passage of the 1964 Civil Rights Act, which included provisions that prohibited racial discrimination in all "public accommodations" such as restaurants and hotels. What made that landmark legislation possible was a broad interpretation of the term *commerce* so that it applied to any product or activity that was involved in the flow of commerce across state lines. Thus, the fact that a Heinz Ketchup bottle manufactured in Pennsylvania sat on the table of an Alabama diner meant that the owners of that diner could not refuse to serve anyone on the basis of race—a blow to the segregationist behavior that was prevalent in the South in those days (see the discussion of rights and liberties in Chapter 4).

Constitutional construction involves actions taken by public officials to fill in the institutional "blank spaces" left by the Constitution. For example, the term *executive privilege* is applied to a president's assumed right to refuse to provide Congress with information that the White House claims the legislators have no right to see. This privilege was first claimed by George Washington, who refused a request to provide the House of Representatives with information about a controversial treaty negotiation. Washington noted that only the Senate had a right to request that information, since it was the Senate alone—and not the

Constitutional interpretation A process of constitutional change that involves attempts to discover the meaning of the words used in the different provisions of the Constitution as they might apply to specific situations.

Constitutional construction A form of constitutional change that occurs as public officials fill in the institutional "blank spaces" left by the Constitution.

House — that played a role in treaty ratification. When the Senate asked for the relevant document, Washington complied. Although not provided for in the Constitution, executive privilege is regarded as a constitutionally protected right of the presidency.

There are many other constructions that play an important role in our constitutional system, from judicial review and the creation of congressional committees to the creation of the U.S. Postal Service and the opening prayer at each daily session of the U.S. House of Representatives. Some of these emerge from custom and practice over time, while others are the result of congressional action or executive orders. The fact that they have been in place for a long time does not keep them from being controversial, however. In 2002, for example, the comptroller general of the United States, an appointee of the U.S. Congress (see Chapter 10, on Congress), filed suit in federal court to obtain access to documents regarding energy policy discussions at the White House that President George W. Bush claimed were covered by executive privilege.

What the Framers Accomplished

Critical Thinking

What is the most effective way to bring about constitutional change?

There is little controversy over the assertion that the framers fulfilled their obligations as constitution makers. They provided a foundation for the American constitutional system through the establishment of "We the People" as a source of constitutional legitimacy, and they put into place the basic structures necessary to make, enforce, and adjudicate laws. Just as important, they established an elaborate system of powers that distributed the functions of governing among different branches and levels of government, while addressing the need to limit those powers or their abusive exercise. Moreover, they allowed for both formal and nonformal (e.g., through constitutional interpretation and construction) means of bringing about constitutional changes that gave the system a chance of surviving over the long haul.

But after all that, what did they actually accomplish? Did they deal with the basic issues of the day, such as slavery or the need for national economic development? Most historians agree that the compromises on slavery at the convention did little more than put off the question for several decades. The answers were eventually worked out on the battlefields of the Civil War. As for national economic development, most would say that the framers accomplished a great deal by providing Alexander Hamilton and others the constitutional authority that they needed if they were to address economic concerns at the national level.

More important is the question of whether the framers succeeded in establishing a constitutional system that would survive over time. Initially, this question took the form of asking whether the framers had built government machinery that would operate effectively in the relatively homogeneous and stable environment that characterized pre–Civil War America. Eventually, the question became whether the framers' handiwork would prove to be adaptable to the tumult and demands that characterized the industrialized and urbanized America that emerged in the late 1800s. As noted earlier, the myth of the living constitution was part of the response to that concern.

Those who adhere to the myth of the living constitution credit the framers with creating more than just the machinery of government. In their view, the framers also created a constitutional system that is endowed with the capacity to withstand all kinds of adverse conditions and challenges, including changing technologies, public values, and mores. To adherents of this myth, the Constitution does more than allow for change; it thrives on it, becoming stronger and more effective in dealing with modern problems as time goes on.

Copyright A constitutionally sanctioned legal right to protection of creative works afforded under law.

For example, consider the question of **copyright** in the Internet age. Copyright is the legal protection given to published and unpublished literary, scientific, and artistic works. The first copyright laws were written in England in the early 1700s, and the U.S. Constitution gives the Congress power over copyright protection in Article I, Section 8. Originally applied to books, copyright now extends to creative works that are fixed in a tangible or material form — that is, if you can see it, hear it, and/or touch it, it may be protected. While the specifics vary, a copyright is now valid from the date of a work's creation until seventy years after the death of the copyright holder. Under current law, if you wish to reproduce or show the copyrighted work you must seek permission from the copyright holder. There are rules, however, that allow for "fair use" of the works — for example, you may legally quote a single sentence from a book for your research paper without seeking the permission from that work's copyright holder. As long as you give credit to the author you do not have to seek explicit permission.

But what happens in the age of the Internet when you can access a copyrighted work just by hitting your computer's search button? There is nothing in the Constitution about the World Wide Web or a Google search, so the question arises about whether copyright law applies to this modern technology. The courts have addressed this in a number of cases, and they have used the approach of the "living Constitution" to do so. In one case, a photographer sued to assert his copyright over "thumbnail" images that were showing up in a search engine. A U.S. circuit court ruled in 2002 that the use of the image in the search process was "fair use" (*Kelly v. Arriba Soft Corporation*). For the advocates of the "living Constitution" perspective, a more adaptable view of the Constitution and its laws is critical in an age when technologies and values are constantly changing.

But there are those who would argue otherwise. Some see today's constitutional system as too adaptable and too flexible. They argue that we have paid too great a price for the changes brought about through the "living constitution" approach. They argue that the value of the framers' Constitution lies not in its capacity to adapt, but in its ability to provide a firm foundation upon which problems can be solved and controversies can be resolved. "The Constitution that I interpret and apply is not living but dead," states Supreme Court Justice Antonin Scalia, "or—as I prefer to call it—enduring." The Constitution "means today not what current society and much less the Court thinks it ought to mean, but what it meant when it was adopted."[44] This can be considered the *myth of the timeless and perfect Constitution.*

Still others look at the so-called living constitution and claim that it has not really adapted well to the demands of modern times. For them, the framers' Constitution reflects the antidemocratic biases and fears of its authors, and was established to limit change rather than promote adaptation to changing conditions.[45] From this perspective, the Constitution is a political document that has been used to promote the interests of those in power, and it is only through political movements that relevant constitutional changes can be made.[46] (See the section "Applying the Principles" later in this chapter for more on these interpretations of the Constitution's role in modern government.)

The Principles of American Constitutionalism

FOCUS QUESTION WHAT ARE THE MAJOR PRINCIPLES OF AMERICAN CONSTITUTIONALISM?

If there is a point of agreement among these three views of the Constitution, it is that over the years the framers' work has been associated with several basic principles that are central to any understanding of the American constitutional system: rule of law, republicanism, separation of powers, checks and balances, and national supremacy.

The Rule of Law

Rule of law The principle that there is a standard of impartiality, fairness, and equality against which all government actions can be evaluated. More narrowly, the concept that no individual stands above the law and that rulers, like those they rule, are answerable to the law.

Although the words **rule of law** are never used in the Constitution, this idea is one of the most important legacies of the framers. As a general concept, the rule of law has its roots deep in Western civilization, but it emerged in its modern form in Europe during the 1600s. According to the rule-of-law concept, there exists "a body of rules and procedures governing human and governmental behavior that have an autonomy and logic of their own." Under such rules and procedures, government and public officials are bound by standards of fairness, impartiality, and equality before the law.[47]

The rule-of-law principle is found in a number of constitutional provisions and implies that those provisions limit the powers of both national and state governments. For example, in Article IV of the Constitution, the framers included a provision that the "Citizens of each State shall be entitled to the Privileges and Immunities of Citizens in the several states." The privileges and immunities clause was intended to prevent any state from using its legal powers to discriminate against out-of-staters. Similarly, states are prohibited from passing any "Law impairing the Obligation of Contracts," thus preventing any governing group from arbitrarily voiding earlier agreements. That last provision was especially important to those among the framers who feared the passage of debtor-relief laws. The Bill of Rights added strength to the rule-of-law principle through the Fifth Amendment by requiring "due process of law" and "just compensation" whenever government initiates adverse actions against a citizen. The "equal protection of the laws" clause in the Fourteenth Amendment is still further evidence of how important this principle has been throughout our history.[48]

Another way of thinking about the rule-of-law principle is that in American government, the rulers, like those they rule, are answerable to the law. No individual stands above the law, regardless of that person's background or the office that he or she holds. Just as there are laws that address the behavior of general citizens, so there are laws that focus on the behavior of public officials. Those laws generally set limits on the powers of these officials or prescribe the procedures they must use in carrying out their duties. Under the rule-of-law principle, those limits and prescriptions must be adhered to if the American constitutional system is to function properly.

How important is this constitutional principle? The rule of law has its greatest impact on the day-to-day operations of American government. Almost every action that government agencies undertake, from the routine task of issuing monthly social security checks to dramatic efforts to help the survivors of earthquakes and other disasters, is carefully designed to meet the requirements of due process of law and other constitutional standards that are the foundation of the rule of law. Violations of those procedures or standards are likely to lead to legal challenges. In fact, both state and federal courts are constantly hearing criminal cases and civil lawsuits in which possible violations of the rule of law are at issue.[49]

No one is exempt from the rule-of-law principle. The most powerful political officials have had to bend to its force. In August 1974, for example, President Richard M. Nixon resigned in the face of charges that he took part in a criminal cover-up of White House involvement in a break-in at the Democratic party's national headquarters at the Watergate office complex in Washington, D.C. Although Nixon and many of his supporters perceived the Watergate cover-up as a relatively minor offense, the president's attempt to circumvent the law resulted in enough political pressure to bring about the first presidential resignation in American history. Nixon and others learned that no public official, not even the president, stands above the law. This lesson in the rule-of-law principle was reinforced twenty-five years later when President Bill Clinton was impeached by the House and tried in the Senate on charges that he had committed the crime of perjury (see the discussion of impeachment later in this chapter).

Republicanism

Republicanism A doctrine of government in which decisions are made by elected or appointed officials who are answerable to the people, not directly by the people themselves.

Federalist Papers A series of editorials written by James Madison, Alexander Hamilton, and John Jay in 1788 to support the ratification of the Constitution in New York State. Now regarded as a major source of information on what the framers were thinking when they wrote the Constitution.

Despite the phrase "We the People," the Constitution's framers had questions about the ability of the American people to rule themselves directly. In turning to **republicanism**, the framers created a government in which decisions are made by elected or appointed officials who are ultimately answerable to the people. The framers opposed a direct democracy because they distrusted human nature and the capacity of ordinary citizens to govern themselves.

We know something about the framers' views on democracy thanks to documents such as the ***Federalist Papers***, a series of editorials that James Madison, Alexander Hamilton, and John Jay wrote in 1788 in support of ratification of the Constitution. In "Federalist No. 10" (which is reprinted in the Appendix), for instance, Madison argued that democracies "have ever been spectacles of turbulence and contention; have ever been found incompatible with personal security, or the rights of property; and have ever been as short in their lives, as they have been violent in their deaths."

What did the framers see in republicanism that they did not see in direct democracy? Again we turn to "Federalist No. 10," where Madison argued that the problems of government can be traced to the "mischiefs of faction." He defined a faction as a group that puts its shared interests ahead of the rights of others or the interests of the community as a whole. These self-serving factions can be small or large; they can even include a majority of the people. According to Madison, all factions pose a threat to the general well-being of society. Because the causes of faction are basic to human nature, eliminating them is impossible. Thus, if any government is to serve the general interest of the people, it must be designed so that the potentially destructive power of factions can be eliminated or controlled.

Critical Thinking

Is the U.S. constitutional system democratic enough? If not, what changes should be considered to make it more democratic?

Madison and the framers favored a republican form of government, in which the people had some voice, but that voice was filtered through their representatives. The community was to be governed "by persons holding their offices . . . for a limited time or during good behavior." And although all officials would be answerable to the people, some would be more insulated from public pressure than others. Members of the House of Representatives were to have the most exposure: They alone would be elected directly by the American voters, and they would have comparatively brief terms, two years. Senators and the president were assigned longer terms, and, under the original provisions of the Constitution, the people did not elect them directly. Instead, state legislators selected senators, and the electoral college, with members selected by the states, chose the president. These methods were later changed by constitutional amendments and by the action of state legislatures. Supreme Court judges received additional protection from the whims of constantly changing public opinion: They were given lifetime appointments and could be removed only through the lengthy and difficult process called impeachment (see the discussion later in this chapter).

Although the framers felt impelled to take these precautions, they never lost sight of the basic principle of republicanism: that the ultimate responsibility of government officials is to the American public.

Separation of Powers

Separation of powers
The division of the powers to make, execute, and judge the law among the three branches of American government: Congress, the presidency, and the courts. This principle was adopted by the framers to prevent tyranny and factionalism in the government.

The principle of the **separation of powers** is also linked to the effort to control factions. By splitting governmental authority among several branches of government and giving each an area of primary responsibility, the framers sought to minimize the possibility that one faction could gain control. "The accumulation of all powers, legislative, executive, and judiciary, in the same hands," states Madison in "Federalist No. 51" (see the Appendix), "may justly be pronounced the very definition of tyranny." Thus, to help avoid tyranny, the power to make, to execute, and to judge the law was divided among the three branches: Congress, the presidency, and the courts.

This principle was an important one for the framers, who debated for many hours about the design of the national government. The idea was to distribute powers among the three branches not in order to increase the efficiency of the government, but to prevent efficiency, which they regarded as potentially dangerous.[50] Each branch was to be independent of the others when exercising its governmental authority. In this way, the American public would be protected against the tyranny that Madison and others so feared.

The framers reinforced this principle in several ways beyond just giving each institution a distinct role in government. The Constitution makes certain that those holding a position in one branch will not serve in either of the others at the same time. Over the years, this prohibition has been both tightened and loosened in practice. During the 1960s, for example, Supreme Court Associate Justice Abe Fortas withdrew from his nomination to be chief justice after it was revealed that he had provided advice to his old friend Lyndon Johnson and that he had sat in on political meetings at the Johnson White House.[51] At the same time, members of Congress have been allowed to serve as reserve officers in the U.S. military—a situation that places them under the command of the president while they are in uniform.[52]

The separation of powers was also reinforced by the framers through the different constituencies and term lengths assigned to the various branches of the national government. Members of the House of Representatives, for example, are directly elected by the eligible voters of their respective districts every two years. U.S. senators, on the other hand, were originally selected by the legislatures of their states for six-year terms, implying strongly that they represented the interests of the state governments that sent them to Washington. The design of the electoral college that was to select the president (see the discussion earlier in this chapter and that in Chapter 7, on campaigns and elections) was intended to guarantee that the winner would regard the entire nation as his or her constituency during a four-year term in office. Along with the lifetime appointment, the elaborate process set up for naming federal court judges — nomination by the president and confirmation by the Senate — was intended to guarantee that those positions were filled by people who were more accountable to the law than to shifting political moods.

Checks and Balances

Checks and balances
The principle that lets the executive, legislative, and judicial branches share some responsibilities and gives each branch some control over the others' activities. The major support for checks and balances comes from the Constitution's distribution of shared powers.
Veto The president's power to reject legislation passed by Congress. Vetoes can be overruled by a two-thirds vote of both chambers of Congress.
Signing statements Comments and clarifications that presidents attach to congressional acts when they sign them into law. In recent years controversy has surrounded the presidential use of these as directives to agencies about how the law is to be interpreted and implemented.
Congressional authorization The power of Congress to provide the president with the right to carry out legislated policies.

While separation of powers provides independent roles for Congress, the presidency, and the courts, the principle of **checks and balances** forces them to work together. By giving each institution the capability of counterbalancing the authority of the other branches, the Constitution makes these institutions interdependent.

The key element in the system of checks and balances is the distribution of shared powers among the three branches of government. Each branch depends on the others to accomplish its objectives, but each also acts as a counterweight to the others (see Figure 2.3). The president's power to **veto**, or reject, legislation checks the legislative actions of Congress. The veto, in turn, can be overridden by a two-thirds vote of both chambers of Congress.

While the veto can be a powerful presidential tool, some have complained that it is of limited value because it leaves the president with no alternative but to either sign or veto an entire bill. The president has no option for dealing with a specific provision of a bill that he finds troublesome. Many state constitutions give their governors "line-item veto" power, which permits them to strike a particular clause of a bill that comes before them. In 1995, Congress passed a limited version of a presidential line-item veto, but in June 1998 the U.S. Supreme Court declared the act unconstitutional. Alternatively, presidents have used **"signing statements"** to deal with the limits of the veto. Traditionally, presidents issued statements when signing a bill into law to clarify legal or administrative issues. Since the early 1980s, however, these statements have been also been viewed as the basis for presidential challenges to specific provisions of congressional acts. By the end of 2006, for example, George W. Bush had used signing statements to issue more than 600 such challenges that acted as directives to members of his administration about how to implement the law.

Congress can restrict presidential power in a variety of other ways. Beyond the powers granted to the president in the Constitution, presidents must have **congressional authorization** to undertake any official course of action. In recent decades, Congress has often allowed the White House considerable flexibility in many areas, especially in the foreign policy field (see Chapter 15, on foreign and defense policy). At times, however, Congress may pass laws that place narrow limits on presidential authority.

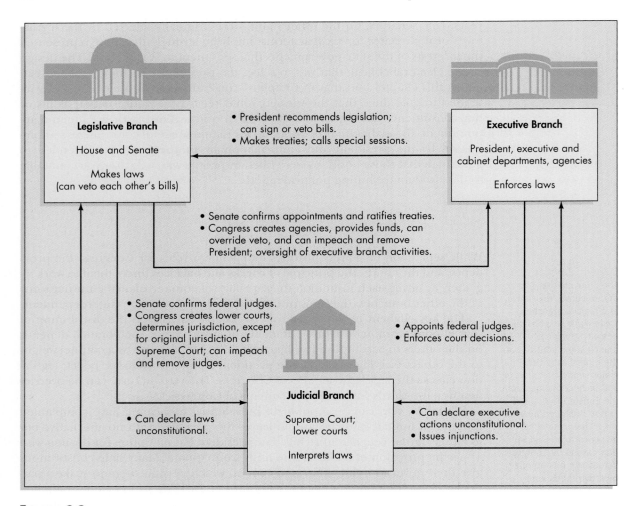

FIGURE 2.3

Separation of Powers and Checks and Balances

Under separation of powers, governmental authority is divided among the three branches: Congress exercises the power to make laws, the president exercises the power to execute laws, and the courts have the power to judge disputes arising under the laws. A system of checks and balances provides each branch with a means to counterbalance the authority of the other two, thus making the three branches interdependent.

Confirmation The power of the U.S. Senate to approve or disapprove a presidential nominee for an executive or judicial post.

    The Senate may also check the president's power by using its right to confirm or reject presidential nominees for judicial and executive positions. Although the Senate rarely says no during these **confirmation** procedures, many such nominations have been withdrawn (or have never been submitted) because they were unlikely to get the necessary votes. The Senate also has the authority to

Treaty ratification The power of the U.S. Senate to approve or disapprove formal treaties negotiated by the president on behalf of the nation.

Appropriation of funds The actions taken by Congress to authorize the spending of funds.

Impeachment A formal charge of misconduct brought against a federal public official by the House of Representatives. If found guilty of the charge by the Senate, the official is removed from office.

Critical Thinking

Is impeachment an effective check on presidential power?

Judicial review The power of the courts to declare acts of Congress to be in conflict with the Constitution. This power makes the courts part of the system of checks and balances.

approve or disapprove treaties through its **treaty ratification** powers (see Chapter 15, on foreign and defense policy).

The control of the public sector's purse strings by Congress is another powerful check on presidential power. Although the president can recommend a budget for Congress to consider, the actual **appropriation of funds** is in the hands of the House and Senate.

The ultimate restraint on presidential (and also judicial) authority, however, resides in the power of Congress to remove a president or other public official from office. **Impeachment** is based on Article II, Section 4, of the Constitution, which holds that "The President, Vice President and all civil Officers of the United States, shall be removed from Office on Impeachment for, and Conviction of, Treason, Bribery, or other high Crimes and Misdemeanors." Such removals involve two steps. First, the House of Representatives votes articles of impeachment, or formal charges, against the official. Once impeached, the official is tried by the U.S. Senate. If found guilty by a vote of the Senate, the official is removed from his or her position.

Charges of impeachment have been considered by the House against more than sixty officials, including nine presidents.[53] Of those more than sixty instances, only seventeen have resulted in the House voting articles of impeachments that led to Senate trials. Most impeachments have been against sitting judges (twelve), and to date seven of these judges have been removed.[54] Only two of the trials have involved presidents.[55] In an 1868 trial, the Senate failed to convict President Andrew Johnson by just one vote. In the 1999 Senate trial of President Bill Clinton, a sharply divided Senate failed by at least twelve votes to convict the president, thus ending a crisis that began when the House voted to impeach Clinton on December 19, 1998.

The most significant check that the courts have is found in their power of **judicial review**, by which they can declare acts of Congress to be in conflict with the Constitution. While not explicitly provided for in the Constitution, the power of judicial review was established in the case of *Marbury v. Madison* (1803) (see the discussion of this concept in Chapter 13, on courts, judges, and the law). Because they can hear lawsuits challenging the actions of public officials, the courts also have an influence on the behavior of officials from the executive branch. At the same time, the president's power to appoint federal judges with the advice and consent of the Senate gives the White House some power over the courts. The power of Congress over the courts derives in part from its constitutional authority to create or abolish any court other than the Supreme Court. Congress can also impeach and remove judges and has recently done so in several cases.

The principle of checks and balances is strengthened by the different methods of selecting officials, which the framers believed would ensure that the different branches represented different public perspectives. Variations in terms of office were intended to add a further check. For example, senators, responding from the perspective of their six-year terms in office, were expected to act in a more measured and conservative way than their peers in the House, who had only two-year terms.

The Clinton Impeachment Trial
With Chief Justice Rehnquist presiding, the U.S. Senate conducted an impeachment trial of President Clinton in 1999.

In setting up the elaborate system of checks and balances, the framers pitted the three branches of government against one another. This has resulted in a slow and ponderous system that often frustrates officials who are trying to deal quickly with critical issues. Too rapid decision making was what the framers feared, however. More often than many of us like, the system works the way they planned it to — deliberately and with care.

National Supremacy

Earlier we pointed out that the U.S. Constitution provides for a federal system in which national and state governments divide the authority of American government. Such a complex arrangement can work only if there is some principle that helps government officials settle fundamental disagreements among the different levels of government. If such a principle did not exist, then "the authority of the whole society" would be "everywhere subordinate to the authority of the parts." That, argued Madison, would have created a "monster" in which the head was under the control of its member parts.[56]

National supremacy
The principle — stated in Article VI, the "supremacy clause" — that makes the Constitution and those laws and treaties passed under it the "supreme law of the land."

In the American constitutional system, that principle is **national supremacy**. As noted earlier in this chapter, the supremacy clause of Article VI of the Constitution makes the Constitution and those laws and treaties passed under it the "supreme Law of the Land." As you will see in Chapter 3, on federalism and intergovernmental relations, that principle has been a central factor in the evolution of the American federal system. It is impossible to understand the operations of American government today without grasping the meaning of federalism and the role of the national supremacy principle in American government.

	The Living Constitution	The Enduring Constitution	The Political Constitution
Views principles as:	Means for adapting to social, political, and economic change.	Fundamental precepts derived from the Framers to be applied to issues.	Rules to be used or changed.

FIGURE 2.4

Three Views of the Constitution

The question of how to apply the basic principles found in the U.S. Constitution has been subject to debate among public officials and scholars.

Originalism An approach to interpreting the Constitution that seeks to rely on the words of the framers.

Textualism An approach to interpreting the Constitution that relies on a literal, "plain words" reading of the document.

Applying the Principles

The role that these basic principles play in the American constitutional system is subject to much debate (see Figure 2.4). For those who rely on the myth of the living constitution, each of these principles is viewed as a means or mechanism through which government is able to deal with ever-changing challenges. During the 1950s and 1960s, for example, policies rooted in the principles of national supremacy and the rule of law were relied upon in the fight to end state government–supported segregation in many southern states, and during the Watergate scandals of the mid-1970s, the system of checks and balances (involving congressional investigations and judicial proceedings) were put to use as a means for thwarting the abuse of presidential authority.

Alternatively, those opposed to the living constitution perspective can also rely on these constitutional principles. Justice Scalia and others who regard the Constitution as enduring (they can be said to operate under the *myth of an enduring constitution*) would see these principles as ends rather than means. For this group, constitutionalism involves acting according to the meaning of these principles as they were developed by the framers, treating them as fundamental precepts to be applied to today's problems. Among lawyers, adherents to this view are said to follow one of two legal philosophies. The first is usually labeled **originalism**, to reflect reliance on the original understanding of the framers when they wrote the Constitution. Originalists, for example, would argue that to the framers, the idea of national supremacy did not mean that the national government could do whatever it wanted in areas that were traditionally left to the states, for example, setting education standards, speed limits, and so on. Instead, originalists would focus on how the framers understood the powers of the state and national governments and thus shape their policies accordingly.

Alternatively, other jurists associated with the "enduring Constitution" view adhere to a position labeled **textualism**. According to this approach, the meaning of the Constitution should be derived literally from a "plain reading" of the words used in the document. One of the most outspoken advocates of this approach was Supreme Court Justice Hugo Black who, when ask to explain his position on First Amendment rights, would read aloud from his copy of the Constitution ("*Congress shall make no law . . .*") and note that "No law means no law!" While this position led to Black's association with the "rights revolution" of the Warren Court (through 1950 and 1960s), it also explains his adamant opposition to the

Critical Thinking

How closely should we adhere to the words of the framers when applying constitutional principles to today's problems?

idea that the Constitution included a "right to privacy"—a point shared today by Justice Scalia.

The third perspective, which regards the Constitution as a political document, views the principles as if they were a set of fundamental "rules" under which government operates. Among today's Supreme Court justices, Justice Stephen Breyer has explicitly taken this position by adhering to a standard of interpretation that favors what he terms "active liberty." For him, taken as a whole, the Constitution establishes a standard for judicial interpretation that requires deference to the "right of the majority to embody their opinion in law." In making decisions, judges should reflect an attitude that favors public will. For example, Breyer would find Hugo Black's literal stand that Congress can make "no law" restricting free speech to be harmful to the right of the public to regulate the right of tobacco companies to market cigarettes to minors. The liberty-protecting stand of textualists like Black, Breyer argues, must be balanced against the right of the public to make "substantive economic (or social) regulatory choices."[57]

It is these differences in perspective among Supreme Court justices that have made debates over the appointment of new members to the High Court so politically sensitive in recent decades (see Chapter 13, on the judiciary). Between Justice Breyer's appointment in 1994 and the summer of 2005, no vacancy had occurred in the Court and no particular constitutional view seemed to dominate. During that period Justice Sandra Day O'Connor emerged as a pivotal "swing vote" on the Court that could determine how a particular question would be resolved. With Justice O'Connor's resignation and the death of Chief Justice Rehnquist, however, two seats opened on the Supreme Court and were filled by a new chief justice (John Roberts Jr.) and new associate justice (Samuel Alito Jr.). Both men have reputations for having views that would likely place them closer to Justice Scalia's position on constitutional issues, but it will probably take two or three Court terms to see what impact their presence will have on U.S. constitutional interpretation.

Conclusion: Living, Enduring, and Political

Americans have developed a complex relationship with our Constitution. In public opinion polls and in other forums, Americans continue to express a reverential pride in our constitutional system, and few advocate radical changes in the structure of government established by the Constitution. For most, in fact, the document represents the American people as a nation.[58] Yet in recent years that support has sometimes seemed less than overwhelming, with a relatively significant minority of about 40 percent of poll respondents favoring a major overhaul of the Constitution.[59] In one poll conducted in July 2000, a bare majority of 51 percent said that they would vote in favor of renewing the current Constitution if it were put to a vote—an increase of two percentage points from the results when the same question was asked two years earlier.[60] But despite these results and a notable ignorance of or indifference to the details of the nation's fundamental law,[61] Americans' general support for the Constitution remains very strong.

In an important sense, what many (perhaps most) Americans have developed over the years is what Sanford Levinson has called "constitutional faith"—that is, a "wholehearted attachment to the Constitution as the center of one's (and ultimately the nation's) political life."[62] As an act of faith, this attachment does not need to be justified with clear reasons linked to some benefits gained from it, nor can it be easily undermined by the expressed dissatisfactions with the inequalities and injustices that sometimes result from the constitutional exercise of authority. That is why myths play such a significant role in how we relate to the American constitutional system. Believing in a "living constitution" not only helps us understand how a document written more than two centuries ago is able to operate as well as it does today, but also allows us to have some faith in the system's ability to deal with the uncertainties of the future.

But it would also be a mistake to give in to blind faith, which is why there are powerful and credible alternatives to the myth of the living constitution. Those who see the fundamental principles of the framers as an enduring anchor believe in a Constitution that provides for sound and time-tested guidance in an era of constant turmoil and change. Their constitutional faith is not weaker; it is just based on a different myth. The same can be said of those whose constitutional faith is based on the hope that through open political deliberation, the system's rules can be used to make American government more democratic and more just in the future.

Tying It Together

FOCUS QUESTIONS RECAP

* What were the circumstances surrounding the framing of the Constitution?
* Who were the framers of the Constitution?
* What were the important traditions underlying the Constitution?
* What do the various provisions of the Constitution accomplish?
* What are the major principles of American constitutionalism?

CHAPTER SUMMARY

1. The framers of the Constitution came together to solve fundamental problems that had arisen under the Articles of Confederation.

2. The framers were mainly well educated, white males who were distinct personalities who shared a common historical and intellectual tradition.

3. The roots of the Constitution can be found in the British legal tradition, including the principles that government officials, as well as ordinary citizens, must obey the law and that there exists a higher (constitutional) standard against which laws made by legislatures can be measured. The colonial experience of self-government and the political philosophy of the Enlightenment espoused by such writers as Hobbes and Locke also helped guide the Constitution's framers.

4. The Constitution's framers accomplished a number of purposes including (a) establishing the legitimacy of the government of the United States as coming directly from the people, (b) dividing authority within the new national government among the legislative, executive, and judicial branches of government, (c) describing the delegated and implied powers of the national government while also (d) setting limits on both national and state power, and (e) specifying the rules for amending the Constitution.

5. The framers established in the Constitution the following fundamental principles of American government: the rule of law, republicanism, separation of powers, the system of checks and balances, and national supremacy.

6. From the perspective of the myth of the living constitution, those principles have been the primary means by which the framers' handiwork has been adapted to deal with the challenges of today's world. Alternatively, those principles can be regarded as enduring precepts of the framers that should be used to guide government officials in turbulent times, or as the basic rules through which the constitutional system can be made to serve the political urge for greater fairness and justice and enhanced democratic participation.

Key Terms

Articles of Confederation (26)
Feudalism (29)
Charter (29)
Magna Carta (29)
Common law (29)
Mayflower Compact (30)
Enlightenment (31)
Popular sovereignty (31)
Declaration of Independence (32)
Legitimacy (33)
Confederation (36)
Unitary system (36)
Federation (36)
Bicameral (37)
Unicameral (37)
Great Compromise (37)
Electoral college (37)
Delegated powers (39)
Concurrent powers (39)

Necessary and proper clause (39)
Implied powers (40)
Reserved powers (42)
Writ of habeas corpus (42)
Bill of attainder (43)
Ex post facto law (43)
Bill of Rights (44)
Full faith and credit (45)
Privileges and immunities (45)
Supremacy clause (45)
Constitutional interpretation (50)
Constitutional construction (50)
Copyright (52)
Rule of law (54)
Republicanism (55)
Federalist Papers (55)
Separation of powers (56)
Checks and balances (57)
Veto (57)

Net Work

Do you need to find a copy of the U.S. Constitution? The Declaration of Independence? How about the Mayflower Compact or the Magna Carta?

- Many of the key historical documents related to American government can be found at the National Archives website: **www.archives.gov/ national-archives-experience/charters/charters.html**.

- Yale University provides online access to many of the documents that preceded the American constitution: **www.yale.edu/lawweb/avalon/constpap .htm**.

- The Government Printing Office provides an on-line copy of the Constitution that is annotated with relevant Supreme Court cases and commentary: **http://www.gpoaccess.gov/constitution/browse .html**.

If you really want to get into the history of the American constitutional system, the Web offers a number of options.

- Congress established the National Constitution Center in 1988, and its website is a good starting point, not only for studying the U.S. Constitution, but also to download some interesting podcasts of events held at the Center that relate to historical and contemporary constitutional issues: **www.constitutioncenter.org**.

- An online history of the U.S. Constitution and its evolution can be found at **http://odur.let.rug.nl/ ~usa/GOV/chap1.htm**.

- Conflicts involving interpretations of the Constitution are reviewed at **www.law.umkc.edu/faculty/ projects/ftrials/conlaw/home.html**.

As an exercise, use a search engine such as Google to see how much you can find on the Internet about some recent constitutional issues. For example, you can focus on the impeachment process and its history. When President Bill Clinton was impeached in 1998 and put on trial in early 1999, dozens of websites appeared to help inform the public. Some of them have disappeared from the Web, but others remain. For example, questions about the impeachment process are answered at the American Bar Association education website: **www.abanet.org/ publiced/impeach2.html**. Can you find some other good sites that explain the impeachment process?

Another issue to explore is whether the electoral college should be changed. For general documents and background on the electoral college, see the U.S. State Department site: **http://fpc.state.gov/c9814 .htm**. For a discussion about "Presidential Elections Reform," see **http://www.fairvote.org/?page=1729**.

3

Federalism and Intergovernmental Relations

MYTH & REALITY

Do the individual states retain constitutional sovereignty?

FOCUS QUESTIONS

* How has federalism changed over the past two centuries of American constitutional development?

* Who are the major actors in the U.S. federal system, and what roles do they play in the federal system?

I n Washington, D.C., they call it the Nuclear Waste Policy Amendments Act of 1987. In Carson City, Las Vegas, and Reno, Nevada, it is called the "Screw Nevada Act."

It is legislation that all but guaranteed that Nevada would be the site of this nation's only repository for spent nuclear fuel and high-level radioactive waste. And despite a concerted fifteen-year effort to stop the process by almost all of Nevada's elected officials and political leaders from both parties, in July 2002 the U.S. Congress gave final approval to start construction of the facility at Yucca Mountain, just a hundred miles northwest of Las Vegas.

Yucca Mountain does not look like what most Americans think of as a mountain. Instead of snow-covered peaks rising majestically thousands of feet into thin air, Yucca is a 6-mile-long volcanic ridge running from north to south that reaches no higher than 1,200 feet from the desert floor, although at its crest it stands 4,950 feet above sea level. It is situated at the edge of an unpopulated area (the nearest year-round residents are 14 miles south of the site) that was used for more than 900 nuclear weapons tests during the Cold War. Under the current law, the U.S. government plans to store 77,000 tons of high-level radioactive waste and spent nuclear fuel at the site, although it is estimated that Yucca Mountain can eventually hold much more. The plan calls for storing the waste 1,000 feet below the surface for at least 10,000 years. By all estimates, the repository will be ready to receive its first shipment of nuclear waste in 2010.

The story of how the Yucca Mountain site was selected dates back to the early 1950s, when the federal government assumed control over the domestic use of atomic energy and responsibility for overseeing the disposal of radioactive

Yucca Mountain

The nation's only high-level radioactive waste dump at Yucca Mountain (near Las Vegas) is being placed there despite strong opposition from the state officials and the people of Nevada.

waste. The new Atomic Energy Commission turned to the scientific community for advice, and the result was a plan to create permanent repositories where the waste could be safely buried for thousands of years. A salt mine in Lyons, Kansas, was initially selected, but this site was eventually abandoned for technical and safety reasons. By the late 1960s and early 1970s, public concerns over health and safety issues were making it increasingly difficult to find a suitable site. Sites in thirty-six states were examined, but Americans were increasingly likely to say **"not in my backyard"** (**NIMBY**) whenever their state or region was mentioned as a possible location for a repository. By the late 1970s, finding a site was no longer merely a technical problem; it now involved politics at the state and local levels.

NIMBY ("not in my backyard") A phrase used to describe the tendency of communities to reject proposals to locate undesirable public facilities in their area

In 1982, Congress passed the Nuclear Waste Policy Act, which required the U.S. Department of Energy (DOE) to evaluate alternative sites for three national repositories that would begin receiving high-level nuclear waste in 1998. In 1983, the DOE focused on nine potential sites, but in the face of political pressures and criticism, its preliminary recommendations were withdrawn and the DOE began a more deliberative assessment of possible sites. By the time the DOE issued its next report, in 1986, the list for the first waste facility had been pared down to five potential sites, all in the West, and then the list was reduced again to three "finalists" in Texas (Deaf Smith County), Washington State (Hanford), and Nevada (Yucca Mountain). Faced with a budget crisis in 1987, Congress decided that it would be too costly to conduct studies of all three sites, and so it changed the process by passing the Nuclear Waste Policy Amendments Act (NWPAA).

By this point the process was definitely more political than technical, and politically Nevada was in the least powerful position of the three states involved since key members of the congressional leadership came from Texas and Washington. Not surprisingly, the DOE was directed to study only the Yucca Mountain site. Under provisions of the NWPAA, if at any point in the assessment this site was found to be unsuitable, the DOE was to stop its study, restore the area to its preassessment condition, and come back to Congress for guidance. However, if the DOE found the Nevada site to be suitable, the secretary of energy would issue a recommendation to the president, who would either approve or disapprove it. Once presidential approval was obtained, construction could start unless Nevada's governor objected; if he did, then both houses of Congress would have to approve the site selection in order for the project to proceed.[1]

There were other provisions in the bill that were intended to make it easier for Nevadans to accept what was being imposed on them, but none of those "sweeteners" made Nevadans any happier with the decision. Public opinion in the state was overwhelmingly against the decision from the outset,[2] and the state legislature immediately passed resolutions expressing its opposition and legislation outlawing the siting of any such nuclear waste facility in the state of Nevada. In addition, state officials used the money granted to it under the 1987 act (which had been granted for the purpose of overseeing and facilitating the project) to establish an "oversight" agency to lead a coordinated fight *against* the Yucca Mountain facility. In fact, from 1987 onward, Nevada took every possible opportunity to halt or slow down the project, including refusing to issue the necessary state permits to drill or make use of water rights at the site. These and other efforts were thwarted by court decisions against the state. Then, in 1996, the DOE decided to cut off funding to the state's oversight agency because the grants were being used to oppose the project. Nevada sued to overrule this decision and lost. Nevertheless, joined by environmental groups and others opposed to the repository project, Nevada's public officials kept raising issues about the safety and security of the Yucca Mountain location and made their views and concerns known at formal hearings held by the DOE in accordance with the 1987 act.

But in the end, the intent of the "Screw Nevada Act" was fulfilled. In 2002, the secretary of energy issued his recommendation to President George W. Bush, who almost immediately gave his approval, despite objections from Nevada's governor. As set forth in the law, on April 8, Governor Guinn submitted his formal notice of disapproval to Congress on behalf of the state. As expected, both houses of Congress overrode Guinn's notice, and the siting was approved on July 8.

The battle over Yucca Mountain is far from over. State officials continue to press ahead on both the legal and public relations fronts, and it remains a sensitive political issue. During the presidential election in 2004, Democratic candidate John Kerry promised to reverse the decision if he was elected. In addition, critics have challenged the credibility of various reports on the safety of the storage site.

In the process of doing battle over the Yucca Mountain project, the citizens of Nevada learned a good deal about the realities of the American constitutional system, and especially about the "truth" behind one of the system's most powerful myths: *the myth of state sovereignty.* According to the myth of state sovereignty, a fundamental and enduring characteristic of the American constitutional system is a division between the national and state governments in which each is capable of exercising some authority over certain matters under its jurisdiction. Although seemingly a very abstract idea, sovereignty was an important legal concept for the framers.

Technically, **sovereignty** is the ultimate source of authority in a constitutional system. While legislation and policy can be made by many decision makers in different constitutional systems—parliaments, congresses, presidents, prime ministers—there must always be a point of sovereignty, an authoritative source from which all formal power emanates.

Historians and legal scholars who study the 1787 Constitutional Convention note that the question of sovereignty was central to all the key compromises made by the framers, from the Great Compromise dealing with representation to the decision to rely on an electoral college to select the president.[3] They were constantly trying to deal with the question of how to establish a viable and authoritative national government while maintaining the autonomy and rights of the member states. As discussed in the previous chapter (see pp. 36–39), their solution was a hybrid structure that stood somewhere between a confederation (where all sovereign authority is retained by the member states) and a unitary system (where sovereignty is located in one central source, such as the monarch or the parliament). This mixed system was a *federation* (see the definition in

Critical Thinking

Should the citizens of Nevada be forced to host the Yucca Mountain facility?

Sovereignty The ultimate source of authority in any political system.

Chapter 2, on constitutional foundations),[4] and (as we will see in the pages that follow) for more than two centuries it has been at the heart of some of the most controversial developments in the constitutional system.

The myth of state sovereignty has been an important part of many of those controversies. Like the other myths discussed in this book, it is neither inherently true nor inherently false; rather, it has been regarded as more or less true by different interests over the decades. For the people of Nevada who oppose the Yucca Mountain project, it has been their fervent hope that state sovereignty is in fact true, and that ultimately they will be victorious in their efforts to be the ones to decide on the future of that site. For those who are convinced that Yucca Mountain is the best solution to a national problem, the idea of state sovereignty on this particular issue makes no sense. Both sides are following in a long tradition.

The Evolution of American Federalism

FOCUS QUESTION   HOW HAS FEDERALISM CHANGED OVER THE PAST TWO CENTURIES OF AMERICAN CONSTITUTIONAL DEVELOPMENT?

Critical Thinking

What did the framers have in mind when they created the federal system?

As the product of constitutional compromise among the framers, federalism had only a vague form when it was implemented in 1788. The proceedings of the convention were held behind closed doors, and the framers had agreed that no one would discuss what took place that summer in Philadelphia—a promise that most of them kept for decades. During the debates over ratification, however, many expressed their opinions about the proposed arrangement, and some did so in response to comments and questions made by opponents of the new government. And so, without a clear idea of how the attempt to mix national and state sovereignties should be worked out, the nation's new rulers engaged in an ongoing debate from the outset.

Battles Over Meaning (1790s–1860s)

At first, the debate focused on the question of which of the two levels of government should take precedence when the two were in conflict: Was the national government primary, or could states ignore the laws of Congress when they chose? Two competing answers emerged, one centered on the states and the other on the nation.[5]

Supporters of **state-centered federalism** wanted to allow the national government only limited powers. Led by Thomas Jefferson and James Madison, they argued that states could overrule national laws if they believed that those laws violated provisions of the U.S. Constitution.[6]

Proponents of **nation-centered federalism** argued that the authority of the national government goes beyond the responsibilities listed in Article I, Section 8,

State-centered federalism The view that the Constitution allowed the national government only limited powers and that the states could overrule national laws if they determined that those laws were in violation of the Constitution.

Nation-centered federalism The view that the authority of the national government goes beyond the responsibilities listed in Article I, Section 8, of the Constitution; it is based on the necessary and proper clause and the principle of national supremacy.

Interstate commerce Trade across state lines; in contrast to intrastate (within state boundaries) trade and foreign trade.

Police powers The powers of state governments over the regulation of behavior within their borders. These police powers were used to justify state jurisdiction over economic matters.

of the Constitution. They contended that the necessary and proper clause and the principle of national supremacy give the national government additional powers to act. Alexander Hamilton and, later, Daniel Webster took this position, as did Chief Justice of the Supreme Court John Marshall in *McCulloch v. Maryland* (1819) (see the discussion of that case in Chapter 2, on constitutional foundations). Five years later, in *Gibbons v. Ogden* (1824), the Supreme Court dealt another blow to the proponents of state power. It held that a New York law establishing a steamboat monopoly between New York City and New Jersey was not constitutional. Only the national government, the Court ruled, could regulate "commercial intercourse" (**interstate commerce**) between states.

The supporters of the state-centered approach did get some relief when, starting in the late 1830s, the Supreme Court made a number of rulings that established the existence of sovereign **police powers**, which a state could exercise as part of its duty "to advance the safety, happiness and prosperity of its people."[7] The existence of these police powers was used to justify state jurisdiction over economic matters.

The debate between advocates of state-centered and nation-centered federalism was also conducted on the floor of Congress. Much of it focused on the issue of slavery, and at times the heated discussions turned bitter and even violent. In one particularly notable episode in the period leading up to the Civil War, a senator from Massachusetts was beaten unconscious with a cane on the Senate floor by an angry member of the House.[8] Ultimately, the conflict over slavery was settled on the battlefields of the Civil War. Out of that bloody confrontation between the North and the South, nation-centered federalism seemed to emerge victorious. The Civil War, it seemed, made it formally possible for the national government to claim a dominant position in the federal system. In reality, however, the story was quite different. As we will see, the myth of state sovereignty was not killed by the Civil War.

From Separation to Cooperation (1860s–1920s)

Instead of domination by the national government, what developed after the Civil War was a system of dual federalism, under which the national and state governments were regarded as equal partners, i.e., as equally sovereign. Under **dual federalism**, each level of government is perceived as being responsible for distinct policy functions, and each is barred from interfering with the other's work. Thus, whereas earlier cases had established that the states could not interfere with the national government's regulation of interstate trade, post–Civil War decisions held that the national government could not interfere with the power of the states to regulate the sale or manufacture of products or services within their own borders. Starting immediately after the Civil War, the Supreme Court declared in a series of rulings that insurance, fishing, lumbering, mining, manufacturing, building, banking, and a variety of other economic activities were not subject to federal regulation, but rather could be regulated under the police powers of individual states.

Dual federalism The perspective on federalism that emerged after the Civil War. It saw the national and state governments as equal but independent partners, with each responsible for distinct policy functions and each barred from interfering with the other's work.

Brooks Beating Sumner in Senate
Prior to the Civil War, disputes over federalism and slavery were taken quite seriously. Senator Charles Sumner, an ardent abolitionist from Massachusetts, was nearly caned to death on the Senate floor by Preston Brooks, a member of the U.S. House of Representatives from South Carolina. Brooks had taken exception to remarks Sumner had made about some proslavery members of Congress.

Grant-in-aid programs
Federal appropriations that are given to states and localities to fund state policies and programs. The Morrill Act (1862) was the first instance of such a program.

The most explicit statement of dual federalism was issued in 1871, when the Court held that within the borders of each state there are "two governments, restricted in their sphere of action, but independent of each other, and supreme within their respective spheres." Neither, the Court said, can intrude on or interfere with the other's actions.[9] Then in *Hammer v. Dagenhart* (1918), the Court declared that those powers "not expressly delegated to the National Government are reserved" to the states.[10] The Court's use of the word *expressly* was important, for it is not a term found in the Constitution; in particular, it is not found in the Tenth Amendment. In fact, when the Tenth Amendment was debated in the U.S. Congress in 1789, the inclusion of this term was voted down.[11] But the myth of state sovereignty was an important feature of the way many people were viewing federalism at the time of the *Hammer* case. Thus, the decision was an expression of dual federalism at its height.

Despite the Court's reliance on dual federalism during this period, the formal separation between the two levels of government was breaking down in the world of practical politics. The first step in this process was **grant-in-aid programs**, through which state policies and programs were partially funded or given other support. The Morrill Act (1862) gave federal land grants to states for the purpose of establishing agricultural colleges.[12] Later, cash grants helped states with agricultural experiment stations, textbook programs for the blind, marine schools, forestry programs, agricultural extension services, state soldiers' homes, vocational schools, road construction, and a variety of other projects. By 1927 these grant programs were bringing state governments $123 million in national funds annually.[13]

Toward Cooperation and Local Participation (1930s–1950s)

The Great Depression of the 1930s significantly altered the relationship between Washington and the states. Demand for public services grew. At the same time, state and local governments were in an extremely tight financial situation because tax revenues had fallen as the economy declined. The national government was expected and willing to respond. There was an explosion of new and cooperative programs in which the national and state governments shared an increasing number of functions. A new kind of relationship had emerged that recognized the interdependence of Washington and state and local governments. Called **intergovernmental relations**, or IGR, it is a system in which the various levels of government share functions, and each level is able to influence the others.

The emergence of intergovernmental relations was an important development in the history of American federalism. It meant that the formal and highly legalistic form of federalism that had previously existed was being replaced by a more flexible and informal approach to nation–state relations. Furthermore, once interactions among various levels of government were treated as IGR rather than as federalism, the door was open for greater participation by many more actors on the federalism stage. Local and regional governments and even private and community groups could now find a role to play.

Under the new system, a variety of grant-in-aid programs were offered, covering a wide range of policy concerns. The number and size of these programs grew dramatically during this period, increasing from $100 million in 1930 to $6.8 billion in 1960.[14] The emergence of intergovernmental relations was the foundation for this period of **cooperative federalism**. Conflict between Washington and the states diminished as public officials worried less about what level of government performed certain functions and more about their specific program responsibilities. State and national officials began to see each other as "allies, not as enemies."[15]

At the heart of the system of intergovernmental relations were a variety of grant-in-aid programs that financed highways, social and educational projects, and other programs. Many were **categorical, or conditional, grants-in-aid**, under which state governments received federal funding for specific purposes only if they met certain general requirements. For example, state highway departments were expected to operate in an efficient and businesslike fashion, free of corruption and undue political influence. Similar standards were applied to welfare programs. If states failed to meet those standards, federal support was withdrawn, or sometimes the program was taken over. Thus, during the Depression, Washington took charge of public assistance programs in six states where officials could not meet federal requirements. Public welfare programs in other states were closely watched to make sure that they were following federal rules.

Under other federal programs, states received **formula grants** based on population, the number of eligible persons, per capita income, or some other factor. One of the largest of these grants, the Hill-Burton program, used a formula that was heavily weighted to favor states with substantial low-income populations. By

Intergovernmental relations The style of federalism that recognizes the interdependence of Washington and state and local governments. The various levels of government share functions, and each level is able to influence the others.

Critical Thinking

How do intergovernmental relations differ from federalism?

Cooperative federalism A period of cooperation between state and national government that began during the Great Depression. The national government began to take on new responsibilities, and state and local officials accepted it as an ally, not an enemy.

Categorical, or conditional, grants-in-aid Money given to the states and localities by Congress to be used for limited purposes under specific rules.

Formula grants Grants given to states and localities on the basis of population, the number of eligible persons, per capita income, or other factors.

Project grants Grants awarded to states and localities for a specific program or plan of action.

Matching grants Programs in which the national government requires recipient governments to provide a certain percentage of the funds needed to implement the programs.

1986 more than $3 billion of Hill-Burton funds had been used to construct and modernize health-care facilities throughout the United States.

Project grants are awarded only after submission of a specific proposal for a project or plan of action. The Housing Act of 1937 was one of the earliest and largest of these programs. Under the provisions of that act, local governments could obtain funds to build public housing. By the 1960s, there were more than 4,000 such projects, with more than half a million dwelling units. In many instances, the national government required recipient governments to provide a certain percentage of the funds needed to implement the programs. Among these **matching grants** was a program that provided aid to dependent children under the Social Security Act of 1935 and one that gave states $9 for every dollar spent to build interstate highways.

Cities and other local governments also became participants in the federal system during this period. Before the 1930s, American cities were regarded as merely subdivisions of the states. Grants or other forms of support came from state capitals, not from Washington. In 1932, for instance, only the nation's capital received aid from the national government. By 1940, however, the situation had changed. That year, the national government handed out $278 million in direct grants-in-aid to local governments for a variety of public housing and public works programs. In the 1950s, the national government expanded the types of projects it would support to include slum clearance, urban renewal, and airport construction. By the start of the 1960s, local governments were receiving $592 million worth of direct grants.[16]

The Urban Focus (1960s–1970s)

Critical Thinking

Should the federal government be required to funnel all aid to local governments through the states?

The intergovernmental relations system continued to grow during the 1960s and 1970s, and by 1980 grant-in-aid programs to state and local governments had surpassed $85 billion. Starting in 1960, other notable changes also took place.[17] For example, grant systems expanded into new policy areas. The percentage of funds devoted to highways and public assistance declined, and funding for programs in the areas of education, health care, environmental protection, worker training, housing, and community development increased significantly.

In a shift in the flow of funds, a growing number of intergovernmental programs were targeted at local, rather than state, governments. President Lyndon B. Johnson's Great Society policies included dozens of new and innovative grant programs with an urban focus. For the first time, community-based programs for feeding the urban poor, training the unemployed, and educating the children of low-income families received support. One important initiative, the Model Cities program, was designed to help cities develop projects addressing a variety of economic and social problems. In 1974, many of these and related programs were consolidated under community development grants. By 1985, the national government was disbursing nearly $5 billion directly to local governments through these programs.

Until the early 1960s, Washington used federal grants simply to help states and localities perform their traditional government functions. State and local governments might be asked to modify their personnel policies or their methods of bidding for contracts, but they rarely had to take on new policy responsibilities as a requirement for receiving federal funds. In contrast, the grant programs of the 1960s and 1970s were increasingly designed to involve these governments in achieving national policy objectives. States or localities that initiated new or special programs promoting national goals received substantial grants. The Model Cities program, for example, encouraged cities to institute programs for improving the quality of life for poor and low-income groups. In other instances, Washington threatened to reduce or cut off funding to governments that failed to change their old policies or to adopt new ones that complied with national standards. It was during this period, for example, that the national government used the threat of withholding highway funds from states that did not lower their maximum speed limits to 55 miles per hour.[18]

Reforming and Devolving (1970s–1990s)

Critical Thinking

Can the national government trust states and localities to effectively implement the programs it funds through grants-in-aid?

Inevitably, the rapid spread of grant programs and their requirements led to problems. Local recipients criticized federal officials for administering programs without regard for the unique circumstances and dilemmas that they were facing. State officials complained that the national government ignored them in designing and implementing many new programs. Both state and local officials complained about the increasing number of strings attached to federal grants, especially policy mandates, which many recipient governments regarded as costly, irrelevant, and inappropriate. At the same time, members of Congress reacted impatiently to the poor coordination and cooperation in the massive intergovernmental relations system. As a result, there was almost constant pressure to reform the grant system.

Responding to pressures for an increased role for state and local officials, Washington took a number of steps designed to loosen its control over grant programs and to enhance state and local authority. During the early 1970s, for instance, the federal government provided funds to support the formation of local and regional **councils of governments**. These associations of local governments helped their member governments contend with such common problems as coordinating local applications for federal grants. In addition, President Johnson and his successor, Richard M. Nixon, reorganized the administration of the grant system, increasing the power of federal regional offices in order to ease the burdens on both state and local governments.

Councils of governments Local and regional bodies created in the early 1970s with federal funds to help solve problems such as coordinating applications for federal grants.

In two additional reform efforts, the national government introduced new funding systems designed to further reduce its control and make procedures more flexible. Most of the programs established before this time had been based on categorical, or conditional, grants, in which money given to the states and localities was to be used for limited purposes under specific rules. In the

Block grants Money given to the states by Congress that can be used in broad areas and is not limited to specific purposes, as categorical grants are. They were introduced in the mid-1960s as a means of giving states greater freedom.

General revenue sharing A small but innovative grant-in-aid program, used in the 1970s and 1980s, that had no significant conditions attached to it. State and local governments received funds according to a formula based on population and related factors.

mid-1960s, however, Congress introduced block grants. **Block grants** were a way of consolidating categorical grants in a given area so that the recipients would have greater freedom in their use of funds and so that paperwork would be reduced. By 1974, there were seven major block grants covering such areas as health, education, and other social services. These grants gave state and local officials more freedom in running their programs and freed them from some of the annoying mandates attached to categorical grants. Nevertheless, in financial terms, they represented only a small portion of the total amount of federal aid flowing to states and localities.

The other new form of federal aid was called **general revenue sharing**. This small but innovative grant-in-aid program had no significant conditions attached to it. State and local governments received funds according to a complex formula based on population and related factors. In the late 1970s, the program was modified considerably, and its funding was reduced. By 1988 it had disappeared from the intergovernmental system.

The late 1970s and early 1980s produced major changes in intergovernmental relations. Most obvious was the reduction in federal funding to states and localities through grants-in-aid. Grant money began to decline in 1979, but the most significant drops occurred during President Ronald Reagan's first years in office. It was nearly a decade before federal aid returned to its pre–Reagan administration levels.[19]

In addition to reducing federal funding, Reagan also attempted a major overhaul of the intergovernmental system. He formally proposed to Congress that many government functions be returned to the states. In exchange, the national government would assume most public welfare programs. When that strategy failed, Reagan administration officials tried to bring about changes by adjusting the way in which grant-in-aid programs were administered. These efforts had a major impact on the federal system.[20]

At the same time, Congress was consolidating more categorical programs into broad block grant programs. During the first half of the 1980s, Congress converted dozens of categorical programs into about a dozen block grants. Despite these efforts, however, hundreds of categorical grant programs remained on the books. By 1988 — the last year of the Reagan administration — the national government was spending an estimated $116 billion on grants-in-aid to states and localities.

There is little dispute, however, that the Reagan administration significantly changed the direction of intergovernmental relations, at least for the short term. Although the absolute amount of federal dollars going for grant-in-aid programs increased through most of the 1980s (from $91.3 billion in fiscal year [FY] 1980 to $121.9 billion in FY 1989), the total amount in constant-dollar terms (adjusted for inflation) declined during most of that period, actually dropping from $168.5 billion in FY 1980 to $148.1 billion in FY 1989 (in 1996 dollars). Only after Reagan left office did grant expenditures increase in both absolute and constant terms.[21]

More important, during this period states and localities were becoming less dependent on federal dollars for carrying out their work. For example, in 1978,

**Denver
International
Airport**

**Denver
International
Airport**
During the 1950s and
1960s, many cities
built major airports
with the help of large
grants provided by the
federal government.
However, the contro-
versial and expensive
Denver International
Airport, opened in
1995 after much delay,
was the first major fa-
cility to be built since
the early 1970s.

26.5 cents of every dollar spent by state and local governments came from the national government. By 1990, however, only 17.9 cents of every dollar spent by states and localities could be linked to a federal grant-in-aid. As one observer put it, the Reagan years represented the years of "fend-for-yourself" federalism.[22]

President George H. W. Bush launched no major initiatives in the area of intergovernmental relations. Nevertheless, two factors emerged that gave cause for concern. First, the combination of cutbacks in federal funding and an extended economic recession created fiscal crises in states and localities throughout the nation. Because many states and localities were required to have balanced budgets, the fiscal crises of the early 1990s had an immediate impact and could not be resolved through government borrowing. States from Connecticut to California were forced to take the unpopular steps of cutting budgets and/or raising taxes. However, the flow of federal grant-in-aid money to states and localities picked up once again, and by the time Bush left office the amount had increased from $121 billion in fiscal year 1989 to $193 billion in FY 1993.

A second factor shaping intergovernmental relations during the early 1990s was the growing number of policy pressures and federally mandated costs that states and localities had to shoulder. The policy pressures came primarily from the White House as President George H. W. Bush made education and a war on drugs two of his top priorities. Although Bush called for major reforms and initiatives in these specific areas, he made no request for additional federal funding for the states and localities that would have to carry out many of the policy changes he was suggesting. Thus, while he held conferences and made speeches on the need for local schools to engage in costly educational reforms, President

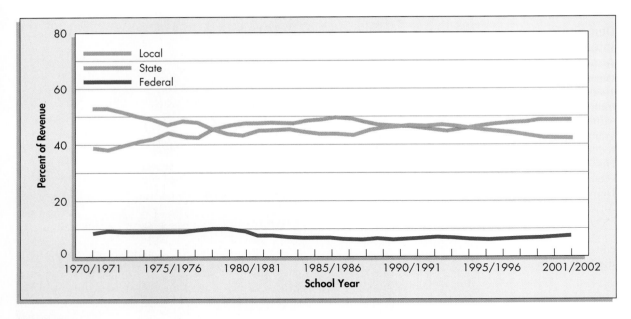

FIGURE 3.1

Sources of Revenue for Public Elementary and Secondary Schools: 1970–1971 to 2001–2002

Source: U.S. Department of Education, National Center for Education Statistics, *Revenues and Expenditures for Public Elementary and Secondary Education*, 1970–1971 through 1986–1987; and the NCES Common Core of Data (CDD), "National Public Education Financial Survey," 1987–1988 through 2001–2002.

Unfunded mandates
Required actions imposed on lower-level governments by federal (and state) governments that are not accompanied by money to pay for the activities being mandated.

George H. W. Bush did not support funding for any major new or special programs to accomplish those objectives. Similarly, his much-touted "War on Drugs" required nearly $500 million in federal funds, but most of the money was earmarked for federal law enforcement efforts and aid to foreign countries. State and local officials complained bitterly that they needed more money if they were to do their part. After all, they argued, it was the states and localities that had to deal with drug use and its consequences.

Congress was also a source of problems. Members offered and passed well-intentioned legislation requiring state and local action but failed to deal with the associated costs of the new programs. In addition to the previously passed requirements for environmental cleanup, Congress in 1990 passed the much-heralded Americans with Disabilities Act, which included provisions for greater public access to services, transportation facilities, and so forth, that would require millions of dollars in additional state and local expenditures for years to come.

Known as **unfunded mandates**, these unfinanced or under-financed burdens on states and localities became a major issue in national politics and policy-making. By 1994, federal lawmakers had developed greater sensitivity to these burdens. The debates on legislation, such as that dealing with clean water, increasingly included consideration of those responsibilities and who should pay for them. A bill addressing the issue of unfunded mandates—one part of the Republican party's "Contract with America" agenda that the Clinton administration supported—became the first substantive item passed by the 104th Congress in January 1995. Clearly, the days when Congress could impose mandates on states and localities without addressing the critical problems that those requirements caused were gone (see the discussion about Congress that follows).

President Bill Clinton was also sensitive to the growing demands being made on states and localities when he came into office in 1993. As governor of Arkansas for twelve years, he had developed a national reputation as an innovative leader who understood and appreciated the role of states in the federal system.[23] After less than two weeks in office, Clinton held a meeting with the nation's governors to hear their complaints and suggestions. While his administration did not propose any major reforms of the intergovernmental system, Clinton did establish a policy that permitted federal officials to loosen program requirements in order to allow states and localities greater flexibility to innovate. This approach of giving states and localities more room to determine the policies they were to enforce became part of a more general movement toward devolution in the intergovernmental relations system. **Devolution** involved having the national government turn over more functions with greater responsibility to state and local governments. During the Clinton years, federal outlays for state and local grants continued to climb, even as welfare programs were reformed and other responsibilities were devolved (see the discussion in Chapter 14). By fiscal year 2001, the final budget of Clinton's term in office, the national government was spending $317.2 billion on grants—more than double what it had been sending to states and localities a decade earlier. As important, in constant-dollar terms (again based on 1996 dollars), the value of those grants had risen to $285.3 billion in FY 2001 from $173.6 billion in FY 1991.

Devolution A term indicating the effort to give more functions and responsibilities to states and localities in the intergovernmental system.

Twenty-first-Century Challenges (2001 and Beyond?)

The presidency of George W. Bush began with plans to continue the efforts at devolution,[24] but also to bring about at least one major change in intergovernmental relations. Early in his term, Bush endorsed an effort to allow **faith-based organizations (FBOs)** to play a major role in the delivery of social and community services that were funded through the federal government. The idea was to remove the legal and administrative obstacles that stopped federal funding of church-related organizations such as the Salvation Army and local African American congregations that were effectively providing social services in local communities. Bush created a high-profile White House Office of Faith-Based and Community Initiatives,[25] but the initiative immediately ran into opposition from those who feared that it would violate the separation of church and state (see the discussion of First Amendment rights in Chapter 4) and also from some religious leaders, who regarded it as a threat to church autonomy.

Faith-based organizations (FBOs) Church-related social service organizations.
Homeland security Domestic programs intended to prevent and, when necessary, deal with the consequences of terrorist attacks on U.S. soil.

Critical Thinking

Would the use of faith-based organizations to carry out federal social policies be a violation of the separation of church and state?

But then the events of September 11, 2001, put all those efforts on hold: Instead, the first priority of the Bush Administration's federalism agenda was to strengthen **homeland security** in the fight against terrorism. As discussed in Chapters 12, 14, and 15, the war on terrorism has had a major impact on the policies and programs of American government. While initially most attention was given to military responses, by the spring of 2002 attention had turned to domestic security concerns. State and local authorities played a central role in dealing with homeland security issues, from providing security at airports to making plans to guard and protect water supplies and other major public facilities. A request for billions of dollars of federal assistance to "first response" agencies—that is, state and local law enforcement, emergency management, and firefighting units—was high on the list of priorities, as were plans to help improve communications and cooperation among governments at all levels.

The faith-based initiatives of pre–September 11, however, were continued and it was estimated by the White House that in the FY 2005 budget, $2.15 billion—or nearly 11 percent of domestic competitive bid grants offered by major federal agencies—went to FBOs. In March 2006, the Bush administration made an effort to reestablish the priority of its FBO program with a special initiative to increase faith-based organizations' involvement in many of the homeland security programs established after September 11.

But most of the major changes having taken place in federalism over the past several years have come from the U.S. Supreme Court. Until relatively recently, the Court seemed to be staying away from any major role on the federalism stage (see the discussion later in the chapter). Starting in the late 1980s, however, observers at the Supreme Court began to notice an emerging trend in the cases and decisions being heard by the nation's top judicial body. It was well known that the late chief justice, William H. Rehnquist, had long favored having the Court reconsider that body's propensity to favor a nation-centered view of federalism. Over his many years on the Court, he had been able to form a slim majority bloc that tended to lean in the direction of reviving a more state-centered view that took the constitutional concept of state sovereignty seriously. The influence of that majority became evident in 1999, when the Court issued several decisions that indicated that it would play a major role in shaping the federalism of the future. The trend has continued. Within the Court, at least, the myth of state sovereignty has been taken more seriously with each passing year. This was reflected in a 2002 decision that overturned an effort by a federal agency (in this instance, the Federal Maritime Commission) to hear a private citizen's complaint against a state agency (the Ports Authority of South Carolina). "Dual sovereignty is a defining feature of the Nation's constitutional blueprint," wrote Justice Clarence Thomas in the majority opinion. "States, upon ratification of the Constitution, did not consent to become mere appendages of the Federal Government. Rather, they entered the Union 'with their sovereignty intact.'"[26]

Critical Thinking

Can we rely on state and local law enforcement to provide enough security for homeland defense?

Critical Thinking

Is the Supreme Court effort to reinvigorate state sovereignty justified in light of the demands for more effective governance?

The Actors of American Federalism

FOCUS QUESTION   WHO ARE THE MAJOR ACTORS IN THE U.S. FEDERAL SYSTEM, AND WHAT ROLES DO THEY PLAY IN THAT SYSTEM?

While the issues surrounding federalism and intergovernmental relations have long histories, they have never been as complicated as they are today. This is in part due to the very nature of modern life, but it is also a result of the number of people and institutions involved in the system. Today's federalism is an intergovernmental relations system involving a cast of hundreds of agencies, thousands of political and administrative personnel, and millions of citizens who depend on government for daily public services. In short, the underlying story is that the American federal system has grown wider and deeper as interactions among the different levels of American government have increased and become more complex. Here we briefly describe the many actors who occupy the modern stage of American intergovernmental relations.

National Government Actors

Formally, there is only one national government in the American federal system. In practice, however, dozens of national-level actors play out daily dramas on the intergovernmental relations stage.

The Supreme Court. In the two centuries of American federalism, no national institution has been more important than the U.S. Supreme Court. We have already seen how in *McCulloch v. Maryland* the Court helped establish the national government's dominant role and how the post–Civil War Court supported the notion of dual federalism.

As noted previously, until recently Supreme Court rulings seemed to be reducing the role of the states as effective policymakers.[27] In the late 1980s, however, some Supreme Court decisions indicated a growing willingness to give state and local governments more power to shape public policies on a wide range of issues, from abortion rights and the right to die to local campaign financing and the use of sobriety tests for drivers suspected of drunk driving. In other areas, such as civil rights, however, the Court seemed more reluctant to defer to states. Then, in a 1992 case (*New York v. United States*), the Supreme Court held that the national government could not "simply compel" a state to take policy actions. New York found itself unable to live up to provisions of a congressional act mandating that it establish a site for low-level radioactive waste disposal within its borders. The federal government's deadline passed, and New York found itself threatened with legal action unless it assumed responsibility for regulating the waste material in the manner prescribed by the law. In this case, the Court reasserted an earlier principle of federalism that Congress may not simply "commandee[r] the legislative processes of the States by directly compelling them to enact and enforce a federal regulatory program."

Four years later, in the case *Seminole Indian Tribe of Florida v. Florida* (1996), the Court declared unconstitutional a law that authorized individuals to sue state governments in federal court for violations of national laws. Similar cases followed. In 1997, the Court overturned a law that required local law enforcement officials to implement provisions of a federal handgun control law (*Printz v. United States*). This was followed by a 1999 decision in which the state of Florida was held to be immune from lawsuits brought against it under the provisions of a federal law dealing with patent rights and false advertising. In another, the Court held that the state of Maine was not subject to federal Fair Labor Standards legislation. In

January 2000, the Court went even further, specifically exempting states from provisions of federal laws aimed at preventing age discrimination (*Kimel v. Florida Board of Regents*). With its decision in the Federal Maritime Commission case (discussed earlier), the Court has made it clear that it is once again a significant factor in shaping both the present and future of federalism.

Congress. Although presidents often receive credit for major policy innovations, Congress has always played a central role in the evolution of the federal system. This has been especially true in the past forty years, during which Congress has increased its authorization of grant programs.

Some students of Congress point to strong incentives for members of the House and Senate to create and fund federal grant-in-aid programs for state and local governments.[28] These programs give almost every state and local government an opportunity to obtain federal funding. Therefore, members of Congress can claim credit for passing and supporting their constituents' grant applications. As a result, even fiscally conservative members of Congress often find it hard to avoid supporting requests for new and larger intergovernmental grant programs. "Philosophically, I have not been one to jump rapidly to new programs," commented one member of the House of Representatives from Virginia. "But if programs are adopted, my district is entitled to its fair share. And I do everything I can to help — if they decide to apply for aid."[29]

The White House. American presidents have proposed new federal grant programs and worked to reform the intergovernmental system. Johnson's Great Society agenda, for example, emphasized the Model Cities program and other new and innovative projects. As previously noted, the administrations of both Johnson and Nixon strove to improve the coordination of federal grant programs. In the late 1970s, President Jimmy Carter issued several executive orders aimed at simplifying grant application and reporting procedures, which by then had grown very complex.

Other White House initiatives have sought to expand the role of state and local governments in the federal system. Johnson called for the establishment of a "creative federalism" involving a partnership of all levels of government as well as community and private organizations. Nixon proposed a "new American Revolution" that would give "power to the people" by turning many national domestic programs back to state and local governments. Reagan announced a "new federalism" that would have revamped the intergovernmental grant system over a ten-year period. Clinton ordered members of his administration to administer programs that allowed states to experiment with innovative ways of dealing with the nation's health and welfare problems.[30] Some changes in the American federal system resulted from each of these presidential initiatives, but none led to radical alterations in intergovernmental relationships. Instead, it has been changes in specific programs that have had the greatest impact on the federal system.

For example, when he ran for the presidency in 1992, Bill Clinton promised that if he were elected, he would bring about "an end to welfare as we know it." On August 22, 1996, he signed into law perhaps the most sweeping changes in

Critical Thinking

Are we in the midst of a major change in American federalism? If so, what kind of change is it?

welfare programs since the early 1960s. The Personal Responsibility and Work Opportunity Reconciliation Act of 1996 significantly altered the system of assistance to the needy, which had generated criticism from both sides of the political spectrum (see the discussion of welfare policy and reform in Chapter 14, on domestic policy and policymaking). The new law was aimed at ending the cycle of poverty and dependence that had caused concern among even the most ardent supporters of government assistance to the poor. But for those who administered the vast web of federal programs that had developed over several decades, the law represented even more important changes. For them, in many respects, the new welfare law meant an end to the intergovernmental relations system as they had known it for more than half a century.

Before the passage of the reform legislation in 1996, assistance to the poor was effectively a set of national programs administered by the states. Thus, despite the significant role played by the states, there was an unmistakable national flavor to the welfare system. As in many other policy areas — from education to environmental protection to highway construction and maintenance — states and localities had taken on significant financial and administrative burdens but were severely limited in deciding on such matters as who was eligible for the programs or how the funds would be spent. After the 1996 reforms supported by the Clinton administration, the role of the states in welfare policy was radically transformed, as they took on most of the responsibility for determining the kinds of assistance programs they would administer.

The Federal Bureaucracy. Perhaps the greatest increase in the number of national-level actors on the intergovernmental stage has taken place in the bureaucracy, especially in such agencies as the U.S. Departments of Housing and Urban Development, Health and Human Services, Agriculture, Interior, Transportation, and Education. Some bureaucrats in these agencies determine the eligibility of state and local grant applicants and the appropriateness of their proposals. Others monitor the use of grant-in-aid funds and constantly consult with other actors in the intergovernmental system about the need to modify specific grant programs.

The emergence of these intergovernmental bureaucracies has added a new dimension to U.S. government. On the one hand, the bureaucrats in these agencies are expected to disburse funds and assist state and local government officials in making effective use of those resources. On the other hand, they are expected to ensure that state and local programs meet federal standards and live up to federal requirements. In other words, the growing federal bureaucracy assigned to intergovernmental programs is supposed to both facilitate the grant process and regulate state and local grant recipients. These bureaucrats are actors on the intergovernmental stage with dual, and often contradictory, roles (see Chapter 12, on the bureaucracy).

Two developments are likely to shape the role of the federal bureaucracy in the federal system in the future. The first is the continued trend toward devolution and program reform, especially in welfare, health care, environmental protection, and education (see Chapter 14, on domestic policy and policymaking). Although the national government is unlikely to withdraw from these areas, its role will be increasingly linked to the work of state, local, nonprofit, and (sometimes) private-sector agencies. The second is the emergence of homeland security as a high priority for the national government. If the Bush administration and its successors are to make any headway in this area, an enhancement of the intergovernmental system will necessarily be required, with a special emphasis on such basic public services as police and fire protection.

States in the Federal System

Even during periods when the national government has seemed to be playing the leading role in the federalism drama, the states have remained important and active participants in the intergovernmental arena. Through all the various changes that have taken place, they have been sustained by the myth of state sovereignty and have retained significant responsibilities in the areas of education, public health, criminal justice, and the regulation of gambling and liquor. They also play major roles in enforcing environmental, safety, and health regulations. For years they have been the chief regulators of public utilities and savings banks.

An important but often unappreciated legal fact about states is that they empower and determine the organization of local governments.[31] Legally, local governments are created by the actions of state legislatures. Thus, theoretically, they can be legally terminated by state officials acting in their constitutionally sovereign role. In practice, however, states rarely use this life-and-death power over the legal existence of local governments, although they have on occasion eliminated entire city governments through legislative action. City governments cannot impose their own sales or income taxes unless state laws grant them that authority. There are examples of state governments taking over or shifting local government functions because of severe financial problems or unbridled corruption and inefficiency. In Missouri, for instance, the state assumed control of the police forces in both Kansas City and St. Louis during the twentieth century because of widespread corruption.[32] And in the 1970s, the state of New York helped New York City deal with its critical financial problems by assuming responsibility for all four-year colleges in the city's municipal university system. In recent years, some states have taken control of inner-city school districts that were failing to perform up to state standards.

The states have also made their mark through creative and innovative approaches to solving public problems and meeting challenges; in fact, the states have often led the way in these areas. For example, Wisconsin regulated railroads and democratized the political nomination process long before such policies were adopted nationally. California led the way in developing building construction standards to help reduce energy costs and in establishing auto-emission standards to help reduce air pollution. Such state-initiated innovations are common in almost every major area of domestic policy.[33] In discussions about welfare and education reform, one of the strongest arguments for giving more responsibility to the states has been their ability to come up with novel and effective programs, even in the face of budgetary cuts.

Critical Thinking

Should the states be abolished and replaced with regional governments?

Most important today, however, is the states' pivotal role as liaison in the intergovernmental relations system. As noted earlier, the national government uses state agencies to administer its grants in a wide variety of policy areas. Furthermore, local governments rely on state officials for technical assistance, as well as for financial aid. In short, state governments may be the key link — and not necessarily the weak link — in the U.S. federal system.

The role of the states in the intergovernmental relations system is always changing. When their influence wanes, students of American government tend to pronounce their doom. According to one prominent observer in the 1930s, the American state was "finished." He said, "I do not predict that the states will go, but affirm that they have gone."[34] At other times, the states have been so important that some can hardly imagine how American government could operate without them, while others are extremely critical of their importance.[35]

What accounts for these gains and losses in power? First, the states' authority changes dramatically as the Supreme Court shifts between strict and flexible interpretations of the Constitution. As noted previously, the current Court majority has signaled its intent to decide in favor of a state-centered view of federalism when issues come before it. Second, the states' role depends on the actual political power they can mobilize. During certain periods of American history, state officials have managed to exercise considerable influence in Washington through their representatives in the House and Senate. At other times, state governors and legislators have carried relatively little weight either at the White House or in the halls of Congress.

Third, public opinion plays a role in determining the extent of states' influence. Although state governments have always been important policymakers, the American public has not always looked to the states for solutions to its collective problems. At times the public has depended on local governments, and more recently it has expected Washington to help. The question of public support for state government is complicated by citizens' attitudes toward their state governments, which tend to vary over time. Over the past three decades, public opinion regarding the capacity of states and localities has become more positive.[36]

Fourth, the role of the states in the federal system depends on their administrative capabilities. If states lack the administrative resources and managerial talent to deliver the goods and services demanded by the public, then they cannot play a major role for very long. Most observers believe that the administrative capabilities of the states have improved markedly since the 1960s. Ironically, much of that improvement has come about as a result of pressures imposed by Washington through the requirements attached to grant-in-aid programs.

Local Governments

When you think of local governments, you probably picture city halls and county courthouses occupied by small councils of elected officials and a few offices occupied by record-keeping clerks, who collect taxes and issue dog tags and automobile licenses. American local governments are much more than

POLITICS & POPULAR CULTURE

The Political "Image" of the South

In this chapter we have emphasized that federalism can be understood as a stage upon which differences among the states are played out. But it is not the only such stage. Modern popular culture also reflects America's regional differences in a variety of forms and formats. Despite the natural cleavages that separate Californians from New Englanders and westerners and Midwesterners from easterners in the United States, it has been the North/South differences that have drawn the public's attention for many decades. Most often it has been the American South that has fascinated us, and we have seen that region portrayed in a variety of ways over the past century, from a region victimized and embittered after the Civil War to a hostile place where bigotry and racism run rampant.

In 1915, D. W. Griffith released *Birth of a Nation*, arguably one of the great cinematic achievements of the silent film era—but also one of the era's most controversial movies, given its extremely sympathetic narrative about how whites had suffered during the Reconstruction era. In 1939, it was the image of a defeated South pillaged and plundered by Northern forces that emerged from the classic movie *Gone with the Wind*. From the 1940s through the 1950s, films portrayed a culturally distinct South, stressing the region's innocence and backwardness. This image had turned quite negative by 1960, when the Broadway hit play *Inherit the Wind* was made into a movie. A fictionalization of the famous "Scopes Monkey Trial," held in Tennessee during the 1920s, it pictures the South as a bastion of backward fundamentalist thinking—more to be pitied than hated.

The image of a South confronting its racism has also been a subject for moviemakers. In the 1967 film *In the Heat of the Night*, a local police chief (Rod Steiger) grudgingly accepts the reluctantly given help of a black police detective from Philadelphia (Sidney Poitier). Both the film and Steiger won Academy Awards, and the show's plot later turned up as a television dramatic series. In 1988, director Alan Parker revisited that era and image of the South in a critically acclaimed movie, *Mississippi Burning*. The film dramatized the 1964 FBI investigation into the disappearance of four civil rights workers.

In popular music, rock singer Neil Young wrote two songs ("Southern Man" in 1970 and "Alabama" in 1972) reflecting the negative image of the racist South. In both he pointed an accusatory finger at the region as the home of racists who needed to change their ways. The members of one southern band, Lynyrd Skynyrd, wrote a musical response in their 1974 hit song, "Sweet Home Alabama," making clear reference to efforts of Southerners to overcome the race-driven politics ("Now we all did what we could do . . .") while pointing to the growing Watergate scandal as an indication that there are problems with politics in the rest of the country as well.

Images such as these in movies and song lyrics are directly related to the changing myths of American government and politics in the federal arena. Just as southern politicians emerged during and after the 1970s as leading "liberals" in the Democratic party (e.g., Jimmy Carter and Bill Clinton), so the popular image of a racist, ignorant, and backward South has significantly changed. The first indications of a change came during the late 1970s with the cinematic image of a "New South" comprising hard-working blue-collar Americans; for instance, Burt Reynolds starred in two box office hits—*Gator* and *White Lightning*—in which progressive "New South" southerners worked with federal agents to triumph over corrupt "Old South" southerners, represented by the local sheriff and other officials. The music also changed, with southern bands like Lynyrd Skynyrd becoming part of the mainstream of the popular sounds that emerged during the 1980s.

that, however, and their role in the intergovernmental relations system is a major one.

As noted earlier, all local governments are creations of the individual states. Under the formal provisions of the federal system established in the Constitution, governmental powers are divided between the national government and the states. Local governments, in other words, have no formal constitutional standing except as subdivisions of the states. Their very existence and legal authority are derived from charters granted to them under state laws. This does not mean that they are powerless or insignificant actors in the federal system, for states often give local government considerable authority. Just how powerful these local governments can be was made clear in 2005 when the Supreme Court issued a decision that upheld the authority of local governments to take private property for public purposes. In that particular case (*Kelo v. City of New London* [125 S. Ct. 2655]), the city of New London, Connecticut, used its power of "eminent domain" to force 115 private home owners to sell their residences so that the city could give the land to a private developer, who had offered to construct a hotel and conference center complex in that economically depressed city. The power of **eminent domain** — or the right of a sovereign government to take property for public purposes for just compensation, even if the owner of that property objects — is a power that most states give to local governments in their charters so they can acquire real property needed for such public purposes as building roads and highways or constructing public facilities such as schools or a city hall. Local governments have also been given the authority to use eminent domain to clear areas of urban blight or to replace slums with public housing. In recent years, a growing number of localities have used eminent domain to promote economic development, and it was for that purpose that New London sought to take possession of those 115 residences. The home owners took the city to court, and in a controversial 5–4 decision, the U.S. Supreme Court sided with the city. Like it or not, the Court majority ruled, local governments do possess whatever power of eminent domain their state charters grant them, and they have wide discretion in determining what is or is not a valid public purpose. Any limits on that power have to come from the state, so the federal courts may not interfere.

Even though local governments formally depend on the state for their legal authority, in practice Americans have always treated local governments as if they had separate and legitimate standing in the federal system.[37] As of 2002, there were 87,849 local governments in the United States. This figure includes county (3,034), municipal (19,431), township (16,506), and other **general service governments**, which provide a wide range of public services to those who live within their borders. It also includes 13,522 school districts and 35,356 other **special district governments** dealing with one or two distinctive government functions, such as fire protection, public transportation, or sewage treatment. Each of these local governments can participate in some way in the intergovernmental relations system — and a great many do.[38]

The problems of local governments are not all alike because those governments reflect a variety of physical, social, cultural, political, and economic conditions. Between the extremes of small, rural, sparsely populated townships and

Eminent domain The right of a sovereign government to take property for public purposes for just compensation even if the owner objects.

General service governments Local governments, such as counties, municipalities, and townships, that provide a wide range of public services to those who live within their borders. **Special district governments** Local governments that deal with one or two distinctive government functions, such as education, fire protection, public transportation, or sewage treatment.

huge, densely populated metropolitan areas are cities, towns, counties, and districts of every conceivable size and shape. To understand the distinctive role played by local governments in the intergovernmental system, we need to perceive their differences.

Of particular importance are the wide economic disparities among various local governments. These differences in wealth influence the way community leaders approach the intergovernmental system. For example, according to recent estimates, the per capita income in Laredo, Texas, is less than half the per capita income of Tulsa, Oklahoma, or Bremerton, Washington, and barely one-third the per capita income of residents of Naples, Florida. A city such as Laredo or Newark, New Jersey, would want more federal aid programs targeted at job training, public housing, public health, and similar needs of the urban poor. Naples's government, in contrast, would seek more federal funding for new highways, construction of new recreation facilities, and other such amenities.

Not only the economic status of the citizenry but also their age and ethnic background bear on local problems and needs. The interests and concerns of Bradenton, Florida, are different from those of many other communities because more than a fourth of Bradenton's residents are over sixty-five years old. In Bakersfield, California, a fourth of the population is fourteen years old or under. Thus, the people of Bradenton would seek federal and state help in funding special programs for the elderly, whereas the citizens of Bakersfield would be more interested in state and federal aid for elementary and secondary school programs. Ethnic concerns can also be a factor. The existence of a very large Hispanic community in El Paso, Texas, is relevant to what that city wants from Washington. The intergovernmental relations system, for instance, can offer El Paso's schools funding for bilingual education programs. Such funds might not be available if the schools had to depend on local resources.

These and other factors make it difficult to generalize about the roles played by local government actors on the intergovernmental relations stage. Nevertheless, local officials have undoubtedly become major participants in the federal system during the post–World War II period and will remain important. They exercise much of their influence through local members of Congress, who are responsive to the needs of their constituents back home. They also exert influence through membership in intergovernmental lobbying groups, which make up an increasingly important set of actors in the federal system.

Nongovernmental Actors

Intergovernmental Lobby. The **intergovernmental lobby** includes individuals and groups that have a special interest in the policies and programs implemented through the growing intergovernmental relations system (for more on interest groups, see Chapter 8). Some of these lobbyists represent private interests that hope to benefit from or expect to be harmed by some intergovernmental program. For example, environmental lobbyists push for effective state and local enforcement of national air-quality and water-quality standards. Other intergovernmental lobbyists support social regulations to strengthen automobile safety,

Critical Thinking

Why have Americans created so many local governments? Are they necessary or justifiable?

Intergovernmental lobby The many individuals and groups that have a special interest in the policies and programs implemented through the growing intergovernmental relations systems. These lobbyists represent private, consumer, and business groups.

consumer protection, or occupational health. Representatives of businesses seek to reduce these regulations and to weaken state and local enforcement.

Lobbyists for the poor and the disabled are also active on the federalism stage. In many instances, their goal is to ensure continued federal funding of social welfare and educational programs. In June 1994, for example, the National Associations of Community Health Centers (NACHC), representing 2,000 medical clinics that serve the health-care needs of nearly 7 million poor Americans, sued the Clinton administration to halt efforts to allow state governments to experiment with the way they provide health care to the poor through Medicaid, the federal program designed to provide health care for America's poor.

In their lawsuit, NACHC officials contended that the waivers being granted by the Clinton administration were illegal because the experimental programs effectively reduced the health care provided to Medicaid recipients in those states.[39] By bringing suit in federal court, the NACHC was pitting one major federal institution (the judiciary) against another (the White House) to draw attention to an intergovernmental issue that has an impact on millions of Americans.

In recent years, a new kind of intergovernmental lobby has emerged: **public-sector interest groups**, who represent the interests of elected officials and other major governmental actors involved in the intergovernmental relations system. For example, the National Governors' Association and the U.S. Conference of Mayors are two of the most active groups in Washington that lobby on domestic policy issues. The American Society for Public Administration and the International City and County Management Association represent the interests of public administrators and other nonelected public-sector workers. Still other groups—such as the National League of Cities, the National Association of Counties, and the Council of State Governments—lobby on behalf of their own government jurisdictions.

Individual governments also hire lobbyists to represent their interests. In 1969, Mayor John V. Lindsay of New York City took the brash step of opening a Washington, D.C., office to lobby on behalf of the Big Apple. Two decades later, New York City had eight full-time lobbyists looking after its interests in Washington. Similar offices have been opened by just about every major government in the United States.

The increase in the number of public-sector interest groups, as well as their political influence, paralleled the growth of the intergovernmental system itself during the 1960s and 1970s. In recent years, however, the reduction in federal aid for states and localities has led several of these public-sector interest groups to reconsider their priorities and roles. Many have cut back their Washington-based staffs and focused more of their attention on lobbying state legislatures or on providing technical assistance to their members, who must adapt to Washington's reductions in grant-in-aid funding.[40]

Citizens. The largest group of potential participants in the intergovernmental system is the citizens of the United States—the intended beneficiaries of all the policies and public services of American government. Hardly an area of American domestic policy remains untouched by the intergovernmental relations system, yet many Americans remain unaware of the role of intergovernmental

Critical Thinking

Does the proliferation of public-sector interest groups help or obstruct the operations of U.S. governments?

Public-sector interest groups A lobby that represents the interests of elected officials and other major governmental actors involved in the intergovernmental relations system. An example is the National Governors' Association.

relations. Every person who drives a car on the highways, attends public schools, uses city buses, or receives emergency care at a community hospital benefits from intergovernmental programs.

Of course, the American people are more than just the beneficiaries of the many goods and services provided through the intergovernmental system. As taxpayers, citizens also pay for those programs, often indirectly. Most intergovernmental programs are paid for with general tax revenues collected by the various levels of government. However, a portion of the money comes from special trust funds established for a particular program. For instance, each time you purchase a gallon of gasoline for your car, you pay a special federal tax. That tax is deposited in the Highway Trust Fund, which is used primarily to pay for the construction and maintenance of interstate highways and other roads (see "Asked & Answered," p. 91).

Most important, the American people generate the demand for intergovernmental programs. The pressures that the public can bring to bear on the system

Federal Aid for Public Works

Some local public works projects require significant support from all levels of government. With federal government support, the state of Massachusetts launched the Central Artery Project in 1982 to deal with the Boston area's traffic problems. Known locally as the "Big Dig," the project was initiated in the early 1980s and neared completion in 2006.

ASKED & ANSWERED

ASKED: Which level of government is responsible for the construction and maintenance of the nation's highways?

ANSWERED: In 2002, the federal government spent nearly $80 billion on the nation's roads. Most of that money came from a special trust fund that motorists pay into through a tax imposed on every gallon of gas purchased at the pump. But despite all the federal money that goes toward the construction and maintenance of roads and highways, it is more likely that, to get a pothole fixed, you would have to call your local road department or state highway agency.

Consider the following statistics: of the 3.9 million miles of roads and highways in the United States, about 3.1 million — a full 77.5 percent — are controlled by local governments, including cities, towns, counties, local special districts, and so forth. Another 776,000 miles are designated as state roads, and a relatively small number of miles — a little over 120,000 — are under the jurisdiction of federal agencies that operate national forests, parks, military reservations, and other federal government lands.

The Constitution does give the national government a potentially powerful source of authority over roads and highways in Article I, Section 8, when it empowers it "to establish post offices and post roads." But from the outset the federal government has avoided assuming too much responsibility for the building or maintenance of roads. In-

stead, it left that task up to states and localities, and instead focused attention on designating certain state and local routes as post roads and providing some advice and support for new forms of transportation such as canals and railroads. The result is that today the construction and maintenance of the country's major roads and highways are intergovernmental responsibilities shared by local, state, and national governments, as well as some private companies.

In the nineteenth century, there were many privately owned and maintained toll roads, mostly access roads and privately financed bridges crossing private property. Although at one time these were all but eliminated by the modern government-financed highway systems, today privately owned highways are making a reappearance in many states. The 14-mile Dulles Greenway that stretches between Leesberg, Virginia, and Dulles International Airport is one such road, as is the 22-mile Camino Colombia Toll Road in Texas. Other privately funded and operated roads are now found in Florida, Colorado, and California, and several more are under construction. Even so, the role of private roads is likely to remain very minor, and to get any potholes filled you will likely have to speak with your local government.

are most evident when popular grant programs are threatened with major cuts or when a community faces a crisis that cannot be handled with local resources. Consider, for example, social service programs for the elderly or handicapped. When members of the Reagan administration suggested cutbacks in social security in 1982, the public reacted so negatively that President Reagan felt compelled to promise never to cut those benefits.

And when a crisis or tragedy strikes some community — when a tornado or flood devastates a small town, or when buried hazardous wastes contaminate a community's soil and water supply — the call for action goes out to Washington as well as to the state capital and city hall. These are the kinds of actions that generate intergovernmental activity regardless of concerns over the constitutional niceties of federalism. The massive mobilization of public-sector resources from all levels of government in response to the tragic events of September 11, 2001, was a case in point, and that effort received generally favorable marks. But there are also examples of terrible failures of this system, the most notable being the response to Hurricane Katrina in 2005, discussed in Chapters 1 and 12.

Conclusion: The Principles and Pragmatism of Federalism

Before embarking on a political career that eventually led him to the governorship of Maryland, Parris Glendening was a scholar who wrote books about federalism. What he observed as a scholar — and attempted to put into practice as an elected public official — is an approach that he calls "pragmatic federalism." From his perspective, intergovernmental relations "are constantly changing, fashioned to address current needs while emphasizing problem solving with minimal adherence to rigid doctrine."[41]

The type of federalism that Glendening and others practice on a day-to-day basis is indeed pragmatic and practical — a type of federalism quite different from the contentious interactions that marked the first years of this institution. The old form of federalism resulted in confrontation rather than cooperation. This new form of federalism took decades to evolve into a system of intergovernmental relations, and most of those engaged in it find debates over such things as state sovereignty quite unproductive and irrelevant.

This is not to say that there are no problems with the intergovernmental relationships that are at the heart of today's pragmatic federalism. Depending on the issue, you will always hear people in city hall or the state capitols complaining about too much interference from Washington; and in the federal bureaucracy, the administrators of various programs feel constantly challenged by local and state officials who they feel are unwilling or unable to meet the minimal requirements established for specific programs. Those outside the system have other issues as well. Some complain about the inequities and inefficiencies that result from having national programs implemented by local and regional governments, while others express frustration at the "one-size-fits-all" mentality reflected in some federal programs. Nevertheless, in the day-to-day world of intergovernmental relations, the question of state sovereignty seems abstract and insignificant.

But today's intergovernmental relations cannot ignore its roots. The legacy of the seemingly ancient debates over sovereignty and authority lingers in the form of the myth of state sovereignty, and it manifests itself in cases before the Supreme Court and controversies such as that surrounding Yucca Mountain. If we are to truly understand the institution of federalism, we need to take into account both the realities of daily government operation and the myths from the past.

Tying It Together

FOCUS QUESTIONS RECAP

＊ How has federalism changed over the past two centuries of American constitutional development?

＊ Who are the major actors in the U.S. federal system, and what roles do they play in the federal system?

CHAPTER SUMMARY

1. The institution of federalism was created through compromises made by the framers of the Constitution, and its exact form has always been ambiguous.

2. The evolution of the American federal system has been shaped by debates over the meaning of federalism, especially the issue of whether it was intended to be nation-centered or state-centered. It has also been shaped by the distinctive challenges that have faced the United States during the past two centuries. Out of that evolution has emerged a complex system of intergovernmental relations based on a variety of grant-in-aid programs. The intergovernmental relations system has been characterized by periods and episodes of conflict and cooperation.

3. There are many different actors engaged in the federal system, all of them contributing to the complexity of the system. In addition to the major branches of the national government (the Supreme Court, the White House, and Congress), there are states, local governments, the intergovernmental lobby, and the citizens of the United States — each with a role and stake in the system.

Key Terms

NIMBY ("not in my backyard") (68)
Sovereignty (69)
State-centered federalism (70)
Nation-centered federalism (71)
Interstate commerce (71)
Police powers (71)
Dual federalism (71)
Grant-in-aid programs (72)
Intergovernmental relations (73)
Cooperative federalism (73)
Categorical, or conditional, grants-in-aid (73)
Formula grants (73)
Project grants (74)

Matching grants (74)
Councils of governments (75)
Block grants (76)
General revenue sharing (76)
Unfunded mandates (78)
Devolution (79)
Faith-based organizations (FBOs) (79)
Homeland security (79)
Eminent domain (87)
General service governments (87)
Special district governments (87)
Intergovernmental lobby (88)
Public-sector interest groups (89)

Net Work

Do you want to know what is going on in the inter-governmental relations arena?

- One of the most widely read periodicals among state and local officials is *Governing* magazine (**www.governing.com**), published by Congressional Quarterly, Inc. The magazine also maintains a list of useful links related to state and local government concerns at **www.governing.com/govlinks/glinks.htm**.

- The Urban Institute (**www.urban.org/center/anf/index.cfm**), a well-respected Washington think tank, has been monitoring changes in federal social and health policies that involve states and localities.

- The American Enterprise Institute has an ongoing project devoted to issues of federalism; see **www.federalismproject.org**.

- Some people advocate the application of the federalist model to international relations. See the website of the World Federalist Movement at **www.wfm.org/html/079ikc_a.html**.

To appreciate the role of federalism in our constitutional system, you should familiarize yourself with the websites of state and local governments. As an exercise, find the website for your home state, your hometown, or the city in which you now reside. Also, since every major airport maintains a website, find the site for the airport nearest your college. How useful or informative are these sites?

4

The Heritage of Rights and Liberties

Is liberty, as defined by the U.S. Constitution, absolute?

FOCUS QUESTIONS

* How has the Bill of Rights been applied to the states?

* What balances have been struck in applying the First Amendment?

* What constitutional rights do those accused of crimes have?

* Does the Constitution provide a right to privacy?

* What types of discrimination violate the constitutional guarantee of equal protection?

As part of its coverage of the Supreme Court's ruling that flag burning is a protected form of free speech, the *Today* show invited a representative of the American Legion (the nation's largest veterans' organization) to appear and explain the group's reaction to the decision. Not surprisingly, the American Legion spokesman denounced the Court's decision. The interview did not end there, however. Jane Pauley, one of the show's hosts, asked the legionnaire to explain what the flag meant to him and other veterans. In response, the guest simply noted, "The flag is the symbol of our country, the land of the free and the home of the brave." Not satisfied with the answer, Pauley pressed him further, asking, "What exactly does it symbolize?" Puzzled and perhaps a little annoyed by the question, the guest responded, "It stands for the fact that this is a country where we have a right to do what we want."[1]

Obviously the legionnaire did not mean exactly what he said, because, taken literally, his statement would have supported the right to burn the flag. Nevertheless, he was expressing the commonly held view that in America, the guarantee of civil liberties means that we can do what we want. (**Civil liberties**, most of which are spelled out in the Bill of Rights, protect individuals from excessive or arbitrary government interference.) As we will see, that belief is a myth, the *myth of absolute or complete liberty.* Liberty is not absolute, nor did our founders think it could be. Moreover, few Americans really believe in complete liberty when it comes to unpopular groups. When asked general questions about First Amendment liberties, Americans almost universally support them. But support for these liberties drops significantly in regard to flag burners, for instance. As you read this chapter, notice how our understanding of liberty has changed. It is not just a static concept enshrined in the Bill of Rights and other constitutional provisions. Instead, like the Constitution, it has been altered by time and circumstances.

Public attitudes toward **civil rights** for individuals or groups (guarantees of protection by government against discrimination or unreasonable treatment by other individuals or groups) tend to reflect a second widely held myth, the *myth of guaranteed political and social equality.* According to that myth, participation in the political and social system is open equally to all. Yet discrimination is still a feature of American society. Indeed, national, state, and local governments have often enforced discrimination instead of guaranteeing civil rights. The rights of minorities have often been ignored in favor of the interests of the majority. Our understanding of civil rights — like our understanding of civil liberties — is constantly changing. Even as our nation struggles to live up to the promise of political equality for African Americans and women, there are new demands for civil rights.

In this chapter, we consider how choices are made regarding the way in which rights and liberties are protected. We briefly explore the expansion and contraction of liberties as the courts have interpreted and reinterpreted the Bill of Rights. We also look at the way in which the Supreme Court has treated minorities, noting particularly its interpretation of the Fourteenth Amendment as it affects the rights of African Americans and women.

Civil liberties Freedoms, most of which are spelled out in the Bill of Rights, from excessive or arbitrary government interference.

Civil rights Guarantees of government protection of individuals against discrimination or unreasonable treatment by other individuals or groups.

Applying the Bill of Rights to the States

FOCUS QUESTION HOW HAS THE BILL OF RIGHTS BEEN APPLIED TO THE STATES?

The original U.S. Constitution, unlike several state constitutions, made no mention of a bill of rights. Why no such protection was specified is unclear. Most historians argue that the framers simply felt that a listing of rights and liberties was unnecessary. The national government was to have only the powers granted to it, and the Constitution did not give the new government any power to infringe on people's liberties. Therefore, many delegates reasoned, there would be no problem. No doubt they also assumed that the separation of powers and the system of checks and balances would thwart any effort to diminish individual liberties.

The failure to include a bill of rights in the Constitution caused clashes at state ratifying conventions. State after state ratified the Constitution only on the understanding that the new Congress would strengthen the document with a guarantee of certain personal liberties. Consequently, the First Congress, meeting in September 1789, proposed twelve amendments to the Constitution; within two years the states had ratified ten of them. These ten amendments, collectively referred to as the Bill of Rights, constitute a list of specific limits on the power of the national government.

Originally, the provisions of the Bill of Rights were understood to limit only the actions of the national government. States were restricted only by the provisions of their individual constitutions. The Supreme Court decision in *Barron v. Baltimore* (1833) clarified that view.[2] Baltimore city officials had decided to redirect several streams that fed into the city's harbor. John Barron, the owner of a wharf in that harbor, sued. After the streams were redirected, large deposits of sand had built up, making Barron's wharf inaccessible to ships. Because the city had destroyed his business, Barron claimed, the city was required by the Fifth Amendment to provide just compensation.

After reviewing the precise wording of the Bill of Rights and the historical justification for adopting it, Chief Justice John Marshall, writing for a unanimous Court, ruled against Barron. According to Marshall, the Bill of Rights applied only to the national government. That is why, Marshall argued, the first word of the First Amendment is *Congress.* That position remained unchallenged until the ratification of the Fourteenth Amendment in 1868.

Drafted chiefly to provide equality before the law to the recently emancipated slaves, the Fourteenth Amendment contains much broader language. Its very first paragraph includes the statement "nor shall any State deprive any person of life, liberty, or property, without due process of law." This statement is critically important for understanding the role of the Bill of Rights in modern society. To some, this "due process" clause clearly indicates that the framers of the Fourteenth Amendment intended to reverse the *Barron v. Baltimore* decision. For instance, throughout his long career, Supreme Court Justice Hugo Black steadfastly maintained that the Fourteenth Amendment *incorporated* (that is, made applicable to the states) the entire Bill of Rights.[3]

Selective incorporation
The Supreme Court's practice of making applicable to the states only those portions of the Bill of Rights that a majority of justices felt to be fundamental to a democratic society.

Although a majority of the Supreme Court has never fully accepted Black's sweeping interpretation of the Fourteenth Amendment, most provisions of the Bill of Rights have since been applied to the states. Beginning in 1925, the Supreme Court slowly increased the number of provisions applicable to the states. It did so through **selective incorporation** — the application to the states of only those portions of the Bill of Rights that a majority of justices believed to be fundamental to a democratic society. The 1937 case of *Palko v. Connecticut* illustrates that approach.[4]

Frank Palko was found guilty of second-degree murder and sentenced to life in prison. The prosecutor, desiring a conviction for first-degree murder, successfully appealed the trial court's decision and retried Palko. This time, Palko was found guilty of first-degree murder and sentenced to death. He then appealed his case to the Supreme Court, claiming that the second trial was unconstitutional because the Constitution protected an individual from double jeopardy, or being tried twice for the same crime. Writing for the Court, Justice Benjamin Cardozo acknowledged that the Bill of Rights contains guarantees that are so fundamental to liberty that they must be protected from state as well as national infringement. He did not, however, include among these guarantees the protection against double jeopardy. Cardozo granted that this protection was valuable and important, but he concluded that it was not "the essence of a scheme of ordered liberty." Consequently, Frank Palko was executed.

The *Palko* decision was overturned in 1969, and by the early 1970s the Supreme Court had incorporated almost all the provisions of the Bill of Rights. Still unincorporated is the Fifth Amendment's guarantee of indictment by grand jury "for a capital, or otherwise infamous crime." More controversial is the unincorporated status of the Second Amendment, which provides that "a well-regulated Militia, being necessary to the security of a free State, the right of the people to keep and bear Arms, shall not be infringed." Although the United States Supreme Court has handed down only three decisions interpreting the Second Amendment, the federal courts have consistently ruled that the right is qualified by the clause stating that it is "necessary for the security of a free State." To the federal courts, this clause has meant that the amendment protects a collective right, preventing the national government from abolishing state militias, not an individual right of gun ownership. Attorney General John Ashcroft has taken issue with this interpretation. In a 2001 letter to the National Rifle Association, Ashcroft assured the organization that his reading of the Second Amendment differed from that of his predecessors. According to Ashcroft, the administration views the amendment as clearly intended to protect individual rights, not just collective rights. Thus, in any future litigation, the Department of Justice can be expected to weigh in on the side of gun owners and against government regulations.

Incorporating the Bill of Rights is one thing, but defining the scope of its provisions is another. We turn now to the Court's interpretation of several provisions of the Bill of Rights, beginning, naturally, with the First Amendment.

Pry It from My Cold Dead Hand

For some time now, the interpretation of the Second Amendment has been controversial, as some have argued for tighter control on guns while gun owners have decried the efforts to restrict gun ownership. Pictured here is actor and former president of the National Rifle Association (NRA) Charlton Heston addressing the association's membership. As president of the NRA, Heston has been a powerful voice for those opposed to limitations on firearm ownership. He has repeatedly opposed gun control by saying that his guns would be taken from him only if pried from his cold dead hand.

The First Amendment Freedoms

FOCUS QUESTION **WHAT BALANCES HAVE BEEN STRUCK IN APPLYING THE FIRST AMENDMENT?**

Because the First Amendment is written in absolute terms ("Congress shall make no law . . ."), it is more likely to be subject to the myth of absolute liberty than the other amendments. But as we will see, the exercise of First Amendment freedoms often conflicts with other highly desirable goals of society. Most justices have realized that it is impossible to protect all liberties without qualification. Therefore, the issue has been one of balance. Sometimes the Court has interpreted the safeguards of the First Amendment strictly, giving maximum protection to individual liberties. At other times, it has allowed the government great latitude in pursuing its interests. Drawing the lines has never been easy, but it has always been necessary.

Freedom of Speech

Freedom of speech is essential for a democracy. As Justice Black observed, "Freedom to speak and write about public questions is as important to the life of our government as is the heart to the body."[5] The First Amendment states that "Congress shall make no law . . . abridging the freedom of speech or of the press."

Nevertheless, the freedom to speak has often been the target of government regulation. No matter how highly we value free speech, each of us is likely at some time to see its exercise as dangerous. This is simply a recognition that ideas have consequences—consequences that we may disapprove of or even fear.

Changing Standards. Although the phrasing of the First Amendment seems to prohibit any limitations on speech, the Supreme Court has never viewed freedom of speech as immune from all government restriction. Justice Oliver Wendell Holmes once noted that freedom of speech does not protect someone who is "falsely shouting fire in a crowded theater." The Court has tried to define the circumstances under which the government may limit speech. To that end, it has employed a series of tests designed to strike a balance between the constitutional protection and the need for public order or security.

The first of these tests was developed by Justice Holmes in *Schenck v. United States* (1919).[6] Charles T. Schenck had been convicted under the Espionage Act of 1917 for distributing leaflets urging young men to resist the World War I draft. Writing for a unanimous Court, Justice Holmes rejected the proposition that speech was always protected from government restriction and instead expounded the **clear and present danger test**. The question, Holmes said, was whether speech would cause evils that the government had a right to prevent. If the speech could be shown to present a grave and immediate danger to the government's interests, the government had a right to punish it. In ordinary times, the justice admitted, the defendant would have been within his constitutional rights, but these were not ordinary times. Urging young men to resist the draft during a war was, Holmes said, a serious threat to the nation's safety.

Very soon after the *Schenck* decision, the majority of the Court began to substitute for clear and present danger the **bad tendency test**. That test allowed the government to punish speech that might cause people to engage in illegal action. Announced in *Gitlow v. New York* (1925),[7] the bad tendency test removed the need to prove a close connection between speech and the prohibited evil. To justify a restriction of speech, the government needed to demonstrate only that the speech might, even at some distant time, present a danger to society. Thus Benjamin Gitlow, a member of the Socialist party, could be convicted under a criminal anarchy law that prohibited anyone from advocating the overthrow of the government, even though there was no evidence showing that his efforts had had any effect

During the 1960s, questions of free speech became numerous as the civil rights movement and the movement against the Vietnam War generated a succession of mass protests. Sit-in demonstrations, protest marches, and draft-card burnings raised new issues of free speech. The Supreme Court of that era, led by Chief Justice Earl Warren, rejected the bad tendency test of the earlier period. It substituted the **preferred freedoms test**, which proposed that some freedoms—free speech among them—are so fundamental to a democracy that they merit special protection. The government can restrict these freedoms only if some particular exercise of them presents a grave and immediate danger to the larger society. Theoretically, then, government may limit speech, but in practice

Clear and present danger test The proposition, proclaimed by the Supreme Court in *Schenck v. United States* (1919), that the government has the right to punish speech if it can be shown to present a grave and immediate danger to the country's interests.

Bad tendency test The principle that the Supreme Court began to prefer, in First Amendment cases, over the clear and present danger test. It allowed the government to punish speech that might cause people to behave illegally.

Preferred freedoms test The principle that some freedoms—such as free speech—are so fundamental to a democracy that they merit special protection. The test was instituted by the Warren Court of the 1960s.

it is difficult to design a law that passes the test. The preferred freedoms doctrine comes close to banning all government restriction of speech.

Symbolic Speech. Not all speech is verbal. In fact, one may engage in what is called *symbolic speech* without uttering a word. Gestures or even the wearing of a certain type of clothing may convey an opinion, perhaps even more effectively than speech. Because symbolic speech is a form of communication, the Supreme Court has generally accorded it the protection of the First Amendment. In 1989, for instance, the Court upheld the right of protesters to burn the American flag. Writing for the majority in *Texas v. Johnson,* Justice William Brennan argued that laws that prohibit the burning of the flag infringe on a form of constitutionally protected speech.[8] Brennan's opinion was greeted by a storm of outrage. Saying that "flag burning is wrong, dead wrong," President George H. W. Bush called for a constitutional amendment to overturn the decision. Although Bush's proposed constitutional amendment failed in the Senate, Congress did pass the Flag Protection Act of 1989, which provided criminal punishments for anyone

Burning Old Glory

The congressional act of 1989 banning desecration of the flag prompted several protests challenging the law. Pictured here is a man, identified only as Dred Scott, being arrested by Capitol Hill police after he set fire to a flag on the steps of the Capitol.

who knowingly "mutilates, defaces, physically defiles, burns, maintains on the floor or the ground, or tramples upon any flag of the United States." In 1990, however, with Justice Brennan again writing the majority opinion, the Court, in *United States v. Eichman,* ruled that the new law also violated the Constitution's guarantee of freedom of speech.[9] Since 1990, several constitutional amendments outlawing flag desecration have been introduced in Congress, but none has received the necessary two-thirds vote in both houses. In 1999, the proposed Flag Desecration Amendment passed the House by the necessary two-thirds vote, but it fell four votes short of passage in the Senate.

Not all symbolic acts have gained protection from the Court, however. In 1994, for instance, the Court upheld a lower court's order prohibiting protesters from blocking the entrance to an abortion clinic. Writing for the Court in *Madsen v. Women's Health Center,*[10] Chief Justice William Rehnquist argued that the state's interest in protecting the well-being of the clinic's patients justified the restraint on free speech. This ruling was further extended in 2000 when, in *Hill v. Colorado,* the Court upheld a Colorado law restricting any speech-related activity within a hundred feet of any health-care facility. The law at issue made it a crime to "knowingly approach" within 8 feet of another person without consent, "for the purpose of passing a leaflet or handbill to, displaying a sign to, or engaging in oral protest, education or counseling." Calling the law "an exceedingly modest restriction," Justice Stevens upheld the law as a legitimate means of protecting persons attempting to enter health-care facilities.[11]

Critical Thinking

What kinds of symbolic actions might be considered speech?

The First Amendment's guarantee of free speech, including symbolic speech, also covers the freedom *not* to engage in symbolic action, such as saluting the flag. This freedom not to speak, in words or symbols, was first articulated by the Court in *West Virginia State Board of Education v. Barnette* (1943). In that case, Walter Barnette, a parent of school-aged children, challenged a West Virginia statute that required all teachers and schoolchildren to recite the Pledge of Allegiance while maintaining a stiff arm salute. Barnette, a Jehovah's Witness, claimed that the action violated a religious commandment against worshiping graven images. Speaking for the majority, Justice Robert Jackson held that the state could not compel any student to salute the flag. To those who argued that a compulsory flag salute was necessary to foster national unity, Jackson answered: "If there is any fixed star in our constitutional constellation, it is that no official, high or petty, can prescribe what shall be orthodox in politics, nationalism, religion, or other matters of opinion, or force citizens to confess by word or act their faith therein."[12]

Freedom of the Press

The same language protects the freedom of the press, which is closely linked with freedom of speech. Because the rights that are at stake are so similar, many of the lines of reasoning that apply in free speech cases also fit freedom of the press. As with free speech, however, the majority of Supreme Court justices have rejected the proposition that freedom of the press is an absolute.

Prior Restraint. Even though the Supreme Court has never accepted complete freedom of the press, it has repeatedly struck down laws imposing prior restraint. **Prior restraint** means blocking a publication from reaching the public. The First Amendment has stood as a strong check against would-be censors. The first significant prior restraint case, *Near v. Minnesota* (1931), illustrates the point.[13]

At issue in *Near* was a state statute that provided for the banning of "malicious, scandalous and defamatory" newspapers or periodicals. After he had printed a series of articles criticizing the local police department, Jay Near, the publisher of the Minneapolis-based *Saturday Press*, was ordered to cease publication of the weekly scandal sheet. In addition to his attacks on city officials, there was a constant anti-Semitic, pro–Ku Klux Klan theme in each issue of the paper.

Clearly, the *Saturday Press* was malicious, scandalous, and defamatory. Yet the Supreme Court lifted the ban on publication, with Chief Justice Charles E. Hughes observing that prior restraint could be applied only in "exceptional cases." Hughes admitted that under some circumstances the government might prohibit the publishing of truly harmful information — for example, information about troop movements in wartime. But in ordinary circumstances, the presumption should be in favor of publication.

A more serious challenge to freedom of the press arose in *New York Times v. United States* (1971), also known as the Pentagon Papers case.[14] Both the *New York Times* and the *Washington Post* published portions of a classified report on the history of American involvement in Vietnam. Citing a breach of national security, the government sought an order preventing further publication of the material by the two newspapers. A divided Court (six to three) ruled that the newspapers could continue publishing the report because the government had not justified the need for prior restraint. However, only Justices Black and William Douglas took the position that the government could never restrain publication. The four others in the majority assumed that in extreme cases, national security could justify an injunction, thus raising the possibility of a constitutional exercise of prior restraint.

The great leeway that the Court has granted the press in the area of prior restraint does not mean that the press is free to do as it pleases without regard to consequences. The press can be punished *after* publication. Two forms of expression, libel and obscenity, are particularly open to punishment.

Libel. **Libel** is the use of print or pictures to harm someone's reputation, whereas **slander** is injury by spoken word. Traditionally, these actions have not received First Amendment protection; therefore, they have been punishable under criminal law and subject to civil prosecution for damages.

Until 1964, a plaintiff could win a libel suit simply by proving that the statements in question were substantially false. In 1964, however, the Court expanded protection of the press by requiring public officials who claimed to have been libeled to prove that the statements were made with "actual malice."[15] In order to recover damages, an official must prove not only that the accusation is false but also that the publisher acted "with knowledge that it was false or with reckless disregard of whether it was false or not." This "actual malice" standard

---

Prior restraint The government's blocking of a publication before it can be made available to the public. The Supreme Court has repeatedly struck down laws imposing prior restraint on publications.

Critical Thinking

What might justify prior restraint?

Libel The use of print or pictures to harm someone's reputation; it is punishable by criminal law and subject to civil suits for damages.

Slander Injury by spoken word. Like libel, it is outside First Amendment protection and punishable by criminal law and civil suits.

was later extended to cover public figures—private citizens who, because of their station in life or their activities, are newsworthy. Actual malice is very difficult to prove, and therefore the Court's decisions virtually immunized the press against libel suits by public officials and public figures.

Perhaps the Court sensed that it had gone too far in protecting the press at the expense of private individuals who had been victimized by irresponsible attacks, because in 1976 it narrowed the category of public figures. In *Time, Inc. v. Firestone* (1976), the Court awarded damages against the news magazine *Time*.[16] A *Time* article about a divorce proceeding referred to the divorcée as an adulteress, a finding that was not substantiated in the trial court's decree. Ruling against the magazine, the Court redefined a public figure as one who voluntarily enters "into the forefront of public controversies." Because parties to a divorce do not meet such a test, Mary Alice Firestone did not need to prove actual malice, but only negligence—a lack of care in checking the facts. In 1988, however, the Court reaffirmed its "actual malice" standard for public figures when it ruled that the Reverend Jerry Falwell was not entitled to compensation for the emotional distress he suffered as a result of a vulgar parody of him published in *Hustler* magazine.[17]

Obscenity. Obscenity has never been considered to be deserving of First Amendment protection. Any work that is judged obscene may be banned. But what is obscene? Again and again the Court has confronted that question, and each time the justices have struggled to give meaning to the elusive concept. Indicative of the difficulty is Justice Potter Stewart's admission that he could not define hard-core pornography, but "I know it when I see it."

In the first of the modern obscenity cases, *Roth v. United States* (1957),[18] Justice Brennan observed that sex and obscenity are not synonymous. Consequently, Brennan tried to formulate a legal test for obscenity that would protect the right to deal with sexual matters and yet reserve to the government the power to prohibit what was truly obscene. The test he proposed was "whether to the average person, applying contemporary community standards, the dominant theme of the material taken as a whole appeals to prurient interest." Later cases attempted to clarify this test by describing the community standards as national standards, not local ones, and requiring proof that the work was "utterly without redeeming social value."[19] This latter aspect of the test made it virtually impossible for prosecutors to obtain pornography convictions.

As a presidential candidate in 1968, Richard M. Nixon vigorously criticized the Court's rulings on pornography as overly permissive. Thus, it came as no surprise when the Supreme Court led by Chief Justice Warren Burger, which included four Nixon appointees, moved to limit the spread of sexually explicit materials. In *Miller v. California* (1973), the Court ruled that prosecutors no longer need demonstrate that the work is "utterly without redeeming social value."[20] From *Miller* on, prosecutors have had to prove only that the work "lacks serious literary, artistic, political, or scientific value."

In the *Miller* decision, the Court also rejected the previous rulings that community standards mean national standards. Arguing that it is unrealistic to require

POLITICS & POPULAR CULTURE

What Does a Wardrobe Malfunction Cost?

Long after even the most fervent football fans have forgotten which team won the 2004 Super Bowl (New England), Janet Jackson and Justin Timberlake will be remembered as providing one of the most memorable moments in Super Bowl history. During the halftime show, Timberlake, in what the CBS television network carrying the event referred to as a "wardrobe malfunction," exposed one of Jackson's breasts to some 90 million television viewers. Although the exposure was so brief that many viewers did not actually see it, members of the Federal Communications Commission (FCC) were not amused. Citing federal law prohibiting indecent broadcasts, the commissioners fined CBS a record $550,000.

As it turns out, the "wardrobe malfunction" was the catalyst that emboldened the FCC to more vigorously enforce decency standards. One month after imposing the Super Bowl penalty, the FCC commissioners fined the 169 Fox TV stations $7,000 each for an airing of a single episode of the short-lived reality show *Married by America*. The episode in question featured sexually explicit scenes of bachelor and bachelorette parties. Although the nudity was pixilated, the sexual nature of the activities was clear and thus to the FCC indecent. Then in 2006, the FCC commissioners struck again, leveling fines totaling almost $4 million involving nine television programs. The largest of these fines, $3.6 million, was levied against the 111 CBS affiliate stations that broadcast a particular episode of the CBS drama *Without a Trace*. Depicted in the show were scenes of teenagers engaged in apparent sexual activities. Again, there was no nudity in the show, but the FCC concluded that the portrayal of sexual activities, especially as those activities involved minors, constituted a violation of the decency rules. Public Broadcasting did not evade punishment, either. In the case of PBS, a $15,000 fine was assessed because the documentary *The Blues: Fathers and Sons* contained numerous obscenities.

All of these fines were levied based on the FCC's interpretation of indecency, defined as any reference to sexual or excretory function aired between the hours of 6:00 a.m. and 10:00 p.m. But the law applies only to over-the-airwaves television and radio broadcasters. Although other forms of communications may be subject to prosecution for obscenity, they are not held to such a strict standard of indecency. Cable television programming and satellite radio (e.g., Sirius and XM) are exempted from the standards because as subscriber-based services not using the public airways, they are not licensed by the FCC. (Indeed, the frequently fined radio personality Howard Stern moved his highly popular show to Sirius Satellite Broadcasting to avoid FCC regulations.) Moreover, the Internet remains free of indecency restrictions. In 1996 Congress attempted, through the passage of the Communications Decency Act, to apply the indecency standard to Internet transmissions. But the Supreme Court struck down that portion of the act relating to decency requirements as suppressing too much speech.

Ironically, the FCC is aggressively pursuing over-the-airwaves broadcasters at the very time that they are losing substantial numbers of their audiences to competitors not licensed or regulated by the FCC.

the same standard in Maine or Mississippi as in Las Vegas or New York, Chief Justice Burger expressed faith in the ability of jurors to draw on the standards of their local community. Nevertheless, the question of what constitutes obscenity remains a perplexing judicial and social issue, with the Court's decisions allowing considerable variability among communities.

Freedom of Religion

The freedom to worship was one of the dominant motives behind the founding of the American colonies. Yet, surprisingly, the original Constitution makes only one mention of religion. Article VI states in part: "No religious test shall ever be required as a qualification to any office or public trust under the United States." Not until the First Amendment do we find guarantees of religious freedom. The amendment begins: "Congress shall make no law respecting an establishment of religion, or prohibiting the free exercise thereof."

As we have seen, the myth of absolute liberty has seldom been upheld because First Amendment rights have often conflicted with other rights and important social values. The problem is particularly acute in the case of religious freedom. The guarantee of the free exercise of religion clearly means that the state must avoid coercion with regard to religious beliefs. But what should be done when social policies offend particular religious beliefs? Does the state have the right to require school attendance and vaccination of public school students whose religious beliefs forbid such practices? Of course, the easy answer is to make an exception, but exceptions run the risk of violating another First Amendment provision — the establishment clause — by showing favoritism to one religion.[21]

Establishment of Religion. What does the establishment clause mean? Years of debate have produced two distinct opinions. One view, known as the **accommodationist interpretation**, holds that the clause was meant to be interpreted narrowly, merely barring Congress from establishing an official, publicly supported church, like the Church of England. Proponents of this view contend that nothing in the establishment clause forbids state support of religion as long as all religions are treated equally.

Others see the establishment clause as a broad-based prohibition against any governmental support of religion. Accordingly, they read the First Amendment as banning government involvement in all religious affairs, even in a completely even-handed way. Advocates of this view claim that the First Amendment requires a complete separation of the government and religion, or, as Thomas Jefferson put it, a **"wall of separation"** between church and state.

The Supreme Court has consistently espoused the "wall of separation" view. Yet in many cases the Court's decisions appear contradictory. They indicate that the justices have not completely rejected the idea of government aid to religious institutions so long as the government does not favor one religion over others. Thus, intense debate continues over the establishment clause. It usually focuses on two questions: aid to religious schools and prayer in public schools.

Accommodationist interpretation A reading of the establishment clause that bars only the establishment by Congress of an official public church. Accommodationists agree with state support of religion so long as all religions are treated equally.

Wall of separation An interpretation of the establishment clause that requires a complete separation of government and religion.

**Critical
    Thinking**

Does the Constitution
require a "wall of sepa-
ration"?

The question of government aid to church-supported educational institutions has long been a knotty problem for the Court. In 1947, the Court allowed to stand a New Jersey plan that provided free bus transportation for children attending parochial schools.[22] Justice Black, writing for the Court, reasoned that the plan was designed to aid the children and their families, not the religious institutions. Using this so-called child benefit theory, the Court has sustained state programs providing parochial schools with textbooks on secular subjects, school lunches, and public health services that are normally available in public schools.

In *Lemon v. Kurtzman* (1971), however, the Court declared unconstitutional state programs that used public funds to supplement the salaries of teachers in parochial schools.[23] Chief Justice Burger argued that supplementing teachers' salaries would require an "excessive entanglement" of government with religion.

Currently, the Court seems divided over establishment clause questions. Some members seek an accommodation of secular and religious practices, whereas others are intent on maintaining a high wall between church and state. A third group on the Court seeks to present a middle position. As a result, the Court has had difficulty drawing a clear line between permissible and impermissible aid programs.

Until 2002, this difficulty in assembling a coherent majority on the Court had left open the question of the validity of voucher programs — programs that provide state funds to parents who want to send their child to a school other than the assigned public school. In 2002, however, the Supreme Court seemingly settled this issue. Writing for a sharply divided Court, Chief Justice Rehnquist upheld Ohio's Pilot Project Scholarship Program. Under this program, parents of Cleveland schoolchildren can receive up to $2,250 for tuition at any public or participating private school in the city. Any private school in the city, including religious schools, is eligible to participate as long as it meets state standards and pledges not to discriminate on the basis of race, religion, or ethnicity. The effect of the program, at least in the short term, is to provide state funds through the parents to religious schools. In the first year of the program, 3,700 Cleveland students participated, and 96 percent of the vouchers went to religious schools. Nevertheless, the chief justice, writing for the five-member majority, ruled that the program was "entirely neutral with respect to religion" and therefore was constitutional. Arguing that the program allowed parents a true choice between public and private, secular and religious education, the chief justice found no violation of the establishment clause.[24]

With regard to the second question, the Court's decisions on prayer in public schools have created intense controversy. In 1962, public protests followed a ruling that a nondenominational prayer of twenty-two words composed by the New York State Board of Regents for daily recitation by New York schoolchildren violated the establishment clause.[25] One year later, the Court added to the controversy by declaring unconstitutional a Pennsylvania law requiring public schools to begin each day with a short reading from the Bible.[26]

Despite the fierce opposition of many religious and political leaders, the Court has maintained its stance that government-sponsored prayers in the classroom violate the First Amendment. In fact, the Court has never prohibited prayer in public schools; rather, it has forbidden government encouragement of or involvement in prayer. However, none of the frequent efforts to institute voluntary prayer in schools has met with the Court's approval. Indeed, the 2000 case of *Santa Fe Independent School District v. Doe* carried these decisions a step further when the Court struck down a Texas school district's practice of permitting a student, elected by the student body, to deliver an invocation before all home football games. According to Justice John Paul Stevens, "the religious liberty protected by the Constitution is abridged when the state affirmatively sponsors the particular religious practice of prayer."[27]

We must stress, though, that the Court has not opposed all exercise of religion in public life. For example, the Court has sustained the practice of opening sessions of Congress and state legislatures with a prayer.[28] Similarly, using what critics have called the "St. Nicholas, too" test, the Court ruled in 1989 that communities may erect Nativity scenes and other religious symbols as long as they are part of a larger display that includes secular objects, such as Santa's house and reindeer.[29]

Free Exercise of Religion. The First Amendment also guarantees that Congress shall not prohibit the free exercise of religion. This sounds like a straightforward statement that religious practice and belief must be free of government interference. The Court has consistently refused to examine the content of religious beliefs. Thus, we are free to adopt any set of beliefs and to call anything a religion.

Freedom to believe, however, is not the same as freedom to act. You can believe in a religion that demands human sacrifice, but the state has a right to make such sacrifices a crime. Following this reasoning, the Court has upheld a law that made it a crime to have more than one husband or wife at the same time, despite objections from Mormons.[30] It has also sustained Sunday-closing laws that have caused problems for Orthodox Jews[31] and laws that require children to be vaccinated despite their parents' religious objections.[32] In each of these cases, the Court argued that the guarantee of free exercise cannot be absolute. The justices did, however, recognize that laws that apply to the general population but unduly burden the free exercise of religion violate the First Amendment, unless the state demonstrates an especially important and compelling interest in the regulations. Illustrative of this approach was the Court's 1972 decision in *Wisconsin v. Yoder,* which exempted Amish children from compulsory school attendance laws.[33] Writing for the Court, Chief Justice Burger concluded that Wisconsin's general interest in an educated population did not justify restricting the free exercise of Amish religious beliefs.

Radically departing from this precedent, in *Employment Division v. Smith* (1990), the Court ruled that state drug laws need not make exceptions for the sacramental use of drugs by religious sects.[34] Specifically, the Court concluded that the state of Oregon did not have to provide unemployment benefits to a worker who was fired for violating state drug laws because he had ingested peyote as part of a ceremony of the Native American Church. Although the Oregon

Supreme Court reasoned that the use of the hallucinogenic plant was protected by the free exercise clause, the U.S. Supreme Court disagreed. Such restrictions on the exercise of religion were, according to Justice Antonin Scalia, permissible, as they were "merely the incidental effect of a generally applicable and otherwise valid provision." In other words, so long as the restrictions applied to all persons and were not intended to deny the free exercise of religious belief, the states needed to offer no compelling justification for the restraints. Under this reasoning, the states were given far more latitude in regulating religious institutions. Following the *Employment Division v. Smith* decision, for instance, Catholic teaching hospitals in Maryland lost their accreditation for refusing to perform abortions.

Critical Thinking

What other regulations may have an "incidental effect" on institutions?

Distressed by the ramifications of the decision, a nearly unanimous Congress passed the Religious Freedom Restoration Act of 1993 (RFRA). Under the terms of the act, government may not "substantially burden" a person's religious practices, even if the burden results from a generally applicable law, unless the government can demonstrate that the law (1) is in furtherance of a compelling governmental interest (e.g., health or safety) and (2) is the least restrictive means of furthering that compelling interest. With this act, Congress directly overturned the *Smith* case.

Congress did not have the last word on the subject, however. In the 1997 case of *City of Boerne v. Flores*, the Court considered the constitutionality of the RFRA.[35] In *Boerne*, the Roman Catholic church in Boerne, Texas, sought to overturn a local zoning ordinance that prevented it from expanding its original building. Claiming that the ordinance substantially burdened the free exercise of religion, the church argued that the RFRA exempted it from the zoning ordinance.

In his opinion in *Boerne*, Justice Anthony Kennedy delivered a stinging rebuke to Congress, declaring that the lawmakers had seized power that was not granted to the legislature. Congress had justified the passage of the RFRA under Section 5 of the Fourteenth Amendment (which empowers Congress to enforce the provisions of the Fourteenth Amendment by legislation). However, Justice Kennedy argued, Congress had not attempted to enforce a right guaranteed by the Fourteenth Amendment. Instead, he charged, it had attempted to create a right by changing the meaning of the free exercise clause. In passing the RFRA, Justice Kennedy declared, Congress had attempted to determine "what constitutes a constitutional violation." In other words, Congress had sought to overturn a Supreme Court interpretation of the Constitution by simple statute. This, he argued, is not within its powers.

In ruling the RFRA unconstitutional, the Supreme Court guaranteed that the issue of religious freedom will remain a contentious issue in American politics. Despite promises by religious leaders, Congress, and the president to find a way to reverse the decision, nothing has happened and the ruling remains the final word on the free exercise clause.

Due Process and Crime

Like the liberties discussed earlier, the rights of persons accused of crimes are rooted in the Bill of Rights, especially the Fifth Amendment's guarantee of "due process of law." These rights are meant to protect the individual from the arbitrary use of police power. When it comes to criminal suspects, however, there is little public support for the myth of absolute liberty. The Court has tried to balance the majority's demand for protection from criminals against the individual's need to be protected from excessive governmental power.

Right to Counsel

The Sixth Amendment to the Constitution guarantees an accused person the right to representation by a lawyer. For most of our history, however, the states were not required to provide attorneys to poor defendants, even though most prosecutions occur in state courts. In 1932, the Supreme Court did declare that in capital offenses—those carrying the death penalty—the state was obligated to provide a lawyer to those unable to afford one (*Powell v. Alabama*).[36] The occasion for the ruling was a famous trial known as the Scottsboro case. In that trial, which lasted only one day, Ozie Powell and seven other young black men were charged with and convicted of raping two young white women. Before the trial, the local magistrate had appointed all members of the local bar as counsel for the defendants. Not surprisingly, none of these lawyers stepped forward to mount an actual defense, and the eight were sentenced to death without ever having had adequate time to secure effective counsel.

Not until 1963 did the Supreme Court extend the state's obligation to provide a lawyer to everyone charged with a felony (*Gideon v. Wainwright*).[37] Nine years later the Court broadened the guarantee to cover any penniless defendant being tried for an offense for which the penalty is a jail term.[38] Considerably more controversial, and some would say more effective, were the Court's decisions providing for the right to counsel before trial. Even the most gifted lawyer is unlikely to be of much help to a client who has made incriminating statements during police questioning. In view of that fact and the likelihood that a fearful and ignorant suspect may say more than he or she intended, the Warren Court expanded the right to counsel to include the investigative stages preceding the trial. Justice Arthur Goldberg, speaking for the Court in *Escobedo v. Illinois* (1964), announced that the right to counsel applied whenever the investigation turned from a general inquiry to a focus "on a particular suspect."[39]

Two years later, the Court bolstered the *Escobedo* decision by requiring that police officers inform suspects of their constitutional rights. In overturning the rape-kidnapping conviction of Ernesto Miranda, the Court, in *Miranda v. Arizona* (1966), created specific guidelines for police interrogations.[40] Accordingly, suspects must be told that (1) they have the right to remain silent; (2) anything

The Scottsboro Defendants

Pictured here with Sam Leibowitz, an out-of-state lawyer provided by a labor organization, are the Scottsboro defendants. The young men underwent four trials, and the last of the group remained in jail in 1950.

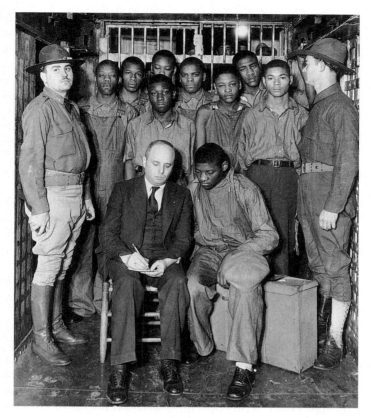

they say may be used against them in a court of law; and (3) they have the right to the presence of an attorney, and if they cannot afford an attorney, one can be appointed prior to any questioning. These warnings do not have to be given in this exact form, however. Police officers need only provide their equivalent.[41]

These so-called *Miranda* rights have become a basic part of police practices, but subsequent Supreme Court decisions have allowed several exceptions to the rule. For instance, the Court let stand the rape conviction of Benjamin Quarles in 1984. Before the *Miranda* warnings were read to him, Quarles, at the request of the police, implicated himself in the crime by pointing to the place where the weapon he had used in the attack could be found. In upholding Quarles's conviction, the Court argued that considerations of public safety may outweigh the need to strictly adhere to the *Miranda* decision.[42] Carving out an even more important exception, the Rehnquist Court ruled that the admission of an illegally coerced confession at a trial does not require overturning the conviction if, given all the other evidence, the impact of the confession was harmless.[43] The admission of an illegally acquired confession may be considered simply a harmless error if other evidence, gathered independently of the confession, substantiates a guilty verdict.

The Court's willingness to allow exceptions to the *Miranda* rule encouraged many opponents of the ruling to believe that, if properly asked, the Court would overturn its own precedent. The hopes of *Miranda*'s detractors were dashed in 2000, however, when in *Dickerson v. United States* the Court reaffirmed its previous decision, ruling unconstitutional a 1968 federal law that attempted to overturn *Miranda*. Chief Justice Rehnquist dashed all hope that the precedent could be overturned by statute when he ruled that "*Miranda* is a constitutional decision," and thus could not be overturned by a simple statute.[44]

Searches and Seizures

The Fourth Amendment states that "the right of the people to be secure in their persons, houses, papers, and effects, against unreasonable searches and seizures, shall not be violated." Notice that only unreasonable searches are prohibited. Unfortunately, the amendment does not tell us what is reasonable, making an absolute application of the amendment impossible.

As a general rule, a search may be conducted after a neutral magistrate issues a **search warrant**, which grants written permission. The authorities must fill out an application describing what they expect to find and where they expect to find it. In addition, the officers must set out facts that enable the magistrate to conclude that there is "probable cause" to justify issuing the warrant. Over the years, however, the Court has recognized certain exceptions to the warrant rule.

If a suspect consents, a warrantless search is legal, even if the suspect was unaware of his or her right to refuse.[45] Recognizing that cars are mobile and relatively public places, the Court has allowed them to be searched without a warrant if the officer has probable cause. In 1991, the Court significantly expanded that exception by ruling that police officers may conduct warrantless searches of closed containers found in automobiles if they have probable cause to believe that those containers conceal contraband or evidence. A suitcase being carried down the street may not be subjected to a warrantless search. But, somewhat paradoxically, that same suitcase may be searched without a warrant if it is found in an automobile.

Instances of hot pursuit also constitute an exception to the warrant requirement. Thus, police officers who are chasing a suspect need not turn back and acquire a warrant. In 1989, the Court created an additional exception by allowing drug agents, without warrants or probable cause, to use "drug courier" profiles to stop and search people who look like possible drug dealers. Finally, a police officer need not ignore evidence that is accidentally discovered; the officer may seize that which is in plain sight.

Before 1961, there were few effective checks on police searches. An individual who was subjected to an illegal search could sue the police for civil damages, but juries rarely sympathized with criminal suspects. Evidence found through a search was admissible in state trials even if it had been gathered illegally. Thus, in 1957, police officers in Cleveland, Ohio, broke into the home of Dollree Mapp and seized pornographic materials while looking for a fugitive. Mapp was

Search warrant A written grant of permission to conduct a search issued by a neutral magistrate to police authorities. Police must describe what they expect to find and must show "probable cause."

Exclusionary rule The principle that evidence, no matter how incriminating, cannot be used to convict someone if it is gathered illegally. Established by the Supreme Court in *Mapp v. Ohio* (1961).

convicted of possession of the pornographic materials seized in the warrantless search. On appeal, the Supreme Court overturned Mapp's conviction, ruling that evidence that was gathered illegally was inadmissible in state trials (*Mapp v. Ohio*, 1961).[46] This **exclusionary rule** means that evidence, no matter how incriminating, cannot be used to convict someone if it is gathered illegally. (See "Asked & Answered," p. 114, for more on the legality of police entering a private home.)

Perhaps no other criminal law ruling has stirred up as much controversy as the exclusionary rule. Law enforcement officials and political leaders around the country accused the Court of coddling criminals. The exclusionary rule provoked such a furor precisely because it dramatizes the conflict between the due process rights of individuals and society's interests in controlling crime. Despite the intense controversy, the Court has continued to enforce the exclusionary rule, although the justices have limited its reach by creating some broad exceptions. In 1984, for instance, the Court adopted what is called an "inevitable discovery exception": It permits the introduction of evidence that was collected illegally when such evidence would have been discovered anyway.[47] More important, that same year the Court allowed what is called the "good faith exception." If the police conduct a search using a warrant that later turns out to be invalid, the evidence discovered during the search is admissible at trial.[48]

In the 2006 case *Hudson v. Michigan*, the Supreme Court provided yet another exception to the exclusionary rule. Although *Hudson* involved an illegal no-knock search, Justice Scalia's opinion was a broadly written critique of the exclusionary rule. Noting that police officers are more professional than was the case in 1961, when the Court handed down the *Mapp* decision, Scalia argued that there is "increasing evidence that police forces across the United States take the constitutional rights of citizens seriously." Given this level of professionalism, Scalia suggested that administrative discipline and threats of lawsuits for damages would deter illegal police conduct, negating the need for the exclusionary rule. Moreover, Justice Scalia noted that the social costs incurred by throwing out of court otherwise valid evidence was too high a price to be paid for the small gain in privacy protection resulting from the knock-and-announce rule.

Cruel and Unusual Punishment

In the 1962 case *Robinson v. California*, the Supreme Court made the Eighth Amendment's protection against the imposition of "cruel and unusual punishments" applicable to the states.[49] But beyond noting that the punishment must fit the crime, the justices did little to explain what the terms *cruel* and *unusual* meant. Lawrence Robinson had been convicted under a statute that made it a misdemeanor to be addicted to narcotics. Robinson was not under the influence of narcotics at the time of his arrest, nor were any narcotics found on him. The police officer made the arrest after observing needle marks on Robinson's arms. Likening this situation to being punished for having an illness, the Court argued that even one day in jail would be excessive.

ASKED & ANSWERED

ASKED: Do police officers conducting a search have to knock and announce their presence before entering a home?

ANSWERED: Under English common law, "a man's home is his castle." This age-old maxim, known as the Castle Doctrine, provides that a home owner may use all manner of force, including deadly force, to protect his or her house and its occupants. In the 1995 case *Wilson v. Arkansas*, the Supreme Court, relying on this doctrine, ruled that the police may not enter a home without first knocking and announcing their presence.

But the Court has acknowledged exceptions. Under certain exigencies, officers may acquire so-called "no-knock" search warrants, whereby police officers may forcibly enter a home without warning. It has been generally acknowledged, for instance, that officials may obtain a no-knock warrant from a judge if they reasonably believe that announcing their presence will endanger the lives of police officers or others in the home. No-knock warrants may also be issued if police have reason to believe that evidence may be destroyed if advance notice of the search is given. Additionally, courts have commonly accepted the evidence garnered from no-knock searches conducted without a specific no-knock warrant, if police can demonstrate that unanticipated exigencies existed at the scene of the search that demanded quick entry into the home.

Still, the Supreme Court has continued to rule that no-knock searches should be the exception and not the rule. In *Richards v. Wisconsin* (1977) the Court invalidated a conviction based on evidence (drugs) seized as the result of a no-knock search, because the state had legislated a blanket exception to the need to knock and announce in all felony drug cases. Writing for the majority, Justice John Paul Stevens made it clear that the valid-ity of a no-knock search would have to be made on a case-by-case basis and not by legislating the use of such searches for whole categories of crimes.

Conversely, in 2003 the Supreme Court ruled that federal agents executing a search warrant were constitutionally justified in waiting only 15 or 20 seconds after knocking and announcing before forcibly entering a home. Writing for a unanimous Court in *United States v. Banks*, Justice David Souter argued that it was not how long it could reasonably take for someone to answer the door that mattered, but rather how long it might take the occupants to dispose of any evidence that dictated how long the police have to wait before entering.

In principle, this 15- to 20-second standard still applies, but the Court's 2006 decision in *Hudson v. Michigan* suggests a greatly diminished importance for the standard. The *Hudson* case involved a search by Detroit police in which they knocked and announced their presence, but waited no more than 5 seconds before entering the property. A search of Mr. Hudson's home produced substantial quantities of cocaine. He was subsequently convicted. Since the lower courts in Michigan ruled the police had conducted an illegal no-knock search, the Supreme Court did not reexamine the question of how long police officers had to wait before entering the house. Nevertheless, the Supreme Court upheld Mr. Hudson's conviction ruling that the evidence gathered from an illegal no-knock search is not subject to the exclusionary rule and thus can be admitted at trial. Even though police officers executing a search warrant still need to wait, at least 15 seconds after knocking and announcing their presence, failure to do so does not invalidate any evidence they may seize.

Critical Thinking

Must the punishment fit the crime?

Recent Court decisions, however, have cast doubt on whether the punishment must fit the crime. In 1991, for instance, a majority of the Court upheld a Michigan law that mandated a prison term of life without the possibility of parole for a defendant found guilty of possessing 650 grams of cocaine.[50] Writing for Chief Justice Rehnquist and himself, Justice Scalia argued that nothing in the text or the history of the Eighth Amendment supported the belief that the harshness of the penalty must be proportional to the severity of the crime. According to Justice Scalia, the Court's Eighth Amendment analysis should be limited to death penalty cases. Justices Sandra Day O'Connor, Anthony Kennedy, and David Souter agreed that the Eighth Amendment did not require proportionality, but they did conclude that it prohibited extreme sentences that are "grossly disproportionate" to the crime. It is unclear what constitutes a grossly disproportionate sentence, but the Court will certainly revisit that issue as litigants begin to appeal the state and federal laws requiring mandatory life sentences for repeat offenders — the so-called three-strikes-you're-out statutes.

In 1972 the Court addressed the most controversial of punishments: the death penalty. In *Furman v. Georgia,* a divided Court concluded that capital punishment was, in that particular case, a violation of the Eighth Amendment.[51] The Court did not reject the death penalty itself as unconstitutional; instead, the Court focused on what one justice referred to as the "wanton and freakish" pattern of the penalty's imposition. Thus, although the Court declared Georgia's death penalty unconstitutional, it also encouraged states to draft more precise laws that would guide judges and juries.

After the *Furman* decision, several state legislatures rewrote their death penalty statutes in an effort to conform to the Court's guidelines. This turned out to be difficult, however, as the Court seemingly zigzagged through the cases, allowing one statute to stand while ruling another unconstitutional. The justices continued to demand precise standards for the application of the death penalty and yet declared unconstitutional a state law that mandated capital punishment for specific crimes because it denied judges and juries the ability to consider mitigating circumstances.[52]

Moreover, in the past few years the Court has struck down some of its own post-*Furman* precedents. In 1989, the Court ruled that states could execute the mentally retarded, as long as the jury was allowed to consider the defendant's retardation as a mitigating factor. In 2002, however, the Court reversed itself and ruled that executing the mentally retarded violated the ban on cruel and unusual punishment. Writing for the majority, Justice Stevens relied upon what he saw as an emerging national consensus that mentally retarded defendants are different from ordinary offenders in that they are less blameworthy.[53] That same year the Court overturned another precedent when it ruled that the death penalty may be imposed only by a jury or a judge acting on the recommendation of a jury. Judges may not independently impose capital punishment.[54] In 2005, the Court, in *Roper v. Simmons,* overruled its sixteen-year-old precedent by concluding that the Constitution prohibits execution for crimes committed before the age of 18.

Privacy

FOCUS QUESTION   DOES THE CONSTITUTION PROVIDE A RIGHT TO PRIVACY?

In a classic law review article published in the 1890s, Charles Warren and Louis Brandeis first articulated the notion of a right to privacy.[55] They hoped to establish the "right to be let alone," but the concept did not easily find a place in American law. In fact, the Supreme Court did not recognize or create such a right until its 1965 decision in *Griswold v. Connecticut*.[56] Dr. Estelle Griswold had been convicted under a Connecticut law that made it illegal to provide birth control devices or even give instruction on their use. When the case was appealed to the Supreme Court, Justice William O. Douglas, writing for the majority, argued that the law unduly interfered with married couples' right to privacy. Because the Constitution does not specifically mention a right of privacy, Douglas took great pains to demonstrate that, taken together, several provisions of the Bill of Rights created such a right.

Abortion

In one of the most controversial decisions it ever delivered — *Roe v. Wade* (1973) — the Supreme Court extended the right of privacy to cover abortions.[57] The Court ruled that in the first trimester of a pregnancy, the decision about abortion rested with the woman. In the second trimester, the state could, in order to protect the health of the woman, dictate general rules governing the procedure, such as requiring that it be performed in a hospital. Only in the third trimester could the state prohibit abortion altogether.

For sixteen years the Court continued to apply the trimester approach developed in *Roe*. In 1989, however, the Court signaled a clear change in direction. Writing for a five-member majority in *Webster v. Reproductive Health Services*, Chief Justice Rehnquist let stand state regulations that significantly limited a woman's right to an abortion.[58] The Missouri law that was at issue in *Webster* required doctors to conduct tests of viability — tests to determine whether the fetus could survive outside the womb — whenever there was reason to believe that the woman was twenty or more weeks pregnant. Because twenty weeks is within the second trimester, the Court, by upholding the law, placed the trimester structure developed in *Roe* in grave doubt. Another provision that the Court let stand banned the use of public facilities for abortions and prohibited state employees from performing abortions. Although the Rehnquist decision stopped short of overturning *Roe*, the case demonstrated that the majority was willing to uphold a wide array of restrictions. Moreover, four justices made it clear that the trimester formula of *Roe* was, in their view, unworkable and unacceptable.

The *Webster* decision led many to assume that a constitutionally protected right to abortion could not survive further Court scrutiny. Expecting a definitive overturning of *Roe*, both supporters and opponents of abortion rights anxiously

Critical Thinking

What kinds of regulation constitute an undue burden?

awaited the Court's 1992 decision in *Planned Parenthood of Southeastern Pennsylvania v. Casey*.[59] The Court disappointed both sides. The five-to-four decision in *Casey* upheld several restrictions on abortions, including a requirement that a woman first be counseled on the risks of and alternatives to abortion and then wait at least twenty-four hours after the counseling to have the abortion. The narrow majority also upheld the state's ban on abortion after twenty-four weeks of pregnancy unless it was necessary to save the woman's life. More importantly, the Court rejected the trimester framework developed in *Roe*. Nevertheless, the Court fell short of overturning *Roe*, declaring that a woman's right to terminate her pregnancy "is a rule of law and a component of liberty we cannot renounce." In place of the trimester formulation of *Roe*, the Court substituted the "undue burden" test. An undue burden is any law that "has the purpose or effect of placing a substantial obstacle in the path of a woman seeking an abortion of a nonviable fetus." Thus, states were granted substantial new powers to regulate abortion but were prohibited from outlawing it entirely. Nevertheless, in 2006 South Dakota outlawed all abortions except when the life of the mother was at risk. Before the statute could be challenged, however, the voters repealed the statute in a public referendum.

Doctor-Assisted Suicide

Closely related to the abortion issue is the equally controversial question of doctor-assisted suicide. Through the advocacy of organizations like the Hemlock Society and more dramatically by the actions of a Michigan doctor, Jack Kevorkian, state laws making assisted suicide a criminal offense have come under attack.

This growing turmoil over euthanasia has once again thrust the Supreme Court into an intensely divisive moral issue. For now at least, the Court has denied that there is a constitutional right to doctor-assisted suicide. In 1997, Chief Justice Rehnquist, writing for a unanimous Court, rejected a lower court decision that the right to die with dignity, like the right to terminate a pregnancy, was an aspect of liberty protected by the Fourteenth Amendment. The state, Chief Justice Rehnquist argued, has "an unqualified interest in the preservation of human life." The state also has an interest in protecting vulnerable groups (the poor, the disabled, the elderly) from the risk of "subtle coercion and undue influence in end-of-life situations."[60] These interests, Rehnquist argued, outweigh whatever interests individuals may have in assisted suicide. In a second case decided in 1997, the Court rejected a lower court's ruling that banning doctor-assisted suicide constituted a denial of equal protection of the laws. The lower court had reasoned that since the terminally ill have a right to discontinue life-support systems and therefore end their lives, it is a denial of equal protection to prohibit terminally ill patients who are not on life-support systems from choosing immediate death. Again speaking for a unanimous Court, the Chief Justice wrote, "Unlike the court of appeals, we think the distinction between assisting suicide and withdrawing life-sustaining treatment, a distinction widely recognized and endorsed in the medical profession and in our legal traditions, is both important and logical."[61] Nevertheless, five justices clouded this distinction by conceding that patients are entitled to pain relief, even if the doses needed to relieve the pain might result in the death of the patient.

Far from resolving the issue, these cases are only the beginning of the debate. The Court has ruled that states may prohibit doctor-assisted suicide, but nothing in its decisions requires states to make the practice illegal. As the chief justice noted, "Throughout the nation, Americans are engaged in an earnest and profound debate about the morality, legality and practicality of physician-assisted suicide. Our holding permits this debate to continue, as it should in a democratic society." Currently, only three states (Nevada, Utah, and Wyoming) have no laws pertaining to doctor-assisted suicide. In 1994, Oregon voters approved an initiative that provides limited rights to doctor-assisted suicide. After years of court battles, the Oregon law took effect in 1998.

Equal Protection of the Laws

FOCUS QUESTION   **WHAT TYPES OF DISCRIMINATION VIOLATE THE CONSTITUTIONAL GUARANTEE OF EQUAL PROTECTION?**

The Declaration of Independence tells us that all men are created equal, and the Fourteenth Amendment provides for equal protection of the laws. The fact is, however, that all laws discriminate. Discrimination in its broadest sense involves treating particular categories of people differently, and that is what most acts of public policy do. The important question, then, is, what categorizations are constitutionally impermissible? Invidious or unconstitutional discrimination occurs when a category is based on characteristics that are not fundamentally related to the situation. As you will see, race is now recognized as such a category. That recognition has come slowly to a society dedicated to the myth of guaranteed equality, and so racial discrimination persists. Can the same conclusions be drawn with regard to distinctions based on sex? Here the answer given by the Court is not so clear.

The Continuing Struggle Against Racism

An important element of post–Civil War Reconstruction was the adoption of three key amendments: the Thirteenth, Fourteenth, and Fifteenth. The Thirteenth Amendment abolished slavery and involuntary servitude. The Fourteenth, as we have seen, addressed several aspects of individual freedom, but its key provision on civil rights is the clause declaring that no state shall "deny to any person within its jurisdiction the equal protection of the laws." The Fifteenth states that the right to vote cannot be denied on "account of race, color, or previous condition of servitude."

Jim Crow

Under the various statutes known as the Jim Crow laws, racial separation was required in all aspects of life. Nothing was too trivial to escape their reach, not even, as this picture shows, drinking fountains.

These three amendments, plus the congressional acts passed under their authority, promised the recently freed slaves a future of political and civil equality. Indeed, as C. Vann Woodward pointed out in his classic study, *The Strange Career of Jim Crow*, the period immediately following the Civil War was a time of great progress in assimilating the former slaves.[62] But the gains did not last.

In 1883 the Supreme Court struck down the Civil Rights Act of 1875, which forbade the separation of the races in places of public accommodation — transportation, hotels, and theaters. Congress had assumed that the equal protection clause of the Fourteenth Amendment gave it the power to pass the act. In disagreeing, the Court argued that the Fourteenth Amendment applied only to state-imposed segregation, not to discrimination practiced by private individuals. This interpretation implied that Congress could act if a state affirmatively discriminated, but not if it simply allowed segregation to exist. Thirteen years later, the Court dealt another blow to those seeking an end to racial distinction when it ruled, in *Plessy v. Ferguson*, that the Fourteenth Amendment did not even prohibit segregation.[63] On the contrary, the Court argued, separation of the races is permitted as long as they receive equal treatment. This is the infamous "separate but equal" doctrine.

The Court's narrow ruling on the Fourteenth Amendment, along with presidential lack of interest in racial equality, gave rise to Jim Crow laws. Community after community decreed the separation of the races, and almost no aspect of life was too trivial to escape the reach of these laws. Not only did states require separate drinking fountains and public bathrooms for blacks and whites, but some went so far as to require different courtroom Bibles.[64] The stress was on separation. Even the Court paid little heed to equality. Three years after *Plessy*, the Court let stand as a local matter a Georgia school board's decision to close the black high school while leaving open the all-white high school.[65] "Separate but equal," then, simply meant separate.

Public Education. Despite such setbacks, the struggle to end segregation in American society continued. The National Association for the Advancement of Colored People (NAACP), formed in 1909, became the driving force in these efforts. At first, the NAACP tried to persuade Congress to pass federal legislation forbidding segregation. Failing in the legislative arena, the organization created a separate unit, the Legal Defense Fund, directed by Thurgood Marshall (who later became a justice of the Supreme Court). The primary tactic of the Legal Defense Fund was to attack segregation in the courts.

In the late 1930s, the Legal Defense Fund began a series of court battles that challenged segregation in all areas of American life. It was most successful in the realm of education. As a result of the fund's efforts, the Court struck down a Missouri law that reimbursed black law students for out-of-state tuition rather than admitting them to the University of Missouri.[66] Then, in 1950, the Court ruled that a separate University of Texas law school for blacks was not equal to the University of Texas law school attended by whites because the former lacked certain intangible factors such as prestige and reputation.[67] Although the Court failed to overturn the "separate but equal" doctrine in its Texas decision, it came close to doing so.

Finally, on May 7, 1954, the Supreme Court startled the nation by a unanimous decision, in *Brown v. Board of Education of Topeka*, that the Fourteenth Amendment prohibits a state from compelling children to attend racially segregated public schools.[68] In a brief opinion that specifically overturned *Plessy v. Ferguson*, the Court simply declared that "in the field of public education the doctrine of 'separate but equal' has no place." No other conclusion was possible, the justices argued, because "separate educational facilities are inherently unequal."

Pronouncing segregation unconstitutional was one thing; compelling desegregation was another. Recognizing that fact, the Court set the case for reargument the following term in order to consider remedies, and *Brown II* (1955) required desegregation of public schools to proceed with "all deliberate speed."[69] "All deliberate speed," however, was interpreted by many school districts and lower courts to mean "all deliberate delay."

Between 1955 and 1969, little change occurred in public schools in the South, and the progress that was made came at a high cost. For instance, in 1957 President Dwight D. Eisenhower used federal troops to protect black students enrolled in a Little Rock, Arkansas, high school. The admission of the University of Mississippi's first black student sparked riots that resulted in the deaths of two men. Responding to this resistance, the Court proclaimed in 1969 that "'allowing all deliberate speed' is no longer constitutionally permissible." Every school district was "to terminate dual school systems at once."[70]

Implementing the *Brown II* decision in southern schools was hard enough, but in the 1970s the Court began to confront seemingly more difficult problems of segregation in the North. By that time, many urban school systems in the North were more segregated than their counterparts in the South, but this segregation was the result of housing patterns rather than state laws. Having ruled that courts could order remedial action, such as busing, only to correct instances of state-imposed segregation,[71] the Supreme Court had made it extremely difficult to remedy segregation caused by the movement of white families from the central cities to the suburbs. This movement created in the North a pattern of largely white suburban school districts surrounding increasingly black and Hispanic city schools. Thus, public school integration remains an elusive goal in many cities.

Critical Thinking

What power has Congress used to prohibit discrimination in public accommodations?

Public Accommodations. The *Brown* decision had little bearing on the widespread practice of private discrimination in public accommodations. As court efforts to eliminate discrimination against blacks continued, public protest against discrimination began to mount. In December 1955, Rosa Parks, a seamstress in Montgomery, Alabama, was arrested for refusing to give up her seat on a bus to a white man. Her arrest sparked a yearlong boycott of the Montgomery bus system — a boycott led by Dr. Martin Luther King Jr. Eventually the system was integrated, but not before Dr. King's home was bombed and he and several others were arrested for "conspiracy to hinder the operations of business."

The Montgomery bus boycott was only the beginning, however. In the early 1960s, unrest grew among the opponents of segregation: Blacks and white sympathizers increasingly turned to public protest. Marches and sit-in demonstrations received wide publicity as police reacted to the protests with increasing force. In 1963, President John F. Kennedy proposed legislation to desegregate public accommodations, which Congress finally passed at the urging of Kennedy's successor, President Lyndon B. Johnson.

The Civil Rights Act of 1964 made it a crime to discriminate in providing public accommodations. It barred racial discrimination in hotels, restaurants, and gas stations; at sporting events; and in all places of entertainment. The act also included provisions against discrimination in employment. Though the ground it covered was similar to that of the Civil Rights Act of 1875, the 1964 statute invoked congressional power over interstate commerce rather than the Fourteenth Amendment. To justify an attack on discrimination on the grounds that it interfered with the flow of interstate commerce may seem strange and even dehumanizing, but it was an effective way of getting around the narrow reading of the Fourteenth Amendment given by the Supreme Court in the Civil Rights Cases of 1883.

Voting Rights. As we noted earlier, the Fifteenth Amendment states that the right to vote cannot be denied on account of race. Nevertheless, after 1877 — the year the federal government stopped supervising elections in the South — southern states excluded the vast majority of blacks from the voter registration rolls. They did so through diverse and inventive means that commonly involved the use of some type of highly subjective test. Potential voters might, for instance, be given portions of the Constitution to read and explain. Because the examiners had complete freedom in selecting questions and answers, rejecting applicants was an easy matter. Even black lawyers sometimes failed the Constitution test. So effective were these efforts that in 1961 less than 10 percent of the black population was registered to vote in 129 southern counties.

To address this situation, Congress passed the Voting Rights Act of 1965. In states and subdivisions covered by the act, all literacy tests were banned, and the attorney general was empowered to assign federal registrars to enroll all applicants meeting state requirements. Extensions of the act in 1970 and 1975 banned literacy tests nationwide and broadened coverage to areas where large numbers of citizens spoke languages other than English — both languages spoken by immigrants, such as Spanish and Asian languages, and those spoken by Native Americans and the Inuit.[72] After a protracted struggle between Congress and the White House, in 1982 portions of the act were extended for twenty-five years. Finally, in 1991, the Supreme Court expanded the reach of the act by ruling that its provisions covered the election of state and local judges as well as legislative and executive officials.[73]

Sex Discrimination

White women have always held citizenship in the United States, but for a long time it was citizenship without political rights. Women could not vote, and married women were recognized by law as subservient to their husbands. They could not own property, contract debts, or even keep any money that they might earn. In return for a woman's giving up her separate existence, the law guaranteed that her husband would provide for her necessities. He was not responsible, however, for anything beyond what he decided were the necessities of life.

The first time American women organized politically was in the effort to abolish slavery. This first generation of feminists, led by Lucy Stone, Elizabeth Cady Stanton, Susan B. Anthony, and others, were dedicated abolitionists. In the organized opposition to slavery, these feminist leaders developed political skills that laid the foundation for the first women's movement.

Crucial to the movement was the first women's rights conference, held in 1848 in Seneca Falls, New York. However, suffrage — the most dramatic of the many reforms proposed by the Seneca conference — was submerged in the Civil War effort and then in the struggle over the post–Civil War amendments. Although some feminists wanted to add sex to the Fifteenth Amendment's list of attributes that could not be used to deny the right to vote, others opposed such an effort. Many supporters of the Fifteenth Amendment maintained that the issues of race and sex had to be treated separately if they were to be successfully resolved.

Among the many groups that continued to press for suffrage, none was more dedicated than the Congressional Union. Using techniques that would become more common in the 1960s, its members held marches, picketed the White House, and staged hunger strikes. Several members were jailed and beaten for their protests. Finally, in 1920, the Nineteenth Amendment was ratified. After years of struggle, the Constitution now contained the guarantee that "the right of the citizens of the United States to vote shall not be denied or abridged by the United States or by any State on account of sex."

After the adoption of the Nineteenth Amendment, the women's movement lost steam. The movement had always been broader than the issue of suffrage, but the long and difficult battle for the vote had displaced most other issues. Not until the early 1960s did the women's movement revive. This "second wave" has been seeking the eradication of sexism in all areas of life.

Paternalism and Discrimination. The ratification of the Nineteenth Amendment did not eliminate sex discrimination from American society, in part because sex discrimination, even more than race discrimination, stems from a strong tradition of paternalism. Discrimination against women has been routinely defended as a means of protecting them, even when the goal was exploitation.

For many years the Supreme Court rather uncritically accepted distinctions based on sex if they appeared to benefit women. The Court's 1948 decision in *Goesaert v. Cleary* illustrates that approach.[74] The Court upheld a Michigan law that prohibited a woman from working as a bartender unless she was the wife or daughter of the bar's owner. Women could, however, work as waitresses. The Court accepted the argument that the statute protected women from the unwholesome elements encountered by bartenders. The exception for wives and daughters was reasonable because the woman's husband or father would protect her. What the Court overlooked was that the statute maintained male domination of the better-paying jobs, while women were relegated to the less lucrative role of server.

Even the Warren Court, which did so much to open American society to racial minorities, accepted the paternalistic treatment of women. In *Hoyt v. Florida*, the Court upheld the conviction of a woman charged with murdering her husband. Gwendolyn Hoyt claimed that her conviction by an all-male jury violated her rights under the Fourteenth Amendment. Florida law made both men and women eligible for jury service, but it also provided that no woman would be called for jury duty unless she had previously registered with the clerk of the court her desire to be placed on the jury list. In declaring the Florida statute constitutional, Chief Justice Earl Warren noted that "woman is still regarded as the center of home and family life."[75] In other words, a woman had a right but not a duty to serve on a jury. Any vitality that *Hoyt* may have had as precedent was eliminated in *J. E. B. v. Alabama* (1994), in which the Court ruled that lawyers may not exclude people from a jury based solely on sex.[76]

In the past twenty years or so, the Court has been less tolerant of statutes that supposedly benefit women. Thus, the Court struck down an Oklahoma law that set a lower drinking age for women than for men.[77] Nevertheless, the Court continues to accept some classifications that treat men and women differently. For instance, the Court accepted as constitutional Florida's tax exemption for widows but not widowers. Noting the economic inequality that existed between men and women, the Court argued that the law was designed to compensate for past discrimination.[78]

Despite the Court's willingness to include sex discrimination under the equal protection clause of the Fourteenth Amendment, it has traditionally not received the same strict scrutiny as racial and ethnic discrimination. That may be changing, however.

Indications of a change in the Court's approach appeared in its 1996 decision on the status of the Virginia Military Institute (VMI) as an all-male school. VMI is a state-supported, four-year institution of higher education providing a unique experience. Students at VMI are subjected to an environment emphasizing "physical rigor, mental stress, absolute equality of treatment, absence of privacy, minute regulation of behavior, and indoctrination in desirable values." In order to stave off a constitutional challenge to the all-male admissions policy, the state of Virginia proposed the creation of a parallel military leadership program at nearby Mary Baldwin College. This Virginia Women's Institute for Leadership (VWIL) would not offer the same rigor that characterized VMI, but it would, the state argued, provide women with an education as citizen soldiers.

Critical Thinking

Does sex discrimination deserve the same protection as racial discrimination?

When this matter was appealed to the Supreme Court, Justice Ruth Bader Ginsburg, writing for the seven-member majority in *United States v. Virginia*, ruled that the all-male policy violated the equal protection clause of the Fourteenth Amendment.[79] Furthermore, Justice Ginsburg argued, the establishment of the VWIL fell far short of the necessary remedial action required. Virginia could comply with the equal protection clause only by opening VMI to women.

More important than the immediate case was Justice Ginsburg's apparent elevation of the level of review employed by the Court. Although the justice denied that classifications based on sex were to be treated like classifications based on race or national origin, she went on to announce a very high standard of review. Accordingly, Ginsburg noted that when reviewing classifications based on sex, "the reviewing court must determine whether the proffered justification is 'exceedingly persuasive.'" To most observers, "exceedingly persuasive" seems to be another way of saying "strictly scrutinized." Whether or not this is true only future cases will determine. It may be that in the future, questions of sex discrimination will receive the same scrutiny as those involving race and national origin.

Women in the Work Force.   One of the most dramatic changes in society has been the growing importance of women in the work force. In 1987, for instance, the Census Bureau reported that for the first time in American history, more than half of all women with children under the age of one were either working or actively seeking employment. Yet women's wages still lag behind those of men. To some extent, the wage gap between men and women represents employers' failure to abide by the Equal Pay Act of 1963, which requires "equal pay for equal work." Economists disagree over how much of the wage gap is the result of such discrimination and how much is the result of other factors. What cannot be denied is that women are now a vital part of the work force and that expectations of equality of the sexes in the workplace will not subside.

Although Title VII of the Civil Rights Act of 1964 prohibits discrimination in employment on the basis of "race, color, religion, sex, or national origin," the application of this provision to women has been slow in coming. Initially, the national government was reluctant to apply the act to cases of sex discrimination. In fact, Herman Edelsberg, a former executive director of the Equal Employment Opportunity Commission, portrayed the ban on sex discrimination in the workplace as a "fluke . . . conceived out of wedlock."[80] The federal courts often tolerated discrimination based on sex plus some other characteristic. For example, the Court used the "sex-plus" distinction to justify company policies that provided for compensation for all non-job-related disabilities except pregnancy. Such policies, the Court argued, do not constitute sex discrimination because they are not based simply on sex but rather on sex plus the characteristic of pregnancy.[81] Congress overturned that decision, however, by passing the Pregnancy Discrimination Act of 1978.

Critical Thinking

On what grounds is sexual harassment illegal?

Title VII also eventually became the vehicle used to attack sexual harassment in the workplace, but judicial acceptance of harassment as discrimination was slow in developing. Initially, courts ruled that harassment was a private matter that was not covered by Title VII. In 1974, for example, the District Court for the District of Columbia dismissed a case brought by an employee of the Environmental Protection Agency who claimed that her job had been abolished because she refused to have an affair with her supervisor. According to the court, the supervisor's actions did not constitute sex discrimination because they were motivated not by her sex but by her refusal to have sexual relations with him. Title VII, the court concluded, did not prohibit that kind of sex-plus discrimination.

Slowly, however, courts began to accept that at least some types of sexual harassment constituted sex discrimination. In the 1976 case of *Williams v. Saxbe*, the District Court for the District of Columbia became the first court to rule that sexual harassment could violate Title VII.[82] Diane Williams brought suit against the U.S. Department of Justice, alleging that she was fired less than two weeks after refusing her supervisor's sexual advances. In finding in Williams's favor, the district court ruled that the type of sexual harassment known as *quid pro quo* constituted sex discrimination. (*Quid pro quo* harassment occurs when a supervisor demands sexual favors from an employee in exchange for some employment advantage.)

Although several lower courts followed the *Williams* decision and permitted Title VII suits for sexual harassment, the U.S. Supreme Court did not rule on the issue until 1986. Writing for the majority in *Meritor Savings Bank v. Vinson*, Chief Justice Rehnquist argued that sexual harassment need not involve questions of promotion or job loss to be prohibited.[83] The creation of an offensive or hostile working environment, Rehnquist said, is sufficient to satisfy the definition of sex discrimination. Not every instance of offensive or annoying behavior in the workplace constitutes harassment, but the Court argued that a pattern of behavior that includes such things as requests for sexual favors, sexual innuendoes, or sexual insults creates a condition of employment disparity that Title VII prohibits. The Court's 1993 decision in *Harris v. Forklift* broadened this ruling. The Court decided that a woman claiming sexual harassment need not prove that she was psychologically injured in order to receive a damage award. She need only prove that the work environment was such that a reasonable person would find it hostile or abusive.[84]

Emerging Issues of Discrimination

Among the groups that are starting to seek coverage under the equal protection clause of the Fourteenth Amendment, none are more controversial than homosexuals and illegal immigrants. For over a decade, gay rights organizations and the Christian right have waged an ideological battle over the constitutional rights of homosexuals. The results, at least in the courts, have been mixed. Similarly, a growing anger over illegal immigration has prompted a national reexamination of U.S. immigration policy and the rights accorded immigrants.

Equal Protection and Sexual Orientation.   Initially, the Supreme Court was reluctant to extend judicial protection to homosexual acts. In the 1986 case of *Bowers v. Hardwick*, the Court ruled that state laws prohibiting homosexual sodomy, even between consenting adults, did not violate the constitutional right to privacy.[85] Writing for the five-member majority, Justice Byron White argued that whatever residual rights to the privacy of the bedroom existed were clearly outweighed by the majority's belief that homosexual sodomy is "immoral and unacceptable." Although the *Bowers* case, based as it was on the right to privacy, did not involve an equal protection claim, the decision did not suggest that the Court would be open to the advocates of gay rights. After all, if the majority's belief in the immorality of homosexuality outweighs the right to privacy, it stands to reason that it may also constitute grounds for discrimination.

Critical Thinking

Is discrimination based on sexual orientation protected by the Fourteenth Amendment?

Thus, the Court surprised both sides on this issue when, in the 1996 case of *Romer v. Evans*, it struck down an amendment to the Colorado constitution that prohibited any law protecting homosexuals from discrimination.[86] The amendment (known as Amendment 2) was the voters' response to ordinances in three Colorado cities that made it illegal to discriminate against homosexuals, as well as women and racial minorities, in housing, education, employment, and health and welfare services. Ignoring the *Bowers* decision, Justice Anthony Kennedy argued that Amendment 2 violated the Fourteenth Amendment by depriving homosexuals of the right to seek legal protection against any form of discrimination except by the extraordinary method of a constitutional amendment. In overruling Amendment 2, Justice Kennedy very carefully avoided defining homosexuals as a constitutionally protected class that was entitled to strict judicial scrutiny. Discrimination against homosexuals could, Kennedy argued, be justified so long as it served a legitimate government interest. But the justice went on to argue that the majority's "animus" toward a group does not constitute a legitimate government interest. No group, Kennedy argued, could be put at an electoral disadvantage simply because a majority disapproved of it. Therefore, as Justice Antonin Scalia pointed out in a biting dissent, the juxtaposition of *Bowers* and *Romer* means that a practicing homosexual may be jailed but not put at an electoral disadvantage. This apparent anomaly was eliminated in 2003, however, when the Supreme Court overruled *Bowers*, and declared existing sodomy laws in 12 states unconstitutional.[87]

Even as the courts were struggling with the question of discrimination against homosexuals, Congress entered the fray, this time to minimize the effects of a

Demanding Equal Treatment

Following the path laid out by previous civil rights movements, gay and lesbian rights supporters have, in recent years, begun to speak out against discrimination. Demonstrations such as the one pictured here have become more frequent as gays and lesbians have become more vocal in their demands for equal treatment.

decision of the Supreme Court of Hawaii. Like the other forty-nine states, Hawaii had limited marriage to two people of opposite sexes, but in 1996 the state's Supreme Court ruled that the law was unconstitutional. Even before the Supreme Court of Hawaii announced its decision, Congress rushed through and the president signed the 1996 Defense of Marriage Act. The act defines marriage as "the legal union between one man and one woman as husband and wife." More important, the act relieved the states of the legal responsibility — under the full faith and credit clause of the Constitution (Article IV, Section 1) — to recognize same-sex marriages performed in any other state. Nevertheless, the issue of same-sex marriages remains a hotly contested issue, particularly following the Massachusetts' Supreme Judicial Court ruling overturning the state ban. In several states constitutional amendments have passed prohibiting same-sex marriages and President George W. Bush has advocated an amendment to the U.S. Constitution, defining marriage as between a man and a woman.

Equality and Citizenship Status. Although it may seem ironic in a nation of immigrants, immigration policy and the legal status of immigrants have often been hotly debated in American politics. In recent years, the debate over the rights of both legal and illegal immigrants has gained new urgency. The state of California, a major destination for both legal and illegal aliens, has spearheaded this reexamination of the legal status of immigrants. On November 8, 1994, California voters opened a nationwide debate over the rights of illegal aliens by adopting Proposition 187. Among its many provisions, Proposition 187 required police officers, health-care professionals, social service workers, and teachers in public schools to verify the immigration status of persons with whom they came in contact and to report to state and federal officials any individuals who lacked proper documentation. The proposition also denied health care, education, and social services to those who were in the country illegally. This broad denial of benefits and services to illegal aliens raised legal issues that had never before been fully addressed. In 1982 the U.S. Supreme Court, in *Plyler v. Doe*, had ruled unconstitutional a Texas law that allowed local school districts to deny educational services to children who were in the country illegally.[88] Proposition 187 went well beyond the law that led to the *Plyler* decision in denying public services. Virtually all the provisions of Proposition 187 were declared unconstitutional by a federal district court in 1998.

Many of the goals embodied in Proposition 187 were given federal expression by the Welfare Reform Act of 1996. Hailed as "the end of welfare as we know it," the act, among other things, terminated Supplementary Security Income and Medicaid benefits to both legal and illegal aliens. A year later, Congress restored these benefits for most legal immigrants who were in the country when the legislation went into effect. The legal problems surrounding citizenship and immigration status continue to make this a highly divisive issue.

Affirmative Action

Affirmative action
A set of procedures that attempts to correct the effects of past discrimination against minority groups. It can include specific goals and quotas for hiring minority applicants.

Affirmative action is a set of procedures that attempts to correct the effects of past discrimination against members of racial minorities and women. In its least controversial form, affirmative action seeks only to ensure that members of minority groups are fairly considered for educational and employment opportunities. Much more subject to dispute are affirmative action plans that establish specific goals and quotas for hiring minority applicants. Attacked by opponents as reverse discrimination, such plans have increasingly provoked criticism.

In its first full review of the affirmative action issue, *Regents of the University of California v. Bakke* (1978), the Court sent mixed signals as to the constitutionality of affirmative action measures. In 1973 and 1974, Alan Bakke had sought admission to the medical school at the University of California at Davis. Both times he was denied admission, even though the school accepted others with lower test scores under its special admissions program for disadvantaged students. Bakke finally sued the school, claiming that he was a victim of reverse discrimination.

A majority of the justices agreed with Bakke and ordered the school to admit him. They argued that because the medical school did not have a history of racial discrimination, it could not establish numerical quotas for minority students. It could not, as had been done on the Davis campus, set aside seats for minority candidates. The Court held, however, that the school could take minority status into account when deciding on admissions; to ensure a diverse student body, the university could treat the applicant's status as a member of a minority group as a plus.[89]

Even though in the *Bakke* case the Court seemed to conclude that affirmative action was constitutional, the confusion surrounding the decision encouraged opponents to continue challenging affirmative action programs. In 2003 the Supreme Court reentered the fray over affirmative action in education by deciding a pair of cases from the University of Michigan, one involving its law school and the other its undergraduate admissions policies. Writing for the Court in *Grutter v. Bollinger,* Justice Sandra Day O'Connor upheld the law school's program of using race as a factor in admissions. Justice O'Connor noted that the law school had no quota for minority students and that each applicant was considered individually. Furthermore, the justice noted that the law school frequently rejects nonminority students with lower grades and test scores than minority applicants who are rejected. The justice did point out, however, that the Court expects that within 25 years' time, the use of racial preferences would no longer be necessary. On the other hand, the Court rejected the university's affirmative action program for undergraduate admissions. Students applying to the College of Literature, Science, and Arts were rated on a 150-point scale, with 100 points necessary to guarantee admission. Minority applicants were automatically awarded 20 points, and the Court found this discriminatory. This mechanistic approach of automatically awarding some students 20 points amounted, the Court majority concluded, to a quota system, a practice banned as far back as *Bakke.*[90] In spite of, or perhaps because of, these decisions, affirmative action will continue to be a highly divisive issue because it represents a basic conflict that is inherent in Americans' ideas about equality.

Conclusion: Absolutes and Qualifications

In this chapter, we have seen how inaccurate and inappropriate the myth of absolute liberty is. As we have noted, the Supreme Court — the federal institution that is most directly responsible for reconciling conflicting values — has never accepted this myth. For many citizens, however, the myth lives on with regard to First Amendment freedoms and occasionally inspires movements to thwart the Supreme Court by amending the Constitution.

There is little public belief in this myth when it comes to the liberties of criminal suspects, however. The Court has tried to balance the majority's demand for protection from crime against appropriate constitutional protections for suspects. A society that disregards the rights of defendants risks creating a police state that ignores all individual rights. Yet all societies must be able to prevent lawless behavior.

Finally, we have seen how in recent years the Court has recognized the reality behind the myth of guaranteed equality. Using the equal protection clause of the Fourteenth Amendment, it has done much to ensure civil rights for African Americans, although equality is yet to be achieved. But the Court has not expanded the concept of equality to cover other minority groups. Thus, women, the aged, the handicapped, homosexuals, and others still face considerable discrimination.

Tying It Together

FOCUS QUESTIONS RECAP

* How has the Bill of Rights been applied to the states?
* What balances have been struck in applying the First Amendment?
* What constitutional rights do those accused of crimes have?
* Does the Constitution provide a right to privacy?
* What types of discrimination violate the constitutional guarantee of equal protection?

CHAPTER SUMMARY

1. Civil liberties are the protections that individuals have against excessive or arbitrary government interference. Civil rights are guarantees by the government of protection against discrimination or unreasonable treatment by other individuals or groups.

2. Originally, the Bill of Rights did not restrict the actions of state governments. Through a process known as selective incorporation, however, the Supreme Court has made most of its provisions applicable to the states as well as to the national government.

3. Rejecting the position that all forms of speech are protected, the Court has attempted to balance conflicting interests, using a series of tests that consider the impact of the speech. Sometimes the Court has favored comparatively few restrictions on free speech, but at other times it has permitted more restrictions.

4. As with freedom of speech, the Court has rejected the argument that freedom of the press is an absolute; however, the justices have been unwilling to permit prior restraint, that is, blocking a publication from reaching the public. After publication, the press can be punished for libel or obscenity.

5. The First Amendment prohibits the government from establishing a religion, and it also guarantees the free exercise of religion. The Supreme Court's interpretation of these provisions has generated considerable controversy in American society.

6. Although it has made some exceptions recently, the Court continues to require that a person suspected of a crime be allowed representation by counsel and be informed of that right, as well as of the right to remain silent. Evidence seized illegally cannot normally be used to convict, although the Supreme Court has recently made broad exceptions to that rule.

7. Although neither the Constitution nor any of the Amendments specifically mention a right to privacy, the Supreme Court has decided that taken together, several provisions of the Bill of Rights created such a right.

8. Racial and sexual discrimination has burdened many in American society. The struggle for equality has led to the end of the separate-but-equal doctrine and some decreases in discrimination, particularly in education, public accommodations, and voting. But African Americans and women are still subject to discrimination.

9. Even as Americans struggle with racial and sexual discrimination, new equal protection claims command the nation's attention.

10. Among the most controversial of the equality issues is affirmative action. Though many view it as an essential means to ensure equality, others attack it as reverse discrimination.

Key Terms

Civil liberties (96)
Civil rights (96)
Selective incorporation (98)
Clear and present danger test (100)
Bad tendency test (100)
Preferred freedoms test (100)
Prior restraint (103)

Libel (103)
Slander (103)
Accommodationist interpretation (106)
Wall of separation (106)
Search warrant (112)
Exclusionary rule (113)
Affirmative action (128)

 ## Net Work

Do you want to research court decisions?

- One of the best places to start is **www.findlaw.com**. This site provides the full text of all federal court decisions, including those of the U.S. Supreme Court, and also includes the decisions of selected state courts.

- Cornell Law School's Legal Information Institute (**www.law.cornell.edu/opinions.html**) is another useful source for recent federal and state court opinions.

As an exercise, explore a particular civil rights or civil liberties issue that interests you. Take the following steps to research your issue of choice:

- Begin by familiarizing yourself with the positions of legal interest groups. You might, for instance, look at the arguments advanced by the American Civil Liberties Union (ACLU) (**www.aclu.org**).

- Next check out the Southeastern Legal Foundation (**www.southeasternlegal.org**). Because this

organization and the ACLU litigate many of the same issues, often in opposition to each other, you can compare and contrast their arguments.

- For further information, check out the position taken by the U.S. Department of Justice. If the issue you have chosen was argued before the U.S. Supreme Court, you can find the full text of any briefs submitted by the U.S. government at **www.usdoj.gov/05publications/05_2.html**. If the issue was litigated by a U.S. court of appeals, you can also find the government's brief before that court at **www.usdoj.gov/05publications/05_2.html**.

- Finally, if you go to the FindLaw site (**www.findlaw.com**), you can, for any recent case, click on all the briefs (including third-party briefs) submitted on behalf of both sides. Read these briefs and use the Web to locate the parties preparing them. How much can you learn about these groups?

5

Public Opinion and Political Participation

Is there such a thing as majority opinion?

FOCUS QUESTIONS

* How do we define political public opinion?

* What agents of political socialization help to shape and influence our opinions about government and politics?

* What factors contribute to a well-designed and effective poll? What factors contribute to a poorly designed poll?

* Do the findings from public opinion polls suggest that Americans question the principles of democracy and representative government?

* How does public opinion vary within and among different ethnic, religious, racial, and age groups?

* What are the different ways in which Americans participate in the political system?

A re you afraid of snakes? Do spiders and insects give you the creeps? What about mice? These are strange questions, no doubt, for an American government textbook. But they are questions that have been asked by reputable polling organizations, and that Americans have opinions on. (You may find it interesting that 51 percent of Americans are afraid of snakes; 27 percent share a fear of spiders and insects; and 20 percent are frightened by mice.[1]) And while attitudes about snakes, spiders, and mice may have relatively little to do with American government and politics, public opinion and polls do play a central role in the shaping of politics and policy in the United States.

The role that public opinion plays in public policy decisions often presents a complex problem for elected officials. In general, policymakers feel compelled to pay close attention to public opinion on an issue, whether that opinion is held by a majority of the public (more than 50 percent) or simply by a plurality (the largest percentage among those polled, but not a majority). Yet public opinion is often difficult to assess. More often than not, pluralities rule the day. This has certainly been the case in recent years regarding the issue of supporting the use of biotechnology in agricultural and food production. One recent poll found that 45 percent of the public supported the use of biotechnology in food production, while 45 percent of the public felt it was wrong.[2] The diversity in public opinion on this issue has made any attempt by Congress to regulate in this area highly controversial and open to considerable debate.

Polls have become ingrained in the political process—not only for predicting election outcomes, but also as a tool that politicians, scholars, and the media use to measure and assess the public's opinions on everything, from its favorite presidential candidate to its attitudes toward specific issues or laws. This reliance on polls comes about, in part, because of the widespread misconception that public opinion is majority opinion. Elected officials who claim that they are following majority opinion when they vote on legislation share this misconception. This view of public opinion is strongly influenced by a widely held myth: the myth of majority opinion.

The *myth of majority opinion* occasionally surfaces in high school civics books. According to that myth, public opinion "is generally used to refer to the opinion held about any issue by a majority of the people."[3] In reality, the public cannot be viewed as a monolith with a single, or even a majority, viewpoint. Rather, the public must be viewed more realistically as a mixture of groups with varying viewpoints that typically arrive at a consensus through compromise. Such compromise potentially allows government to produce reasonably satisfactory public policies. On many issues, public officials must balance a diverse set of opinions voiced by a variety of groups. In effect, "majority opinion" is often unclear, unstable, or nonexistent.

In this chapter, we look at the origins of public opinion and its content. By understanding the facts behind the myth of majority opinion, you can gain a sense of how the public influences the decisions made by government.

We also examine different forms of participation in the political system, for it is often the strength and intensity of public opinion that lead to political

Critical Thinking

Is the absence of a clear majority opinion on many issues in our political system good or bad?

Acting on Political Beliefs and Opinions

Americans hold opinions on many issues, opinions that often vary in intensity, salience, stability, and direction. On April 10, 2006, thousands of demonstrators took part in the National Day of Action for Immigrant Justice in Washington, D.C., calling for congressional action on immigration rights and justice.

activism and participation on the part of citizens. Many journalists, social scientists, and others argue, on the basis of low voter turnout, that citizen participation in politics in the United States is very low. However, participation in politics can take many forms other than the act of voting, from joining the school board, the PTA, or other community groups to attending political rallies and discussing politics with family and friends. It is important to examine not only the origins and content of public opinion but also the many ways in which Americans act on their beliefs and opinions.

First of all, however, we define public opinion and describe its characteristics. Then we discuss the way political beliefs develop and the use of polls in measuring public opinion. We next turn our attention to different avenues of political participation and the factors that promote activism in the political system. Finally, we examine how public opinion can and does have an impact on public policy.

What Is Public Opinion?

FOCUS QUESTION   HOW DO WE DEFINE POLITICAL PUBLIC OPINION?

V. O. Key, a respected scholar of public opinion, said that "to speak with precision of public opinion is a task not unlike coming to grips with the Holy

Political public opinion
The collective preferences expressed by people on political issues, policies, institutions, and individuals.

Opinion intensity The strength of one's opinion about an issue.

Opinion saliency One's perception of the relevancy of an issue.

Opinion stability The degree to which public opinion on an issue changes over time.

Opinion direction One's position in favor of or against a particular issue. Much of the time there are various shades of support for an issue, with no clear and precise direction of public opinion.

Critical Thinking

Can you think of various political issues on which the intensity, saliency, and stability of your opinions vary?

Ghost."[4] And yet no democratic government can afford to ignore public opinion, for it is public opinion that links the values, demands, and expectations of the citizens of any country to the actions of their government. What, then, is this elusive concept? Stated formally, **political public opinion** is the collective preferences expressed by people concerning political issues, policies, institutions, and individuals. In using the term *collective*, we are arguing that public opinion is not "majority" opinion but, more precisely, a collection of opinions that generally reflect a variety of beliefs on a given issue or problem.

Public opinion varies in **intensity, saliency, stability,** and **direction**. Not every issue evokes intense feelings, and not every issue is equally salient or stable. In addition, public opinion varies in terms of direction, that is, whether it is in favor of or against a particular issue. Much of the time there are various levels of support for an issue, with no clear and precise direction of public opinion.

For example, many Americans share a concern about the treatment of laboratory animals. But few feel intensely about this issue, and many may not view it as a salient or relevant issue, either because it matters little in their everyday lives or because they believe that other issues are more important to focus on. In contrast, most people feel strongly, or intensely, about unemployment and high interest rates. These issues are salient, or important, to them because they affect them directly. On other issues — for example, abortion — there are so many shades of opinion among those who are generally in favor of or against that the policy direction supported by the public is unclear.

Public opinion also varies in stability. For example, one poll dealing with national health care found that 61 percent of those surveyed were "willing to pay higher taxes so that all Americans have health insurance that they can't lose, no matter what." A survey taken just one week later found 65 percent of the respondents to be against "raising additional money from taxes" to pay for a national health-care plan.[5] The stability of public opinion over longer periods of time also fluctuates. In 1966, 42 percent of Americans favored the death penalty for individuals convicted of murder. By 1986, that percentage had grown to 70 percent. Today, that percentage has declined to 64 percent.[6] Thus, far from being stable, public opinion on many issues, especially on difficult issues, may be vulnerable to the expectations and demands of the people. On less complex and confusing matters, however, such as public funding of congressional campaigns or federal funding of higher education, public opinion has remained generally stable and favorable over the years.

Many public officials use measures of intensity, saliency, stability, and direction as a guide to the public's political preferences. If a majority, or even an active minority, of the public seems indifferent, or if opinions are unstable and shifting, officials may discount the public's views or not act at all. In contrast, salient issues that arouse intense feelings and popular passions are likely to generate action.

How We Develop Our Beliefs and Opinions

WHAT AGENTS OF POLITICAL SOCIALIZATION HELP TO SHAPE AND INFLUENCE OUR OPINIONS ABOUT GOVERNMENT AND POLITICS?

What factors influence the intensity and stability of public opinion? People's long-term political convictions—particularly whether they think of themselves as Democrats or Republicans—constitute one important factor. Some of the other key determinants are people's views on the role of women and minorities in politics, the value of compromise in the political process, the appropriate use of money in political campaigns, and the effectiveness of the democratic process. When we recently asked our students about their views on terrorism, we found that most based their opinions on such long-term values as the sanctity of life, concern about the random killing of innocent human beings, and faith in the democratic process. These beliefs were strongly reinforced with the loss of thousands of lives after the terrorist attacks on September 11, 2001, on the World Trade Center in New York City and the Pentagon in Washington, D.C.

How do long-term political values and beliefs develop? According to social scientists, they are based on the different experiences that people undergo throughout their lives. Single historical events like that of September 11, 2001, can have a lasting impact on citizens' values and beliefs. There are also subtle long-term impacts on our political beliefs and attitudes. Growing up or living in Boston, Tampa, Pittsburgh, Houston, Cincinnati, San Diego, or Oklahoma City is very different from growing up or living in rural Wyoming, Texas, Vermont, or North Carolina. These differences translate into regional variations in what people believe and value; further differences in opinion derive from gender, race, class, and other factors.

As we indicated in Chapter 1, political ideologies frequently shape our attitudes and opinions about specific political issues and institutions. As the political scientist Max Skidmore suggests, "**Political ideology** is a form of thought that presents a pattern of complex political ideas simply and in a manner that inspires action to achieve certain goals."[7]

Most Americans have a common, or core, **political culture**—that is, a set of shared values, beliefs, and traditions with regard to politics and government. These shared values include a general faith in democracy, in representative government, in the free-market system, in freedom of speech, and in the rights of individuals. The process by which people acquire these important values and gain knowledge about politics is known as **political socialization**. It is strongly influenced by persons with whom an individual has contact from early childhood through adulthood.

Political ideology
A pattern of complex political ideas presented in an understandable structure that inspires people to act to achieve certain goals.
Political culture A set of values, beliefs, and traditions about politics and government that are shared by most members of society. Political culture in the United States includes faith in democracy, representative government, freedom of speech, and individual rights.
Political socialization The process by which individuals acquire political values and knowledge about politics. It is strongly influenced by people with whom an individual has contact from early childhood through adulthood.

Agents of Political Socialization

Children are influenced by many variables as they grow up and are exposed to the political world around them. They learn from songs, the celebration of holidays, the honoring of heroes, and a variety of patriotic rituals that we as Americans practice. Some institutions play a particularly strong role in our acquisition of political values and knowledge.

Family and Friends. Families, especially parents, transmit to their children basic attitudes, beliefs, and values that mold the children's views of the political world. These general values include perceptions of right and wrong and attitudes toward authority figures—parents, teachers, police officers, judges, and political officeholders. They also include perceptions of one's **political efficacy**, that is, one's ability to have an impact on the political system. Family and friends also have an impact on our attitudes about the political system, including how trusting or cynical we may be toward government and politicians, and how alienated from government we may feel.

One specific belief often passed from parent to child that is particularly important in understanding political opinions and behavior is **party identification**, or whether people think of themselves as Democrats, Republicans, or independents. Many studies have found that children have a strong tendency to adopt the party identification of their parents. Despite the significant number of eighteen- to thirty-year-olds who call themselves political independents, children tend to choose the same party as their parents when both mother and father share the same identification.

Peer groups and friends have relatively little influence on a person's party identification or voting behavior at the age of eighteen. As we get older, however, our peers tend to reinforce our already established beliefs because we tend to associate with friends and colleagues who share similar values and attitudes.

Political efficacy The perception of one's ability to have an impact on the political system.

Party identification The tendency of people to think of themselves as Democrats, Republicans, or independents.

I Pledge Allegiance

Like schoolchildren all over America, these second-grade students in Austin, Texas, begin their day with a recitation of the Pledge of Allegiance. Schools are an important influence in learning about politics, often reinforcing such political virtues as patriotism and support of our government system.

School. Another institution that potentially has a great impact on political socialization is the school. At any given time, about a quarter of the population is enrolled, full or part-time, in degree-granting educational programs. Public schools teach such political virtues as patriotism, compliance with the laws, the importance of voting, and the peaceful changeover of presidential administrations. By repeating many of the lessons about government that we learn at home, the school reinforces many of the values we already hold about politics and government.

The amount of schooling a person has greatly influences the way that person forms opinions and views the political world. There are differences between the better educated and the less well educated on a wide range of attitudes and behavior. Better-educated men and women generally know more about politics. Those who have been to college are more likely than others to hold liberal views on civil liberties and rights, foreign policy, and social questions. Education also brings confidence that one can affect political and government policy—what we earlier called political efficacy—which leads to a relatively high level of participation in politics.[8]

The Media. The media, particularly television, are also important socializing agencies. Ninety-eight percent of households in the United States have at least one television. The average child watches close to three hours of television a day, and 58 percent of families watch television during meals.[9] Because the average family television is on about seven hours a day, its potential effect as an agent of political socialization is enormous. But what is its actual influence?

Although television teaches and reinforces general beliefs and attitudes, it has limited political impact, chiefly because such a small proportion of programming has direct political content. For example, in 1952, television network coverage of the Republican and Democratic conventions averaged about sixty hours. During the 2004 conventions, the average coverage had been reduced to a total of only three hours for each of the three major networks.[10]

Clearly, the media in all their forms, including broadcast and print, play an important role in the socialization of Americans. But a careful examination of that role suggests that its impact is varied and is dependent on our viewing and reading habits. (We say more about the impact of the media, including the press, in Chapter 9.)

Religion. Religion can often serve, both directly and indirectly, as an important agent of political socialization. Indirectly, religion teaches morality and values—values that are often also learned from family, schools, and the media—that can apply to the way we think about government and politics. Later in life we may view the acts of politicians through the "value lenses" afforded us by attending a church, synagogue, or mosque of our choice. Religious institutions also take overt positions on political issues that may affect our political beliefs. Some denominations, for example, strongly oppose abortion and voice that position in political campaigns. Others support a woman's right to choose an abortion. An individual's religious training can influence his or her attitudes about many political issues and thus have an impact on the political socialization process.

Critical Thinking

Does television play too great a role in shaping and influencing our opinions about politics?

Political Culture. Although Americans share a common political culture, a variety of political subcultures flourish in this vast country.[11] Individuals who grow up and live in one region have different religious, ethnic, and racial backgrounds and customs and undergo different economic and social experiences from those living in other parts of the country. A carpenter who grew up and still lives in the rural poverty of West Virginia is far less likely to view the political system as responsive than is a lawyer who grew up and prospered in Florida, a state that has experienced great economic growth. Such influences help shape the way a person views the political world.

Indeed, variations in life experience inevitably result in differing political, social, and economic views. The work of pollsters and public officials would be made easier if the myth of majority opinion were true. But reality, it seems, is never that simple.

Adult Socialization

Critical Thinking

Is it OK that Americans tend to be cynical about many aspects of the political system and process?

Not surprisingly, political socialization is not just a childhood experience. As parents' influence declines, coworkers, neighbors, and friends reinforce—and sometimes shape—adults' opinions. Television, of course, affects adults' political views more than children's because adults rely on it for the news more than children do. And a variety of additional media—newspapers, magazines, and radio—provide wider exposure to political information.

In addition, adults bring their own established ideas to their assessment of new situations. They are also likely to be influenced by the current conditions of their life. For example, parents may see more merit in a tax increase to support local schools than do childless adults. Events such as the September 11, 2001, terrorist attack on the United States or the impact of Hurricane Katrina in 2005 on New Orleans, the Gulf Coast, and the rest of the nation continue to shape the values and opinions of millions of adult Americans who view our national security as well as our social welfare as major public policy issues. Thus, the development of public opinion is clearly a process that continues throughout adulthood.

How Polls Work

FOCUS QUESTION WHAT FACTORS CONTRIBUTE TO A WELL-DESIGNED AND EFFECTIVE POLL? WHAT FACTORS CONTRIBUTE TO A POORLY DESIGNED POLL?

Informal public opinion surveys date at least as far back as 1824, when a reporter from the *Harrisburg Pennsylvanian*, standing on a street corner in Wilmington, Delaware, asked 532 men whom they planned to vote for in the presidential race that year. But it was not until the 1930s that George Gallup and Elmo Roper began to experiment with scientific measures of public opinion. By taking into account differences in age, gender, ethnic background, race, religion, social class, and region, pollsters such as Gallup and Roper were able to measure opinion on many issues with a high degree of accuracy.

POLITICS & POPULAR CULTURE

Public Opinion, Participation, and Rock 'n' Roll

Popular music has long been used as a tool to bring attention to political movements. Folk singers such as Woody Guthrie and Pete Seeger in the 1940s and 1950s sang about what they felt were social injustices. More recently, we've seen artists take up causes ranging from African famine relief to Tibetan freedom. Entertainers have increasingly attempted to influence public opinion in support of particular political candidates. As recent presidential campaigns indicate, many musicians have become active participants in the election process, encouraging voters to take part in the election in support of Democratic and Republican candidates.

In particular, music's political "great divide" seems to have arisen between the worlds of country and rock. Whereas the pro-Kerry (or at least anti-Bush) Vote for Change tour in 2004 featured the likes of rock mainstays Bruce Springsteen, R.E.M., and Pearl Jam, country music stars such as Ricky Skaggs, Brooks & Dunn, and Toby Keith hit the road that summer in support of President Bush. Both sides were also involved with voter registration initiatives that claimed to be nonpartisan—from "Punk Voter" to "Your Country, Your Vote"—though the ideological preferences of those in charge of these movements often wound up being forcefully impressed upon the young people they reached out to. (Back in 1992, Soundgarden front man Chris Cornell initially was quite enthusiastic about recording promos for MTV's "Rock the Vote" campaign, but he later backed out when he concluded that the organization was supporting the Democratic party.)

On occasion, participation by musicians in politics may backfire on them. What happens when a musical artist professes support for a political cause that runs counter to the ideology of some of their fans? Country stars the Dixie Chicks found that out in 2003 when, while America was gearing up for an invasion of Iraq, their lead singer stated that she was "ashamed the President of the United States was from Texas."[1]

Shortly thereafter, the group members apologized for being "disrespectful" toward Bush, but continued to state their opposition to the war, even in the face of boycotts of their music by some fans and country radio stations. The group has since toured successfully in America, but has stated that they "don't feel a part of the country scene any longer" and wound up joining Bruce Springsteen on the Vote for Change rally in the fall of 2004.[2]

Interestingly enough, similar splits are found on the opposite side of the political spectrum. Punk legends the Ramones are nothing if not antiestablishment heroes, yet guitarist Johnny Ramone was a lifelong Republican who, when the band was being inducted into the Rock and Roll Hall of Fame in 2002, took the podium and proclaimed, "God bless President Bush, and God bless America."[3] When later questioned about his conservative beliefs, he replied, "I believe Ronald Reagan was the best president of our lifetime."[4] But the Ramones were long finished as an active band—their last album was recorded in 1996—when Johnny Ramone made his comments, so the remarks drew comparatively little reaction from the rock community or the public.

Do musicians actually influence public opinion or sway anyone's vote? The answer is unclear, but evidence would seem to indicate that any impact is marginal at best. None of the battleground states that were venues for the Vote for Change tour voted in a manner different from that predicted in preelection polls, and Ohio—despite hosting six concerts—turned out to be one of Bush's most critical victories. Former metal rocker Alice Cooper commented during the summer of 2004 that "if you're listening to a rock star in order to get your information on whom to vote for, you're a bigger moron than they are."[5] While that statement might be overly harsh, the truth is that we've yet to see platinum record sales and the participation and attempts to influence the political beliefs by celebrity musicians translate into political influence.

1. *Guardian Unlimited*, September 12, 2003, http://arts.guardian .co.uk/reviews/story/0,,912236,00.html
2. *Der Speigel*, September 20, 2003, http://arts.guardian.co.uk/ reviews/story/0,,912236,00.html
3. *Washington Times*, March 12, 2004, http://www.washingtontimes .com/entertainment/20040311-085521-1823r.html
4. *Washington Post*, September 17, 2004, http://www.washingtonpost .com/Wp-dyn/articles/A27587-2004Sep16.html
5. *Washington Post*, August 24, 2004, http://www.washingtonpost .com/wp-dyn/articles/A27098-2004Aug23.html

Kevin Fullam contributed to this essay.

Random probability sampling A method by which pollsters choose interviewees, based on the idea that the opinions of individuals selected by chance will be representative of the opinions of the population at large.

Pollsters choose their interviewees by the method of **random probability sampling**, in which every person in the population theoretically has an equal chance of being selected. While that system of sampling is not perfect (in any population, some individuals have little or no chance of being selected for an interview), and the procedure is fairly complicated (how, for example, do you assure that cell phone users will be included in a telephone survey?), the basic idea—that the opinions of individuals selected by chance will be representative of the opinions of the population at large—is highly effective and reliable. Since 1936, for example, the Gallup poll has correctly predicted the winner in all but one presidential election and has been within a few percentage points of the actual results each time.[12]

Straw polls Polls that rely on an unsystematic selection of respondents. The respondents in straw polls frequently are not representative of the public at large.

In contrast, **straw polls** rely on an unsystematic method of selection. People are questioned in shopping centers or on street corners, with little or no effort being made to ensure that respondents are representative of the population at large. The results are often inaccurate and unreliable. For instance, in 1936, a highly respected magazine, the *Literary Digest*, using a straw poll of 2.5 million people, predicted that Republican Alfred Landon would defeat Democrat Franklin D. Roosevelt in the presidential election; Roosevelt won overwhelmingly. The *Digest* poll failed because it selected its respondents from telephone directories and automobile registration lists. In the midst of the Great Depression, that sample had too many middle- and high-income individuals and excluded voters who could not afford telephones or cars. Gallup's survey for the same election—his first presidential poll—was quite accurate.

Currently, polls are essential to high-visibility campaigns, including presidential, congressional, and gubernatorial races, and increasingly to many lower-profile state and local campaigns. Candidates who can afford the high cost typically survey prospective voters to learn their concerns. In fact, a national or statewide candidate who does not use polls is probably not a serious candidate, or at least does not face serious opposition.

Major television stations and newspapers also survey the public on issues and candidates. When elections are under way, poll results are frequently the bread

Critical Thinking

Do you think that polls and surveys are an important source of information for our elected officials?

and butter of the evening news and the daily newspaper. In the months before major elections — and on election night — these reports often have a horse-race quality; that is, they focus on who is ahead or behind in a contest. That was true in the 2004 presidential and the 2006 congressional elections, when the media spent significant amounts of time and money tracking voter preferences. How people feel about the real issues of the campaign often goes unreported or underreported in election coverage.

Many elected officials, including the president, use polls to assess the public's views on a variety of issues. President George W. Bush employs pollsters and uses the results to help increase support for his positions or to fine-tune or eventually abandon policies.

The fact that public officials use polls, however, should not imply that presidential or congressional decision making is based solely on evaluation of public opinion. Although polls are an important source of feedback in making policy decisions, representatives also rely on their own values and on both their own and others' experience, knowledge, and expertise. In effect, polls provide one glimpse — a snapshot — of the public's attitudes at the time that the poll is taken. Events, both personal and public, may have a significant impact on those opinions a day, week, month, or year later, making opinions susceptible to change.

What makes a good poll? As the failure of the *Literary Digest* poll demonstrates, the sample must be chosen with care. In addition, questions must be worded in such a way that their form or content does not influence the response. For example, starting a question on a farm issue with the phrase "Most people believe that farms should be family owned" will increase the likelihood that a respondent will agree with what "most people" believe. A more neutral, unbiased opening phrase, such as "People have different beliefs regarding support for family-owned farms," avoids the suggestion on the part of the pollster that there is a right and a wrong answer to the question.

Good questions are another important ingredient. Many surveys ask many questions and allow for only brief answers, often a simple yes or no. Although such questions may improve the efficiency of the survey, they do so at the expense of more thorough information. Consequently, the intensity, saliency, stability, and direction of opinion may be distorted and complex shades of opinion may be obscured, giving support to the myth of majority opinion when, in fact, there is no such view.

Finally, pollsters must measure what people know about an issue, as well as what their opinions are, in order to distinguish between informed and uninformed responses. Many Americans recognize the difficulties of keeping up with the issues and also find government often baffling and mysterious. In a recent poll, 60 percent of the public indicated that government was "so complicated that a person like me can't understand what's going on."[13] Still, lack of knowledge and failure to understand do not keep people from answering questions. In a poll taken at the beginning of President George H. W. Bush's administration in 1989, 83 percent of those interviewed rated the president's cabinet appointments as excellent, good, fair, or poor. Yet when asked to name a cabinet member, four out of five could not name a single appointee.[14] Even when the public knows nothing about an issue, it is hardly shy about expressing an opinion.

Public Opinion and Trust in Government

While Americans strongly support our democratic form of government, many citizens remain skeptical about the honesty of government officials. On September 28, 2005, U.S. House of Representatives Majority Leader Tom DeLay (R-TX) makes a brief announcement in Washington, D.C. that he is stepping down from his leadership position. DeLay was indicted on felony conspiracy and illegal money-laundering charges in connection with campaign financing in his home state of Texas.

Poorly designed and poorly administered polls provide inaccurate and misleading findings. The level of confidence we have in a survey may depend on who conducted the poll. Polls commissioned by a candidate are generally more suspect then those conducted and reported by a reputable media outlet. But when carefully done, professional polls can help to link citizens with the officials who represent them, amplifying, not distorting, the public's voice.

The Paradox of Public Opinion

 Do the findings from public opinion polls suggest that Americans question the principles of democracy and representative government?

In the 1950s and early 1960s, Americans viewed government optimistically. Seventy-eight percent of Americans felt that the national government tended to improve conditions in the nation.[15] The nation had triumphed in World War II, the economy was flourishing, and no domestic or foreign policy problem seemed too difficult to solve.

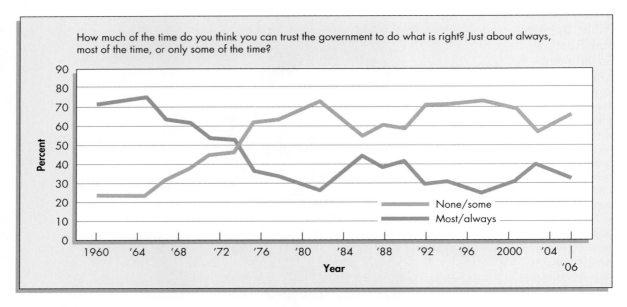

How much of the time do you think you can trust the government to do what is right? Just about always, most of the time, or only some of the time?

FIGURE 5.1

How Much Do You Trust the Government?

Over the past three decades, Americans' trust and confidence in their government's ability have decreased.

Source: University of Michigan National Election Study (NES) for years 1960–1992, 2000; 1996 data from the CBS/*New York Times* poll, December 1996; 1998 and 1999 data from Wake Swell Perry and Associates, November 1999; 2002 data from Center for Public Service, The Brookings Institution, 2002; 2005 data from the CNN/USA Today/Gallup Poll, June 2005.

Starting in the early 1970s and continuing into the twenty-first century, however, Americans gradually lost confidence in government. The Watergate scandal and the resignation of President Richard Nixon, the impeachment and trial of President Bill Clinton, and the disapproval by the public of President Bush's handling of the Iraq War and problems caused by Hurricane Katrina in 2005 all served to fuel the high level of cynicism concerning government and politics held by many Americans.

In 1964, 76 percent of the American people claimed that they trusted and had confidence in "the government in Washington to do what is right" most of the time. By 2006, only 32 percent expressed such confidence (see Figure 5.1). Indeed, two-thirds of Americans are critical of the way that the federal government does its job.[16] While some reports shortly after the terrorist attack on the World Trade Center on September 11, 2001, indicated that there was an increase in public trust and confidence in the government, analysis by a number of prominent political scientists contended that fundamental levels of public trust had not increased and that "there was no sudden affection for big government."[17]

The decline in confidence and trust in government has been matched by a rise in cynicism among many Americans regarding the ethics of elected officials. A 2004 poll found that 35 percent of the public—as against 24 percent in 1958—felt that "quite a few of the people running the government are crooked."[18] By the year 2006, the low confidence in government leaders matched the low levels of trust in government.[19] The cumulative impact of a number of government missteps and scandals at the local, state, and national levels seems to have taken its toll.

Critical Thinking

Do you have confidence and trust in our government and political leaders?

Do these findings suggest that the public no longer believes in democracy and representative government? Interestingly, the answer is no. Most citizens are proud to be Americans. In a poll taken not long after the September 11, 2001, terrorist attacks, 92 percent of Americans said they were proud or extremely proud to be Americans, with 65 percent indicating that they display the American flag on a daily basis.[20] In fact, the legitimacy of the system — that is, the acceptance by the people of the authority of government — has been in serious jeopardy only once in the nation's history: during the Civil War.

Most Americans today believe that no other country or government provides the opportunities found in the United States. When Americans were recently asked to look ahead to the twenty-first century, 79 percent said that they thought government would be more important or equally important, relative to the previous century, in terms of improving the lives of the American people.[21]

Group Opinion: Diversity and Uniformity

FOCUS QUESTION HOW DOES PUBLIC OPINION VARY WITHIN AND AMONG DIFFERENT ETHNIC, RELIGIOUS, RACIAL, AND AGE GROUPS?

The differences both among and within groups in our society further fragment opinion. Political views may differ between men and women, African Americans and whites, young and old. Of course, not all women or all African Americans or all members of any group are necessarily unified in their views. Nevertheless, some generalizations are possible.

Gender. Compared with men, women express greater concern about the problems of poverty and hunger, drug abuse, moral and religious decline, genetic engineering, and international tensions. Historically, men are more concerned about the budget deficit, the cost of living, and the trade deficit. A larger percentage of women than of men consider themselves Democrats, although approximately an equal proportion of men and of women support the Republican party.

Surprisingly, there are no strong gender differences regarding welfare reform, the death penalty, and the right to choose abortion; a majority of men as well as of women support the three positions. In the 2004 presidential elections, Democrat John Kerry received an overall advantage over his Republican opponent, George W. Bush, of 7 percentage points from female voters.

College Students and "Twentysomethings." Despite popular images of youthful extremism, most college students and people in their twenties hold middle-of-the-road political views (see Table 5.1).[22] Their interest in political affairs is relatively weak, however. A recent survey of freshman college students found that only about 27 percent discussed politics with friends and family (although 46 percent did indicate that they discussed politics in their high school classes), and only 36 percent thought it was important to keep up-to-date with political affairs.[23]

TABLE 5.1

The Political Orientation of College Freshmen: The Class of 2009

	AVERAGE	MALE	FEMALE
Far left	3.4%	3.9%	3.0%
Liberal	27.1	24.1	29.6
Middle of the road	45.0	44.8	45.1
Conservative	22.6	24.5	21.0
Far right	2.0	2.7	1.2

Source: Data from John H. Pryor, Sylvia Hurtado, Victor B. Saenz, Jennifer A. Lindholm, William S. Korn, and Kathryn M. Mahoney, *The American Freshman: National Norms for Fall 2005*. Los Angeles: Higher Education Research Institute, UCLA, December 2005, pp. 35, 55, 75.

Critical Thinking

How do your political beliefs and opinions compare with those of other college students?

As Figure 5.2 makes clear, the opinions of college students, like those of the rest of the population, present a diversified picture.[24] (See "Asked & Answered," p. 150, for more about college students and participation.)

Race and Ethnicity. Diversity and divergence also hold true when people are grouped by race and ethnicity, although whites, African Americans, Hispanics, and others manifest some group consciousness on important issues.

A slight majority of African Americans, 56 percent, feel that they are making economic and social progress.[25] Compared with whites, African Americans favor greater government participation in resolving economic and social issues. For African Americans, federal programs, including affirmative action programs, remain a key strategy in dealing with civil rights and other pressing problems. When Hurricane Katrina devastated the city of New Orleans in 2005, whites and nonwhites strongly disagreed with each other over the role of race in the government's response to the tragedy. Sixty-five percent of nonwhites felt race accounted for the slow response to those trapped in New Orleans, while 64 percent of whites said that race played no role.[26]

There is agreement across race on many issues. For example, a majority of African Americans and whites agree that government is often wasteful and inefficient. Both groups think positively about the role and contribution of immigrant groups in equal numbers, both support action to protect the environment, and both are concerned about the concentration of corporate power in the United States.[27]

Among whites, Republicans hold an edge over Democrats, whereas African Americans have been more heavily Democratic since the 1940s. Approximately 28 percent of both whites and African Americans described themselves as "independents."[28] In the 2004 presidential election, George W. Bush received 11 percent of the African American vote; 88 percent voted for John Kerry.[29]

Hispanic opinion is difficult to characterize because the label serves as an umbrella for Mexican Americans, Puerto Ricans, Cuban Americans, and others

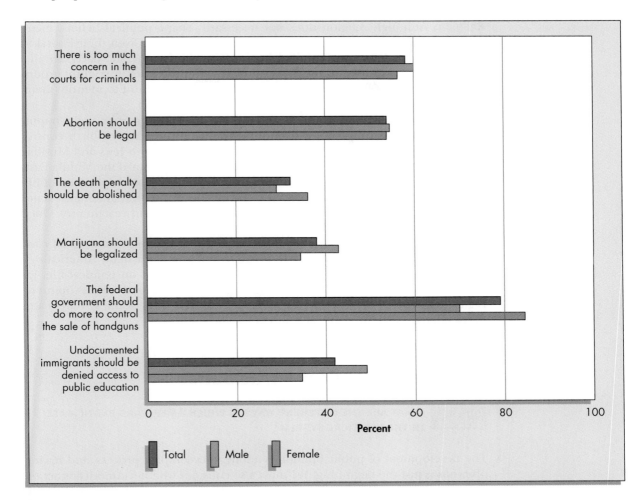

FIGURE 5.2

What Do College Freshmen Think?

Source: Data from John H. Pryor, Sylvia Hurtado, Victor B. Saenz, Jennifer A. Lindholm, William S. Korn, and Kathryn M. Mahoney, *The American Freshman: National Norms for Fall 2005*. Los Angeles: Higher Education Research Institute, UCLA, December 2005, pp. 35–36, 55–56, 75–76.

who trace their origins to the diverse cultures of Central and South America. Except for Cuban Americans (a majority of whom identify with the Republican party), Hispanics tend to be Democratic in their politics. Over the past decade, Democratic presidential candidates received, on average, 68 percent of the Latino vote; Republicans received 28 percent. However, in 2004, Republican George W. Bush received 40 percent of the Hispanic vote.[30]

Mexican Americans, Puerto Ricans, and Cuban Americans have played a growing role in local and state politics in Texas, California, New York, New Jersey, Florida, Illinois, Colorado, Arizona, Nevada, and New Mexico. It is interesting to note that "collectively, Hispanics, blacks, Native Americans, and Asians are currently a majority of the population in California, Hawaii, and New Mexico, while Texas and New York are projected to achieve 'minority-majority' status by 2010."[31] Minorities will certainly gain political strength in many regions of the nation as we move through the twenty-first century.

Religion. Although religion does not necessarily shape political beliefs, members of a particular religious group often share opinions. Given their liberal to moderate bent, Jews and Catholics lean toward the Democratic party, an allegiance stemming from the party's recruitment and support of immigrant groups during the late 1800s and early 1900s. White Protestants tend to identify themselves as Republicans.

Within each religious group, however, there are differences on many important issues. Catholics are divided on abortion, public support of birth control programs, and the public funding of parochial schools. Both Jews and Muslims are divided over the Israeli-Arab conflict and U.S. policy toward the Middle East. A number of Protestant fundamentalist groups oppose a broad spectrum of liberal government policies, but other Protestants decry the fundamentalist stand on social welfare and nuclear policy as too conservative and reactionary. Once again, majority opinion is difficult to define within groups.

In recent years, some observers have argued that economic and social class influences are more important than religious influences for many Americans.[32] Nevertheless, religion continues to have an indirect effect on political life, influencing tolerance toward disadvantaged groups, moral and ethical opinions regarding political behavior, and conformity with the rules of the system — attitudes related to all the political issues of the day.[33]

Avenues of Political Participation

FOCUS QUESTION WHAT ARE THE DIFFERENT WAYS IN WHICH AMERICANS PARTICIPATE IN THE POLITICAL SYSTEM?

Political participation
Taking part in any of a broad range of activities, from involvement in learning about politics to engagement in efforts that directly affect the structure of government, the selection of government authorities, or the policies of government.

Civil disobedience
Refusal to obey civil laws that are regarded as unjust. This may involve methods of passive resistance such as sit-ins and boycotts.

The development of public opinion is a long and complex process, and having opinions is just the beginning. We must also consider whether Americans act on their opinions by participating in the political system. **Political participation** encompasses a broad range of activities, from learning about politics to engaging in efforts that directly affect "the structure of government, the selection of government authorities, or the policies of government."[34]

Most Americans participate in limited ways — for example, by discussing politics with family and friends and by following campaigns, elections, and other political events on television and in the newspapers. Others are more active; they write letters to government officials (the number of letter writers has more than doubled since the 1960s), attend community meetings and legislative hearings, and join in interest-group activities. In 2004, approximately 60 percent of the eligible electorate voted in the presidential election. In 2006, an estimated 40 percent of the eligible electorate voted in the congressional elections. Those who are deeply involved in politics contribute money to campaigns, attend political rallies and speeches, take part in campaigns, and run for political office. A smaller but growing number of people bypass traditional avenues of action and engage in **civil disobedience**, the willful, and at times violent, breach of laws that these people regard as unjust.

Indeed, one study found "a populace in the United States [that] is highly participatory in most forms of political activity and even more so in nonpolitical public affairs (from a vast variety of organizational memberships to charitable giving and volunteer action)."[35] Nevertheless, participation varies depending on the particular activity. During the 2004 presidential election, one survey found that relatively few individuals attended a political meeting (7 percent), gave money to help a campaign (13 percent), or worked for a party or candidate (3 percent). However, 67 percent indicated that they had read about the campaign in newspapers, 28 percent said they had read magazine articles about the election, 86 percent of those surveyed watched programs about the campaign on television, and 51 percent listened to campaign radio programs.[36] Interestingly, if you look at participation at all levels of campaigns and elections, the intensity of political participation has significantly improved. A recent survey found that during one current two-year election cycle, 46 percent of the public attended a public hearing or meeting, 45 percent contacted an elected official, 34 percent contributed time or money to a political campaign, and 27 percent participated in a police-sponsored community-watch program. Indeed, in the age of the Internet, 34 percent of the public visited a government website for information.[37] Research tends to support the idea of relatively high levels of participation by the American people.

Critical Thinking

Should Americans be more active in politics?

For some individuals, however, political inactivity does not necessarily indicate a lack of interest. Threats of violence have kept some groups out of politics; in particular, African Americans in the South were kept out of politics until the 1960s. Work and family responsibilities can also leave little time for political involvement. For people between the ages of eighteen and twenty-six, adjusting to new academic challenges or to being independent, self-supporting adults undoubtedly contributes to political inactivity. Still others either feel that their participation will have no impact on government or are satisfied with what they see and therefore feel they have no reason for action.

Acting on Opinions

Those who do act on their opinions fall into six general categories, according to political scientists Sidney Verba and Norman Nie.[38] Inactives participate by occasionally casting a vote. Voting specialists vote regularly in presidential, state, and local elections but seldom join in other political activities. Parochial activists vote and contact public officials only when their own self-interest is involved. Community activists work to solve problems in their localities and vote regularly, but do not otherwise participate in party activities or elections. Campaigners, the mirror image of the community activists, immerse themselves in partisan politics and campaigns rather than in community organizations. Complete activists engage in activities ranging from community affairs to voting, campaigning, and running for political office.

Verba and Nie's categories represent traditional forms of political participation. What happens when such tactics do not work? In the early 1960s, African Americans in the South organized sit-ins at segregated lunch counters, boycotted

ASKED & ANSWERED

ASKED: Are college students inattentive and inactive in the political process?

ANSWERED: For many years, most people gave this answer: Eighteen- to twenty-four-year-olds did not participate in significant numbers in the political process. College students were not excluded from this generalization; the general belief was that many were preoccupied with their studies, busy with jobs to help fund their education, and generally caught up in planning for the future.

Historically, research supported the finding of low levels of voting among the eighteen- to twenty-four-year-old cohort. In no other age group, including those seventy-five years old and older, did a lower percentage of eligible citizens turn out on election day. But recent elections may have marked a significant change in the participation of college students in the political process — and not just in voting.

College students turned out in significantly higher numbers in the 2004 election than they had in any previous presidential election year. One study found that "based on [a] national exit poll . . . turnout of 18–24 year olds was approximately 42.3% . . . a 5.8% increase in turnout from 2000."[1] In fact, that may be an understatement of eighteen- to twenty-four-year-old turnout, since a third of college students reported voting by absentee ballot and so were not counted in the exit poll data. Previous studies found participation hovering at around 30 to 35 percent. A not insignificant 10 percent of the voters in 2004 were eighteen- to twenty-four-year-olds. It was also the only age cohort in the 2004 election that favored Democratic candidate John Kerry over Republican George W. Bush, by 56 percent to 43 percent.

But college students do more than vote. An impressive 25 percent of college students donated time, money, or both to the 2004 election. In turn, two-thirds of college students indicated that they were more likely to participate in politics in the future. A person's level of civic engagement —

participation in community activities and programs — is often linked by scholars to increasing participation in the political system. If this is the case, then we may have additional support for a growing role by college students in the political system. One recent survey conveyed a strong picture of engagement by students: "47% claimed to have worked on a community problem; 28% suggested that they had contacted an elected official about a public issue; and 24% offered that they had protested."[2]

If this evidence were not enough to suggest an emergent participation by college students in the political process, UCLA's highly regarded annual survey of entering undergraduates for the class of 2009 provides further evidence of an activated student body. An all-time high of 83 percent volunteered during high school and two-thirds of the college-bound students believed that it is vital to help others who are in difficulty, "the highest this figure has been in the past 25 years."[3]

The evidence is clear. We are seeing a rise among college students in civic responsibility and engagement including participation in the political process. Contrary to their counterparts over the past five decades, today's college students "are thinking about politics, willing to get involved, and care about the implications of elections."

1. Unless otherwise cited, data and quotes in this box were abstracted from the Harvard University Institute of Politics' Survey of Student Attitudes: The Global Generation, "Election 2004: College Students Are Involved and Motivated for the Future," April 19, 2005, and CIRCLE — Center for Information & Research on Civic Learning & Engagement, www .civicyouth.org/PopUps/FactSheets/FS-PresElection04.pdf.

2. Sharon E. Jarvis, Lisa Montoya, and Emily Mulvoy, "The Political Participation of Working Youth and College Students," Working Paper 36, August 2005, Center for Information & Research on Civic Learning & Engagement (CIRCLE).

3. UCLA News, Office of Media Relations, www.newsroom.ucla .edu.

buses, and engaged in other acts of civil disobedience. Antiwar protests were a common occurrence during the Vietnam War in the 1960s and 1970s. Since that time, protest has become an increasingly common form of participation among those who find traditional avenues of action ineffective or closed. In the 1990s and early 2000s, both pro- and antiabortion groups marched in cities and towns around the nation, arguing their policy positions. Many of these individuals had never been active in politics before, often not even voting in elections. In at least one case, the antiabortion group Operation Rescue has advocated violent disobedience, including physically blocking access to health clinics that perform abortions; other antiabortion groups have called for nonviolent protest. As you may recall from Chapter 4, many of these groups have also gone to court to try to influence the political system.

Finally, the impact of even limited participation should not be overlooked. As we indicated earlier in this chapter, in the most recent presidential election, 86 percent of the electorate watched programs about the campaigns on television, more than 67 percent of voters read about the presidential campaign in a newspaper, and close to 50 percent of the electorate engaged in persuading others to vote for or against one of the parties or candidates.[39] These forms of political activity may be less direct than voting or running for office, but they represent an important form of participation in the political process.

Despite this evidence, there is certainly room for skepticism, as well as for improvement of Americans' activism. Relatively few people work for parties or candidates. Even though the 2004 presidential election saw the highest turnout since 1960, turnout for presidential elections has been relatively low over the past thirty years, averaging around 50 percent of the eligible voters. We cannot ignore the reality that active political participation in the United States is lower than many political observers believe it should be.

Yet this apparent apathy is balanced by activity. When election time rolls around, many political meetings are jammed with people, campaign buttons and bumper stickers decorate lapels and automobiles, and money pours into campaign headquarters. Political parties, particularly at the national level, thrive on millions of small contributions — most under $50; increasingly, many of these contributions are being made to candidates via the Internet. Tens of thousands of people participate in social and political movements aimed at affecting policy on issues that range from government involvement in Iraq and the Middle East to abortion rights. In addition, volunteerism in the United States is alive and well. Americans feel that volunteering time to community service is an essential or very important obligation of citizens. Two recent polls found that 73 percent of college students and 83 percent of college freshmen stated that they had participated in some form of volunteer work, ranging from helping the homeless to teaching, religious service, social work, and environmental and health care. Polls also found that 43 percent of college students had volunteered more than ten times and that 50 percent of college freshmen had participated in organized demonstrations.[40]

In fact, historically, Americans have engaged in at least as much campaign and community activity as citizens of many other nations. In a study comparing participation in five democracies—the United States, the Netherlands, Great Britain, Germany, and Japan—the United States ranked first in a variety of activities, including signing political petitions, attending public meetings, contacting officials or politicians, and writing to newspapers.[41] In terms of volunteering and giving money to nonpolitical public affairs programs, Americans significantly outdistanced French and Germans in the amount of time and financial support contributed.[42]

What Influences Participation?

Why do people participate in politics? After all, an individual act of participation rarely has much impact. One answer is that people participate if the action does not take much effort. Sending a check or watching the nightly news is easy. People also participate if they care a lot about the outcome. Black college students who took part in sit-ins at lunch counters and marched in demonstrations in the 1960s had a big stake in the success of the civil rights movement. Likewise, during the 1970s and 1980s, many women (and men) participated in demonstrations and marches for equal rights and opportunities for women. Finally, participation depends on life circumstances. Thus, recent increases in political participation in the South can be attributed to rising educational and socioeconomic levels, as well as to enforcement of voting rights laws; in the past, poll taxes, literacy tests, and other barriers to registration prevented African Americans from voting.

Participation breeds more participation. For example, people who work in community and fraternal organizations are more likely than the average citizen to participate in politics. A strong sense of party identity also seems to encourage activism. Indeed, even such passive participation as having an interest in politics or holding strong opinions on issues and candidates can serve as a catalyst for political action.

Political activism also depends on age. Those between eighteen and twenty-four are less likely to vote or engage in other forms of political participation—for example, discuss politics, work for a political party, or run for political office—than those in any other age group through the age of seventy-five. A higher percentage of people ages forty-five and older than of those younger than forty-five register and vote in national elections, although the 2004 presidential election saw a significant increase in the voter turnout of people between the ages of eighteen and twenty-four[43] (see "Asked & Answered," p. 150). As we indicated earlier in this chapter, these statistics often reflect the unsettled lives of young people, who are working, starting families, attending school, or adjusting to their status as independent, self-supporting adults. To some extent, too, political activism is a function of the responsibilities of age. As taxpayers, parents, and homeowners, older people have more immediate reasons to get involved in politics.

Critical Thinking

What factors would make you a more active participant in politics and government?

A Closer Look at Women, African Americans, Hispanics, and Asian Americans

Women. Women have a long history of activism in local and community work; it goes back to Abigail Adams and Judith Sargent Murray during the 1780s and 1790s. Nineteenth-century feminists who fought for equal rights, economic opportunity, and the right to vote included Sarah Grimké, Elizabeth Cady Stanton, Lucretia Mott, and Charlotte Perkins Gilman. Yet women's roles in the partisan political arenas of the time were somewhat limited. In recent years, barriers against women in national and state politics have diminished. Currently, as party leaders, candidates, voters, and community organizers, women are entering politics in greater numbers. The percentage of female voters has exceeded the percentage of male voters in every presidential election since 1980.[44] Their activity at the state and national level has increased significantly.

Since 1975, the number of women holding local or state office has risen dramatically. The 1984 nomination of Geraldine Ferraro as the Democratic candidate for vice president was apparently a breakthrough for women in politics. Two years later, an unprecedented 130 women were contesting national and state offices. In the 110th Congress (2007–2009), 88 women serve in the House of Representatives and the Senate. After the November 2006 elections, women held an estimated 25 percent of the statewide elective executive offices across the nation, including nine female governors (six Democrats, three Republicans). There were more than 1,600 women serving in the fifty state legislatures (although that constituted just under 25 percent of the state legislators in the United States).[45]

Women in Public Office

Although women are still underrepresented in politics, proportional to their numbers in the general population, their participation in government has increased significantly over the past twenty-five years. Secretary of Labor Elaine Chao, the first Asian American woman to serve in a president's cabinet, holds a press conference in Washington, D.C.

Of the delegates to the 2004 Democratic National Convention, 50 percent were women. Female delegates to the Republican National Convention in 2004 totaled 43 percent. In 2006, four women served in President Bush's cabinet.

With regard to the appointment of women as federal court judges, however, progress has been slow. In recent years, the percentage of women appointed to the federal courts has ranged from a high of 29 percent during the Clinton administration to 8 percent during the Reagan administration. Twenty-one percent of George W. Bush's appointments to the federal bench have been women.[46] One woman now serves on the U.S. Supreme Court: Ruth Bader Ginsburg.

No doubt, women's activism will keep growing as female elected and appointed officials become role models for other women, and as barriers to the inner circles of politics continue to break down.

African Americans. Discrimination, along with alienation from and lack of faith in the electoral process, has historically contributed to African Americans' low rates of participation in politics. African American voter turnout has increased greatly during the past three decades — in good part because of voting rights laws, key Supreme Court decisions, registration drives, and a rise in educational achievement and economic well-being. In 1960, only 29 percent of African Americans in the South were registered to vote, compared with 61 percent of whites. By the 2004 presidential election year, approximately two-thirds of African Americans across the nation reported being registered to vote; the percentage for whites was 68 percent.[47]

Since the 1970s, increasing numbers of African American candidates have won political office. In 1970, there were 1,469 African Americans holding local, state, and national offices. By 2001, that number had increased to 9,101, although this still represented less than 2 percent of elected officials in the United States.[48] Not only have the numbers of African Americans serving as city council members, sheriffs, and county officials significantly increased, but African Americans have also won mayoral races in Atlanta, Chicago, Dallas, Denver, Detroit, Gary (Indiana), Los Angeles, Newark, New Orleans, Oakland, Philadelphia, Richmond, Seattle, and Washington, D.C. In 1989, David Dinkins became the first African American mayor of New York City, and Douglas Wilder of Virginia became the first African American governor in the United States. Prominent present or past black officials include Democratic U.S. Senator Barack Obama of Illinois and Congresswoman Sheila Jackson Lee of Texas, and Republicans Kenneth Blackwell, Ohio secretary of state, and former congressman J. C. Watts of Oklahoma.[49] Blackwell unsuccessfully ran for governor in Ohio in 2006. There are 43 African Americans serving in the 110th Congress (2007–2009). In 2004, 18 percent of the delegates to the Democratic National Convention and 6 percent of those attending the Republican National Convention were African American. In 2006, President George W. Bush's cabinet included two African Americans; one of them, Condoleezza Rice, was the first black female secretary of state. As with women, however, the record is mixed. Although there are growing numbers of African Americans on the federal bench (almost 12 percent of President George W. Bush's appointments and more than 13 percent of President Clinton's appointments to the federal appellate courts were African Americans), the number of appointments over the past twenty years has represented a relatively small proportion of the total appointments (1.3 percent of President Reagan's appointments and 5.4 percent of President George H. W. Bush's).[50] The only African American serving on the Supreme Court is Clarence Thomas.

Hispanics. Mexican Americans and Puerto Ricans have also faced major barriers to participation, including language problems, low levels of education and income, literacy tests, and residency requirements. Recently, registration drives in Florida, Texas, and California, where many Cuban Americans and Mexican Americans live, have produced increases in voter turnout. In the 2004 presidential elections, 58 percent of eligible Latino voters were registered to vote in the United States.[51] There are twenty-seven Hispanics serving in the 110th Congress. Two Latinos serve in President Bush's cabinet, including Attorney General Alberto Gonzales. After the November 2006 elections, Hispanics held an estimated 30 percent of the more than 7,000 state legislative seats. Almost 9 percent of George W. Bush's appointments to the federal appellate courts have been Latinos; more than 11 percent of President Clinton's appointments were Hispanic.[52] Although Hispanic participation is still limited in the United States, the twenty-first century will very likely see dramatic increases in Hispanic activism, particularly in states such as California, Arizona, New Mexico, Texas, Colorado, New York, Florida, and New Jersey, which are experiencing significant increases in the number of Latino and Latina voters. Candidates for office in many parts of the nation recognize the growing size and importance of the Hispanic vote.

Asian Americans. Although only limited data are available regarding the political participation patterns of different Asian American groups, some tentative conclusions can be drawn. Most Asian Americans, including Japanese, Korean, Vietnamese, and Filipino Americans, are less likely than either whites or African Americans to participate in the political system. Chinese Americans, however, are as likely to vote as white Americans. It is also true that "members of Asian American ethnic groups are less likely to contact public officials than are whites, but Japanese Americans are more likely to contribute money than are whites."[53] In the 2004 presidential elections, members of Asian American ethnic groups supported Democrat John Kerry with 74 percent of their vote. President George W. Bush received 24 percent of the Asian American vote.[54] A recent study argued that factors contributing to the relatively low voter turnout of many Asian American groups include limited English proficiency among voters and real and perceived biases against Asian Americans by poll workers.[55]

At present, eight members of the U.S. Congress have Asian or Pacific Island backgrounds. As of 2006, no Asian Americans had been appointed by President Bush to the federal appellate courts (although 6 percent of his appointments to the federal district court were Asian Americans).[56] As members of various ethnic groups from Asia and the Pacific Basin settle in the United States, learn the language, and assimilate into the political system, it is likely that we will see increases in their political participation. Elaine Chao serves as secretary of labor in President George W. Bush's administration.

Conclusion: Many Minorities, Much Activity

In this chapter we have looked at the myth of majority opinion. What is the reality behind this myth? Is there a majority opinion? The answer is yes—and no. Many Americans do share certain beliefs about the political system, including the importance of democracy and representative government, majority rule, and concern for minority rights. An overwhelming majority—in most polls, much more than 90 percent of the respondents—support a democratic form of government. And public officials pay attention to public opinion when it has strength and direction on a given issue.

The myth, however, obscures an important attribute of public opinion: that it is often difficult to define clearly. Public opinion is often fuzzy and unstable; it is also frequently uninformed and sometimes does not exist at all. It rarely comes packaged in neat, easy-to-understand categories. In this vast and varied nation, differences in religious background, region of residence, education, class, gender, race, and ethnicity produce a broad spectrum of views about the political world. To complicate matters further, even when people have similar backgrounds, they often do not share the same views.

Thus, in defining majority opinion on any issue, policymakers must tread carefully. Often the answers to a single survey question or even a series of such questions do not capture the diversity or ambiguity of public opinion. Clearly, for many issues, the generalization that there is a majority opinion in the United States is a myth.

In this chapter, we also discussed political participation in the United States. Americans are frequently criticized for their lack of participation in the political process. That criticism often focuses on the relatively low voter turnout in the United States, particularly when compared with higher turnout figures in many other nations.

We agree that if activism is defined by voting, then the American public seems apathetic indeed. But if we broaden the definition to include many other activities, including such forms of participation as political discussions, we depict a reality of a more politically and socially concerned citizen, a citizen who is more active in the political system than was previously thought.

Critical Thinking

Do you accept the myth of majority opinion?

Tying It Together

FOCUS QUESTIONS RECAP

✳ How do we define political public opinion?

✳ What agents of political socialization help to shape and influence our opinions about government and politics?

✳ What factors contribute to a well-designed and effective poll? What factors contribute to a poorly designed poll?

✳ Do the findings from public opinion polls suggest that Americans question the principles of democracy and representative government?

✳ How does public opinion vary within and among different ethnic, religious, racial, and age groups?

✳ What are the different ways in which Americans participate in the political system?

CHAPTER SUMMARY

1. Public opinion is defined as the shared evaluations expressed by people on political issues, policies, and individuals.

2. Four important characteristics of public opinion are its intensity, saliency, stability, and direction.

3. Political socialization is the process by which people acquire political values and opinions about the political world. The socialization process is strongly influenced by people and events from early childhood through adulthood. Family and friends, school, the media, religion, and political culture are five important factors that mold our political beliefs and opinions.

4. Polls are a major instrument for measuring public opinion. Poorly designed and administered public opinion polls can provide inaccurate and misleading findings. When carefully designed and administered, however, professional polls offer sound and meaningful information about public opinion. Nevertheless, on many issues, a clear and unambiguous majority opinion is often difficult to assess from polls.

5. Factors that contribute to a well-designed poll include random sampling; questions whose form and content do not sway the respondent one way or another; both short-answer questions and the opportunity for the respondents to provide more detailed answers; and questions that distinguish between informed and uninformed responses. Poorly designed polls do not fulfill these minimal requirements.

6. Although Americans show a lack of confidence and trust in government and politics, they still have an overwhelming faith in the political system in general, and in the principles of democracy and representative government.

7. The opinions of Americans are often influenced by age and sex and by ethnic, religious, racial, regional, and educational backgrounds, although opinions can and do vary widely within any group.

8. Political participation can range from activities that involve taking part in the learning process about politics to activities that directly influence the structure of government, the selection of government authorities, or the policies of government. Participation in politics in the United States is more extensive if we include not just voting, but also all forms of political participation.

9. Minority groups have made some important gains but still do not have opportunities proportional to their numbers. It is likely that we will see increases in political participation and activism by members of many of these groups as we move into the new millennium.

10. While there can be majority opinion as well as well-defined, stable, and easily understood issues, public opinion is often difficult to define clearly and can be fuzzy and unstable, often uninformed, and sometimes doesn't exist on a given issue.

Key Terms

Political public opinion (135)
Opinion intensity (135)
Opinion saliency (135)
Opinion stability (135)
Opinion direction (135)
Political ideology (136)
Political culture (136)

Political socialization (136)
Political efficacy (137)
Party identification (137)
Random probability sampling (141)
Straw polls (141)
Political participation (148)
Civil disobedience (148)

 ## Net Work

Do you want to find out more about public opinion on politics and government?

- Three excellent sources for public opinion polls dealing with politics and government are the Gallup Organization (**www.gallup.com**), the Pew Research Center for the People and the Press (**www.people-press.org**), and the Roper Center (**www.ropercenter.uconn.edu**). These sources are among the most respected polling and survey institutions in the nation.

- News services are also excellent sources of political information on both public opinion and polit-

ical participation. Three very good sources are the Polling Report (**www.pollingreport.com**), *Roll Call*, the Capitol Hill newspaper (**www.rollcall .com**), and *Slate*, a magazine on politics and popular culture (**www.slate.com**).

———

As an exercise, visit any two of the websites listed above and select a similar poll from each one. Do both of the polls report similar results? What might explain differences in results between the polls? Consider the importance of the wording of the questions and the dates when the polls were taken.

6

Political Parties

MYTH & REALITY

Is there little difference between the Democratic and Republican parties?

FOCUS QUESTIONS

* What are the three parts of the party that we refer to as the "three-headed political giant"?

* What are some of the key differences between the Republican and Democratic parties?

* What are some of the reasons why we have a two-party system in the United States?

* What are the different roles of party organizations at the local, state, and national levels?

When we teach about political parties in our American government courses, we often start off by asking our students what single word comes to mind when they think about political parties. While the initial response is often just "Republican" or "Democrat," the words that next come to mind are pretty consistent — "unnecessary," "corrupt," "one-sided," "bad," "untrustworthy" — and suggest a negative image of political parties in the United States and what they stand for. What do you think of political parties? Do you support one party and hate the other? Do you think the two parties are both basically the same? Or have you never really thought about them before?

It may come as a surprise to you that, like many Americans today, the Founding Fathers were distrustful of political parties. In his farewell address to Congress, George Washington warned his fellow politicians about the "baneful effects of the spirit of party." John Adams, his vice president, complained, "There is nothing I dread so much as the division of the Republic into two great parties, each under its own leader." And in the early 1790s, Thomas Jefferson, who is often referred to as the father of the American party system, declared, "If I could not go to heaven but with a party, I would not go there at all." The men who helped shape the American democracy felt strongly about this indeed.

Not surprisingly, given that the framers held such strong antiparty feelings, there is no mention of political parties in the Constitution. Today, many college students share the belief of many other citizens that there's "not a dime's worth of difference between the two major parties." Even though a majority of Americans identify to one degree or another with either the Democrats or the Republicans, more often than not they claim that such identifications don't influence their vote for specific offices.

Critical Thinking

Do you think that most people see a difference between Democrats and Republicans on the major issues?

Political Party Appeal

One of the most important tasks of a political party is to recruit new members. Here, both Republicans and Democrats vie for the attention of prospective party loyalists.

What is the source of this hostility toward political parties? Americans' views of the Republican and Democratic parties seem to stem from two misconceptions: that the parties are alike and that they have little impact on domestic and foreign policy. Indeed, when asked to evaluate the Democratic and Republican parties, approximately 45 percent of the respondents in one survey had unfavorable attitudes about parties.[1] Apparently, many Americans see parties as having limited value even at election time, when two-thirds of the voters indicate that they typically split their ticket, voting for candidates from different parties.[2] Furthermore, approximately one-third of the public regard themselves as political independents.[3] In the words of one observer of political parties, "the public is highly skeptical of the parties and their activities."[4]

How can we explain this deep-seated skepticism about parties? We argue that public criticism of the Democrats and Republicans reflects the *myth of party irrelevance*. This myth holds that the Democratic and Republican parties are unnecessary, perhaps even worthless, in our political system. If that is a myth, what is the reality? In this chapter, you will learn that the two major parties are different in several important respects and that parties still matter in the country's politics, even though fewer people now strongly identify with them.

What Parties Are and What They Do

FOCUS QUESTION   **WHAT ARE THE THREE PARTS OF THE PARTY THAT WE REFER TO AS THE "THREE-HEADED POLITICAL GIANT"?**

Political parties differ from country to country. In most Western European democracies, for example, parties are highly centralized, stable, and tightly knit coalitions of men and women with commonly held opinions and beliefs. In these countries, parties take clear-cut, sometimes extreme, ideological positions. (As you may recall from Chapter 1, ideologies are coherent sets of beliefs about what government should do.) For example, in a number of the European nations, where you often have a multiparty system with more than two parties successfully competing in elections (see "Global Politics," p. 171), socialist parties on the Left face a spectrum of ideologically conservative parties on the Right.

In the United States, some minor parties are strongly ideological—for example, the Libertarian party, the Conservative party, and the Socialist Workers party. However, historically, the two major parties, the Democrats and the Republicans, have not based their positions strictly on ideology; rather, they have followed a set of guiding principles, most of which focus on the role that government should play in supporting and enhancing our democratic system. Each party's positions reflect a wide range of beliefs about what government should do in particular areas, and each party seeks to attract a broad spectrum of supporters. Because some of their beliefs overlap, the Democratic and Republican parties may seem alike, especially since they share a strong democratic, capitalist tradition. But they differ on many economic and social issues, and they draw differing proportions of liberals, moderates, and conservatives into their political folds.

Political party In the United States, a coalition of people organized formally to recruit, nominate, and elect individuals to office and to use elected office to achieve shared political goals.

In the United States, **political parties** are coalitions of people organized formally to recruit, nominate, and elect candidates for public office. In addition to organizing elections, political parties are instrumental in running the government, creating and implementing shared political goals through the election of officials to the executive and legislative branches of government, and bringing stability to the political system. As strange as it may seem to many people who are cynical about political parties, the parties do serve as a major link between the public and government officials.

The Republicans and the Democrats, the two major parties, are decentralized organizations, regulated at the state level.[5] The concept of decentralization is not as confusing as it may seem. In this context, **decentralization** means that many different individuals within the party share the decision-making power. No single individual or organization controls the entire system (as compared, for example, with Great Britain, Germany, and Italy, which have highly centralized party organizations controlled by a relatively few individuals or central committees). The comments of one local party leader perhaps best describe that structure: "No state leader, not even the president of the United States, is going to dictate to us whom we slate for local office. They can't even tell us what issues are important." All state party organizations and most local party organizations operate more or less independently of one another, although the authority of one party organization may overlap that of another. Compared with other nations, the United States has one of the most loosely integrated party systems in the world.[6] The Constitution makes no mention of parties, and Congress has passed few laws regulating party activities. By and large, individual states are free to set the rules for their own state parties' operation, although recent Supreme Court decisions have enhanced the power of the national parties to regulate some aspects of state party activity.

Decentralization A term used to describe the Republican and Democratic parties, meaning that decision-making power is dispersed, the party is regulated at the state level, and no single individual controls the system.

The Three-Headed Political Giant

In describing political parties, we might best characterize them as "three-headed political giants."[7] The three heads represent three different alliances of members: the party-as-organization, the party-in-the-electorate, and the party-in-government. As in our relationships with brothers, sisters, or friends, sometimes these three alliances cooperate, and sometimes they pull in different directions.

The **party-as-organization** is small and relatively informal. American party organizations consist primarily of state and county chairpersons and ward and precinct captains (sometimes paid, but more often volunteers) who work for the party throughout the year, recruiting candidates and participating in fundraising activities.

The **party-in-the-electorate** includes all those who identify with the particular party and tend to vote for that party's candidates; some of these may also contribute to its campaigns. Anyone of voting age can choose to be a member of the party-in-the-electorate. American parties depend on such public support for their electoral strength.

Party-as-organization An entity with few members, primarily consisting of state and county chairpersons and ward and precinct captains, who work for the party throughout the year, recruiting candidates and participating in fundraising activities.

Party-in-the-electorate The coalition of everyone who identifies with a particular party and tends to vote for that party's candidates; these people may also contribute to its campaigns.

Party-in-government
The individuals who have been elected or appointed to a government office under a party label. They play a major role in organizing government and in setting policy.

The **party-in-government** comprises the individuals who have been elected or appointed to a government office under a party label. Contrary to the myth of party irrelevance, parties play a major role in organizing government and in setting policy. For example, in the U.S. House of Representatives and the U.S. Senate, the Republican party supports policies different from those supported by Democrats.

If a party is going to be successful, it must attract people like you and me to its fold. Parties need paid and volunteer workers to ring doorbells, distribute campaign literature, register voters, and staff party headquarters. They need voters who will support the party's candidates, donate money to campaigns, and volunteer their services around election time. Finally, parties need candidates who can successfully run for office and, once elected, work to attain the party's policy goals.

Who Belongs to Major Parties and Why?

FOCUS QUESTION WHAT ARE SOME OF THE KEY DIFFERENCES BETWEEN THE REPUBLICAN AND DEMOCRATIC PARTIES?

Given the high level of skepticism about parties in the United States that we've discussed thus far, it may seem strange for us to ask you the question, "Do you belong to either the Democratic or the Republican party?" Interestingly, for many college students, even those who are cynical about the role of parties, the answer is often yes, although the attachment may be weak. Despite the widespread belief that the two major parties are alike, more than 60 percent of the population identifies with one or the other. As you can see in Figure 6.1, attachment to the Democratic party is slightly stronger than attachment to the Republican party, although the percentages tend to fluctuate from month to month between elections.[8]

What difference does party identification make? Clearly, it often determines citizens' political choices. In a typical election, for example, a voter may face a ballot listing candidates for ten, twenty, thirty, or more offices. Because no one can thoroughly study every issue and every office seeker's record, many voters select candidates on the basis of party affiliation. Not surprisingly, one of the reasons individuals who identify with a political party are more likely to vote in an election is that the party label often serves as a shortcut or cue to how to vote, allowing an individual to vote for a candidate he or she may know little or nothing about. These voters rely on a candidate's party label to help guide their choice. Self-declared independents are less likely to vote because they don't have a party label cue to rely on when they know little or nothing about a candidate other than her or his party identification.

Sometimes voters find, to their disappointment, that a candidate does not represent their views, but the party label often indicates a candidate's political philosophy and positions on issues with reasonable accuracy. As one party loyalist in Michigan recently put it, "If you are a Democratic candidate in this state and don't support labor, you won't be a Democratic candidate for very long."

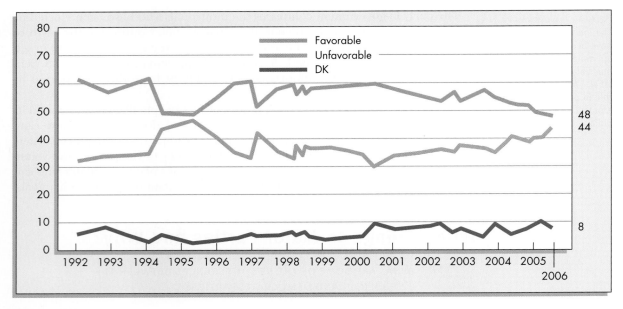

FIGURE 6.1

Democratic Party Favorability

While the gap between favorable and unfavorable views toward the Democratic party has narrowed in recent years, Democrats still maintain a favorable public opinion rating with the American people.

Source: Pew Research Center.

In the Driver's Seat: Democrats and Republicans

Who are the Democrats and the Republicans? The parties tend to attract different groups of supporters. Democrats maintain their greatest strength among African Americans and Hispanics, Catholics and Jews, women, members of the working class, and individuals over the age of fifty. White southerners were once a critical part of the Democratic coalition, but a majority of them have voted for the Republicans in recent elections, although Democrats still maintain a foothold in the South through the support of African Americans. Republicans are scattered across the country. They tend to be white, Protestant, and middle to upper class, and their views are comparatively conservative.

After the September 11, 2001, terrorist attacks in the United States, Republicans and Democrats, both partisan supporters and officeholders, came together to present a united front against our enemies. In a time of crisis, this is not surprising. It has historically been the case in wartime and during national emergencies. But partisanship has strong roots in our nation, and six months after September 11, many traditional partisan divisions were evident in Congress and state legislatures. The issue that most sharply divides Democrats and Republicans is the role of government. Since the 1930s, Democrats have favored a large government role in such policy areas as social welfare and business regulation. For example, in the 1930s, Democrats took the lead in supporting the social security program. They are also more willing than Republicans to support nonmilitary foreign aid programs and domestic environmental initiatives. Republicans, on the other hand, are more likely to favor reducing taxes and, as a result, government services, including aid to minorities and social welfare programs. They

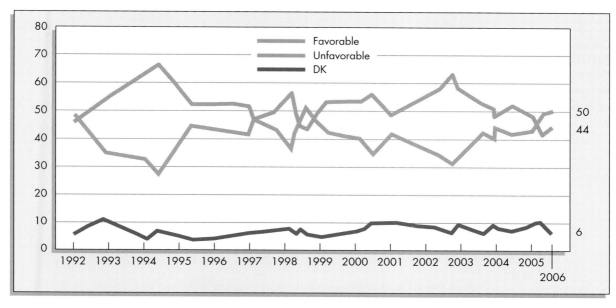

FIGURE 6.2

Republican Party Favorability

Public opinion ratings of the Republican party have fluctuated in recent years with the Republicans seen today as more unfavorable than favorable by the American people.

Source: Pew Research Center.

Critical Thinking

How important is a candidate's party label to you when you vote?

also prefer that government have less of a role in regulating business but are more likely than Democrats to support government spending on the military.

Although the polling data presented at the beginning of this chapter describe a public that feels that political parties are irrelevant in the political system, when it comes to the question of which party can best handle a variety of national issues, people tend to view Republicans and Democrats differently (see Table 6.1).[9] How do your values and issue concerns match up with the party lines suggested by these recent poll findings in Table 6.1?

A Back Seat in Politics? Independents

Independents—individuals who do not identify with any party—often claim that their voting patterns are influenced by issues and leadership qualities, not by party labels. The increase in the number of independents during the 1960s and 1970s, particularly among young voters between the ages of eighteen and twenty-four, and the leveling off of this trend in the 1980s and 1990s parallel the belief in the myth of party irrelevance—that is, the tendency of many Americans to question the ability of parties and government to solve the nation's major problems. The United States has faced a series of major crises in the past three decades, from Watergate, to the impeachment and trial of President Bill Clinton, to the war in Iraq. Many people, including college students, believe that all of these events have contributed to a general feeling that the political system is ineffective and to a corresponding increase in indifference toward both parties.[10]

TABLE 6.1

Comparisons Between the Democratic and Republican Parties on Policy Issues

Do you think the Republicans in Congress or the Democrats in Congress would do a better job of dealing with each of the following issues and problems?

ISSUE	REPUBLICANS	DEMOCRATS	ADVANTAGE
The economy	38%	50%	D+12%
Health care	30	59	D+20
Gas prices	31	51	D+20
Corruption in government	33	44	D+11
Social Security	33	56	D+23
The situation in Iraq	40	46	D+6
Terrorism	49	38	R+11
Taxes	41	49	D+8

Source: Jeffrey M. Jones, "GOP Image Taking a Hit," Gallup News Service, November 7, 2005.

Critical Thinking

Can individuals who regard themselves as independents gather enough information to intelligently vote in elections for all offices at the local, state, and national levels?

Independents make up an important part of the voting population, especially in presidential elections. There is less evidence, however, that they maintain an independent position in state and local elections.[11] In these contests, voters often lack information on candidates' policy positions or leadership qualities. In an average election, voters may be faced with dozens of candidates seeking dozens of offices at all levels of government. It is not easy to learn about and understand all of the issues involved and all of the candidates' positions. Therefore, there are not many voters who are pure independents and totally avoid using party labels to identify the candidates for whom they will vote. For example, independents favor the Republican party on certain issues, including the handling of terrorism and problems related to the Middle East. They favor the Democratic party on other issues, including that party's version of federal support for prescription drug benefits under Medicare.[12] Thus, party label remains one of the best predictors of voter choice in many elections, even for self-declared independents.

A majority of Americans appear to accept the Democratic and Republican parties as relevant symbols, particularly when it comes to voting. In fact, when independents who lean toward one or the other of the two major parties are included, 90 percent of the electorate identify to some extent with either the Democratic or the Republican party.[13]

If Parties Are So Important, What Do They Do?

To no one's surprise, a basic task of political parties is to win elections. Once parties have successfully run candidates for political office, they offer a way to

Critical Thinking

Would voters and elected officials act effectively without political parties?

organize the political world and provide elected officials with a means to organize the government. Had parties not developed as a link between the public and the institutions of government, they would have had to be invented.[14] Let us look more closely at some of the functions of parties.

Simplifying Voting. Many citizens, often voting in dozens of elections at the local, state, and national levels, cannot adequately research all of the candidates and issues. Thus, as mentioned above, many individuals rely on a candidate's party identification to identify his or her positions on general issues and to serve as a shortcut or cue for voting decisions. In a complex world of issues and problems, this shortcut method is probably not a surprising tool for many voters, including college students. This use of party identification also explains why partisans vote more often than self-declared independents do. Independents have fewer useful clues or shortcuts to help them make their electoral choices.

Electoral coalitions Groups of loyal supporters who agree with the party's stand on most issues and vote for its candidates for office.

Building Electoral Coalitions. Parties exist to organize people into **electoral coalitions**: groups of loyal supporters who agree with the party's stand on most issues and vote for its candidates for office. Although individual ties to political parties have weakened over the past fifty years, party labels remain an important electoral symbol in the United States, and for many Americans no other institution or organization embraces as broad a range of issues and goals on the national, state, and local levels as the Democratic and Republican parties.

Developing Public Policy. Parties also play a role in developing positions on what government should do about various problems and in translating those positions into legislation. Research on presidential and state platforms indicates that opposing candidates usually have distinctly different positions on certain issues. **Platforms**, which are statements of party goals and specific policy agendas, are taken very seriously by the candidates and the parties, although they are not binding on either candidates or elected officials.[15] As political scientists Gerald Pomper and Susan Lederman argue,

Platforms Statements of party goals and specific policy agendas that are taken seriously by the party's candidates but are not binding.

> The parties do not copy each other's pledges, but make divergent appeals, thereby pointing to the differences in their basic composition. [The platform] is important because it summarizes, crystallizes, and presents to the voters the character of the party coalition. We should take platforms seriously because politicians seem to take them seriously.[16]

As you can see in Table 6.2, despite some similarities, the Republican and Democratic platforms differed significantly in 2004. While party platforms do serve as a form of propaganda—an attempt to put a positive light on the party's programs and goals—they also represent a serious declaration of policy. The Democrats' positions were relatively liberal, with strong support for social spending, and the Republicans' positions were relatively conservative, with emphasis on individual enterprise.

Winning Elections. A party's ability to recruit the best possible candidates and to win elections determines its success. Party organizations do not monopolize that

TABLE 6.2

2004 Party Platform Comparisons

ISSUE	REPUBLICANS	DEMOCRATS
Patriot Act	"Because it has proved to be instrumental in helping break-up terrorist cells and plots and seizing terrorists' assets, Republicans believe the Congress needs to reauthorize this important law."	Calls for strengthening some provisions, such as on money laundering, while repealing others, such as permission for federal agents to snoop on library or book store records.
War in Iraq	The platform fully supports President Bush's decision to go to war, saying he had a choice: "Trust a madman or defend America. He chose defending America." Calls on America to persevere in Iraq to hold free elections and build a democracy.	The platform says the Bush administration exaggerated prewar claims about Iraq's weapons of mass destruction and ties to al-Qaeda, and in a rush to war failed to build a broad international coalition. Says too few troops were sent. Calls for getting more nations to participate in Iraq and for appointment of U.N. high commissioner to be international community's senior official in Iraq. Attacks no-bid contracts on reconstruction work.
Tax Cuts	Backs making Bush's tax cuts permanent.	Calls for rolling back the cuts for highest income Americans.
Budget Deficit	Says it will fall as "Republicans in Congress work with the president to restrain spending and strengthen economic growth." Goal of halving it in five years.	Calls for cutting it in half over four years. "We will commit to living within tough budget caps—real and enforceable limits on what the government can spend."
Education	Praises Bush for "transforming the debate on education" with passage of the No Child Left Behind Act and calls for expanding its provisions to early-childhood education and high school improvements. Endorses school vouchers.	Says Bush shortchanged his own education act by $27 billion and cut Pell Grants and other college scholarship programs. Calls for full funding of No Child Left Behind, accompanied by reforms. Supports higher public teacher pay and opposes vouchers for private schools. Also calls for a tax credit for four years of college costs.
Gay Rights	Supports a federal constitutional amendment that would define marriage as being between a man and a woman. Also condemns state recognition of civil unions or the granting of domestic partner benefits.	Condemns Bush for pushing the constitutional amendment and says questions surrounding marriage should be left to the states. Calls for "equal responsibilities, benefits and protections" for gay and lesbian families.
Stem Cell Research	Supports President Bush's 2001 decision to bar federal funding for embryonic stem-cell research, except for stem-cell lines that were then in existence and for adult stem cells.	Calls for reversing Bush's decision and pushing ahead with embryonic stem-cell research.
Abortion	Supports a "human life amendment" to the Constitution that would outlaw abortion and hails Bush for signing a ban on so-called partial-birth abortions.	Calls for defending a "woman's right to choose," and voices support for family planning and adoption. Says "abortion should be safe, legal and rare."
Guns	Silent on this point, although in 2000 Bush said he would sign a renewal if Congress passed it.	Calls for renewal of the assault weapons ban, which expires Sept. 13.

Source: Information from the *San Francisco Chronicle*, September 5, 2004.

process; many candidates seek nomination on their own. In recent years, however, parties have offered their candidates a growing list of services. Party organizations, particularly at the state and national levels, offer candidates training and support, help them raise funds, and encourage voter turnout on election day. However, many candidates in highly visible races also rely heavily on paid professional consultants to manage and finance their campaigns.

Primary An election in which party members select candidates to run for office under the party banner.

Today, the nomination of many candidates rests in the hands of those voters who take part in **primaries** — elections to select candidates to run for office under the party banner. (We discuss primaries in detail in Chapter 7, which covers elections.) Although primaries limit the direct role of the party-as-organization in the nomination process, partisanship prevails as the party-in-the-electorate makes its choices. It is important to note, however, that in some parts of the country, local party organizations are still instrumental in assisting candidates in their efforts to serve in government.[17] If you are interested in running for office in your home- or college town, one way of making that a reality is to get involved with the local party you most closely identify with.

Organizing Government. Parties also organize the legislative and executive branches of government. Congress and most state legislatures are structured along party lines. Leadership and committee assignments in those bodies are usually by party, and executives — including mayors, governors, and the president — often work closely with party leaders to pass bills and implement programs.

Although members of Congress often vote along party lines, changes in the internal processes of Congress have in some ways made it difficult for party leaders to control their members. Many members of Congress, looking ahead to the next election, are more committed to their constituents than to their party. In addition, self-recruitment and the use of independent campaign consultants decrease reliance on the party as the source of nomination and campaign support. As a result, members of Congress do not necessarily put their party first and ignore their districts' or their own interests. (See Chapter 10, which covers Congress, for a detailed discussion.)

In short, party control over the vote of a member of Congress is far from absolute, in contrast to the situation in countries such as the United Kingdom of Great Britain and Northern Ireland, where the party's domination of the nominating process often guarantees the loyalty of its legislative members. Nevertheless, most members of Congress have a pronounced sense of party loyalty and share common values and policy positions with their party colleagues. The average Democrat or Republican often votes along party lines on issues on which the party has taken a strong partisan stand.[18]

Mitigating Conflict. Parties also serve to allay and control conflict among and between different groups and interests in our society. When different groups hold different opinions, the Democratic and Republican parties can provide a stage for compromise. It must be noted, however, that strong partisan differences between the Republicans and Democrats can also increase conflict. Such has been the case in recent years in Congress, where the Democrats and Republicans have engaged in very strong and often divisive battles over public policy issues ranging from foreign and military policy to social security funding and funding programs for college students.

American-Style Politics: The Two-Party System

FOCUS QUESTION WHAT ARE SOME OF THE REASONS WHY WE HAVE A TWO-PARTY SYSTEM IN THE UNITED STATES?

As noted earlier, the Constitution makes no mention of parties, and in fact many of the founders viewed them as dangerous. Yet the debate and controversy that evolved as our nation struggled to deal with complex domestic and foreign issues slowly brought about the rise of divisions in the population and in the government—divisions that would lead to the advancement of political parties.

The founders' fear of parties slowly began to diminish, and by 1828, the nation had a two-party system. In the years that followed, parties evolved into a mechanism for expressing public opinion and organizing support among the citizenry. By 1908, New Jersey governor Woodrow Wilson, soon to become president, argued that parties are "absolutely necessary to . . . give some coherence to the action of political forces" and that they "have been our real body politic."[19]

The Winners: The Democrats and the Republicans

The modern Democratic party evolved as a result of the election of 1828 and strongly felt differences of opinion between Andrew Jackson and supporters of Jefferson. By the end of Jackson's presidency in 1837, which drew heavily on the support of farmers and other working people, the Democrats were truly a national party.

The Republican party was born in 1854 in opposition to slavery. It drew its support from businesspeople and merchants, abolitionists, and small farmers in the North and West. With the 1860 election of Abraham Lincoln, the Republicans established themselves as a major party, replacing the Whig party, which had been the other major party from the 1830s to the 1850s, in opposition to the Democrats. Since 1860, the Republicans and the Democrats have alternately dominated party politics.

In recent years, scholars, reporters, and political pundits have raised questions about the future of the two-party system. Is the two-party system viable? Can a third party challenge the Democrats and Republicans for the presidency? Can the Republican and Democratic parties sustain majority status at the presidential level? We turn now to a discussion of these questions.

GLOBAL POLITICS

The Life of the Party

During every American election cycle, the following lament is often heard among voters: "Shouldn't we have more than just two options on the ballot?" Clearly, the Democratic and Republican parties dominate the political system in the United States. In most election years, only between 2 and 5 percent of House seats are deemed "competitive," although a number of analysts argued that as many as forty seats were competitive in 2006.

At the presidential level, our electoral college system helps to undermine independent and third-party candidates (see our discussion of the electoral college in Chapter 7). Consider the following: In 1992, Reform party presidential candidate Ross Perot received 19 percent of the popular vote, but was completely shut out of the electoral college because he failed to win a single state. In a hypothetical parliamentary system with proportional representation (see p. 174 in this chapter), Ross Perot's Reform party might instead have been granted 19 percent of the seats in Congress — imbuing that movement with considerable leverage against the two major parties. Moreover, the citizens who cast their votes for the Reform party might not have felt as if their votes were "wasted" (a common argument against supporting third parties) since they'd have something to show for their efforts. But perhaps this is yet another case of the "grass being greener on the other side of the fence." What are some of the disadvantages associated with multiparty parliamentary systems so often found in other countries around the globe?

- **Unstable government coalitions.** With proportional representation in government, it's often the case that no single party controls a majority of the legislative seats. As such, larger par-

ties are often forced to form coalitions drawing on the support of other smaller parties to create a majority alignment in the legislative body. Depending on how fragile the alignments are, even the exodus of a small, weak party from the coalition may wind up upsetting the entire governmental apple cart. Israel has had repeatedly to call for early elections over past decades due to coalition breakdowns — and often, the entrance of one party into an alliance has meant the exit of another.

- **Party-based campaigns.** When people vote for a member of Congress in the United States — for example, Nancy Pelosi (D-CA) or Dennis Hastert (R-IL) — they have a reasonably good idea of whom they're putting into office. But elections that are centered on the party rather than on the candidates, as is often the case in parliamentary systems, can produce representatives whom the public knows little about — which likely wouldn't sit very well with most American voters.

- **Radical ideologies in government discourse.** France's National Front party would be hard-pressed to gain political representation in a two-party system; its ultranationalistic views (which in the past have included a proposal to expel all French residents not of European descent) would relegate it to the sidelines in national debate, just as extreme candidates in the United States fail to survive the electoral process. But the electoral parliamentary system of France, based on proportional representation, encourages extreme, fascist parties like the National Front to run candidates for office, and frequently allows them to succeed, as they have in recent years. While some political pundits argue that the inclusion of extreme candidates on the Right and the Left siphon off attention from the more "serious" candidates, proponents of parliamentary systems often claim that more political voices equal an increase in voter participation.

In two-party systems, many of the political movements—such as the Christian Coalition in the GOP and environmental activists in the Democratic party—are able to use their political muscle within the primary process. But during general elections, the median voter is the ultimate prize, and thus centrist positions often prevail in our nation. While this may serve to dampen the enthusiasm of the political idealist, this also has the effect of preventing volatile governments and ensuring that administrations generally maintain consistent policies from one regime to the next.

No doubt the issue of a two-party system versus a multiparty system in the United States will continue to occupy the attention of many American voters in the future, especially as we gain new insights into politics at the global level.

Kevin Fullam contributed to this essay.

Realignment of Parties

Party realignment A major shift by voters from one party to another that occurs when one party becomes dominant in the political system, controlling the presidency and Congress, and many state legislatures as well.

Have we been experiencing, in recent years, a major realignment of political parties in the United States as Democrats and Republicans trade off control of the White House and Congress? For a **party realignment** to take place, one party must become dominant in the political system, controlling the presidency and Congress, and many state legislatures as well. Realignments occur either (1) when a political, social, or economic development prompts those groups that have traditionally supported one party to shift their support to another party, or (2) when large numbers of new voters enter the electorate, causing a shift to a new majority party.[20] The democratization of parties in the 1820s, the issue of slavery in the 1850s, and the Great Depression in the 1930s were three economic and social issues that precipitated major party realignments in the past. There have been four major American realignments altogether, marked by the election of Andrew Jackson in 1828, Abraham Lincoln in 1860, William McKinley in 1896, and Franklin D. Roosevelt in 1932.

The realignment that brought the Democrats to power in 1932, for example, was partly the result of a shift in population away from rural small towns, where traditional Republican support rested, and to the big cities, which the Democratic party had cultivated. A new coalition combining immigrants with Catholics, blacks, union members, various ethnic groups, and disaffected Republicans provided a lasting reservoir of support for the Democratic party.

Critical Thinking

Are we undergoing voter realignment— a shifting in party preferences—in the United States?

Do recent electoral victories by Republican presidential and congressional candidates mean that realignment has occurred? Three characteristics of our contemporary political scene warn us against any quick judgments regarding realignment. First, despite the significant Democratic electoral successes in the 2006 elections, particularly in gaining control of Congress, only a handful of seats separated the two parties in both the Senate and the House of Representatives. In neither the 2004 presidential election nor the 2006 congressional elections was there any clear sign of party realignment. Second, realignments tend

National Party Conventions and Hoopla

National party conventions, while serious events confirming the selection of a party's candidate for the presidency of the United States, are filled with celebration and hoopla. Here Texas delegates cheer during the Republican National Convention, August 31, 2004, in New York City.

Party dealignment A period in which the public disassociates itself from both parties and splits its votes between them.

to occur over a period of years, and any permanent realignment will have to face the test of time. Third, some scholars have suggested that we may in fact be going through a period of **party dealignment**, in which the public disassociates itself—that is, dealigns itself—from both parties and divides its votes among them and strong third-party or independent movements.[21] The relative increase in the number of independents over the past thirty-five years and weak party identifiers during the past thirty years tends to support this argument. If this pattern prevails, neither party may be able to regain a solid, long-term hold on the title of "majority party" in the near future.

At present, therefore, no clear realignment has occurred. Although some scholars argue that we appear to be moving through a dealigning period, the concept of dealignment does not satisfactorily explain all citizen sentiment regarding parties and politics in the United States. Certainly no strong third-party challenge to the political system has taken hold in the twenty-first century.

Why Two Parties?

One thing is clear: For most of its history, the United States has had a two-party system. We have many minor parties, but their members are rarely elected to a major office. Why has this been the case? Other democracies, including Israel, Holland, France, and Italy, have several important parties. What factors limit significant party activity in the United States to the Republicans and the Democrats?

Winner Takes All. According to one explanation, the rules that govern the electoral system in the United States are responsible for the two-party system.[22] Early in our history, we adopted what is known as a **single-member district, winner-take-all electoral system**. In all federal and state elections and in most local elections, we elect officials from districts served by only one legislator. In order to gain office, a candidate has to win a plurality—the most votes. (In certain states, a candidate in a given election must win a majority of the votes—that is, more than 50 percent.) Thus, only one U.S. representative or state legislator is elected from each congressional or legislative district, no matter how close the vote.

By contrast, most European nations use a system of **proportional representation**. In this system, each electoral district has a number of legislative seats, and these seats are assigned to the candidates of each party in proportion to the percentage of the vote that that party receives within the district. If a party receives 35 percent of the vote in a district, it is allocated approximately 35 percent of that district's legislative seats. Thus, minor or third parties may accumulate enough votes to gain representation in the legislature even if they are not able to attract a plurality or have only pockets of support.

The winner-take-all system in the United States has worked against the development of minor parties. Because it is so difficult for even the most successful minor parties to accumulate pluralities, their candidates rarely win. Recognizing that minority party candidates have little chance, voters tend to be drawn to the major party coalitions at election time, and those parties try hard to maintain middle-of-the-road positions that will attract voters.[23] The result has been two broad-based party coalitions, such as the Republicans and the Democrats of today.

A Division of Interests. A second explanation, advanced by political scientists V. O. Key Jr. and Louis Hartz, points to a natural division of interests in our nation as the source of the two-party system.[24] From the time of the country's founding until recently, divisions have existed: between eastern manufacturers and western frontier interests, between slaveholders and abolitionists, between urban and rural interests, and among various regional interests. These divisions have stemmed from tensions over the power of the national government and over questions of economic and social policy. That situation, according to Key and Hartz, has fostered the two-party competitive system, which is really a response to the national duality of interests.

A Similarity of Goals. Still another view focuses on the overriding consensus in the United States regarding our political, social, economic, and governmental systems. For example, most Americans believe in capitalism, virtually no Americans want to institute a monarchy, and most Americans believe in some form of free enterprise in the United States. By contrast, in many European countries, the people support a variety of radically different social and economic alternatives, ranging from socialism to anarchy, and differences in social class and religion have given rise to a broad range of parties.

Divisions do exist in the United States, of course—for example, between the poor and the wealthy. But a basic acceptance of the political and governmental

Single-member district, winner-take-all electoral system The system of election used in the United States in all national and state elections and in most local elections; officials are elected from districts that are served by only one legislator, and a candidate must win a plurality—the most votes.
Proportional representation The electoral system used by many European nations in which legislative seats are assigned to party candidates in proportion to the percentage of the vote that the party receives within the district.

system by most Americans makes compromise possible. As a result, according to this view, the two major parties can adequately serve us all, and we do not need a complex multiparty system.

State Laws. As there is no mention of political parties in the U.S. Constitution, the definition of what a party is and the laws that regulate parties have been left, for the most part, to the individual states. Since the two major parties, the Republicans and the Democrats, have dominated the state legislatures, with the exception of that of Nebraska, state laws, in general, have historically made it difficult for third parties to get on the ballot. These restrictive state laws have helped to perpetuate the two-party system in the United States (although recent court challenges have eliminated some of those restrictions in various states).

The Hidden Actors: Third Parties in the United States

Critical Thinking

Do you think we are better off with a two-party system, or would we be better off with a multiparty system with strong third parties?

Despite the strength of the two-party system, minor parties have always existed in the United States. There have been more than 900 of these "third" parties, and occasionally they even do well in national elections, although only one of them — the Republicans in 1860 — has developed into a permanent national party. In 1992, independent candidate Ross Perot mounted a highly visible campaign for the presidency and received 19 percent of the popular vote. In 1996, however, running as the Reform party presidential candidate, he received only about 8 percent of the vote. In 2004, Green party candidate David Cobb and independent candidate Ralph Nader each received less than 1 percent of the presidential vote.

Sometimes a minor party forms around a single issue, such as prohibition, or an ideology, such as socialism. Other minor parties are splinter groups that leave a major party because they feel that their interests are not well represented.

Most of the third parties' electoral successes have come at the state and local levels. But even at those levels, they must overcome many barriers. Dominated by the two major parties, state legislatures have created complicated electoral rules, often requiring petitions, nominating conventions, minimum levels of registered voters, organizational requirements, or a combination of all of these provisions that can make it hard for the minor parties to place their candidates on the ballot.

Federal election laws also work against the minor parties. For example, the major parties automatically receive funding for presidential campaigns. A third party cannot obtain such funding until its candidate has demonstrated the ability to garner a certain amount (5 percent) of the popular vote.

Despite these obstacles, third parties persist, attracting devoted members and serving as a force for change in American politics. These parties put new issues on the political agenda — issues that the major parties may overlook in their search for the broad middle ground, where most voters are perceived to be. For example, social security, unemployment insurance, the five-day workweek, workers' compensation, national health insurance, and government aid to farmers

Third Party and Independent Candidates in a Two-Party System

Third party and independent candidates have been a part of the political landscape in the U.S. for more than 200 years. In the 2004 presidential election, Ralph Nader, a well-known consumer advocate, was able to attract only about 1 percent of the presidential vote.

were first introduced by the Socialist party in its 1932 party platform and only later recognized as important programs by both the Republicans and the Democrats.

Future elections will no doubt provide voters with a number of third-party candidates for the presidency, as well as for Congress and state and local offices. In 2006, dozens of minor parties ran candidates in Senate, House, and gubernatorial races and in many local elections.

Party Structure from the Bottom Up

FOCUS QUESTION WHAT ARE THE DIFFERENT ROLES OF PARTY ORGANIZATIONS AT THE LOCAL, STATE, AND NATIONAL LEVELS?

Decentralization is the key word to remember when you think about the structure of parties. Just as in our governmental system, power in the parties is fragmented among local, state, and national organizations. The two national parties are loose confederations of state parties, and state political parties are loose confederations of city and county political organizations.

Local Parties

Precinct The bottom of the typical local party structure—a voting district, generally covering an area of several blocks.

You may be most familiar with the structure of political parties at the local level. At the bottom of the typical local party structure is the **precinct**, a voting district that generally covers an area of several blocks. An elected or appointed precinct captain may oversee electoral activities in the precinct, including voter registra-

Ward A city council district; in the party organization, this is the level below the citywide level.
Patronage The provision of jobs in return for political support.
Preferments The provision of services or contracts in return for political support. Party committee members use patronage and preferments to court voters and obtain campaign contributions.

tion, distribution of leaflets, and get-out-the-vote efforts. Above the precinct level, several different organizations exist. **Wards**, or city council districts, are important in big cities such as Chicago. Elsewhere, party organizations exist at the city, county, congressional district, state legislative district, or even judicial level. Members of these committees may be elected or appointed. Their responsibilities include raising money, recruiting candidates, conducting campaigns, getting out the vote, and handling **patronage** — that is, jobs for party loyalists—and **preferments** — services or contracts provided to individuals and companies in return for campaign support.

In many places around the country, local parties scarcely exist at all. Nonpartisan elections are the rule, a result of antiparty reforms during the early 1900s, and politics is relatively informal. Indeed, two-thirds of cities with populations of more than 5,000 use the nonpartisan form of election. In many of these communities, formal or informal "political clubs" raise money and run campaigns. These clubs actively compete with each other in elections and may identify with either major party.[25]

Even in communities where partisan elections are the rule, party organization and strength vary tremendously. If one party dominates, the weaker party may find it impossible to recruit workers and candidates and to raise money for elections. Until its recent resurgence, the Republican party had to cope with this kind of handicap throughout a Democrat-dominated South. In communities that show little interest in politics, neither party may be able to put together a strong local organization.

Nevertheless, it is at the grassroots local community level that party organization often finds its greatest strength, and it is at that level that we have seen growth in party organizations in recent years. Indeed, recent research suggests that local party organizations are becoming increasingly active in various aspects of the campaign process in communities.[26]

State Parties

The influence and power of state party organizations vary from state to state. State parties in Alabama, California, and Maryland, for example, have almost nothing to say about which candidates run for office or how they run their campaigns. In contrast, parties in states such as Connecticut, Indiana, and Michigan wield considerable power. Often a good deal of that power is in the hands of the state chairperson. It is not unusual for the governor of a state to control the state's party organization, although, as we shall see in Chapter 7, on elections and campaigns, governors are often motivated to establish their own candidate-centered organization devoted to their campaign for reelection. Party organization varies from state to state, however, and depends on the preferences of officeholders and other influential party members and on state laws and party rules and regulations.

In recent years, state party organizations have assumed an important role on the political scene.[27] State parties have increasingly begun to offer state and local candidates fundraising, polling, and research services as well as technical

POLITICS *&* POPULAR CULTURE

Cartoons and Political Parties: "Stop Them Damned Pictures"

William Marcy "Boss" Tweed, the notorious boss of New York City's Tammany Hall Democratic machine during the 1860s and 1870s, detested political cartoons. Shortly after viewing a cartoon by Thomas Nast, who was highly critical of Tweed's sleaze and corruption in New York politics, Tweed was said to have ordered his lieutenants to "Stop them damned pictures. I don't care so much what the papers say about me. My constituents can't read. But, damn it, they can see pictures!" Nast's cartoons about Tweed were thought to have contributed to Tweed's eventual downfall. In the words of one scholar, they also "established once and forever . . . cartooning as an enduring presence in American [popular] political culture."

Indeed, many an early-rising, coffee-drinking, sleepy-eyed newspaper reader turns every morning to the editorial page, where political cartoons are often featured. One particular editorial cartoonist, Dick Locher, has frequently captured the mood of the nation through his artful and often satirical critiques of politicians and political parties. A good example is a cartoon he drew in 2006 satirizing political parties. Locher's message is clear: During a time when congressional ethics issues were front-page news in the nation, Republicans and Democrats couldn't be trusted to introduce or enforce ethics reforms in Congress. No doubt, many Americans share this opinion.

Yet the idea that political parties exist only to churn out unethical officeholders — a distortion that editorial cartoons like this one often foster — feeds and reinforces an unfair stereotype of U.S. political parties. To be sure, we appreciate Locher's humor and must even acknowledge the partial accuracy of his cartoon. But, as we point out in this chapter, we must also remind ourselves that, while recent scandals have made clear that some party members are unethical, most individuals elected under a party banner bring a high level of integrity and ethics to public office.

Source: Roger A. Fisher, *Them Damned Pictures: Explorations in American Political Cartoon Art* (North Haven, Conn.: Archon Books, 1996), especially chaps. 1 and 6. The quotations are from pp. 2 and 3. The cartoon is from the *Chicago Tribune*, 2006.

help in establishing candidate websites. They may also provide computer analyses of voting behavior. In addition, most state party organizations help orchestrate the state presidential campaigns.

National Parties

The national party organizations come into their own every four years when they organize the national conventions and support candidates for major office. Although the national parties are less visible the rest of the time, their staffs, directed by the national chairpersons and the national committees, which include representatives from all the states, are hard at work. They raise money for national and state elections, run workshops on campaigning and fundraising techniques for congressional candidates, and maintain the loose, decentralized structure that is the national party. The Democrats and the Republicans, by devoting greater resources to their national party organizations, have undergone a national resurgence during the past fifteen years.

> **Political action committee (PAC)** An independent organization that can be established by interest groups, officeholders, and political candidates for the sole purpose of contributing money to the campaigns of candidates who sympathize with its aims. PACs are the result of federal laws that prohibit most interest groups from donating money to federal political campaigns.

The electoral role of the national party organizations has been challenged in recent years by interest groups and their **political action committees (PACs)**. Because federal laws, as well as many state laws, prohibit various interest groups from donating money to political campaigns, such groups have set up affiliated PAC organizations for the purpose of contributing money to the campaigns of candidates who sympathize with their aims. (See Chapter 8, on interest groups, for a more detailed discussion of the role of PACs.) The involvement of professional consultants and the media in the campaign process has also challenged the role of the national organizations. (See Chapter 7, on elections, for more on this topic.)

Despite these challenges, the national organizations have refused to accept a secondary role in national politics and during the past twenty-five years have worked to revitalize themselves.[28] Both the Republican and Democratic parties have strengthened their fundraising and candidate support systems. They now provide sophisticated technical campaign expertise to state and local parties in addition to providing financial support for campaigns. In addition, the Democrats have redefined the rules governing the selection of presidential convention delegates to make the party's decision-making structure more democratic and to increase grassroots participation in the party.

Conclusion: Decline or Transformation of Political Parties?

What is the future of the Democratic and Republican parties? Some scholars insist that both parties are in a period of decline and see them as weak, inconsistent in their policies, lacking accountability for their actions, disorganized in

Party-centered campaign A campaign in which the party coordinates activities, raises money, and develops strategies.

Candidate-centered campaign A campaign in which paid consultants or volunteers coordinate campaign activities, develop strategies, and raise funds. Parties play a secondary role.

Critical
Thinking

Do you agree or disagree with the myth of party irrelevance?

pursuing their goals, and less effective in organizing government than in the past.[29] In recent presidential campaigns, we have seen both the Democratic and the Republican parties faced with contentious battles over which faction of the party—moderate, liberal, or conservative—will control the nomination of candidates and the writing of the party platform. We seem to be moving from **party-centered campaigns** to **candidate-centered campaigns**, reflecting the shift in control over the candidate recruitment and campaign process from the political parties to candidate-controlled campaign organizations. Given the decrease in party identification and the weakening of party control over some aspects of the campaign and election process, it is not surprising that many people believe in the myth of party irrelevance.

Are the parties identical? It often seems that way because in some areas their policies can be difficult to distinguish. On certain broad issues, such as supporting reductions in the national deficit, and certain narrow issues, such as social security for the elderly, their positions are often the same. To confuse matters further, groups of legislators from both parties occasionally join forces to support or oppose legislation.

Nevertheless, the evidence suggests that the parties are not irrelevant. The fact that they attract different coalitions of voters and office seekers and that Democrats and Republicans in the electorate and in government tend to view many issues differently attests to their relevancy in the political system.

The significant number of independents, along with the increase in ticket splitting, suggests that parties may be less relevant than they have been in the past, as does the takeover of some traditional party roles by interest groups, political action committees, the media, and professional political consultants. These issues will be discussed further in Chapters 7, 8, and 9. However, the parties have changed in response to such challenges. Furthermore, although parties attract fewer strong supporters, particularly among college students, a significant majority of voters still feel some attachment to either the Democrats or the Republicans and believe that one party can do a better job than the other in tackling the nation's most serious problems.

If parties are still viable, what kind of change is taking place? How can we explain, for example, the growing independence of political candidates and legislators from their parties? Some scholars have suggested that a transformation is taking place in the roles and functions of parties in our society.[30]

Although parties are now sharing many traditional functions with other groups, they have also taken on new tasks, as our discussion in this chapter has shown. Both national and state organizations have enhanced their roles in the campaign process, and parties continue to play an important role at the local level. In fact, most of the elections held in our nation during the four years between presidential races—and they number more than 500,000—are not touched by any other organized group. Party influence in the Senate and House remains strong, and on many partisan issues the members vote along party lines more often than not. This pattern is also typical of state legislators.

Thus, despite the myth of party irrelevance, parties remain a key institution in American politics and are still one of the most important cues for voters making electoral decisions. They also play a dominant role in organizing and coordinating public policy on literally thousands of issues. Finally, parties represent many individuals and groups that are not adequately served by other organizations. These groups include the poor and minorities. All of them have benefited from strong party platforms and legislative action. Challenged by the entry of new and competing institutions into the electoral process, parties have increasingly adapted to these challenges and have maintained their unique role in our political system.

Tying It Together

FOCUS QUESTIONS RECAP

* What are the three parts of the party that we refer to as the "three-headed political giant"?

* What are some of the key differences between the Republican and Democratic parties?

* What are some of the reasons we have a two-party system in the United States?

* What are the different roles of party organizations at the local, state, and national levels?

CHAPTER SUMMARY

1. American political parties are coalitions of people organized formally to recruit, nominate, and elect candidates for public office and to use elected office to achieve shared political goals.

2. Parties represent three different alliances of members, what we sometimes refer to as the "three-headed political giant": the party-as-organization, the party-in-the-electorate, and the party-in-government.

3. There are some key differences between the Republican and Democratic parties. Ideologically, Republicans tend to be more conservative; Democrats, more liberal. They attract different supporters. Democrat support comes more from African Americans and Hispanics, Catholics and Jews, women, members of the working class, and citizens over the age of fifty. Republican supporters tend to be white, Protestant, and middle to upper class, and this group may now include white southerners.

4. Although many Americans' identification with the Republican or Democratic party seems to be weak, the parties continue to be relevant symbols, particularly when it comes to voting.

5. Parties organize citizens into electoral coalitions, develop policy positions, work to win elections, and organize government.

6. Parties developed slowly in the United States, but by the 1860s the Republicans and the Democrats had laid the foundation for the two-party system. There have been four major party realignments, or major shifts in party coalitions, in U.S. history. Currently, scholars are debating whether we are in a period of realignment or dealignment.

7. Explanations for the existence of the two-party system include winner-take-all electoral rules, a division of social and economic interests, a basic consensus on political goals, and restrictive state laws regarding third parties.

8. Despite the strength of the major parties, minor parties thrive and present program alternatives that are often adopted by the Democratic and Republican parties.

9. Both local and state political parties have grown in importance in recent years. Although the national party organizations have been challenged by competing groups, they have responded to the challenge and, in changing, have revitalized themselves.

10. The party organizations at all levels play a number of roles. Local party organizations raise money, recruit candidates, and conduct campaigns. State party organizations also raise money, recruit candidates, and conduct campaigns and increasingly offer state and local candidates polling and research services. They also provide technical assistance and help maintain candidate websites. In addition, they provide support for the national party organizations for presidential campaigns. The national party organizations, in addition to supporting all of the types of services provided by local and state party organizations, organize and support the national convention every four years, the place where the party's presidential and vice-presidential candidates are confirmed and where the national party platform is written.

11. The key roles that political parties play in our political system include organizing and coordinating public policy on literally thousands of issues, providing the American electorate with different ideological orientations, and serving as a cue for voters who don't know very much about the candidates or the issues they stand for. In addition, political parties act as an organizational structure for our legislative bodies, and represent hundreds of millions of Americans, including many individuals and groups that are not adequately served by other organizations.

Key Terms

Political party (162)
Decentralization (162)
Party-as-organization (162)
Party-in-the-electorate (162)
Party-in-government (163)
Electoral coalitions (167)
Platforms (167)
Primary (169)
Party realignment (172)
Party dealignment (173)

Single-member district, winner-take-all electoral system (174)
Proportional representation (174)
Precinct (176)
Ward (177)
Patronage (177)
Preferments (177)
Political action committee (PAC) (179)
Party-centered campaign (180)
Candidate-centered campaign (180)

Net Work

Political parties, while not mentioned in the Constitution, are one of the most important institutional arrangements in our political and governmental system. To find out more about the two major parties in the United States, visit their homepages:

- Democratic National Committee (**www.democrats.org**)
- Republican National Committee (**www.rnc.org**)

Both parties have party organizations affiliated with each of the houses of Congress:

- Democratic Congressional Campaign Committee (House of Representatives) (**www.dccc.org**)
- Democratic Senatorial Campaign Committee (**www.dscc.org**)
- National Republican Congressional Committee (House of Representatives) (**www.nrcc.org**)
- National Republican Senatorial Committee (**www.nrsc.org**)

Not surprisingly, a number of minor or third parties also maintain websites. They include the following:

- Libertarian Party (**www.lp.org/lp.html**)
- Reform Party (**www.reformparty.org**)
- Green Parties of North America (**www.greens.org**)
- Democratic Socialists of America (**www.dsausa.org**)
- United States Taxpayers Party (**www.ustaxpayers.org**)

Third parties offer different policy positions that are often opposed to those of the two major parties. As an exercise, select three of the third parties listed above and compare their positions on one or more issues to those of the Democrats and the Republicans.

7

Campaigns and Elections

Do politicians always break their campaign promises?

FOCUS QUESTIONS

* What roles do party caucuses, primaries, and conventions play in the nomination process?

* What impact does money have on political campaigns?

* What recent changes have been made in federal election campaign finance laws?

* How do the media have an impact on political campaigns?

* What have been the consequences of the shift from party-centered campaigns to candidate-centered campaigns?

* What factors influence the way people vote in an election?

* How does the electoral college function? What alternatives have been suggested as a replacement for the electoral college?

* Do candidates, when elected to office, try to keep their campaign promises?

T he election campaign was exhilarating. Millions of people turned out to see and hear the presidential candidates as they traveled around the nation speaking on the issues of the day. Between July and November, the Democratic candidate "made five hundred speeches . . . addressing thirty to forty million people . . . traveling 18,000 miles in four swings around the country."[1] One scholar wrote of the Republican candidate that his was a classic case of a "modern advertising campaign." Cartoons, posters, and inscriptions were turned out by the carload, more than "120 million campaign documents" were distributed to the people, and "an army of 1,400 trained speakers" was engaged to speak in favor of the candidate.[2] The Republicans canvassed voters and targeted specific ethnic groups with campaign literature written in German, Spanish, French, Italian, and Yiddish, as well as other languages.[3]

That campaign story may seem familiar. The campaign strategies and hoopla may remind you of recent races you have witnessed or seen on television. Yet the campaign took place more than 110 years ago, in 1896, when William Jennings Bryan was the Democratic presidential candidate, running against Republican William McKinley.

Rallies, use of the media, and appeals to special interests remain a basic part of modern-day campaigns and elections, and the intensity and excitement have stayed the same. The electoral system itself is quite different, however. An array of regulations, restrictions, and constitutional amendments has changed the way candidates are nominated, how campaigns are run, and who is eligible to vote. Unlike McKinley or Bryan, today's candidates for president have to contend with presidential primaries, campaign spending limits, and an expanded voting population. In 1896, most voters were middle- and upper-class white men. Today, candidates must appeal to men and women, minorities and whites, rich and poor, and young and old. Furthermore, in recent years candidates for every office from city council member to president have had to deal with new technologies, including the World Wide Web and the Internet.[4]

Despite the excitement of the campaigns and the widespread media coverage, the American public has some misgivings about the election process. While voter turnout for the 2004 presidential election approached 60 percent of eligible voters, it was still lower than it was for the Kennedy-Nixon race in 1960, which attracted 63 percent of the vote. There are no data to suggest that the trend of overall low voter turnout in the United States will be reversed in the near future.[5]

Poll findings also suggest that many Americans do not believe that our elected representatives respond to their demands and expectations. For example, about two-thirds of Americans "don't think public officials care much about what people like me think." Almost 60 percent feel that they can trust government in Washington to do what is right only some of the time or never.[6]

The public also strongly disapproves of the way candidates run their campaigns, particularly the way they finance them. Such views are reinforced when, for example, the public learns that presidential candidates spent more than $1 billion on the 2004 primary and general election campaigns. Congressional candidates spent an estimated 1.2 billion on the 2006 elections. Expenditures on

Hoopla and Campaigns

Every campaign has included advertising posters, cartoons, and campaign literature. When William McKinley ran for president in 1896, his campaign literature emphasized his link to prosperity, prestige, and economic well-being.

individual races also attract a great deal of attention. In 2004, South Dakota Republican and Democratic Senate candidates spent a total of $36 million. That comes to $60.87 per voter. In a highly contested House of Representatives race in Texas's Thirty-Second District, the two candidates combined spent more than $9 million.[7]

Why have so many Americans come to doubt the usefulness of elections? Why do so many of us stay home on election day? One myth seems to be at the root of public criticism of the electoral process. The *myth of broken promises* holds that elections do not affect government policies—that candidates, once they are elected, fail to keep the promises they made during their campaigns.

The reality of the election process, however, differs from that myth. We demonstrate in this chapter that politicians seek to achieve not only their own career goals but also the social and political goals put forth in their campaigns. In addition, we show that although money is very important in campaigns because it pays for television time, polls, consultants, and the like, a variety of other factors also have a significant impact on who is elected.

Nominations: The Selection Process

FOCUS QUESTION WHAT ROLES DO PARTY CAUCUSES, PRIMARIES, AND CONVENTIONS PLAY IN THE NOMINATION PROCESS?

Every year thousands of individuals decide to run for political office. In many cases, before they can get on the ballot, they must be selected, or nominated, by a political party, often after a costly, time-consuming, and exhausting primary campaign. What motivates these individuals?

Why Do People Run?

"The stakes are too high for government to be a spectator sport," former member of Congress Barbara Jordan from Texas told a commencement audience. Few of those who run for office would disagree. Public service, personal ambition, and policy goals motivate people to enter the proverbial election ring.[8] These factors often drive politicians to climb what Joseph Schlesinger refers to as the **opportunity structure**: the political ladder of local, state, and national offices that brings one greater prestige and power as one moves toward the presidency at the very top.[9]

Opportunity structure The political ladder of local, state, and national offices that brings greater prestige and power as one moves toward the presidency.

The Caucus: Old-Fashioned Politics

Ambition and commitment alone are not enough to ensure election, however. Anyone who wants to run for political office in most partisan elections, including the presidency, must first secure a party nomination. One of the oldest methods of nomination is the **caucus** (the word means "meeting"). A diary entry written by John Adams in 1763 gives a less-than-flattering description of the process:

Caucus A forum for choosing candidates that was closed to the public until the Progressive Era; contemporary caucuses are local party meetings, open to all who live in the precinct, in which citizens discuss and then vote for delegates to district and state conventions.

> This day learned that the caucus club meets at certain times in the garret of Dawes. . . . There they smoke tobacco till you cannot see from one end of the garret to the other. There they drink flip* . . . and they choose a moderator who puts questions to the vote regularly; and selectmen, assessors, collectors, fire wardens, and representatives are regularly chosen before they are chosen in the town.[10]

Until the Progressive Era, a period of political reform starting around the end of the nineteenth century, most party nominations were decided by caucuses or conventions. These meetings were closed to the public, and party leaders usually

---

*For the curious and those with a cast-iron stomach, flip is a hot mixture of beer, cider, sugar, egg, and nutmeg—an excellent eye opener.

chose the nominees. Most contemporary caucuses are local meetings that are open to all who live in the precinct. These citizens "caucus"—that is, meet and discuss—and then vote for delegates to district and state conventions. These delegates then nominate candidates for congressional and statewide offices. In about 20 percent of the states, delegates to the national presidential conventions are chosen by the caucus/convention method. Many of these delegates are committed in advance to a particular presidential candidate. Some, however, choose to run as uncommitted delegates, awaiting the national convention to declare their candidate preference.

The most celebrated of modern presidential caucuses takes place every four years in Iowa, where candidates compete for the Democratic and Republican presidential nominations. Traditionally, the Iowa caucus is the first of the presidential campaign cycle, and candidates are anxious to do well in order to demonstrate their appeal both to the voters and to potential campaign contributors who want to support a winner.

Primaries: New Kid on the Block

Except in presidential contests and when minor political parties select their candidates, caucuses are relatively uncommon in contemporary politics. As we pointed out in Chapter 6, most Democratic and Republican nominees, whether at the national, state, or local level, are chosen in a **primary**: an election in which party members (for the most part—in some states, nonparty members may participate) select candidates to run for office under the party banner. The first recorded primary was held in Crawford County, Pennsylvania, in 1842, but the first statewide primary system was not enacted until 1901, in Florida. In 2004, the Democrats held presidential primaries in 38 states, and the Republicans did so in 27 states.*

In an **open primary**, any qualified registered voter may participate, regardless of party affiliation. Upon entering the polling place, voters select a Democratic, Republican, or other party ballot and choose among the names on the ballot to select that party's candidates for the various offices. A variation on the open primary is the blanket primary, in which voters do not disclose their party affiliation at the polling place and may participate in the Democratic primary for one office and the Republican primary for another office. However, in a decision delivered on June 26, 2000, the U.S. Supreme Court declared the blanket primary in California unconstitutional, arguing that it violated a political party's First

Critical Thinking

Do you think primaries or caucuses are a better means for nominating party candidates for political office?

Primary An election in which party members select candidates to run for office under the party banner.

Open primary A primary election in which any qualified voter may participate, regardless of party affiliation. The voter chooses one party ballot at the polling place.

---

*It is difficult to say exactly how many states use a primary system because the two parties in a particular state do not necessarily use the same system. In Delaware, Idaho, Virginia, and Washington, the Democratic party uses a caucus/convention system to select delegates to the national convention, whereas the Republican party uses a primary. In Texas, the Democratic party selects its delegates using a combination primary/caucus system, whereas the Republican party employs a primary system. In addition, the number of presidential primaries held by a party may vary from one election year to the next. For example, in 2004, Republican presidential primaries were canceled in Connecticut, Florida, Mississippi, New York, and South Dakota because the only qualifying candidate in those five states was George W. Bush.

Closed primary A primary election in which a voter is allowed to obtain only a ballot of the party in which he or she is registered.

Partisan primary A primary in which candidates run for their own party's nomination.

Nonpartisan primary A primary in which candidates are listed on a ballot with no party identification.

Runoff primary An electoral contest between the top two vote getters in the primary that determines the party's candidate in a general election. Such primaries are held in the ten southern states in which a majority of the vote is needed to win the primary.

Amendment right of association.[11] In a **closed primary**, used in a majority of the states and in Washington, D.C., voters are allowed to obtain only a ballot of the party in which they are registered.

In a **partisan primary**, candidates run for their own party's nomination. In a **nonpartisan primary**, candidates are listed on a ballot with no party identification. All presidential primaries are partisan, but many local primaries and the Nebraska state primary are nonpartisan.

In most states, the winning candidate is the one who receives the most votes. In ten southern states, however, a majority (more than 50 percent) of the vote is needed to win; if no candidate receives a clear majority, a **runoff primary** between the top two vote getters determines the party's candidate in the general election.

In presidential contests, the first presidential primary is always held in New Hampshire. Although the state is small and its population is not representative of the nation's population as a whole, this primary plays a significant symbolic role in the nomination process, as New Hampshire citizens are given the first opportunity to express their preferences for Republican and Democratic presidential hopefuls. Like victory in the first caucus, held in Iowa, victory in the New Hampshire primary brings the candidate a great deal of media coverage, which helps in attracting campaign donations. From New Hampshire's point of view, having the first primary draws the candidates, their entourage, and the media into the state. This means not only prestige and honor, but additional revenue, too. It is no wonder that New Hampshire jealously guards the honor of initiating the primary season.

Historically, presidential primaries were spread out over the first six months of the calendar year in which the presidential election took place, beginning

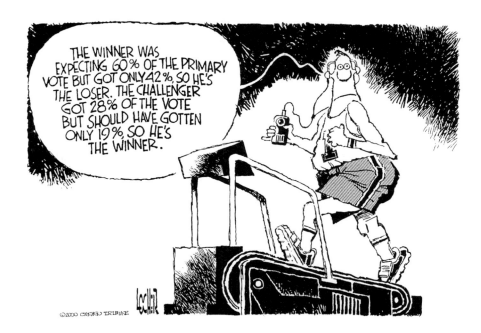

with the New Hampshire primary in February and culminating with several state primaries in June. In 2000 and again in the 2004 presidential primary races, however, many states, eager to have an early influence on the Republican and Democratic nominating process, moved their primaries ahead. As a result of this **front-loading** phenomenon, by the end of March 2004, 80 percent of the delegates to both the Democratic and the Republican conventions had been selected. Why is front-loading important? It tends to give the candidates who are the front-runners at the beginning of the primary season an advantage: With a shorter primary season, underdogs have only a brief window of opportunity to overtake the front-runner. In the past, with primaries spread out over a six-month period, a candidate who was not initially favored could still theoretically build momentum through the later primaries. Now, candidates must demonstrate that they have public support very early in the primaries if they are going to have any chance of getting their party's nomination. In addition, with the primaries clustered so close together, campaign money must be raised early and in large amounts if a candidate is to compete successfully. In 2004, ten Democratic presidential aspirants and President George W. Bush spent more than $660 million on their nomination campaigns.[12] Money raised after the March primaries is unlikely to have any significant impact on the nomination race. Clearly, the front-loading of primaries has had a significant impact on strategies for winning the Democratic or Republican presidential nomination.

> **Front-loading** The scheduling of primaries very early in the campaign season by states eager to have an early influence on the Republican and Democratic nomination process, as occurred in 2004.

Both the Democratic and Republican parties are considering alternative proposals for spacing primaries to avoid front-loading. However, because each of the fifty states decides individually when its primaries and/or caucuses are held, there is no guarantee that the parties will be able to reduce the impact of front-loading on the nomination process.

The Changing Role of Nominating Conventions

When Hubert Humphrey was nominated by the Democratic party in 1968, he had entered no primaries, counting instead on support from President Lyndon B. Johnson and other party leaders. His defeat in the November election ended a century-old tradition in which the presidential and vice-presidential candidates were in effect chosen at their party's national convention by delegates from the fifty states, the District of Columbia, and (in the case of the Democrats) offshore territories and Democrats abroad.

The rise of the presidential primary has meant that the national party conventions no longer select the candidates, but rather ratify the choices that have already been made in statewide primaries and caucuses.[13] Conventions still serve a number of traditional functions, however. They give the party faithful a place to transact business, which includes changing rules and writing the party platform. When a convention is run smoothly, with minimal disputes and conflicts, it serves as an important "media event," publicizing the party's candidates and issues to a nationwide audience.

Until the rule reforms of the late 1960s and early 1970s, state and local party leaders appointed most convention delegates. The delegates were largely well-educated, white, male professionals. One survey in the 1940s found that nearly 40 percent of them were lawyers.[14] In 2004, a majority of the delegates to the Democratic and Republican conventions were elected through primaries. Delegates still tend to come from elite groups, however: They tend to be well educated and predominantly white, with relatively high family incomes. The Democrats attract more African Americans, young people, union members, and women to their conventions, whereas Republican delegates tend to be older, white, and predominantly Protestant. Loyal supporters of one of the major candidates, most delegates stand for election in a primary or caucus in that candidate's name.

Although for both parties the nomination process is critical to the success of any presidential aspirant, it apparently matters less to most voters. In most primaries, fewer than 30 percent of the eligible voters turn out to vote; often the percentage is under 20 percent.

Who Gets Nominated?

In the past, almost all the Democratic and Republican presidential nominees have been white, male, wealthy Protestants. The barrier against Catholics fell with the Democratic nomination of Al Smith in 1928 and the nomination and election of John Kennedy in 1960, but Protestant candidates still remain the rule. Furthermore, with the exception of General Dwight D. Eisenhower, a World War II hero who was elected in 1952, all successful presidential candidates for the past hundred years have previously held some high elective office — the vice-presidency, a seat in the U.S. Senate, or the governorship of a state.

Growing Numbers of Women in Politics

Women are playing a growing role in politics in the United States. Pictured here are Senator Debbie Stabenow (D-MI), Senator Dianne Feinstein (D-CA), host Barbara Lee, Senator Hillary Rodham Clinton (D-NY), and Senator Marie Cantwell (D-WA) participating in a Democratic Senate fundraising event in Boston on October 28, 2005.

These elected positions give candidates the visibility and prestige necessary to attract campaign financing and to mount a national campaign.

Social barriers to the nomination of women and of African Americans, Jews, and other ethnic candidates seem to be weakening. In 1984, Congresswoman Geraldine Ferraro was the Democratic vice-presidential nominee. In 2000, the Democratic party nominated the first Jewish vice-presidential candidate on a major party ticket, Senator Joseph I. Lieberman. It is at least possible that in the not-so-distant future a woman, African American, or member of a minority religious denomination will successfully compete for a major party nomination for the presidency.

The Race for Office

FOCUS QUESTION
WHAT IMPACT DOES MONEY HAVE ON POLITICAL CAMPAIGNS? WHAT RECENT CHANGES HAVE BEEN MADE IN FEDERAL ELECTION CAMPAIGN FINANCE LAWS?

Campaign watching is a favorite pastime for many Americans. A controversial candidate, a close race, or any presidential campaign brings headlines, television interviews and debates, and other media coverage. The public may be skeptical about the value of elections and the way they are financed, but it still enjoys the excitement of campaigns.

Financing Campaigns: The Buying and Selling of Office?

Critical Thinking

Do you think that money buys elections?

Much of the public regards the way many, if not most, campaigns are financed as suspect. The feeling prevails that campaigns consume far too much money. This perception is not just a modern impression. In 1895, Senator Mark A. Hanna, a Republican from Ohio who was regarded as one of the most powerful party leaders in the nation, said, "There are two things that are important in politics. The first is money, and I can't remember what the second one is."[15] While reality tells us that Hanna's observation is an exaggeration, campaign financing, particularly in federal elections, remains a major of concern among the American public.

Candidates can be offered large campaign contributions in return for favors. No doubt, some candidates accept such offers; others do not. One would-be contributor to Edmund Muskie's 1972 presidential campaign offered $200,000 with the following stipulation: "You understand, . . . I want to be an American ambassador. Not a big country, you understand, not France or England. I couldn't afford those anyway. But can you give me a little one, Switzerland or Belgium?"[16] Muskie summarily declined the offer.

Of course, financing campaigns is an expensive proposition, especially given the cost of television and the high fees charged by pollsters and campaign strategists. In 2004, presidential candidates spent more than $1 billion on campaigns and national conventions.[17] In congressional elections that year, candidates for the House of Representatives and the Senate collectively spent more than $1.1 billion.[18] And, as is evident from viewing Table 7.1, presidential hopefuls also spent a great deal of money in the 2004 presidential election.

Act I: The Federal Election Campaign Act. In 1971, and again in 1974 and later, Congress stepped in to limit the amount of money presidential candidates could receive and spend. The problem that Congress was trying to solve was not the overall size of campaign expenditures, but rather the imbalances created when some individuals and groups could afford to contribute far more than others. The new law ensured that a single individual would no longer be able to do the kind of thing that W. Clement Stone did in 1972: The Chicago businessman directly contributed $2.1 million to Richard Nixon's presidential campaign.

TABLE 7.1

Candidate Spending in the 2004 Presidential Election

PRESIDENTIAL CANDIDATES

George W. Bush	$345,259,155	Republican party
John Kerry	310,013,730	Democrat party
Ralph Nader	4,563,877	Independent candidate
Michael Badnarik	1,073,940	Libertarian party
Michael Peroutka	708,221	Constitution party
David Cobb	385,707	Green party

CANDIDATES WHO DROPPED OUT OF THE RACE PRIOR TO THE GENERAL ELECTION

Carol Moseley Braun	623,869	Democratic party
Wesley Clark	29,586,661	Democratic party
Howard Dean	52,113,785	Democratic party
John Edwards	33,596,064	Democratic party
Richard Gephardt	21,091,591	Democratic party
Robert Graham	5,489,902	Democratic party
Dennis Kucinich	13,143,419	Democratic party
Lyndon LaRouche	9,988,895	Democratic party
Joseph Lieberman	18,839,280	Democratic party
Al Sharpton	696,347	Democratic party

Source: Center for Responsive Politics.

The Federal Election Campaign Act (FECA) of 1971, as amended in 1974 and later, created a system to monitor the flow of funds and set limits on contributions made by individuals. It also provided for public financing of campaigns and restricted total spending by those candidates who accept federal funding. The spending limits, however, applied only to presidential campaigns. Congress has never restricted its own election expenditures.

The act, along with its amendments, had four key features:

- It set up the Federal Election Commission, a bipartisan, six-member commission, to administer and enforce federal regulations regarding the contribution and expenditure of campaign funds.

- It limited individual contributions to primary, runoff, and general elections, as well as contributions to any one political action committee (PAC) or national party committee. The total amount of contributions per year by an individual could not exceed $25,000. PACs could contribute up to $5,000 per candidate per election. The limits on contributions applied to congressional as well as presidential candidates. In 1976 the Supreme Court ruled in *Buckley v. Valeo* that, under the First Amendment right of freedom of speech, no limitation could be placed on contributions to the campaign by candidates or their families.

- It provided for public funding of the major parties' presidential election costs, including the Democratic and Republican national conventions.

- It placed important controls on the amount of money that could be spent in presidential primaries and general elections. In primaries, presidential hopefuls who received federal funding were required to conform to a number of federal regulations, including both a ceiling on the amount of money they could spend in each state and a ceiling on the amount they could spend on the entire pre-convention campaign (an amount that was lower than the sum of the state limits). Candidates had to record all donations of $50 or more. In return, the federal government matched individual contributions of up to $250 each, with a ceiling on total expenditures by a candidate. In 2004, the successful Republican (George W. Bush) and Democratic (John Kerry) presidential candidates turned down the federal matching grants in the primaries and raised their own campaign funds. Thus, they were free of any restrictions on the amount of money they spent in the primaries. However, in 2004, both the Democratic and Republican candidates for the presidency each received approximately $75 million in federal funding for the general election. By accepting this funding, the candidates agree not to spend any additional funds on the campaign, although, as we shall shortly see, other organizations and individuals can spend money supporting or opposing a presidential candidate.

In implementing the Federal Election Campaign Act, Congress did not intend to reduce the importance of money in the election process, however. As we've seen, in 2004 candidates for the House of Representatives and the Senate collectively spent more than $1 billion. In 2006, approximately $2.8 billion was spent by all sources (PACs, 527s, individuals, and candidates) on House and Senate races. Expenses covered by campaign funds included the rental and furnishing of campaign headquarters, communication and transportation, polls, television and newspaper advertisements, political consultants, and, of course, accountants to keep track of how the money was collected and spent. In a competitive Senate race, one political observer has estimated that between 70 and 80 percent of campaign expenditures go for television advertisements.

While the campaign expenditure figures that we have discussed are, indeed, quite substantial, keep in mind that the advertising budgets for many corporations are much higher. In past years, the advertising budget for General Motors has approached $4 billion a year; Ford Motor Company, drug company Pfizer, Philip Morris, and Procter & Gamble have each spent more than $2 billion a year to advertise their products. The cost of a 30-second advertisement for the 2006 Super Bowl was $2.5 million (and that didn't include the cost of producing the advertisement, which can run well over $2 million). The 2006 blockbuster film *King Kong* cost more than $200 million to film and tens of millions of dollars to promote. By comparison, over the past two and a half years, the Bush administration has spent $1.6 billion on advertising and public relations contracts covering everything from military recruitment to various promotions (the Air Force spent $35,000 for promotional materials for a golf program, for example).[19] Furthermore, no matter how much a candidate spends, he or she may still lose. For example, in 1994, California Republican challenger Michael Huffington spent more than $30 million on a race for the Senate but still was defeated by the Democratic incumbent, Senator Dianne Feinstein, who spent about $12 million.[20]

Where does the money come from? Some wealthy candidates finance their own campaigns or lend themselves the needed funds. This can give them a significant advantage over their opponents. Most candidates, however, must solicit gifts and loans from interested individuals, their party, or other groups, including PACs.

One major consequence of the Federal Election Campaign Act has been the rise of the PACs. They were set up to bypass a provision of the act that prohibits unions, corporations, and other groups from contributing directly to candidates for national office. (This is nothing new; loopholes made a 1907 law prohibiting corporations from contributing to national elections and the Smith-Connally Act of 1944 placing similar prohibitions on labor unions essentially unenforceable.) PACs distribute voluntary contributions from such groups to candidates. During the 2004 election cycle, PACs contributed more than $294 million to congressional candidates. In 2006, PACs were estimated to have contributed more than $317 million to congressional candidates, thus continuing to have a significant impact on the financial resources available in federal elections.

PACs (and individuals) can legally spend any amount of money on a candidate as long as they do not coordinate their spending efforts or otherwise cooperate with the candidate's campaign. Thus, their participation can circumvent the spending and contribution limits of the campaign act. As important as PACs have become, however, they are still overshadowed by individual contributors, who supply the bulk of election funds: over $690 million in the 2004 congressional elections.

Critical Thinking

How would you reform the financing of campaigns at the federal, state, and local levels of government?

Soft money Unrestricted contributions to political parties by individuals, corporations, and unions that can be spent on party-building activities such as voter registration drives and get-out-the-vote efforts. The problem is that loopholes in the law allow soft money to also be spent in support of party candidates as long as key words such as "elect," "vote for," or "vote against" do not appear in the ads.

Act II: The Bipartisan Campaign Finance Reform Act. Although money may not be the only important factor in a successful campaign, many people believe that even the appearance of improprieties on the part of candidates in raising campaign funds is reason enough for reforming the system. The millions of dollars in soft money contributed to political parties by individuals, corporations, and unions have also made voters uneasy about the role of money in campaigns. For many Americans, the campaign funding system is broken and needs to be replaced.

Many reforms have been suggested. They have ranged from spending limits for candidates and the elimination of soft money to restrictions on PAC contributions, an increase in the size and enforcement powers of the Federal Election Commission, and the public financing of elections (for other strategies, see "Global Politics," p. 198, for a look at campaign finance in Western Europe). The issue of **soft money** had become particularly problematic by 2002. Soft money is unrestricted contributions by individuals, corporations, and unions that could, under FECA regulations, be spent on party-building activities such as voter registration drives and get-out-the-vote efforts or on campaign issue advertising, but not in support of a specific candidate. The problem was that loopholes in the law allowed soft money to be spent in support of party candidates as long as key words such as "elect," "vote for," or "vote against" a candidate did not appear in the ads.

Under growing pressure from the public and the media, Congress enacted and President Bush signed into law the Bipartisan Campaign Finance Act of 2002 to further reform federal campaign financing. This act focuses on weaknesses in the existing law that were targeted for change by Senators John McCain (R-AZ) and Russell Feingold (D-WI) and Representatives Christopher Shays (R-CT) and Martin Meehan (D-MA).

The act, which took effect after the November 2002 elections, has four key features that modify some of the provisions of the Federal Election Act:

- It bans soft money contributions to the national political parties. The national parties were not able to accept soft money after November 6, 2002, and had to dispose of all soft money in their accounts by December 31, 2002.

- It increases the limits on hard money contributions by individuals to individual candidates and total overall contributions to all candidates and political parties. Individual contributions are limited to no more than $2,000 per candidate per election (primary, runoff, and general elections are regarded as separate elections), $5,000 per year to any one political action committee (PAC), and $25,000 per year to a national party committee. The total amount of contributions per two-year election cycle by an individual cannot exceed $95,000, of which only $37,500 may be contributed to candidates over the two years. In addition, individuals may contribute up to $10,000 per state or local party committee per year. Contributions are keyed to inflation and thus can increase from one election year to the next.

- PACs can contribute up to $5,000 per candidate per election, $5,000 to other PACs per year, $15,000 per national political party committee per year, and $5,000 per state or local party committee per year. There is no ceiling on the total contributions that a PAC can make.

- The act prohibits corporations, unions, and trade associations from paying for broadcast advertising if the ads refer to a specific candidate and run within sixty days before a general election or thirty days before a primary. Such ads can be paid for only with regulated hard money through a political action committee.[21]

A number of problems concerning campaign finance reform at the federal level remain. The Federal Election Commission, which was given the responsibility for implementing "the new law's candidate and party soft money provisions . . . has opened loopholes that could allow elements of the current state party soft money system to continue."[22] These provisions would allow contributors to continue to make indirect soft money contributions to federal campaigns. As one political observer has noted, "The States have been the backdoor to American politics for years," and they may very likely continue in this role.[23] Proponents of campaign finance reform argue that actions taken by the Federal Election Commission may distort and undermine the spirit of the act.

There is another major concern, this one regarding the growth of **527 committees**, which aren't regulated by the Federal Election Commission (FEC). These committees are tax-exempt groups "organized under section 527 of the Internal Revenue Code to raise money for political activities including voter mobilization efforts, issue advocacy and the like."[24] Unless the 527 committee is also a political party or PAC specifically engaged in advocating the election or defeat of a federal candidate, it is not required to file disclosure reports with the FEC. In effect, 527 committees can raise unlimited soft money to mobilize targeted voters for the election and for certain types of issue advocacy, as long as there is no expressed support for or against a specific candidate. The use of 527 committees to spend millions of dollars in the 2004 presidential election — $177 million, to be precise — illustrates that candidates in federal elections can circumvent federal laws designed to reform the campaign finance process.

The future of campaign finance reform remains uncertain; what is clear is that the issue will not disappear. Only time will tell whether pressures from the public for reform will continue to have an impact on elected officials at both the state and national levels of government.

Does Money Buy Victory? Since 1976, the federal government has funded presidential campaigns, giving the Democratic and Republican candidates equal support. As a result, the major party candidates have entered the race for president, at least initially, on a more or less equal financial footing. In 2004, the Republican and Democratic candidates for the presidency each received close to $75 million in federal funding for their campaigns. This has reduced the amount of money spent in presidential campaigns but has not entirely controlled it because, as we have seen, spending by private individuals and groups is still permitted as

527 committees Tax-exempt groups that can raise unlimited soft money to be used to mobilize targeted voters and for issue advocacy if there is no expressed support for or against a specific candidate. These 527 committees are not regulated by the Federal Election Commission.

GLOBAL POLITICS

The World of Money and Campaigns

American politicians have quarreled over various proposals for campaign and election reform since the inception of the country, but no aspect of reform has drawn more attention than that of campaign finance. Some observers believe campaign-spending limits could positively reform the system, while others argue that these limits would restrict freedom of speech and serve to increase the power of incumbency rather than to diminish it (since whatever the limits, incumbents tend to receive a larger share of campaign contributions than challengers). Will there ever be a campaign finance solution that satisfies all parties? Might other democracies employ strategies that could be successful in America? For an alternate perspective, let's take a look across the Atlantic to see how countries in Western Europe are dealing with similar issues.

- **Length of political campaigns.** It's harder to burn through huge sums of money when you don't have much time to spend it. Whereas American presidential candidates often start establishing bases in New Hampshire and Iowa at least a full year before the general election, by comparison, British campaigns last roughly just four weeks from beginning to end. That's just one month's worth of print advertisements, television commercials, and massive voter outreach efforts to pay for.

- **Size of the voting population.** There's simply no way to get around the fact that the United States is a huge country, and campaigning before 300 million Americans who are spread out over dozens of states is much more difficult than reaching, for example, 60 million French citizens residing in a smaller, much more densely populated area. Even at the U.S.

congressional level, the number of House seats has remained constant since 1911, which means that each representative is responsible for reaching an increasing number of constituents with each passing year. At present, the average congressional district numbers about 650,000 citizens.

- **Party-centered vs. candidate-centered campaigns.** American political campaigns are based on the individual, with messages tailored to detail specific points on why a candidate is the most qualified to represent her or his particular district or state. In Western European parliamentary elections, campaigns are focused on the parties, and it's much more efficient for a party to coordinate a single, national message than it is to run 100 variations on the same theme. This, of course, leads to the question of whether our country would actually have to modify its style of government in order to overhaul the way that campaigns are financed.

- **Television ad time.** As already discussed, the United States is a much larger country than any of its Western European counterparts. Even running a statewide race can be prohibitively expensive, given the need to buy commercial airtime. However, many parties in Western European countries are given free television time, drastically reducing the obligation to raise huge sums of money. Some in America have called for television networks to assume more responsibility for the public's civic education by granting free access time to candidates. However, others view this practice as yet another example of government "overstepping its bounds" and potentially limiting the free flow of ideas.

For all the talk of upwardly spiraling campaign spending in the United States, some political scientists believe that this isn't a pressing concern for our democratic institution, pointing out that the advertising budgets of some Fortune 500 companies greatly dwarf what is spent on politics each year. Still, as the costs of campaigns spiral up — the chairperson of the Federal Election Commission predicts that for the 2008 presidential races, serious prospective candidates should be prepared to raise $100 million[1] — we may well want to look to our global neighbors for answers to the complex issue of campaign finance reform.

1. Thomas B. Edsall and Chris Cillizza, "Money's Going to Talk in 2008," *Washington Post*, March 11, 2006, p. A1.

Kevin Fullam contributed to this essay.

long as those efforts are not coordinated with the candidate's campaign. Clearly, the Bipartisan Campaign Finance Reform Act of 2002 does not resolve all the issues and problems regarding campaign financing in presidential campaigns. The public remains justifiably skeptical of laws that supposedly limit the influence money has on campaigns and eliminate "fat cat" contributors.

Money also plays a large part in congressional campaigns, which are not funded by the federal government. In 2004, for example, campaign spending for all congressional races was more than $1.1 billion. In 2006, that figure approached $2.8 billion. For many candidates, especially challengers of incumbents, money is a passport to visibility — or at least to the television exposure needed to mount an effective challenge.

Money is unquestionably a very important factor in many campaigns, and it affects more than just the election outcome. First, both incumbents and challengers must spend a considerable amount of time raising funds for a congressional election, time that takes them away from campaigning and, for incumbents, from governing and policymaking. An average competitive Senate race will cost in excess of $5 million, requiring a senator who is running for reelection to raise a minimum of $20,000 every week of her or his six-year term. In many Senate races, the price of victory or defeat is considerably more than $5 million. In 2004, the combined amount spent by both the Republican and Democratic candidates in the ten most costly Senate races ranged from more than $16 million in Wisconsin to more than $36 million in South Dakota. The other eight states were Pennsylvania, North Carolina, Florida, California, Washington, New York, Colorado, and Illinois. Second, the need to raise large sums of money to campaign for Congress (as well as many other offices) prevents many citizens from even contemplating a run for political office. Third, the large sums of money spent on campaigns often give the public the impression that contributors can buy the favor of elected officials.

However, it is important to recognize that money is not the only factor determining the outcome of congressional elections. Who wins also depends on the circumstances of the race, particularly whether one of the candidates is an **incumbent** — that is, in office at the time of the election. Incumbents are hard to beat because they are usually well known to voters and because they have

Incumbent A candidate who holds the contested office at the time of the election.

already served the state or district. The retention rate of incumbent members of the House of Representatives who were running for reelection in 2006 was more than 94 percent.

Furthermore, incumbents often find it relatively easy to raise funds. Indeed, incumbents get the lion's share of campaign contributions. Still, a strong, competitive challenger may have a chance against an incumbent,[25] although the race may be lost before it begins unless the challenger can raise enough money to create name recognition. Spending has the greatest impact on an election in which there is no incumbent in the race — known as an **open race** — and the outcome is uncertain.

Open race An election in which there is no incumbent in the race.

Thus, the reality is that money is a necessary, but not a sufficient, factor in a successful bid for many political offices. As Gary C. Jacobson has pointed out,

> Money is not sufficient because many factors quite apart from campaigns . . . affect election outcomes: partisanship, national tides, presidential coattails, issues, candidates' personalities and skills, scandals, incumbency, and many others. Money is necessary because campaigns do have an impact on election results, and campaigns cannot be run without it.[26]

Organizing Campaigns: The Old and the New

In Boston and its suburbs, in the weeks before any election, busy street corners and highway overpasses are crowded with silent partisans holding signs that promote their candidate. This ritual, unusual elsewhere in the country but commonplace in Boston, assures the wavering voter that the candidate has support. Campaign tactics range from such homey local traditions to highly sophisticated media shows. Even though most state and local campaigns are unorganized or underorganized and lurch from one improvisation to another as the year unfolds, the most visible campaigns — including those for the presidency, the Senate, and many House seats and governorships — are highly organized.

Campaign Organizations. John Kennedy's 1960 presidential campaign was the first to make significant use of an organization recruited from outside the party structure. Kennedy relied heavily on a personally selected team of advisers and staff, including his brother Robert, to take on the major burdens of running the campaign. That model has been followed in most presidential campaigns since the 1960s, and in many state and local races as well.

Candidates assemble personal staffs because the parties historically have been slow to develop polling and media consulting programs and other support systems. The existence of such staffs also reflects the growing sophistication of campaigns. Staff members write speeches, schedule appearances, plan strategy, and recruit additional talent as needed. In recent years, however, both major parties, but especially the Republicans, have made considerable progress in providing these services. Major state and local candidates now receive sophisticated training and support from the parties. Nevertheless, presidential candidates and many congressional and statewide candidates still seek the guidance of their own professional consultants as well as that of their personal advisers.

Campaign Strategy. A critical part of the campaign process is the development of themes (reasons why the public should support the candidate) and campaign strategies. The plausibility of these themes is critically important to a candidate's success. If voters do not believe that a candidate will fulfill his or her campaign promises — if the candidate's words evoke the myth of broken promises — the election game is lost.

In most presidential, House, and Senate races, campaign strategy depends on whether the candidate is an incumbent or a challenger. Congressional incumbents generally have the advantage of name recognition and a record of accomplishments. They often start with a loyal constituency, and, as we have noted, their established position and visibility make it relatively easy for them to raise funds. Not surprisingly, then, most incumbents in the House — between 80 and 99 percent since World War II — have succeeded in their quest for reelection.

Incumbency is also important in presidential elections. No other officeholder in the United States has as much visibility, name recognition, prestige, and opportunity to speak to voters on the issues, and incumbent candidates take full advantage of these assets. Incumbency does not guarantee a second term, however. Since the end of World War II, six out of eleven incumbent presidents have not served second terms.

Differences among election outcomes reflect something more than incumbency, however. Winners and losers alike are profoundly affected by the political environment: the partisan leanings of the electorate; the candidates' experience, personality, personal values, and leadership skills; and the candidates' positions on policy issues. Most candidates try to ensure that none of these factors polarizes the electorate and drives away potential supporters. Thus, they are generally unlikely to take either strongly conservative or strongly liberal stands, although on balance Republican candidates are more conservative than Democratic ones. In 2006, this was particularly the case.

The New Campaign Style. The tools, and consequently the style, of campaigns have changed over the years. One major innovation has been the use of polls, an expensive campaign tool that can dramatize or establish proof of a candidate's viability for major office.[27] In Chapter 5, on public opinion, we looked at the way candidates use polls to evaluate their strengths and weaknesses, assess the relevance of specific issues, and determine the campaign's impact on the voters. Positive poll results can energize a campaign and draw new support and funding.

Professional pollsters have established strong reputations for the accuracy of their estimates of candidates' standings and the voters' views on the issues. Pollsters' services are now almost universally used by candidates in presidential races and are used in many congressional and statewide races as well. Costs depend on the size of the state and the kind of polling. A statewide poll can run from $25,000 to $100,000.

Another "miracle" of modern campaign technology is the use of computers. All of the major party candidates seeking the presidential nomination in 2004 created an electronic version of their campaign brochure on a personalized Internet webpage, posting everything from their personal leadership qualities and their policy positions to baby pictures and favorite Bible passages. This was true of most congressional candidates in 2006 as well as many state and local candidates running for a variety of political offices. In addition, many candidates have engaged in online fundraising, seeking financial contributions from supporters who click on to their website. Millions of dollars for the 2004 presidential primaries and the 2006 congressional races were raised through the Internet. There is every indication that these new campaign tools will have a growing role in future presidential, congressional, state, and local races.

Technological changes over the past three decades have been accompanied by the rise of a new political animal — the **political consultant**. These individuals, often trained in public relations, media, or polling techniques, have replaced the traditional campaign manager in the most visible elections. Some consultants organize all aspects of the race, from the physical appearance of the candidate to the strategies that he or she adopts in presenting his or her positions on issues. Most consultants specialize in certain aspects of the campaign, such as polling, fundraising, or the media,[28] and most generally work for either Democratic or Republican candidates exclusively. David Axelrod, a prominent Democratic campaign consultant based in Chicago who has worked on many statewide and national campaigns, exemplifies the modern-day campaign consultant who serves as a "hired gun." His record of successful campaigns suggests either that he associates with many likely winners or that campaign consultants can be effective managers of campaigns. In all probability, his success and that of other campaign consultants result from a mixture of both.

> **Political consultant** An individual, often trained in public relations, media, or polling techniques, who advises candidates on organizing their campaign.

The Media and Campaigns: Are We Brainwashed?

FOCUS QUESTION   HOW DO THE MEDIA HAVE AN IMPACT ON POLITICAL CAMPAIGNS?

Use of the media, particularly television, has become almost a way of life in recent presidential, congressional, and gubernatorial races, and many mayoral contests as well. A campaign is often organized around media coverage. Candidates make decisions about trips, rallies, and press conferences with an eye to attracting the press and meeting its schedules. Because advertising costs so much, campaign managers work hard to maximize free coverage by television news as well as radio and newspapers to promote their candidates' virtues. Consequently, a candidate's speeches and rallies before large crowds are often scheduled so that they can appear on the evening local and network news programs.

Candidates and the Media

The modern-day campaign for high-visibility offices is often marked by a wide and varied use of the media. Here, Republican Senator Rick Santorum (left) and Democratic challenger Bob Casey, in their 2006 Pennsylvania race for the U.S. Senate, debate the issues on the popular Sunday morning news program "Meet the Press." Casey went on to win the seat by a sizable margin.

Congressman Harold Ford, Democratic candidate for the U.S. Senate in Tennessee, appears before his supporters as cameras capture his image and his comments for the evening news and newspapers. Ford later lost the election to Republican candidate Bob Corker.

The media also manipulate the coverage of important campaigns in order to maximize the attention of their audience. Media people try to structure election news so that it will attract and hold the biggest audience possible. Often that means highlighting and even promoting conflict. Candidates are encouraged to attack one another's policies, and television debates, especially among presidential candidates, have become contests, with "winners" and "losers." The Kennedy-Nixon debates in 1960 marked the beginning of face-to-face discussion between presidential candidates. In the 2004 presidential campaign, three presidential debates were held, as well as one debate between the vice-presidential candidates.

Of course, candidates do not rely on free coverage alone. Advertising is also a crucial part of campaigns. Media consulting firms such as Greer, Margolis, Mitchell, Burns & Associates and Stevens, Reed, Curcio & Company provide their clients with a full range of services, from the production of television spots — which can average as much as $350,000 — to the purchase of advertising time on local and network stations. Television advertising is expensive — a thirty-second political campaign spot that airs on a local station in a top ten market can cost anywhere from $4,000 during a movie to $45,000 during a highly rated show. Network television will charge anywhere from $80,000 to $600,000 for a thirty-second spot on a prime-time television program. Not surprisingly, television advertising is used primarily in visible and well-funded campaigns.

The high cost of network television advertising has been tempered somewhat in recent years by the significant growth in cable television. Many cable outlets provide candidates with relatively inexpensive access to the public with television spots as inexpensive as $5 during prime time.[29] Instead of paying for a political advertisement that may reach hundreds of thousands of viewers outside their election district, local candidates can use cable television to limit their campaign advertising to their prospective constituents. Such access can be cost-effective when cable television advertising rates are relatively low.

The evidence regarding the impact of the media on campaigns and elections is still very sketchy. Clearly, the use of television has increased the costs of running presidential, congressional, and gubernatorial campaigns, as well as campaigns for other highly visible public offices. Do the media brainwash us into voting for specific candidates? Media advertising is probably more effective in motivating and encouraging a candidate's supporters to go to the polls than in changing the minds of already committed opponents of a candidate. With marginal voters, media news coverage and advertisements are both effective. Because such voters lack strong or even moderate commitment to a candidate, they are more open than partisan voters to the opinions and influence of a news anchorperson or reporter or to the appeals of a paid political advertisement. Finally, the media help to shape the issues that candidates focus on in an election, thus serving as an agenda-setting force in a campaign. This can have a dramatic effect by determining the quality of debate throughout the race. (See Chapter 9 for a more far-reaching discussion on the role of the media in politics.)

Campaigns and Political Parties

FOCUS QUESTION WHAT HAVE BEEN THE CONSEQUENCES OF THE SHIFT FROM PARTY-CENTERED CAMPAIGNS TO CANDIDATE-CENTERED CAMPAIGNS?

By using the media, as well as independent campaign consultants, computers, and polls, many high-visibility office seekers have been able to bypass the political parties, which traditionally played a major role in the campaign process. Presidential, congressional, gubernatorial, and mayoral candidates are now no longer dependent on party volunteers or party campaign-funding events to jump-start their campaigns. That change has shifted the focus from **party-centered campaigns** (where the party coordinates activities, raises money, and develops strategy) to **candidate-centered campaigns** (where paid consultants or volunteers perform those tasks).

However, as we suggest in Chapter 6, the role of parties in the campaign process is still evident at most levels of government. In recent years, parties have learned to adapt to the changing campaign strategies, providing candidates at the national, state, and local levels with consultants, advisers, and workshops on campaign funding and strategy, and, as political brokers, with access to PACs and individual contributors who seek out the party's advice on their campaign contributions. That last function is critical for candidates who rely on the party to direct individual and PAC contributions to their campaigns.

Political parties are unlikely to return to the center stage of many political campaigns, but evidence suggests that the parties have adapted to the new campaign style, including the "new kids on the block" — the political consultants who play a central role in the shaping of that style.

Party-centered campaign A campaign in which the party coordinates activities, raises money, and develops strategies.

Candidate-centered campaign A campaign in which paid consultants or volunteers coordinate campaign activities, develop strategies, and raise funds. Parties play a secondary role.

Voting and Elections

FOCUS QUESTION WHAT FACTORS INFLUENCE THE WAY PEOPLE VOTE IN AN ELECTION?

Voting rules and regulations have changed considerably in the past 200 years. Until 1920, women could not vote in most states. African Americans and women faced voting restrictions for much of the country's history. Although the vote has now been extended to all adult citizens, not everyone chooses to exercise that prerogative. Therefore, it is important to look at who votes and why.

Critical Thinking

Does it make more sense, when voting at election time, to identify as a Democrat or Republican or to be an independent?

Who Is Allowed to Vote?

The Constitution originally left the decision on voting qualifications to the individual states. Article I, Section 4, specifies that Congress may regulate by law only the time, place, and manner of federal elections. Any extension of voting rights by the federal government must come in the form of a constitutional amendment or a federal law.

State leaders in the 1780s had little sympathy for the idea of universal voting rights. Indeed, John Jay, a New York delegate to the Constitutional Convention, summed up the view of many of the Founding Fathers when he wrote in 1787 that "the mass of men are neither wise nor good—those who own the country ought to govern it."[30]

All of the original thirteen states restricted voting rights to white males, and only three of these states—New Hampshire, Pennsylvania, and Georgia—admitted adult males into the electorate without a property requirement. Even in those states, however, the voter without property had to be a taxpayer. As a result, in 1789, only some 10 percent of the population could cast ballots.[31]

Over the past two centuries, voting rights have been extended to those who do not own property and to African Americans, Native Americans, women, and young people ages eighteen to twenty. But equality was not achieved without an intense struggle. It took a civil war to give citizenship to African Americans. And although passage of the Fifteenth Amendment in 1870 gave African American males the right to vote, they had to struggle for another hundred years before most barriers to voting came down.

Women fought for half a century for voting rights. In 1878, human rights activist Susan B. Anthony managed to introduce in Congress a proposed constitutional amendment that said, "The right of citizens of the United States to vote shall not be denied or abridged by the United States or any state on account of sex." That is the wording eventually used in the Nineteenth Amendment, which became part of the Constitution in 1920.

In 1971, passage of the Twenty-sixth Amendment lowered the voting age in national, state, and local elections from twenty-one to eighteen. Several states had already lowered the voting age. There is nothing in the Constitution that prohibits states from setting their own voting standards, as long as these regulations do not violate the Constitution or federal law. Thus, women in Wyoming had the vote some forty years before the Nineteenth Amendment enfranchised women in other states. For the same reason, a state can establish any minimum voting age, so long as it is not above the national one.

Congress has intervened several times to break down barriers set up by the states to prevent African Americans and others from voting. The 1970 extension of the 1965 Voting Rights Act banned the use of literacy tests and similar qualifying devices. Then the 1975 extension of the act increased the opportunities for participation for Hispanics. When the act was strengthened and extended for twenty-five years in 1982, it resulted in increased electoral participation by African American voters in the South and by other minorities, including Inuit. Poll taxes were eliminated in 1964 with the adoption of the Twenty-fourth Amendment. Finally, Supreme Court decisions have laid the remaining voting restrictions to rest. During the 1960s, the Supreme Court struck down property ownership requirements and shortened residency requirements. Today, a citizen needs only to have resided in a state for thirty days in order to vote in national elections and in most state elections.

Who Votes?

Americans are proud of their electoral system. Indeed, many citizens would argue that the freedom to select political leaders is one of the most important differences between a democracy and a dictatorship or a communist government. Yet, as we saw in Chapter 5, on public opinion and political participation, relatively few Americans vote. On the average, since 1964, about 50 percent of Americans can be counted on to take part in presidential elections. While close to 60 percent of eligible voters participated in the 2004 presidential elections, it is not clear whether that level of participation will be sustained in the future. In the 2006 elections, 40 percent of the electorate voted. Primary elections tend to attract even fewer voters. For example, only 16 percent of eligible voters went to the polls during the 2006 primary elections. By contrast, 95 percent of Australians regularly go to the polls, and the turnout in other democracies ranges from 59 percent in Great Britain to 92 percent in Belgium. These comparisons are not entirely fair, however, because voting is easier and simpler in other nations. Americans face much longer ballots and relatively brief and inconvenient polling schedules. In many European countries, voting takes place on weekends. Many European nations also have automatic universal registration, which is not widespread in the United States. As a final incentive to ensure voting, some European countries levy fines on stay-at-homes.

Demographics and Voter Turnout. In Chapter 5, we also learned about the social and economic factors that influence political participation patterns, particularly voter turnout. Individuals who vote regularly are likely to have higher levels of education, higher incomes, and better jobs than nonvoters. Education seems to be the key to voter turnout.[32] As political scientists Raymond Wolfinger and Steven Rosenstone point out, education "imparts information about politics . . . and about a variety of skills, some of which facilitate political learning. . . . Educated people are more likely to be well informed about politics and to follow the campaign in the mass media."[33] In addition, for non-English-speaking citizens, including those of Puerto Rican, Mexican, Cuban, Russian, Eastern European, and Vietnamese extraction, education provides fluency in English, a necessary tool for following and participating in the electoral process.

Older Americans (except those who are handicapped and therefore have difficulty getting to the polling booths) are more likely to vote than younger ones. The reasons for that pattern are complex. Young people are frequently preoccupied with the demands of school, military service, or new careers. They also tend to believe that they have little impact or influence on the political system.

In the past, turnout for women trailed that for men. Today, however, the percentage of women voting is slightly higher than that for men.

The Disappointed Electorate. As indicated earlier, barriers such as preregistration requirements and long ballots reduce the numbers of citizens who vote. But another obstacle is the myth of broken promises. Many Americans do not take part in elections because they do not believe that government in general and elected officials in particular can solve the country's problems. They also question the honesty and integrity of many political leaders. This lack of confidence in government is relatively new. The Watergate scandal in the early 1970s and the subsequent resignation of President Richard Nixon undermined confidence in government. In 1999, President Bill Clinton was impeached by the House of Representatives and became only the second president in our history to be tried for misconduct by the Senate. Although he was acquitted of all charges brought against him, the events surrounding the impeachment and the Senate trial were seen as bringing discredit not only on President Clinton but also on the political and governmental system in general. (The impeachment and trial are discussed in more detail in Chapter 11.) In 2000, the highly controversial election of President George W. Bush, who received a majority of the electoral college vote but lost in the popular vote to Democratic candidate Al Gore by more than 500,000 votes, also weakened many Americans' confidence in the political process, as has the protracted war in Iraq.

In this atmosphere of cynicism, many potential voters doubt that their vote matters and simply stay home on election day. Several studies have clearly documented the reasons for failure to vote. First, many people believe that government cannot solve the nation's problems. In addition, as we pointed out in Chapter 6, people are less likely than before to strongly identify with one political party, an identification that once got out the vote. Finally, some people have even questioned whether it makes any difference who wins elections.[34]

Should we be concerned about the disappointed voter? Some observers say yes, arguing that low turnout undermines representative government, which, they argue, depends on full electoral participation. Others disagree, suggesting that people who are ill informed may make poor choices when they vote. It has even been argued that low levels of voter turnout are a sign of a healthy system — that is, they show that people are satisfied with their government.

Why Do People Vote the Way They Do?

Critical Thinking

What factors influence the way you vote? Why?

What draws voters to the polls? What influences their choices of candidates? How did voters make their choices for president and Congress in 2004 and for Congress in 2006? Obviously, the supporters of the various candidates thought that their man or woman was the better candidate, and that he or she would better serve their interests. But a number of factors influence voter choice.

Issues. Political observers often accuse American voters of focusing on frivolous aspects of campaigns. In fact, many American voters do pay attention to issues and take them into account in making their choices. Of course, no one can review all the positions of every candidate who is running for office. Given that hundreds of issues arise at the local, state, and national levels each year, no one could possibly follow them all, or even have an interest in most of them.

However, in presidential elections, there seems to be some relationship between the issues that citizens support and the candidates whom they vote for.[35]

In the 2004 presidential election, voters viewed the policy positions of the Democratic and Republican contestants differently. Domestic issues that were most important to voters included the candidates' stands on homeland security policy, Iraq, the environment, crime, illegal drugs, education, and health care.[36]

Candidate Image. The candidate's personal qualities, particularly her or his experience and leadership, also count. Furthermore, voters ask themselves how well the candidate represents voters' own interests and whether the candidate is honest, trustworthy, and approachable by the electorate. One observer labels this process "politics by psychoanalysis." (For voter attitudes toward celebrity candidates, see "Politics & Popular Culture," p. 210.)

In the 2004 presidential elections, the American voters clearly were seeking a president with leadership qualities. Both George W. Bush and John Kerry also came under strong scrutiny by the public with regard to their honesty and trustworthiness.

Party Identification. As we saw in Chapter 6, party identification gives voters a general sense of how candidates are likely to approach various issues and policies. This identification can be misleading, as opinions within the parties are quite diverse. Nevertheless, in a world in which voters may know little or nothing about many of the candidates, the party label serves as an indication of their policy positions. Indeed, the results of surveys often show that many individuals vote along party lines in making their presidential choice.

Retrospective voting
Individuals basing their votes on the candidates' or parties' past record of performance.

Retrospective Voting. When individuals base their votes on the candidates' or parties' past performance, we say that they are engaging in **retrospective voting**.[37] Incumbents are judged on their records in office; challengers may be judged on what they did in the offices they previously held. In effect, voters are looking at the past to help them evaluate the future — one rational way to make judgments.

Is retrospective voting common? Evidence suggests that it is and that it can have an important impact on voting behavior. In the 2004 presidential race, research findings suggest that "[a]lthough Kerry was favored on prospective evaluations," that is, how voters felt the candidates would perform in the future, "that was offset by Bush's slight advantage based on retrospective evaluations."[38] Bush's response, specifically to September 11 and the threat of terrorism, and his stance on homeland security, were important factors for many voters in supporting the incumbent president.

Group Support. People of different genders, races, age groups, and educational and political backgrounds vote in predictable and yet divergent ways for political candidates. In the 2004 election, for example, George W. Bush drew strong support from conservatives, who are traditionally allied with the Republican party, while, not surprisingly, John Kerry drew deep support from liberals. Republican George W. Bush received a majority of the vote from males, whites, college graduates, and people of the various Protestant faiths. In addition to these

POLITICS & POPULAR CULTURE

Celebrity Politics and the Run for Office:
Movie Stars, Talk Show Hosts, Wrestlers, and Ballplayers

American culture is built on the concept of celebrity. We happily support our favorite television and movie stars by watching the television shows and movies in which they star. When that's not enough, we can follow their daily exploits by reading about them in print and by watching what they do on television magazine "news" shows.

So what's new? Candidates for political office are arising from this pool of actors and sports figures. The entrance of celebrities into the realm of public office is a relatively recent phenomenon. Former president Ronald Reagan had spent time in Hollywood prior to his political career, but his movies were B-level productions, and Reagan—much like current California governor Arnold Schwarzenegger—laid the groundwork for his foray into public service with decades of GOP campaigning. However, today's celebrities are often embraced as candidates for high-level offices, despite their having little or no political experience. Let's take a look:

- Radio talk-show host Howard Stern ran for governor of New York in 1994 after capturing the Libertarian party nomination by swarming its primary with throngs of his fans. Galvanizing support under a platform that included the reinstitution of the death penalty—his slogan was "A Volt For Every Vote"—Stern polled surprisingly well in a three-way race before dropping out over a refusal to divulge information about his personal finances. Stern later endorsed Republican candidate George Pataki, who went on to narrowly defeat Democratic incumbent Mario Cuomo.

- In one of the most shocking political upsets in recent memory, former Navy SEAL and professional wrestler Jesse "the mouth" Ventura captured Minnesota's governorship in 1998. Running under the mantle of the Reform party, Ventura waged an Internet campaign (believed to be one of the first of its kind) that emphasized his desire to return the state's tax surplus to its citizens. Despite Ventura's low initial polling numbers, both Republican Norm Coleman and Democrat Hubert Humphrey III allowed him to participate in gubernatorial debates, each thinking that Ventura's presence in the campaign would erode the support of their opponent. This strategy backfired when Ventura served as a lively, refreshing contrast to his stodgy opponents, generating a surge of momentum even while admitting that he had yet to form clear positions on various policy questions. In addition, Ventura was buoyed by Minnesota election laws that let voters register on the day of the election. A surprising 28 percent of his support came from residents who claimed they wouldn't have voted at all were Ventura not on the ballot. Once in office, however, without fellow members of his party in the Minnesota legislature, he found it difficult to advance his agenda and his vetoes of legislation were often overturned. In addition, Ventura's off-the-cuff comments demeaning the media and particularly organized religion drew national criticism and he did not seek reelection when his term expired in 2002.

- The 2006 Republican candidate for governor of Pennsylvania was none other than former Pittsburgh Steelers football star Lynn Swann, who coasted to his party's nomination despite having virtually no political experience . . . or even a regular voting record. Swann didn't register to vote until age thirty-two and had participated in fewer than half of the elections held since 1984. Swann was defeated in 2006, failing to join a group of athletes-turned-politicians that includes Heath Shuler (D-NC and former quarterback for the Washington Redskins) and Senator Jim Bunning (R-KY and Philadelphia Phillies baseball Hall of Famer).

As it becomes increasingly expensive to fund competitive campaigns, it's not hard to see why celebrity status has become so valuable. Celebrity candidates don't have to spend huge amounts of money promoting name recognition, and some people have favorable impressions of them, regardless of what they have or have not accomplished in political arenas. That's why it's often the case that these candidates will try to avoid expounding upon their platforms while running for office — extra details simply provide voters with more opportunities to see just what it is they have to say.

Kevin Fullam contributed to this essay.

groups, Bush also drew strong support from the wealthy (those with family incomes over $75,000), gun owners, and evangelical Christians. Democrat John Kerry received strong support from a majority of African Americans, Hispanics, young voters, union members, Jews, and working-class Catholics.[39] The gender gap was evident in the 2004 presidential election, with a 7 percent overall advantage for Kerry among female voters. Bush showed similar strength among male voters, winning a clear majority of that vote.

The Electoral College

FOCUS QUESTION HOW DOES THE ELECTORAL COLLEGE FUNCTION? WHAT ALTERNATIVES HAVE BEEN SUGGESTED AS A REPLACEMENT FOR THE ELECTORAL COLLEGE?

Electoral college The system set up by the Constitution under which the people in each state elect a number of electors equal to the number of senators and representatives for that state. In most states, the presidential candidate winning a plurality of the vote in that state receives all its electoral college votes.

The constitutional environment in which presidential campaigns take place is the **electoral college**. Although the founders believed in representative government, they hesitated to place the selection of the president directly in the hands of the people. The system that they devised provides for the election by the people of each state of a number of electors equal to the number of senators and representatives representing that state in Congress. For example, the congressional delegation of Texas includes two U.S. senators and thirty-two members of the House. Thus, in presidential elections, that state's voters elect thirty-four electors to the electoral college. North Dakota, with two U.S. senators and one member of the House, has a total of three electoral college votes.

Until the drama of the 2000 presidential election, when George W. Bush had a minority of the popular vote but was elected to the presidency with a slight majority of the electoral college vote, most Americans understood little about the electoral college, but assumed that when they cast their ballots, they are voting directly for the presidential candidate of their choice. Instead, they are really voting for a slate of electors (equal to the size of the state's congressional delegation) who have committed their support to that presidential candidate. In only twelve states do the names of the actual electors appear on the ballot next to the presidential candidate's name. State law determines how a person becomes an elector. In Pennsylvania, the presidential candidates select their electors. In thirty-eight states, the electors are nominated at state party conventions. In most of the remaining states, electors are selected in primaries or by state party committees.

In most states, the presidential candidate who wins a plurality of the vote in the state receives all its electoral college votes. (The two exceptions are Maine and Nebraska. Maine awards two of its electoral college votes according to the statewide vote and two according to which candidate wins in each of the two congressional districts. Nebraska, with five electoral college votes, has a similar system.) The members of the electoral college chosen in the November general election in each state meet in December and vote for the president. The votes from each state are forwarded to Congress, where an official count takes place on the first day of the congressional session in January. Only after completion of that vote count is the official winner of the presidential election declared. A total of 538 electoral college votes are cast in the fifty states and the District of Columbia; the presidential candidate receiving the majority of these votes wins the election. The vice president is selected in the same manner. (If no candidate receives a majority of the electoral college vote, the House of Representatives selects the president while the Senate selects the vice president in special sessions.)

At least two problems with this system have been noted. First, in twenty-one states, the electors whose party candidate wins a plurality of the state's popular vote are required to vote for that candidate. In the remaining twenty-nine states, however, an elector is not required by law to support the candidate who has won the popular vote in the state. Disloyal electors have voted for a candidate other than the winner of the popular vote in seven elections since World War II, although the final outcomes of those presidential elections were not affected by their actions. In 1988, one disaffected West Virginia Democrat who was a member of the electoral college voted for Lloyd Bentsen for president. Bentsen was the running mate of the Democratic presidential candidate, Michael Dukakis.

A second problem is that a president can be elected by a majority of the electoral college without having a majority of the national popular vote. That was the case in 2000, when George W. Bush was elected president with 271 electoral college votes, although his opponent, Al Gore, received more popular votes. A number of reforms have been proposed to deal with this problem, including the selection of the president by direct popular vote (see Table 7.2). Yet no consensus for a constitutional amendment has emerged, and thus the indirect election of presidents through the electoral college has remained intact.

When they are campaigning for the presidency, candidates are well aware that gaining a majority of the popular vote is not enough. A candidate must be successful in garnering pluralities in a sufficient number of states to ensure receiving a majority of the electoral college vote (see Figure 7.1). Not surprisingly, most candidates focus much of their attention on the larger states, such as California, New York, Texas, Pennsylvania, Illinois, Ohio, Florida, and Michigan — states that have significant numbers of electoral college votes.[40]

Critical Thinking

Does the electoral college make any sense as a way of selecting a president? What alternative plan, if any, would you support?

TABLE 7.2

Eight Modern Presidential Election Outcomes Under Alternative Plans

ELECTION	ELECTORAL COLLEGE	DIRECT ELECTION	PROPORTIONAL PLAN*	DISTRICT PLAN	BONUS PLAN
2004	**Bush wins**	**Bush wins**	**Bush wins**	**Bush wins**	**Bush wins**
	Bush 286	Bush 51.0%	Bush 274.0	Bush 320.5	Bush 388
	Kerry 252	Kerry 48.1%	Kerry 257.8	Kerry 217.5	Kerry 252
		Others 0.9%	Others 6.2		
2000	**Bush wins**	**Gore wins**	**No one wins a majority**	**Bush wins†**	**Gore wins**
	Bush 271	Gore 48.4%	Bush 259.4	Bush 271	Gore 368
	Gore 266	Bush 47.9%	Gore 258.4	Gore 266	Bush 271
	One blank vote	Others 3.7%	Others 20.3	One blank vote	One blank vote
1996	**Clinton wins**	**Clinton wins**	**No one wins a majority**	**Clinton wins**	**Clinton wins**
	Clinton 379	Clinton 49.2%	Clinton 262.1	Clinton 345	Clinton 481
	Dole 159	Dole 40.7%	Dole 222.0	Dole 193	Dole 159
	Perot 0	Perot 8.4%	Perot 45.2	Perot 0	Perot 0
1992	**Clinton wins**	**Clinton wins**	**No one wins a majority**	**Clinton wins**	**Clinton wins**
	Clinton 370	Clinton 43.0%	Clinton 231.1	Clinton 324	Clinton 472
	Bush 168	Bush 37.4%	Bush 202.2	Bush 214	Bush 168
	Perot 0	Perot 13.9%	Perot 101.8	Perot 0	Perot 0
1988	**Bush wins**	**Bush wins**	**Bush wins**	**Bush wins**	**Bush wins**
	Bush 426	Bush 53.4%	Bush 288.1	Bush 377	Bush 528
	Dukakis 111	Dukakis 45.6%	Dukakis 245.1	Dukakis 159	Dukakis 111
	Others 1	Others 1.0%	Others 4.5	Others 0	Others 1
1976	**Carter wins**	**Carter wins**	**Unclear‡**	**No one wins a majority**	**Carter wins**
	Carter 297	Carter 50.1%	Carter 269.5	Carter 269	Carter 401
	Ford 240	Ford 48.0%	Ford 258	Ford 269	Ford 240
	Others 1	Others 1.9%	Others 10.5	Other 0	Others 1
1968	**Nixon wins**	**Nixon wins**	**No one wins a majority**	**Nixon wins**	**Nixon wins**
	Nixon 301	Nixon 43.4%	Nixon 233.8	Nixon 289	Nixon 403
	Humphrey 191	Humphrey 42.7%	Humphrey 223.2	Humphrey 192	Humphrey 191
	Wallace 46	Wallace 13.5%	Wallace 78.8	Wallace 57	Wallace 46
1960	**Kennedy wins**	**Kennedy wins**	**No one wins a majority**	**Nixon wins**	**Kennedy wins**
	Kennedy 303	Kennedy 49.7%	Kennedy 264.8	Nixon 278	Kennedy 405
	Nixon 219	Nixon 49.6%	Nixon 263.5	Kennedy 245	Nixon 219
	Others 15	Others 0.7%	Others 7.7	Others 15	Others 15

Electoral college plan: The existing system of selecting a president. The candidate winning a majority of the electoral college vote (at least 270 votes) wins the election (see page 211).

Direct election plan: The candidate receiving a majority of the popular vote wins the election.

Proportional plan: The electoral college vote is kept, but candidates receive a proportion of each state's electoral college vote based on the percentage of the popular vote they win in each state.

District plan: The electoral college vote is retained in each state, but it is apportioned according to the plurality popular vote winner in each congressional district, plus two votes for winning the state (the plan presently used by Maine and Nebraska, see page 211.

Bonus plan: This plan keeps the electoral college system but awards 102 extra votes to the candidate who wins the national popular vote (originally proposed by the Century Fund).

*Divided to the nearest tenth.

†These are preliminary results based on unofficial aggregation of counties to congressional districts. See Tom Squitieri, "Changes to Electoral College Would Not Alter Outcomes," *USA Today* (December 15, 2000): 8A.

‡Whether there is a winner or not depends on the definition of a majority. If a majority is defined as any number higher than 269.1, then Carter wins; otherwise the race remains undecided.

Source: This table appears in Robert L. Dudley and Alan R. Gitelson, *American Elections: The Rules Matter* (New York: Longman, 2002), pp. 150–151. The table is an updated version of a table constructed by Nelson W. Polsby and Aaron Widavsky, *Presidential Elections: Strategies and Structures of American Politics* (New York: Chatham House, 2000), p. 251.

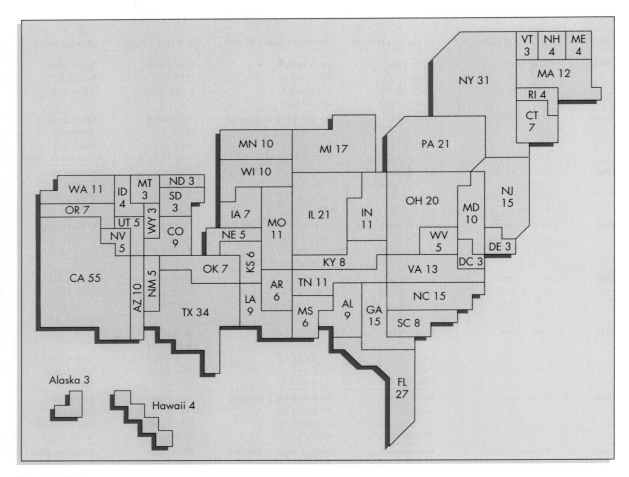

FIGURE 7.1

The United States According to Electoral College Votes

This distorted map will give you a sense of the electoral power of the most populous states, such as California, New York, Texas, and Pennsylvania.

Source: U.S. National Archives and Records Administration, Washington, D.C.

Promises, Promises: The Link Between Campaigns and Public Policy

FOCUS QUESTION   DO CANDIDATES, WHEN ELECTED TO OFFICE, TRY TO KEEP THEIR CAMPAIGN PROMISES?

As we noted earlier, poll results show that the public doubts whether the promises a candidate makes in a campaign have any bearing on the policies that candidate promotes once in office. We believe that this perception of broken promises is a myth — a simplification of the facts.

Critical Thinking

Do you agree or disagree with the myth of broken promises? Why?

Of course, candidates do not fulfill all the promises they make. How could they? The collective wish list of Americans, let alone the candidates, is endless. But candidates try hard to keep many of their promises.[41] Party platforms are, in effect, their agreements with the electorate. It is as if they were saying: "This is what I think. This is what I will try to do. If you agree with what I think, at least on many of the issues, then vote for me." (A slight variation of that invitation is, "Even if you don't agree with me, give me a chance. I'm right.")

Recent presidents have been reasonably successful at fulfilling the promises in their party platform and persuading Congress to act on those promises.[42] For example, during the Clinton administration, the president pledged to shore up the economy, appoint moderates to the federal court system, and pass welfare reform. He accomplished all those goals. George W. Bush promised to reduce taxes and appointed conservatives to the Supreme Court, which he accomplished during his presidency.

All presidents make some promises that they fail to keep—but not for want of trying. Why did they fail? Why was George W. Bush unable to get a social security reform package passed during the initial years of his administration? A president's programs can fail because they are poorly conceived or ineffective. They can also fail because Congress refuses to cooperate. Bush faced opposition from Congress, including members of his own party, regarding social security reform. Sometimes one or both houses are controlled by the opposition party. Sometimes the president is not able to persuade his own party to support his programs. Regarding their campaign promises, then, presidents are successful in some areas and unsuccessful in others.

In short, the politics of implementation is complex, but successful candidates try and often manage to deliver on many of their promises. These promises are not made in a vacuum, and more often than not they represent the genuine intentions of the candidates. While voters are often disappointed by the slow processes of government and the incomplete realization of platform agendas and campaign promises, they also often "win" when they place their wishes, desires, and expectations in the hands of our elected officials. For the voters, elections do more than just select our representatives. They provide for citizen empowerment.

Conclusion: Do Elections Matter?

Americans are ambivalent about elections. They acknowledge the importance of elections in the democratic process but take part in them in relatively low numbers, compared with many Western European democracies. To understand the election process better, we have examined in this chapter the facts behind the myth that candidates break their campaign promises. Although that myth contains some truth, it is by and large inaccurate and misleading.

What is the reality? First, although some campaign promises are not fulfilled, many are. Furthermore, although candidates run for office for personal reasons — power is a strong motivator — they also run in order to implement their promised policies. And they are often successful in achieving that goal. An analysis of presidential performance, for example, shows that recent presidents have managed to fulfill many of their promises either partially or completely.[43]

We also examined the relationship of a number of variables to election campaigning and voting behavior, particularly the influence of money. Money is a very important — indeed, a necessary — part of most campaigns, but it is not the only important factor in most elections. Other elements, such as incumbency, issues, personalities, skills, national trends, and partisanship, strongly influence election outcomes. The voters' characteristics — religion, ethnic identity, race, age, and so forth — also appear to affect how they view the political world and for whom they cast their ballots.

Tying It Together

Focus Questions Recap

✳ What roles do party caucuses, primaries, and conventions play in the nomination process?

✳ What impact does money have on political campaigns? What recent changes have been made in federal election campaign finance laws?

✳ How do the media have an impact on political campaigns?

✳ What have been the consequences of the shift from party-centered campaigns to candidate-centered campaigns?

✳ What factors influence the way people vote in an election?

✳ How does the electoral college function? What alternatives have been suggested as a replacement for the electoral college?

✳ Do candidates, when elected to office, try to keep their campaign promises?

Chapter Summary

1. Elections begin with the nomination of candidates. Those who run for office are motivated by personal ambition and by a commitment to policy goals.

2. Candidates are nominated in open meetings (caucuses) or, most commonly, in primary elections. While some states and minor political parties still use conventions to nominate candidates, the most prominent conventions are at the national level. Presidential nominations take place at national conventions, which today generally ratify the outcome of primary and caucus campaigns where delegates to the national conventions are selected.

3. While money is not the only important variable affecting the outcome of an election, it is often critical in the success of many campaigns. The escalation of campaign costs led Congress to pass the 1971 Federal Election Campaign Act, which set limits on contributions and expenditures in federal elections. The law gave rise to a new source of funds, political action committees (PACs). Congress enacted and President Bush signed into law the Bipartisan Campaign Finance Act of 2002 to further reform federal campaign financing. This act focuses on weaknesses in the existing law, although it did not eliminate all of the loopholes that allowed campaigns to legally circumvent the intent of the

law through the establishment, for example, of 527 committees.

4. Most highly visible election campaigns — including those for the presidency, the U.S. Senate and House, governorships and many other statewide offices, and many large-city mayoralties — are highly organized, with staffs that include professional consultants and personal advisers. A campaign's outcome can depend on whether the candidate is an incumbent and on other factors in the political environment, particularly the presence of the media. Campaigns have increasingly become candidate-centered instead of party-centered.

5. The media can have an impact on political campaigns because they can serve as an important and effective tool in motivating and encouraging a candidate's supporters to go to the polls on election day, influencing a voter who is undecided, and helping shape the issues that candidates focus on in an election. Thus, the media can have an impact on the quality of the debate throughout a race.

6. The shift from party-centered campaigns to candidate-centered campaigns has weakened the role of political parties and placed more control over many campaigns in the hands of candidates and their political consultants. Nevertheless, the role of parties in the campaign process is still evident at most levels of government.

7. Women and nonwhite males have faced voting restrictions for most of the nation's history. Voting rights have been extended to these groups and to young people between the ages of eighteen and twenty by constitutional amendment and by federal and state laws.

8. Voter turnout for U.S. elections is low compared with that in other countries. Wealthy, well-educated, older individuals are more likely to vote than members of other groups. Low turnout has been attributed to laws and institutional factors (such as preregistration requirements and long ballots), as well as to voters' loss of faith in government.

9. Factors that influence our vote include issue preferences, the personal qualities and past records of the candidates, and our party and social identities.

10. Although the founders believed in representative government, they hesitated to place the selection of the president directly in the hands of the people. The system they devised, the electoral college, provides for the election by the people of each state of a number of electors equal to the number of senators and representatives representing a state in Congress. With the exception of Maine and Nebraska, in most states, the presidential candidate who wins the popular vote also wins the state's electoral college votes. The electoral college vote determines the winner of the presidential election. Alternative methods of selecting the president include the direct election, the proportional plan, the district plan, and the bonus plan.

11. The candidates' positions are not idle promises. Once elected, candidates try to fulfill many of their campaign pledges.

12. Elections matter because they provide for citizen empowerment. While Americans are often ambivalent about elections, they acknowledge the importance of elections in the democratic process.

Key Terms

Opportunity structure (187)
Caucus (187)
Primary (188)
Open primary (188)
Closed primary (189)
Partisan primary (189)
Nonpartisan primary (189)
Runoff primary (189)
Front-loading (190)

Soft money (196)
527 committees (197)
Incumbent (199)
Open race (200)
Political consultant (202)
Party-centered campaign (205)
Candidate-centered campaign (205)
Retrospective voting (209)
Electoral college (211)

Net Work

Do you want to find out more about campaigns and campaign funding? Helpful websites include:

- The Federal Election Commission (**www.fec.gov**), which provides data on campaign funding for federal elections

- Project Vote Smart (**www.vote-smart.org**), which provides candidate profiles, campaign finance information, issue positions, and other information on candidates running for office at the national, state, and local levels as well as ballot measures in the various states

- Public Agenda (**www.publicagenda.org**), which provides research on major issues in a nonpartisan venue

- The Center for Responsive Politics (**www.crp.org**), which provides extensive campaign contribution information

- Campaign Finance (**www.campaignfinance.com/ states/index.html**), which provides information on campaign contributions for state races

- Voter and registration demographics from the Census Bureau (**www.census.gov/population/www/ socdemo/voting.html**)

- The Polling Report (**www.pollingreport.com**), which provides polling data on elections and campaign events

- The Center for American Women and Politics/Rutgers University (**www.rci.rutgers.edu/ ~cawp**), which provides data and reports on women and women's voting behavior

Most candidates for office at the national or state level (and even some local candidates) post websites. There you can find information about the candidate's positions on issues, read or listen to recent speeches, and see a schedule of upcoming events. As an exercise, find out about the candidates in an upcoming national, state, or local election. Using a search engine, find the websites for the Democratic and Republican party candidates and any minor party candidates. What positions has each candidate taken?

As a second exercise, find out more about campaign financing in your area. Go to the Federal Election Commission website to see how much money is being raised and spent by candidates for the House of Representatives in your congressional district, and to learn more about PAC spending and contributions to federal candidates. For more about campaign financing in your state elections, visit the Campaign Finance website or use a search engine to find information about campaign finance laws in your state.

8

Interest Groups

Are all interest groups corrupt and self-serving?

FOCUS QUESTIONS

* What are the differences between interest groups and political action committees (PACs)?

* What factors determine the power of an interest group?

* What tools do interest groups use in attempting to influence the policymaking process?

* Do interest groups play a role in the representative process?

T he headline on the front page of the *Washington Post* didn't mince words: "K Street's New Ways Spawn More Pork." It wasn't referring to a drove of hogs making their way down K Street in the nation's capital. It referred, instead, to the street in Washington that is home to many high-powered interest groups and lobbyists, and to "pork," meaning the "pork barrel," or the government support lobbyists hope to garner for the special projects of the interest groups they represent. Beginning in 2005 and continuing into 2006, a major pork barrel scandal unfolded in Washington, D.C., leading to the conviction of two Republican members of the House of Representatives, Randy "Duke" Cunningham of California and Bob Ney of Ohio, as well as former GOP lobbyist Jack Abramoff. As the *Washington Post* article put it, "At issue is a symbolic relationship between lawmakers well positioned to slip special-interest projects into legislation, and wealthy lobbying groups that raise large sums of campaign funds or provide trips and other benefits to those lawmakers."[1]

Indeed, big money is always at stake when the president and members of Congress are debating the national budget, and many institutions hire lobbyists to represent their interests and to seek benefits. These interest groups range from large corporations and labor unions to universities and colleges like the one you attend.

Some 38,000 registered lobbyists work in Washington, representing the interests of various groups and individuals before the members of Congress and their staffs and before executive branch officials.[2] Although some special-interest groups, such as universities and colleges, are seen as being as American as apple pie, many Americans see most interest groups and lobbyists in a different and harsher light. They see lobbyists as wheeler-dealers and government as being influenced by a relatively few big interests. They suspect interest groups of dishonesty and of corrupting the political process by unduly influencing government, most often by "buying" members of Congress through campaign contributions. Polls often reflect such skepticism. One recent poll found that 77 percent of the public believed that "recent reports that lobbyists may have bribed members of Congress [is] the way things work in Congress." While Republican members were more likely than Democrats to be perceived by the public "as likely to accept bribes or gifts that affect their votes" (28 percent versus 13 percent), 36 percent felt members of both parties in Congress were equally likely to accept bribes or gifts.[3] These public sentiments are not new. Concerns over interest groups have been around since the government was formed. Many Americans continue to question the roles of special-interest groups and lobbyists in government activities.

Critical Thinking

Do you think that all interest groups are corrupt and self-serving?

Apparently, a majority of Americans believe in the *myth that interest groups are a corrupting influence in politics.* Though interest groups are undoubtedly playing a bigger role in the American policymaking process, whether they are a corrupting influence is open to question. We take up this issue at the end of the chapter. Before we can evaluate the myth and reality of interest groups, however, we must look at the role they play in American politics and at the resources and techniques that they use to influence politics.

Interest-Group Lobbying

Whenever Congress is in session, you will find lobbyists seeking access to our elected officials in order to try to influence their decisions. Here, hundreds of interest-group representatives wait outside a congressional hearing room awaiting the results of their lobbying efforts.

Movers and Shakers: Interest and Other Advocacy Groups

FOCUS QUESTION WHAT ARE THE DIFFERENCES BETWEEN INTEREST GROUPS AND POLITICAL ACTION COMMITTEES (PACs)?

Our first task is to define three key terms: *interest groups,* *lobbies,* and *political action committees (PACs).*

Interest Groups

Interest group Any organized group of individuals who share common goals and seek to influence government decision making.

A political **interest group** is any organized group of individuals who share common goals and who seek to influence government decision making.[4] Such diverse groups as the National Rifle Association, the Sierra Club, the U.S. Chamber of Commerce, and the League of Women Voters all fit this definition. Even college students are represented by interest groups — for instance the United States Student Association (see "Asked & Answered," p. 227).

Interest groups differ from political parties.[5] In Chapter 6, on political parties, we emphasize that parties are broad-based coalitions, with policies on a wide range of issues. A party's ultimate goal is to contest and win elections in order to control and operate government. In contrast, interest groups put forth a limited set of demands.* Although they sometimes try to affect the outcome of certain elections, they do not run candidates for office or attempt to control or operate government. Their primary concern is to influence policy in their own area of interest.

Interest groups differ in size and makeup and pursue varying objectives. They also serve as an important link between their members and elected and appointed government officials. What justifies the existence of interest groups in a democratic, representative form of government is their role in making members of the executive, legislative, and judicial branches of government more aware of the needs and concerns of various groups in America. Many people join interest groups to promote their own economic well-being or to effect political and social change. They believe that their goals are best served by acting together with other citizens. Indeed, while we regard ourselves as a very individualistic society, we also join groups fairly frequently. We are far more likely to join organizations and groups than the English, French, Italians, and Germans, for example.

Economic Interest Groups. Among interest groups, business, labor, professional, and agricultural groups are the most enduring and powerful types. That fact is hardly surprising, given the intensity of most people's preoccupation with their own economic welfare.

Thousands of individual corporations and businesses employ lobbyists, or spokespersons for the corporation or business, in Washington.[6] The concerns of these organizations depend on the business in question and on the political climate. Tax laws, government subsidies, antitrust laws, tariffs on imported goods, and consumer product and environmental regulations may all affect the cost of doing business. In recent years, issues like minimum wage legislation and a national health insurance program have led to increased lobbying efforts on the part of the business community.

Business and trade associations are another type of economic interest group. Under the umbrella of business associations are the large and influential U.S. Chamber of Commerce, with a membership of more than 250,000 individuals and companies; the Business Roundtable, made up of approximately 200 of the largest industrial, commercial, and financial businesses in the nation; and many other groups. These associations represent some of the most powerful interests of corporate America.

Trade associations, which represent entire industries, also have widely divergent interests, ranging from government regulation of food and drugs to regulation of the import of beef from Argentina. These groups are interested in government regulations that may affect the way their members do business. The National Cable Television Association, for example, closely monitors government regulations covering the cable industry—regulations that may have an impact

Critical Thinking

What kind of interest groups might a college student belong to? For what reasons?

---

*Some interest groups, such as Common Cause and the Liberty Federation, have positions on a wide range of issues. Even these two groups, however, usually focus on a few key issues and direct their resources toward them.

on how much you and I have to pay for cable television service. Even lobbyists have a trade association, the American League of Lobbyists.

Another important type of economic interest group is labor organizations. The American Federation of Labor and Congress of Industrial Organizations (AFL-CIO) is an umbrella organization of fifty-eight labor unions. Overall, the number of union members in the United States is approximately 15.5 million, although this figure represents a significant decline in membership over the past four decades.[7] The AFL-CIO, along with large unions such as the United Auto Workers and the Teamsters, has for many years represented the interests of labor in the state capitals and in Washington. Smaller individual labor unions also lobby independently. For example, the Independent Federation of Flight Attendants keeps on top of airline industry issues, and representatives of the International Brotherhood of Boilermakers, Iron Ship Builders, Blacksmiths, Forgers & Helpers focus their attention on legislation related to their interests, including shipbuilding, tool making, and construction of nuclear and fossil-fuel plants.

Professional associations also bring the economic interests of their particular membership to the government's attention. Two of the most powerful, the American Bankers Association and the Association of Trial Lawyers of America, have large lobbying budgets and maintain full-time staffs in Washington and in many state capitals. Smaller, less-powerful associations, such as the Clowns of America, have fewer resources but also try to protect their members' interests with regard to workers' compensation, tax laws, and other legislation affecting their professions.

Farmers, as an economic interest group, are a relatively strong economic force in contemporary American politics, as upward of 20 percent of the work force is directly or indirectly employed in agribusiness. One of the major goals of agricultural interest groups is protection from fluctuating prices for meat, grain, fruit, and other agricultural products, which affect the income of the groups' members.

Citizen Activist Groups. Not all interests are purely economic. In the past three decades, there has been an increase in the number of citizen activist groups. These groups often try to represent what they deem to be the interests of the public and so are referred to as **public interest groups**.[8] Other organizations focus on specific causes or serve as advocates for those who are not able to represent themselves.[9]

Public interest groups
Citizen activist groups that try to represent what they deem to be the interests of the public at large.

Public interest groups such as Common Cause (a grassroots organization supported by member dues), Public Citizen, Inc. (a loose affiliation of consumer groups supported by foundation grants), and the Christian Coalition (a group seeking to protect the values of Christian America) were part of an explosion of citizen lobbies beginning in the 1960s. Public interest groups have tried to represent what they see as the public's interests on such issues as civil rights, consumer protection, campaign reform, environmental regulation, and family values.

Single-issue group An activist group that seeks to lobby Congress on a single issue or a narrow range of issues.

An activist group with an extremely narrow focus is known as a **single-issue group**. For example, the major goal of the Bass Anglers' Sportsman Society is to further the interests of bass fishing. The National Rifle Association (NRA) and the Gun Owners of America work to preserve the right of Americans to own handguns and rifles. NARAL Pro-Choice America fights for legislation and court decisions that protect the right of women to have abortions.

Some citizen activist groups serve as advocates for people who may be unable to represent their own interests individually.[10] For instance, the National Association for the Advancement of Colored People (NAACP), the Child Welfare League of America, and the American Cancer Society assist their target populations by lobbying, providing the public with information, and taking cases to court.

Government Interest Groups. Not only do governments receive pressure from lobbyists, they also lobby other governments. San Francisco, Baltimore, Chicago, Chattanooga, and Newark are only a few of the cities that have lobbyists representing their interests in Washington on such matters as budget and appropriation legislation, Medicare, housing, and transportation. Indeed, the offices of hundreds of cities and states are listed in the *Washington Representatives Directory*. The efforts of these cities are directed toward ensuring that they receive their share of federal funding—funding that can ease the burden of local taxes. Cities also heavily lobby their state capitals for financial aid, as well as in support of or against legislation that affects them. With many programs and policies being jointly implemented or funded by local and state governments as well as by the federal government, many government lobbying groups find that they have

Interest-Group Protests

One tactic that interests groups use to win support and to encourage legislative action is the protest. Here, pro-choice and pro-life demonstrators hold up signs expressing their strongly held positions on the issue.

to lobby all three levels of government on policy issues ranging from environmental pollution to workplace safety.

Critical Thinking

Do you think that local governments should be allowed to lobby their state capitals for state aid and resources? Should state governments be allowed to actively lobby the federal government for federal aid and resources?

Public-Sector Interest Groups. In addition to lobbying by governments, there are a number of associations of governments and government officials that represent the collective interests of their members. These organizations include the U.S. Conference of Mayors, the International City Management Association, the National League of Cities, the National Association of Counties, the Council of State Governments, and the National Governors' Association. Local and state governments have come to depend on Washington for funds to pay for everything from public roads to new airports and schools. Public-sector interest groups (collectively made up of mayors, governors, state legislators, or other associations of elected or appointed government officials) will often lobby for those funds.

Foreign Nation Interest Groups. Even foreign nations have lobbyists looking after their interests. Nations such as Turkey, Jamaica, Guinea, and the African Republic of Transkei have lobbyists in the United States that represent their interests before Congress and the executive branch. Those interests can range from military and economic assistance programs to technical advice on how to build an electric power plant. This globalization of interest-group activity extends to the private sector, too. Groups like Amnesty International, a worldwide watchdog organization, lobby against any government's repression and torture of its citizens. Amnesty International has offices in the United States, Great Britain, and throughout the world.

Lobbyists

Lobbyist An individual who works for a specific interest group or who serves as the spokesperson for a specific set of interests.

Who does the work for an Interest group? A **lobbyist** is an individual who works for a specific interest group or who serves as the spokesperson for a specific set of interests. Lobbyists engage in the act of lobbying—that is, they try to affect government decision making by influencing legislators and members of the executive branch to support or reject certain policies or legislation.

Although some interest groups maintain their own staffs of full-time lobbyists, other groups hire a lobbying firm to represent them in Washington or in various state capitals. Increasingly, lobbying has become a professional, full-time occupation. Many lobbyists are lawyers, former members of the executive branch or of Congress, or former employees of one of the hundreds of federal agencies. Government experience and contacts, along with accumulated expertise, are valuable assets in the lobbying game.

As we shall see later in this chapter, when we discuss the tactics of interest groups, the effectiveness of the lobbyist as spokesperson for an interest group is generally central to that interest group's success in achieving its goals.

Political Action Committees and 527 Committees

Political action committees (PACs) Organizations set up solely for the purpose of contributing money to the campaigns of candidates who sympathize with particular goals. A PAC need not be affiliated with an interest group but can be unaffiliated, representing an ideological position or even a candidate or officeholder.

If the myth of corruption has tainted interest-group politics in recent years, a major source of that concern has been **political action committees (PACs)**. As you learned in Chapter 7, on campaigns and elections, these are independent organizations set up to collect campaign contributions from individuals who support their goals and to pass those contributions on to candidates. PACs resulted from a change in campaign finance laws designed to limit interest groups' financial involvement in elections.[11]

This change came about in the 1970s, when Congress passed the Federal Election Campaign Act. The act provides for a rigid reporting system covering money raised and spent for campaigns, and it restricts campaign contributions and prohibits corporations and labor unions from directly raising funds for or making contributions to political campaigns. However, Congress permitted unions and corporations to set up and administer independent organizations designed to collect and disburse campaign contributions (see the section on electioneering and policymaking later in this chapter, p. 235).

Unions invented PACs, but as you can see in Figure 8.1, PACs sponsored by corporations rapidly surpassed union-sponsored PACs in numbers. Now almost every kind of group uses PACs. Trade and professional groups (for example, the American Institute of Certified Public Accountants), unions (such as the American Federation of Teachers Committee on Political Education), corporations and businesses (for example, the American Dental Political Action Committee), and cooperative groups (such as the Committee for Thorough Agricultural Political Education of Associated Milk Producers, Inc.) have PACs that solicit money and contribute it to political campaigns. There are more than 4,200 PACs registered in Washington, D.C.[12]

Critical Thinking

Are political action committees (PACs) a positive or a negative force in American politics?

A PAC need not be affiliated with an interest group. Unaffiliated groups (such as the Fund for a Conservative Majority and Voters for Choice), often representing strongly held ideological positions on the political spectrum, have grown in numbers over the past twenty-five years. The number of personal PACs has also grown; these are established by officeholders or would-be officeholders to raise money for their own campaigns or for self-promotion, or to assist in the election or reelection of partisan or ideological colleagues. Two of the leading personal PACs are the Keep Our Majority PAC (Representative Dennis Hastert, R-IL), and Committee for a Democratic Majority (Senator Edward Kennedy, D-MA). Many personal PACs are funded by friends and supporters of the individual or by other PACs.

As we discussed in Chapter 7, on campaigns and elections, many groups effectively bypassed the limitations placed on PAC contributions by establishing 527 committees, which aren't regulated by the Federal Election Commission (FEC) or covered by the reforms in the Bipartisan Campaign Reform Act of 2002. The 527 committees are tax-exempt groups "organized under section 527 of the Internal Revenue Code to raise money for political activities including voter mobilization efforts, issue advocacy and the like."[13] Unless the

ASKED & ANSWERED

ASKED: Are college students represented by interest groups?

ANSWERED: With almost 33,000 lobbyists registered in Washington, D.C. (and many more not registered because the rules are unclear and the penalties for not registering are small), you'd assume that college students would have interest group representation in the nation's capital. After all, billions of dollars are spent every year by the federal government on higher education and many laws enacted by Congress have a direct (or often an indirect) impact on college students.

Indeed, groups in Washington represent college students on campuses across the country. As Philip Sharp, director of Harvard University's Institute of Politics has suggested, college students are "rising activists and rising players in the political system." With activism often comes organization, and with organization can come formal interest-group representation.

One specific group that represents college students is the United States Student Association (USSA). The USSA is, in its own words, "the country's oldest and largest national student organization, representing millions of students." Founded in 1947, USSA regards itself as the major voice of college and university students from around the nation, a voice most likely to be heard at the White House and in Congress. The tools used by the USSA are similar to those employed by many other interest groups. "The organization tracks and lobbies federal legislation and policy, and organizes students from across the country to participate in the political process, through testifying in official Congressional hearings, letter-writing campaigns, and face-to-face lobby visits between students and their elected officials." In addition, employing the traditional tactics and tools of lobbyists, the USSA trains and organizes students on campuses, focusing on issues including school fee hikes, recruitment and retention of underrepresented students, and lobbying to improve campus safety.

The tactics don't always work. The USSA, along with many other interest groups representing universities and colleges, was unsuccessful in preventing federal legislation that cut $12 billion from student loan programs for fiscal year 2007. The legislation also increased interest rates on Stafford loans and Parent Loans for Undergraduate Students (PLUS loans). In reaction to the budget cuts, the USSA and other groups claimed that they would make their voices of concern heard at the ballot box in the next congressional elections.

The USSA is not the only interest group whose lobbying has had an impact on college students. Recently, efforts by interest groups representing commercial for-profit universities such as the University of Phoenix were successful in lobbying for federal rules changes that will allow online distance learning institutions to be eligible for federal funding, including student loans and grants. Thus, students taking online education courses at for-profit universities can now qualify for student aid. The effort to bring about this change (a change challenged by many traditional colleges and universities) was supported by a significant lobbying effort by the for-profit universities and colleges. As Representative Michael Castle (R-DE) put it, "The power of the for-profits has grown tremendously. They have a full-blown lobbying effort and give lots of money to campaigns. In 10 years, the power of this interest group has spiked as much as any you'll find."

Indeed, examples like these make the answer to our original question crystal clear. Are college students represented by interest groups? They are, most definitely.

Source: United States Student Association press release, February 1, 2006, homepage, www.usstudents.org. Source for the for-profit colleges and universities discussion is Sam Dillon, "Online Colleges Receive a Boost from Congress," *New York Times*, March 1, 2006, p. A1.

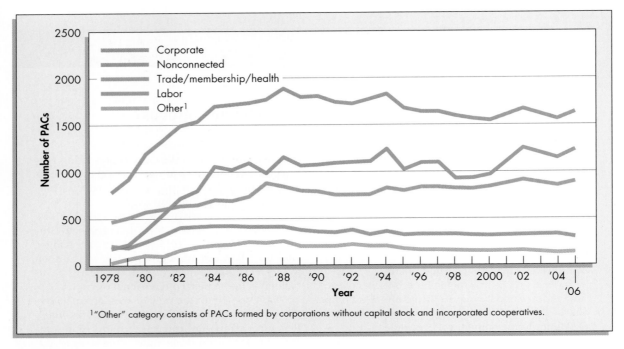

[1]"Other" category consists of PACs formed by corporations without capital stock and incorporated cooperatives.

FIGURE 8.1

An Explosion of PACs

Unions invented PACs, but corporations forged ahead with them when they were in their infancy. Corporate, union, and trade PACs have tended to support candidates, whereas nonaffiliated PACs have worked on negative campaigns.

Source: Federal Election Commission press release, February 23, 2006.

527 committee is also a political party or PAC specifically engaged in advocating the election or defeat of a federal candidate, it is not required to file disclosure reports with the FEC. In effect, 527 committees can raise unlimited soft money to mobilize targeted voters to turn out for the election and for certain types of issue advocacy, as long as there is no expressed support for or against a specific candidate. By using 527 committees, federal candidates and PACs are able to skirt federal laws meant to reform the campaign finance process. United Parcel Service, the Republican Governors Association, the Democratic Governors' Association, Promoting American Values for Everyone, and the Christian Coalition Fund are all examples of groups registered with the IRS as 527 committees.

What Makes an Interest Group Powerful

FOCUS QUESTION WHAT FACTORS DETERMINE THE POWER OF AN INTEREST GROUP?

What accounts for the success of interest groups? What problems do they experience or create? In this section, we focus on six factors that strengthen or weaken interest-group activity: size, unity, leadership, information and expertise, money, and monopoly.

Size

Size is a major factor affecting an interest group's power. Large organizations, such as the AFL-CIO or the U.S. Chamber of Commerce, have the potential to mobilize vast resources of money, information, time, and energy in the service of an issue. The success of unions' support of the minimum hourly wage is a measure of the importance of size as a component of political power. The success in the mid-1990s of the U.S. Chamber of Commerce's efforts in support of the North American Free Trade Agreement with Mexico and Canada is an indication of the political impact of the chamber's membership and size.

The importance of the size of a group's membership varies among interest groups. Corporate interest groups that are not membership organizations and trade associations, which generally have relatively few members, obviously need not pay much attention to membership size. On the other hand, unions and citizens' groups, which traditionally claim large memberships and mass representation, do place a high value on membership size.[14]

In evaluating the impact of size, the key word is *potential*. Many large interest groups have little or no influence over the political opinions and participation of their membership. Indeed, a large membership is often difficult both to manage and to influence.[15] But if the leaders of large interest groups such as the

An Interest Group in Action

Students call for increased higher education funding during a rally sponsored by the U.S. Student Association.

AFL-CIO or the U.S. Chamber of Commerce can convince elected officials, administrators, and congressional staff that they can mobilize their membership behind a policy, size becomes very important. Elected officials are often impressed and influenced by interest groups that have a large membership.

Unity

A group's power is also strongly affected by the unity of its members. In recent legislative battles to reform the Social Security and Medicare systems, the American Association of Retired Persons (AARP) was sure that its large membership was united. Such unity gave the AARP enormous strength in overcoming changes it did not support. Congress, the president, and the bureaucracy cannot ignore the preferences of millions of organized individuals who are united by a common goal.

When an interest group lacks unity on an issue, its influence on the policy-making process drops considerably, even if the group is large. Internal disagreements often work against a group's interests. For example, agreement is rare across the petroleum industry, where companies differ in size from giants such as Exxon Mobil to the smaller, independent "wildcat" companies. One lobbyist for the American Petroleum Institute, a trade association representing oil interests, suggested that consensus on some issues was a "long time coming." When such consensus is lacking, the institute often takes "no stand" at all, even if the issues affect its membership across the board.[16]

Leadership

Size and group unity do not necessarily ensure success, however. Interest groups must also have leaders who command respect and who can articulate and represent the issues and demands of the organization. Without such leadership, the interest group is "headless" and, more often than not, is ineffective in pushing its goals.

One example of effective leadership is provided by Marian Wright Edelman, head of the Washington-based Children's Defense Fund, which lobbies on health and social service issues on behalf of children. Highly respected by many members of Congress, she and her organization have been very successful in supporting programs that have a beneficial impact on the lives of children.

Information and Expertise

What lobbyists know—their ability to collect information, evaluate its importance, and pass it on to appropriate government officials—is critical to their success. Faced with the need to make decisions on a variety of issues, public officials need credible and trustworthy information. Thus, an interest group that can present its expertise cogently and convincingly has a distinct advantage over less-informed and less-articulate organizations. Patrick Healy, who was powerful and successful as chief lobbyist for the National Milk Producers' Federation, argues that facts are the major resource of lobbying and that being able to provide accurate information to members of Congress and their staffs is the key to a lobbyist's success. Few of his colleagues would disagree with him.

The effectiveness of a group's expertise and the delivery of its information also depend on the perception of the group's motives. The American Medical Association's position on smoking is presumed to be economically disinterested and hence is heeded by Congress and the public. But its stand against national health insurance for all citizens is viewed with some skepticism, as it may stem from doctors' economic self-interest.

Money

Lobbying, collecting information, and other such activities cost money. In addition to the lobbyists' salaries, there are expenses for office space, support staff, telephones, office equipment, and travel. Some groups hire professional lobbying firms, and the costs of these services can be significant. A large budget may not be an interest group's most critical resource, but adequate funding is essential.

Fundraising tactics differ from group to group. Many citizen activist groups, such as the Sierra Club, rely on an annual membership fee. For these groups, finding enough members to maintain the organization can be a problem. A hiker or camper need not join the club in order to benefit from its achievements in improving environmental conditions and preserving national parks. To get around this problem of **free riders** — those who benefit from the actions of interest groups without spending time or money to aid them — groups may seek funding from foundations that favor an interest group's goals. Groups may also offer special services and resources to help recruit members.[17] They may provide members with free publications, technical journals, informative newsletters, reduced insurance rates, and even the opportunity to combine business with pleasure at annual meetings held in vacation resorts. For example, the AARP provides its members with low-cost health insurance policies and a money market fund.[18] The members of the National Rifle Association can buy ammunition, handguns, and rifles at discount prices.

Economic groups often have easier access to funds. Groups such as the U.S. Chamber of Commerce and the National Association of Manufacturers receive dues from their corporate and individual members. Many companies use corporate funds to cover the cost of maintaining a staff lobbyist or hiring a lobbying firm. Organizations that people must join in order to keep their jobs can certainly count on financial support from their members. This is typical of many trade and industrial jobs and even some professions. Carpenters and plumbers must join their unions, and physicians, lawyers, and other professionals find themselves under pressure to join professional associations.

Free riders Those who benefit from the actions of interest groups without spending time or money to aid those groups.

Monopoly

Whether an interest group is challenged effectively by one or more other interest groups can have a significant impact on the influence and power of that interest group. In effect, the larger and more powerful the countervailing forces are, the less power an opposing interest group will have. Few or no countervailing forces can provide an interest group with a monopoly in influencing the policies and programs linked with that interest group. The American Boiler Makers Association can often monopolize policy regarding its industry (construction of commercial boilers), for example, because of the absence or near-absence of any rival forces to oppose them.

Interest-Group Tactics: "You Don't Lobby with Hundred-Dollar Bills and Wild Parties"

FOCUS QUESTION   **WHAT TOOLS DO INTEREST GROUPS USE IN ATTEMPTING TO INFLUENCE THE POLICYMAKING PROCESS?**

Interest groups are as powerful as their size, unity, leadership, expertise, and funds enable them to be. A group need not have all of these resources, but the more of them that it has, the better. Of course, no single resource will make or break a group. More often than not, success comes from effectively combining organizational resources and the tactics used to influence policymaking.

"You don't lobby with hundred-dollar bills and wild parties. You lobby with facts," says former lobbyist Patrick Healy. As you will see, however, money counts, although it is only one of many tools used by interest groups to influence government.

Lobbying

Lobbying The act of trying to influence government decision makers; it is named after the public rooms in which it first took place.

As you learned earlier in this chapter, **lobbying** is the act of trying to influence government decision makers. Named after the public rooms, lobbies, in which it first took place, lobbying now goes on in hearing rooms, offices, golf courses, and restaurants—any spot where a lobbyist can gain a hearing and effectively present a case.

Lobbyists' stock in trade is their relationships with government officials and their staffs (see Table 8.1). There is no question that there are unscrupulous lobbyists who use bribes to curry favors from dishonest and corrupt government officials in the form of favorable support. But for most lobbyists, for the more than 520,000 elected U.S. officials, and for the administrators in the more than 87,000 units of government in the nation, relationships are maintained not with bribes and favors, as the myth of corruption implies, but with data—the technical information that members of Congress and bureaucrats need in order to

TABLE 8.1

What Lobbyists Do   Despite the myth of corrupting influence, lobbyists do not spend all of their time "endorsing candidates" or contributing to political campaigns. As these data demonstrate, disseminating information is a major focus of their work.

TYPE OF TECHNIQUE	PERCENTAGE OF ORGANIZATIONS USING TECHNIQUE	
	REGULARLY	OCCASIONALLY
Contacting Congress personally	96	4
Talking with the press	76	22
Testifying in Congress	70	30
Presenting research to government	68	32
Contacting agency personnel	67	33
Mobilizing group members	56	38
Contributing to campaigns	54	10
Presenting research to the press	49	49
Testifying at agency hearings	39	49
Participating in litigation over policy	22	51

Source: Ken Kollman, *Outside Lobbying: Public Opinion and Interest Group Strategies* (Princeton, N.J.: Princeton University Press, 1998), p. 35.

carry out their committee and administrative assignments. Their work demands a level of expertise on a wide range of topics that few can muster, and so they come to depend on lobbyists' information and recommendations regarding the thousands of issues on which they must decide. Lobbyists even draft legislation, write speeches, and help plan legislative strategy. For most lobbyists, however, presenting research results or technical information to public officials is the most important and time-consuming part of their jobs.[19]

Once an interest group proves itself as a source of dependable information, it has easier access to officials. Lobbyists also share that expertise at congressional hearings, presenting research or technical information or discussing the impact of a bill on national, state, or local interests. Knowing how important constituents' concerns are to legislators, lobbyists are quick to point to the impact of a bill on a representative's home district or state. Whenever they can, interest groups mobilize the folks at home to write and call members of Congress to stress the importance of particular issues.

Clearly, there are unethical lobbyists, and their existence supports the myth of corruption. In the early years of the republic, presenting gifts to or bribing willing legislators was a not uncommon way of influencing the passage of a specific bill. Indeed, in 1833, as prominent a senator as Daniel Webster was on retainer to the Bank of the United States, which was fighting for its survival.

POLITICS & POPULAR CULTURE

Sleazy Lobbying and Special Interests

If you wanted to dramatize the corruption of politicians and interest groups, you couldn't do a better job than that done by Gary Markstein, an editorial cartoonist for the *Milwaukee Journal-Sentinel*. Markstein satirized a major congressional scandal in 2005 and 2006 that contributed to the downfall of Texas Republican representative Tom DeLay and his resignation from the House of Representatives. DeLay was alleged to have received favors from lobbyist Jack Abramoff in exchange for supporting legislation favoring Abramoff clients. In Markstein's cartoon, a Republican-controlled Congress is portrayed, ironically, as seeking the advice of lobbyists to clean up the "sleazy lobbying system."

As we noted in "Politics & Popular Culture" in Chapter 6 (p. 178), the editorial cartoon remains one of the most creative instruments in popular culture for satirizing politics and government; as with all myths about politics, cartoon portrayals contain a certain amount of undeniable truth. While this particular cartoon depicts Republican members of Congress as puppets of special-interest groups (Democrats don't fare very much better in public opinion polls on relationships between elected officials and lobbyists), in reality, most lobbyists serve the important function of providing legislators with important and accurate information on a given policy, and they also often represent the legitimate interests and concerns of a lawmaker's constituents. That interest groups can and do influence the policymaking process, sometimes detrimentally, is indeed true. That they are a constant and overwhelming force of corruption in the policymaking process is a myth that is generated and reinforced by cartoons like the one reprinted here.

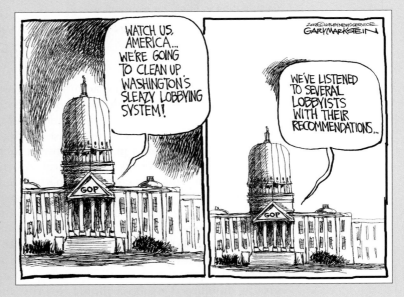

Webster wrote to the bank president: "My retainer has not been renewed or refreshed as usual. If it is wished that my relation to the Bank should be continued, it may be well to send me the usual retainer."[20]

Despite their reputation for bribery and corruption, however, most interest groups today function within the law. Nevertheless, Congress has found it necessary from time to time to pass laws regulating these groups and their representatives. It was in 1887 that Congress first required lobbyists to register with the House of Representatives. Additional laws since that time have mandated that lobbyists file reports listing their clients, describing their activities, and recording the amount of money spent. Recent legislation, including the 1995 Lobbying Restrictions Act, has sought to regulate lobbying in Washington, although there are still many loopholes in the law that prevent effective overall control over lobbying activities.[21] The lobbying scandal discussed in the opening paragraphs of this chapter has prompted many members of Congress to call for new laws placing greater restrictions on lobbying members.

In their relations with government officials, lobbyists' actions are governed by one major rule: A lobbyist should never lie. This may seem to you to be strange or untrue, but it is the way most lobbyists work. As one member of Congress put it, "It doesn't take very long to figure which lobbyists are straightforward, and which ones are trying to snow you. The good ones will give you the weak points as well as the strong points of their case. If anyone ever gives me false or misleading information, that's it—I'll never see him again."[22] When 175 lobbyists were asked what resources were most important to their success, an overwhelming majority singled out the reputation for being credible and trustworthy.[23]

Electioneering and Policymaking

Electioneering Participating in the election process by providing services or raising campaign contributions.

Participating in the election process — **electioneering** — is an important tactic of many interest groups. As part of that tactic, both interest groups and political action committees have become very important to candidates.

During the 2004 election cycle, PAC contributions to federal candidates totaled $310.5 million in contributions and other costs related to Senate and House races. Few congressional candidates, incumbent or not, refuse PAC funding of their expensive campaigns. (See Table 8.2 for a list of major PAC contributors.)

PACs' patterns of giving reflect their partisan persuasions. In 2006, for example, labor-sponsored PACs, which are traditionally strong supporters of the Democratic party, channeled their contributions primarily to Democratic candidates. Corporate-sponsored PACs, on the other hand, directed much of their support to Republican candidates.

Do PAC contributions influence politicians' decisions? Do the recipients of campaign funds support the donors' programs? Interest groups apparently think they do. In one study, 58 percent of interest-group representatives said that they used campaign contributions as a means of influencing the policymaking process.[24] Despite that belief, there is limited evidence that campaign contributions guarantee support of a lobbyist's position or votes on a bill. In general, what a

TABLE 8.2

Top Ten PACs:
Contributions to
Congressional and
Presidential
Candidates During
the 2004 Election
Cycle

RANK AND ORGANIZATION	AMOUNT
1. National Association of Realtors Political Action Committee	$3,771,083
2. Dealers Election Action Committee/National Automobile Dealers Association	2,584,800
3. International Brotherhood of Electrical Workers Committee on Political Education	2,304,600
4. National Beer Wholesalers Association Political Action Committee	2,289,000
5. Laborers' Political League-Laborers' International Union	2,249,000
6. Build Political Action Committee of the National Association of Home Builders	2,221,500
7. Association of Trial Lawyers of America Political Action Committee	2,170,499
8. United Parcel Service Inc. Political Action Committee	2,139,929
9. American Medical Association Political Action Committee	2,077,899
10. UAW Voluntary Community Action Program	2,065,200

Source: Federal Election Commission, 2005.

gift may do is ensure that representatives of an interest group will have easier access to elected officials or their staffs. This is important in itself, for such access allows lobbyists to present and argue their positions and to influence the agenda of Congress. However, while the list of the top ten PAC contributors in 2004 in Table 8.2 is impressive, don't be misled. A majority of the more than 4,200 registered PACs in Washington donate little or nothing to political campaigns, but keep a safe arm's-length distance from the financing of the campaign process.

While some studies claim that campaign contributions by PACs influence the policymaking process, other studies assert that there is no clear link between money and policymaking. Many legislators argue that PAC funds are not intended to buy congressional votes; rather, their purpose is to support legislators who are already committed to the PAC's positions. As Representative Jack Fields said in responding to allegations of PAC influence through financial contributions, "I haven't changed my philosophy in the fifteen years I've been in Congress. My philosophy has always been free enterprise and to support whatever creates jobs, and those who want to contribute to me are free to do so."[25] Nevertheless, the 2004 presidential and congressional elections and the 2006 congressional elections saw both record PAC contributions and a growing skepticism on the part of citizens about the role that money plays in the campaign and policymaking process.

According to the Federal Election Campaign Act (left unchanged by the Bipartisan Campaign Finance Reform Act of 2002), PACs can donate no more than $5,000 per candidate per election (primaries and general elections count as separate elections), a restriction motivated by a history of interest-group contributions that sometimes reached tens of thousands of dollars for a single candidate. Because candidates must now seek out more contributors to their campaigns to ensure sufficient funding, a single group may have less influence on a candidate than it expects. However, the $5,000 per candidate restriction makes it possible for PACs to support more candidates, for the number of campaigns to which a PAC may contribute is unlimited. This outcome is disturbing to many reformers, who had hoped to restrict, not increase, the involvement of interest groups in campaigns.

Interest-group activity in campaigns has given rise to other concerns as well. As we discussed in Chapter 7, recent campaign finance reforms at the federal level prohibit "corporations, trade associations, and labor unions from financing 'electioneering communications' within 60 days of a general election and 30 days of a primary election using 'treasury money.' An electioneering communication is one that refers to a clearly identified federal candidate and is targeted to the candidate's state or district." A corporate, trade association, or union PAC, however, "may still run or finance such ads because its funds are, by definition, *hard money*" (*hard* money is money that is regulated by the Federal Election Commission).[26] The role of PACs in funding federal elections through contributions at the state level also continues to provide PACs with a very powerful campaign financing tool. Clearly, interest groups and their respective PACs will continue to have a significant impact on the election process.

Interest groups support campaigns in other ways besides PAC contributions. Labor, trade, and professional associations supply candidates with volunteers and offer public endorsements. The AFL-CIO, Americans for Democratic Action, and the American Conservative Union are just three of the many interest groups and PACs that provide their members and the public with voting scorecards on candidates they support or target for defeat. By listing key votes, the cards can praise or damn the candidate. The National Congressional Club PAC specializes in the so-called negative campaign, or putting down the opposition. This group has spent large sums in the past, particularly on television advertisements, in an effort to defeat liberal candidates. In turn, the AFL-CIO has financed expensive television advertising campaigns that have both directly and indirectly supported Democratic candidates for Congress as well as financing campaigns against candidates who have not been pro-labor.

Interest groups do not limit their activities to congressional races. Besides pressuring the major parties to include the interest group's goals in the presidential party platforms, a group may turn out in force at the national conventions. Of the 4,322 delegates to the 2004 Democratic National Convention, 25 percent were members of labor unions. Not surprisingly, the party took strong platform positions on labor concerns. The pro-business, antiregulation platform of the Republican party was no doubt influenced, in part, by the strong representation of self-declared conservatives, 63 percent of the 2,509 delegates, that attended the 2004 Republican National Convention.[27]

Building Coalitions

Coalition building The bringing together of diverse interest groups in a common lobbying effort.

An interest-group tactic that has gained increasing importance is **coalition building** — the bringing together of diverse interest groups in a common lobbying effort. In the past, various groups have formed coalitions to support or prevent the passage of congressional, state, or local legislation. Increasing the forces in favor of or against legislation can add legitimacy to the lobbying effort and attract the attention of elected officials.

Most signs point to increasing use of coalition building by interest groups and PACs in an effort to influence the policymaking process.

Grassroots Pressure: Power to the People

Grassroots pressure Lobbying by rank-and-file members of an interest group who use such tactics as letter writing and public protests to influence government.

The word *grassroots* is a people-centered term. In interest-group politics, **grassroots pressure** refers to lobbying by rank-and-file members of an interest group — often just ordinary citizens — who use such tactics as letter writing and public protests to influence government.

When the National Beer Wholesalers Association wanted to be exempted from antitrust legislation, it mobilized grassroots support for a massive letter, telephone, and telegram campaign. Truly a "bottoms-up" effort to stimulate pressure from the grassroots level, the campaign was supported by political contributions from the association's political action committee — which, as you have no doubt guessed, is often called SIXPAC.[28]

Grassroots activity includes face-to-face meetings between members of Congress and selected constituents, as well as demonstrations and protests. When interest groups mobilize grassroots mail and telephone campaigns, they tend to focus on narrow issues and to direct their efforts toward specific members of Congress. On any given issue, "lobbyists understand intuitively what political scientists have demonstrated empirically: members of Congress are more influenced by their constituents than by Washington lobbies."[29] For that reason, many interest groups stress grassroots efforts.

Indeed, grassroots mobilization has evolved into a highly professional undertaking. In an article appearing in the late 1990s, *Campaigns & Elections* magazine estimated that "professional grassroots lobbying has become an $800 million industry. . . . The planned orchestrated demonstration of public support through the mobilization of constituent action is . . . one of the hottest trends in politics today. . . . Interest groups that don't play the game risk becoming political eunuchs."[30] Today, professional grassroots lobbying is a billion dollar industry. An interest group representative may call members of the public and solicit their opinion on a topic; if their opinion coincides with the position of the interest group, the individuals are offered an immediate and direct telephone hookup with their representatives in Congress. In this way, interest groups try to ensure that grassroots opinions favorable to them reach the appropriate legislators. As *Washington Post* correspondents Haynes Johnson and David Broder point out, "there's nothing spontaneous about this kind of operation." It has been called "astroturfing"—a reference to the synthetic grass used on many football, soccer, and baseball fields.[31] Unlike spontaneous grassroots activity generated by citizens who are concerned about an issue, astroturfing is "public opinion" that is systematically organized and generated by an interest group.

Litigation

Many pressure groups, particularly public interest and advocacy groups, also use the courts to influence policy. They bring direct suits, challenge existing laws, or file briefs as "friends of the court" to support one side in cases that are already before the court.

Though it is expensive and time-consuming, litigation can bring about remarkable political change. Perhaps the outstanding example is the use of the courts by the National Association for the Advancement of Colored People (NAACP) in the 1940s and 1950s. In a series of cases, culminating in the *Brown v. Board of Education* decision in 1954, NAACP lawyers argued and the Supreme Court affirmed that school segregation was illegal in the United States. Women's groups, consumer groups, environmental groups, religious groups, and others have followed the lead of the civil rights movement in taking their causes to the courts. Corporations and trade associations have also engaged in litigation.

Lobbying Gone Wrong
While most lobbyists conduct their business within the boundaries of the law, there are exceptions. Here, Jack Abramoff (center), a well-connected Republican lobbyist, leaves the federal courthouse in Washington, D.C., on January 3, 2006, having pleaded guilty to fraud, tax evasion, and conspiracy to bribe public officials. He will be required to provide evidence about the possible illegal behavior of members of Congress.

However, the high cost restrains many groups. One interest group, the Women's Equity League, was unable to appeal a court ruling against it in an important case because it could not afford the $40,000 necessary to pay for copies of the trial transcript.[32]

In another approach, groups try to influence the composition of the Supreme Court by opposing or supporting judicial nominees. In 2005, President George W. Bush's nominee to the Supreme Court, Harriet Miers, was strongly opposed by both conservative and liberal groups. Miers was President Bush's chief White House counsel and a long-time ally, dating back to the time he was governor of Texas. Many prominent conservatives opposed the nomination, questioning her qualifications and her judicial philosophy, which they felt was not conservative enough. Liberal groups charged cronyism and expressed the belief that Miers was not qualified to be on the Supreme Court. President Bush eventually withdrew the nomination as support in Congress faded and public opinion turned against the nomination.

Hard-Line Tactics

In recent years, a number of interest groups have used hard-line tactics, including civil disobedience and illegal action, to further their cause. In the 1980s and 1990s, groups like ACT UP drew public attention to the plight of AIDS victims by disrupting public events, and organizations like Operation Rescue received a great deal of attention because they advocated illegally blocking access to abortion clinics. Hard-line tactics appear to be a growing mechanism for presenting an interest group's cause. Recent demonstrations and protests aimed at meetings of the World Bank and the International Monetary Fund, on the funding of social security and Medicare and the war in Iraq, have all focused on placing pressure on elected officials to respond to one or another interest group's cause.

Interest Groups and Democracy

FOCUS
QUESTION   DO INTEREST GROUPS PLAY A ROLE IN THE REPRESENTATIVE PROCESS?

Interest groups pose a number of problems for a democratic society. In "Federalist No. 10," James Madison argued that the rise of factions is inevitable in a democracy. Although he believed that factions could destroy the policymaking process, he did not want to prohibit them, for that would undermine the basic tenets of a participatory republic. Instead, Madison hoped that the divisiveness of factions would be tempered both by built-in checks and balances and by a political system that would ensure the creation of competing factions.

Interest groups do distort the democratic process to some degree, mainly because their membership is clearly biased toward the upper half of the socioeco-

Critical Thinking

Do interest groups distort the democratic process?

nomic ladder. To the extent that business, labor, and professional groups have exceptional influence, policy is distorted.

However, many groups, including some of the public interest groups that we discussed earlier in this chapter, seek to help and represent less affluent and underserved citizens, including the homeless and the poor. While the distribution of representation by interest groups in the United States remains distorted, with the advantaged being better represented than the disadvantaged, there is reason to believe that the public increasingly recognizes the need for broad representation in a society based on strong interest-group representation.

Conclusion: Corrupt or Constructive?

Unquestionably, interest groups have come to wield increasing political power, and Americans' fear of these groups as a corrupting influence in politics has some basis in reality. With large treasuries to disburse and an inside track with public officials, they are potentially a distorting influence on the functioning of the political system. Broad national interests can be lost in the clamor of pressure-group activity and narrow self-interests. Interest groups also work out of public view, thus encouraging the popular belief that the public cannot adequately scrutinize their activities.

Not every group with a shared interest is self-interested, however. Like the proverbial concept of beauty, an interest group's "goodness" or "badness" is often in the eye of the beholder. To see only the biasing effects of interest groups is to perpetuate the myth of corrupting influence. Interest groups are also a healthy feature of and a positive force in the political process. They are organizations that give voice to the voiceless and represent the unrepresented. Advances for many minority groups, for the poor, the young, the aged, and others who are disadvantaged, and for farmers, laborers, and owners of small businesses, can be attributed in part to the effective activities of interest groups. Increasing numbers of interest groups support and fight for programs that benefit and contribute to our democratic process. They serve to supplement our representative body of elected officials by giving citizens an additional voice in government.

Critical Thinking

Is it a myth that interest groups are a corrupting influence in politics?

Few, if any, citizens are not represented either directly or indirectly by one or more interest groups, whether those groups are concerned with economic, social, or environmental issues.

Madison appropriately warned of the pitfalls of interest groups. He also argued that they are inevitable in any democratic system. We argue that the groups link citizens and public officials through corporate, labor, trade, and professional associations and through citizen activist groups. Such linkages may be worth the price of the real (and imagined) distortions that inevitably occur when interest groups are active in the policymaking process. Certainly, the groups are too useful to simply dismiss by invoking the myth of corrupting influence.

Tying It Together

FOCUS QUESTIONS RECAP

✳ What are the differences between interest groups and political action committees (PACs)?

✳ What factors determine the power of an interest group?

✳ What tools do interest groups use in attempting to influence the policymaking process?

✳ Do interest groups play a role in the representative process?

CHAPTER SUMMARY

1. Interest groups are organized groups of individuals who share one or more common goals and who seek to influence government decision making. Political action committees (PACs), cousin organizations of interest groups, serve as affiliated or independent organizations with the prime function of collecting and disbursing campaign contributions.

2. Political parties deal with both specific and general policy development. Interest groups usually focus on narrow policy areas. Although they may attempt to influence the outcome of certain elections, interest groups, unlike political parties, do not run candidates for elective office, their names do not appear on the ballot, and they do not attempt to control or operate government.

3. Types of interest groups include economic interest organizations, citizen activist groups, and government-related interest groups.

4. A lobbyist is an individual who works for a specific interest group or who serves as the spokesperson for a specific set of interests. Lobbyists engage in the act of lobbying—that is, they try to influence government decision making by persuading legislators and members of the executive branch to support certain policies or legislation.

5. A number of factors determine the power of an interest group. These factors include size, degree of unity, quality of leadership, information and expertise, money, and the degree to which the interest group monopolizes the policy area. In general, however, given different issues and different political environments, no single resource determines the success of an interest group. A group's influence is usually strongest when a combination of organizational resources is brought to bear on the policymaking process.

6. Tools used by interest groups in attempting to influence the policymaking process include the use of grassroots pressure as well as lobbying, electioneering (which includes financing and supporting campaigns through affiliated PACs), coalition building, and litigating.

7. Interest groups can pose problems for a democratic society because they often represent narrow interests that are biased toward the higher economic groups. Interest groups are important to the political process because they can and do focus our attention on important issues.

8. While interest groups can be a distorting influence on the political and governmental process, they are also a positive force, giving voice to the voiceless and representing the unrepresented. They serve to supplement the representative process by providing an additional voice in the policymaking process.

Key Terms

Interest group (221)
Public interest groups (223)
Single-issue group (223)
Lobbyist (225)
Political action committees (PACs) (226)

Free riders (231)
Lobbying (232)
Electioneering (235)
Coalition building (238)
Grassroots pressure (238)

 ## Net Work

Interest groups come in all shapes and sizes, including advocacy groups on hundreds of different issues representing different ideologies. For two sites that often have competing viewpoints on issues, see **www.aclu.org** and **www.conservative.org**.

Other interest-group sites dealing with specific issues that you may want to explore include the following:

Abortion

- National Right to Life Committee (**www.nrlc.org**)
- NARAL Pro-Choice America (**www.naral.org**)

Environment

- Sierra Club (**www.sierraclub.org**)
- Environmental Defense Fund (**www.edf.org**)

Gun control

- Center to Prevent Handgun Violence (**www.handguncontrol.org**)
- National Rifle Association (**www.nra.org**)

Women

- Eagle Forum (**www.eagleforum.org**)
- National Organization for Women (**www.now.org**)

As an exercise, select one issue from the above list and examine it from the point of view of two different interest groups. In what ways are the positions of the two groups the same as or different from each other? What are the merits of the opposing arguments?

9

Media and Politics

MYTH & REALITY

Do the media have the power to influence public opinion?

FOCUS QUESTIONS

* How have the media evolved over the past decade?
* What is news?
* How does media coverage affect people's attitudes?
* How do government officials shape the news?

Media and Politics   245
J ust two months before election day 2004, CBS broadcast a controver-
sial story about President George W. Bush on its *60 Minutes* Wednesday
newsmagazine. Dan Rather, the reporter on the story, claimed to have
documented proof from an anonymous source that a young George
Bush had used his political connections to join the Texas Air National Guard,
thereby avoiding the draft, and then again used his connections to cover up the
matter. As damaging as the story might have been to Bush's reelection, however,
it turned out to be far more damaging to CBS and Dan Rather. Within minutes
after the story had aired, authors of online journals went to work discrediting it.
In very short order, these "bloggers" demonstrated that the document was a
fake, a fact that CBS was forced to admit in the end.

To political conservatives, this was proof that CBS, Dan Rather, and, for that
matter, most of the mainstream media, were dominated by liberals intent on defeating the president. Even before this incident, more than 70 percent of self-
identified conservatives viewed news coverage as biased. What may have come as
a surprise to conservatives, however, was that their liberal counterparts shared
a similar assessment of the media: At the time, 66 percent of self-identified liberals saw a great deal or fair amount of bias in media coverage of politics. Of
course, even though the two groups agreed on the fact that there was bias, they
disagreed on the direction of that bias.[1]

In their attacks on the media, both sides in the dispute implicitly agreed that
the press plays a crucial role in American politics. But in what ways? In part, the
popular view of the power of the media rests on the *myth of media manipulation*:
the idea that television, radio, and the print media dominate and direct the
public's thinking about politics. The myth of media manipulation is not confined to any particular group in society; it is shared by Americans with widely
varying political perspectives. Conservatives worry about the effects on the public of what they see as a liberal conspiracy, and liberals often describe the media
as a capitalist plot serving the interests of the wealthy. In their own defense,
journalists say that they are simply reflecting the world as it is — serving as a mirror to society. They just cover the story. Thus, Roan Conrad, political editor for
NBC News, argued over two decades ago that "the news is what happens. . . .
The news is not a reporter's perception or explanation of what happens; it is
simply what happens."[2]

As you will see in this chapter, although the media's choice of stories does
much to define public concerns, the relationship between the media and public
opinion is not as straightforward as the myth, or Conrad, suggests. The media
cannot dictate the political beliefs of the country. At the same time, journalists
are not simply passive instruments through which events, called news, are transmitted. Interestingly, the standards by which journalists decide what is newsworthy often work to the advantage of officials and candidates who know how to use
the media to achieve policy and electoral goals.

The Rise of the Media

FOCUS QUESTION   HOW HAVE THE MEDIA EVOLVED OVER THE PAST DECADE?

Americans buy nearly 60 million newspapers and keep their television sets on for an average of more than six hours each day. They can choose from among 10,000 or so weekly and monthly periodicals, and there are almost 9,000 radio stations in the country. Moreover, the growth of the Internet is opening up an uncountable number of media sources for those who have access. The attentive media watcher faces an incessant flow of information on topics ranging from foreign affairs to domestic scandals. Yet it has not always been this way. A mere 170 years ago, news from Washington or the state capital arrived days, weeks, or even months after the events occurred, if it arrived at all.

The Early Days

Before 1830, the American press consisted of specialized publications designed to reach elite audiences. Many papers were simply organs of political parties or individual candidates. Appearing once or twice a week, these partisan papers rallied the party faithful and denounced political opponents, often through vicious personal attacks. The only alternative sources of news were commercial papers, which were designed for merchants and traders. The commercial papers provided extensive accounts of business activities, such as shipping dates, commodity prices, and business transactions, but they were short on politics and made no attempt to reach a wide audience.

With the publication in 1833 of the *New York Sun*, American publishing entered the age of mass journalism. Capitalizing on technological advances that made printing relatively fast and cheap, the *Sun* was the first paper to appeal successfully to the public at large. It was sold on street corners for a penny a copy, and it and its many imitators (together they became known as the **penny press**) cultivated readerships in the thousands. A breezy style and an emphasis on local news, especially scandalous events, ensured the papers' popularity. Each vied fiercely with the others to produce the most sensational stories. At one point the staff of the *Sun* came up with a hoax about life on the moon.[3]

Toward the end of the nineteenth century, the emphasis on sensationalism became even more pronounced. Joseph Pulitzer, a crusading spirit who owned the *New York World*, and William Randolph Hearst, owner of the *New York Journal*, created **yellow journalism** — named for the "Yellow Kid" comic strip, which appeared first in the *World* and then in the *Journal*. Yellow journalism utilized large, bold headlines, illustrations, cartoons, and color features to promote its tales of scandal and corruption. Not content with reporting the news, both Pulitzer and Hearst often made news by committing the considerable resources of their papers to various political causes. For instance, Hearst is usually credited with arousing in the American public the strong anti-Spanish feelings that led to the Spanish-American War. Just before the war, Hearst sent an artist to Cuba to cover

Penny press The term for the first generation of newspapers with mass popular appeal. The name comes from the *New York Sun*, which was sold for a penny a copy in the mid-1800s.

Yellow journalism A type of journalism that flourished in the late nineteenth century and whose popularity was based on sensationalized stories of scandal and corruption.

Read All About It

The modern mass media were born in America with the creation of the penny press. Sold on street corners by young boys and girls, like those pictured here, the penny press specialized in sensationalism.

Critical Thinking

Is yellow journalism making a comeback?

the conflict between Spain and Cuba. When the artist wired that war did not seem likely, Hearst replied, "Please remain. You furnish the pictures. I will furnish the war."[4] Many people believe that he did just that.

While Hearst and Pulitzer inflamed public opinion with their sensational appeals, a new style of journalism was developing. A conservative paper, the *New York Times*, attacked the excesses of yellow journalism as indecent and stressed objectivity in its reporting. Newspapers, according to Adolph Ochs, owner of the *Times*, had the responsibility to "give news impartially, without fear or favor, regardless of any party, sect or interest involved."[5] Although its circulation was small compared with that of the yellow press, the *Times* became a standard by which journalism was judged, and objectivity became the goal of serious journalists. As any trip to the supermarket will show, however, yellow journalism did not die; it just became less mainstream.

The Broadcast Media

Even as newspapers were undergoing change, the technology of the broadcast media was being developed. The first regularly scheduled radio station, KDKA in Pittsburgh, began operation in 1920. Its owner, Westinghouse, the nation's leading manufacturer of home receivers, initially viewed it as a means of creating a market for its products. Most of the early radio stations were owned by nonprofit institutions and were seen as public service entities designed to educate citizens for life in a democratic culture. In 1928, however, the newly created Federal Radio Commission (the predecessor to the Federal Communications Commission) reallocated frequency assignments in a way that greatly favored commercial owners. The commission reasoned that nonprofit owners would not act in the public interest because they were not motivated by profits. Nonprofit stations quickly disappeared, to be replaced by commercial broadcasters that linked advertising to immensely popular and profitable entertainment programs.

Critical Thinking

Is news and public affairs programming compatible with for-profit media ownership?

Although broadcasters stressed entertainment, government leaders were quick to grasp the political potential of radio. During the Great Depression, President Franklin D. Roosevelt employed the medium skillfully to deliver his famous fireside chats. Speaking in a warm and informal manner, Roosevelt sought to reassure his millions of listeners by making his broadcasts sound like friendly discussions. Roosevelt demonstrated the vast possibilities of radio, as well as its potential for overt manipulation. During the 1944 election campaign, for instance, Roosevelt learned that his opponent, Thomas Dewey, had purchased airtime immediately following his own. Although he was scheduled to speak for fifteen minutes, Roosevelt stopped after fourteen. Millions of puzzled listeners turned their dials away from the silence and missed Dewey's address.

Despite the interest shown by political leaders, most broadcasters resisted programming news shows until the fledgling CBS network entered the business. Its owner, William Paley, saw news as a cheap source of programming and a means of competing with NBC, the more established radio network. His team of journalists, including Edward R. Murrow and Eric Sevareid, quickly established a reputation for superior news coverage. Murrow's broadcasts from London during World War II captured the imagination of the entire country, making Murrow a national celebrity.

Like radio, television was from the beginning a commercial venture that stressed entertainment and advertising. (Appropriately, Philo T. Farnsworth, the inventor of television, used a dollar sign as his first test pattern.) Throughout the 1950s, each of the three television networks — CBS, NBC, and ABC — provided one fifteen-minute news program five evenings a week. Even CBS, which had pioneered radio news, was reluctant to use valuable television airtime for news and public affairs, preferring the popular and extraordinarily profitable quiz shows.

The situation changed in 1960, however, when all three networks televised the debates between presidential candidates John F. Kennedy and Richard M. Nixon. Although there is still disagreement over which candidate won, the debates definitely demonstrated the commercial potential of news and public affairs programming by drawing an audience of 60 to 75 million viewers. News programs ceased to be viewed simply as a means of improving a network's public image. Instead, the networks began competing to produce the most highly rated news programs, using such advanced technology as small hand-held cameras, wireless microphones, and satellite transmissions. As news coverage broadened, the audiences grew into the millions, and a majority of Americans came to depend on television as their prime source of news. Moreover, for the majority of Americans, television is the most believable source of news.[6]

Diversity and Concentration

Although the media offer a staggering array of choices, merely reciting the number of outlets can be deceiving. The real issue, say media critics, is the increasing concentration of ownership in a few hands—a change that threatens to limit diversity of expression. About 80 percent of all daily newspapers published in the United States are owned by one of the large chains. The largest of all, Gannett, owns ninety-nine newspapers, including *USA Today*. (Gannett also owns twenty-two television stations.) Furthermore, even though the number of newspapers has stayed about the same in recent years, newspaper competition has decreased markedly. Only 2 percent of American cities have more than one newspaper.[7]

Concentrated ownership and influence are even greater in the television markets. About 85 percent of the nation's commercial over-the-air television stations are affiliated with ABC, CBS, or NBC.[8] The three major networks, in turn, are owned by large conglomerates with multiple media interests that combine publishing, broadcasting, and Hollywood production studios.

All is not well for the networks, however. The rise of the Fox network and, more importantly, the growth of cable television have substantially eroded network dominance. Where once the network news programs were the major source of political information for most Americans, they now trail local news and cable news programming as regular sources of information about public affairs.

The enormous growth of cable, direct satellite transmission, and a host of developing technologies that combine video and computer processing with microwave transmissions suggest a future of almost infinite choices. But who will control these outlets? Many observers believe that the technological revolution is destroying the centralized and concentrated media, which are exemplified by the major networks, and paving the way for a more democratic means of information production.[9] Others, however, expect the future to be much like the past, with major corporations becoming multimedia giants that will control the worldwide production, distribution, and technology of the new media.

During the past few years, a new medium, the Internet and the World Wide Web, has grown to challenge the old alignment of media sources. Many Internet enthusiasts assume that as the technology goes digital, the ability of users to produce high-quality programming at minimal cost will simply overwhelm the current media. Thus, John Perry Barlow dismisses the rise of huge entertainment conglomerates like Disney and AOL Time Warner, arguing that they are "merely rearranging deck chairs on the *Titanic*."[10]

Certainly the Internet is a revolutionary technology with unparalleled potential, but its potential has not been lost on media owners. Increasingly, a key component of media conglomerates is the ability to provide content for the World Wide Web. Disney already owns a substantial interest in the popular Infoseek search engine, for example.

Even blogging (posting an online weblog), assumed by many to be a check against these mainstream conglomerates, has become increasingly mainstreamed itself. The medium catapulted onto the national scene in 2003 after bloggers

Critical Thinking

What will happen to the Internet if the media conglomerates come to dominate it?

TOLES © 2000 The Washington Post. Reprinted with permission of Universal Press
Syndicate. All Rights Reserved.

circumvented traditional media channels to report on controversial, seemingly
pro-segregation remarks made by Senate Majority Leader Trent Lott. When
these reports, which were eventually picked up by the mainstream press, forced
Senator Lott to give up his leadership position, bloggers were hailed as pioneers
in democratizing the delivery of news to the American people. But these days,
the bloggers' world is increasingly populated by those with ties to the mainstream media — think tanks, interest groups, trade associations, media outlets,
and even politicians have their own online diaries. Moreover, as more and more
blogs begin to accept advertising, the blog sphere has started to look increasingly familiar.

At this point it is simply too early to tell whether the Internet will challenge
the current media or simply become an arm of the media conglomerates. What
is clear, however, is that the Internet is a target of media owners, who are working to integrate it with their other holdings.

Government Regulation

The American mass media are freer from government restrictions than the mass
media in any other nation. Nevertheless, the government exercises some control, especially over radio and television. In the case of printed materials, regulation applies only to obscenity and libel (see Chapter 4, on rights and liberties).

POLITICS & POPULAR CULTURE

Fake News

For many Americans, especially those under the age of thirty, comedy programs have become an important source of news about politics and political campaigns. Indeed, in 2003 the Pew Research Center released a poll that indicated that, for this age group, comedy programs rival traditional news outlets as sources of information about candidates and elections. Among those under thirty, 21 percent reported that they regularly learn about presidential candidates from comedy shows. Additionally, 50 percent of those under thirty professed that they sometimes learn about the campaigns from comedy shows.

That presidential candidates and election year activities would be the subject of comedy is hardly new. Political leaders have long been the butt of comedians' jokes. Late-night talk show hosts Jay Leno and David Letterman often pepper their monologues with jokes and barbs aimed at politicians, but neither of them devotes an entire show to satirizing our leaders. Not so with Comedy Central's *Daily Show*, however. In a thirty-minute show four nights a week, Jon Stewart portrays the acerbic anchor of a mock news program. Using comic interviews and video clips drawn from mainstream news programs, Stewart lampoons politicians, punctuating the segments with a cutting wit and a bag of clever deadpan facial expressions. The satire and political parody are often biting and the show's victims are inevitably portrayed as buffoons. Through it all, Stewart maintains the poise that has earned him the title "the most trusted man in fake news." Indeed, Stewart eagerly embraces the description of his show as fake news—

his news is meant to entertain, even if people do learn a thing or two in between laughs.

But what happens when the line between real and fake news becomes blurred? Several years ago, the U.S. Department of Education released a video designed to promote the Bush administration's "No Child Left Behind" education act. Aired by more than 300 television stations, the video was structured like a news report, complete with a voice-over narrator who claimed to be reporting from Washington. Local television stations were also provided with a recommended lead-in speech introducing the narrator and her story. This arrangement clearly implied that the voice was that of a (presumably objective) reporter, and that viewers were watching a genuine news story. Meanwhile, at about the same time, it came to light that the department had also paid Armstrong Williams, a nationally syndicated journalist, $240,000 to promote the same law on his television show. The department failed to inform the public that the video information came from a government source, and neither the government nor Williams made it clear that he was being paid to promote the law on air.

In truth, such activities are not new—previous administrations have wandered into similar gray areas before—but these activities do raise interesting questions about what we see and where it comes from. Indeed, the next time you turn on your television you may find yourself wondering: What is the real fake news?

Source: Pew Research Center poll; www.gao.gov/decisions/appro/304228.pdf.

Government Licensing. Because of the limited number of frequencies over which radio and television signals can be transmitted, Congress created the Federal Communications Commission (FCC) in 1934 to monitor and regulate the use of the airwaves. Besides assigning frequencies so that stations' signals do not interfere with one another, the FCC issues licenses, which must be renewed every five years for television and every seven years for radio. According to statute, license renewals depend on "satisfactory performance" that "serve[s] the public interest, convenience, and necessity." The vagueness of that mandate gives the FCC tremendous discretion in awarding or denying license renewals, but as a matter of practice it has denied few applications and has exercised little control over the content of broadcasts. Illustrative of the FCC position is its refusal, in the face of heavy lobbying by advocacy groups, to require television broadcasters to present only family programming during the early evening hours; instead, it accepted a rating system created and managed by the networks.

Equal-time rule A Federal Communications Commission rule that requires a broadcaster who permits one candidate to campaign on the station to provide all other candidates for the same office with equal time at identical rates.

Equal Time. The most significant FCC requirement is the **equal-time rule**. This provision stipulates that broadcasters who permit a candidate for political office to campaign on the station (including through paid advertisements) must allow all other candidates for the same office equal time at identical rates. Recently, industry leaders and others have pushed for the relaxation or elimination of this rule, arguing that the increased competition among the numerous radio and television stations ensures access for all points of view. Indeed, critics of the rule note that electronic media are far more competitive than newspapers. Very few cities in the United States are served by more than one newspaper, but most citizens have several choices among stations, especially since the introduction of cable television. Although the Reagan administration supported this argument for deregulation, Congress has not significantly altered the equal-time rule.

Making News

FOCUS QUESTION   WHAT IS NEWS?

Prominently displayed on the front page of the *New York Times* is the company motto: "All the News That's Fit to Print." Admirable as this sentiment may be, it is not, nor can it be, true. Indeed, a more accurate rephrasing of the motto provided by wags is "all the news that fits." The argument that the news is simply what happens is unrealistic. No form of mass media can carry every newsworthy event; all are constrained by costs and by the availability of space and time. For instance, the average daily newspaper fills approximately 62 percent of its space with advertising, leaving a mere 38 percent (called the news hole) to be shared by news accounts, human-interest stories, and pure entertainment features.

Network television news is even more limited. Each half-hour program contains only eighteen minutes of news and human-interest stories. Thus, the news is not simply what is happening out there; it must be picked from a multitude of events, only a few of which will be covered. What, then, is news? Perhaps the best explanation is that "news is what reporters, editors, and producers decide is news."[11]

Although the basis of news judgment often seems vague and unarticulated, it is possible to identify the criteria that are most often used in selecting stories.[12]

Critical Thinking

What are the consequences of defining news as conflict?

- Newsworthy stories must be *timely and novel*. They must be what reporters call *breaking stories*. The routine is considered unworthy of coverage, even though it may have a significant impact on people's lives. As a former editor of the *New York Sun* put it, "When a dog bites a man, that is not news, because it happens so often. But if a man bites a dog, that is news."

- Newsworthiness is heightened by *the presence of violence, conflict, disaster, or scandal*. Violent crime, for example, was a staple of the penny press and continues to dominate contemporary news. Even nonviolent conflict makes news. Larry Speakes, deputy press secretary during the Reagan administration, once noted that no one pays attention when 100 members of Congress come out of a White House meeting and say that the president's program is great. "But if one says it stinks, that's news."

- *Familiarity* is also an important element of newsworthiness. Events are more likely to be covered if they involve individuals whom the public already knows. Approximately 85 percent of the domestic news stories covered by television and news magazines involve well-known people — mostly those holding official positions.13 Unknown people are most newsworthy when they are victims of crime or natural disasters.

To this list might be added the availability of individuals for interviews. Reporters rely heavily on interviews rather than printed documents. This dependence on the interview results partly from the need to personalize the news. Interviews with adversaries also increase the sense of conflict, adding a dramatic element to the narrative while preserving the reporter's image of objectivity by presenting the story in the familiar point-counterpoint format. Whatever the cause, the result is a bias in favor of those who are willing and able to provide the pithy comment.

Critical Thinking

Has the growth of news programming improved the quality of reporting?

These criteria mainly stress ways of keeping the audience interested. Because media outlets make their profits from selling their audience to advertisers, they must keep their ratings or circulations high. Indeed, cynics often claim that news is "that which is printed on the back of advertisements."[14] Ironically, with the growth of cable and the Internet, the fierce competition produced by the proliferation of twenty-four-hour news programming has led to a relaxation of the standards for determining what constitutes news. As Tom Brokaw of NBC News said, "We get one crack, we've got to get them, they've got to stay with us."[15] To attract them and keep them, media outlets increasingly rely on feature stories, or the so-called soft news. In the case of NBC, this has meant an increasing emphasis on health and science stories. Moreover, the need to attract and hold an audience has blurred the line between newscasts and entertainment programming. Most of the programming for the all-news outlets is provided by talk shows and infotainment programs that stress opinion, not news. These shows are not designed to report news or explore issues. As Chris Matthews, the host of CNBC's *Hardball*, admitted, "People aren't tuning me in for news. They are tuning me in as an alternative to *Friends*."[16] Shows like *Hardball* and *Entertainment Tonight* are entertainment shows with the feel of tabloids that sometimes masquerade as news outlets. Even the major networks are increasingly relying on entertainment features by, for instance, using news programming to promote their reality shows. As you will see, this concern for audience appeal has an impact on the way politics is conducted in the United States.

The Effects of the Mass Media

FOCUS QUESTION   HOW DOES MEDIA COVERAGE AFFECT PEOPLE'S ATTITUDES?

For many citizens, concern about media manipulation stems from a belief that the media have an extraordinary effect on public opinion. Critics of television have been particularly prone to view it as dictating the attitudes of a largely passive audience. Indeed, the argument goes, if the media were not influential, why would companies spend so much money on advertisements? Social scientists who have examined the issue are far less certain of the media's impact. In fact, contrary to the myth, most research suggests that the media by and large fail to change people's settled political beliefs. More precisely, individuals who already hold beliefs on particular issues or candidates are unlikely to change their minds as a result of what they are told by the media.

The media's power to change established political beliefs is limited because people exercise selective exposure, absorbing only information that agrees with their existing beliefs.[17] Such information is more easily incorporated than data that contradict preconceived ideas; those data may be dismissed or entirely ignored. Existing beliefs also influence the way people interpret what they see — a process known as selective perception. Thus, a candidate's actions may be perceived by supporters as demonstrating complete integrity, while being perceived by opponents as demonstrating complete dishonesty.[18]

Nevertheless, the media are capable of swaying individual beliefs. In matters where a person has neither experience nor a firmly held opinion, the information and interpretation supplied by the media may shape that person's political attitude. Citizens who lack knowledge on a particular subject often adopt the views expressed by media commentators.[19] More importantly, television news is a particularly significant force in shaping the public's attribution of responsibility. Whom the public blames when things go wrong is influenced by the way television frames (presents) the issues. For instance, televised coverage of a particular political issue will be predominantly either episodic or thematic. Episodic coverage of an issue, which is exemplified by live, on-the-scene reporting that focuses on the individual (e.g., a homeless person or the victims of terrorism), encourages the public to attribute responsibility to the private individuals involved. Thematic reporting, on the other hand, puts the issue in a larger, more abstract context and provides in-depth background on it. Stories that are framed

Covering One of Its Own

In the fall of 2005, media attention turned inward as *New York Times* reporter Judith Miller, shown here speaking to her colleagues outside a U.S. District Courthouse, became not the reporter but the subject of reports. Miller became the subject of a federal investigation for reporting a leak on Central Intelligence Agency information. After refusing to identify the source of the leak, Miller spent twelve weeks in prison, released only after her source waived the pledge of confidentiality.

in the thematic style lead the public to attribute responsibility to societal forces or the motives and actions of public officials. Thus, perceptions about whether public officials should be held responsible for problems are influenced not only by what television reports but also by how it covers the issue.[20]

Setting the Agenda

Critical Thinking

What do we know about the world that we do not learn from the media?

Increasingly, the media also influence the political agenda and the conduct of politicians. When deciding what to cover, journalists focus on some aspects of public life and ignore others. Because the media are often the public's only source of knowledge, what journalists do not report as news might as well not have happened. As Austin Ranney suggests, the appropriate riddle for the media age may well be this: "If a tree falls in a forest but the event is not videotaped or broadcast on the nightly news, has it really happened?"[21]

When the public knows events and issues well, the media have less impact on its attitudes. For example, in a study conducted in 1981 and 1982, individuals who were exposed to stories alleging that the nation's defenses were weak grew more concerned about national defense. Stories about inflation, however, had little effect on their opinions, undoubtedly because inflation affects everyone personally.[22] Thus, the media wield the most influence in shaping the public agenda when the events and issues are either outside an individual's experience or new to the society.

Priming The capacity of the media to isolate particular issues, events, or themes in the news as the criteria for evaluating politicians.

Of particular importance is the effect that the media's agenda setting has on the public's evaluation of candidates and public officials. Studies examining the effect of media have identified a process called **priming**, which "refers to the capacity of the media to isolate particular issues, events, or themes in the news as the criteria for evaluating politicians."[23] The more attention the media give to an issue, the greater that issue's weight in the formation of public evaluations of candidates and public officials. By highlighting some issues and ignoring others, the media influence the standards by which people judge governments, public officials, and candidates.

Conducting Politics in the Media: Old and New

Politicians are much more attuned to the media than the public is. The conduct of politics in the United States is changing as candidates and public officials increasingly tailor their activities to meet journalists' needs. Thus, they plan and time speeches, rallies, and personal appearances to win maximum media coverage, especially on television. To further facilitate coverage, campaign staffers supply the media with daily schedules, advance copies of speeches, and access to telephones and fax machines. If the campaign is managed well, it exploits the reporters' need for a story and influences the content of news coverage.

Pseudo-events Events, such as speeches, rallies, and personal appearances, that are staged by politicians simply to win maximum media coverage.

All these efforts are in vain, of course, if the campaign cannot get reporters to cover the candidate. Therefore, to attract reporters, campaigns routinely create **pseudo-events**—staged events that are intended to produce media coverage. Pseudo-events are often presented with the special needs of television in mind. Knowing that television producers dislike "talking heads" (footage of the candidate simply delivering a speech), campaign organizers work to provide interesting and symbolic visuals for the evening news. Whether candidates visit farms to indicate their concern for the family farmer or visit retirement centers to emphasize their commitment to aging Americans, the picture is the thing.

Even with all the planning, candidates have become increasingly frustrated with media coverage. Although the coverage is extensive, the established media give candidates little direct access to the public. As political scientist Thomas Patterson has pointed out, the candidates have become voiceless. For every minute that the candidates spoke on the three major networks' evening news shows in 2000, the reporters covering them talked for seven minutes. In 2000, between Labor Day and election day, George W. Bush and Al Gore spoke on the three networks for a combined total of twenty-three and twenty-two minutes, respectively. Most of this time was in increments of seven seconds or less, known as sound bites.[24]

In order to reach the public directly, political candidates have adopted a variety of techniques designed to bypass the established media. One such technique, the video news release (VNR), is a newslike report or interview paid for by the candidate and delivered to local television stations. By renting time on a satellite transponder, the candidate can be interviewed by local television reporters all over the country without leaving a studio. The local stations get the chance to interview a national political figure at no cost to themselves, and the candidate covers several cities quickly. This technique also has the advantage that local anchors are seldom as hard on candidates as the national reporters covering the campaign and are more likely to let the candidate talk directly to the audience.

Besides making extensive use of VNRs, the presidential candidates are turning to what have been called "the new media": radio call-in shows, early morning television programs, televised town meetings, and late-night entertainment productions. The significance of this for candidates can be seen by looking at Al Gore and George W. Bush's appearances in 2000 on the *Late Show with David Letterman.* Both candidates talked for approximately thirteen minutes on the show. Those thirteen minutes were, for both candidates, more time than the three networks combined gave them for the entire month of September. Candidates are also increasingly making use of the Internet. Every major candidate now has a homepage outlining his or her background and positions on the issues, and giving instructions for making an online contribution.

For the candidates, these new media offer irresistible opportunities to circumvent the press and speak directly to the American people. President Clinton described the advantages of the new media best in March 1993 when he told a group of radio and television correspondents, "You know why I can stiff you on press conferences? Because Larry King liberated me by giving me to the American people directly."[25]

Besides affecting the candidates' conduct, media-oriented politics also diverts attention from issues and draws it to campaign strategies. Because, as we have seen, journalists define news as involving conflict and personalities, they pay special heed to the "horse-race" characteristics of elections. Media attention focuses on who is winning and why. During the 2000 presidential election, a full 80 percent of the televised news stories focused on candidates' changes in tactics, which candidates had the most money, and internal troubles in the candidates' campaign organizations. When issues are discussed, the question is how the candidate's position on these issues will help or hurt the campaign. For reporters, elections are simply games in which candidates devise tactics to defeat their opponents. Foremost among the tools for reporting campaign strategy is the public opinion poll. Even though polls are of little value to voters other than those making book on the election, the media saturate their audience with frequent and often hyped poll results. The public opinion poll is the press's version of the pseudo-event; the press creates and pays for polls and then covers them as news.[26]

Critical Thinking

Is the public well served by the horse-race coverage of elections?

Of course, journalists defend this preoccupation with strategy by arguing that the audience prefers to hear about the campaign rather than about the issues. Whether or not they are correct about that, it is apparent that discussions of campaign strategies appeal to reporters, editors, and producers for several reasons. These stories are easier to do than more substantial reports because reporting on campaign tactics requires little knowledge of complex political issues. Indeed, horse-race stories can easily be reduced to the simple question of who is winning and who is losing. More importantly, reporting on strategy and mechanics provides the kind of dramatic themes that keep an audience interested.

Campaigning in Cyberspace

The Internet has increasingly become an important tool for reaching voters. Here Howard Dean launches his bid for the Democratic party's presidential nomination standing before a banner clearly displaying his website. For Dean, as well as other candidates, cyberspace in the 2004 election was a crucial way of attracting voters and campaign contributions.

Although there is no unanimity of opinion on the effects of horse-race coverage, many observers believe that the emphasis on elections as games has a detrimental effect on public opinion. By highlighting tactics and strategies, the media present a consistent image of candidates as political opportunists who are interested only in winning elections. According to many observers, the constant repetition of that vision simply increases the public's mistrust of candidates.

The Uneasy Alliance Between Government and the Media

FOCUS QUESTION   HOW DO GOVERNMENT OFFICIALS SHAPE THE NEWS?

Government officials and journalists are often portrayed as adversaries locked in combat, each trying to best the other. This is an accurate picture when their goals conflict — when, for instance, journalists, wanting the big scoop on governmental waste, fraud, or incompetence that will bring them instant fame, confront government officials, who want the press to present their actions in the most favorable light possible. At other times, however, journalists' and officials' goals overlap, and the two groups cooperate. Journalists court officials to obtain the information that is their livelihood, and government officials woo the media in order to build public support for their policies. As veteran newscaster Walter Cronkite once remarked, "Politics and media are inseparable. It is only the politicians and the media that are incompatible."[27]

Furthermore, government officials are avid consumers of journalism — more so than the general public — and this fact creates additional incentives for cooperation. The mass media provide an important communication link among officials, informing them of what others in and out of government are doing and saying. When, for instance, King Hussein of Jordan wanted to respond to American criticism that he was favoring Iraq in the 1991 Gulf War, he bypassed normal diplomatic channels and responded to President George H. W. Bush by appearing on CNN.

Given this mutual dependence, the media and government form an uneasy alliance. Journalists report the actions of government officials, particularly the president and the more prominent members of Congress, while government officials attempt to shape the content of news.

Covering the President

Nowhere is the uneasy alliance between the media and government more apparent than in the coverage of the White House. Almost everything the president does becomes news. Even trivial events receive wide coverage. For presidents, this extensive coverage represents a valuable means of reaching the American public on a daily basis, but it is also a source of frustration. The frustration undoubtedly increases throughout a president's term. As political scientist Fred Smoller has demonstrated, television portrayals of a president become more negative as the president's term progresses.[28] John Kennedy undoubtedly spoke for all presidents when, in response to a question concerning some particularly critical accounts of his administration, he claimed to be "reading more and enjoying it less."[29]

Because the media provide the vital link between the president and the public, and because, from the president's perspective, journalists cannot be counted on to get their stories right, the White House goes to great lengths to put its view across to the media. Indeed, about one-third of the high-level White House staff are directly involved in media relations.[30]

Most of the responsibility for dealing with the media falls to the president's press secretary, who gives a daily briefing to some seventy-five reporters and photographers who regularly cover the White House. Under constant pressure from their editors to file stories on the president, these reporters rely extensively on these briefings and on press releases provided by the press secretary. On occasion, the press secretary may also arrange interviews with the president or provide photo opportunities — a chance to take photographs of the president, although not to ask questions. Most White House reporters simply repeat the information given them by the press secretary. According to Bill Moyers, who was press secretary during Lyndon Johnson's administration, the White House press corps "is more stenographic than entrepreneurial in its approach to news gathering."[31] As a result, presidents are less subjects of news coverage than they are sources of news.

Press Conferences. Presidents communicate with the public through press conferences. Although press conferences often seem spontaneous, they are in fact highly structured events that allow the president a great deal of control. Typically, these thirty-minute affairs begin with a short statement. This enables the president to speak directly to the public. It also reduces the time available for questioning and focuses the audience's attention on a subject of the president's choosing.

Careful preparation and rehearsal further strengthen presidential control of press conferences. Days, or even weeks, before a press conference, the president's staff prepares a list of the questions that are most likely to be asked and then provides written answers so that the president can study and rehearse them. Ronald Reagan, for instance, held mock news conferences. Furthermore, presidents can and do frequently call on reporters who are known to be friendly to their administration. Such reporters are far more likely than others to ask easy questions, or even to ask questions furnished (planted) by the White House. At Reagan press conferences, reporters thought to be sympathetic to the administration, called the "known friendlies," were seated in front and to the president's right. If a line of questioning became uncomfortable, Reagan needed only to "go to the right."[32]

Though press conferences can be a valuable tool, they still pose risks. Even though they have a high level of control over what questions are asked and by whom, presidents cannot avoid embarrassing or politically charged queries. Few presidents are satisfied with press conferences as an institution, and most take part in them with some misgivings. Indeed, during his first year in office, President Clinton sought to avoid the traditional press conference by combining new technologies and the new media, which had proved so useful in the election campaign. For instance, the White House quickly implemented methods of making the full text of speeches and presidential proposals available electronically (through the Internet) to circumvent the filtering influence of press summaries. The administration also made frequent use of satellite press conferences with local journalists across the country and satellite media tours during which top administration officials gave five-minute interviews to local reporters.

Going Public. In addition to making use of a large staff dedicated to managing media relations in Washington, presidents increasingly try to shape press coverage by taking their policy proposals directly to the public. This strategy, known as "going public," has the president and often senior members of the administration fanning out across the country to give policy speeches. Most importantly, however, the strategy involves circumventing the national media by providing local reporters, not used to covering national politics, with opportunities to report firsthand on national political figures. Not surprisingly, the local press tends to be far less critical of presidents than are the national media.

Done well, going public can be a very effective strategy, garnering not only good press but also public support. In 2001, President George W. Bush, for instance, skillfully used this strategy to convince Congress that his proposed tax cuts were necessary. On the other hand, a president who calls for public response

ASKED & ANSWERED

ASKED: What are leaks and where do they come from?

ANSWERED: We have all read or heard stories of a brewing White House scandal, an impending resignation from the administration, a policy proposal under consideration, or a disagreement among policymakers that gets attributed to some unnamed source. Sometimes the source is described as "knowledgeable," "close to the decision makers," or even a "high White House official," and, whomever the source, the information he or she provides is often described as a "leak." But what exactly is a leak, and why would someone use this method to convey information to the press?

Although there is no precise definition of a leak, Stephen Hess best defines the term as the "premature unauthorized partial disclosure" of information. To understand why individuals leak information requires an examination of motive. Some leaks (ego leaks) come from people who want to demonstrate how important they are, how much they are "in the know" in the political world. Other leaks (goodwill leaks) are an attempt to curry favor with a reporter in hopes that in the future the favor will be repaid. Alternatively, still others (animus leaks) may be part of an ongoing conflict between policymakers and as such are designed to embarrass an adversary. Finally, some leaks (whistle-blower leaks) may be the result of a person's frustration at his or her inability to use proper channels to correct what is perceived as a wrong being done by the government. Of course, there are many variations on these basic types and often a leak serves more than one purpose.

Although presidents have long decried leaks, they, or people authorized by them, are often the sources of stories from unnamed officials. The information they provide is called a "plant," which Hess defines as a "premature authorized partial disclosure" of information. Presidents authorize the release of information this way for a variety of reasons. Often, presidents use reporters to send up "trial balloons." For example, a story about a proposal under consideration is planted with a reporter. If the public or Congress reacts negatively, the president can disclaim the story and drop the proposal, all the while denying that there was any basis to the story. This gives the president what is called "plausible deniability." Alternatively, a president, or someone authorized by the president, may plant a story in order to discredit a competing policy proposal or a political opponent. Plants, like leaks, have many justifications.

Washington is rife with both leaks and plants, which is not always a bad thing: While leaks and plants always serve the purposes of those who release the information, they can also serve the democratic process by opening up matters of public concern for debate and discussion. But whatever the benefits or drawbacks, we can be certain that leaks and plants will continue to be part of American government; as the late journalist James Reston so famously said, "A government is the only known vessel that leaks from the top."

Source: Stephen Hess, *The Government/Press Connection: Press Officers and Their Offices* (Washington, D.C.: The Brookings Institution, 1984).

too often may find the public losing interest. This may be what happened to President Bush in 2005 when he and several top administration officials crisscrossed the nation in a "60 Stops in 60 Days" tour to promote his Social Security reform plan. Although his views were well covered by the local press, the tactic failed to move the plan in Congress.[33]

Covering Congress

The media do not seem to pay as much attention to Congress as they do to the executive branch. To some extent, this apparent imbalance is due to the nature of the institution itself. Unlike the administration, Congress has no single leader who can be expected to speak authoritatively, although its members are generally more willing to talk and far less secretive than officials of the executive branch. Reporters cope with the multiple voices of Congress by concentrating their attention on party leaders, committee chairs, and others who hold key leadership positions or who are clearly identified as experts on a particular issue. As a result, many senators and representatives receive little or no national media attention. To political scientist Stephen Hess, such focus suggests that "where you sit determines how often you will be photographed."[34]

Illustrating the standards for defining news, coverage of Congress emphasizes partisan conflict and scandal. Policy accomplishments are generally ignored or trivialized. Debates over policy questions are most often described as power struggles, and compromise is characterized as unprincipled behavior motivated by electoral concerns.

Despite these constraints, individual members of Congress often receive favorable attention from parts of the media, especially their home-state media, which often depend heavily on their local senators and representatives to provide a regional perspective on national issues. Many members even become regular contributors to their local media, writing news columns and producing broadcast-quality radio and television tapes for distribution within their constituency.

Critical Thinking

Do the media present an accurate picture of Congress?

Covering the Courts

The branch of government that is least covered by the media is the courts. Although specific decisions of the U.S. Supreme Court may receive substantial media attention, most decisions go unreported. When decisions are reported, the discussion is often superficial, concentrating, again, on who won and who lost.

The complex nature of judicial decisions and the specialized knowledge necessary to interpret them make judicial opinions particularly subject to misinterpretation by journalists, and justices often complain about such misinterpretation. Nevertheless, justices also remain indifferent to the needs of journalists. For instance, they do not hold press conferences or grant interviews to explain their decisions. Reporters are expected to read the decisions and draw their own conclusions. Most justices accept Justice William Brennan's observation that their opinions "must stand on their own merits without embellishment or comment from the judges who write or join them."[35]

Critical Thinking

Should the federal courts be open to television coverage?

Meet the Press

Although most members of Congress receive little national media attention, congressional leaders are frequently featured. Pictured here is Senate Democratic Minority Leader Harry Reid speaking at a press conference held by a bipartisan group of Senate leaders, who used the press conference to announce an agreement on an overhaul of U.S. immigration laws.

Conclusion: The Great Manipulator?

We began this chapter by noting the general belief that the mass media have dramatically altered the conduct of American politics. But the increasingly sophisticated technology that made possible inexpensive newspapers and then the transmission of voice and images over the airwaves also changed the media. Slowly, newspapers began to emphasize objective reporting of public events. Similarly, radio and television turned into important sources of news, but only after it became apparent that there was an audience for such programming.

Along with the development of the mass media has come the fear, expressed as the myth of the manipulative media, that Americans are in danger of being indoctrinated by journalists. This myth exaggerates the power of the mass media to alter established political opinions. Citizens are not so susceptible to being told what to think as the myth suggests; they are not uncritical receptors of the media product. Nevertheless, the media do play an important role in framing the issues and setting the political agenda. Journalism may not change political attitudes, but it does have a significant effect on what people think is important and how they form political judgments. In many cases, the choices that journalists make define the political reality.

Furthermore, the mass media have greatly affected the conduct of political campaigns and government business. The media do not simply hold up a mirror to these processes; the reporters and cameras are not invisible observers. On the contrary, media coverage introduces distortions. However, there is little evidence that these distortions are journalistic attempts to manipulate the news. In fact, journalists often feel that they are the ones being manipulated when political candidates and public officials attempt to use them to get their stories across to the public.

Tying It Together

FOCUS QUESTIONS RECAP

✳ How have the media evolved over the past decade?

✳ What is news?

✳ How does media coverage affect people's attitudes?

✳ How do government officials shape the news?

CHAPTER SUMMARY

1. Early American newspapers were either organs of the political parties or commercial papers that reported business news to merchants. True mass media did not come into being until the 1830s, with the rise of the sensationalist penny press. Radio and then television developed initially as entertainment media. Only slowly did they come to be purveyors of news and public affairs programming.

2. The American mass media consist of thousands of alternative outlets. Nevertheless, critics worry that the increasingly concentrated ownership of media outlets threatens the diversity of information. Few cities have more than one newspaper and more than 85 percent of the local television stations are affiliated with one of the three major networks, which in turn are owned by huge conglomerates, comprising media outlets that combine publishing, broadcasting, and Hollywood studios.

3. Television and radio are subject to government regulation by the Federal Communications Commission (FCC), which has been reluctant to control the content of broadcasts. They do, however, require that stations that provide campaign airtime to a candidate for political office must allow all other candidates for the same office equal time at identical rates.

4. News is what editors and reporters say it is. There are, however, several identifiable criteria for selecting stories. Events are more likely to be considered news if they contain conflict, involve people who are already well known, and are timely or novel. It also helps if there are

people to interview, and, for television, it is important that the event provide good visuals.

5. The power of the media to change public opinion is limited because many people accept only information that confirms the beliefs they already hold. The less familiar the issue, the more likely it is that the media will have an impact on people's attitudes.

6. That which reporters and editors say is news, is often the only source of knowledge that the public has. By highlighting some events and ignoring others, the media have the capacity to influence what people think are the important issues.

7. American political candidates arrange their campaigns to ensure media exposure. Candidates also create pseudo-events solely for the purpose of attracting media attention. Journalists, in turn, are more likely to cover the horse-race elements of political campaigns than they are the policy issues.

8. Political candidates have become increasingly frustrated with media coverage that gives them very little direct access to the American public, while giving reporters and commentators a great deal more time on the air. To counter this, political candidates are turning to what has been called the new media.

9. Although government officials often view reporters as adversaries who must be controlled, they use the media to build public support for their programs. Press conferences, media interviews, going public, and planting information

are some of the ways they convey information to the public.

10. The president is the prime focus of media coverage. Presidential administrations expend a great deal of time and effort on dealing with the media. Presidents commit substantial staff resources to media relations and plan their appearances before the public with the media in mind.

11. Congress is a more difficult institution for the national media to cover, but members of Congress receive a great deal of local media coverage.

12. The Supreme Court is the least covered institution in American government, in part because the justices are not particularly attentive to the needs of journalists.

Key Terms

Penny press (246)
Yellow journalism (246)
Equal-time rule (252)

Priming (256)
Pseudo-events (256)

 ## Net Work

Since the Web itself is an increasingly important part of the media, there is no shortage of relevant sites for you to examine.

- You can use a search engine to identify several mainstream news organizations (e.g., the *New York Times* or the major television networks) and to compare how these different organizations treat the same stories. You can also search for additional news sources that are not sponsored by the mainstream outlets.

- To put the role of journalism in perspective, check out the Freedom Forum's interactive museum of journalism (the Newseum) at **www.newseum.org**. The site's historical materials examine how the reporting of news has changed over the years.

- To research how people react to journalism, the Pew Research Center for the People and the Press at **www.people-press.org** is a valuable source. The site includes surveys measuring the extent to which people follow particular stories, so you can determine how your interests compare to those of Americans in general.

- To match the reported public interest in a particular story with the coverage that the story actually received, visit the Annenberg Public Policy Center at **www.appcpenn.org**. The site regularly conducts and reports on studies of television's coverage of politics.

- A very good source of commentary and studies on modern journalism by journalists can be found at **www.journalism.org**. This site, sponsored by the Committee of Concerned Journalists, is an especially good source for information about local television news practices. You can use the information on this site to see how your local station stacks up against stations around the country in its coverage of news.

As an exercise, develop a short list of political blogs that interest you. If you have trouble getting started look at the webpages of the major newspapers and television networks. They increasingly cite blogs and they are a good place to start exploring this world.

10

Congress

Is Congress ineffective and buried under partisan bickering?

FOCUS QUESTIONS

* Who serves in Congress?

* What are the major functions of Congress?

* What role do the parties play in organizing Congress?

* How do the procedures for passing legislation in the House and Senate differ?

* What are the important influences on members' voting decisions?

During the spring and summer of 2002, Wall Street and Main Street alike were shocked by a series of high-profile financial collapses. As ImClone, Enron, WorldCom, and a number of other previously high-flying companies reported record losses and then filed for bankruptcy, the crisis deepened. On Wall Street, stock prices tumbled as stockholders rushed to sell. Meanwhile, employees of these companies saw their retirement savings evaporate. Even more troubling was the sense that these financial collapses were the product of a series of illegal activities. Executives of the companies were accused of cooking the books in order to overstate company profits, engaging in insider trading, using phony companies to siphon off millions of dollars, and extending themselves generous stock options.

As investors lost confidence in the markets, calls for reform became louder. Even cable television's financial talk shows, the cheerleaders for corporate America throughout the 1990s, began to focus on the necessity for regulatory control as the only means of restoring trust in the markets. As one financial analyst after another appeared on the shows to call for government regulation, their discomfort was obvious. Although they recognized the need for regulations, they also shared a suspicion of government. Indeed, one guest on an MSNBC show in July captured this angst perfectly when, after calling for reform, he expressed a fear of congressional action. He said that he was apprehensive because "Congress could mess up a three-car funeral." He simply did not trust Congress to do the job.

The image of Congress as paralyzed by its own internal bickering and lack of effective leadership pervades almost all discussions of the institution. Consequently, public opinion polls routinely find that the American public lacks confidence in Congress. It is rare to find a poll that reports that even half the people approve of the way Congress is doing its job.

Consequently, a rather widely held *myth of Congress as the broken branch*, an institution incapable of effective action, is hardly surprising. That image of Congress seems easy to support by listing the pressing national problems that remain unsolved. The huge national debt, homelessness, sagging educational performance, a troubled health-care system, and the countless other problems plaguing society at any given time could be solved, so the myth assumes, if only Congress were more effective. Putting aside the possibility that, in the short run at least, the problems may be insolvable, the myth does an injustice to the complex nature of Congress as an institution.

As you will see, the myth rests on the perception that Congress is solely a policy-making body, but that view ignores the full range of congressional responsibilities and their often contradictory nature. For instance, it is important to note at the outset that Congress is a representative institution as well as a policymaking one. It does not just make laws for the nation; its members are also expected to represent the interests of the states and districts that they serve. Congress must find ways to reconcile these different interests in the course of producing national policy. Moreover, Congress was designed as a deliberative body that would act to change the status quo only if a broad consensus favored change. Efficiency was never the goal. A look at how Congress is organized should help illustrate these points.

A Portrait of Congress

FOCUS QUESTION WHO SERVES IN CONGRESS?

Article I of the Constitution specifies only three criteria for membership in the U.S. Congress. To be eligible to serve as a senator, a person must have reached the age of thirty by the time he or she takes office, must have been a citizen of the United States for at least nine years, and must reside in the state from which he or she is elected. Representatives may enter office at the age of twenty-five and after only seven years of citizenship. Members of the House must also reside in the states from which they are chosen, but the Constitution does not require them to reside in the districts they represent.

Who Serves in Congress?

Despite these rather minimal requirements, a group portrait of Congress reveals an institution composed primarily of individuals drawn from the upper levels of American society. The typical member is a middle-aged, highly educated white male who was previously employed in a high-status occupation that earned him an income well above the national average.

Education and Occupation. As befits an elite, virtually all members of Congress hold a college degree, and a majority have completed some form of graduate work or professional study. Senators and representatives come from many different occupations, but lawyers outnumber the members of any other profession; they currently constitute about 40 percent of the membership. Although that percentage is lower than it was in the 1970s, the legal profession is still a steppingstone to Congress. Next to law, business and banking are the most common occupations of legislators. Members of such occupational groups as manufacturing workers, farm laborers, and domestic servants are rarely found in Congress.

Critical Thinking

Does it matter that there are few women or members of minority groups serving in Congress?

Race and Sex. In the period immediately after the Civil War, more than twenty blacks (all of them Republicans) served in Congress. By the late nineteenth century, however, restrictions on the voting rights of blacks had eliminated their congressional representation entirely. No black Americans served in Congress from 1900 until 1928, when Oscar DePriest, a Republican from Chicago, was elected to the House of Representatives. During the next twenty-five years, only three more blacks entered Congress.

In the 1970s, the number of black legislators increased significantly, and forty-two blacks had seats in the House after the 2006 midterm elections. There is only one African American senator. Despite these recent gains, blacks, who constitute about 11 percent of the population, are still underrepresented in Congress.

A Minority of One

Although African Americans have made substantial gains winning seats in the U.S. House of Representatives, only one African American, Senator Barack Obama, serves in the U.S. Senate. Pictured here is Senator Obama speaking to constituents in Jacksonville, Illinois.

The Hispanic community is faring slightly better, with almost 5 percent of the seats in the House. This is a fivefold increase since 1980, when the House contained only four Hispanics. The 1992 elections produced the first Native American senator in sixty years.

The first woman to serve in Congress, Representative Jeannette Rankin, a Montana Republican, was elected in 1916, four years before the Nineteenth Amendment guaranteed women nationwide the right to vote. Although she was defeated in 1918 when she sought the Republican nomination for a Senate seat, she returned to Congress for one term in 1940. Since Rankin's election, slightly more than a hundred women have served in Congress.

During the 1970s and 1980s, women made only incremental gains in number of congressional seats held. Between 1980 and 1991, for instance, women gained only seven seats. But in 1992, which many dubbed the "Year of the Woman," women won a record-breaking forty-seven House seats. Since then the pace has slowed again, but women continue to make some gains. After the 2006 midterm elections, seventy-two women had seats in the House and sixteen were serving in the Senate. (For an international perspective on the number of women serving in legislatures, see "Global Politics," p. 273.)

Getting Elected

Despite the myth of Congress as the broken branch, the American public demonstrates considerable faith in individual members by consistently reelecting incumbents — proving, as Albert Cover put it, that "one good term deserves another."[1] Since 1946, more than 90 percent of the House incumbents who have sought reelection have won and slightly more than 80 percent of the incumbent senators seeking reelection have been victorious.

Remarkably, incumbents did well even in 1994. The 1994 election marked a historic change in Congress as the Republicans gained fifty-three seats and took control of the House for the first time in forty years. Several highly prominent members of the House were defeated, including Thomas S. Foley, the Speaker of the House in the 103rd Congress. (Foley became the first Speaker defeated in a reelection bid since 1860.) But the election was not simply the product of anti-incumbent fever. House members who sought reelection generally did well—overall, slightly more than 90 percent of them won. Of course, the losses were not distributed equally between the parties. Not one incumbent Republican was defeated, whereas thirty-five incumbent Democratic representatives and two Democratic senators lost their seats. Yet even in that seemingly bad year for Democratic incumbents, 84 percent of them were returned to Congress.

Subsequent elections trimmed the size of the Republican majority in both houses. The 2000 elections resulted in a Senate tie, with each party controlling fifty seats, until Senator James Jeffords changed his affiliation to independent and decided to caucus with the Democrats, giving them a one-seat advantage in the Senate. Then in 2002, the Republicans reversed the tide by gaining seats in the House and taking back control of the Senate. This long run of Republican successes sparked pundits to talk about a "permanent majority," with Republicans entrenched by the advantages of incumbency and Democrats perpetually in the minority. All of that talk evaporated in the wake of the 2006 midterm elections, however. In the middle of an increasingly unpopular war in Iraq and a series of congressional scandals, Democrats gained thirty seats in the House and six in the Senate. When the dust settled on the election of 2006, the Democrats, for the first time since 1994, controlled both houses of Congress. Even so, as in the 1994 elections, incumbents generally did well. The incumbent losses were limited to Republican candidates, but even the vast majority of Republican incumbents held onto their seats.

Despite the incumbents' success in keeping their seats, Congress has experienced substantial turnover. More than half of the current representatives and 40 percent of the senators have arrived since 1992. High reelection rates notwithstanding, many members decide against seeking reelection. Some retire because of age, others are weary of the workload or wish to return to private life for some other reason, and still others believe that they cannot win reelection.

Just why incumbents do so well is the subject of much speculation. One frequent explanation is that House incumbents are "safe by design"—that is, that their districts have been drawn to maximize their party's strength among voters. The process of designing districts does, in fact, have a major impact on political power within Congress. Every ten years, in response to the census, House seats are redistributed among the states (see Figure 10.1) and House districts are redrawn by state legislatures. The Supreme Court has held that in drawing the new boundaries, state legislatures must create districts that are approximately equal in population.[2] Furthermore, the districts may not be designed to dilute minority voting strength.[3] However, in *Miller v. Johnson* (1995), the Supreme Court ruled that so-called majority-minority districts, districts that create a political majority for a racial or ethnic minority, are unconstitutional if race was the "predominant factor" in drawing the boundaries. Thus, if districts are designed with the intent of giving a particular racial or ethnic group an advantage, they are likely to be unconstitutional. Nevertheless, legislatures have considerable freedom to engage in the practice of **gerrymandering** — the drawing of district boundaries in ways that provide political advantage.

> **Gerrymandering** The practice by the party controlling the state legislature of drawing congressional and other district boundaries to maximize the number of seats it can win.

Indeed, the Supreme Court's 2006 ruling in *League of United Latin American Citizens v. Perry* increased this freedom. The *Perry* case arose out of the failed effort of the Texas legislature to draw new districts following the 2000 census. With the state senate controlled by Republicans and the House controlled by the Democrats, Texas was unable to agree on a single plan. As a result, the Texas congressional districts were redrawn by a federal court. The court-imposed plan produced a congressional delegation composed of seventeen Democrats and fifteen Republicans. In 2002, however, Republicans took control of both houses of the state legislature and promptly set about to redraw the state's congressional districts. Led by then Majority Leader in the U.S. House of Representatives, Tom DeLay, the Republicans produced a plan that eventually resulted in a seven-seat gain for the party. Opponents of the newly drawn plan sued, claiming that a mid-decade redistricting of congressional seats out a desire to increase partisan representation violated the Constitution. But the Supreme Court disagreed with that contention. Although the seven justices in the majority gave varying reasons for rejecting the challenge to the law, they agreed that a mid-decade redistricting plan, even one designed to increase the number of seats held by a party, did not violate the Constitution. It remains to be seen how many states will adopt the strategy, but the Court's decision is clearly an incitement to gerrymandering.

The party that controls a state government generally attempts to draw boundaries that maximize the number of House seats it can win. It tries to concentrate the other party's supporters in the fewest possible districts (a practice called packing) and to create majorities of its own supporters in as many districts as possible. Alternatively, the party in power may try to spread the other party's supporters over several districts in a way that makes them the minority party in each of those districts (this practice is called cracking).

Clearly, some incumbents benefit from these practices, but gerrymandering alone cannot explain the success of incumbents. Incumbents have been receiving larger percentages of the vote even in states that did not redistrict.[4] With or without gerrymandering, they have a variety of resources on which to draw. They find it easy to get their names before the public, and they are almost always better known and viewed more favorably than their challengers. Former Speaker of the House Jim Wright may have been correct when he said that outside their districts, members of the House are individuals of "widespread obscurity," but within their districts they are conspicuous.[5] This visibility is the result of hard work and the skillful use of the resources of office. As one observer noted, "When we say Congressman Smith is unbeatable, we mean Congressman Smith is unbeatable as long as he continues to do the things he is doing."[6]

Members of Congress have a wide array of official resources that they can use in pursuing reelection. For example, incumbents can send out mail free of charge. Using this **franking privilege** to send out newsletters or questionnaires enables them to cultivate a favorable image among constituents. Shared use of a completely equipped television studio, an allowance to maintain district offices, and a travel allowance sufficient to permit weekly visits to their districts further help incumbents enhance their name recognition. The dollar value of these services and privileges is conservatively estimated at more than $1 million over a two-year House term.

Sitting members of Congress also have opportunities to engage in "credit claiming" — taking credit for benefits that their constituents receive from the national government.[7] When a representative or senator announces an award of federal money for a new dam, a highway extension, or an important defense contract, the effect is to portray him or her as someone who is working hard for the district and getting results. Legislation appropriating funds for local projects is often referred to as **pork-barrel legislation**. Securing such benefits for one's district is "bringing home the bacon."

Finally, incumbents' success depends on what political scientist Richard Fenno has called their **home style**, or the way they present themselves to their constituents. As Fenno observed, "It is the style, not the issue content, that counts most in the re-election constituency."[8] Although incumbents may differ in how they present themselves, their purpose is the same: to win the voters' trust. This kind of bond does not develop overnight; it takes time and constant attention, but the rewards can be great. An incumbent who is trusted by the voters is relatively safe from political attack and is likely to find constituents understanding of occasional political mistakes. In the brief time span of a campaign, challengers find it difficult to establish this kind of relationship.

Although incumbents have a strong advantage, they are not invincible. Challengers can win, but they generally have to spend a great deal of money; just how much varies from race to race. As we mentioned in Chapter 7, on campaigns and elections, money does not buy elections, but it may buy the name recognition that is essential for competing against a well-known incumbent.[9] Unfortunately for challengers, incumbents have a decided advantage in attracting campaign contributions, particularly those from political action committees.

The electoral advantage enjoyed by incumbents has given rise to a call for term limits. Since 1990, twenty-three states have passed legislation or amended their constitution to limit the tenure of members of Congress. In 1995, however, the Supreme Court declared such limits unconstitutional. Writing for a sharply divided court in *U.S. Term Limits, Inc. v. Thorton,* Justice John Paul Stevens argued that the states do not have the constitutional authority to regulate the tenure of federal legislators. Limiting congressional terms, the majority ruled, requires a constitutional amendment. Proposed constitutional amendments setting term limits failed in Congress in both 1995 and 1997, and voters continue to demonstrate approval of their members by reelecting them.

Franking privilege The power of members of Congress to send out mail free of charge; this allows incumbents to cultivate a favorable image among their constituents.

Pork-barrel legislation Legislation that appropriates funds for local projects in an area that a member of Congress represents.
Home style The way in which incumbent members of Congress present themselves to their constituents in an attempt to win the voters' trust.

Critical Thinking

Should congressional terms be limited?

GLOBAL POLITICS

Gender Equality in Legislative Bodies

While the movement toward democratization gains increasing velocity around the world, women have made little progress in gaining political power in the world's legislative bodies. Globally, only about 14 percent of the world's legislators are women. Ironically, in some countries undergoing democratization, the number of women legislators has actually declined.

It is easy to dismiss these global numbers by pointing to countries where culture, and even law, restricts the freedoms of women, but the underrepresentation of women is not limited to countries with these restrictions. Underrepresentation of women is also common in many older, affluent democratic nations, including our own. Consider the following statistics: While some longstanding democracies post impressive numbers — in Sweden, for instance, women hold 43 percent of the parliamentary seats — the percentage of national legislative seats held by women in the United States only slightly exceeds the world average, yet still tops the percentages in Japan, France, and Greece.

To equalize representation along gender lines, some nations have tried an active approach: implementing gender quotas. In 1991, for example, Argentina instituted a quota system for parties contesting elections. Thirty percent of each party's list, at minimum, must be women, and noncompliance results in a disapproval of the entire list. A decade after the implementation of the quota system, women constituted almost 31 percent of the national assembly, up from less than 5 percent before implementation.

But comparable laws in other Latin American countries and in Europe have not produced such a dramatic effect; results varied, but on average the gains were slight. In 1999, for example, France passed a parity law similar to Argentina's requiring that 50 percent of party nomination lists be women. Failure to reach parity now results in a loss of government financial support for party activities. Unlike the Argentine experience, however, the French law has produced only a small gain for women, less than a 2 percent increase in women legislators. Likewise, Belgium passed an act in 1994 requiring that no more than two-thirds of the candidates nominated by a party may be of the same gender, but it produced only modest gains in the seats held by women.

Why is it that even with legal quotas, gender parity in legislative seats is so difficult to achieve? The answer involves several characteristics of culture and politics, but the most important element seems to be the electoral system itself. Key to increasing the number of legislative seats held by women seems to be the use of multimember districts (elections in which voters choose multiple candidates to represent the district) as opposed to the typical U.S. single-member district election in which only one candidate is selected. After controlling for cultural norms and laws mandating parity, the use of multimember districts is the most important factor increasing women's success in winning legislative seats. Evidence from the United States confirms this: The percentage of women holding legislative seats in states using multimember districts is higher than in those using single-member districts, and states that have shifted from multimember to single-member districts have generally seen a decline in the percentage of women legislators.

Just why multimember districts promote more gender diversity is unclear, but there are some possible explanations. First of all, in single-member districts elections tend to be candidate centered, with the personal qualities of the candidates playing a considerable role in the voters' decision, while voters in multimember districts cast their vote for a group of candidates from the same party, which usually includes women candidates. Second, single-member districts are notoriously advantageous for incumbents, allowing them, as the only representative from the district, to develop a personal relationship with constituents. Because most incumbents are men, the success of women candidates in single-member electoral systems is limited. Candidates, female or male, have considerable difficulty beating incumbents.

Source: Pippa Norris, *Electoral Engineering: Voting Rules and Political Behavior* (Cambridge, U.K.: Cambridge University Press, 2004).

The Work of Congress

FOCUS QUESTION   WHAT ARE THE MAJOR FUNCTIONS OF CONGRESS?

Even though the Constitution establishes a government in which three branches share power, the framers were united in the belief that the legislature should play the central role in governing. As a result, Congress is charged with several different kinds of duties.

Making Laws

Article I of the Constitution charges Congress with making laws. In addition, Section 8 of Article I lists a series of specific congressional powers, known as the *enumerated powers*—for example, the power to establish post offices and to coin money. Section 8 also gives Congress the power "to make all laws which shall be necessary and proper for carrying into Execution the foregoing Powers, and all other Powers vested by this Constitution in the Government of the United States." This "necessary and proper" clause has been interpreted by the Supreme Court in such sweeping terms that Congress can now legislate in nearly every aspect of American life.[10]

The Power to Tax

Foremost among the duties of Congress is the setting of taxing and spending policies for the nation. According to the Constitution, bills raising revenue (taxes) are to originate in the House, but because the Senate may amend these bills, the distinction is not particularly significant.

It was evident that tax policies were a top priority early in George W. Bush's tenure when he proposed a $1.6 trillion tax cut. In 2001, the president got most of the tax cut that he wanted, but the cuts were spread out over several years. For instance, increased deductions for married couples do not take effect until 2008. This guarantees that tax policies will remain a perennial issue of dispute, as future Congresses may repeal some of the cuts before they ever take effect. What makes tax policies so contentious is that they go to the very heart of the role of government. Many Republicans, for example, see tax cuts as a way of shrinking the size and scope of government by starving it of financial resources.

Producing the Budget

Equally controversial are the spending decisions (appropriations) that Congress makes each year and incorporates as the federal budget. Throughout most of the nation's history, Congress made no attempt to coordinate the federal budget. The budget was simply the total of the separate appropriations for each department of government. For nearly three decades, however, Congress has attempted to centralize the budget process and place restraints on overall spending levels.

With the passage in 1974 of the Budget and Impoundment Control Act, Congress established a new budget committee in each house. These committees receive the president's budget and an analysis provided by the Congressional Budget Office (CBO), which was created to provide Congress with expertise equivalent to that possessed by the executive branch. The CBO analyzes the president's budget, identifies changes in spending levels, and estimates the expected revenue from taxes and other sources. It also projects the cost of **entitlements**, which are payments that automatically go to any person or local governmental entity that meets the requirements specified by law—social security benefits and military pensions are examples. On the basis of that information, the budget committees recommend to their respective houses spending ceilings for major funding categories. These recommendations constitute the **First Concurrent Budget Resolution**, which must be passed by both the House of Representatives and the Senate by April 15 each year.

In formulating the funding bills for specific departments and programs, the various appropriations committees of the two houses are expected to follow the overall spending guidelines set by the budget resolution. If these guidelines are exceeded, either the appropriations must be reduced or the House and Senate must agree to amend the amounts in the first budget resolution.[11] This process, known as *reconciliation*, has to be completed by the passage of a second budget resolution in September.

The act gave the budgeting process a new sense of coherence, but it did not reduce the budget deficit. It was simply too easy for Congress to ignore the first budget resolution and pass a second one that merely totaled the various appropriations bills. In the 1980s, combinations of tax cuts and spending increases brought record deficits. In response, in 1985 Congress passed the Gramm-Rudman-Hollings law, which set a series of deficit reduction targets that were supposed to produce a balanced budget in 1993.

Central to the workings of Gramm-Rudman-Hollings was the assumption that the threat of sequestrations, or the withholding of funds that had already been appropriated, would force Congress to make the tough decisions necessary to

Entitlements Payments that automatically go to any person or local governmental entity that meets the requirements specified by law; examples are social security benefits and military pensions.

First Concurrent Budget Resolution The recommendation for spending ceilings in major funding categories. It is submitted to the House and Senate by their respective budget committees and must be passed by April 15.

reduce the deficit. However, in 1990, the sequestrations demanded by the law were so drastic that the process lacked credibility. According to one estimate, the sequestration process demanded by Gramm-Rudman-Hollings would have required "a halving of military forces, the closing of many air traffic control installations, the end of meat inspections for five months, a halt in new cleanups of toxic waste sites, and cancellations of vaccinations against childhood diseases for one million children."[12]

After months of battling between Congress and the president, Congress avoided the sequestration by passing the Budget Enforcement Act of 1990, which once again reformed the budgeting process. This new act largely displaces Gramm-Rudman-Hollings. Instead of focusing on deficit targets, it divides discretionary spending into three categories (defense, domestic, and international), with a spending cap on each. If spending in any of the categories exceeds the cap, it will trigger automatic cuts within that category. Moreover, savings in one category may not be used to offset expenditures in another. Finally, the 1990 act stipulates that changes in eligibility requirements for entitlement programs that increase expenditures must be offset by either decreases in other entitlement programs or tax increases. This pay-as-you-go feature of the new act was invoked in 1991, when Congress extended eligibility requirements for unemployment compensation. In accordance with the act, Congress included in the extension new taxes to pay for the benefits.

In 1997, Congress and the president agreed to a bipartisan plan to balance the budget by 2002. Aided by a rapidly growing economy, the goal of a balanced budget was actually achieved by fiscal year 1999, and subsequent years produced budget surpluses. This dramatic reversal of economic circumstances led to new controversies over what to do with the excess revenues, but this situation did not continue for long. Although the government began 2001 predicting a surplus for the next decade, by the end of the year the surplus was gone and the government had returned to deficit spending. The dramatic downturn in the economy, especially after the terrorist attacks of 2001, the collapse of stock prices, and, to some extent, the tax cuts of 2001 combined to substantially reduce government revenue, even as spending for defense and education was being appreciably increased.

Critical Thinking

Should the Constitution be amended to require a balanced budget?

Casework

In addition to representing constituents on policy questions, members of Congress are expected to provide their constituents with personal services, called **casework**. Senators, representatives, and their staffs spend a great deal of time and energy helping constituents through the maze of federal programs and benefits. For instance, are you leaving the country and need a passport in a hurry? Contact your representative. Maybe you need help with a Small Business Administration official who will not return your phone calls. Or maybe you're having problems getting a Veterans Administration or social security check. Per-

Casework Work done by members of Congress to provide constituents with personal services and help them through the maze of federal programs and benefits.

haps you have a son or daughter in the army who has not written home in several weeks. Call the district office of your representative or senator.

Many members of Congress complain that casework reduces them to errand runners, but few refuse to do the work. Instead, most members have accommodated the demand for casework by enlarging their district or state offices. Between 1972 and 1987, for instance, the total number of staff assigned by members of the House to their district offices more than doubled, and the number of Senate staffers located in the state offices more than tripled.[13]

Though it may be tiresome, casework is good electoral politics. As Morris Fiorina has pointed out, "The nice thing about casework is that it is mostly profit; one makes many more friends than enemies."[14] But casework is more than simply good politics; it is also a form of representation. Richard Fenno reminds us that constituents may want "good access or the assurance of good access as much as they want good policy."[15] Contrary to the myth of Congress as the broken branch, members of both the House and the Senate are quite effective at providing that access.

Congressional Oversight

The passage of a law rarely ends congressional involvement in the matter. Congress is responsible for overseeing the activities of the executive agencies that are charged with implementing policy. This process of legislative oversight, which has become a crucial aspect of congressional work, takes many forms. For instance, casework can sometimes bring the weakness or ineffective administration of a program to a member's attention.[16] Congress may also require executive officials to prepare periodic, detailed reports of their activities. In the 1996 Department of Defense appropriations act, for instance, Congress mandated so many reports that it took the Pentagon 111 pages just to list them. Often, however, the oversight function is performed as part of the appropriation process. The hearings that are held to consider agency budgets give members of both houses an opportunity to question executive officials extensively. As one member of the House Appropriations Committee remarked, "You keep asking questions just to let them know someone is watching them."[17]

More dramatically, Congress may exercise oversight by conducting committee investigations. A committee of either house can compel testimony and evidence from government officials and private citizens for the purpose of proposing new legislation. In 2002, Congress used this committee oversight function to investigate the financial dealings of Enron officials and the government agencies that were responsible for regulating the financial markets.

In the 1970s, Congress increasingly relied for oversight on the **legislative veto**—a device in a bill that allowed Congress or a committee of Congress to veto the actions of an executive agency or the president in an area covered by the bill. To establish the legislative veto, Congress would pass a statute granting the president or an administrative agency wide discretion in formulating specific

Legislative veto
A device in a bill that allowed Congress or a congressional committee to veto the actions of an executive agency or the president in an area covered by the bill. It was declared unconstitutional by the Supreme Court in 1983.

Reporting to Congress

In performing its oversight function, Congress often requires executive branch officials to come before it to report on administration activities. Here U.S. Attorney General Alberto Gonzales appears before the U.S. House of Representative's Judiciary Committee to explain and answer questions regarding the administration's controversial use of wiretaps in the war on terror.

policies, but these policies would be subject to congressional approval. Thus, in the War Powers Resolution of 1973, Congress gave the president the authority to send troops into a hostile situation for sixty days. The troops would have to leave at the end of that period unless Congress declared war or provided specific statutory authorization.

In 1983, the Supreme Court declared the legislative veto unconstitutional.[18] Nevertheless, Congress has been reluctant to give up this form of oversight. Because the language of the Supreme Court opinion is not entirely clear, Congress has continued to include the legislative veto in statutes. Whether federal courts will declare these laws unconstitutional remains to be seen.[19] Even if the laws are declared unconstitutional, Congress has devised other informal means of holding agencies accountable. The most popular of these methods is to provide only short-term appropriations, so that the agency has to come back to Congress again and again.

The Organization of Congress

FOCUS QUESTION WHAT ROLE DO THE PARTIES PLAY IN ORGANIZING CONGRESS?

Bicameral Refers to a legislature that is divided into two separate houses, such as the U.S. Congress.

The U.S. Congress is a **bicameral** legislature—a legislature that is divided into two separate houses. Our Congress, however, differs markedly from most bicameral legislatures in other countries in that the two houses have nearly equal power. That arrangement was set up in order to divide power and to strike a balance

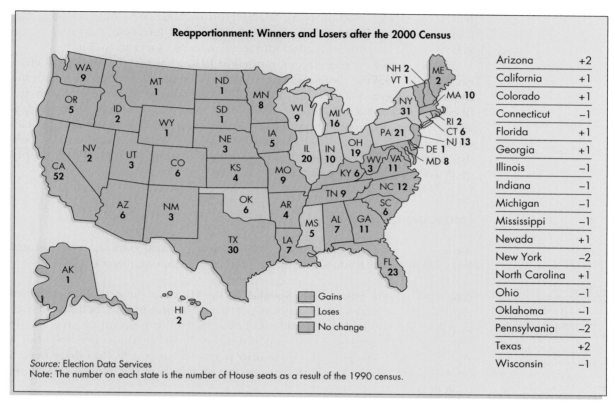

Reapportionment: Winners and Losers after the 2000 Census

Arizona	+2
California	+1
Colorado	+1
Connecticut	−1
Florida	+1
Georgia	+1
Illinois	−1
Indiana	−1
Michigan	−1
Mississippi	−1
Nevada	+1
New York	−2
North Carolina	+1
Ohio	−1
Oklahoma	−1
Pennsylvania	−2
Texas	+2
Wisconsin	−1

Source: Election Data Services
Note: The number on each state is the number of House seats as a result of the 1990 census.

FIGURE 10.1

Reapportionment: Winners and Losers After the 2000 Census

between the large and the small states. Furthermore, Congress is "an assembly of equals,"[20] in which each senator or representative has his or her own constituency to represent, and consequently each member of Congress has an equal claim to legitimacy. The effect of this egalitarianism in Congress is to fragment and decentralize power, which must be structured in some manner if the institution is to make policy.

Bicameralism

The founders designed the two houses to represent different elements in American society. The House of Representatives, with its membership based on frequent and popular elections, was to be the voice of current public opinion. James Madison saw the House as "the grand repository of the democratic principles of government." In contrast, senators, who were originally chosen by state legislatures, were expected to curb the radical tendencies of House members. George Washington gave what may be the best description of the purpose of the Senate. When asked by Thomas Jefferson why the Constitutional Convention had agreed to the second body, Washington replied, "Why did you pour that coffee into your saucer?" "To cool it," responded Jefferson. "Even so," said Washington, "we pour legislation into the senatorial saucer to cool it."[21]

The Seventeenth Amendment, ratified in 1913, changed the method of electing senators, making them also chosen directly by the electorate. Although the founders' expectations for the two bodies may not have been completely fulfilled, the bicameral structure is still an important feature of the American legislative system. Because the two houses are nearly equal in power, public policies are the product of two distinct legislative processes, with two sets of rules, politics, and internal dynamics. These differences fragment power and give Congress a decentralized organization.

Congressional Leadership

Although the Constitution does not mention political parties, congressional leadership is party leadership, for the political parties organize Congress.

Leadership in the House. The **Speaker of the House** is the presiding officer of the House, the leader of its majority party, and second in line, behind the vice president, to succeed the president. The only House position created by the Constitution, the Speaker was supposed to be elected by the entire body but is actually chosen by a vote of the majority party. Not since 1923 has there been a floor battle over the Speaker, because the members of the House vote along straight party lines.

Because the Speaker serves as leader of the majority party and presides over the House, the position is the most powerful in Congress. Nevertheless, the Speaker's power has greatly diminished since the early 1900s, when Speakers dominated the business of the House. The last of the truly powerful Speakers, Joseph "Uncle Joe" Cannon, assigned members of both parties to committees, appointed and removed committee chairs at will, controlled the flow of bills to the floor, and exercised complete authority over which members were recognized to speak on the floor. Cannon's almost dictatorial control of the House precipitated the 1910 "revolt against the Speaker," which stripped the office of all committee assignment powers and drastically limited the power of recognition. Modern Speakers have regained a great deal of power.

The holder of the second-ranking position in the majority party, the **majority leader**, schedules floor action on bills and guides the party's legislative program through the House. The majority leader also works with the Speaker and other party leaders to develop the party's legislative agenda. The majority leader generally succeeds the Speaker.

The **minority leader**, chosen by a vote of the minority party, heads the opposition party in the House and represents its interests. The minority leader also consults with the Speaker and the majority leader on the scheduling of bills and rules for floor action. The most important job of the minority leader is to work to win back control of the House. Like their counterparts in the majority party,

Speaker of the House The only House position created by the Constitution. The Speaker is chosen by a vote of the majority party and is the presiding officer of the House, the leader of its majority party, and second in line to succeed the president.

Majority leader The second-ranking party position in the House (and the first in the Senate). The majority leader schedules floor action on bills and guides the party's legislative program through the House.

Minority leader The head of the minority party in the Senate. Also the leader of the minority party in the House, who represents its interests by consulting with the Speaker and the majority leader on the scheduling of bills and rules for floor action.

Party whips Members of Congress who support the party leaders in the House and Senate by communicating the party's positions to the membership and keeping the leaders informed of members' views.

minority leaders are generally seasoned legislators. The majority and minority leaders have the assistance of the **party whips**, who support the party leaders by communicating the party's positions to the membership and keeping the leaders informed of members' views. In recent years, both parties have expanded their whip systems by creating the positions of deputy and regional whips. Expanding the whip systems allows the parties to bring more members into the leadership ranks, giving more members an incentive to support the party leadership.

Senate Leadership. The Constitution makes the vice president of the United States president of the Senate. This is largely a ceremonial position; the Senate's presiding officer votes only to break a tie. The positions of majority and minority leader are of greater importance. Vice President Cheney has reportedly brought new energy to the role, however. Shortly after taking office, then-Speaker of the House, Dennis Hastert, offered the vice president an office near the House chamber, making him the first vice president to have office space on both sides of the Hill. The vice president has also been extremely active in lobbying both houses. He has established a legislative liaison office separate from the president's, focused on both the House and the Senate. Additionally, the Constitution provides for a president pro tempore to preside over the Senate in the vice president's absence. Traditionally, the president pro tempore is the majority party senator with the longest continuous service.

Much like their counterparts in the House, the majority and minority leaders of the Senate are expected to organize support for party initiatives. Furthermore, the majority leader is expected to manage floor activity, while the minority leader represents the "loyal opposition." When the majority leader is a Democrat, he or she heads the party in the Senate and chairs the committees that assign members to committees and schedule floor debates. When the Republicans are in the majority, these tasks are assigned to three different senators. The Senate also has whips, although they have fewer responsibilities than House whips.

The Committee System

Critical Thinking

Why does Congress need standing committees?

Party leaders in both houses struggle to bring organization to a fragmented institution. In their efforts to manage the Congress, they must contend with a committee system that distributes power to many others, because work in the modern Congress is mostly carried out in committees and subcommittees. These "little legislatures," as Woodrow Wilson referred to them, screen the thousands of bills that are introduced during each session and decide which should be recommended for consideration by the larger body. The few bills that the committees recommend for floor action define the congressional agenda. Bills that are passed over by committees rarely reach the floor.

It has not always been this way. In the early days of Congress, temporary committees considered specific legislative proposals and then disbanded.[22] These committees had little independent power and could not withhold a bill from

A First for the House

After the Democrats gained control of the House in the November 2006 elections, former Minority Leader Nancy Pelosi of California became the first woman to hold that body's most powerful position: Speaker of the House.

floor consideration. Only gradually did Congress come to rely on permanent committees.

Types of Committees. The most important committees in Congress are the **standing committees**. These are permanently established committees that consider proposed legislation in specified policy areas and decide whether to refer it to the larger body. It is to the standing committees that nearly all legislation is sent. Table 10.1 lists the standing committees of the 109th Congress.

Most of the standing committees also have subcommittees, each of which covers a portion of the policy area controlled by the larger committee. Throughout the 1980s, the number and power of subcommittees grew to the point that congressional scholars began to describe the policy process as being dominated by subcommittees. In 2001, however, the new Republican majority moved to rein in subcommittee power. The number of subcommittees was reduced. All committees except Appropriations and Government Reform were limited to six subcommittees. House rules also limit members to serving on no more than four subcommittees.

Select, or special, committees are temporary committees that are established by the House or the Senate to study particular problems. For instance, in 1986, both the House and the Senate created select committees to investigate the Reagan administration's sale of arms to Iran and the diversion of funds from the sale to forces seeking the overthrow of the government of Nicaragua. Select or special committees usually last for no more than two years and are disbanded at

Standing committees Permanently established committees that consider proposed legislation in specified policy areas and decide whether to recommend its passage by the larger body.

Select, or special, committees Temporary committees established by the House or Senate to study particular problems.

TABLE 10.1

Standing Committees of the House and Senate, 109th Congress (2005–2006)

Almost all of these committees have subcommittees. The number of members ranges from ten to sixty-one.

House	Number of Subcommittees	Senate	Number of Subcommittees
Agriculture	5	Agriculture, Nutrition, and Forestry	4
Appropriations	10	Appropriations	12
Armed Services	6	Armed Services	6
Budget	None	Banking, Housing, and Urban Affairs	5
Education and the Workforce	5	Commerce, Science, and Transportation	10
		Energy and Natural Resources	4
Energy and Commerce	6	Environment and Public Works	4
Financial Services	5		
Government Reform	7		
Homeland Security	6	Homeland Security and Governmental Affairs	3
House Administration	None	Finance	5
International Relations	7	Foreign Relations	7
Judiciary	5	Judiciary	8
Resources	5	Health, Education, Labor, and Pensions	4
Rules	2		
Science	4		
Small Business	4	Rules and Administration	None
Standards of Official Conduct	None	Small Business and Entrepreneurship	None
Transportation and Infrastructure	6		
Veterans Affairs	4	Veterans Affairs	None
Ways and Means	6		

Source: www.thomas.gov.

Joint committees
Congressional committees that are usually permanent and consist of an equal number of members from each house.

the end of the congressional session. Unlike the standing committees, select or special committees generally have no authority to receive bills and are primarily investigative bodies, although in extraordinary circumstances they may be empowered to initiate legislation. There are also four permanent **joint committees**, composed of an equal number of members from each house. The leadership of these committees rotates between the House and the Senate each Congress. One of these is the Joint Library Committee, which oversees the activities of the

**Conference commit-
tees** Temporary joint
committees that are
formed to reconcile
differences between
the House and Senate
versions of a bill. Such
committees often play a
critical role in shaping
legislation.

Library of Congress. Finally, temporary **conference committees** are formed to reconcile differences between the House and Senate versions of a bill. Sometimes called the "third house of Congress," conference committees are composed of members of both bodies. Because a bill may be sent to the president only if it has been passed in identical form by both houses, the conference committees often take on great importance in giving legislation its final form.

Committee Size and Membership. Questions concerning the size of a committee and the number of Democratic and Republican members it has are settled by negotiations between the party leaders. Each house can adjust the size of its committees from session to session.

The ratio of majority to minority party members on each committee causes far more controversy than the size of the committee. Generally, the allocations reflect the strength of each party in the full House or Senate. The question of the partisan ratio on committees briefly took on added importance after the 2000 elections. With the Senate tied at fifty Republicans and fifty Democrats, the Republicans technically controlled the body because the Constitution gives the vice president the power to break ties. However, the split gave the Democrats substantial power to deadlock the Senate. After weeks of negotiations, the two parties agreed to allocate an equal number of seats on committees to each party and to share the staff resources of the committees evenly. Under this unprecedented power-sharing agreement, the Republicans were allowed to retain the committee chairs, but in the event of a tie vote on a bill or nomination, either party leader could move them to the floor for a vote. This agreement ended in June 2001, when Senator James Jeffords resigned from the Republican party, declaring himself an Independent but caucusing with the Democrats. Jeffords's defection made the Democrats the majority party in the Senate, and the Democrats then took over the leadership of all the committees in the Senate.

Committee Assignments. The House and Senate rules specify that the full membership is responsible for electing individuals to committees. By custom, however, the parties make the assignments, and the chambers simply ratify their choices.

Because of the key role that standing committees play in controlling the flow of bills to the floor of Congress, competition for places on these committees is often keen. Junior members struggling for a desirable assignment seek allies among the senior members and among outsiders who have an interest in the committee's area. Members will often mount intense campaigns to win a desirable committee assignment. For instance, House Democrats who are desirous of a seat on the Education and Workforce Committee often entreat leaders of organized labor to intervene on their behalf.

Individual goals also play an important part in committee assignments. Legislators worried about reelection and placing their main priority on constituent service choose committees that serve their districts' interests. Not surprisingly, for example, representatives from rural districts are usually desirous of a seat on the Agriculture Committee. Members who want to acquire influence in the

Presiding Over the Senate

The Constitution makes the Vice President of the United States the President of the U.S. Senate. Here Vice President Dick Cheney, thought by many to be the most powerful vice president in history, awaits the arrival of President Bush and his State of the Union Address.

House or Senate have a different set of committee preferences. They may prefer appointment to the Rules Committee in the House or one of the Budget Committees. Still others may pick committees that allow them to pursue certain policy objectives.[23] Of course, these goals are not necessarily contradictory, and each member's preferences may result from a mix of goals.

Committee Leadership. Following the principle that the parties organize Congress, chairs of committees and subcommittees are always members of the majority party in the body. Furthermore, the committee leadership reflects the **seniority system**, a tradition that provides that the member of the majority party with the longest continuous service on a committee becomes its chair. Similarly, the most senior member of the minority party is generally the ranking minority member. Senate Republicans observe this rule strictly. A Republican chair is always the party member with the longest continuous service on the committee. Similarly, if the Republicans are in the minority, the ranking minority member on a committee is always the one with the most seniority. In the House, neither party applies seniority as strictly as the Senate Republicans do. Although seniority remains an important criterion, it is not the sole standard.

A series of Republican party reforms in 1995 shifted the locus of control over House committee assignments, giving the party leadership more power over the

Seniority system The tradition that provides that the member of the majority party with the longest continuous service on a committee automatically becomes its chair.

Critical Thinking

How does the seniority rule conflict with the party leadership's control of Congress?

selection of committee chairs. The reforms also put a six-year term limit on committee and subcommittee chairs. Although seniority remained a factor in selection of chairs, other characteristics, especially record of consistently supporting the party leadership and a history of raising campaign contributions for the party, became important. These rules applied only to the Republican party procedures, so the Democrats were not bound by them in organizing the 110th Congress.

The Congressional Staff

At the beginning of the twentieth century, representatives had no personal staff and all the senators collectively had only thirty-nine personal assistants. By 1987, however, the number of personal assistants allocated to members had mushroomed to more than 11,000.[24] Although most of these assistants spend their time providing constituent service and casework, staffers also participate in the legislative process. Members of both the House and the Senate have come to rely heavily on their personal staff to conduct research, write questions to be posed to witnesses in committee hearings, write speeches, draft bills and amendments to bills, and prepare briefs on pending legislation. Moreover, much of the negotiation among members is conducted not by the members themselves but by staff assistants representing their respective employers.

In addition to the members' personal staff, more than 2,000 people are assigned to the various committees and subcommittees of Congress. With little, if any, responsibility for constituent service, committee staffers are involved purely in drafting legislation and conducting committee investigations. Because they provide needed technical expertise, committee staffers often play a vital role in forming policy. In fact, committee staffers often act as policy entrepreneurs, developing new initiatives and then persuading the committee to accept them.

Congress has also created three major support agencies to furnish technical advice. The staffs of the Congressional Research Service, the General Accounting Office, and the Congressional Budget Office are responsible for providing detailed policy analysis.

With all these staff resources, Congress has become better informed on technical matters and far less dependent on the expertise of the executive branch. Moreover, individual members, faced with more complex issues and busier schedules, naturally find their staffs invaluable. But the growing size of the staff also has a cost. As the pool of politically relevant participants grows larger, Congress becomes further decentralized. As Senator Fritz Hollings, a South Carolina Democrat, put it, "Everybody is working for staff, staff, staff, driving you nutty, in fact. It has gotten to the point where the senators never actually sit down and exchange ideas and learn from the experience of others and listen."[25]

Having campaigned on the promise to streamline Congress, the Republicans of the 104th Congress reduced the number of staff positions by a third. Significantly, however, the reductions came entirely from committee and subcommittee staff. No cuts were made in members' personal staffs. Thus, the members' constituent service function was not affected by the cuts.

How a Bill Becomes Law

FOCUS QUESTION HOW DO THE PROCEDURES FOR PASSING LEGISLATION IN THE HOUSE AND SENATE DIFFER?

The most obvious congressional function, lawmaking, is also the function that Congress has the most difficulty performing. For those who wish to pass legislation, the congressional process is an obstacle course.[26] The maze of complex rules and multiple points of power overwhelmingly favors the opponents of legislation. Ignoring the old saying that the public should never see the making of sausages or legislation, we now will look at the making of laws. Figure 10.2 shows the process schematically.

Any member of Congress — but only a member — may introduce legislation. To aid in this important task, each house has an Office of Legislative Counsel that assists in the actual drafting of legislation; members need only present their ideas to this office. Some of the bills that are introduced may in fact have been drafted elsewhere — by constituents, interest groups, or the presidential administration.

Regardless of a proposal's source, the formal process of introduction is the same. Representatives simply drop the proposal into a box called the "hopper." Senators hand the proposed law to a clerk for publication in the *Congressional Record*. After the initial action is taken, the bill is numbered (by order of introduction) and sent to the Government Printing Office, which makes multiple copies. An "HR" preceding the number identifies bills introduced in the House; Senate bills are marked with an "S."

Committee Consideration

After a bill has been properly introduced, the Speaker of the House or the Senate's presiding officer refers it to a committee. Because both houses have elaborate rules that restrain the leaders' choice of committee, most proposed bills automatically go to the committee that specializes in the area the bill deals with. On occasion, however, the presiding officer may be able to choose among rival committees. Perhaps the most notable example of the exercise of this option occurred in 1963, when the Kennedy administration's civil rights bill was referred to the Senate's Commerce Committee rather than to the Judiciary Committee, which had a predominantly southern membership. In the House, however, the bill was given to the House Judiciary Committee, whose chair strongly supported civil rights legislation.

If the subject is broad enough, proposed bills may need to be referred to more than one committee. However, under the rules, the Speaker may refer a bill to only one committee at a time. On rare occasions, a special or select committee may be created to deal with a single bill. This is what happened in the House when President George W. Bush asked for the authority to create a Department of Homeland Security. Since the president proposed consolidating

FIGURE 10.2

**How a Bill
Becomes Law**

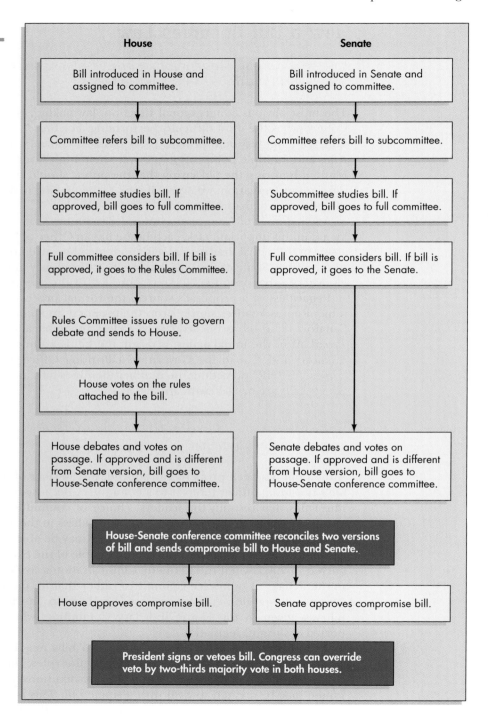

FIGURE 10.2

**How a Bill
Becomes Law**

House

Bill introduced in House and assigned to committee.

Committee refers bill to subcommittee.

Subcommittee studies bill. If approved, bill goes to full committee.

Full committee considers bill. If bill is approved, it goes to the Rules Committee.

Rules Committee issues rule to govern debate and sends to House.

House votes on the rules attached to the bill.

House debates and votes on passage. If approved and is different from Senate version, bill goes to House-Senate conference committee.

Senate

Bill introduced in Senate and assigned to committee.

Committee refers bill to subcommittee.

Subcommittee studies bill. If approved, bill goes to full committee.

Full committee considers bill. If bill is approved, it goes to the Senate.

Senate debates and votes on passage. If approved and is different from House version, bill goes to House-Senate conference committee.

House-Senate conference committee reconciles two versions of bill and sends compromise bill to House and Senate.

House approves compromise bill.

Senate approves compromise bill.

President signs or vetoes bill. Congress can override veto by two-thirds majority vote in both houses.

employees from many different agencies, the bill would have had to be referred to the several committees overseeing all the agencies affected. Sequential assignment of the bill to so many committees would have delayed action on it interminably. To speed up the process, in 2002 the House passed a resolution creating the Select Committee on Homeland Security. The resolution directed the committee to propose comprehensive legislation establishing a Department of Homeland Security, after which it was to dissolve.

When a bill reaches a committee, it is usually referred to the subcommittee that has jurisdiction in the matter. For the vast majority of bills, that is the final resting place. Woodrow Wilson best described the fate of bills in committee when he said, "As a rule, a bill committed [to committee] is a bill doomed. When it goes from the clerk's desk to a committee room, it crosses a parliamentary bridge of sighs and dim dungeons of silence whence it will never return."[27]

If the subcommittee chooses to hold hearings, then members of the president's administration, congressional colleagues, representatives of interest groups, and (time permitting) private citizens are invited to testify. Afterward, the subcommittee meets in what is called a *markup session*, in which it votes on amendments to the bill and settles on the bill's precise language. Sometimes that process involves a line-by-line analysis of the bill, with debate on the language or intent of virtually every sentence. In other cases, the subcommittee may substitute an entirely new version of the bill. Subsequently, most bills go to the full committee; at this point, the process of hearings and markup may begin again, or the full committee may accept the subcommittee version. The full committee may also take no action, thus killing the bill, or send the bill back to the subcommittee for further work.

If the committee orders the bill reported — that is, votes to approve it — the bill is sent for consideration to the full originating body (the House or the Senate). A committee report explaining the bill and justifying the committee's action accompanies it. These reports are crucial because for some members of Congress, they are the main source of information about a bill. Senators and representatives who are not on the committee that approved the bill are unlikely to have a great deal of expertise in the subject matter. Thus, they often look to the committee reports for guidance.

Floor Action

When a committee orders a bill reported, it is placed on a calendar. What happens next is different in the House and in the Senate.[28]

The House Floor. In the House, the Rules Committee determines the scheduling of controversial bills that are unlikely to receive unanimous consent from the floor and bills that require the expenditure of public funds. This committee specifies the time allocated for debate and may set limitations on amendments. The committee may, for instance, attach a rule prohibiting amendments from the floor; such a rule is known as a *closed rule*. In formulating the rules for a bill, the committee may conduct hearings of its own or kill the bill by doing nothing.

The actions of the Rules Committee with regard to a particular bill are stated in a resolution that must be approved on the House floor before the bill can be considered. Often the battle over this resolution is the most important floor action. In 1981, for instance, a fierce struggle developed over the rule for Reagan's budget cuts. A Democratic-sponsored rule would have required the House to vote on individual spending cuts separately. Republican leaders opposed it, fearing that a majority would not vote to cut popular social programs if they were separated from the larger package. With the help of conservative Democrats, Republicans managed to defeat the resolution and substitute one that permitted the cuts to be voted up or down as a whole.

Once a rule is accepted, the House can begin debate, which is strictly limited by the rules adopted. The time allotted for debate ranges from an hour or two for a noncontroversial bill to ten hours for difficult legislation. Votes on amendments, if these are permitted under the rules, are crucial because they can alter the bill sufficiently to attract or lose supporters. Once debate is over, the full House votes on the bill and any amendments that have been attached to it.

The Senate Floor. Because the Senate is a smaller body than the House, the floor procedures are considerably more casual. The Senate has no counterpart to the House Rules Committee. Bills come off the Senate's calendar when the majority leader schedules them. The Senate also allows its members to engage in unlimited debate. This privilege of unlimited debate can lead to a **filibuster**—a prolonged debate that is intended to prevent a vote on a bill and thus kill it. Filibusters can be broken, but only with difficulty, because the rule for **cloture**, or ending of debate, requires that at least sixty senators vote to cut off the discussion. When it comes to the filibuster, no one has yet topped the performance of South Carolina Republican Strom Thurmond, who, while leading the opposition to the 1957 Civil Rights Act, held forth for twenty-four hours and eighteen minutes.

Conference Work

Before a bill can be sent to the president, it must be passed by both houses of Congress in identical form. Usually this requirement poses little difficulty. If the last house to act on the bill makes only slight changes, the bill is generally sent back to the originating house for approval. When the two versions differ significantly, however, a conference committee is appointed to work out the differences.

If the members of this committee cannot reach agreement, the legislation may die in conference. More commonly, the committee reports a compromise bill, which must then be accepted by both houses. The compromise, may, however, include provisions not in any previous version of the bill. Conference committee members may add or delete anything from the two bills in order to produce a single bill. Thus, conference committees are sometimes referred to as the "third house of Congress." So much work has gone into producing the legis-

Critical Thinking

Is the filibuster antidemocratic?

Filibuster A prolonged debate in the Senate that is intended to kill a bill by preventing a vote on it.

Cloture The rule for ending debate in the Senate; it requires that at least sixty senators vote to cut off discussion.

lation that rejection of the bill and the committee report is rare. The bill is then sent to the president, who either signs or vetoes it.

As we noted earlier, the lawmaking process is an obstacle course studded with complex rules and multiple points of power. In fact, many of these rules reflect the original intent of the founders, which was to create a legislative system that works slowly and is not unduly influenced by the passions of a few. As it has evolved, the system is best designed for preventing the passage of legislation and so has reinforced the myth of Congress as the broken branch. Yet Congress does make the system work, and not just in small matters. One has only to think of the civil rights bills of the 1960s to recognize that Congress can and does respond when a consensus forms in society.

Congressional Voting

FOCUS QUESTION WHAT ARE THE IMPORTANT INFLUENCES ON MEMBERS' VOTING DECISIONS?

Members of Congress cast thousands of votes every year on a staggering array of issues. Understanding how they vote and why they vote as they do has long been a preoccupation of students of Congress. This task is made difficult because each vote represents not one choice but a set of choices. As one observer noted, "The predicament of the legislator is that every vote is a dozen votes upon as many issues all wrapped together, tied in a verbal package, and given a number of this bill or that."[29] In addition, legislators are routinely asked to vote on bills covering an incredibly broad range of subjects.

Except in selecting its leaders, Congress rarely engages in straight party-line voting. Nevertheless, a member's party remains the single best predictor of how that member will vote. On the average, the members support their party's positions on better than two out of three votes. Given the extensive party organizations within Congress, this outcome is not surprising. Of course, since the members of a party are likely to attract the same kinds of supporters, they may be voting alike more because of loyalty to these constituents than to party loyalty.

Do the members' constituencies influence legislative decision making? The answer is difficult to determine, in part because constituents' views are not clearly expressed. When an issue arouses deep feelings, the constituency may well sway a senator's or representative's decision. In most instances, however, members of Congress receive little or no instruction from their districts. In such cases, members of Congress often work to shape or rally public opinion, rather than simply reacting to what they think the public wants.[30] Nonetheless, a district's majority usually exerts at least an indirect influence because most members of Congress share their constituents' views. That is why they were elected to begin with.

The threat of electoral defeat also ensures a measure of constituency influence. A single vote in Congress rarely ends a senator's or representative's career. In general, a representative or senator who has cultivated an effective home style can now and then take a position that is at odds with constituents' views.

Critical Thinking

Do party-line votes prove the power of the party or of the electoral constituency?

POLITICS & POPULAR CULTURE

Good and Evil in the U.S. Senate

Few movies made about the U.S. Congress have reached the status of cinema classic, but director Frank Capra's *Mr. Smith Goes to Washington* is most certainly of that caliber. Although the film was made more than sixty years ago, it is still acknowledged as one of the great movies of all time. The film's appeal is founded on Capra's inspired direction, a brilliant lead performance by the late Jimmy Stewart, and a strong supporting cast.

But the film has also lasted because it touches on widely held views about the U.S. Congress. As the movie opens, Mr. Jefferson Smith (Jimmy Stewart), a naive young man who leads an organization of children called the Boy Rangers, is appointed to fill the unexpired term of a deceased U.S. senator. Given his inexperience and naiveté, Mr. Smith is expected to give unquestioning support to the senior senator from his state.

Initially, awed by Washington, Mr. Smith behaves as expected. Because he is truly an innocent, the new senator supports his colleague, completely unaware that he is being used by a corrupt political machine in his home state. Oblivious to the nature of politics, the idealistic Mr. Smith does not see that he is surrounded by crooked senators interested only in reelection. Even his only staffer, a holdover from the previous senator, is jaded and corrupted by congressional politics. That Mr. Smith has no idea how Congress works is, the movie assures us, proof of his goodness; it demonstrates that he has not been debased by Washington. Mr. Smith is simply too good and too honest for Washington.

Of course, eventually even Mr. Smith figures out what's going on. When his plan to build a summer camp for children conflicts with the party bosses' desire to build a dam, Mr. Smith takes a stand. Shocked by the corruption around him, he vows to fight the bosses and stand up for the children of the nation. Unable to convince him to go along with their scheme, the bosses frame Mr. Smith by forging his signature on land deeds that make it appear that he plans to make a profit off the camp.

Disgraced before the very children he sought to help, Mr. Smith prepares to depart Washington without a fight. At the last minute, however, his now loyal staffer persuades him to stay and fight. What follows is a classic confrontation of good versus evil, as one man takes on the sinister forces of the U.S. Senate. Mr. Smith blocks Senate action on the dam by launching a filibuster. As his speaking marathon drags on, the children of America begin to rally around him and even the cynical press corps begins to side with the heroic senator. Rather than the obstruction of majority will by a minority, the filibuster is described by the movie characters as "democracy's finest show" and "democracy in action."

In the end, of course, good triumphs. Mr. Smith collapses in the twenty-fourth hour of his filibuster, and the senior senator from his state, overcome with remorse, confesses to the scheme to debase Mr. Smith. Evil is defeated, but, according to the movie, it takes an outsider to restore goodness to Capitol Hill.

But some issues are a danger for every member. Few members of Congress relish votes on particularly controversial issues because such issues may in fact be very costly to their reelection efforts. Issues such as abortion and gun control may well spell defeat for members who go against the views of their constituency, or at least those of the organized elements in their constituency. Moreover, members are constantly concerned with what use future opponents may make of their floor votes. As Senator Thomas Daschle, a Democrat from South Dakota, said, "I dare say the first thing that comes to my mind in a vote is: Can it [the issue] pass the 30-second test, [and] how successful will my opponent be in applying it to a 30-second ad? It's a screen that comes up whenever there is a vote."[31] Hence few members of Congress frequently vote against the wishes of their districts.

Given the time constraints under which senators and representatives operate, no member can be fully informed on every issue. Therefore, members turn to one another for information and guidance on how to vote. Most members develop a set of colleagues with whom they are in general agreement and who can be trusted to provide them with honest and knowledgeable advice. These experts are often members of the subcommittee or committee in charge of the area in question. Thus, members are usually extremely well informed on the narrow range of issues with which they are familiar but heavily dependent on trusted colleagues with regard to other legislation.

Conclusion: Is Congress the Broken Branch?

We began this chapter by noting that Congress is generally perceived as the broken branch. This is not a recent perception, but rather a long-standing complaint. For instance, the nineteenth-century House of Representatives struck Woodrow Wilson as "a disintegrated mass of jarring elements."[32]

Yet individual members of Congress seem to satisfy their constituents. While bemoaning the condition of Congress in general, voters return the same members to that institution election after election. Despite the myth of Congress as the broken branch, then, voters seem satisfied with the incumbents. That situation is no accident. Incumbent members of Congress are safe because they work hard at carrying out their constituents' wishes for personal services. In that area of activity, Congress surely cannot be deemed a failure.

Part of the reason that Congress works slowly is that it was designed that way. Its complex rules and maze of procedural hurdles were set up to frustrate immediate responses. George Washington's talk of cooling legislation in the Senate might well describe the entire legislative process. But the lawmaking function of Congress is also filtered through the representational function. Responding to the demands of constituents enhances the representative nature of Congress, but it also diminishes the capacity of members' ability to engage in policymaking. Moreover, the representative function encourages members to view policy in local rather than national terms. Nevertheless, Congress is capable of fomenting great change when a nationwide consensus develops.

Tying It Together

FOCUS QUESTIONS RECAP

* Who serves in Congress?

* What are the major functions of Congress?

* What role do the parties play in organizing Congress?

* How do the procedures for passing legislation in the House and Senate differ?

* What are the important influences on members' voting decisions?

CHAPTER SUMMARY

1. Members of Congress tend to be wealthier and better educated than the public they represent. Furthermore, Congress includes proportionately fewer minority group and women members than the general population.

2. Despite the public's seeming dissatisfaction with Congress, incumbents are greatly favored in congressional elections. Incumbents use the opportunities and resources available to them to win the voters' trust.

3. Members of Congress perform many roles. For example, Congress is responsible for the creation of taxing and spending policies for the nation. The members are also expected to represent the interests of their constituents and oversee the actions of the executive branch.

4. As a bicameral institution, Congress is highly decentralized. The two houses of Congress have developed their own rules and internal dynamics.

5. The political parties organize congress and staff the leadership positions.

6. The most powerful position in the House of Representatives is that of the Speaker of the House. Elected by the majority party, the Speaker is assisted by the majority leader and the majority party whip. Leadership of the minority party in the House falls to the minority leader and the minority party whip.

7. Although the Constitution makes the vice president the presiding officer of the Senate, the majority and minority party leaders are of greater importance.

8. Most of the work of Congress is done in its committees and subcommittees. This reliance on committees and subcommittees results in decision-making by highly specialized members.

9. Committee leaders are generally those members of the majority party who have the greatest seniority on the committee. The reforms of 1994 gave the leadership more power in selecting committee chairs and displaced the seniority rule for selection of chairs. Although seniority remained a factor in the selection of chairs, other support for the party and a record of raising campaign contributions for the party also became important criteria in the selection of committee chairs. Because these rules applied to Republican party procedures, the Democrats were not bound by them in organizing the 110th Congress.

10. A bill becomes law only after it has passed through a maze of complex procedures. Though they resemble an obstacle course, these rules and procedures are in keeping with the founders' intent that Congress not act in haste.

11. Because the Senate is a smaller body than the House, the floor procedures are more casual. The Senate has no counterpart to the House

Rules Committee. Moreover, the Senate allows its members to engage in unlimited debate, creating the possibility of filibusters.

12. Members of Congress make decisions on a broad range of issues. In so doing, they take into account the desires of party leaders and those of their constituents. The members also accept and seek out the advice of trusted colleagues who have expertise in the subjects under consideration.

Key Terms

Gerrymandering (271)
Franking privilege (272)
Pork-barrel legislation (272)
Home style (272)
Entitlements (275)
First Concurrent Budget Resolution (275)
Casework (276)
Legislative veto (277)
Bicameral (278)
Speaker of the House (280)

Majority leader (280)
Minority leader (280)
Party whips (281)
Standing committees (282)
Select, or special, committees (282)
Joint committees (283)
Conference committees (284)
Seniority system (285)
Filibuster (290)
Cloture (290)

Net Work

Do you want to learn more about Congress, its members, and recent legislation?

- For a comprehensive look at Congress past and present, try the congressional website Thomas (**http://thomas.loc.gov**). In addition to a wealth of information about the current activities of Congress, Thomas provides a set of important historical documents on American government.

- If you want to learn more about a particular representative or senator, there are several valuable sources. The House of Representatives maintains its own website at **www.house.gov**. Similarly, the Senate website can be found at **www.senate.gov**. Both of these websites provide access to the homepages of individual representatives and senators.

- As an additional source, you might try CapWeb, the Internet guide to the U.S. Congress (**www.capweb.net**). In addition to offering access to representatives' and senators' individual homepages, CapWeb offers a complete set of district maps, so that you can examine the electoral district of each U.S. representative.

- Are you interested in how particular House members or senators voted on an issue? Project Vote Smart (**www.vote-smart.org**) explains current legislation in easy-to-understand language and reports the recorded votes in both the House and the Senate. You can follow the path of a piece of legislation as it moved through Congress, identify which committees dealt with the legislation and who sponsored the bill, and determine the vote totals in the House and the Senate.

As an exercise, learn more about your own representative and senators and the legislation they support. Locate the homepage of your representative or one of your senators. On what committees does he or she serve? Using the Project Vote Smart site, research how he or she has voted on recent bills. Are you pleased with your official's voting record?

11

The Presidency

Is the president all-powerful?

FOCUS QUESTIONS

* How has the presidency evolved into a powerful office?

* What are the various roles that presidents are expected to play and what are the constitutional foundations for these roles?

* Who are the president's most important advisers?

* How do presidents differ in their management styles?

* What tools does the president have to influence other decision makers?

Three days after terrorists destroyed the World Trade Center towers in New York City, President George W. Bush toured the site of the wreckage. Accompanied by Governor George Pataki, Mayor Rudy Giuliani, and New York's two senators, the president climbed a pile of rubble and began to address the hundreds of rescue workers at the site. Barely audible over the din of the ongoing rescue work, the president greeted the workers and began telling them, "I want you all to know that America today, America today is on bended knee in prayer for the people whose lives were lost here, for the workers who work here, for the families who mourn." The president then went on to say, "This nation stands with the good people of New York City and New Jersey and Connecticut as we mourn the loss of thousands of our citizens." At this point, a voice called out from the crowd, "George, I can't hear you!" Responding to the challenge, the president roared back, "I can hear you! And the people who knocked these buildings down will hear all of us soon!" With this, the crowd began the chant "U.S.A.! U.S.A.!" No writer could have scripted it better, for here stood an American president in the heroic pose that we so like. Here was a president appearing presidential.

Presidents are set apart not only from average citizens but also from other leaders in our society because, for many citizens, the president *is* American government. When things go well, it is because the president is exercising leadership; when they go badly, it is because the president is weak or incapable. If we could just get the right president—perhaps another Lincoln or Roosevelt—all would somehow be well. Whether it is called the "textbook presidency,"[1] the "imagined presidency,"[2] or the "savior" model of the presidency,[3] that view projects the *myth of the all-powerful president.* Its imagination fueled by legends of great presidents, the public has come to believe that all of the country's problems—social, economic, and international—can be solved by the immense power available to the president. Even presidents themselves can succumb to this myth. Jimmy Carter once contended that "the President is the only person who can speak with a clear voice to the American people and set a standard of ethics and morality, excellence and greatness."[4]

In this chapter, we consider the expectations placed on presidents and the powers at their disposal. We begin by examining the evolution of the presidency, for even though the Constitution has changed little with respect to presidential power, the modern presidency is a far different institution from that in the eighteenth century.

The Growth of the Presidency

FOCUS QUESTION HOW HAS THE PRESIDENCY EVOLVED INTO A POWERFUL OFFICE?

On April 30, 1789, General George Washington stood before the assembled Congress and repeated the oath of office administered by Robert Livingston. The oath completed, Washington lifted the Bible to his lips as Livingston cried out, "It is done." But just what had been done must have been a mystery to all

The Heroic President

Nothing confirms Americans' expectations of the presidency as the leader in times of crisis. Pictured here is President George W. Bush addressing the workers amidst the rubble of the World Trade Center in New York.

present, for no one could be sure what shape the presidency would take or what influence presidents would have. Nor did the character of the modern presidency develop in an instant. Rather, the office has evolved over the course of two centuries, and during that period the balance of power has moved back and forth between the presidency and Congress.

The First Presidents

As the first president, Washington was keenly aware that he was building a new institution and that his every act created a precedent. Although he respected the need to cooperate with others, he was careful to protect the dignity and strength of the office. Once, while on a visit to Boston, Washington was informed that John Hancock, the governor of Massachusetts, was ill and would be unable to call on the president. Believing that governors should defer to the office of the president, Washington canceled his dinner engagement at the governor's mansion and proceeded to outwait Hancock. The next day an apologetic Hancock, carried by four men, appeared at Washington's door to pay his respects.

During his presidency, Washington developed a notably broad interpretation of executive power. Although he stayed aloof from congressional politics, he was quite active in formulating legislation. Using his secretary of the treasury, Alexander Hamilton, to build congressional support, Washington successfully steered his program of economic development through Congress.

Washington also established a number of presidential roles and customs, including the practice of meeting with the heads of his executive departments as a cabinet. His response to international threats established a dominant role in foreign affairs for the president. Finally, by refusing to seek a third term, Washington eased fears that the presidency might become a monarchy; in the process, he created the precedent, not broken until 1940, of a two-term limit.

Washington's strength contrasted sharply with the weakness of his successor, John Adams. Although Adams was one of the great American patriots (during the American Revolution, he was known as the "Atlas of Independence"), his presidency was marked by failure. At odds with the opposition party (the Jeffersonians) and with members of his own Federalist party, Adams lasted only one term as president. He lost his reelection bid to Thomas Jefferson.

As the leader of the Jeffersonians (the predecessors of the modern Democratic party), Jefferson advocated restrictions on the national government. Yet as president, he enlarged the powers of the office and skillfully used his political party in Congress. During his presidency, he planned his party's legislative strategy and worked diligently to elect party faithful to Congress. By these actions, he greatly enhanced the president's effectiveness as a legislative leader. Furthermore, without consulting Congress, he doubled the landmass of the United States through the Louisiana Purchase of 1803.

Jefferson's immediate successors were comparatively unsuccessful at leading their party. The so-called era of good feeling (1812–1824) was a period of congressional and one-party governance.

The Jackson Presidency. With the election of Andrew Jackson in 1828, the United States had its first president who was truly elected by the people. Until then the state legislatures had appointed most members of the electoral college, but by 1828 only Delaware and South Carolina refused to select delegates by popular vote. At the same time, the elimination of the requirement that only property owners could vote had significantly expanded the eligible electorate.

Capitalizing on his personal popularity, Jackson established a popular base for the presidency and strengthened the executive's role. He styled himself as the only representative of all the people and went over the heads of congressional leaders to appeal directly to the public, which supported him in his confrontations with Congress. He vetoed twelve acts of Congress, more than all his predecessors combined. More important, he claimed the right to veto legislation simply because he disagreed with Congress; previous presidents had vetoed bills only when they thought them unconstitutional. Commenting on Jackson's battles with Congress, critics complained that the presidency had become an elected monarchy. The president, claimed Daniel Webster, "carries on the government; all the rest are subcontractors."[5]

Congress Reasserts Power

Although Jackson offered little in the way of policy initiatives, he profoundly influenced the office by demonstrating that a strong and independent presidency could be based on popular support. Few of his successors could apply these lessons, however. For the next hundred years, presidents, with a few exceptions, remained in obscurity.

As soon as Jackson retired, Congress reestablished its power over the less flamboyant Martin Van Buren (1837–1841) — a man so famous for his political evasiveness that the noun *noncommittalism* was coined to describe his usual public stance.[6] Van Buren, a Democrat, was no match for his opponents in the Whig party. The Whig theory of presidential power held that Congress is the center of government and that the president's job is simply to execute the laws.

Van Buren was not alone in his failure to maintain a strong and independent presidency. The years between Jackson's presidency and Lincoln's were marked by a string of remarkably mediocre presidents. Even their names are difficult to remember. The reputation of Millard Fillmore (1850–1853) illustrates the lack of power of these presidents; his only claim to fame, that he installed the first bathtub in the White House, is not even true. The one exception to this general mediocrity was James Polk (1845–1849), who annexed Texas through war with Mexico and obtained the Oregon Territory from the British by peaceful means. When he left office, the nation was half again as large as it had been when he entered it.

In Abraham Lincoln (1861–1865), however, the nation found a president of immense influence. Although Lincoln was a Republican when he was elected president, he had earlier been elected to Congress from the Whig party. As a Whig, he had continually challenged executive authority, even attacking the war with Mexico as an unconstitutional act initiated by Polk. (Indeed, Polk had provoked the Mexican army into an attack.)

On taking office, Lincoln used the powers of the presidency in new and extraordinary ways. He blockaded southern ports, called up the militia, closed opposition newspapers, ordered the arrest of suspected traitors, closed the mail to "treasonable correspondence," and issued the Emancipation Proclamation — all without prior congressional approval. Throughout the Civil War, Lincoln did whatever he thought was necessary in order to win the war. In doing so, he demonstrated that in times of national emergency the American presidency possessed virtually unlimited powers.

Lincoln, like Jackson, was followed by a series of weak, readily forgotten presidents — known collectively as the Bearded Presidents — who were easily dominated by Congress. So complete was congressional control that for the next forty years all-important legislation, including the decision to enter the Spanish-American War (1898), was initiated in Congress.

Only the vigorous administrations of Theodore Roosevelt and Woodrow Wilson briefly interrupted the era of congressional government. Viewing the presidency as a "bully pulpit" from which he could appeal to and educate the American public, Roosevelt skillfully used public opinion to build support for

Critical Thinking

Is the president the only official capable of representing the entire nation?

his actions. He articulated the "stewardship theory" of presidential power: that the president, as the only official elected by the entire nation, has the duty to take whatever action is necessary as long as it is not specifically forbidden by the Constitution or by law. Taking a similar view of the presidency, Wilson was the first president to propose a comprehensive legislative program.

The Modern Presidency

Theodore Roosevelt argued for a strong presidency, but it was Franklin D. Roosevelt who gave the office the power it now has. Confronting the Great Depression and then World War II, the second Roosevelt rallied the American people to accept his leadership and, in the process, the legitimacy of the powerful presidency. Immediately after his inauguration in 1933, Roosevelt called Congress into special session and in the First One Hundred Days introduced fifteen major pieces of legislation. A willing Congress passed all of them. (One of the most important of these bills, the administration's banking bill, passed in just seven hours.)

World War II helped to expand Roosevelt's power still further. The mobilization effort needed to fight a total war led to such spectacular growth in the size and authority of the federal government that the government became involved in every aspect of life. Struggling to deal with the emergency of war, Congress willingly turned to the president for policy leadership. By the end of the war, political power had dramatically shifted from Congress to the White House, and the Whig model of the active Congress dominating the passive president was dead. More important, the heroic image of Roosevelt rescuing the nation so changed the presidency that the nation came to expect action from a vigorous president as the norm. As one scholar put it, rather than being a threat to democracy, the strong executive was its "savior."[7] The argument was simple: The more power the executive had, the more good he could do. Ironically, the "savior" quickly turned into what one critic called a "Frankenstein monster"[8] when Lyndon B. Johnson and Richard M. Nixon used their power to prosecute an increasingly unpopular war in Southeast Asia. Revelations of secret bombings of Cambodia and the Watergate scandal led to a general disenchantment with the presidency. Suddenly, presidential government seemed harmful to the republic. Many of the same scholars who had glorified the expanded presidency of Franklin D. Roosevelt began to argue that the office had grown too strong. Arthur M. Schlesinger Jr., whose biographies of Andrew Jackson, Franklin D. Roosevelt, and John F. Kennedy had done so much to build myths around the presidency, began to warn of the dangers of the *imperial presidency*—the increased authority and decreased accountability of the presidency in the 1960s.[9]

In the wake of these concerns, leadership passed to two successive presidents who were anything but imperial. Gerald Ford assured the nation that he was "A Ford, not a Lincoln," and Jimmy Carter, with his cardigans and blue jeans, sought to reduce the pomp surrounding the president. Failing to project the image of a strong leader, both were rejected by the voters, and presidential observers began to worry about the *tethered presidency*—a presidency that was too constrained to be effective.[10]

The election of Ronald Reagan in 1980 seemed to confirm the concern over the tethered presidency. Elected on the promise to dismantle much of the federal government, Reagan seemed unlikely to manifest the characteristics of a strong president. His first term saw major legislative victories on tax and budget reductions, but deepening economic problems soon overshadowed these triumphs. Midway through Reagan's first term, the number of unemployed reached 11 million, and the president could command only a 37 percent approval rating in the Gallup poll.

Yet those who wrote off Reagan as another one-term president obviously misjudged the situation. Riding the wave of an economic recovery, Reagan scored a landslide victory in 1984. At the beginning of his second term, he garnered higher public opinion approval ratings than had the popular Dwight D. Eisenhower, the last president to serve two full terms. Often defying the image of a lame-duck president, Reagan took strong positions on some issues, backing them up with vetoes and threats of vetoes. However, his second term was also marred by the Iran-Contra affair—which resulted in the forced resignation and criminal conviction of some of the president's closest advisers—and a much-enlarged federal deficit.

As Reagan's political heir, Vice President George H. W. Bush benefited directly from Reagan's popularity in his campaign for the presidency. But Bush, unlike Reagan, was forced to begin his administration with both houses of Congress controlled by the Democrats. Recognizing this, President Bush called for a "new engagement" between the president and Congress, one characterized by cooperation and mutual respect. The public perceived both the invasion of Panama and the war with Iraq as great successes, and Bush's popularity soared. Buttressed by approval ratings as high as 90 percent, Bush aggressively assailed Congress with a series of vetoes that Congress could not override. In his fourth year, however, his popular approval dropped below 40 percent as the economy suffered a recession. As a result, Bush became another one-term president.

Although he was elected with only 43 percent of the popular vote, President Bill Clinton initially had the advantage of taking office with his party controlling both houses of Congress. That advantage, however, was more apparent than real. The administration did have some early successes in Congress, most notably the passage of the North American Free Trade Agreement, but the president was also rebuffed by Congress on several occasions. As Clinton fell in the polls and, after the 1994 elections, had to cope with a Republican-controlled Congress, his reelection seemed doubtful. However, he dealt with Congress skillfully and even succeeded in blaming its extremist elements for the two government shutdowns. As a result, Clinton was able to win reelection in 1996 with 49 percent of the popular vote. Despite the scandals that resulted in his impeachment, Clinton left office with an unprecedented 65 percent approval rating. But Clinton's approval ratings did not ensure continued control of the White House, as the Republicans recaptured the office with the election of George W. Bush.

Given the elongated election of 2000, decided only when the Supreme Court barred further recounts in Florida, and the fact that George W. Bush received fewer votes than Al Gore, many expected the new Bush administration to be weakened and even timid in its approach to governing. That was not to be the case, however. George W. Bush began his tenure with a quick congressional victory on tax cuts, but the real change for the administration came in the wake of the terrorist attacks of September 11, 2001. His response to the events, including the wars in Afghanistan and Iraq, elevated his public approval ratings and strengthened his leadership.

Riding the wave of strong public approval, George W. Bush won reelection in 2004. Shortly after the election, the president made it clear that he did not intend to be a lame duck. He began his second term pressing forward on several major initiatives, including tax cuts and major reforms in health care and social security. But the lengthy war in Iraq, the flawed relief efforts following Hurricane Katrina, and rising fuel prices stalled action on much of his agenda. By the middle of his sixth year in office his public approval ratings had plummeted to the mid–30 percent range and Republicans began to worry about their fate in the midterm elections of 2006. It turns out their concerns were well founded: the Democrats won majorities in both houses of Congress, and the day after the election the president attempted to defer criticism of the war in Iraq by replacing Donald Rumsfeld as Secretary of Defense.

Presidential Roles

 WHAT ARE THE VARIOUS ROLES THAT PRESIDENTS ARE EXPECTED TO PLAY, AND WHAT ARE THE CONSTITUTIONAL FOUNDATIONS FOR THESE ROLES?

Tethered or free, presidents are perceived as being central to American politics. Perhaps the strongest evidence of their eminence is the variety of roles that they are expected to play. Taken together, these roles create the appearance of what has been called "the awesome burden" of the presidency. Indeed, as one scholar has pointed out, "All that is missing is Mover of Mountains and Raiser of the Dead."[11] (For a look at the roles of executives around the globe, see "Global Politics," p. 304.)

Chief of State

Presidents are not just celebrities; they are the American version of royalty.[12] Lacking a royal family, Americans look to the president to symbolize their government.

In their role as chief of state, presidents entertain foreign dignitaries and prominent Americans, throw out the first baseball of the season, review parades, issue proclamations, and carry out other ceremonial duties. To some people, these activities may seem like a waste of valuable time, but presidents view them as enhancing their prestige. Ever mindful of the value of pageantry, George

GLOBAL POLITICS

Multiple Executives

Americans entrust the roles of chief of state and chief executive to one office. After all, in the U.S. system the president is not only the chief of state who symbolically represents the nation, he (or she) also serves in a political and policymaking role as the chief executive. However, in much of the rest of the world, these functions are separate. Indeed, although it is true that some countries in Central America, South America, Asia, and Africa have adopted the presidential system and the blending of these roles, it still remains the minority governmental arrangement in the world today.

Most nations use some version of the parliamentary system, which has a multiple executive arrangement—one official serves as the chief executive, the other as the chief of state. In parliamentary systems, the chief executive (usually called the prime minister) is a member of the legislature, designated by it to form a government, because he or she is a member of the largest party. The prime minister serves at the pleasure of the parliament and can be removed by a vote of no confidence.

On the other hand, in parliamentary systems the chief of state is generally limited to ceremonial duties, having little or no policymaking authority. Under such systems, the chief of state may be selected in one of several ways. In some parliamentary systems, the chief of state is selected by succession from an imperial family. The United Kingdom, with its royal family, famously illustrates this method. It is the Queen, rather than the prime minister, who symbolizes the nation and performs the ceremonial functions, which in America are performed by the president. But the United Kingdom is not alone in relying on heredity. Japan's head of state, for example, is its emperor, a male member of an ancient ruling family.

But the chief of state in parliamentary systems is not always a hereditary position. Indeed, most nations use some type of electoral system for selecting the chief of state, usually election by a legislative body. The chief of state in India, for instance, is elected by the parliament. Similarly, the chief of state in Germany is elected for a five-year term by a special federal assembly composed of the entire *Bundestag* membership (the German parliament) and an equal number of members from the legislatures of the sixteen states (*Landers*). Usually, the individual selected for the job is a distinguished long-term politician. As if to answer the age-old question, "What's in a name?" the chief of state of both of these countries, and many others, is called the president, even though he or she performs only the ceremonial functions.

Interestingly, France has a hybrid system that combines elements of the presidential and parliamentary system, with both a president and a prime minister. The president is elected by popular vote to a seven-year term, with no limit on reelection. The president then appoints the prime minister and the entire cabinet. Unlike the United Kingdom, for example, the prime minister need not be a member of the parliament. In fact, any member of the parliament accepting the post of prime minister must immediately give up the legislative seat. Under this system, the prime minister acts at the direction of the president and thus has little independent power. Thus, even though France has a prime minister, the French president, like the U.S. president, is both chief of state and chief executive.

Source: Gregory S. Mahler, *Comparative Politics: An Institutional and Cross-National Approach*, 2nd ed. (Englewood Cliffs, N.J.: Prentice Hall, 1995).

Washington regularly rode through the streets of Manhattan (New York then being the nation's capital) in an elaborate carriage pulled by six cream-colored horses. On the days when he chose to ride horseback, he mounted a white steed draped in leopard skin with a saddlecloth bound in gold. Washington's flair for pomp and circumstance was such that John Adams once said of him, "If he was not the greatest President, he was the best actor that we ever had."[13]

Chief Executive

Article II of the Constitution clearly specifies that "the executive power shall be vested in a President of the United States of America" and that the president shall "take care that the laws be faithfully executed." On the surface, then, the president appears all-powerful as a chief executive. After all, no other official shares executive authority. Yet the notion that one person can manage an executive branch that has grown to some 3 million civilian employees is an illusion. Modern presidents quickly discover that management is a considerably more difficult and time-consuming function than they had imagined. Indeed, they often neglect management functions in favor of more immediate and rewarding political concerns.

Powers to Appoint and Remove. Given the president's role as chief executive, it stands to reason that he would possess enormous power to staff the executive branch. Such is not the case, however. Because the vast majority of federal employees are protected by the civil service (see Chapter 12, on the bureaucracy), there are fewer than 2,000 positions that the president can fill by appointment. Moreover, many of these appointments require senatorial approval, which may on occasion be denied. The fate of President Clinton's nomination of Anthony Lake to head the CIA illustrates the Senate's power. After days of grueling questioning about his role in foreign policymaking during Clinton's first term, his personal stock investments, and his management abilities, Lake, the former national security adviser, asked the president to withdraw his nomination.

Likewise, the president has limited power to remove officials—an issue on which the Constitution is silent. The president can hire and fire agency heads and others who perform purely executive functions. Officials who perform quasi-legislative or quasi-judicial functions, however, are protected by Congress from presidential discharge, although the line between purely executive functions and those that are quasi-legislative or quasi-judicial is somewhat unclear.[14]

Power to Pardon. The president's power to grant pardons and reprieves is one of the few executive powers that Congress may not limit. This power may be used to correct what the president sees as mistaken convictions or, as Alexander Hamilton put it, to "restore the tranquility of the commonwealth." President Reagan demonstrated the first of these uses when, in 1981, he granted pardons to two FBI agents who had been convicted of burglarizing the homes of Americans suspected of harboring terrorists. Reagan claimed that the agents had acted in

The Appointment Power

As chief executive, presidents make appointments of key advisers, with Senate approval. Here President George W. Bush walks across the White House lawn with his choice for secretary of state, Condoleezza Rice.

good faith, believing that their actions were legal. In the second category, after the Civil War, President Andrew Johnson used this power to restore tranquility to a divided nation by granting full amnesty to all Confederate veterans except those guilty of treason or felonies. Similarly, President Ford justified his pardoning of Richard Nixon as necessary to shift national attention away from what he referred to as our "long national nightmare" and toward the economic problems of the nation. As controversial as these and other pardons have been at times, the president's power to pardon is such that Congress has no meaningful way of limiting presidential actions in this area.

Executive Privilege. Even though the Constitution makes no mention of it, presidents from Washington onward have claimed **executive privilege** — the right to withhold information from the legislature. Justifying their claims either by the need for secrecy in foreign affairs or by the necessity of keeping advice confidential, presidents exercised this power sparingly without serious congressional challenge for almost 200 years.

The use of executive privilege became an issue, however, when the Nixon administration attempted to greatly expand the meaning of the term. As the events of Watergate began to unfold, Nixon tried to deflect inquiry by claiming that executive privilege applied to all executive officials. At one point, he even

Executive privilege The right, claimed by presidents from Washington onward, to withhold information from Congress.

Critical Thinking

On what grounds can executive privilege be justified?

claimed executive privilege for all those who had previously worked for the executive branch.

The confrontation came when the Watergate special prosecutor requested tape recordings of White House conversations. The president, citing executive privilege, refused to turn over the tapes, and the special prosecutor pursued the matter in federal court. In the case of *United States v. Nixon* (1974), the Supreme Court ruled that presidents could rightfully claim executive privilege, but not when facing a criminal investigation.[15] In the Clinton administration, the courts further limited executive privilege by ruling that it could not be invoked to avoid or delay civil proceedings for actions taken prior to assuming the presidency.[16] Moreover, the courts made it more difficult for presidential aides to invoke executive privilege.[17] Even the president's Secret Service protectors can, in the future, be compelled to testify.[18] Thus, although the Court has recognized the need for executive privilege, it has also set limits on this power.

George W. Bush is fighting these limits, however. Intent on reinvigorating presidential powers, the administration has invoked executive privilege in several high-profile situations. Illustrative of this is President Bush's executive order effectively rewriting the Presidential Records Management Act of 1978, which mandates the release of unclassified presidential records twelve years after the president leaves office. George W. Bush's executive order allows former presidents to delay the release of these materials indefinitely. Former presidents may even assign the right to invoke executive privilege to anyone of their choosing, delaying the release of papers even after the former president's death. The Bush administration has also sought to expand executive privilege by conveying the power to vice presidents. Thus, when Congress sought records of Vice President Dick Cheney's meetings with energy company officials, the White House, citing executive privilege, refused to turn them over. Whether the president's claims will stand remains to be seen, but it is clear that George W. Bush is intent on defining presidential power broadly.

Chief Diplomat

According to Article II of the Constitution, the president is authorized to make treaties with the advice and consent of the Senate; to receive foreign ambassadors and ministers; and, with the advice and consent of the Senate, to nominate and appoint ambassadors, ministers, and consuls. As chief diplomat, the president plays a leading role in shaping U.S. foreign policy, although he is seldom free to do as he wishes. While President Harry Truman once claimed, "I make foreign policy," presidents have found their role as chief diplomat far more constrained than the constitutional provision suggests.

Treaties. The power to make treaties illustrates the limits of the role. A literal reading of the Constitution suggests that both the president and the Senate are to take part in all phases of the treaty process. Such was President Washington's initial understanding, but he soon changed his mind. While negotiating a treaty with the Indians, Washington appeared before the Senate and requested advice on certain provisions. The Senate, however, withdrew to discuss the matter without Washington. Angered by the Senate's refusal to engage in face-to-face discussions, Washington reversed his position.

Since Washington's time, no president has appeared before the entire Senate seeking advice on treaty provisions. Nevertheless, presidents do consult prominent senators. As former secretary of state Dean Acheson said, "Anybody with any sense would consult with certainly some of the members of the ratifying body before he got himself out on the very end of a limb from which he could be sawed off."[19] At times, individual senators are even included in the delegation appointed by the president to negotiate a treaty. For example, the 1963 nuclear test ban treaty was negotiated in the presence of a panel of senators. In contrast, at the end of World War I, President Woodrow Wilson did not include senators in the delegation to the conference that created the League of Nations, and many observers believe that this oversight angered members of both his own and the opposition party and led the Senate to reject U.S. membership in the new international organization.

Consulting leading senators is imperative because every treaty must be approved by two-thirds of the Senate before it can take effect. Even if the Senate does not reject the treaty, it can modify it in ways that the president may find hard to accept. President Carter, for instance, won the necessary Senate support for his Panama Canal treaties only after agreeing to several Senate modifications that he had initially opposed.

Executive Agreements.   To avoid the uncertainties associated with treaty ratification, presidents frequently turn to **executive agreements**, agreements with other nations that are made by the president without the Senate's consent. Such accords have all the legal force of treaties while they are in effect but, unlike treaties, are not binding on succeeding presidents.

> **Executive agreements**
> Agreements with other nations that are made by the president without the Senate's consent. They have all the legal force of treaties but, unlike treaties, are not binding on succeeding presidents.

Even though the Constitution does not provide for executive agreements, presidents from Washington onward have used them for both trivial and important matters. Because executive agreements can be made quickly and secretly, presidents use them to avoid rejection by the Senate. Thus, in 1905, when Senate Democrats, fearful of foreign commitments, blocked consideration of a proposal for American operation of customhouses on the Caribbean island of Santo Domingo, Theodore Roosevelt implemented the proposal as an executive agreement.[20]

Legally, anything that the president and the Senate can do through treaties can be done by the president alone through executive agreements. The political reality is sometimes quite different, however, since the implementation of an executive agreement often requires congressional action. For instance, executive agreements generally need appropriated money, which means that both the House and the Senate become involved in the implementation.

> **Congressional-executive agreement**
> An agreement with a foreign nation that is negotiated by the president and then submitted to both houses of Congress for approval.

Congressional-Executive Agreements.   Presidents have also started using a method known as the **congressional-executive agreement** — an agreement (usually a trade pact) with a foreign nation that is negotiated by the president and then submitted to both houses of Congress for approval. By submitting the agreement to both houses, the president can win assent for the agreement while avoiding the constitutional requirement of a two-thirds vote in the Senate for treaty ratification. (Congressional-executive agreements need only a majority vote in each house for approval.) President Clinton successfully used this procedure to win approval for the North American Free Trade Agreement (NAFTA), which probably would not have received the necessary votes in the Senate had it been submitted as a treaty.

Critical Thinking

Should presidents be prohibited from concluding congressional executive agreements?

Power of Recognition. As an element of their constitutional power to receive foreign ambassadors and ministers, presidents possess the power of recognition. The simple act of receiving a foreign diplomat signifies the official recognition of the sponsoring government. As one observer noted, "Throughout the entire course of our national history the President has performed dozens of acts of recognition of new governments without consulting, or being expected to consult, Congress."[21] Thus President Washington granted recognition to the new French Republic without consulting Congress. Similarly, within hours of Soviet President Mikhail Gorbachev's resignation, President George H. W. Bush extended recognition to Russia and five other republics of what had been the Soviet Union.

Diplomatic Appointments. A final aspect of the president's role as chief diplomat is the power to make diplomatic appointments. According to Article II of the Constitution, the president "shall nominate, and by and with the advice and consent of the Senate, shall appoint ambassadors, other public ministers and consuls." By and large, the Senate automatically approves such nominations, allowing the president to fill diplomatic posts with people who share his views. On occasion, however, members of the Senate delay and even obstruct a confirmation as a way of expressing displeasure with administration policy. In reaction to Nixon's efforts to normalize relations with the People's Republic of China, several senators used confirmation hearings to block the administration's initiative. Nevertheless, David Bruce and George H. W. Bush, Nixon's liaisons to Beijing, were eventually confirmed.

Commander in Chief

Of all the president's roles, the most controversial is that of commander in chief. Under the provisions of Article II of the Constitution, the president is the "Commander in Chief of the Army and Navy of the United States, and of the Militia of the several States, when called in the actual service of the United States." The Constitution, however, clearly assigns the power to declare war to Congress, not to the president. Alexander Hamilton, in "Federalist No. 69," stressed this division of responsibilities when he said of the role of commander in chief, "It would amount to nothing more than the supreme command and

Making Foreign Policy

As chief diplomat, presidents depend heavily on an array of advisors to keep them abreast of world affairs. Pictured here is George W. Bush meeting with the National Security Council. Among the participants in the meeting are Secretary of State Condoleezza Rice (left), then-Secretary of Defense Donald Rumsfeld (second from left), and Vice President Dick Cheney (right).

direction of the military and naval forces, as first general and admiral of the confederacy." Thus, the president was to command the troops once they were committed to battle, but Congress was to make the decision to wage war.

Although the founders restricted the role of commander in chief, presidents have come to view this power quite expansively. In fact, presidents have regularly committed troops to action without asking Congress to formally declare war. Usually these actions have been small in scale, as when Jefferson sent ships against the Barbary pirates in 1805. Sometimes, however, presidents have unilaterally embarked on major war efforts. Convinced that he possessed all the powers necessary to win the Civil War, Lincoln undertook a series of extraordinary actions that included the blockade of southern ports, the expenditure of $2 million that had not been appropriated by Congress, and the drafting of 300,000 militiamen. All of this was done without explicit statutory authorization, although Congress did later approve most of the president's actions.

In the period preceding America's entry into World War II, Franklin D. Roosevelt issued several orders that were of doubtful constitutionality. The most famous of these was his "shoot at sight" order to U.S. naval vessels transporting military material to Great Britain. Roosevelt's directive, issued without congressional approval, empowered U.S. naval forces to fire at German submarines even though the United States had not yet entered the war. A formal declaration of war did not come until three months later, after the attack on Pearl Harbor.

Roosevelt's successor, Harry S Truman, went a step further in exerting presidential power when he ordered U.S. troops to repel an attack on South Korea by North Korean troops. Upon learning of the North Korean assault, Truman

Critical Thinking

What is the proper role of the president as commander in chief?

did not seek a congressional declaration of war; instead, he immediately committed thousands of American soldiers to combat in what was called a "police action." Truman moved with such speed that his order to the troops preceded both South Korea's and the United Nations' requests for intervention. Later, the administration justified this action as necessary to fulfill the U.S. commitment to the United Nations. However, a State Department publication noted at the time that the dispatching of military forces was really based on the "traditional power of the president to use the Armed Forces of the United States without consulting Congress."[22]

Presidents took over the power to make war because Congress and the public, particularly in the face of the perceived Soviet threat during the Cold War, let them do so. Even though specific presidential actions at times generated controversy, Congress was willing to surrender its constitutional authority to the president. Not until the U.S. involvement in Vietnam divided the nation did Congress begin to reassess its own role.

Johnson's and Nixon's continuation of the Vietnam war led Congress and the public to question presidential power in this area. Yet the initial commitment of American military forces to Vietnam had followed a familiar pattern of executive leadership and congressional docility. In August 1964, Johnson reported to Congress that the USS *Maddox* had been attacked while patrolling in international waters off the coast of North Vietnam. At the president's request, Congress responded to the event by passing, with only two dissenting votes, the Gulf of Tonkin Resolution, which authorized the president "to take all necessary measures to repel any armed attack against the forces of the United States and to prevent further aggression." Thus, with little knowledge of the actual events and only nine hours of debate, Congress provided the president with a blank check to increase American involvement as he saw fit.

Nine years after the Gulf of Tonkin Resolution, Congress moved to limit the president's war-making powers by passing the War Powers Resolution of 1973. Enacted over Nixon's veto, the War Powers Resolution provided that the president could send troops into hostile territory for a period not to exceed sixty days (Congress can provide a thirty-day extension). If Congress did not approve the actions within that time or if by resolution it voted to withdraw the troops, they must be removed. Another important provision of the resolution required the president "in every possible instance" to consult with Congress before dispatching troops into hostile or potentially hostile situations.

Years after the enactment of the War Powers Resolution, its effectiveness remains questionable. In 1982, President Reagan detailed a "peace-keeping" force of marines to Lebanon. Initially, Reagan refused to acknowledge the validity of the resolution and therefore did not formally notify Congress. One year after the introduction of the marines, however, the president and congressional leaders worked out a compromise that allowed the troops to stay in Lebanon for eighteen months on the condition that the president recognize the legitimacy of the resolution.

Reagan thus became the first president to invoke the resolution, but only in this one instance. In 1983, he informed Congress about the invasion of Grenada after it was over, and late in his term he refused to invoke the resolution in his decision to provide U.S. naval escorts for foreign ships operating in the Persian Gulf, even though these ships often engaged in hostilities.

Most telling of all, however, is the insignificant role that the War Powers Resolution played in the first war with Iraq. Following the Iraqi invasion of Kuwait, Bush deployed troops to Saudi Arabia without informing Congress. As the mission changed from defending Saudi Arabia to driving Iraq out of Kuwait, some members of Congress began to protest. Bush eventually requested and received congressional authorization for his actions, but only after he became convinced that he had strong support in Congress. By joint resolution in January 1991, Congress approved what amounted to a declaration of war when it authorized the president to use "all means necessary" to force Iraq out of Kuwait. Neither Congress nor the president, however, invoked the War Powers Resolution, and the president claimed, even as Congress was voting on the joint resolution, that he needed no congressional authorization. For some analysts, the minor role played by the War Powers Resolution in the Gulf War suggests that it is no longer viable.[23]

Prior to the invasion of Afghanistan, George W. Bush did request action from Congress, as his father had done before the invasion of Iraq. The joint resolution, known as the "Authorization for Use of Military Force," empowered the president to use all necessary and appropriate force against nations, organizations, or person(s) that planned, aided, authorized, or committed the terrorist acts of September 11, 2001. The resolution made it clear that it was intended to constitute specific authorization as defined by the War Powers Resolution. Nevertheless, George W. Bush, like his predecessors, denied that he needed congressional authority. Indeed, in 2002, even as the president was asking Congress to authorize the invasion of Iraq, the administration released a legal opinion prepared by the Department of State that dismissed entirely any need to consult with Congress.

Chief Legislator

These days, the mass media, the public, and even members of Congress look to the president as a kind of grand legislator who initiates public policy and then guides it through Congress. As soon as they take office, presidents are expected to formulate and present a well-defined legislative program that promises to solve all the problems that ail the nation. As the chairman of the House Foreign Affairs Committee told an Eisenhower administration official in 1953, "Don't expect us to start from scratch on what you people want. That's not the way we do things here. You draft bills and we work them over."[24]

These assumptions would suggest that the president possesses broad legislative powers, but such is not the case. Article II of the Constitution gives the president only four rather narrow legislative duties: (1) to "convene both Houses, or either of them" in special sessions, (2) to adjourn Congress if the two houses cannot agree on adjournment, (3) to "from time to time give Congress Information of the State of the Union," and (4) to recommend such measures "as he shall judge necessary and expedient." In addition, Article I arms the president with a veto.

The president no longer uses his powers to convene and adjourn Congress, mostly because of the extended length of the legislative year. Congress was last called into special session on July 26, 1948 — the day turnips are planted in Missouri. President Truman barraged this so-called Turnip Congress with one reform proposal after another. When, as expected, Congress failed to act, Truman had the issue he needed for his 1948 campaign. Running against the "do-nothing, good-for-nothing" Eightieth Congress, Truman defeated his Republican opponent, Thomas E. Dewey, and scored the biggest political upset of the century.

Recommending Legislation. The weak presidents of the 1800s offered Congress few specific policy proposals for fear of appearing to meddle with the legislative process. Modern presidents show no such reluctance, and this attitude certainly contributes to the myth of their unlimited power. The State of the Union message delivered each January illustrates the change in presidential dealings with Congress. During the 1800s, presidents typically offered nothing more than a routine report on the work of the previous year. Today this message is a major political statement that is addressed to the entire nation. The president exalts the administration's achievements and presents legislative goals for the coming year. Carefully crafted to hold the attention of the radio and television audience (a detailed written report is provided a few days after the oral message), the contemporary State of the Union message gives the president an opportunity to mobilize congressional and public support.

The president presents legislative proposals in less conspicuous ways as well. Numerous statutes require the president to submit detailed reports and even specific legislation. Each year, for instance, the president, as directed by the Budget and Accounting Act of 1921, presents a proposed federal budget for congressional consideration. Similarly, the president reports annually on the nation's economic condition, as required by the Employment Act of 1946. As you will soon see, initiating legislation and mobilizing sufficient support to secure its passage are two different matters. Members of Congress expect presidential initiatives; they even demand them. That does not mean, however, that the president's program will pass.

The Veto Power. The president's ultimate weapon is the veto. After passing both houses of Congress, bills are submitted to the White House for the president's signature. A presidential signature is not necessary for a bill to become law, however. If the president fails to act within ten days of receiving the bill (Sundays excepted), it becomes law without presidential approval.

Pocket veto A decision by the president not to sign a bill during the last ten days of a term, effectively killing the bill.

During the last ten days of a session, however, the president's failure to sign has the opposite effect: It kills the bill. This action, known as a **pocket veto**, is particularly effective because Congress, having gone out of session, has no way to fight back. When presidents exercise their ordinary veto power by sending bills back to the originating house, these vetoes can be overridden by a vote of two-thirds of those present in both houses.

In practice, Congress overrides few vetoes, giving presidents a substantial advantage. Nixon's veto of the War Powers Resolution at the height of the Watergate scandal shows how hard it is for Congress to muster its forces for an override even when a president is in disgrace. Though the scandal had seriously undermined the president's public support, the House was able to override his veto by only a four-vote margin.

Because Congress succeeds in overriding vetoes so rarely, presidents can wring concessions from it through the threat of a veto. In such instances, the House and Senate may drop provisions that run counter to White House priorities and will sometimes even withhold entire bills rather than face a certain veto. But to make the threat credible, the president must occasionally use the veto. At one time Franklin Roosevelt is said to have pleaded with his staff to "give me a bill that I can veto" so that Congress would be convinced of his willingness to use this power.[25]

In recent years, presidents have complained that the veto power is too blunt an instrument to prevent wasteful spending. Since the president must sign or veto the entire bill, Congress has often attached **riders** (provisions, usually unrelated to the main purpose of the bill) opposed by the administration to a bill that the president wants. When this happens, the president must either accept the objectionable parts or veto the entire bill. In most cases the president signs the bill.

Line-Item Veto. After years of debate, Congress finally passed the Line Item Veto Act of 1996, giving the president a **line-item veto**: the power to veto portions of a bill while signing the rest. Under the terms of the act, the president was empowered to sign a bill but to strike out individual spending provisions. The president was also given the authority to cancel any tax breaks that applied to a hundred or fewer taxpayers. Congress could restore these provisions by passing a bill disapproving the cuts, but the president was allowed to veto that legislation, forcing Congress to override that veto by a two-thirds vote.

Two months after the bill became effective, President Clinton used the line-item veto to cancel a spending provision and two portions of a tax bill giving special relief to small groups of taxpayers. But Clinton's use of the line-item veto was immediately challenged in court. In the 1998 case of *Clinton v. City of New York*, the Supreme Court ruled the act unconstitutional. According to the Court, the act violated the presentment clause of the Constitution, which requires that a bill be passed by both houses of Congress in exactly the same language and then sent to the president for signature or veto. The Court reasoned that allowing the president to veto a portion of a bill was to allow the president to create a different law, one that had not been passed by either the House or the Senate. (Another method of bypassing Congress, the signing statement, is discussed in "Asked & Answered," p. 316.) If Congress wanted to create a new procedure, the Court said, it must do so by constitutional amendment.

Impoundment. Since the Line Item Veto Act did not pass constitutional muster, presidents are left to fashion a weak version of the line-item veto by **impounding** (withholding) funds appropriated by Congress. As far back as Jefferson, presidents have claimed the right to impound funds, either by deferring spending to

---

Riders Provisions, usually unrelated, that are attached to a bill; in general, these are provisions that Congress knows the president opposes that are attached to bills that the president otherwise desires.

Line-item veto The power to veto portions of a bill but sign the rest of it. The president was given this power in 1997, but the act giving him this power was ruled unconstitutional.

Critical Thinking

What effect would giving the president a line-item veto have on the balance of power between the executive and legislative branches?

Impoundment Withholding by a president of funds that have been appropriated by Congress. Used in place of a line-item veto.

A Focus on Education

During his presidential campaign, George W. Bush promised to be the "Education President," vowing to recommend laws to reform the nation's education system.

some later date or by forbidding agencies to spend the money. Jefferson postponed spending $50,000 on gunboats in 1803 so that he could purchase a more advanced model the following year.

Traditionally, presidents have used impoundment cautiously to avoid confrontation with Congress; in most cases the money was eventually released. However, Richard Nixon took impoundment further than any previous president had done. After failing to get Congress, which was controlled by the Democrats, to agree to cut spending, Nixon simply impounded appropriated funds, arguing that he had a right not to spend money that he had not requested. Nixon used the technique to eliminate whole programs that he disliked. By signing the bills that created the programs but refusing to spend the money to implement them, he fashioned a veto that could not be overridden. His strategy was more than a method of controlling spending; it was a means of controlling Congress.

Congress responded by limiting the president's impoundment power. In the Budget and Impoundment Control Act of 1974, it set forty-five days as the maximum time that funds could be impounded. If during that time Congress did not pass a new act—a rescission bill (as in *rescind*, or repeal)—to cancel the spending, the funds must be spent.

The Seamless Web

For the sake of easier discussion, we have partitioned presidential responsibilities into distinct roles. Yet presidential activity is not so neatly divided. In fact, the various roles form a "seamless web" of endless combinations, and doing well in one

ASKED & ANSWERED

ASKED: What is a signing statement?

ANSWERED: When presidents are presented with a bill passed by both houses of Congress, they have the option of either signing it or vetoing it. Vetoed bills are sent back to the house that originated the legislation with a statement explaining the president's objections, while the signing of bills is frequently marked by a public ceremony. Often, however, the signing and ceremony mask the reality of the president's intentions for the bill, and just how willing he is to implement its provisions. To make these intentions more clear, for several years now presidents have taken the opportunity to add to their formal approval a *signing statement*, a document explaining the administration's interpretation of and concerns about the new law.

These signing statements are not simply a president's general musings on the law in question; they are calculated efforts to enhance presidential powers. By providing an alternative interpretation of a law, the president may in effect rewrite the law according to his own specifications. Signing statements also routinely instruct executive branch officials on how the administration wants the new law implemented.

Although several presidents have used signing statements, President George W. Bush has been the most aggressive to date. Ironically, although the president issued no vetoes in his first term, he produced a record-breaking 107 signing statements in those four years, and he has continued that trend into his second term. In 2006, for instance, the president signed the extension of the Patriot Act, praising Congress for its work. However, he then released a signing statement indicating that his administration felt free to ignore important provisions of the law, specifically those requiring that the president disclose to Congress how several of its powers were being used. The president's sign-

ing statement simply noted that, despite the congressional mandates that he provide reports, the president retained the right to withhold information when, in his judgment, it was in the national interest to do so. Likewise, the president signed the Defense Authorization Act, which included a controversial provision forbidding the torture of anyone in the government's custody. Although the president publicly applauded the provision, and its sponsor, Senator John McCain, his signing statement asserted that he could and would circumvent the law to protect national security.

What makes signing statements so attractive to presidents is that they are difficult to challenge. These presidential objections are frequently justified on the vague grounds that the legislation interferes with the executive's constitutional obligation to faithfully execute the laws. The vagueness of such justifications makes it difficult to challenge the president's interpretation as a violation of presidential authority. Moreover, unless the implementation instructions to executive officials are quite specific, it is often impossible to link the signing statement to specific problems that may result from the law's application. This is especially problematic, since implementation of a law's provision may come long after passage of the law itself.

In the end, signing statements constitute a form of line-item veto, but without any procedures for congressional override. Whether future presidents will continue the vigorous use of the signing statement remains to be seen. However, the effectiveness of signing statements in challenging Congress suggests that their popularity will continue.

Source: Phillip J. Cooper, "George W. Bush, Edgar Allan Poe, and the Use and Abuse of Presidential Signing Statements," *Presidential Studies Quarterly*, 35 (September 2005).

role may be helpful, or indeed essential, to performing another.[26] For instance, successful performance as chief of state can often benefit a president in other roles. Similarly, when diplomatic actions involve the threat or use of force, the distinction between chief diplomat and commander in chief may all but disappear.

The Institutional Presidency

FOCUS QUESTION WHO ARE THE PRESIDENT'S MOST IMPORTANT ADVISERS?

According to the standard organizational charts reproduced in textbooks, the president is the boss of some 3 million civilian employees — the largest administrative organization in the country. Obviously, no single person can control an organization of that size, yet that is exactly what presidents are expected to do. But the president does not perform the task alone, for the modern president is surrounded, perhaps even engulfed, by layers of presidential advisers, known collectively as the institutional presidency.[27] Included in that group are members of the cabinet and of the Executive Office of the President, the White House staff, and the vice president.

The Cabinet

The original advisory group is the cabinet. Not provided for in the Constitution, the cabinet by tradition comprises the heads of the major executive departments and other officials whom the president designates. George Washington created the cabinet by meeting frequently with his attorney general and the secretaries of state, treasury, and war. (James Madison gave those meetings with Washington the title of the "president's cabinet.") By law, the modern cabinet consists of the fifteen department heads. The vice president is also accorded a place in the cabinet. Presidents may also elevate others within their administration to cabinet-level rank. In 1996, for instance, President Clinton elevated the director of the Federal Emergency Management Agency (FEMA) to cabinet-level rank. George W. Bush, on the other hand, downgraded the director of FEMA, but after September 11, 2001, he granted his new Director of Homeland Security cabinet-level rank. Other officials with cabinet-level rank include the director of the Environmental Protection Agency, the director of the Office of Management and Budget, the director of Office of National Drug Control Policy, the U.S. Trade Representative, and the president's chief of staff.

As a unit, the cabinet has seldom functioned as an effective advisory body for the president. Because it is not provided for in the Constitution, its role in decision making is defined by the individual presidents, who rarely find it useful. Many presidents have undoubtedly found themselves in the position of Lincoln when he asked his assembled cabinet for advice. As Lincoln went around the table, each member voted against the president's position. Undisturbed, Lincoln announced, "Seven nays and one aye; the ayes have it."

**Critical
    Thinking**

Can the cabinet ever
be an effective advisory
body?

Even though collectively the cabinet does not often act as an effective advisory body to the president, its members may perform important advisory functions. In any cabinet, there are likely to be individuals who are close to the president. (John F. Kennedy's reliance on his brother, Attorney General Robert Kennedy, is an obvious example.) By virtue of the departments they head, members of what Thomas Cronin calls the "inner cabinet" (the attorney general and the secretaries of state, defense, and the treasury) are most likely to serve as important counselors to the president. The secretaries of the clientele-oriented agencies (that is, health and human services, education, labor, housing and urban development, the interior, agriculture, commerce, transportation, energy, and veterans affairs) generally constitute a kind of "outer cabinet" whose members often have little direct contact with the president.[28] Indeed, the pressures to represent the interests of their clientele often put secretaries of these departments at odds with the president.

The Executive Office of the President

In 1939, the President's Commission on Administrative Management reported: "The President needs help." Acting on the commission's recommendations, Franklin D. Roosevelt issued an **executive order**—a rule or regulation that has the effect of law—creating the Executive Office of the President (EOP). The EOP is not so much an office as an umbrella for a hodgepodge of organizations performing a wide variety of tasks for the president. Currently, it is composed of ten separate organizations, the most important of which are the Office of Management and Budget, the Council of Economic Advisers, and the National Security Council.

Executive order A rule
or regulation issued by
the president that has
the effect of law.

The Office of Management and Budget. The Office of Management and Budget (OMB), until 1971 known as the Bureau of the Budget, is the largest of the organizations within the Executive Office of the President. Although the OMB was originally viewed as a professional organization producing independent analysis, in recent years it has become an institutional advocate for the president's initiatives, a status that often puts it in direct conflict with other departments, particularly those that compose the "outer cabinet." The OMB's primary function in recent years has been to prepare the president's budget for presentation to Congress each January. Each of the departments and agencies of the executive branch submits its budget request to the OMB, which screens these requests for fidelity to the president's spending priorities and impact on the economy. Because no agency can request appropriations from Congress without clearance from the OMB, the director of the office, who is appointed by the president with senatorial confirmation, serves as an important means of controlling the budget and making policy through budgetary power.

In addition to its budgetary responsibilities, the OMB routinely reviews all legislation proposed by the executive departments and agencies to make sure that the proposals are consistent with the president's program.[29] Agencies proposing laws and regulations with projected costs of $100 million or more must justify the expense. The OMB cannot reject a proposal on the basis of such a cost-benefit analysis, but it can recommend that the president do so. Increasingly, the OMB even conducts cost-benefit analyses on its own. Although these procedures may help the president gain information, they heighten tension between the departments and the Executive Office of the President.

The Council of Economic Advisers. Legislated into existence by the Employment Act of 1946, the Council of Economic Advisers (CEA) consists of three members, generally professional economists, who are appointed by the president with senatorial confirmation. Its small but highly competent staff advises the president on the full range of economic issues: unemployment, inflation, taxes, federal spending levels, and the value of the dollar abroad. The council also prepares an annual report that contains analyses of current economic data and economic forecasts. Given its wide-ranging responsibilities, the council often finds itself competing for influence in economic policymaking with the director of the Office of Management and Budget, the chairman of the Federal Reserve Board, and the secretaries of the treasury, commerce, and labor.

The National Security Council. Created by the National Security Act of 1947, the National Security Council (NSC) advises the president on foreign and defense policy. By statute, the NSC consists of the president, the vice president, and the secretaries of state and defense. In addition, the heads of the Central Intelligence Agency and the Joint Chiefs of Staff are statutory advisers. The president may also request the attendance of other officials.

The role of the NSC depends greatly on the president's preference. President Eisenhower met weekly with the council, but succeeding presidents have preferred to rely on informal groups of advisers and the special assistant for national security affairs. Originally, the special assistant for national security affairs was little more than the secretary of the NSC. But President Kennedy, in order to limit his dependence on the State Department, gave greater authority to McGeorge Bundy, the special assistant, encouraging him to create a "little State Department." President Nixon's special assistant, Henry Kissinger, using an enlarged staff and his considerable political skills, soon eclipsed Nixon's secretary of state, William P. Rogers, as foreign policy adviser to the president. Ultimately, Rogers resigned, and Kissinger took on the second job as well.

During Reagan's second term, the National Security Council became the subject of controversy because of its direction of undercover operations in Iran and Nicaragua. In an effort to secure the release of Americans held hostage in the Middle East, NSC employees arranged for the sale of weapons to Iran. Profits from these sales were then diverted to Contra rebels who were attempting to overthrow the government of Nicaragua, despite a congressional ban on such aid. In this instance, rather than serving as an advisory body, the NSC engaged in policy implementation.

The White House Office: Two Management Styles

FOCUS QUESTION   HOW DO PRESIDENTS DIFFER IN THEIR MANAGEMENT STYLES?

Technically, the White House Office is part of the Executive Office of the President, but in an important sense the two organizations are separate. The White House Office is composed of staff members who are located in the White House and serve the president's political needs. Smaller than the Executive Office of the President, it is nevertheless a sizable organization in its own right—for example, in the Clinton administration it employed more than 400 people. The White House Office includes assistants, special assistants, counselors, special counselors, and consultants with varying titles who function almost totally in the service of the president. Originally, the staff's function was limited to coordinating executive branch activities, but presidents, frustrated by their inability to control the bureaucracy, have increasingly come to rely on the White House Office to develop and implement policy initiatives. Indeed, cabinet secretaries, much to their chagrin, often find that policies affecting their departments are developed in the White House Office.

The actual structure of the office depends on the president's organizational preferences. Some presidents have favored a rather loose structure in which several aides report directly to the president. Sometimes referred to as the "wheel," this highly personalized approach is designed to assure the president access to information.

Most modern presidents, however, have favored a tight structure, with staff responsibilities and reporting procedures clearly detailed, and subordinates reporting to a chief of staff. Under this organizational style, which resembles a pyramid, only one or two key aides have access to the president. Eisenhower, with his military background, preferred this type of arrangement and delegated much authority to his chief aide, Sherman Adams. Unless Adams initialed it, nothing could come to the president. Carrying the pyramid style a step further, Nixon used his chief of staff, H. R. "Bob" Haldeman, and his domestic adviser, John Ehrlichman, to seal him off from the rest of the government. Haldeman had such tight control over the president's daily schedule that not even members of the president's family could see him without Haldeman's permission.

Pyramid structures can reduce the president's burden, allowing him to concentrate on those issues that truly require his time. But the relief may come at some cost. The top aides may limit their communications to what the president wants to hear, cutting off dissenting viewpoints. And they may make important decisions before the questions reach the president. As two critics have observed, "presidential assistants can become assistant presidents."[30]

The Vice President

Benjamin Franklin once suggested that the vice president be called "His Superfluous Majesty," and Daniel Webster, saying that "he did not propose to be buried until he was already dead," refused to accept nomination for the office.[31] Although fourteen vice presidents have later become president, esteem for the office has never been high. The reason rests with the Constitution, which provides the vice president with little to do. The vice president's only constitutionally prescribed task — presiding over the Senate — offers little real power, except in the rare case of a tied vote. The vice president has no role in the day-to-day business of that body.

The vice president does, of course, become president if the president dies in office, resigns, or is impeached and removed from office. Furthermore, since the adoption of the Twenty-fifth Amendment, the vice president can assume the presidency if the president decides that he is disabled, or if the vice president and a majority of the cabinet declare the president to be disabled. For instance, before undergoing cancer surgery, President Reagan wrote a letter empowering Vice President George Bush to take over the functions of the presidency while Reagan was under the anesthetic.

Critical Thinking

What role was originally intended for the vice president?

An Expanding Role
For most of our history, vice presidents have played only a small role in national politics. Recent vice presidents have become more influential, however. Still, no vice president has been more powerful than Vice President Dick Cheney, pictured here with President George W. Bush.

Because the Constitution does not specify the vice president's duties, they are determined by the president. Typically, presidents send their vice presidents to advisory panels and ceremonial occasions that they themselves want to avoid. Perhaps the most striking example of a distant relationship between a president and a vice president was provided in 1945. Although it had been known for months that President Roosevelt was dying, Truman was not briefed on the existence of the atomic bomb until after he became president, a mere four months before he made the decision to use it.

In part, presidents have been reluctant to delegate too much power to their vice presidents for fear of creating a political rival. Generally, a vice-presidential candidate is chosen with an eye to drawing additional supporters to the ticket; thus, the vice president is a potential competitor for the limelight. The vice president is also a constant reminder of the president's mortality. Indeed, Lyndon Johnson likened the vice president to "a raven hovering around the head of the president."[32]

Recently, however, presidents have delegated more responsibilities to their vice presidents. Carter signaled the change by allowing his vice president, Walter Mondale, to influence the selection of several high officials in the administration. Presidents since Carter have continued to give their vice presidents expanded responsibilities and greater visibility. No vice president has matched the power and presidential access possessed by Vice President Dick Cheney, however. From the beginning, George W. Bush publicly assigned Cheney wide-ranging responsibilities. Indeed, Vice President Cheney has publicly taken the lead in representing the administration's position on its most important initiatives.

Presidential Influence

FOCUS
QUESTION   **WHAT TOOLS DOES THE PRESIDENT HAVE TO INFLUENCE OTHER DECISION MAKERS?**

To those outside the office, the myth of the all-powerful president seems compelling. Yet presidents themselves stress the frustrations of holding office. Truman, describing what it was going to be like for his successor, Eisenhower, said: "He'll sit here, and he'll say, Do this! Do that! And nothing will happen. Poor Ike — it won't be a bit like the army."[33] Similarly, Lyndon Johnson once complained that the only power he had was nuclear, and he could not use it.

The point of these remarks is that the president's desires are not automatically translated into government policy. In the American system, power is shared. Congress, with its different constituency interests, often checks presidential initiatives. The bureaucracy has endless opportunities to circumvent presidential directives. According to political scientist and former presidential adviser Richard Neustadt, for a president to be effective, he must become adept at persuasion, convincing others that what he wants of them is in their own interest.[34]

Persuading Congress

Perhaps the greatest and most persistent problem facing any president is working with Congress. According to Lyndon Johnson, "There is only one way for a President to deal with Congress, and that is continuously, incessantly, and without interruption. If it's really going to work, the relationship between the president and Congress has got to be almost incestuous."[35] As you may recall from Chapter 10, on Congress, presidential initiatives are only a starting point for congressional action. Obtaining congressional support is crucial. In pursuing this goal, presidents have three primary resources: party loyalty, staff lobbyists, and personal appeal.

Critical Thinking

What are the consequences for the president of having Congress dominated by the opposition party?

Party Loyalty. At the heart of a successful strategy for dealing with Congress is the political party. Presidents must retain the support of members of their own party while gaining the support of as many members of the opposition party as possible. Historically, party loyalty has been fairly strong among congressional Republicans and less so among congressional Democrats. Presidents cannot take members of their own party for granted, but they must assume that most members of the opposition party will oppose them. Having a majority of seats in Congress is therefore no guarantee of an administration's success, but it is easier than dealing with a Congress controlled by the opposition.

Staff Lobbyists. Before 1953, contacts between the president and Congress were informal and largely based on personal relationships. Some presidents relied on frequent social events to discuss their concerns with members of Congress. Jefferson used that tactic with particular success. His elaborate dinner parties were planned as much for their lively talk as for their superb cuisine. In 1953, however, Eisenhower created the Office of Congressional Relations to formalize the administration's lobbying efforts. (That did not, of course, replace the social events; rather, it provided the president with a structure for coordinating lobbying activities.)

Because Eisenhower offered few major legislative proposals, the office was initially small and mostly concerned with heading off the passage of legislation that he opposed. During the Kennedy and Johnson years, however, the office began to grow substantially as these administrations took a more aggressive legislative posture. Johnson, in particular, used the office to inform members of Congress of the administration's position on issues and to solicit congressional support. More important, Johnson expanded the role of the office by instructing its staffers to help members of Congress with personal services for constituents.

Although talented lobbyists can be quite effective in persuading members of Congress to support administration proposals, they must be close to the president if they are to succeed. According to Bryce Harlow, legislative liaison chief under both Eisenhower and Nixon, "for real effectiveness a White House congressional man must be known on Capitol Hill as a confidant of the president; he must be in the know."[36] As if to underscore the point, Harlow resigned as Nixon's liaison chief because he lacked the necessary access to the president.

Personal Appeal. A president's ability to appeal personally to members of Congress can be vital to his success. A little flattery and attention from a president can go a long way. Reagan used this personal approach to great advantage, offering frequent invitations to breakfast at the White House and gifts of cuff links bearing the presidential seal in his persistent effort to cultivate relations with Congress. On important bills, the president often made phone calls to wavering members, personally soliciting their support. But even Reagan's personal appeal had its limits. Although he had great success in securing congressional support early in his first term, his success rate declined markedly after 1982. A little flattery may go a long way, but too much dilutes its effectiveness.

Public Opinion

Lincoln once said, "Public sentiment is everything. With public sentiment nothing can fail, without it nothing can succeed." Although Lincoln overstated the importance of public approval, popularity is an important tool of persuasion. One political scientist has argued that members of Congress try to predict the public's reaction to their behavior toward the president and often decide what tack they should take on that basis.[37] Lacking precise information about public attitudes, they look to the president's popularity as a guide. Popularity does not guarantee that a president will be successful, however. "When [a member of Congress] is confronted by a choice between supporting a popular president and the clear interests of his constituents, the president's public prestige is a poor match for his or her constituents' interests."[38]

Naturally, presidents are well aware of the importance of public popularity. (When the polls were good, Lyndon Johnson used to carry the results in his breast pocket, ready to show anyone who needed convincing.) President George W. Bush demonstrated a keen awareness of the role of public opinion when, shortly after his reelection in 2004, he announced that the public had given him some capital that he was going to spend pursuing his policy agenda. Unfortunately for presidents, presidential popularity tends to decline during a president's term of office (see Figure 11.1).

At the beginning of a term, presidents traditionally enjoy a honeymoon period of broad public support and favorable media coverage. Indeed, with the exception of Ronald Reagan, a substantially larger percentage of Americans have approved of newly elected presidents than were willing to vote for them. By a president's third year in office, however, public approval declines significantly.

The existence of this decline in presidential popularity is part of what political scientist Paul Light calls the "cycle of decreasing influence." According to Light, as a president's term progresses, his political capital (that is, public approval and partisan support), time, and energy diminish, seriously eroding his influence over public policy.[39] Given this cycle, presidents may even suffer from these initially high ratings. When the inflated ratings drop, as they inevitably will, "the fall can be all the more devastating."[40]

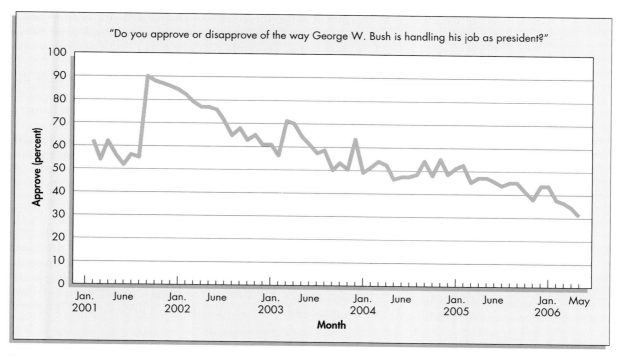

"Do you approve or disapprove of the way George W. Bush is handling his job as president?"

FIGURE 11.1

The Ups and Downs of President George W. Bush

Most presidents experience a decline in public approval as the term of office progresses.

Critical Thinking

Why do presidents' approval ratings fall during the term?

High levels of public approval may also be a trap for modern presidents. As a president's popularity surges, expectations of successful leadership also escalate. Indeed, the more popular the president, the more the myth of the all-powerful president seems a reality. But, as we have seen, presidents are not the government, and while high public approval ratings may give presidents some leeway, they do not automatically translate into power. A highly popular president who does not translate high approval ratings into visible legislative successes runs the risk of looking like a failure.

Conclusion: The All-Powerful President?

According to the myth of the all-powerful president, modern presidents possess awesome powers that, if mobilized, would enable them to solve all the country's problems. Although that myth has not always prevailed, it colored what the public expected of the presidency in the latter half of the twentieth century. As the office evolved to its current state, the course of change has not been smooth. Presidential power has increased at times of grave emergency and great stress. In calmer periods, Congress has generally reasserted its role by reining in the president.

The broad range of roles ascribed to the president further enhances the myth of presidential power. Yet presidents often find that the duties associated with these roles are more difficult than they imagined. And Congress is hardly a silent spectator in the process of governing.

To give him support in his various roles, the president has acquired a multitude of advisers—in the cabinet, the Executive Office of the President, and the White House Office. In fact, presidents are surrounded by a bureaucracy of advisers who constitute the institutional presidency. Thus the president does not lack counsel; instead, the problem has become one of managing the advisers.

Finally, we have examined presidential power as persuasion. Although the office itself is generally seen as all-powerful, presidents find that their wishes do not automatically become policy. In this system of shared powers, the president must convince others that what he wants is in their interest as well. The invoking of party loyalty, effective lobbying, and personal appeal are all potential means of persuasion, but the support of the public is particularly useful. Although popular approval does not guarantee presidential success, it makes it more likely.

Tying It Together

FOCUS QUESTIONS RECAP

* How has the presidency evolved into a powerful office?

* What are the various roles that presidents are expected to play and what are the constitutional foundations for these roles?

* Who are the president's most important advisers?

* How do presidents differ in their management styles?

* What tools does the president have to influence other decision makers?

CHAPTER SUMMARY

1. The powers of the presidency have expanded significantly since the adoption of the Constitution. American history has witnessed periods of presidential dominance, usually in times of emergency, followed by congressional efforts to reassert the power of Congress by placing limits on the powers of the office. In the end, however, the ebb and flow of power have generally benefited the presidency. As new problems and threats have emerged, presidents have been perceived as the most effective source of relief.

2. The importance of the modern presidency is seen most clearly in the variety of roles that the incumbent is now expected to play: chief of

state, chief executive, chief diplomat, commander in chief, and chief legislator.

3. As chief of state, the president is the ceremonial head of the government.

4. As chief executive, the president must "take care that the laws be faithfully executed" and manage an executive branch composed of some 3 million employees. To perform the duties of chief executive, the president has the power of appointment, the power to grant pardons, and the power of executive privilege, but none of these is unlimited.

5. As chief diplomat, the president, with the advice and consent of the Senate, can negotiate treaties and make diplomatic appointments. The president also has the power to extend diplomatic recognition to other countries and can make executive agreements with other nations without Senate approval.

6. As commander in chief, the president is supreme commander of the nation's military forces. Presidents have also used that role to claim the power to make war.

7. As chief legislator, the president can convene special sessions of Congress and adjourn Congress if the two houses cannot agree on a date of adjournment. The president is also required to give Congress "from time to time" information on the "State of the Union" and to recommend measures for congressional action. Furthermore, the president has the power to veto acts of Congress, although the veto is subject to override.

8. The modern president is assisted by several advisory groups—the cabinet, the Executive Office of the President, and the White House Office—and by the vice president. These advisers constitute the institutional presidency.

9. The cabinet, consisting of the fifteen department heads, the ambassador to the United Nations, and other officials whom the president designates, is the original presidential advisory group. But the cabinet does not often function effectively, and most presidents hold cabinet meetings purely for ceremonial purposes.

10. Created by an executive order of Franklin D. Roosevelt, the Executive Office of the President (EOP) contains ten separate organizations, including the Office of Management and Budget, the Council of Economic Advisers, and the National Security Council.

11. Also within the EOP is the smaller White House Office, which includes assistants, special assistants, counselors, special counselors, and consultants who perform a wide variety of personal and political duties for the president.

12. In managing the White House Office, presidents demonstrate different styles. Some presidents have preferred what is called the "wheel." The wheel is a loose organizational structure that has several aides reporting directly to the president. This structure guarantees that the president has access to a wide variety of views. Most presidents, however, prefer the pyramidal style, requiring aides to report to a chief of staff. The advantage of the pyramid style of management is that it reduces the president's burden, allowing him to concentrate on what is truly important.

13. The vice president presides over the Senate but votes only to break a tie. The vice president assumes the presidency if the president dies, resigns, is removed by impeachment, or is unable to function because of a disability.

14. To be effective, presidents must be skilled at persuasion. In dealing with Congress, presidents can rely to some extent on party loyalty, but they must also assemble an effective lobbying staff and use it well. Skillful use of personal appeals to legislators is often effective and necessary.

15. Presidents are more successful at persuasion when their public popularity is high, but popularity often eludes them as their term progresses.

Key Terms

Executive privilege (306)
Executive agreements (308)
Congressional-executive agreement (308)
Pocket veto (313)

Riders (314)
Line-item veto (314)
Impoundment (314)
Executive order (318)

 Net Work

For information on the presidency and the White House, check out the following websites:

- To learn more about the president's historic residence, visit the White House Historical Association site (**www.whitehousehistory.org**). While you are there, take a virtual tour of the White House and check out its china and art collections.

- Are you looking for a specific document from a previous administration? Visit the National Archives and Records Administration site (**www.archives.gov**). Use this source or one of the presidential libraries linked to it to find an example of an executive order, or try finding a presidential veto message.

If your interests are more current, there are a couple of excellent sources for following the day-to-day activities of the president.

- First, you can read daily press releases and briefings, the same ones that reporters use for their stories, by going to the White House Official Source (**www.whitehouse.gov**). If you have the software, you can also listen to the president's Saturday radio address.

- Then, for a more visual experience of the White House, go to C-SPAN's site on the Bush administration (**www.c-span.org/executive**). This site provides audio and video coverage of the goings-on at the White House. Presidential speeches, bill-signing ceremonies, and press briefings can be viewed or heard live.

As an exercise, try comparing a White House press release with a published press account of that release. How true to the original release is the media story?

12

Bureaucracy

MYTH & REALITY

Are Washington bureaucrats unresponsive and incompetent?

FOCUS QUESTIONS

* Who works in the bureaucracy? What do these people do? Where do they work?

* What factors have led to the growth of the federal bureaucracy?

* What are the sources of (and limits on) bureaucratic power?

* What are the major problems with bureaucratic behavior, and what steps have been taken to control them?

T his is the story of a bureaucratic agency that, in 1995, was called "the most dramatic success story of the federal government in recent years. Not only does it provide further evidence that the government can work, it offers a blueprint for what it takes: strong leadership, energetic oversight, and, most importantly, a total reevaluation of its mission."[1]

The agency referred to in that statement is the Federal Emergency Management Agency (FEMA). Ten years later, this agency, charged with overseeing and coordinating government response to disasters, was itself declared a disaster by the media and general public after its failure to deal adequately with the aftermath of Hurricane Katrina in New Orleans and much of the Gulf Coast in late August 2005. On September 12, 2005, two weeks after the storm had made landfall in the New Orleans region, FEMA director Michael Brown submitted his resignation. Months later, in an interview with Chris Wallace of Fox Cable News Network, Brown would call Hurricane Katrina a "catastrophic event of biblical proportions" for which the government was not prepared.[2] Although much of the criticism and blame for FEMA's poor performance was targeted at Brown for not adhering to disaster plans, for being out of touch, and for not following the chain of command, among other faults, he continued to maintain that the problem had more to do with the changes made since September 11, 2001, in the way that government operates. When asked about the future, Brown was not optimistic about the changes made after his departure. "If you look at what's happening in FEMA, they still have . . . hundreds of vacancies they can't fill. There's still this confusion about what FEMA is supposed to do and not do. . . . The partnerships between FEMA and state and local governments have been broken and will continue to be broken by the path that the [current leadership] . . . is headed down. So I think we're worse off today than we were even before Katrina."

How did the successful agency of 1995 deteriorate into the bureaucratic mess of 2005? The story behind the failure of FEMA can be traced back to its formation in 1979. President Jimmy Carter, using authority granted to the White House by Congress in 1932, issued an Executive Order (see Chapter 11, on the presidency) that consolidated the Department of Defense's Civil Preparedness Agency (Civil Defense) with many smaller, related agencies and programs into a new independent FEMA (see the discussion below).

At the outset, half of FEMA's budget and its primary mission were related to "civil defense" functions designed to assure that the nation was prepared to survive a massive nuclear attack. Its role in disaster relief was limited to providing coordination for whatever aid and loans might be made available to parts of the country that had been designated disaster areas after an event (e.g., flood, tornado, hurricane) had taken place.

With such a limited role to play in preventing disasters or even in emergency management, FEMA did not develop the capacity for quick response until the late 1980s, and then did so only slowly. For presidents, the underfunded FEMA became an agency in which they could put their unqualified political appointees, leading some critics to term it "the turkey farm."

Things started to change in 1989 when Hurricane Hugo, a category 5 storm, hit Puerto Rico and both North Carolina and South Carolina. Seventy people

Working Together Before Things Got Worse

Michael Brown (center), head of FEMA at the time Hurricane Katrina hit New Orleans, is pictured consulting with Ray Nagin (left), the city's mayor, and Michael Chertoff, Secretary of the Department of Homeland Security.

died, and FEMA's slow response became an issue. Calling the agency a "bunch of bureaucratic jackasses," South Carolina Senator Fritz Hollings led the call for reforms to make FEMA more responsive. But in 1992, another hurricane (this time Andrew) hit Florida hard. Under the law and agency operating rules in place at the time, FEMA could and would do nothing unless called into an area by state governors, and Florida's governor (unaware at the time of the extent of the damage caused by Andrew) was hesitant to do so since a decision to seek help would require the state to provide matching funds from its own tight coffers for each dollar that FEMA would spend. Once it became evident just how much devastation Andrew had caused, not only FEMA but also the Department of Defense were mobilized to deal with the immediate aftermath as well as the long-term cleanup.

The problems with FEMA were politically costly to the first President Bush. Many analysts believe he lost the 1992 election because of FEMA's failure to effectively respond to Hurricane Andrew and other disasters. It was a lesson taken to heart by Bill Clinton when he entered the White House. He appointed James Lee Witt, the head of emergency management in Clinton's home state of Arkansas, and someone who had gained a good reputation by handling flood relief in that state in 1990 and 1991. Witt took over an agency that was under severe political attack and in which morale was low. By early 1993, influential members of Congress had their staffs develop plans for the radical transformation of the country's disaster response programs — plans that threatened the very existence of FEMA as an independent agency. Witt pleaded for one year's time to allow him to turn the agency around, saying that if he failed to do so he would join in the push for the more radical reforms.

Within a year FEMA was transformed. Its mission and authority were refocused to include disaster prevention as well as response, and its capacity to respond quickly and effectively to all types of catastrophic events was greatly enhanced. Closing unnecessary field offices, eliminating dozens of internal rules, and flattening the organization, Witt also made strategic and pivotal personnel changes by eliminating appointees with no relevant experience and replacing them with those who had appropriate experience with disaster prevention and management at the state and local levels. A complete audit and assessment of the agency followed. As one indication of improvement, kudos rather than criticisms were showered on FEMA after its response to flooding in the Mississippi River basin in 1994. By 1995 FEMA had truly become the model of a responsive and effective bureaucracy.

FEMA was not only responding to natural disasters. On April 19, 1995, less than half an hour after a terrorist bomb destroyed the Murrah Federal Building in Oklahoma City, FEMA's Washington office received a call from Oklahoma City's emergency management director. FEMA's response to him was almost immediate:

> A couple of years earlier he would have been told that his governor needed to file a written request for federal emergency assistance and mail it to Washington. No longer. Four and a half hours after [the] call, at 2:05 p.m., FEMA's advance team got there, complete with damage assessors. At 8:10 p.m., James Lee Witt, FEMA's director, arrived to personally coordinate the federal response. Witt had been a state emergency services director himself and he knew the drill. By 2:30 a.m., FEMA's own search and rescue teams were on the scene to help the city's fire department.[3]

FEMA remained a model agency throughout the Clinton administration, and Witt remained at its helm.[4] However, when George W. Bush became president, he appointed to the post James Allbaugh, a close political associate of his. Under Allbaugh, FEMA was reorganized and downsized, and after September 11, 2001, its focus became dealing with terrorism. After Allbaugh left government to work as a consultant and lobbyist, Bush replaced him with an old school friend of Allbaugh's, Michael Brown. By that time FEMA had become part of the Department of Homeland Security, and much of Witt's accomplishments had been undermined by the time Katrina hit land on August 29, 2005.

The story of FEMA's rollercoaster ride from the "turkey farm" of the 1980s to the model federal agency of the 1990s to today's case study of a bureaucratic disaster can probably be told about many other federal agencies. The federal bureaucracy comprises hundreds of such agencies, some more visible than others, each with a distinct history of successes and failures.

But for the general public, it is the stories of the failures more than of the successes that feed the major myths associated with the inadequacies of U.S. bureaucracy. When Americans think about government bureaucrats, they rarely think of all the efficiencies that characterize a great deal of what governments do. Instead, they picture incompetent or unresponsive pencil pushers, sitting behind their desks in Washington, D.C., wasting the taxpayers' money. Those are the images fed by the popular media and built on a foundation of two pervasive myths: the *myth of bureaucratic incompetence* and the *myth of the unresponsive bureaucracy*.

Behind the myth of bureaucratic incompetence is a widely held belief that the management of government programs need not be significantly different from private-sector management. According to that view, governments can and should be as efficient and effective as businesses. The myth of bureaucratic incompetence has emerged because most government programs do not seem to measure up to private-sector standards. To most Americans, the federal bureaucracy seems too large and cumbersome, bloated by wasteful practices and inefficiencies.

Public opinion polls illustrate the popularity of the myth of bureaucratic incompetence. In a 1958 poll, 85 percent of those surveyed said that they thought government wasted at least some of the money they paid in taxes. The belief that government wastes "some" or "a lot" of taxpayers' money has remained high throughout the past several decades, reaching 98 percent in 1996, and it has not fallen from that level since.[5]

The myth of an unresponsive bureaucracy is also reflected in survey results. In a 1999 survey conducted for the Council for Excellence in Government, a majority of those polled felt "disconnected" from the government and were more likely to think of it as *the* government than as *our* government.[6] A "government responsiveness" index based on public opinion polls showed a decline from its highs in the 1960s (67 and 78 in 1964 and 1966, respectively) to a low of 34 in 1982; however, it rebounded to 57 in 2000 and it was as high as 71 in 2002, perhaps as a result of the greater trust in government generated by the events of September 11. By 2004, however, the index had dropped to 61. Polls also indicate that many Americans assume that individual agencies and bureaucrats are responsive to "big interests" rather than to the general public. The percentage of Americans agreeing with the statement that government "is pretty much run by a few interests looking out for themselves" increased from 29 percent in 1964 to nearly 76 percent in 1994. The figure declined to 61 percent in 2000 and dropped to 48 percent after September 11. In 2004 it was back to 56 percent. In short, a significant number of Americans view their government as unresponsive to their needs. No less disturbing is the finding that 35 percent of those surveyed in 2004 believed that "quite a few of the people running government are crooked." That is a decline from the 52 percent who believed in the corruption of government officials in a poll taken in 1994, but it represents a significant increase from the 29 percent who agreed with that statement in 1964.[7] Given the widespread belief in the myth of the unresponsive bureaucracy, it is little wonder that the American public is suspicious about the work of federal government agencies.

A Profile of the Federal Bureaucracy

FOCUS QUESTION WHO WORKS IN THE BUREAUCRACY? WHAT DO THESE PEOPLE DO? WHERE DO THEY WORK?

The myths of an incompetent and unresponsive federal bureaucracy result in part from a lack of knowledge about the agencies and the people who make up the administrative machinery of our government. We often hear complaints about the bureaucracy as though it were a monolithic entity that could be found in a particular location in the middle of Washington, D.C. — just like Congress or the White House or the Supreme Court. As we shall see, the facts offer an entirely different picture.

Who Are the Bureaucrats?

Bureaucracy Any large, complex organization in which employees have specific job responsibilities and work within a hierarchy. The term is often used to refer to both government agencies and the people who work in them.

Technically, a **bureaucracy** is any large, complex organization in which employees carry out specific job responsibilities within a hierarchy. For most Americans, however, the term *bureaucracy* is commonly used to describe both government agencies and the people who work in them. For our purposes, in 2005 the term applied to the 2.6 million nonelected civilian federal employees working in the United States and abroad. Although we will focus on these civilian federal workers, we should keep in mind that there are another 1.4 million uniformed individuals in the military and that 19 million people work for state and local governments.[8]

As of September 2005, some 89 percent of federal civilian workers were employed in full-time clerical, technical, service, managerial, professional, and other salaried white-collar positions. That includes people working in a wide range of occupations, from hundreds of biomedical engineers and creative arts therapists to thousands of computer specialists, practical nurses, general attorneys, and forestry technicians. The blue-collar federal government work force, which includes carpenters, maintenance workers, and a variety of other skilled and unskilled workers who receive hourly wages rather than salaries, is equally diverse. Among these workers are sheet metal mechanics, electricians, pipefitters, pest controllers, and tool grinders.[9]

In 2005, 44 percent of all federal employees were women, with a significant portion (57 percent) in professional and administrative positions. Within the ranks of blue-collar workers, men held just under 98 percent of the jobs and almost all the supervisory positions.

In 2005, the "typical" federal employee was almost 47 years of age and had been working for the federal government for 15.1 years. Forty-one percent had earned a bachelor's degree or higher, and worked for an annual base salary of $62,123 ($83,870 if the person worked in the Washington, D.C., area). Members of minority groups constituted 31.4 percent of all federal workers in 2004:

Critical Thinking

What are the differences between government bureaucracies and the bureaucracies found in large corporations?

16.9 percent were African American, 7.3 percent were Hispanic, 5.0 percent were Asian American, and 2.1 percent were Native American. Some 7 percent had disabilities. Approximately 25.1 percent were veterans, with almost half having served during the Vietnam War.[10]

Political Appointees. The federal government has adopted several different personnel systems to manage this large and diverse work force. The most visible consists of **political appointees**, who occupy the most strategically important positions in government. At the top of this group are the members of the president's **cabinet**, an official advisory board comprising the heads of the fifteen major departments responsible for carrying out most of the federal government's policies and programs (see Chapter 11, on the presidency). The heads of these departments have the title of secretary, except at the U.S. Department of Justice, where the chief officer is called the attorney general. Below them are assistant and deputy department secretaries, deputy assistant secretaries, counselors, and a variety of other appointive positions.

Technically, in 2005 there were 9,041 positions (out of the 2.6 million federal civilian jobs) that could have been filled by "noncompetitive" processes, which means, in short, that they are outside the normal rules that provide for open and competitive appointment to a federal job. But not all those positions actually go to political appointees. According to the 2004 Plum Book (see "Asked & Answered," p. 336), only 1,137 positions in the Bush administration were political appointments that required Senate confirmation—these jobs are top slots in cabinet departments or ambassadorships, for example. An additional 320 were listed as presidential appointments that do not require Senate approval, and these include a wide range of those who serve in the White House Office (famously portrayed in the TV series *The West Wing*, which is discussed in Chapter 14) to others who serve on various commissions (e.g., the U.S. Holocaust Memorial Council).

Beyond these presidential appointments, there are several thousand others that can be filled by noncareer appointees. For example, every year the Office of Personnel Management designates a certain number of executive and managerial "spaces" for each agency based on an assessment of the agency's needs. In 2004, there were more than 4,500 such "general" spaces, and agency heads could fill these spaces with either career or noncareer personnel within certain limits set out in federal personnel policies. In 2004, there were in excess of 3,000 positions that could be filled outside the career, merit-based civil service system. In other words, in 2004 there were at least 9,051 positions that the Bush administration could fill without relying on merit or competitive examinations.[11]

While this number might sound large to us today, at one time in our history, political appointees made up a vast majority of the federal bureaucracy. **Patronage**—the term generally given to systems in which individuals received government positions through noncompetitive means—was commonplace. Presidents often used patronage to reward their supporters, but just as often they used it to help offset political divisions within the country and provide

Political appointees Government officials who occupy the most strategically important positions in the federal government; most of them are appointed by the president.

Cabinet An official advisory board to the president, made up of the heads (secretaries) of the major departments in the federal government.

Patronage A system of filling government positions in which individuals receive positions through noncompetitive means. It is used both as a means for rewarding supporters and to bridge divisions within the country through access to positions of power.

ASKED & ANSWERED

ASKED: What are the "plum jobs" in the federal government?

ANSWERED: There are many ways to find out about employment opportunities in the federal government. You can visit the U.S. Office of Personnel Management's official job-listing website (www.usajobs.opm.gov/); go to the Fedworld .gov jobs search engine operated by the U.S. Department of Commerce (www.fedworld.gov/jobs/ jobsearch.html); try the Federal Jobs Digest website (www.jobsfed.com/); or look for listings at the federaltimes.com site (www.federaltimes.com/). But what if you are interested in aiming high — that is, looking for one of those "plum jobs" in Washington?

According to the Oxford English Dictionary, one of the figurative definitions of "plum" is a "'good thing' . . . one of the best or choicest things among situations or appointments. . . ." Since 1960, in Washington, D.C., a "plum job" has been one listed in a plum-colored book issued every four years by the U.S. House of Representative's Committee on Governmental Reform.

Under the rather boring title of "United States Government Policy and Supporting Positions," the 2004 Plum Book, as it is known, is one of the most informative documents on the shelves of those who keep track of who's who in the government. It contains the names and positions of all those who hold the "noncompetitive" appointment positions in every agency at the time of publication. Do you want to know who sits on the Corporation for Public Broadcasting's Board of Governors? Go to page 154. Or how about the executive director of the Harry S Truman Scholarship Foundation (p. 174)? Want to know what pay plan the White House Chief of Staff is compensated under (p. 4), or how much the Comptroller General of the United States gets paid (p. 1)? And when does the term of the chairperson of the U.S. Election Assistance Commission expire (p. 207)? All this information is found in the Plum Book.

For those who succeed in getting one of the "plum jobs," there is another book available to make their transition to their new position a bit easier. The Prune Book, a joint publication of the Washington, D.C.–based The Brookings Institution and the Council for Excellence in Government, is also released every four years, typically at the start of each new presidential administration. "A prune," the book's authors explain, "in our lexicon, is a plum seasoned by wisdom and experience, with a much thicker skin" (p. 1).

The Prune Book was first published in 1988, and its early editions profiled the toughest positions in the federal government, and at times the toughest positions in specific areas of government. Over the years, it has moved from giving profiles to giving advice to appointees based on the premise that a "thick skin is essential armament in the politically charged environment in which you will be working." Its chapters are filled with practical lessons drawn from experienced plum job veterans as well as general insights into the major programs and trends that new appointees can expect in their positions. "Lone rangers rarely succeed in Washington," the book warns as it stresses the need for teamwork. And while acknowledging that it is "hard to be humble" when you've been picked by the president to serve in his administration, they note the benefits and importance of "humility" and patience as plum appointees assume their positions. "Communicate, communicate, communicate," the authors advise, and also retain a sense of humor — sage advice for aspiring prunes, to be sure.

Note: To see an online version of the Plum Books for 1996 and later, visit www.gpoaccess.gov/plumbook/index.html. *The 2004 Prune Book: Top Management Challenges for Presidential Appointees*, by John H. Trattner with Patricia McGinnis, is published by The Brookings Institution; you can read about it (and read the first chapter) at www.brookings.edu/press/books/2004prunebook .htm?String=newsrel.

Critical Thinking

Should those who head federal agencies be appointed on the basis of their expertise or their loyalty to the president whom they serve?

access to positions of power in government. George Washington, for instance, included both Alexander Hamilton and Thomas Jefferson in his first cabinet, despite the deep divisions between them. Thomas Jefferson used patronage in 1801 when he replaced many government workers who were loyal to John Adams and the Federalist Party with individuals who would be committed to his political objectives.

However, the first wholesale application of patronage appointments followed Andrew Jackson's election nearly three decades later. Jackson was committed to opening up government positions to ordinary American citizens, and the political appointment process was his means of promoting democracy. Others in the Jackson administration, however, regarded such appointments as a way to reward those who supported him in the election. For them, patronage was not a tool for democracy, but instead a reward for electoral victory. "To the victor goes the spoils" was the phrase used by one defender of this system, and thus the idea of the **spoils system** was born.

The Jacksonian spoils system influenced the design and operation of the federal government for several decades. Under this system, the federal bureaucracy was probably more than usually responsive to the president's wishes, because loyalty to the White House was the key to getting the job in the first place. But there was another important outgrowth of this patronage approach. Because no one stayed in any position for very long, government jobs had to be redesigned and standardized so that anyone could step in to perform the tasks the position required. Thus, the job of being a postal clerk or a customs tax collector was made much simpler and less demanding. Instead of seeking people with special skills for special jobs, government agencies hired less-skilled people and then trained them to do the tasks demanded by the simply designed positions.[12]

Spoils system Taken from the phrase "to the victor goes the spoils," a patronage system in which government jobs at all levels are given to members of the party that has won the top political office.

Merit Systems. But patronage and the spoils system it bred inevitably led to undesirable outcomes, such as widespread political corruption in the administration of Ulysses S. Grant and the assassination of President James Garfield in 1881 by a disgruntled office seeker. These events led to calls for reform, and in 1883 Congress passed the **Pendleton Act**, which reduced the number of political appointments a president could make and established a merit system for about 10 percent of the existing federal jobs. A **merit system** stresses employees' ability, education, experience, and job performance; political factors are not supposed to be considered. Hiring and promotion depend on competitive examinations or job performance evaluations, usually overseen by a civil service commission or a professional personnel office.

The national government's merit system now applies to almost all federal civilian jobs. More than two thirds of federal civilian employees come under the **General Schedule (GS) civil service system**, which covers government positions from weather forecasters to financial analysts and from librarians to civil engineers. Many of these federal workers obtain their jobs through a competitive process, and most are ranked according to a schedule that runs from GS-1 through GS-15 (see Table 12.1).

Pendleton Act A law passed in 1883 that established the first merit-based personnel system for the federal government.
Merit system A system that stresses the ability, education, and job performance of government employees rather than their political backgrounds.
General Schedule (GS) civil service system The merit-based system that covers most white-collar and technical positions in the federal government.

TABLE 12.1

Pay for Meritorious Service: The Salary Scale for White-Collar Federal Employees

Standard salaries for federal workers generally reflect the pay earned by their counterparts in private industry, except at the higher levels, where ceilings on compensation are imposed by Congress.

Grade: Salary Range for 2006

GENERAL CIVIL SERVICE

1: $16,352–20,450	9: $38,175–49,632
2: $18,385–23,134	10: $42,040–54,649
3: $20,060–26,081	11: $46,189–60,049
4: $22,519–29,278	12: $55,360–71,965
5: $25,195–32,755	13: $65,832–85,578
6: $28,085–36,509	14: $77,793–101,130
7: $31,209–40,569	15: $91,507–118,957
8: $34,563–44,931	

SENIOR EXECUTIVE SERVICE (SES) (2006)

Minimum: $109,808 to Maximum: $165,200

Source: OPM website, www.opm.gov/oca/PAYRATES/index.htm.

Senior Executive Service (SES) The highest category of senior level federal employees, most of whom form a select group of career public administrators who specialize in agency management.

At the top of the general civil service and sitting astride the political appointee system is the **Senior Executive Service (SES)**, a select group of career federal public administrators who specialize in managing public agencies. Most of the career (permanent) civil servants in the elite SES have made their mark as effective managers within the particular agency at which they have spent most of their career. In becoming part of the SES, they agree to make themselves available for transfers to other agencies that need their talents. In exchange, they receive higher salaries (see Table 12.1) and the possibility of greater rewards. Before the Civil Service Reform Act of 1978 established the SES, the best executive talent in the federal government occupied "supergrade" positions (GS-16 through GS-18) within their agencies and could not be used efficiently or effectively because moving them from one agency to another was too difficult. Since that time, the supergrade positions in most agencies have been phased out. Now, along with a small group of noncareer senior executive presidential appointees (see the previous discussion), more than 5,200 SES personnel fill most major managerial positions in federal agencies.[13]

Career service personnel systems Separate personnel systems for highly specialized agencies like the Coast Guard and the Foreign Service.

Besides the general civil service and the SES, there are **career service personnel systems** for highly specialized agencies, such as the Forest Service and the Coast Guard; approximately 15 percent of nonpostal federal civilian employees fall into this category. Perhaps the best known of these career service systems is the Foreign Service, which includes more than 13,000 State Department officials who serve in American embassies throughout the world. The Department of Veterans Affairs (formerly the Veterans Administration) operates the largest career service system, employing more than 36,000 physicians and surgeons. Altogether, approximately 125,000 federal civilian employees occupy positions in these career service systems.

Wage Systems. Finally, a little under a million workers can be classified as part of the federal government's **wage systems**. Included in this group are those with blue-collar and related jobs, ranging from pipefitting to janitorial work. More than 764,000 career and noncareer postal workers make up the largest single organized group in this category. Many of the workers in these wage systems are paid by the hour, and a great many are represented by unions or other associations that have limited bargaining rights under current civil service laws.

> **Wage systems** Federal personnel systems covering more than a million federal workers who perform blue-collar and related jobs and are largely represented by unions or other associations with limited bargaining rights.

What Do Federal Bureaucrats Do?

The primary role of the national bureaucracy is to implement the policies of the federal government. In that sense, the work of federal agencies touches almost every aspect of American life. Sometimes these agencies carry out the policies themselves. For example, the Federal Aviation Administration employs air traffic controllers to oversee the growing volume of aviation in America's skies, and federal rangers protect and manage national parks and forests throughout the country. We also deal directly with federal employees when the U.S. Postal Service delivers our mail, when we have questions about social security benefits, or when we have problems with our federal taxes.[14]

At other times, the federal bureaucracy carries out its implementation tasks indirectly, through a variety of arrangements that one analyst has termed "government by proxy." **Proxy administration** of government programs includes such things as government contracts, grants-in-aid, loan guarantees, and the establishment of government-sponsored enterprises to carry out government programs.[15]

> **Proxy administration** The government's use of indirect means to deliver public goods and services, such as contracting, grants-in-aid, loan guarantees, and government-sponsored enterprises.

Many government activities are carried out through *government contracts* with private firms. The U.S. Department of Defense makes use of this approach when it hires private companies to build weapons systems or supply food for the troops. In fiscal year 2004, for example, Lockheed Martin Corporation earned more than $21.3 billion from Defense Department contracts and another $6.9 billion from nondefense agreements with the federal government. While that is a significant amount of business for one company, it must be seen in light of the fact that the federal government purchased nearly $327.8 billion in goods and services from the top 200 private companies during that same year,[16] and billions more from hundreds of smaller contractors.

The role of contractors is looming ever larger in the federal government's budget. According to one estimate, if you consider only those federal funds spent on providing public-sector goods and services (that is, excluding grants, loans, entitlement payments such as Social Security, and so on), approximately 60 percent is spent through contracted agencies. Much of the budget of the National Aeronautics and Space Administration is spent through contracting, as is

Doing the Public's Business
Many private firms conduct the public's business under government contracts. Among the biggest contractors are aircraft manufacturers.

a good portion of the Department of Energy's annual budget. Three-fourths of the national government's spending on research and development is done through contracts to think tanks, university labs, and private industry. The idea of "outsourcing" work to the private and nonprofit sectors is nothing new in Washington, but it has increasingly become the preferred way of doing the government's business. More often than not, today's federal bureaucrat is dealing with contractors rather than directly with the public[17] (See "Global Politics," p. 341, for a look at contracting on a global scale.)

The intergovernmental relations system and its *grant programs*, discussed in Chapter 3, on federalism and intergovernmental relations, offer another indirect means of implementation. For instance, through grants to states and localities, the U.S. Department of Education can get local school districts to offer special-education courses for children with learning disabilities (see the discussion of education policy in Chapter 14, on domestic policy and policymaking). Similarly, the U.S. Department of Transportation provides the states with funds for highway construction and maintenance through a special trust fund.

The federal government also uses other indirect means to carry out some of its policies. Through bank *loan guarantees*, for example, some federal agencies are able to get local financial institutions to lend money to home buyers, students, or farmers who might not otherwise qualify. These guarantees cost the taxpayers nothing until and unless the borrower defaults on the loan — something that was happening with greater frequency for student loans during the 1980s.

In some cases, the federal government has established special **government-sponsored enterprises (GSEs)**, which, among other functions, make credit more easily available to special populations for specific purposes without relying on loan guarantees. Though created by the government, these organizations often operate

Government-sponsored enterprises (GSEs) Federally initiated organizations designed to operate as if they were privately owned and operated, usually established for specific functions that serve targeted populations, e.g., helping to support inexpensive student loans. Many eventually are privatized.

The Reach of U.S. Contractors

Halliburton Company has been in the news a great deal in recent years. Vice President Dick Cheney was its chief executive officer from 1995 until August 2000 when he left to join George W. Bush on the Republican party ticket. Since then the company has been the subject of significant attention as the major private contractor in Iraq during the pre- and post-invasion periods, providing services of every sort to American forces and to the interim Iraqi governments.

As a federal government contractor, in 2004 Halliburton ranked sixth among *Government Executive* magazine's top 200 companies. Almost all of its $8.175 billion worth of business with the federal government (97 percent) was conducted with the Department of Defense, but that is only part of the story. Halliburton, along with its number one competitor, Bechtel Corporation (ranked eighth on the 2004 *Government Executive* list), is in fact a global contractor serving public- and private-sector customers in dozens of other countries (it has offices in 43 countries) offering a wide range of services.

Halliburton is really two distinct companies. The Energy Services division specializes in services to "upstream" energy companies—that is, it specializes in tasks early in the energy exploration and production process, from analysis and exploration of potential oil fields to the "optimization" of production at existing refineries. Its Kellogg Brown and Root (KBR) division "provides a wide range of engineering, construction, operations and maintenance, logistics and project management services to three markets: upstream, downstream and government & infrastructure." In short, Halliburton is the universal contractor who is able to undertake tasks at every point in a project or program.

In the United Kingdom, for example, Halliburton is constructing new access roads and ramps at Heathrow Airport for the British Airport Authority. Several miles away, it is working for the U.K. Ministry of Defence by designing and constructing submarine refueling and refitting areas. It also holds the contract to help the British military handle the logistical aspects of quick deployment.

Halliburton has also become a contractor for former U.S. enemies. In Russia, for example, it has the contract to dismantle and eliminate 350 intercontinental ballistic missiles and their launch silos. In Libya, it is overseeing the construction of that nation's Great Man-made River Project.

In Malaysia, Halliburton is helping to rejuvenate natural gas facilities; in Australia, it is building a rail link between Alice Springs and Darwin and designing and constructing waste-water treatment plants; and in South America, it has been planning and constructing pipeline for the Bolivian and Brazilian petroleum agencies.

Most controversial, however, has been the role Halliburton and other contractors have played in facilitating the global reach of the U.S. military. In addition to its multibillion-dollar contracts tied to the occupation and reconstruction of Iraq, Halliburton holds contracts that help maintain support for U.S. peacekeeping troops in the Balkans and other political hot spots. In a very real sense, these contracts represent the extension of the U.S. bureaucracy to these locations by corporate proxy.

Note: For more information on Halliburton's global projects, visit its "Project Profiles" website at www.halliburton.com/kbr/projectProfiles/index.jsp.

as if they were privately owned and operated, and in some cases they eventually are turned into investor-owned organizations, or are *privatized.* For example, in 1972, the federal government created the Student Loan Marketing Association (known as "Sallie Mae") as a government-sponsored enterprise designed to promote low-cost loans to students by arranging to "buy" student bank loans from lending institutions and then selling them to investors. The success of Sallie Mae and the desire to have it expand its programs led to proposals for privatizing it. A plan for doing so was approved and initiated in 1997 and was fully implemented by 2006.

This was not the first time that a GSE has been so successful. In 1938, Congress created the Federal National Mortgage Association, known as "Fannie Mae." It has since become an investor-owned corporation that is playing a leading role in the American economy. There are also a number of GSEs that are still public-sector corporations, including those that were established to help finance farm-related loans and troubled financial institutions.

These GSEs are not limited to financial support programs. The *Communication Satellite Corporation (COMSAT)* was established by an act of Congress in 1962 to facilitate the launching of telecommunications satellites. During the early days of space exploration, government support was necessary in order to get firms to undertake such a risky enterprise. Private companies were willing to invest in telecommunications, but they needed to have the government as a partner. Initially, up to 50 percent of COMSAT could be owned by the private-sector firms that used the agency's services, and three members of COMSAT's fifteen-member board of directors were appointed by the president. In most other respects, however, the organization was intended to act like a private corporation. Over time, Congress privatized COMSAT by allowing private firms to purchase the rest of the organization, and by the 1990s, it was a wholly private corporation that retained a special relationship with the federal government. Finally, in 1999, Congress voted to end COMSAT's special status, and in 2000, the company was purchased by Lockheed Martin Corporation.

Beyond their role as the implementers of policies and programs, some federal agencies provide expert advice to policymakers, especially in the design of special policies and highly technical programs. Agencies such as the Bureau of Reclamation and the Army Corps of Engineers develop plans for water diversion and storage projects, which then go to the White House and Congress for revision and adoption as official government programs; those agencies often oversee these programs after their approval. At other times Congress and the president establish the general outlines of policies and leave specific policy decisions to designated agencies. That approach is common with defense policies, where program details are left to civilian and military experts at the Pentagon (see Chapter 15, on foreign and defense policy).

Where Do They Work?

Federal civil servants work in literally hundreds of agencies, ranging from those closest to the president to agencies with a great deal of independence from the White House.

Executive Office of the President (EOP)
The collective name for several agencies, councils, and groups of staff members that advise the president and help manage the federal bureaucracy. The EOP was established in the 1930s; the number and type of agencies that constitute it change with each presidential administration.

Office of Management and Budget (OMB)
An EOP agency that acts as the president's principal link to most federal agencies. The agency supervises matters relating to program and budget requests.

White House Office
An EOP agency that includes the president's key advisers and assistants who help him with the daily requirements of the presidency.

Executive Office of the President. Faced with the task of managing the federal bureaucracy, the president relies on several agencies that collectively make up the **Executive Office of the President (EOP)** (see Chapter 11, on the presidency).[18] Among the most important of the EOP agencies is the **Office of Management and Budget (OMB)**. The OMB is the president's principal link to most federal agencies. Almost all federal agencies report to the OMB on matters relating to program and budget requests. A smaller (but no less important) group of EOP employees is located in a variety of offices known collectively as the **White House Office**. These staff members include the president's key advisers, as well as those who help the chief executive deal with the day-to-day business of the presidency.

Also found in the EOP[19] are various councils and staff members specializing in particular policy areas. These agencies include the *Council of Economic Advisers*, the *National Security Council*, a *Domestic Policy Council*, the *Council on Environmental Quality*, and the *Office of National Drug Control Policy*. How many of these agencies there are changes with each presidential administration. For example, in 1981 President Ronald Reagan eliminated the Council on Wage and Price Stability, which had been created ten years earlier by President Richard Nixon to oversee anti-inflation policies. In 1989, President George H. W. Bush established a National Space Council in the EOP to deal with issues related to the nation's space policy; a similar agency had been eliminated by Nixon during his administration, and when Bill Clinton took office, he eliminated the agency once again. However, Clinton created other EOP offices, including a *National Economic Council* to coordinate policy in that area and the *Office of National AIDS Policy* in response to the growing concern about that epidemic. Similarly, upon entering office, President George W. Bush created an *Office of Faith-Based and Community Initiatives* that was designed to promote the use of faith-based organizations (FBOs) (see Chapter 3, on federalism and intergovernmental relations) in the implementation of various social service programs. One of the first responses to the September 11, 2001, attacks was the creation of a White House *Office of Homeland Security (OHS)*; this was followed several months later by the creation of a *Homeland Security Council*, with members drawn from the top echelons of relevant agencies throughout government. The OHS would eventually emerge as the Department of Homeland Security in 2002.

The importance of particular EOP agencies also varies over time. For many years, the Special Representative for Trade Negotiations was an obscure office in the EOP. However, when foreign trade and international economic policy became a major factor in American life during the 1970s and 1980s (see Chapter 15, on foreign and defense policy), the job of the trade representative grew more important. The agency, now called the *Office of the United States Trade Representative*, became increasingly visible, and the choice of a person to head the office became as significant as any cabinet appointment.

EOP agencies are designed to play key roles in formulating public policy, but not in carrying it out. However, the lines between formulation and implementation (see Chapter 14, on domestic policy and policymaking) are sometimes quite blurry. In the Reagan administration, for example, some members of the National Security Council staff seemed to cross the boundary into implementation when they arranged to sell arms to a hostile government in Iran and illegally transfer funds to support rebel groups in Central America. The resulting scandal, which surfaced in 1986, led to several resignations and a political crisis that nearly paralyzed the White House for several months and continued to make headlines through 1992.[20]

The Cabinet Departments. The most visible agencies in the executive branch are the fifteen *cabinet departments* (see the previous discussion and Figure 12.1). The newest department, dealing with homeland security, began operations in early 2003.[21] Each department is headed by a secretary or, in the case of Justice, the attorney general. Some of these departments are in charge of basic government functions, such as defense and foreign relations. Others address the needs of special groups—for example, agriculture, veterans affairs, and labor—or coordinate federal programs in education, energy, health and human services, and other areas.

Each cabinet department is composed of smaller units, called bureaus, offices, services, administrations, or divisions. For example, among the major units in the U.S. Department of the Treasury are the Internal Revenue Service (IRS), the U.S. Customs Service, the Bureau of the Public Debt, the Financial Management Division, the U.S. Mint, the Bureau of Engraving and Printing, the Office of the Comptroller of the Currency, the U.S. Secret Service, and the Bureau of Alcohol, Tobacco, and Firearms. Many of these units are divided into even smaller subunits. The IRS, for instance, has several regional offices, more than sixty district offices, and nearly 200 local offices.

Historically, there has been no particular logic underlying the way in which cabinet departments are organized. The best way to understand their design is to realize that politics plays an important role in determining the organizational form, status, and location of any agency or function of government. In the case of FEMA, for example, its creation by President Carter in 1979 came at the urging of the nation's governors who sought to have the hundreds of programs related to disaster relief—located in different cabinet departments—consolidated in one independent federal agency. Ironically, twenty-five years later, FEMA would end up as part of the Department of Homeland Security (DHS) as a result of similar political pressures. The DHS was reluctantly created by President George W. Bush under strong pressure from the public and key members of Congress who wanted to have the anti-terror resources of the federal government under one agency. Bush's original and preferred strategy was to have the post–September 11 security efforts coordinated from an office in the White House and to avoid the organizational and political problems created by having to integrate and manage literally hundreds of different programs from dozens of different agencies under one roof. But the political pressures were too great, and eventually the White House supported the creation of the DHS, including ending FEMA's status as an independent agency (see p. 332 and Figures 12.2 and 12.3).

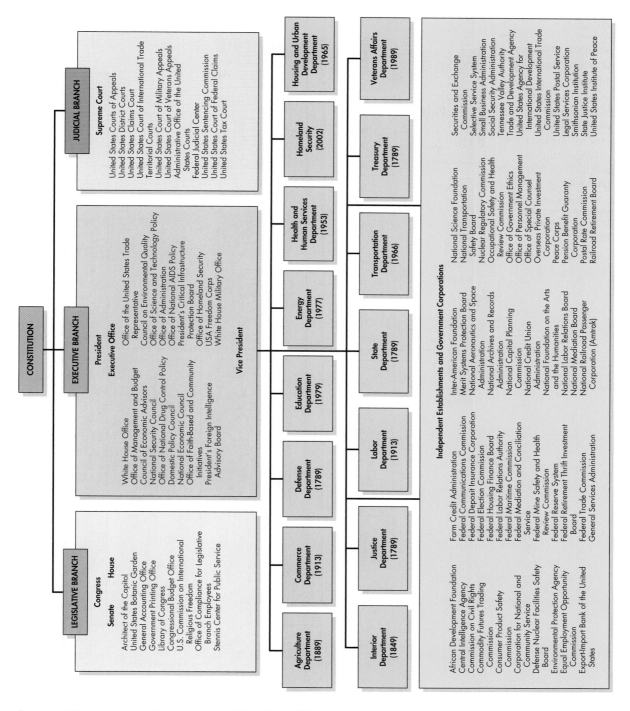

FIGURE 12.1   **Government of the United States**

FIGURE 12.2

The Department of Homeland Security on Paper

Formally, the DHS, like other government agencies, seems like a rational organization of offices and sub-agencies that fit a neat hierarchy.

Source: Information on the Department of Homeland Security can be found at www.dhs.gov.

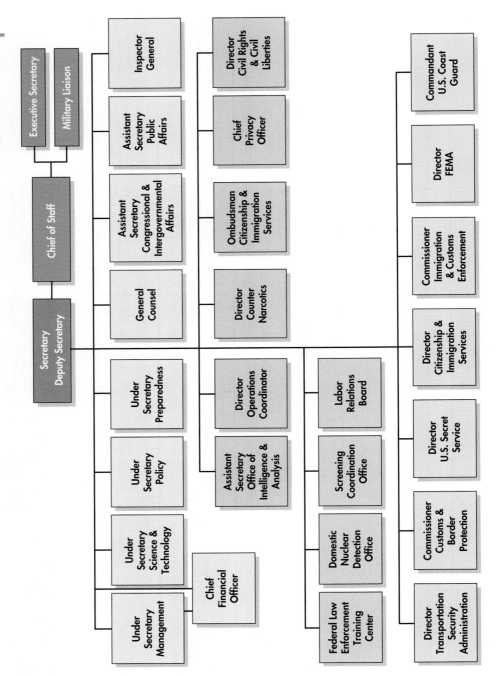

FIGURE 12.3

The Reality of DHS Pipelines

In contrast to the neatly drawn organization chart for the Department of Homeland Security depicted in Figure 12.2, this diagram illustrates the number of agencies involved in a homeland security "threat pipeline"—that is, all the points in the bureaucracy activated by a threat.

Source: Dr. Jay Jakub.

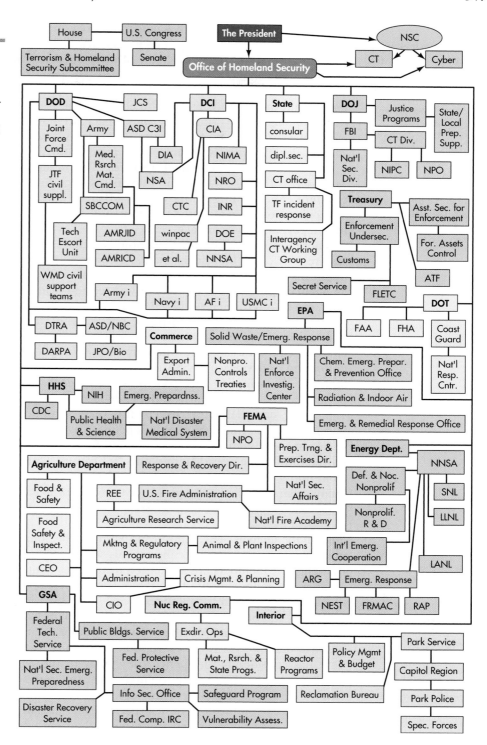

Independent agencies
More than 200 agencies that exist outside the EOP and the cabinet departments. Reporting directly to the president, they perform a wide range of functions, from environmental protection (EPA) and managing social programs (SSA) to conducting the nation's space policy (NASA), and helping the president manage the federal government (GSA and OPM).

Independent Executive Branch Agencies. A great many federal bureaucrats work for the more than 200 **independent agencies** that exist outside both the EOP and the cabinet departments. Many of these agencies carry out important government functions. The *Environmental Protection Agency (EPA)*, for example, regulates air and water quality, as well as the use of pesticides, disposal of hazardous wastes, and other challenges to the ecology. The *National Aeronautics and Space Administration (NASA)* runs the civilian space program. The *General Services Administration (GSA)* is essentially the government's all-purpose "housekeeping" agency, dealing with everything from paper clips to real estate and building management for many federal agencies. The independent *Office of Personnel Management (OPM)* oversees the human resource functions of the federal government. The administrators who head these independent executive branch agencies report directly to the president and do not have to work through a cabinet department bureaucracy.

There is no overall rationale for some agencies to be independent while others are part of cabinet departments. Sometimes the nature of what an agency does calls for this special status. In other instances, the political importance of an agency's programs at the time it was created made the difference. Both factors were involved when the *Social Security Administration (SSA)* was made an independent agency in 1994. Formerly part of the Department of Health and Human Services, SSA implements a variety of important social programs, including federal old-age and disability insurance (see Chapter 14, on domestic policy and policymaking). SSA is a very large and politically important agency, and the financing of SSA programs has been a sensitive issue for several decades.[22] The Social Security Independence and Program Improvements Act — signed on August 15, 1994, exactly fifty years and one day after social security was established — made SSA an independent agency operated under a commissioner of social security who is appointed for a term of six years and can be removed only by the president and only "for cause." Thus, not only was SSA taken from under the jurisdiction of the secretary of the Department of Health and Human Services, but its head was given some protection from being removed from office arbitrarily or for political reasons.

Regulatory commissions Federal agencies led by presidentially appointed boards that make and enforce policies affecting various sectors of the U.S. economy. Formally independent of the White House to avoid presidential interference, these agencies employ large professional staffs to help them carry out their many functions.

Regulatory Commissions. Employing large professional staffs, **regulatory commissions** make policies affecting various sectors of the American economy. Although their members are appointed by the president, regulatory commissions are formally independent of the White House; that is, they exist outside the cabinet departments and have a special legal status (provided by Congress and supported by the Supreme Court) that protects them from excessive presidential interference. For example, the president cannot fire commission members for political reasons — only for corruption or a similar cause. Of course, the president has considerable influence over many of the commissions; he appoints their members and designates their chairpersons, and so he can choose individuals whose views are likely to be in accord with his own.

Regulatory commissions have a special legal status in the federal bureaucracy because they are empowered to do more than enforce the law or implement public policy. Most of them have the authority to formulate rules that regulated

Quasi-legislative functions Lawmaking functions performed by regulatory commissions as authorized by Congress.

Quasi-judicial functions Judicial functions performed by regulatory commissions. Agencies can hold hearings for companies or individuals accused of violating agency regulations. Commission decisions can be appealed to the federal courts.

Government corporations Public agencies that carry out specific economic or service functions (such as the U.S. Postal Service and the Corporation for Public Broadcasting) and are organized in the same way as private corporations.

companies or individuals must adhere to. In this sense, regulatory agencies are performing lawmaking, or **quasi-legislative, functions**.[23] For example, in 1972 the *Federal Trade Commission (FTC)* issued regulations requiring that all billboard and magazine advertisements for cigarettes contain a warning from the surgeon general's office about the health hazards of smoking.

Along with enforcing and making rules, these commissions also have **quasi-judicial functions** because they sit in judgment on companies or individuals that are accused of violating the regulations. Violators of commission rules get their first courtlike hearing before commission officials. For example, in 2001 the FCC levied a fine of $27,500 against Infinity Broadcasting for its broadcast of a segment of radio "shock jock" Howard Stern's show that it determined had violated the commission's regulations against indecency. The Stern saga continued in April 2004, when the FCC issued a $495,000 fine against Clear Channel Communications, another radio broadcaster, as a result of a complaint about an "indecent" Stern broadcast one year earlier. Eventually, Stern was taken off the air, and reappeared in 2006 on satellite radio, which is not subject to the FCC's standards. A company or person that is found guilty of such violations may appeal directly to the federal court system. More recently, the *Federal Communications Commission (FCC)* passed a rule requiring that all television sets sold in the United States be equipped to receive digital television signals by 2007.

Government Corporations. A unique form of bureaucracy, the **government corporation** is designed to act more like a private business than like a part of government. As we have already noted, some of these government corporations are actually *government-sponsored enterprises* that are created and launched by the

Becoming Unregulated

Radio "shock jock" Howard Stern is shown promoting his move to unregulated "satellite radio" in 2005 after fines imposed on his former employers by the FCC made it difficult for him to broadcast on commercial (regulated) stations.

government to perform special functions, but that are effectively private organizations, operating as much in the private sector as in the public sphere.

Other government corporations are located within cabinet departments and operate more like other government agencies, although with somewhat greater independence. For example, the *Commodity Credit Corporation* — the organization through which farm subsidy programs are funded — is part of the Department of Agriculture. Still other government corporations — such as the *Tennessee Valley Authority (TVA)* and the *U.S. Postal Service (USPS)* — exist separately from other federal agencies.

Most government corporations carry out specific functions, such as generating electric power or delivering the mail. Most are intended to be self-financing, but that does not always work out as planned. The *Corporation for Public Broadcasting (CPB)* helps promote and fund the *Public Broadcasting System (PBS)* and *National Public Radio (NPR)*. In the past, the CPB has provided significant subsidies for public radio and television, either through government grants or by raising funds privately. That support has decreased in recent years, leaving PBS- and NPR-affiliate stations with the task of raising money through donations and sponsorships.

The *Federal Deposit Insurance Corporation (FDIC)* insures savings accounts in many local banks. It was intended to be self-funding through the fees it assesses its member banks. In the late 1980s, however, failures of member banks forced FDIC officials to borrow money from the federal treasury and to actually consider asking Congress for tax dollars to help save it from insolvency. To help the FDIC deal with those problems, Congress authorized the creation of still another government corporation, the *Resolution Trust Corporation (RTC)*. From August 1989 until its termination in December 1995, the RTC assumed control of the assets of banks that had been declared insolvent by the FDIC and attempted to reduce the government's losses by selling those assets to private bidders. With the crisis over, the RTC was eventually merged into the FDIC.

Other Agencies. Besides these five types of federal agencies, there are literally hundreds of boards, commissions, institutes, foundations, endowments, councils, and other organizations in the federal bureaucracy. They range in importance from the *Federal Reserve System* (better known in the news media as the "Fed"; see Chapter 14, on domestic policy and policymaking) and the *National Science Foundation (NSF)* to the *National Telecommunications Information Administration* and the *U.S. Metric Board.*

A Diverse Institution

Our profile of the federal bureaucracy makes it clear that we are not discussing a single-minded, monolithic institution. Instead, we see that the federal bureaucracy is composed of hundreds of distinct organizations employing millions of individuals — a powerful institution that is so large and complex that to the uninformed citizen it seems to be a maze of shadowy structures that is to be viewed

Critical Thinking

Should more government corporations that provide public services (like the postal service or public television) be expected to "pay their own way"?

with sharp suspicion. Typically, Americans' suspicions regarding public agencies take the form of concerns about both the growth and the power of the federal bureaucracy. As we see in the sections that follow, those concerns are also built on myths.

Growth of the American Bureaucracy

FOCUS QUESTION **WHAT FACTORS HAVE LED TO THE GROWTH OF THE FEDERAL BUREAUCRACY?**

Many Americans believe that the government bureaucracy has grown too large and has become a burden on the American public. Bureaucratic growth is seen as being an inevitable result of the incompetence and unresponsiveness of government agencies. An incompetent bureaucracy wastes resources. If government workers were more productive, they would use fewer resources, and the result would be smaller but more efficient public agencies. To many Americans, excessive bureaucratic growth is also related to unresponsive government agencies. Unresponsive agencies are more likely to serve their own needs — including the need to grow and expand. A truly responsive bureaucracy would aim to serve the general public's wishes for less, not more, government intrusion.

Has bureaucratic growth been excessive? Is that growth a result of bureaucratic incompetence and unresponsiveness?

Overview of Bureaucratic Growth

The framers of the Constitution said little about how they thought the policies of the newly established republic should be administered. We do know that they considered bureaucracy a vital institution in our constitutional system. For instance, in "Federalist No. 70," Alexander Hamilton acknowledged that a badly administered government "must be . . . a bad government."

The Constitution makes the president responsible for ensuring that the laws and policies of the national government are carried out. The tasks that the framers foresaw for the national government were relatively few and easy to implement. Executing the law meant keeping the peace, defending the country from foreign intruders, collecting import duties and other taxes, and delivering the mail. To the framers, charging a single individual with overseeing the administration of government did not seem unreasonable. Consequently, in Section 2 of Article II, they made the president both commander in chief of the armed forces and the chief executive officer to whom the heads of all administrative departments would report.

Initially, the framers' assumptions about the administration of the government were correct. The federal bureaucracy was small, and its functions were simple enough to permit the president to oversee most of the national government's tasks.[24] In 1802, for example, there were fewer than 10,000 civilian and military federal employees, and almost all the civilian employees were tax collectors or postal workers. But those were simpler times. The country was rural, and the people were more self-sufficient. When Americans did turn to government for help in building roads or establishing schools, they usually turned to state and local governments rather than to the nation's newly settled capital in Washington, D.C.

Of course, the number of federal workers did grow during these early years. By the 1820s, the national government's civilian bureaucracy had more than doubled. However, that growth did not represent a major expansion of governmental activities. No major new agencies were created during this early period. Most of the growth in federal government jobs took place in the Post Office Department, where nearly 75 percent of the federal work force was employed.

A different pattern began to emerge after the Civil War, as Americans demanded more and better government services from elected officials at all levels. During the last half of the nineteenth century, the number of federal agencies doubled. The major agencies established during that period included the Department of Agriculture and the Interstate Commerce Commission. Federal workers were being hired not just to deliver the mail, but also to regulate railroads, assist farmers, manage the federal government's vast land holdings, survey and help settle newly acquired territories in the West, and promote American commerce overseas. The changing nature of government is evident when the relative size of the post office is considered. In 1861, the post office accounted for 80 percent of all federal civilian jobs; by 1901, post office positions made up only 58 percent of such jobs.[25]

Rapid bureaucratic expansion continued through the first decades of the twentieth century. Between 1901 and 1933, the number of major federal agencies increased from 90 to 170. Then, responding to the economic and social problems of the Great Depression, President Franklin D. Roosevelt proposed, and Congress enacted, many new federal programs and agencies, especially in the areas of employment and business regulation. Federal employment jumped under Roosevelt's New Deal, and the demands of World War II led to further growth in the bureaucracy and the expansion of government responsibilities in domestic and foreign affairs.

Putting that growth in perspective, although the federal civilian work force numbers in the millions, it constitutes a relatively small—and shrinking—part of the total U.S. labor force. When viewed as part of the U.S. labor force, the federal bureaucracy does not look quite so big and is in fact shrinking in size each year. For example, the number of civilians employed in the federal executive branch was as high as 15 federal employees for every 1,000 Americans in 1968; by 2005, that figure was 8.9 per 1,000 population.[26]

Nor does the federal bureaucracy seem too big when its work force is compared with the number of civilian workers employed by state and local governments. The federal government employs fewer than one out of every four full-time government workers in the United States. In 2005, for instance, there were 4.1 million federal employees and 19 million state and local workers.

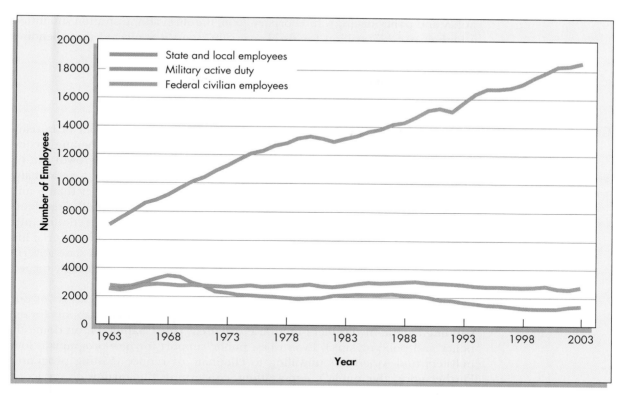

FIGURE 12.4

Relative Size of the Federal Bureaucracy

Contrary to conventional wisdom, the size of the federal bureaucracy has been shrinking, especially in comparison to the growth of the state and local government employment.

Source: U.S. Census Bureau.

When federal military personnel are subtracted from the totals, the federal work force is seen to be even smaller (2.7 million) relative to the work forces at the state and local levels. Furthermore, the relative shrinking of the federal civilian work force has been a significant trend for at least three decades (see Figure 12.4).

In other words, while 2.7 million federal civilian employees may seem like a lot, in relative terms the federal bureaucracy is not as big as it appears to be at first glance. Nevertheless, 2.7 million is a great many people, and the question of why there are so many federal bureaucrats is unavoidable.

Another indicator of bureaucratic expansion is the growing federal budget. George Washington ran the government for about $1.5 million a year. By the time Andrew Jackson took office in 1829, the federal budget had increased tenfold, to more than $15 million. By 1940 the budget had climbed to $9.5 billion, and in 1960 the U.S. government spent a little over $92 billion. The greatest growth in federal expenditures, however, took place over the next quarter century. In January 1987, President Reagan submitted the first trillion-dollar budget proposal to Congress, and federal government spending continued to climb under Presidents George H. W. Bush and Bill Clinton (see Chapter 14, on domestic policy and policymaking). In February 2006, the Bush administration submitted a budget of $2.77 trillion for fiscal year 2007, and it projected that spending would reach nearly $3.24 trillion by the year 2011.

Explaining the Growth of the Bureaucracy

Critical Thinking

Is it reasonable to expect one official, the president, to effectively manage today's vast federal bureaucracy?

What accounts for the growth of the bureaucracy and the number of bureaucrats since the late 1800s? Was all this growth the result of bureaucratic incompetence and unresponsiveness? Many observers believe that the growth can be attributed directly to the expansion of the nation itself. There are a great many more of us—more than 274 million in 2000, compared with fewer than 5 million in the 1790s—and we are living closer together. Not only do the residents of cities and suburbs require many more services than did the predominantly rural dwellers of the early 1800s, but the challenges of urban and industrial life have intensified, outstripping the capacity of families or local and state governments to cope with them. Thus, the American people have increasingly turned to the national government for help.

There is considerable evidence that the growth of bureaucracies is "of our own making."[27] Public opinion polls indicate widespread public support for expanding federal involvement in a variety of areas (see Chapter 14, on domestic policy and policymaking). Even when public support for new programs is low, pollsters find Americans unwilling to eliminate or reduce existing programs. Furthermore, the public's expectations concerning the quality of service it should receive are constantly rising. The public wants government to be more responsive, responsible, and compassionate in administering public programs. Officials have reacted to these pressures by establishing new programs and maintaining and improving existing ones.

The federal bureaucracy has also expanded in response to sudden changes in economic, social, cultural, and political conditions. During the Great Depression and World War II, for example, the federal bureaucracy grew to meet the challenges these situations created. Washington became more and more involved in providing financial aid and employment to the poor. It increased its regulation of important industries, and during the war it imposed controls on much of the American economy. As part of the general war effort, the federal government also built roads and hospitals and mobilized the entire population. When these crises ended, the public was reluctant to give up many of the federal welfare and economic programs that had been implemented during the time of emergency.

Political leaders, too, foster bureaucratic growth. Government bureaucracies are often enlarged by presidents running for reelection so that they can leave their mark on history. We have noted the large expansions of the federal bureaucracy that occurred under Franklin D. Roosevelt's New Deal and Lyndon Johnson's Great Society programs. Congress, however, is no innocent bystander. Bowing to pressure to "bring home the bacon" for the folks back home, even the most conservative members of Congress find themselves voting for new or larger programs to serve their constituents.[28]

There is also considerable evidence that the bureaucracy itself plays a role in developing and expanding government programs.[29] Some analysts point out that expansion of their agency's programs and budgets is among the few personal rewards that bureaucrats can seek, since compensation for public employees is limited and opportunities are very limited. However, the role of bureaucrats in government growth is not merely self-serving. For example, a 1970 report by Department of Labor staff members found that many Americans were being needlessly exposed to work-related illnesses and injuries. Although there were state and national policies to deal with the consequences of work-related disabilities, the staff found no significant program designed to prevent on-the-job ailments or accidents. As a result of that study, Congress created the *Occupational Safety and Health Administration (OSHA)*, which oversees the regulation of workplace conditions.

Thus, a number of factors have contributed to the growth of the federal bureaucracy. Although bureaucratic incompetence and unresponsiveness may play a part in governmental expansion, most of the evidence points to the other factors we have discussed.

Bureaucratic Power

FOCUS QUESTION WHAT ARE THE SOURCES OF (AND LIMITS ON) BUREAUCRATIC POWER?

Bureaucratic power
The power of government agencies, derived from law, external support, expertise, discretion, longevity in office, skill, leadership, and a variety of other sources.

To operate effectively, government must employ qualified personnel and must have the financial resources to enable these employees to carry out their jobs. Another critical ingredient, however, is **bureaucratic power**. Government agencies require power if they are to be competent. This requirement is so great that one student of American public administration has called power the "lifeblood of administration."[30] Without sufficient power, government agencies would certainly live up to the myth of bureaucratic incompetence, for they would not be able to accomplish their tasks effectively or efficiently.

In spite of the importance of bureaucratic power, the public is very suspicious of the role that this power plays in American government. Inherent in the myth of an unresponsive bureaucracy is a fear of bureaucratic power and a widespread belief that federal bureaucrats are misusing or even abusing this power. The U.S. constitutional system is rooted in the idea that the people should govern, if not directly, then at least indirectly, through their elected representatives. Yet over the past two centuries, more and more governmental power has been placed in the hands of bureaucrats. Those who believe in the myth of an unresponsive bureaucracy are likely to worry about the existence and use of bureaucratic power.

The Sources of Bureaucratic Power

Where do bureaucracies get the power they need in order to function? Some of it is derived from the legitimacy of the laws they are required to enforce or the policies they are asked to implement (see Chapter 2, on constitutional foundations).

The Bureaucracy Takes Us to Mars

Federal bureaucracies are capable of undertaking very successful and popular programs. Pictured here is an artist's rendition of a "rover" that has been exploring Mars for years. The Mars Rover Exploration Project is operated by NASA's Jet Propulsion Laboratory in conjunction with scientists and dozens of contractors.

But often the legitimacy of these laws or these policies is not enough. There are other key factors to look for.[31]

External Support. A major source of bureaucratic power is the support that government agencies receive from the general public, special-interest groups, the media, Congress, or the White House. The greater an agency's external support, the more power it is likely to wield. Throughout the 1950s and 1960s, for example, the *Federal Bureau of Investigation (FBI)*, under Director J. Edgar Hoover, had a great deal of support from the general public. After Hoover's death and a series of revelations about questionable actions taken by the FBI, however, the agency's reputation and support declined. The directors who succeeded Hoover had to work for many years to restore public confidence in the agency and to rebuild its power. But these efforts were not always successful, and during the 1990s, the FBI was plagued by a series of well-publicized mistakes. The agency came under severe scrutiny in the post–September 11 period and undertook a major reform of its operations to help regain public support.

Another form of external support comes from coalitions formed between bureaucracies and other actors in the American political arena. Thus, agencies sometimes participate in political alliances that might include their clientele group, other agencies, lobbyists for special interests, and members of Congress who preside over relevant committees and subcommittees.[32] Analysts call these alliances **policy subgovernments** because the actors effectively exercise authority in a narrowly defined policy area.

Policy subgovernments Alliances and relationships among specific agencies, interest groups, and relevant members of Congress that have been capable of effectively exercising authority in a narrowly defined policy area, such as transportation and farm price supports. Powerful alliances often form cozy triangles, like the tobacco subgovernment; looser alliances involving a wide range of actors are called issue networks.

In their most extreme forms, often called *cozy triangles*, these subgovernments can be powerful coalitions (see Chapter 8, on interest groups). The success of any cozy triangle coalition depends on its members' ability to limit participation to a few "insiders" and to maintain a low public profile. Until recently, one of Washington's most successful cozy triangles was the tobacco subgovernment, which focused on policies related to promoting the consumption of tobacco products. The three main sets of actors in that subgovernment were members of Congress from tobacco-growing states (for example, North Carolina, South Carolina, and Kentucky) who sat on the agriculture and appropriations committees; lobbyists representing tobacco growers and cigarette-manufacturing companies; and bureaucrats from tobacco-related programs at the Agriculture and Commerce Departments. Meeting regularly to work out favorable policies, these actors created programs that helped tobacco farmers and the giant tobacco industry to fend off attacks from those who sought policies contrary to their interests.

In 1964, the cozy world of the tobacco subgovernment began to fall apart. That year, the surgeon general of the United States issued a report linking cigarette smoking to lung cancer, heart disease, and emphysema. The report was followed by a Federal Trade Commission proposal that cigarette packages and advertising carry health warnings. The cozy triangle no longer had the low visibility that had made it so effective before the surgeon general's announcement. Nevertheless, the tobacco subgovernment still exists today, although its members can no longer easily set public policies related to tobacco. For years they fought a constant battle to maintain what remained of their subsidy and international marketing programs.[33] More recently, members of Congress and state and local officials, in conjunction with a variety of federal agencies — from the Public Health Service and the Environmental Protection Agency to the Food and Drug Administration — have mounted a direct attack on the tobacco industry, suggesting that there will be greater regulation of cigarette production and consumption in the future.[34]

At the opposite extreme from cozy triangles are subgovernments organized as issue networks. *Issue networks* involve a large number of participants with different degrees of interest in and commitment to the policies and problems that bring them together. An issue network is an open and at times highly visible subgovernment. The individuals taking part in it may come and go, and often they have neither the time nor the leadership to develop consistent shared attitudes toward policy. Bureaucrats also play a role in issue network subgovernments, but that role often depends on their grasp of the issues and their willingness to dive into the open policymaking process.[35]

Environmental policymaking is a classic example of an issue network in action. It has been highly visible since the mid-1960s. The challenge of environmental protection has attracted a multitude of actors, including dozens of members of Congress, hundreds of interest groups with varying points of view, and a host of media and academic observers. In the middle of that issue network sits the Environmental Protection Agency (EPA), which was created in 1970 to coordinate the implementation of federal environmental policy. The

EPA maintained a leading role in the environmental issue network quite successfully during the 1970s. Beginning in 1981, however, the agency's situation changed as it experienced a crisis.

The Reagan administration came to office intent on changing the direction of environmental policy through deregulation and reform. It planned to use the EPA to implement these changes by instituting new agency policies and radically altering the way in which environmental regulations were enforced in established program areas. The administration's strategy basically ignored the interests of some of the major actors in the existing environmental policy issue network. Incensed at the EPA's new positions, environmental interest groups formed alliances to defeat Reagan's initiatives in a variety of program areas. A coalition of conservationists and others who were concerned about environmental policy used direct lobbying and the media to press the White House and Congress for major changes in the Reagan approach. In 1983 the administration acknowledged defeat by replacing the controversial head of the EPA, Ann Gorsuch Burford, with William Ruckelshaus, who was highly regarded by environmental interest groups and who had been the first administrator of the agency when it was created during the Nixon presidency.[36] Ruckelshaus spent two years undoing the administrative changes made during Burford's tenure and reestablishing the EPA's credibility within the environmental issue network.

Whether it takes the form of public support or coalitions with special-interest groups, external support plays an important role in shaping and directing bureaucratic power. The cases of the tobacco and environmental policy subgovernments indicate just how significant that support can be for individual agencies.

Expertise. An agency's power can also stem from its expertise. In matters of national defense, America's top policymakers often turn to experts at the Pentagon for advice. On issues involving public health, they ask the opinion of the surgeon general or the *Centers for Disease Control and Prevention (CDC)*. On international subjects, the *Central Intelligence Agency (CIA)* is regarded as the primary source of expert information. As long as such expert information is deemed accurate and reliable by those who use it, it enhances the power of the agency. But if the credibility of that information is brought into question—as happened to the CIA both in the late 1980s when it failed to accurately predict the collapse of the Soviet bloc and again in 2003 and 2004 when its intelligence on Iraq was brought into question (see Chapter 15, on foreign and defense policy)—the public immediately questions the competence of the agency and its officials. Once the credibility of a bureaucracy's expertise is put in doubt, that bureaucracy's influence and power are likely to deteriorate.

Discretion. Bureaucrats are often permitted to use their own judgment in implementing public policies and programs. Congress and the White House frequently formulate policies in ambiguous and vague terms. When President John F. Kennedy issued a mandate to the National Aeronautics and Space Administration to land an American on the moon by 1970, he could not tell the agency exactly when and how to do it; those details were left to the discretion of NASA officials.

Discretion can be an important source of power, for it gives some individuals within a bureaucracy considerable flexibility in deciding how to do their jobs.

Longevity in Office. The merit system, which protects most federal employees from being fired for political reasons, provides still another source of bureaucratic power. Because it is extremely difficult to dismiss a federal civil servant without a good, nonpolitical cause, civil servants usually stay in their jobs for a long time. Presidents and members of Congress come and go, as do the presidential appointees who head federal agencies, but the average bureaucrat serves through several presidential and congressional terms in office. As a result, elected officials and their appointees often find themselves relying on career civil servants to keep the agencies functioning. Thus, longevity in office can mean considerable power for the experienced bureaucrat.

Critical Thinking

Should we impose a limit on the number of years an individual can serve in a particular government job?

Skill and Leadership. External support, expertise, discretion, and longevity in office will not accomplish much by themselves. Potential wielders of bureaucratic power must have the talents and the will to use those resources. That is as true for agencies as it is for individuals. Without skill and leadership, even the most resource-rich federal agency will not be able to accomplish its objectives.

The Defense Department, for all its potential power and influence, would fail in its search for White House and congressional support if the secretary of defense did not provide effective leadership. During the Reagan administration, for example, Secretary of Defense Caspar ("Cap") Weinberger gained a reputation as a successful advocate for increasing defense expenditures. When some members of the Reagan administration proposed reductions in the defense budget, Weinberger managed to convince the president that defense "is not a budget issue. You spend what you need." In most instances, Weinberger was able to get the president to protect his department's budget.[37]

In short, power is the fuel that gives bureaucracies the energy to carry out their missions. A bureaucracy without power or the potential to exercise power is truly a waste of public resources. The question is not whether bureaucratic power exists or should exist, but whether that power is responsive to the wishes of the American public and its elected representatives.

Limiting Bureaucratic Power

The American political system does provide effective means of limiting bureaucratic power and keeping it responsive. It offers a variety of internal and external checks designed to contain bureaucratic influence and authority within acceptable bounds.

Self-Restraint and Limited Resources. Some of the curbs come from bureaucratic self-restraint. In the mid-1970s, certain regulatory commissions took the initiative in relaxing the controls they had previously exercised over sectors of the American economy. For example, the *Civil Aeronautics Board (CAB)* intentionally eliminated many barriers to competition among the nation's major airlines. That initiative proved so popular that Congress formally deregulated the airline industry in 1978 and eliminated the CAB altogether in 1985. Although no other major regulatory commission has been abolished, most exercised similar self-restraint during the late 1970s and throughout the 1980s.

The quantity and quality of available resources also put limits on bureaucratic power. The *Internal Revenue Service (IRS)*, for example, does not have enough auditors and agents to review everyone's tax return and investigate all suspected cases of tax fraud. In fact, the IRS is able to investigate only a small percentage of the returns filed each year. Therefore, the competence of its auditors and agents determines how effectively the IRS collects taxes, as does the agency's increasing use of computers to process tax returns. Ultimately, however, the IRS's best tool is the individual taxpayer's fear that his or her return might be one of the few that are subjected to a detailed audit.

The White House. As the formal head of the executive branch, the president can exercise considerable control over the federal bureaucracy by carefully selecting the people he appoints to office or promotes. Before taking office in 1981, Reagan established an appointment system that attempted to choose for office only people who would be loyal to him and would be willing to pursue his objective of reduced government activity forcefully.[38] In addition, the Reagan administration functioned through a system of what one observer termed "jigsaw puzzle management," under which agency managers were told to carry out policies and programs while being kept in the dark about the overall strategy being pursued. The impact of these strategies was to reduce the overall effectiveness and influence of federal bureaucrats while enhancing the power of administration officials.[39]

The White House can also influence the funding of federal agencies and their programs. Typically, federal agencies make their budget requests through the Office of Management and Budget, which evaluates the agencies' proposals and often modifies them to conform to presidential priorities. Even after Congress has appropriated funds and other resources for agency programs, the White House retains control over the allocation of funds from the Treasury Department. In addition, the president can require federal agencies to adopt certain management methods and budgetary techniques. In 1965, for example, President Johnson ordered all federal agencies to adopt an agency planning technique that originated in the Department of Defense. When Jimmy Carter became president in 1977, he ordered federal agencies to adopt a "zero-based" budgeting approach that he had used when he was governor of Georgia. In both instances, the new management technique was intended to give the president greater control over agency decisions (see the discussion on presidential reforms later in the chapter).[40]

Congress. Congress can also impose limitations on the power of federal agencies. The Constitution authorizes Congress to establish public programs and arrange for their implementation. Yet Congress has not always been detailed and explicit in its instructions to federal agencies. Vague legislation has led many critics to argue that Congress is not working hard enough to limit or control bureaucratic power, and bureaucrats themselves have complained about the lack of specificity. In 1979 one administrator openly criticized a congressional act that, in a single line of statutory language, required his agency to establish a program to protect the rights of the handicapped—with no details or guidance. "They're frequently very unhappy with what we do after they give us a mandate like that," he noted. "But the trouble is, the mandate is broad, they deliberately are ambiguous where there is conflict on details, and they leave it to us to try to resolve the ambiguities."[41]

Implied in such criticism is the belief that Congress has a right to exercise much more legislative control than it does today by expanding or narrowing an agency's authority to take action. In a few instances, Congress has tried to provide federal agencies with detailed instructions. The Clean Air Act Amendments of 1970, for instance, set a number of specific deadlines for action by the Environmental Protection Agency (EPA). These challenging goals ultimately proved too difficult to reach on schedule. Delays and postponements were common. Critics of too much congressional interference in the implementation process point to those problems when they are asked why Congress often shies away from supplying many details in its legislation.[42]

Although Congress finds it difficult to control or limit bureaucratic power through detailed legislation, it has other tools with which to accomplish these ends.[43] Congress reviews agency budget requests each year, and it can use that opportunity to scrutinize agency operations. Almost every congressional committee has jurisdiction over a group of federal agencies, and these committees sometimes exercise their oversight responsibilities by holding public hearings on agency operations.[44] In 1988, for example, Representative Douglas Barnard Jr. from Georgia, chairman of the House Government Operations consumer subcommittee, launched a two-year investigation of the operations of the IRS. That investigation eventually led to administrative changes within the agency, including the establishment of an IRS ethics program. Similar hearings were held a decade later, again resulting in major changes in agency procedures. The result has been an effort to make the IRS more customer-oriented in its treatment of taxpayers.[45]

Individual members of Congress often intercede with specific agencies on behalf of their constituents. Members of Congress can also order the Government Accountability Office to conduct an audit or investigation of any federal program. Finally, the role of the U.S. Senate in confirming political appointments provides that chamber with a unique opportunity to review bureaucratic actions.

The Courts. The courts also play a role in limiting the power of the federal bureaucracy.[46] In the period before 1937, the judiciary often agreed to hear cases challenging the authority given to federal agencies by Congress. Today the courts are much less likely to entertain such cases; nevertheless, they pay considerable attention to complaints that a federal agency has exceeded its authority or acted in an arbitrary or unreasonable way when carrying out its duties.

Critical Thinking

Should we prohibit members of Congress or their staffs from contacting a federal agency on behalf of a constituent?

Some of the courts' power over the federal bureaucracy stems from specific provisions of the U.S. Constitution, such as the prohibition against "unreasonable searches and seizures" or the guarantee that citizens shall not be deprived of "life, liberty, or property without due process of law." These powers were reinforced by the Federal Tort Claims Act of 1946, which permits (with a few specified exceptions) Americans to sue the federal government for damages incurred through governmental actions. Congress has even made special provisions for taking legal action against specific agencies. Under provisions of the 1988 tax laws, for example, a taxpayer may sue an IRS employee for damages if the agent seeks to collect taxes in a reckless way or with intentional disregard of tax laws. The possibility of being challenged in court has proved to be an effective means of control.

The courts also play a role in shaping the relationships between the bureaucracy and the other branches of government. From time to time in our history, controversies have arisen about whether government agencies were subject to presidential or congressional control. Sometimes these have taken the form of court cases. In some of these cases the courts have sided with Congress, and in others they have deferred to the White House. The Supreme Court has tended to favor the presidency in recent years,[47] but over the past 200 years there has been no consistent answer to the question of who runs the bureaucracy. Thus, the courts remain a major factor in the life of the federal bureaucracy.

Other Restraints. Competition among federal agencies is another source of limits on bureaucratic power. Many agencies have competitors in the federal government — other agencies that vie for the same set of authorizations or appropriations. The different branches of the armed forces, for instance, compete with one another for a bigger slice of the defense budget. Although such competition may seem inefficient, it does help impose restraints on the power of the military bureaucracies by leading each of them to keep an eye on the activities of the others.

A strong sense of professionalism and responsibility on the part of public-sector employees can also act as a brake on bureaucratic power, especially when someone within an agency exposes inappropriate, unethical, or questionable activities. For example, in 1968 Ernest Fitzgerald, a civilian analyst at the Defense Department, went public with his concerns about major cost overruns on the purchase of C-5A transport planes by the U.S. Air Force. His complaints led to an investigation of those cost overruns and several new management policies. People like Fitzgerald, who risk their careers to halt bureaucratic misconduct, are called **whistle-blowers**.

Whistle-blowers Employees who risk their careers by reporting corruption or waste in their agencies to oversight officials.

Whistle-blowers usually pay a high price for their honesty and candor. In many instances, blowing the whistle on an agency can make one an outcast in the organization and end one's career.[48] Today whistle-blowers have some protection under federal personnel laws, and at least one agency (the National Aeronautics and Space Administration) has a special telephone number that

Inspector general An official in a government agency who is assigned the task of investigating complaints or suspicious behavior.

Freedom of Information Act (FOIA) A public disclosure law that requires federal agencies to release information upon written request.

whistle-blowers can call. Each agency also has an **inspector general's** office,[49] which can investigate complaints or suspicious behavior.

By investigating leads that might uncover major problems, an alert press corps can also restrain bureaucratic power. The **Freedom of Information Act (FOIA)** and other public disclosure laws restrain bureaucratic power as well. Under the FOIA, agencies are required to provide citizens with public records upon written request. The law does allow certain material to remain secret and does not apply to the courts or to Congress. Citizen lobbies, such as Common Cause and Ralph Nader's Public Citizen (see Chapter 8, on interest groups), perform much the same function at times.

Limits and Responsiveness. As we have seen, although it is impossible to guarantee that bureaucratic power will not be misused or abused, mechanisms for limiting that power do exist. Thanks to these potential and actual restraints, bureaucratic power in the federal government has a good chance of being controlled.

In many respects, these limits work to make government agencies more, rather than less, responsive. The problem is that being responsive to one constituency group often means being perceived as unresponsive by others. Consumer groups, for example, often criticize the Department of Agriculture for being too supportive of farming interests and not sufficiently attentive to the needs of consumers. Similarly, many businesses complain that the Environmental Protection Agency and other regulatory agencies fail to take their interests and needs into account, whereas those who support regulation believe that the regulators are on the right track.

Bureaucratic Problems and Reforms

FOCUS QUESTION WHAT ARE THE MAJOR PROBLEMS WITH BUREAUCRATIC BEHAVIOR, AND WHAT STEPS HAVE BEEN TAKEN TO CONTROL THEM?

If the myths of bureaucratic incompetence and unresponsiveness do not reflect the reality of government administration, then why do so many Americans continue to complain about the way government operates? This is somewhat mysterious, for students of public administration find that many citizens are quite satisfied with most of their routine encounters with the bureaucracy.[50] The complaints that most Americans have about the federal bureaucracy may reflect more what they hear about others' ordeals than what they have experienced themselves. There are, however, problems with the bureaucracy that help keep the myths alive.

Bureaucratic Pathologies

At its best, the federal bureaucracy serves the public interest. At its worst, it seems to conduct itself in ways that feed the myths of incompetence and unresponsiveness. Students of American government describe these behaviors as **bureaucratic pathologies**—or "bureaupathologies," for short.[51]

Clientelism. In very general terms, public agencies attempt to work in behalf of the public interest. On a day-to-day basis, however, bureaucrats must deal with those who are served by the programs being implemented—the agency's clientele. The Department of Agriculture works with farmers, the Department of Education with educators, and so on. This daily contact with their clientele is an absolute necessity for employees of these agencies if they are to be responsive to the needs of those they serve. But this constant contact can become pathological when bureaucrats begin to display favoritism toward their clientele's interests, even when those interests do not serve the public good.

The tobacco subgovernment discussed earlier is a classic example of clientelism at work. Bureaucrats within the Department of Agriculture who had worked with tobacco farmers for decades supported their clients' interests even though they were contrary to emerging government policies to discourage smoking.

Similarly, the staffs of government regulatory commissions are sometimes accused of being "captured" by those they regulate. For many years the now defunct Civil Aeronautics Board issued policies and decisions that clearly favored the interests of the nation's major airlines rather than those of airline passengers.

Pathological Incrementalism. Federal agencies are created to administer programs, and we expect them to do so with consistency and fairness. But the conditions under which agencies operate competently are not stagnant. Conditions and circumstances change—sometimes quite swiftly. One would expect public-sector agencies to adapt to those changes as quickly as possible, but often they resist change or make only small, incremental adjustments. At times this response may be intentional. For example, Secretary of Defense Richard Cheney and others in the first Bush administration resisted calls for radical reductions in the Pentagon's 1991 federal budget, despite the major changes that were taking place in the former Soviet Union and Eastern Europe.

However, incrementalist behavior can become pathological when it threatens the very program or service that the agency is supposedly providing. The U.S. military has often been plagued by pathological incrementalism. The navy was slow to recognize the importance of air power in the 1920s until, in a widely publicized demonstration of the point, a maverick army general, Billy Mitchell, sank a warship. During that same period, it was equally difficult to convince many army leaders to abandon horse cavalry units. Bureaucracies tend to move cautiously and slowly, and sometimes that snail's pace can prove both dangerous and costly.

Standard operating procedures (SOPs) Regularized procedures used in public agencies to help the agencies conduct administrative business effectively and efficiently.

Arbitrariness. A competent bureaucracy is one that does its job effectively and efficiently. To achieve this condition, an agency often must adopt **standard operating procedures**, often called **SOPs**. There are times, however, when the use of regularized procedures can interfere with responsiveness or replace common sense, and then arbitrariness becomes a factor. For example, there are stories about people losing their welfare or unemployment benefits because they failed to show up for an appointment with a social worker or forgot to file a certain form on time. A bureaucrat who is unwilling to listen to excuses or explanations can hardly be faulted for sticking to the rules, but he or she can be faulted for being too arbitrary and losing sight of why a program or procedure exists. Bureaucracies often serve people with special needs or individuals facing special circumstances. Even if the aim is efficiency, arbitrary behavior can prove harmful under such conditions.

Arbitrariness also arises when a bureaucrat acts without legal authority. While a police officer has the authority to stop a driver whose vehicle is swerving dangerously, he or she cannot use a nightstick to beat the car's driver or occupants without cause.[52]

Parochialism. In order to perform their functions effectively, some government agencies believe that it is necessary to focus attention on the job at hand. Such concentration on getting the job done can result in another pathological behavior — parochialism.

For example, the job of the army's Rocky Mountain Arsenal was to produce and store chemical and biological weapons, and for most of its thirty-year existence that organization carried out its work without paying much attention to the damage it was doing to its surroundings. That parochial attitude had both short-term and long-term effects. During the early 1970s, a series of earth tremors in the Denver region were traced by one geologist to a weapons disposal process being used at the arsenal. After months of denying any link between its activities and the disturbances, the arsenal temporarily halted the operation. The tremors came to an end, and the army finally agreed to discontinue the process permanently. Years later, when the army closed the arsenal, state and federal environmental protection investigators found that the land in and around the weapons facility was so contaminated that it might remain unusable for hundreds of years. Taken to its extreme, this type of pathological behavior can prove deadly.

Imperialism. As we noted earlier, bureaucracies need power in one form or another in order to do their jobs. Therefore, bureaucrats seek to obtain the resources they need if they are to carry out their assignments. At times, this means expanding agency operations and taking on more responsibilities and personnel. In some agencies, this drive for expansion becomes an end in itself — a key sign of the pathological behavior we call *bureaucratic imperialism*.

Imperialism may involve getting a bigger slice of the federal budget pie, or it may mean starting new programs or even taking over another agency's functions.

Whatever form it takes, most Americans do not regard expansion for its own sake as a desirable feature of bureaucratic operations. During the 1950s and 1960s, for example, the U.S. Army built up its "aviation" units through the acquisition of enough helicopters to make it the third-largest air force on earth, after the U.S. Air Force and the air forces of the Soviet Union. The army leadership rationalized the growth of its aviation units as a means of improving the mobility and effectiveness of land troops. This upset air force generals, who constantly argued that they should have exclusive control of all airborne military equipment and personnel.[53]

Calls for Reform

These pathological behaviors help to explain why the myths of incompetent and unresponsive bureaucracies remain popular today. Americans perceive these problems as the rule rather than the exception. It is not surprising, therefore, to hear calls for bureaucratic reform.

Various Approaches. Those who focus on the need to deal with bureaucratic incompetence advocate the elimination of certain government programs and agencies. Others stress the need to reduce agency size and adopt more efficient management techniques. Still others suggest that the work of government agencies should be turned over to the private sector — a strategy called **privatization**.[54]

Privatization The process of turning the work of government agencies over to the private sector.

Ombudsman A person in a government agency who is responsible for hearing citizen complaints or problems related to government programs and policies.

Some reformers believe that government agencies must be made more responsive, more open, and more aware of potential problems. They advocate holding public hearings or establishing an agency **ombudsman** office to hear citizen complaints concerning the agency's programs. Others believe that government agencies would be more responsive if they relied more on marketplace strategies. For example, instead of having a government agency build and operate public housing units, why not provide qualified families with either money or housing vouchers and let them find appropriate rental space themselves within the local private housing market? A similar voucher approach has been advocated for primary and secondary education.[55]

A number of reformers believe that problems of incompetence and unresponsiveness can be solved through agency reorganizations. Some reorganization plans call for increased centralization within federal agencies to enhance coordination and efficiency. Others require agency decentralization in an effort to enhance responsiveness and citizen participation.

Still other reforms focus on agency personnel policies, such as hiring practices or compensation levels. For instance, a major accomplishment of reformers during the past 150 years has been the adoption of a merit-based personnel system and the elimination of political appointments within federal agencies. Reformers have also pressed for increasing the pay of government employees to help the agencies attract more qualified people to public service.[56]

Presidential Reform Efforts. The current efforts to reform the federal bureaucracy have a nearly century-long history. The most visible reforms have been led by the White House — often in an attempt to gain greater control over the bureaucracy.

For example, in 1905 President Theodore Roosevelt asked an assistant secretary of the treasury, Charles H. Keep, to chair a Commission on Department Methods. Over the next four years, the Keep Commission brought about significant changes in the record keeping and accounting procedures used by federal agencies. Between 1910 and 1913, President William Howard Taft's Commission on Economy and Efficiency sought to bring more budgetary and managerial coordination to the federal bureaucracy. Although no major commissions were formed by either President Woodrow Wilson or his immediate successors, major congressional initiatives for reform were enacted and implemented during their terms.

Under Franklin D. Roosevelt, a President's Committee on Administrative Management (known as the Brownlow Committee, after its chair, Louis Brownlow) advocated a major transformation of the federal bureaucracy, one that would greatly enhance the president's role as the chief administrative officer of American government. Under both Harry S Truman and Dwight D. Eisenhower, commissions chaired by former president Herbert Hoover called for still more reforms. Kennedy and Johnson relied more on task forces within their administration to recommend and implement managerial reform. Nixon appointed a council headed by businessman Roy Ash (who later became the head of the Office of Management and Budget) to assess the federal bureaucracy. Gerald Ford was not in office long enough to undertake any significant reform effort, but Carter came into office seeking major changes in the way business was conducted in Washington. Reagan sought advice from a presidentially appointed but privately funded commission chaired by Peter Grace. George H. W. Bush took few initiatives in the area of administrative reform, but his administration did work toward implementing and extending many of the privatization and similar efforts begun under Reagan.

As one of his first acts as president, Clinton put his vice president, Al Gore, in charge of an effort — the *National Performance Review (NPR)* — to improve the performance of the federal bureaucracy. Influenced by the writings of David Osborne and Ted Gaebler,[57] the NPR called for the "reinvention" of the federal bureaucracy. The aim of **reinventing government** was to "put people first" by having agencies cut unnecessary spending, serve their "customers," empower their employees, help communities solve their own problems, and foster excellence in public service.

The NPR effort differed from past presidential reform initiatives in several important ways. First, it did not stress increased presidential power over the bureaucracy. In fact, its emphasis on empowering government employees and communities seemed contrary to past efforts at centralization. Nor did the NPR focus obsessively on cutting the size of government; instead, it sought to improve the government's performance. Furthermore, the NPR's strategy was to

Reinventing government An approach to bureaucratic reform adopted by the Clinton administration that emphasized empowerment and decentralization in order to enhance the performance of government agencies and programs.

push reform from the inside—to make government employees a force for reform instead of trying to impose changes from outside or from the top.

One byproduct of the efforts to reinvent government was passage of the **Government Performance and Results Act of 1993 (GPRA)**, in which Congress, starting in 1999, required each agency to issue annual performance plans and reports. Such regular reporting and the growing use of performance measures in the federal government are likely to have a long-term impact, but it is too early to tell how successful this and related efforts will be in improving the operation of the federal bureaucracy. Some critics have charged that the changes that are being made are superficial and will not have a lasting impact. Others contend that the performance approach will ultimately fail. That is, public-sector agencies have legal and constitutional obligations that must be fulfilled, and some reforms—no matter how sensible or well intentioned—do not fit well into the American legal framework.

With the election of George W. Bush, White House support for reinventing government was replaced by other priorities, such as the push for making greater use of faith-based organizations in delivering public services (see the discussion earlier in the chapter and in Chapter 3). However, the post–September 11 reorganization of the federal government to focus on homeland security has provided a major opportunity to bring about other changes, and the Bush White House has responded with an approach to performance assessment it calls Program Assessment Rating Tool (PART). The primary objective of PART is to make certain that the aims and operations of federal programs are brought in line with the overall priorities of the president's program priorities.[58]

Conclusion: Expectations and Government Operations

Although these efforts to reform the federal bureaucracy are well-meaning, most of them are based on the two myths we have examined in this chapter. The reforms aim at making government agencies either more competent or more responsive, or both. Yet there is little evidence to support the contention that bureaucratic incompetence and unresponsiveness are as pervasive as they are believed to be. Instead, the problems of our national bureaucracy may be rooted in the constant effort of federal employees to respond competently to the diverse and often conflicting demands of politicians, clients, taxpayers, etc.

Americans are demanding citizens. They want government to be efficient and to keep costs to a minimum, while at the same time insisting that agencies spare no resources to get the job done. They want government workers to treat everyone equally, but they feel that bureaucrats should consider the special needs of individual citizens. They want public officials to increase the quantity and quality of public services while insisting that program budgets be cut back. To put it bluntly, the principal problems facing our national bureaucracy lie in what the American people expect from it.

Expectations are important for bureaucrats because they spend most of their time trying to live up to the expectations of others—expectations that are as varied and diverse as the programs they administer.[59] Many of the problems surrounding bureaucratic institutions can be traced to those efforts. If we are going to criticize the performance of our bureaucrats and accuse them of being wasteful or unresponsive, then we must remember that federal employees are often responding to our demands.

Tying It Together

FOCUS QUESTIONS RECAP

* Who works in the bureaucracy? What do these people do? Where do they work?

* What factors have led to the growth of the federal bureaucracy?

* What are the sources of (and limits on) bureaucratic power?

* What are the major problems with bureaucratic behavior, and what steps have been taken to control them?

CHAPTER SUMMARY

1. The federal bureaucracy comprises diverse groups of people who occupy a variety of white-collar and blue-collar positions. They are organized under several personnel systems, including the ranks of political appointees, the general civil service system, career service personnel systems, and wage systems. Much of what federal bureaucrats do is hidden from public view. Nevertheless, they play important roles in the policymaking process—roles that go beyond merely administering government programs. Organizationally, federal bureaucrats work in hundreds of agencies, including the Executive Office of the President, cabinet departments, independent executive branch agencies, regulatory commissions, government corporations, and other types of agencies.

2. The federal bureaucracy has grown in size and changed in nature over the past two centuries, mostly because of increasing demands by the public and changing conditions in American society.

3. Bureaucracies need power in order to function in the American political system. They derive that power from a variety of sources, such as external support, expertise, bureaucratic discretion, longevity, and skill and leadership. There are many limits to bureaucratic power. These limits come from the legal and political controls exercised by the presidency, Congress, the courts, and various other groups.

4. In their operation, bureaucracies sometimes develop pathological behavior patterns. They may give excessive attention to the interests of those they serve (clientelism), oppose change (incrementalism), tend to be arbitrary and capricious (arbitrariness), take an overly narrow view of the world (parochialism), or yield to an urge to expand (imperialism). Pathological behaviors have stimulated a variety of reform efforts, many of which have focused on reorganizations and changes in personnel policies. Ultimately, however, bureaucracies must meet the expectations of the public in carrying out their jobs. In many instances, those expectations are in direct conflict with the standards of businesslike performance.

Key Terms

Bureaucracy (334)
Political appointees (335)
Cabinet (335)
Patronage (335)
Spoils system (337)
Pendleton Act (337)
Merit system (337)
General Schedule (GS) civil service system (337)
Senior Executive Service (SES) (338)
Career service personnel systems (338)
Wage systems (339)
Proxy administration (339)
Government-sponsored enterprises (GSEs) (340)
Executive Office of the President (EOP) (343)
Office of Management and Budget (OMB) (343)
White House Office (343)
Independent agencies (348)

Regulatory commissions (348)
Quasi-legislative functions (349)
Quasi-judicial functions (349)
Government corporations (349)
Bureaucratic power (355)
Policy subgovernments (356)
Whistle-blowers (362)
Inspector general (363)
Freedom of Information Act (FOIA) (363)
Bureaucratic pathologies (364)
Standard operating procedures (SOPs) (365)
Privatization (366)
Ombudsman (366)
Reinventing government (367)
Government Performance and Results Act of 1993 (GPRA) (368)

Net Work

Do you want to learn more about the agencies and people that make up the federal and state bureaucracies?

- Begin by exploring the FirstGov portal (**www .firstgov.gov**), which serves as an excellent introduction to our government's vast data resources. The site includes an alphabetized listing of agencies, state and local information, reference material, and government news, and other useful links.

- After this government overview, find out more about the people who make up the federal work force. All the up-to-date data can be found at using the U.S. Office of Personnel Management website (**www.opm.gov**).

As an exercise, see if you can find answers to the following questions using the resources above:

- What is the average age of the typical federal employee?

- How many federal government employees work in California? How many work in Maine?

- What does a level GS-13 federal employee do when he or she enters government employment? What if she or he works in San Francisco? In New York?

Finally, as another activity, find the website addresses (URLs) for the following federal and state agencies:

- U.S. Department of Commerce

- Internal Revenue Service

- National Park Service

- New Jersey Department of Environmental Protection

- National Aeronautics and Space Administration

- Office of Management and Budget

- Texas Rangers (the state police organization, not the baseball team!)

13

Courts, Judges, and the Law

Are judicial decisions completely objective and final?

FOCUS QUESTIONS

* What are the differences between civil and criminal law?

* How do trial courts differ from appellate courts?

* What are the major components of federal and state court systems?

* How are judges selected in the United States?

* What are the major steps in Supreme Court decision making?

* Why is it that Court decisions are not simply self-executing?

By now, the story of the presidential election of 2000 is a well-known tale that provided unparalleled drama. It was an election so close that the outcome of the electoral college vote came down to a handful of contested votes in Florida. But the 2000 presidential election also demonstrated the centrality of courts in American society. In the thirty-six days that followed the November 7 election, the candidates and their supporters filed more than fifty lawsuits. In the end, it was the U.S. Supreme Court that ended the election when it ordered a halt to the manual recounting of votes in Florida. With the recount stopped, Al Gore conceded the election, and George W. Bush called for national unity. In the early 1800s, the French observer Alexis de Tocqueville noted that in America, all political questions become legal questions. If ever this observation needed verification, the 2000 election provided it.

In large measure, the uniqueness of the American political system stems from the role played by the courts. No other nation grants so much authority and political power to the judiciary, nor are citizens of other nations quite as willing to entrust their fate to courts as are Americans. Yet for all their faith in courts, most Americans know very little about the legal system. They may have had a brush with the local traffic court or been entertained by Judge Judy. They may even be frequent viewers of cable television's *Court TV*. Nevertheless, when pressed to elaborate on what courts do and why they do it, most people fall back on some vague notions about the law.

The courts are shrouded in symbolism and myth. Pomp and circumstance surround even the lowliest of courts. Only in a courtroom will you find a black-robed individual looking down from a raised platform. No other public official is allowed such trappings. In fact, a mayor or senator decked out in a black robe would seem a pompous fool. Yet when a judge puts on those same robes, no one laughs or even thinks it odd; instead, the robes evoke respect. The same is true of the myths that surround the American court system: If they were attributed to any other political institution, they would seem preposterous.

Perhaps the most widespread of the illusions surrounding the courts is the idea that they are above politics. In contrast to the compromise and partisanship of the political world, the *myth of the nonpolitical courts* represents the judiciary as operating with the certainty that comes from the neutral application of a body of specialized knowledge. Presidents and members of Congress may act out of self-interest; judges simply apply the law. It is the fate of courts to be characterized as the defenders of the rule of law as opposed to the rule of ordinary men and women.

As comforting as this myth may be, it distorts reality. In the pages that follow, you will see that even the act of creating the federal courts was fraught with political conflict. Similarly, not only is the process of selecting judges mired in political controversy, but those chosen are often active participants in politics. The idea that courts have special powers also gives rise to the *myth of finality*, which assumes that once a court—especially the Supreme Court—has spoken, the decision is automatically implemented. This tendency to view court decisions as an endpoint in the political process makes courts seem more powerful than they actually are. But courts cannot compel anyone to comply with their decisions.

Their orders become effective only with the aid of others—aid that is not always provided. Final authority does not rest with the Supreme Court, nor should it in a representative democracy.

We begin our discussion of the role of courts in American society by distinguishing the various sources of law. Then we look at the structure of the court system and the way in which judges are appointed and removed. We conclude the chapter with an examination of the workings of the Supreme Court and the question of compliance.

The Origins and Types of American Law

FOCUS QUESTION WHAT ARE THE DIFFERENCES BETWEEN CIVIL AND CRIMINAL LAW?

As you may recall from Chapter 2, on constitutional foundations, the oldest source of law applied by U.S. courts is *common, or judge-made, law*, which dates from medieval England. A comparatively modern and increasingly important source of law is *statutory law*, which originates from specifically designated lawmaking bodies (for example, Congress and state legislatures).

The distinction between civil and criminal actions is also important in understanding the legal process. **Civil actions** involve a conflict between private persons and/or organizations. Typical of these cases are those involving disputes over contracts, claims for damages resulting from a personal injury, and divorce petitions. In a civil case, the person bringing the suit is called the plaintiff, and the person being sued is the defendant.

Criminal law, on the other hand, applies to offenses against the public order and entails a specified range of punishments. Acts that are in violation of criminal law are specifically detailed in governmental statutes. The party demanding legal action (the national, state, or other government) is called the prosecution, and the person being prosecuted is called the defendant. Most of these cases arise in state courts, although there is a growing body of federal criminal law dealing with such issues as kidnapping, tax evasion, and the sale of narcotics.

Civil actions Suits arising out of conflicts between private persons and/or organizations; they typically include disputes over contracts, claims for damages, and divorce petitions.

Criminal law The branch of the law dealing with offenses against the public order and providing for a specified punishment. Most criminal law cases arise in state courts.

The Structure of the Court Systems

FOCUS QUESTION HOW DO TRIAL COURTS DIFFER FROM APPELLATE COURTS?

When most Americans think about courts, the U.S. Supreme Court immediately comes to mind. As the highest court in the land, the Supreme Court symbolizes the American judiciary. Yet it is only one of more than 18,000 American courts, most of which are the creations of the various states. Each state and the Commonwealth of Puerto Rico has its own independent court system. Because most criminal prosecutions and civil actions are governed by state laws, these are the

The Latest Trial of the Century

In 2004, the nation was riveted by the criminal trial of pop singer Michael Jackson. The entertainer was indicted on numerous child molestation charges, but after a media-saturated trial, he was found not guilty. Jackson is shown here leaving the Santa Maria, California, courthouse.

courts that most affect the average citizen. For example, a motorist who is accused of driving under the influence of alcohol will be brought before a court in the state in which the violation occurred.

Obviously, with fifty-two court systems, there is bound to be a great deal of variability; in fact, no two of these systems are exactly alike. Nevertheless, two types of courts can be found in all systems.

Trial courts, the lowest level of a court system, are the "courts of first instance," possessing **original jurisdiction** (the power to be the first court to hear a case). These courts take evidence, listen to witnesses, and decide what is true and what is not. Trial courts handle both criminal and civil cases.

Trial court decisions may be made by a single judge (a procedure known as a *bench trial*) or by a jury made up of citizens selected from the community. The Constitution provides for jury trials in all criminal cases and in civil cases where the value contested exceeds $20. Most state constitutions contain similar provisions for jury trials. Nevertheless, jury trials tend to be the exception rather than the rule. The desire for a quick decision encourages many defendants to waive the time-consuming jury selection process in favor of the faster decision by a judge. Parties to particularly complicated civil litigation may also assume that members of a jury will be less capable of following the detailed arguments than a judge. In criminal cases, a high percentage of defendants enter into plea-bargaining agreements, in which the accused, with the consent of the prosecutor, avoids a trial by pleading guilty to a lesser crime or accepting a less severe punishment.

Trial courts Courts at the lowest level of the system. They possess original jurisdiction. **Original jurisdiction** The authority to hear a case before any other court does.

Critical Thinking

Is justice served by plea bargaining?

Appellate courts Courts that reconsider the decisions rendered by trial courts if the losing party requests it and demonstrates grounds for it.

In contrast, **appellate courts** are charged with the responsibility of reconsidering decisions made by trial courts if the losing party requests it and demonstrates grounds for it. The appellate review is designed to ensure that there is no error in judicial procedures or interpretations of the law. Because appellate courts simply review the written record of lower courts, they do not use juries.

The Federal and State Court Systems

FOCUS QUESTION   **WHAT ARE THE MAJOR COMPONENTS OF FEDERAL AND STATE COURT SYSTEMS?**

On paper, the federal court structure appears to be relatively simple and eminently rational. After all, the system is composed of a single Supreme Court, several appellate and trial courts, and a limited number of specialized trial courts (see Figure 13.1). But behind the judicial system's facade of orderliness is a history of intense political struggle that contradicts the myth of the nonpolitical courts.

Lower Courts

Article III of the Constitution creates only one court, the Supreme Court, giving Congress the power to create such "inferior courts" as it deems necessary. This peculiar approach to court structure was the direct result of the bitter struggle between the Federalists and the Antifederalists at the Constitutional Convention. The Antifederalists, in order to protect the power of the states, wanted a system in which all cases, even those involving the national government, would be heard by the state courts. The Federalists argued for a national court system, which would establish the supremacy of the central government and limit the biases of the local courts.[1] Unable to reach agreement, the delegates finally compromised by creating the Supreme Court and leaving the responsibility for filling in the details of the system to Congress.

The organization of the federal courts remains a divisive political issue. For example, it took twenty years of struggle between conservative white southerners and civil rights groups to split the old fifth circuit court of appeals. (A *circuit* is a judicial territory.) In the 1960s, southerners proposed splitting the circuit and moving southern judges into the new circuit, creating a Deep South court. Convinced that such restructuring would weaken civil rights enforcement, civil rights groups, principally the National Association for the Advancement of Colored People (NAACP), managed to block the reorganization. In 1980 civil rights groups and liberal members of Congress finally agreed to split off a new eleventh circuit from the old fifth circuit. The NAACP withdrew its opposition only after the appointment of some black judges to these circuit courts—demonstrating that even the apparently technical questions of court structure are matters of sharp political conflict.

FIGURE 13.1

Organization of the Federal Court System

The lines and arrows show the routes of cases through appeals and Supreme Court grants of hearings.

Source: From Lawrence Baum, *American Courts: Process and Policy*, 2nd ed., p. 28. © 1998 by Houghton Mifflin Company.

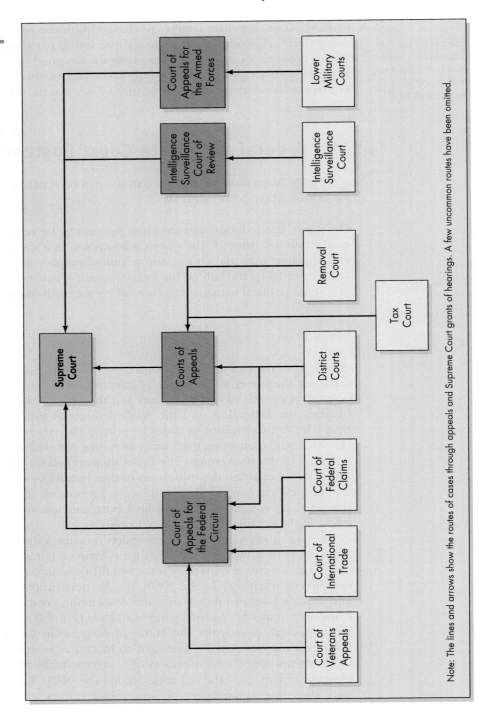

Note: The lines and arrows show the routes of cases through appeals and Supreme Court grants of hearings. A few uncommon routes have been omitted.

U.S. District Courts.

As trial courts of general jurisdiction for the federal system, district courts hear trials in all federal criminal and civil cases. The district courts also hear what are known as *diversity cases*: suits between parties from different states when the amount in controversy exceeds $75,000. In addition to their trial duties, the district courts are also responsible for the naturalization of aliens, the approval of passports, and the granting of parole to federal prisoners.

The Judiciary Act of 1789, the first Senate bill introduced in the First Congress, created a national judiciary that included the district courts. Although the creation of these courts resulted from the Federalist impulse to establish a strong national judiciary, the form they took was shaped by the Federalists' need to compromise with the Antifederalists. Thus, the Federalist forces attained their goal of a national court system, but the Antifederalists insisted on district boundaries that were identical with state borders—which remains true to this day. By requiring district court and state boundaries to be the same, the Antifederalists achieved a decentralized structure that was committed to local political values.

Currently, there are ninety-four U.S. district courts distributed among the fifty states, the District of Columbia, and the four territories. Twenty-four states contain more than one district, and the remaining states and territories have one district court each.

District court cases are usually heard by a single judge, who presides over both civil and criminal trials. The district courts have a total of 632 judicial positions, but the number of judges assigned to a district varies from 1 to 28. The federal territory of Guam, for example, constitutes a single judicial district,

Critical Thinking

Why is it important that district court boundaries never cross state lines?

A Failed Nomination

While presidents nominate justices to the Supreme Court, they must be confirmed by the Senate. Shown here is President George W. Bush introducing his nominee, Harriet Miers, to fill the seat vacated by the retirement of Justice Sandra Day O'Connor. Confronted with strong opposition, Miers eventually asked that her nomination be withdrawn.

staffed by one judge. Among the states, Idaho, North Dakota, and Vermont each contain one district with two judges. In contrast, the Southern District of New York, which includes Manhattan and the Bronx, has twenty-eight judges assigned to it.

To most Americans, the district courts may seem to be the least important of the federal courts. Yet district courts hear more than 200,000 cases each year, and fewer than 10 percent of them are appealed to a higher court. Of those that are appealed, only a small fraction are reversed. For most litigants, the district court decision is the final decision.

Courts of Appeals. Courts of appeals, or **circuit courts**, as they are sometimes called, serve as the major appellate courts for the federal system. They review all cases — civil and criminal — that are appealed from the district courts. Moreover, on occasion these courts review decisions of the independent regulatory agencies and departments. For example, decisions of the Federal Communications Commission involving the renewal of radio and television licenses can be appealed directly to the District of Columbia Circuit.

There are twelve U.S. courts of appeals, one for the District of Columbia and eleven others covering regional groupings of states (see Figure 13.2). Although the circuits include more than one state, no state is divided among circuits. A thirteenth court of appeals, the U.S. Court of Appeals for the Federal Circuit, is an appellate court charged with hearing patent and trademark cases.

The twelve courts of appeals of general jurisdiction have 179 authorized judgeships. But, as in the district courts, these judges are unevenly distributed among the circuits. Individual circuits have anywhere from six to twenty-eight judges assigned to them. The number is determined by Congress and is supposed to reflect the workload of the circuit. Ordinarily, the courts of appeals hear cases in panels of three judges, and the membership of these panels varies from case to case.

Circuit courts Federal courts of appeals that rank above the district courts and serve as the major appellate courts for the federal system. They review all cases, both civil and criminal, and the decisions of independent regulatory agencies and departments.

The Supreme Court

The Constitution is remarkably vague even with regard to the Supreme Court. It is worth comparing Article I with Article III and noticing how detailed Article I is concerning the makeup and duties of Congress, and how lacking in such details about the Court Article III is.

How many justices serve on the Supreme Court? The answer is currently nine, but you will not discover that from reading the Constitution. The Constitution does not designate a size for the Court; that is left up to Congress. Since 1869, the Court has been staffed by a chief justice and eight associate justices. Until 1869, however, Congress made frequent changes in the size of the Court. Often these changes were thinly disguised efforts to promote partisan political objectives. During the Civil War, for instance, Congress created a tenth seat on the Supreme Court, assuring President Abraham Lincoln a solid majority on the Court.

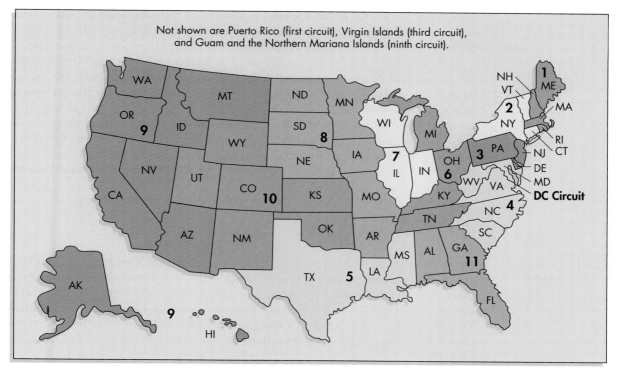

Not shown are Puerto Rico (first circuit), Virgin Islands (third circuit), and Guam and the Northern Mariana Islands (ninth circuit).

FIGURE 13.2

U.S. Circuit Courts of Appeals

According to the Constitution, the Supreme Court has both original and appellate jurisdiction. Original jurisdiction, as stated earlier, means that a court is empowered to make the first decision in a particular kind of dispute; it is the court of first instance. Article III limits the Supreme Court's original jurisdiction to cases involving foreign ambassadors and those in which a state is a party. Suits under original jurisdiction account for a very small portion of the Supreme Court's workload. In 1998, for instance, of the 7,692 cases that the Supreme Court was asked to decide, only 7 were presented under original jurisdiction.

The chief labor of the Supreme Court is appellate. For much of the nation's history, the Court was required by Congress to hear all cases that came to it. Complaints by the justices that the workload was unmanageable finally led Congress to pass the Judiciary Act of 1925. Under the provisions of this act, the Court has tremendous latitude in selecting the cases it wants to hear.

Of the more than 7,000 brought to the Supreme Court each year, approximately 90 percent come by way of a request for a **writ of certiorari** — a request that the Supreme Court order the lower court to send up the record of the case. Cases are accepted for review by means of the *rule of four*; that is, four justices must vote to consider the case. More than 95 percent of requests for writs of certiorari are denied, normally without explanation. The Court simply notes that certiorari is denied and that the decision of the lower court stands. Cases can

Writ of certiorari An order by the Supreme Court that a lower court send up the record of a case.

Appeal A route by which cases can reach the Supreme Court. In such cases, litigants have some right under the law to have their cases reviewed.

also come to the Court by **appeal**, which means that the litigants have some right under the law to have their cases reviewed. In practice, appeals are treated in the same discretionary way as requests for certiorari.

Because the Court receives many more petitions each year than it can possibly process, the freedom to accept only a limited number of cases is essential to its effective operation. But there are also political advantages to the screening process. By carefully selecting cases for review, the justices can and do advance their policy preferences. Moreover, the ability to deny review without explanation can be used to avoid particularly controversial political issues. Thus, the Supreme Court avoided ruling on the constitutionality of the undeclared war in Vietnam by refusing, without explanation, to grant certiorari to cases raising the issue.

Specialized Courts

Critical Thinking

How can the refusal to hear cases advance policy preferences?

In addition to the federal courts that we have discussed, Congress has also created a few specialized courts. One of them is the U.S. Court of Federal Claims, created to litigate disputes involving government contracts. Other special courts include the U.S. Court of Military Appeals, the U.S. Court of International Trade, the Court of Veterans Appeals, and the U.S. Tax Court. Staffed by judges with expertise in a particular area, these courts reduce the workload of the general courts.

Usually these specialized courts attract little attention from the general public, but in 2002 the most specialized and secret of these courts, the U.S. Foreign Intelligence Surveillance Court, suddenly burst into the public limelight. Created in 1978, the Foreign Intelligence Surveillance Court was designed to adjudicate requests for wiretaps designed to secretly obtain information about a foreign government or persons suspected of engaging in sabotage. The court, which is staffed by judges borrowed from the district courts, meets in a windowless office in the Department of Justice. The same congressional act also created the U.S. Foreign Intelligence Surveillance Court of Review to review decisions of the lower court. (The court of review is composed of three judges borrowed from the courts of appeals.) Until 2002, the court of review had never met because the Foreign Intelligence Surveillance Court had never turned down a wiretap request from the Department of Justice. In 2002, however, the trial court refused to permit the Department of Justice to implement new secret rules that would allow criminal prosecutors and counterintelligence investigators to work together. The court ruled that the department was trying to use the powers of counterintelligence agents to conduct normal criminal investigations. Since the standards for securing a wiretap are considerably lower when the target is a foreign government or someone suspected of sabotage, allowing wiretaps in normal criminal investigations under the guise of counterintelligence would greatly loosen the standards for wiretaps. The Department of Justice then successfully appealed the case to the U.S. Foreign Intelligence Surveillance Court of Review.

POLITICS & POPULAR CULTURE

Law and Order

Courtroom dramas have long been a staple of American television, but few series have been as successful as *Law and Order* and its various spinoffs. First broadcast in 1990, the series, which advertises itself as being "ripped from the headlines," engages legions of fans with its realistic stories, a strong cast, and a gritty image. Cinematically groundbreaking, its use of hand-held cameras often gives it that realism missing from earlier crime dramas. Each episode features a high-profile violent crime, sometimes complicated by social issues, whose perpetrator is captured, tried, and convicted during the one-hour show. The prosecution team is often challenged by well-prepared and extremely competent defense attorneys. Indeed, the prosecution is generally forced to change tactics in the face of these tenacious defense attorneys, and on occasion the prosecution even loses cases.

As good as the show is, however, it is Hollywood's version of the criminal trial, and as such has little to do with normal criminal proceedings. Indeed, most criminal defendants do not even go to trial; instead, in more than 90 percent of all cases, they plead guilty. Often the defendants participate in a criminal justice system that has been labeled by its critics as "slaughterhouse justice." As one public defender explained after disposing of seventeen cases, "I met 'em, pled 'em, and closed 'em—all in the same day."

Even when a trial does take place, it rarely resembles the television show trial because few criminal defendants have the resources to hire a phalanx of highly skilled attorneys and investigators. Many defendants are indigent and thus are unable to afford even basic representation. These defendants must depend on court-appointed counsel. Although these lawyers may be highly skilled, they seldom have the investigative resources available to the state or to a wealthy defendant. In

New Orleans, for instance, even before Hurricane Katrina, the public defenders' office had only three investigators to handle more than 7,000 cases a year.

Moreover, the quality of appointed counsel varies tremendously. Most courts provide legal services to indigents by appointing private counsel to serve the defendant—generally only the largest communities have a public defender service. Because the fees paid to court-appointed counsel are commonly less than those attorneys receive for other services, experienced lawyers are reluctant to accept such assignments. Thus, court-appointed counsel are often inexperienced lawyers who have little interest in criminal law but need even the small fees that the court pays. In Philadelphia, for instance, one study found that the appointed counsel were so bad that "even officials in charge of the system say they wouldn't want to be represented in traffic court by some of the people appointed to defend poor people accused of murder." Even more illustrative may be the trial of a woman in Alabama who was accused of murdering her abusive husband. The trial was delayed by a day when the judge found her appointed counsel in contempt for showing up drunk. The following day, the attorney and his client were both led into the courtroom—from jail. The trial proceeded, and the defendant was found guilty and sentenced to death. The court-appointed lawyer never produced hospital records documenting the injuries suffered by the woman and her children.

Thus, we see that, as interesting and timely as the cases presented on television can be, courtroom action on the small screen is far more dramatic than the typical criminal trial.

Source: Quotes from Stephen B. Bright, "Counsel for the Poor: The Death Sentence Not for the Worst Crime But for the Worst Lawyer," *Yale Law Review*, 103 (1994): 1835–1883.

State Court Systems

Each state has at least one appellate court that serves as its highest tribunal. These courts are not always identifiable by title, however. For example, in the state of New York, the highest court is called the court of appeals, and the trial courts are designated as the supreme courts. Whatever the name, nearly every state has one court that reviews the decisions of all other courts. (Both Texas and Oklahoma have two high courts—one for civil litigation and one that handles only criminal appeals.) Slightly more than half the states also make use of an intermediate appellate court to hear appeals from trial court decisions. Such courts permit the parties to appeal without overburdening the highest court.

The most numerous state courts, the trial courts, are divided into two types: those with limited jurisdiction and those with general jurisdiction. Trial courts of **limited jurisdiction** are empowered to hear only a narrowly defined class of cases. These specialized courts often process a large number of routine cases involving minor issues. Among the most common courts in this category are traffic courts and small-claims courts.

Trial courts of **general jurisdiction** have authority over a much broader range of issues. Ordinarily, such courts hear all civil cases involving nontrivial monetary value and all cases involving serious criminal matters. Although the courts of general jurisdiction are not as specialized as the courts of limited jurisdiction, it is not unusual to find courts of general jurisdiction divided into criminal and civil courts, especially in metropolitan areas with heavy caseloads.

> **Limited jurisdiction** The power of certain trial courts that are allowed to hear only a narrowly defined class of cases.
> **General jurisdiction** The power of trial courts to hear cases on a broad range of issues, ordinarily including all civil cases involving nontrivial monetary value and all cases involving serious criminal matters.

Interactions Among Court Systems

The existence of so many court systems obviously complicates the interactions among them. Often the litigants (parties involved in a suit) can choose among several different courts. Indeed, it is common for the plaintiff (the party bringing suit) to shop around for a court, hoping to find one that will be favorable to his or her side.

This complexity is heightened by the fact that both state and national courts may have jurisdiction over the same issues—a situation known as *concurrent jurisdiction.* For example, Congress has granted to the federal district courts the right to hear the so-called diversity cases—cases involving citizens of different states contesting a sum greater than $75,000. In doing so, however, Congress did not deny the state courts the right to hear such cases; it merely established an additional forum for resolving them.[2]

Although the complex network of multiple court systems gives plaintiffs the opportunity to shop around for a favorable court before bringing an action, once the case has been tried, appeals must be made within the same court system. Occasionally, decisions of a state's highest court are successfully appealed to the U.S. Supreme Court, but this can occur only when the state's highest court has rendered a decision interpreting provisions of the U.S. Constitution, a treaty, or a federal law. Decisions of a court in one state may never be appealed to a court in another state, nor is it possible to appeal a federal court decision to a state court.

Recruiting and Removing Judges

FOCUS QUESTION HOW ARE JUDGES SELECTED IN THE UNITED STATES?

In contrast to nations such as Italy (see "Global Politics," p. 389), the United States does not have a career judiciary; there is no special training required for judges. In fact, the U.S. Constitution does not even require legal training as a qualification for service on the Supreme Court. All 110 justices who have served on the Court have been lawyers, but it was not until 1957 that all members of the Court had earned law degrees.

There is an old adage in American politics that a judge is a lawyer who knew a senator or governor. Though something of an overstatement, this saying indicates that beyond the formal requirements of constitutions and statutes lies a selection process that is highly political. The myth of the nonpolitical courts suggests that judicial selections are or should be based solely on merit. The reality is that the choices are always political.

Federal Judges

According to Article II of the Constitution, the president shall nominate and, with the "advice and consent of the Senate," appoint justices of the Supreme Court. The president proposes a candidate to the Senate; if a majority of the Senate approves, the nominee takes office. Of course, these nominations, like any legislative act in the Senate, may be blocked by a filibuster. This same formal method is used to appoint judges to the courts of appeals and district courts. But the constitutional requirements do not describe the political complexity of the selection process. Furthermore, informal methods of selection have evolved alongside the formal process.

Appointments to the District Courts. The president has the power to make nominations to the district courts. Most administrations establish guidelines detailing the qualities the president expects in a nominee and then leave the search for candidates to the U.S. Department of Justice. In Ronald Reagan's administration, for instance, the Justice Department's Office of Legal Policy was chiefly responsible for nominations to the federal district courts. To ensure that the nominees shared the president's political philosophy, attorneys in the Office of Legal Policy reportedly subjected judicial candidates to extensive interviews, said to last six or more hours. The most controversial aspect of the Reagan administration's screening was the reported use of abortion as a litmus test.

Throughout Reagan's term, complaints surfaced that Justice Department officials routinely questioned prospective nominees on their views on abortion and rejected those who did not conform to the administration's position. Though Reagan was certainly not the first president to consider the ideology of his nominees, his administration represents "the most systematic, most coordinated effort at the use of appointment power to maximize the president's agenda and to maximize the president's influence on the appointment process."[3]

In nominating candidates for the district courts, however, the executive branch must always be mindful of the power of individual senators. Under the unwritten rule of senatorial courtesy, if a senator of the president's party from a nominee's state opposes the nomination of a candidate, the Senate as a whole will reject the nomination. In recent years, senatorial courtesy has been exercised at the committee stage by use of the "blue slip." When it receives a nomination to a federal court, the Senate Judiciary Committee notifies the senators by means of a blue slip. If a senator of the president's party from the nominee's state fails to return the blue slip, it kills the appointment. The committee will simply refuse to take any action until the nomination is withdrawn.

Rather than provoke confrontations with the Senate, presidents have as a rule accepted advice from the relevant senators. Often this translates into formal nomination by the president but informal nomination by a senator. In fact, the prominence of senatorial courtesy led one former assistant attorney general to remark, "The Constitution is backwards. Article II, Section 2, should read: 'the Senators shall nominate, and by and with the consent of the President, shall appoint.'"[4]

Appointments to the Courts of Appeals. The president and the Justice Department have a freer hand in making appointments to the courts of appeals than they do in making appointments to district courts. Because each circuit contains more than one state, no senator can unambiguously claim senatorial courtesy. However, because it is generally assumed that each state in a circuit should have at least one judge on that circuit's appellate bench, the president is constrained by having to maintain the proper balance of state representation.

Over the past decade, judicial appointments, especially those to courts of appeals, have become more controversial and thus more difficult for presidents. During the Clinton administration, Republicans refused to even give a hearing to several Clinton nominees, thus dooming any possibility of their nomination. With George W. Bush in the White House, the Democrats replied by obstructing committee action and, in 2005, filibustering five nominees. The Republicans in turn threatened to use an arcane rule to cut off Senate debate and end the filibuster. This so-called "nuclear option" would have allowed the Senate to end the debate, on judicial nominees, with a simple majority vote rather than the 60 votes needed to invoke cloture. In the end, the showdown was avoided when fourteen senators (seven Republicans and seven Democrats) agreed to allow three of the nominations to go forward on the condition that none of the participating senators would support the filibuster of a future nominee except under "extraordinary circumstances."

Appointments to the Supreme Court.

The Supreme Court is a national institution, with no special ties to states or regions. Thus, the president need not worry about individual senators exercising senatorial courtesy, although the senators from the nominee's state are asked to serve as sponsors. The Senate is far from irrelevant to the nomination process, however, and it has considered itself free to reject candidates for a variety of reasons. Reagan's nomination of Judge Robert Bork, for instance, failed in the Senate because of widespread opposition to his restrictive views on the right to privacy and equal rights for women.

Critical Thinking

What criteria should the Senate use in confirming judicial nominees?

In the nineteenth century, the Senate was more likely to disapprove a presidential nomination on purely partisan grounds than it is today. Before the Bork nomination, the two most recent nominations to fail in the Senate, those of Judges Clement Haynsworth and G. Harrold Carswell, were opposed by Senate liberals for ideological reasons, but both candidates had other serious disadvantages. Haynsworth came under attack for having purchased stock in a company that had been a party in a case before him; he had bought the stock after the decision had been made, but before it was announced. Carswell was criticized for lacking the professional qualifications expected of a Supreme Court justice. His fate was probably sealed when one of his defenders, Republican Senator Roman Hruska from Nebraska, argued that "there are a lot of mediocre judges and people and lawyers. They are entitled to a little representation, aren't they, and a little chance?"[5]

None of these battles, however, not even the failed Bork nomination, matched the furor over President George H. W. Bush's 1991 nomination of Judge Clarence Thomas. Nominated by the president to replace Thurgood Marshall, the Court's only African American justice up to that time, Thomas initially appeared assured of Senate confirmation. Like Marshall, he had overcome segregation and poverty. But from the beginning, Thomas's conservatism, particularly on issues of affirmative action, troubled Senate liberals and leaders of the major civil rights organizations.

After five days of hearings, during which Thomas recanted many of his previous writings and refused to discuss his opinions on abortion, the Senate seemed set to confirm his nomination. As the Senate was about to vote, however, allegations of sexual harassment were leaked to the press. Although the allegations made by Professor Anita Hill, who had formerly worked for Thomas, had been presented to the committee, they had not been part of the public record. Embarrassed by the leak, the Senate postponed the floor vote on the nomination, and the Senate Judiciary Committee reconvened for an extraordinary set of weekend hearings, covered live on television. The Judiciary Committee heard testimony from Hill, Thomas, and others concerning the nominee's behavior. Following this second round of hearings, the committee sent the nomination to the Senate floor without a recommendation — the committee had divided seven to seven over whether Thomas should be confirmed. Eventually the Senate confirmed him by the closest vote accorded any successful nominee in the twentieth century, but the battle polarized the nation and left many senators questioning the confirmation process. Several senators, including the chair of the Judiciary Committee, vowed to seek changes in the Senate procedures, but so far no changes have been made.

Breaking the Color Barrier on the Court

After an extraordinary career as a leader in the civil rights movement, a career that included arguing *Brown v. Board of Education* before the Supreme Court, Thurgood Marshall became Justice Thurgood Marshall. Marshall was the first African American to serve on the nation's highest court. His appointment occurred at a time when very few African Americans served on any of the nation's courts.

Because justices of the Supreme Court are appointed for life and occupy such a prominent position in the American system of government, presidents are quite careful to choose justices whose ideological views seem to be in harmony with theirs. If fate provides enough vacancies, a president's appointments can reshape the judiciary to reflect his views, perpetuating the president's philosophical positions long after the administration has left office (see Table 13.1).[6]

In both the 2000 and 2004 presidential elections, George W. Bush promised that he would transform the Supreme Court by appointing individuals similar to Justice Antonin Scalia, perhaps the Court's most conservative justice. During the president's first term, however, the Court membership remained stable, but in July 2005 the Court's makeup began to change when Justice Sandra Day O'Connor notified the president that she intended to retire once her successor was confirmed by the Senate. Shortly thereafter, President Bush nominated Judge John Roberts to fill the O'Connor vacancy. Then on September 3, 2005, as Judge Roberts was preparing for his Senate confirmation hearings, Chief Justice William Rehnquist died. Three days later, the president withdrew the Roberts nomination to fill O'Connor's seat and nominated him to be the new Chief Justice instead. Given his record as a conservative Appeals Court judge, Democrats were wary of the nomination. Nevertheless, Roberts was confirmed by a vote of 78 to 22, with every Republican voting for him and the Democrats evenly divided.

Roberts's confirmation left the O'Connor seat still to be filled. Initially the president, at the urging of Senate Minority Leader Harry Reid, nominated Harriet Miers, his White House Counsel and prior to that his personal attorney. Interestingly, Miers had chaired the committee that recommended Judge Roberts

TABLE 13.1

The Roberts Court

Justice	Year Born	Year Appointed	Appointing President	Political Party
Roberts, John	1955	2005	George W. Bush	Rep.
Stevens, John Paul	1920	1975	Ford	Rep.
Scalia, Antonin	1936	1986	Reagan	Rep.
Kennedy, Anthony	1936	1988	Reagan	Rep.
Souter, David	1939	1990	George H. W. Bush	Rep.
Thomas, Clarence	1948	1991	George H. W. Bush	Rep.
Ginsburg, Ruth Bader	1933	1993	Clinton	Dem.
Breyer, Stephen G.	1938	1994	Clinton	Dem.
Alito, Samuel	1950	2006	George W. Bush	Rep.

for the O'Connor seat. From the beginning, the Miers nomination was controversial. Her lack of judicial experience led senators from both parties to question her suitability for the job. Additionally, conservatives in the president's own party expressed strong concerns about her level of commitment to basic conservative beliefs. After three contentious weeks, Miers asked the president to withdraw her nomination.

The president then nominated Judge Samuel Alito, known to his critics as "Scalito" for his similarity to Justice Scalia. Unlike the Roberts nomination, which was after all appointing a conservative to replace a conservative, the Alito nomination, which appeared to replace a moderate justice with a conservative justice, stirred up significant partisanship. Senator John Kerry announced his intention to filibuster the nomination, but that was quickly ended by a cloture vote of 75-25. In the end the nominee was confirmed by a highly partisan vote of 58-42. Only four Democrats supported his nomination, while only one Republican voted against confirmation. With these appointments, President Bush seemingly edged closer to transforming the Supreme Court into a more conservative institution.

Of course, presidents are not always successful in predicting what a candidate will do once she or he is in office. Perhaps the most famous example of a president who was frustrated by his own appointment is Theodore Roosevelt, who nominated Oliver Wendell Holmes. Before forwarding the nomination of Holmes to the Senate, Roosevelt had assured himself that the candidate shared his views on the antitrust statutes. When Holmes immediately voted against the president's view in an antitrust case, Roosevelt quipped that he could "make a judge with a stronger backbone out of a banana."[7] Similarly, President Dwight D. Eisenhower came to regret his appointment of Earl Warren as chief justice.

Eisenhower had made the appointment expecting Warren to adhere to the president's own middle-of-the-road political views. Instead, the Warren Court (1953–1969) became known as the most liberal Supreme Court in U.S. history. Eisenhower referred to the appointment as "the biggest damned-fool mistake I ever made."[8]

Nominations to the Supreme Court also give presidents a chance to recognize important constituent groups, especially social groups that have previously been unrepresented. President Lyndon B. Johnson broke the Supreme Court's color barrier by appointing Thurgood Marshall, the first black justice. President Reagan appointed Sandra Day O'Connor, the first woman to serve on the Court. Obviously, the appointment of a woman or member of a minority group to the Court is unlikely to have a substantive impact on decisions, but representation for a group that has traditionally been excluded from the process has great symbolic value.

Who Becomes a Federal Judge?

No recruitment system is ever neutral. Any system will favor certain skills and characteristics and downplay others. The process of selecting Supreme Court justices favors individuals from socially advantaged families. As an observer has noted, "The typical Supreme Court Justice has generally been white, Protestant (with a penchant for a high social status denomination), usually of ethnic stock originating in the British Isles, and born in comfortable circumstances in an urban or small-town environment."[9] What is more, almost two-thirds of the justices have come from politically active families. Finally, those appointed to the Court have by and large been politically active themselves, with the vast majority having previously held political office.

When we examine the judiciary in the lower federal courts, we see a similar, although less pronounced, pattern of upper- and middle-class appointees. Compared with Supreme Court justices, judges on the courts of appeals, for instance, are slightly less likely to come from politically active families and more likely to have been educated at less prestigious law schools. These courts also show greater sexual and racial diversity than does the High Court. This diversity peaked under President Jimmy Carter, who appointed more women and minorities to the federal courts than any other president.

Because appointments are for life, the federal courts are an especially rich source of political patronage, and presidents are under some pressure to reward the party faithful with such appointments. Although presidents occasionally nominate a member of the opposition party, most have selected at least 90 percent of their appointees from their own party. Staffing the courts with partisans ensures a party a foothold in the government even when the party is out of favor with the voters. Aside from patronage questions, relying on members of their own party allows presidents to choose judges who are more likely to share their political outlook. Thus the bias toward fellow party members serves two goals, both of which clearly contradict the myth of nonpolitical courts.

GLOBAL POLITICS

Selecting Judges at Home and Abroad

Although all major courts in the U.S. federal system are staffed by judges appointed by the president, with the advice and consent of the Senate, this is not the way judges are selected in most political systems. In fact, even in the United States this manner of executive nomination and legislative consent is atypical. A few states, mostly confined to the Northeast, imitate this model by empowering the governor, usually with legislative confirmation, to appoint judges. Three states (Rhode Island, South Carolina, and Virginia) allow the state legislature to appoint members of the judiciary. In most states, however, judges are elected either in partisan or nonpartisan elections. Alternatively, some states utilize the so-called "merit system." Under this scheme the governor of the state makes the initial appointment from a list of names provided by a nonpartisan nominating commission. The judge serves for a short period and then must stand for election in a retention election in which the voters are asked simply if the judge should be retained or not. The incumbent is retained if a majority of the voters approve. If the voters should decline to retain the judge, the process begins again. To confound the issue, several states use different selection methods for different levels of courts.

The methods of judicial selection in other countries also vary considerably. In Canada, court judges at the national level are appointed by the executive, but there is no legislative confirmation. Additionally, provincial general jurisdiction trial and appellate judges are appointed by the national executive, while provincial judges of limited jurisdiction courts are appointed locally, by the provincial attorneys general.

The British also use an appointment system, but it differs significantly from the U.S. and Canadian styles. The professional judiciary is selected from among the barristers (lawyers who are qualified to work as advocates in court), but the appointments are made by the Lord Chancellor, a position unique to the United Kingdom. The Lord Chancellor is a member of the cabinet, Speaker of the House of Lords, and a judge. Thus, the Lord Chancellor is a member of all three branches of government. More curious is Britain's heavy reliance on lay judges. These judges are not required to have any legal education, and are not compensated for their work. Nevertheless, they preside over the majority of civil and criminal trials.

Continental European nations rely more heavily on examinations and merit-based performance to select judges. Italy, for instance, selects judges from a national competition. Shortly after graduation, students of law desiring to enter the judiciary sit for extensive examinations; only the highest scoring graduates receive appointments. Those selected enter the judiciary either as judges or prosecutors and build their careers within the judiciary. Lateral movement from private practice to a judgeship is rare. The result is that the individuals recruited to the judiciary in Italy are younger than those in the United States, Canada, and the United Kingdom, but they also lack experience beyond the classroom.

The German model attempts to address this lack of experience by requiring an extended training period after law school. Recent graduates of law school desirous of a judicial position take the "first state examination." Those who pass are given a government appointment, with a small salary, to supplement the years of practical training in various legal environments that follows. The prospective judges then must take the "second state examination," which covers much the same material as the first but with a stronger applied focus. Only those with the highest score on this second exam will eventually be chosen as judges.

Source: Carlo Guarnieri and Patrizia Pederzoli, *The Power of Judges: A Comparative Study of Courts and Democracy* (Oxford, U.K.: Oxford University Press, 2001).

Removing Judges

Critical Thinking

Should the Constitution be amended to provide set terms of office for federal judges?

In the early days of the republic, one of the most important problems facing the federal courts was attracting and retaining judges. As strange as it may seem, President George Washington had problems filling positions on the Supreme Court. For example, John Rutledge, one of Washington's first appointees, resigned before the Court ever met to become the chief justice of the South Carolina supreme court—a position he apparently found more attractive. As the prestige of the federal courts increased, recruitment problems diminished, although attracting and retaining lower-court judges is sometimes difficult because the salaries are low compared with what many potential appointees could earn in private law practice.

Because the prestige and power of a judgeship are understandably hard to give up, it is occasionally necessary to remove an ill or incompetent judge who refuses to retire. This problem is particularly thorny in the federal courts because the only constitutional means for removing federal judges is the impeachment process, which requires evidence of "Treason, Bribery, or other high Crimes and Misdemeanors."

Over the years there have been few impeachment trials. In 1986, however, Congress, in its first such trial in fifty years, did impeach and convict U.S. District Court Judge Harry E. Claiborne of Nevada. Claiborne had previously been convicted of evading the payment of more than $90,000 in income taxes. At the time of his impeachment trial, he was serving a two-year sentence in federal prison but was continuing to draw his salary as a federal judge. In 1989 Congress

The Roberts Court
The Supreme Court consists of eight associate justices and the Chief Justice. Seated from left, Anthony Kennedy, John Paul Stevens, John G. Roberts (Chief Justice), Antonin Scalia, and David Souter. Standing from left, Stephen Breyer, Clarence Thomas, Ruth Bader Ginsburg, and Samuel Alito Jr.

impeached and convicted two more district court judges. Judge Walter Nixon of Mississippi was removed from the bench on the grounds that he had committed perjury. At the time of his Senate conviction, he was serving a five-year prison sentence for knowingly making false statements to a grand jury. More controversial was the impeachment and conviction of Judge Alcee L. Hastings of Florida. Hastings was removed for accepting a bribe in a criminal case. Unlike Claiborne and Nixon, Hastings had been acquitted of related charges in a criminal trial, but the Senate concluded that he had lied and presented false evidence at the criminal trial. These two impeachment trials in a single year prompted several members of Congress to seek alternatives to the time-consuming process. Suggested constitutional amendments to provide for an easy removal procedure were introduced in 1990, but no action has been taken on them.

Even if impeachment were easier, it would probably not be deemed appropriate for judges who suffer from illness or senility. A case in point is that of Utah District Court Judge Willis Ritter. Ritter first drew national attention when he ordered court officials to arrest noisy plumbers who were making repairs near his courtroom.[10] He also engaged in such eccentric behavior as hissing throughout an attorney's presentation to the court. But although this behavior is clearly odd, it does not seem to fit the definition of an impeachable offense — "Treason, Bribery, or other high Crimes and Misdemeanors."

Lacking an effective means of removing judges, Congress has turned to providing pension programs as an incentive for them to step down. Under a 1954 act of Congress, a judge can opt for the status of senior judge. Senior judges receive a pension equal to full pay and may participate, where needed, in as many cases as they choose. This option allows a judge to enjoy a reduced workload without completely retiring. Senior judges have become essential to the operation of many of the more overworked lower federal courts. Senior judges typically handle about 20 percent of the appellate and district court cases.

Because judges do not have to accept senior status, Congress has also provided a mechanism for denying case assignments to sitting judges on the lower federal courts.[11] The judge retains the post and the salary but receives no work.

The Supreme Court at Work

FOCUS QUESTION WHAT ARE THE MAJOR STEPS IN SUPREME COURT DECISION MAKING?

The Supreme Court term begins the first Monday in October and runs through June or into early July, depending on the workload. Court terms are designated by the year in which they begin, even though very few decisions will actually be handed down in October, November, or December of that year. Throughout the term, the Court alternates between two weeks of open court, called sessions, and two weeks of recess, the time when the justices read petitions and write opinions.

Oral Argument

During the weeks that the Court is in session, the justices meet Monday through Wednesday to hear oral arguments. These sessions begin at 10 a.m. and last until 3 p.m., with a one-hour break for lunch. Ordinary cases are allotted one hour for arguments, and the time is evenly divided between the parties. If the case is especially important or involves multiple parties raising a variety of issues, the Court may permit longer presentations.

The attorneys presenting oral arguments are reminded of their time limitations by two lights on the lectern. When the white light appears, they know that they have five minutes left. The flash of the red light signals that their time is up, and they must cease speaking unless the chief justice grants an extension. Most often the parties are held strictly to their allotted time. Chief Justice Charles E. Hughes (1930–1941) was so rigid in enforcing the time limit that he is said to have stopped an attorney in the middle of the word *if.*

Because all parties have prepared written **briefs** (documents containing a summary of the issues, the laws applying to the case, and arguments supporting counsel's position), the Court discourages attorneys from reading prepared statements. Indeed, the Court's rules state that "the Court looks with disfavor on any oral argument that is read from a prepared text." Generally, the justices expect the attorneys to discuss the case, not to deliver a lecture. Often the attorneys spend their allotted time answering questions posed by the justices, and the justices often use these questions as a means of debating with one another. On one occasion, as Justice Felix Frankfurter repeatedly questioned a nervous attorney, Justice William O. Douglas repeatedly responded with answers helpful to the attorney. Finally, a frustrated Frankfurter, directing his remarks to the attorney, said, "I thought you were arguing this case." The attorney responded, "I am, but I can use all the help I can get."[12]

In addition to the arguments of the lawyers representing the parties to the case, the Court may also consider the positions taken by interested third parties. Any individual or organization, with the consent of the parties involved in the case or by Court permission, may submit written arguments known as **amicus curiae** (friend of the court) briefs. Occasionally, amicus participation may even include the offering of oral arguments. For instance, in the 1989 abortion case *Webster v. Reproductive Health Services,* seventy-eight amicus briefs were filed, and the Court allowed the federal government, acting as amicus, ten minutes of oral argument.[13] Amicus participation has become an important means of interest-group lobbying before the courts.

Conference Work

Though oral argument may be dramatic, the crucial work of the Court is done in conference. When the Court is in session, the justices gather in the conference room twice a week to discuss and decide cases. No one else is admitted—not even secretaries or law clerks to help the justices. If a justice needs anything from outside the room, the junior justice (the least senior in terms of service, not the youngest) must go to the door and summon a messenger. In the past, the junior justice was even responsible for pouring the coffee, a practice rumored to have ended with the appointment of Justice Sandra Day O'Connor.

Generally, the justices first decide which petitions should be accepted. Before the conference, the chief justice, with the aid of law clerks, prepares and circulates to the other justices a "discuss" list: a list of cases that the chief justice thinks worthy of discussion. Any case that is not on the list will be automatically denied review unless another justice requests that it be added to the list. Apparently, as many as 70 percent of the requests for review are denied without any discussion.[14]

Cases that make the list are not automatically accepted for review, however. Instead, each case is considered and voted on by the justices. Only those cases that receive four votes (the rule of four) are accepted and scheduled for further action, and the number of such cases is usually quite small. In recent years the Court has accepted only about eighty cases a term for review.

After deciding which cases to accept for review, the Court moves on to the cases being argued that week. The chief justice begins the discussion of each case by outlining and commenting on the main issues. Then each justice, in order of seniority, comments on the case. If the votes of the justices are not clear from the discussion, the chief justice calls for a formal vote. Most questions, however, require no vote, since the justices' positions will be clear from their initial comments. These conference votes are only tentative votes, however. As Justice John Harlan explained, "The books on voting are never closed until the decision actually comes down."[15]

After the vote, the chief justice, if in the majority, assigns the writing of the opinion. If the chief justice is not in the majority, then the majority's most senior justice makes the assignment. The assignment of an opinion writer is important because it will determine the grounds for the Court's decision and perhaps even the size of the majority, since the conference vote was tentative. The justice who assigns the writing of the opinion may decide to write the opinion himself or herself, or may give the task to the member of the majority whose views are closest to his or her views. As rumor has it, when Warren Burger was chief justice, he frequently let his turn in the discussion of important cases pass so that he could remain free to join the majority at the end and therefore pick the opinion writer. This practice reportedly became so common that Justice Potter Stewart is said to have drawn a tombstone for Burger with the words, "I'll Pass for the Moment."[16]

Concurring opinions
Opinions written by Supreme Court justices that agree with the conclusion but not with the reasoning of the majority opinion.

Writing and Announcing the Opinion

Once the writing of the opinion has been assigned, the justice who was given this task begins work on a draft that expresses his or her own ideas and also takes into account opinions expressed by others in the conference. At the same time, other justices may be drafting separate **concurring opinions** (opinions that

Dissenting opinions
Legal opinions written by Supreme Court justices that disagree with the majority conclusion.

agree with the conclusion but not with the reasoning of the majority) or **dissenting opinions** (opinions that disagree with the majority conclusion).

As the drafts are completed, they are circulated so that all justices can see them and have an opportunity to comment on them. As justices suggest changes in wording and reasoning, negotiations begin. The justice who has drafted the majority opinion, as well as any justices working on concurring or dissenting opinions, may have to make changes in order to satisfy the others. Sometimes conflicting views among the justices make this process extremely difficult and time-consuming. More important, the need to compromise may produce vague decisions that offer little guidance to lower courts. For instance, many Court observers have attributed the extraordinarily vague command of *Brown v. Board of Education II* (1955) to desegregate with "all deliberate speed" to the chief justice's desire for a unanimous decision.[17]

Occasionally, the justice assigned to write the majority opinion will change her or his position and become a dissenter, or vice versa. Justice William Brennan described the process when he noted: "I have had to convert more than one of my proposed majority opinions into a dissent before the final opinion was announced. I have also, however, had the more satisfying experience of rewriting a dissent as a majority opinion of the Court."[18]

The opinion-writing stage does not end until all the justices have decided which opinion to join. Once they do so, the Court announces the opinion. Throughout much of the Court's history, the justices have read their opinions—majority, concurring, and dissenting—publicly. Currently, the opinion writers read only short statements describing the issues and the disposition.

Interpreting the Constitution

Chief Justice Hughes once quipped, "We are under a Constitution, but the Constitution is what the judges say it is." Of course, as we saw in Chapter 2, on constitutional foundations, judges are not the sole interpreters of that document. Nevertheless, judges, and particularly justices of the Supreme Court, do play a leading role in interpreting the Constitution, largely because of the power of **judicial review**: the power of courts to declare an act of a legislature constitutional or unconstitutional.

Judicial review The power of courts to declare an act of a legislature constitutional or unconstitutional.

Nowhere in the Constitution is the U.S. Supreme Court specifically granted such authority. Instead, judicial review was inferred by the Court in the 1803 case of *Marbury v. Madison.*[19] After the election of 1800, which saw Thomas Jefferson and members of his party win control of the White House and both chambers of Congress, the incumbent president, John Adams, and the Federalist party attempted to maintain a foothold in government by using the time between the election and the inauguration to fill the judiciary with Federalists. First, John Marshall, secretary of state in the Adams administration, was named the new chief justice of the Supreme Court. Congress then created fifty-eight additional judgeships, to be filled by loyal Federalists. (Because these appointments came in the last days of the Adams administration, they became known as the "midnight appointments.")

Critical Thinking

Is there a better justification for judicial review?

So great was the Adams administration's haste that it failed to deliver the commissions of four newly appointed justices of the peace for the District of Columbia. The four undelivered commissions were returned to the secretary of state's office, where James Madison, the new secretary of state, found them. On orders of President Jefferson, Madison refused to deliver the commissions, prompting William Marbury, one of the four whose papers were withheld, to bring suit in the Supreme Court. Marbury requested that the Court issue a writ of *mandamus* (an order to a government official to carry out a duty of his or her office) compelling Madison to deliver the commission. The case was filed with the Supreme Court directly because a congressional statute, the Judiciary Act of 1789, empowered the Supreme Court to issue such writs as an act of original jurisdiction.

Critical Thinking

Should Chief Justice Marshall have removed himself from the case?

Marbury's suit placed the Court in a difficult and politically charged situation. Congress had given the Court a warning by canceling its 1802 term, and so Marbury's case had to be put off until 1803. The Court appeared to be faced with two choices, neither of them attractive. The justices could have issued the writ and ordered Madison to deliver the commission, but that would have been to no avail. Madison would most certainly have defied the writ, making the Court look powerless. On the other hand, the Court could have refused to issue the writ, but that would have amounted to an admission of impotence.

Chief Justice Marshall, however, devised a third alternative. He wrote an opinion that attacked the administration for neglecting constitutional duties, but ruled that the Court could not constitutionally issue the writ of mandamus. The Court was powerless in this instance, Marshall argued, because the provision of the Judiciary Act of 1789 that granted it original jurisdiction to issue such writs was unconstitutional. Article III of the Constitution specifies the circumstances under which the Court possesses original jurisdiction, and the issuance of writs of mandamus is not included. Therefore, argued Marshall, the Judiciary Act of 1789, by adding such writs to the Court's original jurisdiction, was actually attempting to alter the Constitution by simple statute rather than by the prescribed method of amendment. Since Congress may not do this, Marshall concluded that the act was null and void and the Court was without power to grant Marbury a writ of mandamus.

As a political document, Marshall's decision was a masterpiece. By arguing that Madison was obligated to deliver the commission, Marshall attacked the Jefferson administration. Yet by refusing to issue the writ, he avoided a confrontation with the president that the Court would have been sure to lose. More important, Marshall created for the Court the power of judicial review and insulated that power from attack. The only loser in the case was Marbury, who was sacrificed to Marshall's larger political design.

The political brilliance of Marshall's opinion is unquestionable, but to this day the legal reasoning employed remains subject to debate. In a straightforward manner, Marshall simply stated that (1) the Constitution is superior to any statute, (2) the Judiciary Act of 1789 contradicted the Constitution, and (3) therefore the Judiciary Act of 1789 must be unconstitutional. As an exercise in logic, the conclusion seems inescapable.

To many critics, however, Marshall's logic misses the point. Why is it the job of the Court, composed as it is of life-tenured appointees, to decide whether an act conflicts with the Constitution? Why, ask Marshall's critics, should this power not belong to elected officials?[20]

Although judicial review has become a standard element of American politics, it remains controversial. Those judges and legal scholars who find Marshall's reasoning unconvincing advocate **judicial restraint**—the limited and infrequent use of judicial review. Advocates of judicial restraint argue that the frequent use of judicial review substitutes the judgment of unelected, life-tenured officials for that of elected representatives and is therefore undemocratic. Indeed, the frequent use of judicial review, according to some critics, creates an "imperial judiciary," which makes decisions that are best left to the elected branches of a democratic government.[21] Opposing judicial restraint are those judges and legal scholars who believe in **judicial activism**: that the Court has a right, and even an obligation, to exercise judicial review. In our day, activism is usually justified by liberals as necessary for the defense of political minorities, but the frequent use of judicial review and the numerous precedents overturned by the Rehnquist Court demonstrate that conservatives may also be activists.

A more recent judicial argument concerns how the Constitution is to be interpreted. One perspective on its interpretation demands that justices adhere to a literal reading of the Constitution or, if the language is not specific, the intent of the provisions' authors. During the 1980s, this view, known as original intent, was forcefully advocated by President Reagan's attorney general, Edwin Meese. Meese repeatedly argued that the justices should restrict themselves to the Constitution's original intent and not its spirit. Original intent assumes that judges do not make law, but rather find it ready-made by others—those who authored the Constitution.

Opponents of that view—a loose collection of scholars and judges, conservatives and liberals—contend that many of the Constitution's most important provisions are "deliberate models of ambiguity."[22] Although these opponents often disagree among themselves on the preferred interpretation of constitutional provisions, they are united in their belief that judging involves choosing among competing values and not simply finding the law.[23]

Judicial restraint Limited and infrequent use of judicial review. It is advocated on the grounds that unelected judges should not overrule laws passed by elected representatives.
Judicial activism The concept that the Court has both a right and an obligation to engage in judicial review; today it is usually justified as necessary for the defense of political minorities.

The Implementation of Court Decisions

FOCUS QUESTION   WHY IS IT THAT COURT DECISIONS ARE NOT SIMPLY SELF-EXECUTING?

The pomp and circumstance surrounding the announcement of a Supreme Court decision lends credibility to the myth of finality. Yet this ceremony seldom settles the matter. Rather than being the end of the case, the Court's announcement is only the beginning of a long process of implementation.

Court orders are not self-executing, and the Court needs the cooperation of others to carry out the announced policy. It cannot force compliance; it cannot call on an army or police force to carry out its orders, nor can it levy taxes to fund their implementation. Furthermore, if a particular decision is not being implemented, the Court cannot act until someone brings suit in a lower court. Unlike the other agencies of government, courts must await cases; they cannot seek them out. Their only recourse is to signal their willingness to consider cases involving particular issues by the language that they use in deciding cases before them.

Compliance by Other Courts

Compliance is not just a matter of getting the parties in a case to go along with the decision. When the Supreme Court overturns the decision of a lower court, it generally sends (remands) the case back to the lower court for a decision "not inconsistent" with its opinion. But lower courts do not always follow the Supreme Court's wishes.

In some cases, lower courts may find it difficult to carry out an ambiguous Supreme Court decision. If multiple concurring and dissenting opinions accompany a decision, the lower court may find the decision difficult to interpret. In *Furman v. Georgia* (1972), for example, five justices ruled that the death penalty as it was applied in that particular case was unconstitutional, but they could not agree on the reason.[24] Consequently, each justice wrote a separate opinion. Lower courts cannot interpret such a decision easily, and in such situations lower-court judges find it easier to substitute their own values and beliefs.

Because lower federal and state courts are independent of the High Court, they can—and occasionally do—defy the Court's rulings. There is little that the Court can do in such cases. The judges of these lower courts are sworn to uphold the U.S. Constitution but not the opinions of the Supreme Court, and the Court lacks the power to fire even the most disobedient judge. Thus the Supreme Court's power to reverse lower-court decisions is limited both by its inability to police lower courts and by time constraints (it cannot review every lower-court decision).

Critical Thinking

What is the likelihood that a lower-court decision will be overturned?

Reversal sometimes causes difficulties for lower-court judges. Judges who are caught between the mandates of the Supreme Court, located in far-off Washington, and the strong contradictory desires of their neighbors may find the displeasure of the High Court easier to bear than the anger of their community. Elected state judges may be especially reluctant to enforce Court orders that might anger voters, even if they personally agree with the High Court. In the 1950s, federal district court judges were deeply embroiled in the school desegregation issue—a conflict of national versus local values. Many communities resisted Court-ordered desegregation, often vehemently. Those district judges who enforced *Brown v. Board of Education* (1954) found themselves cut off from their own communities, with old friends and colleagues falling away. Many were threatened, and some were even physically harmed.[25]

Congress and the President

Just as the Supreme Court must depend on the so-called inferior courts to implement decisions, so too must it rely on the cooperation of Congress and the president. Both institutions have the power to aid or hinder the implementation of Supreme Court decisions.

The most important power that Congress has is its control of public funds. By providing or withholding the funds necessary to carry out Court policy, Congress can significantly affect implementation, as the history of school desegregation amply illustrates. During Lyndon Johnson's administration, Congress authorized the U.S. Department of Health, Education, and Welfare to withhold federal funds from school systems that refused to desegregate — giving communities a strong incentive to comply with the Supreme Court's 1954 ruling. In 1975, however, Congress, disturbed by court-ordered busing, diminished the incentive by prohibiting the withholding of funds from school districts that refused to implement busing.

Critical Thinking

Should the Supreme Court have the last word on the constitutionality of public policy?

The actions of individual members of Congress may also advance or impede Court policy. Whether important political leaders defend or attack a Court decision may have much to do with the willingness of others to accept that decision. Clearly, the cause of school desegregation was not helped when, in 1956, ninety-six members of Congress signed the Southern Manifesto, a document attacking the *Brown* decision. Those who believed that the Supreme Court was wrong could always point to distinguished members of Congress who shared their view. Furthermore, the support of so many in Congress undoubtedly gave opponents of desegregation hope that the decision would someday be overturned.

Congress may also use its powers to directly counteract Court decisions. Decisions interpreting the Constitution, for example, may be overturned by a congressionally initiated constitutional amendment. Although the process is cumbersome and difficult, it has been used on five occasions. Most recently, the Twenty-sixth Amendment, lowering the voting age to eighteen, overturned the decision in *Oregon v. Mitchell* (1970).[26] (In the *Mitchell* decision, the Court had ruled that Congress could by statute lower the voting age to eighteen in national, but not state, elections.) The Court's decision prohibiting prayer in public schools has generated hundreds of proposals for constitutional amendments. To date none of these proposals has passed both houses of Congress.

Occasionally, Congress tries to pressure the Court into reversing a decision. In 1964, for instance, angered by a series of Warren Court rulings that required reapportionment of state legislatures solely on the basis of population, Congress gave the justices a smaller pay raise than other top-level officials. To underscore the point, Republican Representative Robert Dole of Kansas proposed that the pay increase be contingent on reversal of the decision.[27]

The president and the executive branch can also vitally affect the fate of Supreme Court decisions. On the average, a president appoints a new justice every twenty-two months. Thus a two-term president has the potential to reshape the Court, and it can then negate a troublesome policy. Richard Nixon certainly intended to do just that when, in 1968, he campaigned for the presidency on the promise to appoint justices who would be tough on criminal defendants. Much of Nixon's 1968 presidential campaign was an attack on the liberal Warren Court. His four appointments to the Supreme Court, including a new chief justice (Warren Burger), managed to modify the liberal trend set by the Warren Court and even to reverse some previous liberal decisions.

Similarly, Reagan attempted to alter the direction of the Court through careful selection of nominees. Reagan's appointments of associate justices Sandra Day O'Connor, Antonin Scalia, and Anthony Kennedy, as well as his elevation of William H. Rehnquist to the post of chief justice, were designed to create a Supreme Court that was ideologically compatible with his administration. President George H. W. Bush's appointment of Clarence Thomas to replace Thurgood Marshall was seen by observers as a continuation of the Reagan administration's strategy.

As the most visible public official, the president may influence public opinion by his willingness to accept a decision. His silence, on the other hand, may encourage disobedience or delay implementation. President Eisenhower's initial refusal to endorse the *Brown* decision gave support to those who opposed the Court. Although in 1957 Eisenhower dispatched troops to enforce court-ordered desegregation of the schools in Little Rock, Arkansas, many commentators have argued that his initial reluctance to support the decision had encouraged the avoidance of court orders. Indeed, a Supreme Court justice of that period, Tom C. Clark, observed that "if Mr. Eisenhower had come through, it would have changed things a lot."[28]

As the head of the executive branch, the president may also order the U.S. Department of Justice to prosecute noncompliance vigorously or to make only a token effort. President Johnson's vigorous use of the department to prosecute segregated school districts was very important in implementing *Brown*. President Nixon, on the other hand, slowed the process of desegregation by curtailing the department's prosecutorial activities.

Conclusion: The Courts Are Not What They Seem

This brief discussion of the American legal system demonstrates that, no matter how much we may wish it were otherwise, the courts are political institutions. As soothing as it may be, the myth of the nonpolitical courts simply does not reflect the American legal system. Although the conflict that produced the basic structure of the federal courts occurred long ago, the potential for political discord still exists, and we should not be blind to this fact. Nor can we ignore the link between partisan politics and the courts that is inherent in the system of judicial selection. Because judicial positions go to those who demonstrate faithful service to the party, individuals with considerable political experience staff the courts.

The myth of finality likewise fails to capture the reality of American courts. The implementation of court decisions requires the participation and cooperation of many in the political system. A simple pronouncement from a court does not suffice.

Tying It Together

CHAPTER SUMMARY

1. Civil actions cover conflicts between private individuals or organizations; criminal law concerns wrongs done to the public.

2. Trial courts are courts of first instance — the first court to hear the case. These courts take evidence, hear witnesses, and make determinations of fact. Appellate courts, on the other hand, are responsible for reviewing the decisions of trial courts. Appellate review is designed to ensure that there was no error in judicial procedures or interpretations of the law.

3. The United States has fifty-two court systems, one for the national government, one for each state, and a separate system for the Commonwealth of Puerto Rico.

    The ninety-four U.S. district courts are the trial courts for the federal system. Approximately 200,000 cases a year are heard by the district courts, and fewer than 10 percent of their decisions are appealed.

    The twelve U.S. courts of appeals handle most of the appellate work in the federal system. Organized into state groupings known as circuits, the courts of appeals hear all appeals from the federal district courts and some independent regulatory agencies and departments.

    Cases are appealed to the Supreme Court primarily either by an appeal or by a writ of certiorari. The Court has great latitude in deciding which cases it wants to hear.

4. Each state has at least one appellate court that serves as its highest tribunal, reviewing the decisions of all other courts in the state. (Both Texas and Oklahoma have two high courts — one for

civil litigation and one that handles only criminal cases.) Slightly more than half the states also make use of intermediate appellate courts to hear appeals from the trial courts. The most numerous courts in the states are the trial courts. Trial courts at the state level tend to be divided into two types: those with limited jurisdiction and those with general jurisdiction.

5. The Constitution requires that federal judges be nominated by the president and appointed with the advice and consent of the Senate. Appointment procedures vary considerably, however, depending on the level of the court involved. The nomination of district court judges often originates with the senator or senators of the president's party from the nominee's state. These senators may exercise senatorial courtesy. Because courts of appeals are organized into circuits that cross state boundaries, no senator is entitled to exercise senatorial courtesy over these appointments.

6. Because federal judges are appointed for life, the need to remove an ill or incompetent judge occasionally arises. Because the Constitution provides for removal only by impeachment, Congress has created the position of senior judge as a means of encouraging judges to retire.

7. The public phase of the Supreme Court's business consists of oral arguments presented before the justices. These are very formalized procedures conducted under tight time constraints.

    The most important part of the Court's work takes place in its conferences, which are closed to all but the justices themselves. In these conferences, the justices discuss and vote on the cases.

Once a vote has been taken on a case, the chief justice, if in the majority, or the senior justice in the majority assigns the writing of the opinion. The justice assigned to write the opinion must then circulate drafts of the decision to the other justices. No opinion is final until at least a majority of the Court agrees on it.

Justices who disagree with the majority opinion are free to write dissenting opinions explaining why they cannot accept the majority decision. Justices who agree with the majority opinion but not its reasoning may write concurring opinions.

8. Judges are often involved in interpreting the Constitution, although controversy exists over how aggressively the courts should pursue such judicial review.

9. Lower courts do not necessarily comply with Supreme Court decisions. Often they find the decisions sufficiently ambiguous to make compliance extremely difficult. When Supreme Court decisions conflict with locally held values, lower-court judges may be reluctant to displease their communities by enforcing the High Court's rulings.

Congress also possesses a great deal of power over the implementation of Supreme Court decisions because implementation often requires the appropriation of public funds, a function controlled by Congress. Congress can also propose constitutional amendments to overturn Supreme Court decisions.

The successful implementation of Supreme Court decisions also requires the cooperation of the president, or at least his acceptance of the policy. A president's willingness to accept a particular Court opinion can influence public opinion. More important, a president may seek to reshape the Court through the appointment process.

Key Terms

Civil actions (373)
Criminal law (373)
Trial courts (374)
Original jurisdiction (374)
Appellate courts (375)
Circuit courts (378)
Writ of certiorari (379)
Appeal (380)
Limited jurisdiction (382)

General jurisdiction (382)
Briefs (392)
Amicus curiae (392)
Concurring opinions (393)
Dissenting opinions (394)
Judicial review (394)
Judicial restraint (396)
Judicial activism (396)

 ## Net Work

To learn more about the judicial system, there are plenty of sites you can visit.

- As a general overview of the federal judiciary, the federal judiciary homepage (**www.uscourts.gov**) is extremely helpful. You will find a comprehensive guide to the federal court system, complete with directories of federal judges, court statistics, and a glossary of legal terms.

- Findlaw (**www.findlaw.com**) provides a window to a diverse array of legal sources, including the full text of opinions.

- Cornell Law School (**www.law.cornell.edu**) provides another gateway to many useful law-related resources, including the full texts of U.S. Supreme Court, appellate court, and district court decisions.

As an exercise, to explore the wide range of online legal resources more fully, pick a Supreme Court case that interests you, find the text of that Supreme Court decision, and then follow it back in time. How far can you go in tracing its origins?

14

Domestic Policy and Policymaking

MYTH & REALITY

Are government policies and programs necessary evils?

FOCUS QUESTIONS

* How is public policy made?

* What has been the federal government's role in dealing with issues related to education?

* How does the federal government attempt to manage the American economy?

* What are the issues surrounding the federal government's efforts to enhance overall economic growth?

* How has the federal government used regulatory policies in dealing with economic, social, and environmental problems?

* What does the federal government do to assure the economic well-being of individuals?

When it comes to their views of government, Americans are a conflicted people. On the one hand, we value individualism and abhor the restrictions on our freedom that government often requires. On the other hand, we also value the security, safety, and benefits with which public policies and programs provide us.

Consider, for example, our driving behavior. When we drive at or just below the speed limit on some of our nation's interstate highways, we often feel as if we are standing still while dozens of vehicles pass us at speeds clearly in excess of the posted limits. We have all seen other drivers seemingly expressing their individuality (or indifference) by failing to wear seat belts, littering the highways, failing to signal lane changes, not slowing down in school zones or road construction areas, and committing dozens of other violations. Nevertheless, as a nation we collectively insist on tougher enforcement of the very rules that we are often inclined to break as individuals. We complain about highway and bridge tolls, but we insist that every road be in good repair and wide enough to convey us to our destinations quickly. Or consider our puzzling attitudes toward tobacco and alcohol products. Our per capita consumption of cigarettes, beer, and wine remains among the highest in the world—and yet we insist on strict government regulation of who can buy them and where they can be sold and consumed. We complain about our taxes, while at the same time insisting that government spend more on everything from cleaner air and higher-quality schools to safer streets and more jobs. We openly disparage "welfare" programs and those who use them, but we insist that government provide all Americans with an economic "safety net" to protect individuals and families during hard times.

These conflicting views of public policies are sustained by one of the most powerful myths in the American political culture: the *myth of government as a necessary evil.* Traceable back to the American Revolution, it is a belief that while we need government to protect ourselves from dangers and to accomplish collective goals, we are paying a significant price for those benefits. According to the most popular versions of this myth, the heaviest price we pay is a loss of individual liberty. This position is most directly expressed in libertarian ideologies, which have become increasingly popular in recent years (see Chapter 1).

We have other fears as well, including anxiety over our growing dependence on some anonymous government bureaucracy (see Chapter 12, on bureaucracy). During the heated debate over the Clinton administration's national health-care proposals in 1994, those who opposed the reforms launched a successful campaign that focused on mobilizing Americans' antigovernment feelings and fear of bureaucracy. One of the most memorable elements of that campaign was television advertisements featuring a middle-class, white, fortyish suburban couple (Harry and Louise) who worried aloud about the consequences of letting some government bureaucrat make decisions about their medical care.[1] Economic analysts reinforce these concerns about government solutions by arguing that public solutions to our problems are nearly always wasteful and less efficient than private market solutions.[2]

**Critical
 Thinking**

Do Americans really
hate government, or
do they just find it
annoying?

This myth has had a profound impact, particularly in the negative views of government that it promotes. Historian Garry Wills has examined the government-as-necessary-evil myth and found that its roots run deep in American political history.

> After studying the ways our fear of government has found expression, I was struck by the persistence . . . of [antigovernment] values. At times, these values uphold liberal positions, at other times conservative ones. They can show up on the left or on the right. . . . They can be found in a hippie commune or a modern militia camp. These are all good American values, and it is no wonder that people want to uphold them, especially if they believe (as they often do) that government would weaken or obliterate them. That sincere belief is behind much of the need to oppose any increase in government.[3]

However, there is a positive side to the myth as well: the idea that government actions are often "necessary." Thus, many Americans believe that only government can deal with major crises, such as an economic depression. Stories of the Great Depression of the 1930s tell how the American economy worsened because President Herbert Hoover did nothing to rescue the U.S. economic system after the great stock market crash of 1929. According to this view, only the active intervention of government under President Franklin D. Roosevelt helped to alleviate the worst consequences of the Depression.[4] In contrast, critics of America's welfare policies during the 1960s frequently tell stories of how these programs failed, leaving a legacy of social deprivation among the poor. These critics support their view of government's negative influence by pointing to stories telling of the success of those who avoided or escaped the welfare system, or by citing a link between those programs and high crime rates or civil disorders.[5] For the American public, the decision as to whether the government is more evil than necessary often depends on the specific issue or program being discussed, the language being used, and the way the program is presented. Public opinion pollsters and politicians understand, for example, that Americans will be much more supportive of social programs that are called "assistance to the poor" rather than "welfare" (see Figure 14.1).[6]

**Critical
 Thinking**

How much impact do
the media have on
American attitudes to-
ward public policy?

Are government policies necessary? If so, are they necessarily an evil? Those questions are central to an understanding of much of the ongoing debate about public policies among politicians and policymakers. As we can see in the following discussion of various domestic policy issues, the questions have no definitive answers. Nevertheless, the myth of government as a necessary evil remains important because of the dynamic role it plays in shaping public perceptions and in giving force and direction to the deliberations of public policymakers.

FIGURE 14.1

The Answer Depends on the Question

Americans' attitudes suggest that we are spending too much on "welfare," but too little on "assistance to the poor." This interesting contrast says a great deal about the complex attitudes of Americans toward government and public policies.

Source: Copyright © 1992 by the New York Times Company. Reprinted by permission.

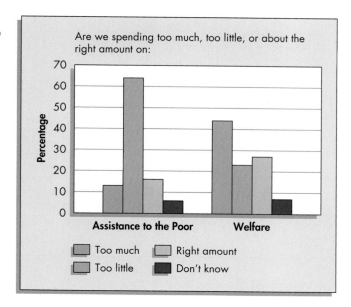

Are we spending too much, too little, or about the right amount on:

Public policies Decisions made and actions taken by government officials in response to problems identified and issues raised through the political system.

Issue identification The first of six stages in policymaking, in which some event, person, or group calls attention to a problem that needs government action.

Making Public Policy

FOCUS QUESTION HOW IS PUBLIC POLICY MADE?

Public policies are decisions made and actions taken by government officials in response to problems identified and issues raised through the political system. At the national level, public policies can emerge from each of the major institutions of government. Congress makes policy by enacting laws, such as the 1964 Civil Rights Act (see Chapter 4, on the heritage of rights and liberties). Presidents can issue executive orders (see Chapter 11, on the presidency), as President John F. Kennedy did in 1961 to create the Peace Corps. As discussed in Chapter 13, on the courts, judges, and the law, judges also make policy through court decisions and orders, such as the famous one in *Brown v. Board of Education* (1954) that led to the desegregation of southern schools. Even bureaucracies are involved in public policymaking through the rules and regulations they develop and publish. None of these institutional actions occurs in a vacuum, however. Each is the product of formal and informal interactions among hundreds of participants both inside and outside government.[7]

Stages in the Policymaking Process

Public policymaking can be pictured as a six-stage process (see Figure 14.2). In the first stage, **issue identification**, some event, person, or group calls attention

FIGURE 14.2

The Six Stages of Policymaking

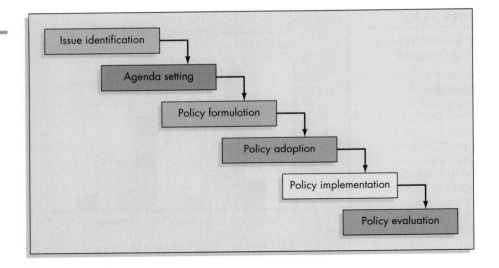

to a problem that needs governmental action. During the early 1980s, for example, the increasing number of deaths attributed to acquired immune deficiency syndrome (AIDS) brought demands for money to fund research into the cause of the deadly disease. Health-care professionals, the surgeon general of the United States, and groups representing homosexual men (who were at high risk for the disease) used every opportunity they could to get the attention of policymakers at all levels of American government.[8]

In the second stage, **agenda setting**, the issue or problem is seriously considered by the policymaking institution. Not all problems identified in the first stage of the process get this far. In mid-November 1953, for instance, a thick cloud of dirty air settled on New York City, causing headaches, itchy eyes, nausea, and other physical ailments. The incident lasted long enough to draw the media's attention, for the clouded atmosphere interfered with football games, astronomical observations, and other outdoor activities. The cloud eventually dissipated, and no action followed, since the immediate impact of the air pollution was not regarded as serious. It was not until nine years later that a review of public health records showed that the incident had been linked to approximately 200 deaths in the New York area.[9] By the early 1960s, however, environmental pollution was on the agenda of national policymakers, and problems similar to New York City's "cloud"—for example, the smog that hangs over Los Angeles and other major cities—began to get serious attention.

The fact that an issue on the government's agenda gets serious attention does not necessarily mean that a policy will immediately emerge. Someone must develop a proposal or program that can address the issue. This third stage of the policymaking process, **policy formulation**, may take years to complete as policymakers and their staffs deliberate the pros and cons of different courses of action.

These policy responses may be formulated within government agencies, in Congress, or by groups outside the national government, working separately or together. Both the White House and Congress looked to the federal Centers for

---

Agenda setting The second stage of policymaking, in which the issue or problem is seriously considered by the policymaking institution.

Policy formulation The third stage of policymaking, in which policymakers and their staffs deliberate the pros and cons of different courses of action, a process that may take years to complete.

Disease Control and Prevention for policy proposals to deal with AIDS. One major reform of the U.S. welfare system, the 1988 Family Support Act, was formulated by a group of governors working with the staff of the National Governors' Association. Five years later, President Clinton appointed a twenty-seven-person task force to develop proposals for even more significant reform. In the meantime, House Republicans had developed their own welfare reform proposals. It was not until 1996, however, that a major reform package emerged from Congress (see the discussion later in this chapter).[10] In 1993, a White House task force involving dozens of government officials took nine months to come up with a comprehensive health-care proposal. As the health-care debate unfolded over the next year, a variety of alternative proposals emerged. By the summer of 1994, anyone who was attempting to follow the debate needed a guidebook to help sort out all the different proposals that had been formulated to deal with America's health-care crisis.[11]

Policy adoption The fourth stage of policy-making, which is usually a fight to gain governmental support for a policy and demands much bargaining and compromise.

The next step, **policy adoption**, includes efforts to obtain enough support to enable a proposal to become the government's stated policy. At this point, most policy proposals — particularly congressional legislation — go through a process of bargaining and compromise and emerge significantly changed. When Congress considers tax reform proposals, for instance, what began as an attempt to close large tax loopholes may wind up creating more or different loopholes.[12] When members of Congress propose amendments to bills, they can radically change the intent of a bill or give it added meaning through the process of adding "riders" or "earmarks" to the legislation (see "Asked & Answered," p. 408). In 1987, a bill funding highway projects included an amendment authorizing states to raise the maximum speed limit on interstate highways to 65 miles per hour in rural areas. In 1988, a bill intended to create a new cabinet post — the Department of Veterans Affairs — became the vehicle for passing a law giving veterans the right to sue the government.[13]

Policy adoption is no less complex in the executive branch. Executive orders, vetoes of legislation, and other presidential actions are not made arbitrarily, for the White House cannot operate in a political vacuum. After President Kennedy used an executive order to set up the Peace Corps in 1961, he did not go to Congress for funding immediately, but rather paid for its operation for nearly six months through a special discretionary account. During that period, administration officials worked to build congressional support for the program. Although Kennedy was eventually successful in gaining this support, some members of Congress questioned his use of executive powers to establish and operate a brand-new program without congressional authority.

Decisions of the Supreme Court are a special type of public policy, for they are often rooted in legal doctrines. Nevertheless, even policy adoption in the Supreme Court involves some political give-and-take among the Court's members, which has an impact on the resulting policies (see Chapter 13, on courts, judges, and the law). In recent years we have learned a great deal more about what takes place when the justices of the Supreme Court decide an important case. Conferences involving all the Court's members are held regularly, and supposedly the discussions in those closed meetings sometimes focus on the political, as well as the legal, implications of a case.[14]

ASKED & ANSWERED

ASKED: What is "earmarking," and what does it have to do with policymaking?

ANSWERED: Among those who deal with cattle and sheep, the common practice of "earmarking" involves placing a tag or other identifying mark on a particular animal, by which the animal can be distinguished from the rest of the herd for special treatment.

In the policymaking process, earmarking involves attaching a "tag" to some special project included in a bill so that it stands out from the other provisions—the herd, if you will—to allow for special treatment. Such special treatment might mean that the project is automatically funded or that it moves to the top of the list of priorities for the agency in charge.

Earmarking by Congress can take place at either the authorization or appropriations stages. An "authorization" occurs when Congress passes a law or creates a program that gives government that authority to take some action. At the appropriations stage, however, Congress is actually providing funding for the authorized program to be implemented.

In very general terms, earmarking by Congress has a long history of being productive. Revenues raised by federal gasoline taxes, for example, are earmarked for deposit in the Highway Trust Fund, which is then tagged for use on highway and mass transit projects. In the past there have been some cases of "special" earmarks where well-positioned members of Congress used their influence to get pet projects authorized and funded for their home districts—demonstrating their power to "bring home the bacon"—but while often widely known, these examples of "pork barrel" projects were relatively few in the general scheme of things. For example, there were only ten earmarks found in the 1982 transportation (authorization) bill, which included approval for all kinds of road and highway construction projects.

In recent years, however, earmarking has become more widely used. In the 1991 transportation

bill, the number of earmarks had grown to 538, and in 1998 it had climbed to 1,800. By the time the 2004 transportation authorization act had passed the U.S. House it had been burdened with 2,881 earmarks valued at nearly $10 billion!

If a member of Congress does not succeed in getting a project through the general authorization process, she or he can try to tag some funds in the annual appropriation bills. Each year Congress passes eleven major appropriations bills, each dealing with a general area of government activity (e.g., agriculture, defense, energy, and water). For 2004, it was estimated that these bills included $14 billion attributed to earmarks for projects covering transportation, labor, education, agriculture, health, and related domestic programs. While that seems like a great deal of money, it amounts to only 2 percent of the federal government's discretionary spending—and discretionary spending (that is, funds that the national government is not mandated to spend, such as interest on the national debt) amounts to only one-third of all federal spending.

The most publicized earmark of 2004 was $175 million tagged for a bridge in Alaska that connected a very small community with an even more sparsely populated island. The project passed intact, but it reemerged as an issue after Hurricane Katrina struck New Orleans and the Gulf Coast in 2005 and Congress had to deal with emergency appropriations for reconstruction of that devastated area. The people of Alaska who would benefit from the bridge made it known that they would gladly give up that piece of pork in favor of the people of the New Orleans area.

Source: Brian Friel, "Transportation: Defending Pork," *National Journal*, May 8, 2004. Also see the analysis of "Reforming Congressional Earmarks" by Scott Lilly at www.americanprogress .org/site/pp.asp?c=biJRJ8OVF&b=1487355.

The policy adoption stage can go on for quite a long time. The first national air pollution laws were passed in 1960, but they did little more than authorize the surgeon general to study the problem. Three years later, Congress set up a technical committee to monitor air pollution problems and to provide assistance to state and local governments that chose to develop and maintain antipollution programs. In 1965 and 1967, Congress required states and localities to develop antipollution programs and required federal agencies to set emission standards for new automobiles. In 1970, President Richard M. Nixon acknowledged the importance of environmental problems by creating the Environmental Protection Agency (EPA). A few weeks later, Congress gave the EPA significant powers to clean America's air. Additional amendments followed during the 1970s and 1980s, and policy adoption in this area continued with passage of Clean Air Act amendments in 1990.

Policy implementation The carrying out of policy mandates through public programs and actions—the fifth stage in the policymaking process.

Critical to the policymaking process is the stage of **policy implementation**—the carrying out of policy mandates through public programs and actions. The national bureaucracy traditionally performs this task, although in recent years it has been using contracting out and other methods associated with proxy administration (see Chapter 12, on the bureaucracy). In addition, many policies require the cooperation of state and local officials and of individuals outside government. For example, when Congress passed an income tax law, it created the *Internal Revenue Service (IRS)* to implement it, but the government still relies on the American people to do most of the paperwork. Washington also depends on state and local officials to enforce a variety of environmental laws. As noted in Chapter 3, on federalism and intergovernmental relations, most domestic policies require the cooperation of either private individuals or the intergovernmental relations system.

Policy evaluation The final stage in the policymaking process: looking at the government's actions and programs to see whether their goals have been achieved or to assess their effectiveness and efficiency.

The final stage in public policymaking is **policy evaluation**—looking at the government's actions and programs to see whether their goals have been achieved or to assess their effectiveness and efficiency. Changes in the policy or program may then be instituted quickly, slowly, or not at all. A major plane crash caused by poorly maintained equipment is likely to result in new directives being issued immediately by the Federal Aviation Administration. A report indicating that public schools are not giving students an education that is appropriate for the changing world economy will not result in quick changes, but it might generate plans for major long-term changes in high school curriculum and instruction. Another report indicating that interstate highway speeds in excess of 40 miles per hour result in thousands of additional deaths each year is unlikely to result in policy changes in most states because of popular pressure to keep or even raise the current speed limits.

Models of Decision Making

The stages of the policymaking process presented here may seem both sequential and logical, but what actually takes place is rarely so neat. During each stage, policymakers must reach many decisions about how the issue will be handled or how an adopted policy will be implemented or evaluated. Ideally, policymakers

Rational model of decision making The ideal process in which a policymaker has a clear objective and all the information needed to make a sound and reasoned decision, with the result being the selection of the best way to achieve the desired goal.

should carefully analyze the issues being addressed, consider all alternative actions that could be taken to address those issues, accurately evaluate those alternatives, and finally select one as the government's policy. This ideal process is called the **rational model of decision making**. It assumes that the policymakers have a clear objective and all the information needed for a sound and reasoned decision, with the result being the selection of the policy alternative that offers the most efficient and effective way to achieve the desired goal.

Few of the conditions required for rational decision making exist in the real world of public policy. Policymakers rarely have enough information to analyze all the alternatives. And no matter how much information they have, there is always some doubt about the future. This uncertainty affects not only members of Congress and people on the White House staff, but also their advisers in the scientific community and elsewhere.

Furthermore, large groups of decision makers usually have trouble reaching a consensus on goals. There are some exceptions, of course. In May 1961, President Kennedy had broad political support when he declared that the aim of U.S. space policy was to land an American on the moon by the end of the decade.[15] With such a clear and widely accepted goal, decision making in the National Aeronautics and Space Administration (NASA) seemed close to the rational model. But the NASA programs of the 1960s were not the norm. In most cases, the objectives of public policies are too vague or too controversial for the rational model to apply.

Is there a different model that explains how policymakers really make their decisions? One possibility is the **incremental model of decision making**. According to this model, public policymaking is a process by which, little by little, decisions add to or subtract from the policies that already exist. Each year, for example, the national government reconsiders the amount of money it will spend on highways and education. However, the White House and Congress rarely start their annual deliberations with a clean slate. Instead, in most cases executive officials and members of Congress begin by assuming that most current highway and education programs will remain intact; usually, the major issues are whether to expand or reduce spending for these programs and, if so, by how much. Sometimes this leads to marginal changes in the policies as well. For instance, each time a major program such as social security comes up for reauthorization before Congress, amendments are added to meet the new or special needs of recipients that have emerged since the law was last revised. Thus public policies and programs develop and change from year to year through marginal adjustments.

Incremental model of decision making A more realistic model of decision making that sees public policy as a process of making decisions at the margins of current policies by adding to or subtracting from those policies.

Other models of decision making trace public policies back to certain groups or classes of people. The **elite model of decision making** holds that public policies are made by a relatively small group of influential leaders who share common goals and points of view. President Dwight D. Eisenhower may have had this model in mind when, in his 1961 farewell address to the nation, he warned against the emerging influence of the "military-industrial complex," in which high-level military and industry leaders make decisions that have widespread effects throughout the rest of the country and the world.

Elite model of decision making The theory that public policies are made by a relatively small group of influential leaders who share common goals and points of view.

Pluralist model of decision making A theory that attributes policy outcomes to pressures exerted by different interest groups.

Critical Thinking

Is the country run by a small, elite group? Or is the policymaking system open to anyone who wishes to get involved?

In contrast, the **pluralist model of decision making** attributes policy outcomes to pressures exerted by different interest groups. Specific policy choices reflect the relative influence of these interest groups at given points in the decision-making process (see Chapter 8, on interest groups). Thus, although environmentalists may have the upper hand in Congress, advocates of deregulation might be more influential in the White House or at the EPA. This model assumes that public policies are the product of bargains and compromises among the various interests and policymakers.

The models may differ, but there is one point on which all observers agree: *Public policies are the result of a dynamic process involving a variety of participants and a wide range of factors that change over time.*[16] One constant feature of the process is the debate between those who believe strongly in the necessity of governmental action and those who fear the consequences of relying too much on government programs. That debate has an impact on almost all domestic policies.

Education Policy

FOCUS QUESTION WHAT HAS BEEN THE FEDERAL GOVERNMENT'S ROLE IN DEALING WITH ISSUES RELATED TO EDUCATION?

Given the antigovernment inclinations of Americans, what kinds of problems lead to the adoption of public policies as solutions? The answer to this question is likely to be found by considering the kinds of issues that emerge in each policy issue area.

Some of the most heated debates about public policy revolve around questions of education. Education is one of the areas in the American federal system where states and localities tend to dominate. Nevertheless, the national government has become a major player in this policy arena, particularly in response to four general issues: access to education, funding of education, content of education, and quality of education.

Access to Education

The national government's involvement in issues of *access to education* actually predates the Constitution. In establishing a plan for the settlement of the northwestern territories (at that time, the region north of the Ohio River and east of the Mississippi River, including the current states of Ohio, Indiana, Illinois, Michigan, and Wisconsin), the congress under the Articles of Confederation passed the *Northwest Ordinance* (1787), which, among other things, required that "schools and the means of education shall forever be encouraged" by the governments formed in that region.[17] Similar provisions were included in all legislation related to the governing of territories and the admission of states for the next two centuries. In addition, federal land grants for the establishment of colleges devoted to "the agricultural and mechanical arts" were granted in the *Morrill Act of 1862* and became the basis for many of today's leading state universities (see Chapter 3, on federalism and intergovernmental relations). In 1914, Congress passed the *Smith-Lever Act*, which promoted the educational missions of colleges and universities through off-campus cooperative extension programs. Access to higher education was a key component of the "GI Bill of Rights" that provided benefits to veterans returning from World War II.

By the 1950s and 1960s, the issue of access had been redefined to stress the need for *equal access* for all Americans. In *Brown v. Board of Education* (1954) (see Chapter 4), the Supreme Court struck down government policies that supported segregated access to public education, and in the civil rights and education policies that followed there were specific provisions making discriminatory policies illegal at all levels of education. Today, the mission of the Department of Education's Office of Civil Rights is to enforce the antidiscrimination policies established in

- Title VI of the Civil Rights Act of 1964 (prohibiting discrimination based on race, color, or national origin)

- Title IX of the Education Amendments of 1972 (prohibiting sex discrimination)

- Section 504 of the Rehabilitation Act of 1973 (prohibiting disability discrimination)

- Age Discrimination Act of 1975 (prohibiting age discrimination)

- Title II of the Americans with Disabilities Act of 1990 (prohibiting disability discrimination by public entities, including public school districts, public colleges and universities, public vocational schools, and public libraries, whether or not they receive federal financial assistance).[18]

Funding of Education

Critical Thinking

Would segregated schools still exist were it not for the actions of the federal government?

The national government's ability to shape educational access policies at the state and local level has long been tied to its ability to deal with *educational funding issues*. The Morrill Act land grants were only the beginning of a historical trend toward making federal funds available to the states for educational programs. Initially, these programs resulted from the fact that the national government was intermittently faced with surplus funds and often used them for education-related purposes. Eventually, however, programmatic objectives (e.g., the promotion of vocation education) led to the creation of small grant programs.

The major breakthrough, however, came with passage of the *National Defense Education Act of 1958 (NDEA)* (discussed in the next section), which focused on higher education programs, and the *Elementary and Secondary Education Act of 1965 (ESEA)*. ESEA was the first major effort to provide a broad range of federal financial support for K–12 education, and its provisions targeted districts that served large numbers of children from low-income families. In amendments added in 1968, Congress extended ESEA's reach to programs for handicapped and other special needs students, as well as to rural areas and bilingual education. The next major revisions came in the 1994 reauthorization of ESEA (called the *Improving America's Schools Act*), in which Congress broadened the financing provisions of ESEA to cover items ranging from school building repair to multicultural education programs. This effort continued under Presidents Bill Clinton and George W. Bush. In 2002, Congress passed the *No Child Left Behind Act*, which significantly modified many provisions of the ESEA by tying funding to achieving national standards (see later discussion).

Educational Curriculum

Federal programs dealing with *content*—that is, with what is taught in schools—are implied in most of the early access and funding policies just discussed. The Northwest Ordinance regarded schools as a means for promoting religion and morality as well as knowledge. The land grants starting with the Morrill Act stressed the need for more education in practical arts, and these efforts were enhanced from time to time with federal grants in support of vocational education. However, it took the Cold War–era fear that the Soviet Union was outdoing the United States in certain critical areas of science to begin a major effort by the federal government to shape the curriculum of America's classrooms. The *National Defense Education Act of 1958* began with the declaration that "an educational emergency exists and requires action by the federal government. Assistance will come from Washington to help develop as rapidly as possible those skills essential to the national defense." While the language of the act emphasized that this was not an attempt to impose federal control of education, the programs that this act established and funded had a major impact on education at all levels. Great stress was placed on enhancing the teaching of foreign languages, science, math, and other areas deemed critical to the Cold War effort. In addition, the NDEA authorized federal spending for programs designed to modernize classroom instruction in key areas.[19]

The first comprehensive federal programs dealing with curriculum issues in K–12 programs were passed in the *Goals 2000: Educate America Act of 1994*. That act linked future funding to specific goals and included provision promoting the adoption of programs in math, the sciences, literacy, and lifelong learning. Along with the *Improving America's Schools Act*, passed the same year, *Goals 2000* proved to be a content-relevant bridge between federal funding and quality education programs.

Critical Thinking

Should there be a national curriculum and national education performance standards? Or should those matters be left up to local schools to decide?

Educational Quality and Accountability

Federal involvement in *educational quality* concerns is increasingly evident. George W. Bush's *No Child Left Behind Act (NCLB)* initiative was a key part of his run for the presidency, and he was in the midst of pushing for the legislation when the events of September 11 occurred. As passed in January 2002, the act stresses the need for states to develop educational standards in specific subject areas and to implement testing programs for assessing how well the schools are helping students meet those standards. In addition, schools that are not achieving those standards are required to provide annual public reports demonstrating that they are making progress toward those goals. In addition, states and schools must demonstrate that they are undertaking programs to assist those with special needs to meet the standards. The NCLB represents an effort to make schools more accountable, and in the process it gives the national government a very prominent role in education policy for the future.

The debate over federal education policy is a prime example of how Americans have increasingly relied on the national government to deal with problems that cannot be handled by state and local officials alone. It is clear that most details of education policy have always been a matter for states and localities to deal with, but it is also clear that federal policymakers have not been reluctant to get involved if the public seems supportive. To establish these various programs, advocates must focus on the necessity of federal involvement because of the inability or unwillingness of state and local officials to take action. Although these various efforts come at a "cost" in terms of reduced local autonomy, they have rarely been regarded as "evil" intrusions. In fact, in many instances, federal programs have been received with open arms in many communities. In the case of No Child Left Behind, at the time of its passage twenty states already had similar or more stringent programs in place, and many other states were ready to adopt such programs.

Managing the Economy

FOCUS QUESTION **HOW DOES THE FEDERAL GOVERNMENT ATTEMPT TO MANAGE THE AMERICAN ECONOMY?**

What should be the government's role in managing the economy? For many Americans, the answer depends on whether one emphasizes the "necessary" or the "evil" part of the dominant myth. Those who stress the "necessary" part of the myth fault government for doing too little. They believe that government must be more active in guiding the American economy, despite the inefficiencies that might result. They argue that because the private marketplace cannot meet the basic needs of many citizens, the government must step in and correct its imperfections. In contrast, others think that government is likely to interfere too much in economic matters. They view most public policies as needlessly restricting the operations of the marketplace and damaging the nation's economic health.

Behind this debate is the fact that the national government has been engaged in economic policymaking for most of its history. Government intervention in the marketplace can be traced to colonial times.[20] Colonial governments offered payments (called bounties) to businesses that made large investments in the manufacture of certain products or increased the exportation of locally pro-

The Economic Puzzle

Economic policymaking is made more difficult by the uncertainties of just what is causing the problems that officials want to solve.

duced goods. In 1640, for example, Massachusetts offered bounties for the production of wool products. In 1661, Virginia awarded bounties of large quantities of tobacco to shipbuilders and ship owners for every vessel they docked in the colony. Other forms of business support were available as well. Many colonies provided public instruction to train young men in tanning, silk production, lumbering, and similar trades. Colonial governments even owned and operated businesses and banks. Many of these activities continued long after the Revolution as states and local governments actively promoted their economies with tax breaks, low-cost loans, grants-in-aid, and franchises to certain businesses.

Alexander Hamilton, the first secretary of the treasury, and others tried to give the national government a major role in the economy during the presidencies of George Washington and John Adams. Hamilton felt that the young nation's future depended on its having a strong economy, and he believed that the national government should play a major role in shaping that economy. In contrast, Thomas Jefferson and his successors (especially Andrew Jackson) strongly opposed any form of central control. They believed that economic policy should be left to local and state governments. This opposition, however, did not stop some national policymakers. Between 1816 and the early 1830s, members of Congress from the northeastern states won passage of banking and tariff legislation that was favorable to their small but growing manufacturing and trade businesses. During the 1830s, the power in Congress shifted toward agricultural interests in the South and West. With that shift came lower tariffs and other economic policies favoring farmers and plantation owners. Railroads were important to agrarian America, and so between 1850 and 1857 Congress turned over more than 25 million acres of public land to railroad companies.

After the Civil War, Congress became much more involved in the nation's economy by promoting westward expansion and the growth of business and by establishing regulatory agencies to control and monitor certain industries. But in spite of these efforts, throughout the late nineteenth and early twentieth centuries, the economy remained subject to boom-and-bust cycles, culminating in the Great Depression of the 1930s.

The Great Depression became a watershed era, as President Franklin D. Roosevelt's administration responded with a series of popular programs, known as the New Deal, to help promote recovery and stabilize the economy. Two major dimensions of national economic policy emerged during this period: monetary policy, involving control of the money supply, and fiscal policy, involving changes in government spending and tax rates.

Monetary Policy

Monetary policy The manipulation of the money supply in order to control the economy. The Federal Reserve System, or the "Fed," is the principal mechanism for making monetary policy.

Economists talk of tight and loose money supplies. A *tight money supply* exists when the amount of money circulating in the economy is low relative to the demand for money by consumers and investors. Basic economics teaches that when the money supply is tight, interest rates (the cost of using someone else's money) tend to be high and the cost of most goods and services is likely to fall. A *loose money supply* exists when the amount of money circulating is high relative to the demand for money. During these periods, interest rates decline and prices of goods and services increase. Thus economists attribute periods of both high and low interest rates, deflated and inflated prices, and a variety of related economic conditions to the supply of money circulating in the economy.

Monetary policy— the manipulation of the money supply in order to control the economy— has become one of the government's major economic management tools. The principal mechanisms for carrying out monetary policy are in the hands of the Federal Reserve System, also known as the "Fed" (see Figure 14.3). The Federal Reserve System, established in 1913, consists of twelve regional banks and a Federal Reserve Board, which is empowered to regulate the circulation of currency in the U.S. economy. When the economy is sluggish— when not enough money is being invested to maintain economic growth or when unemployment is high— policymakers at the Fed will try to stimulate economic activity by increasing the supply of money. With more money in circulation, people will be more likely to make purchases or investments, which, in turn, will generate business activity and jobs. If policymakers think that the economy is overheated and is generating too much inflation, they can reduce the supply of money in an attempt to slow down economic activity.

The Fed's policies are often influenced by recent history.[21] The double-digit inflation of the late 1970s and early 1980s was still fresh in the minds of the monetary policymakers who sat on the Federal Reserve's governing board in 1993 and 1994, when the U.S. economy began to pull out of its long recession. While most Americans welcomed the signs of recovery, the Fed's governors saw them differently. Fearing the return of inflation, they began raising interest

FEDERAL RESERVE BANKS

Twelve banks representing the nation's twelve Federal Reserve districts. The twelve manage the day-to-day needs of the banking system by maintaining a stable flow of money.

The banks, by districts:

1 Boston	7 Chicago
2 New York	8 St. Louis
3 Philadelphia	9 Minneapolis
4 Cleveland	10 Kansas City
5 Richmond	11 Dallas
6 Atlanta	12 San Francisco

What They Do

- Act as lender of last resort to banks, savings associations, and credit unions in trouble
- Keep reserves deposited by depository institutions
- Supply currency and coins to banks
- Destroy worn-out bills, coins
- Operate clearinghouses for checks
- Serve as fiscal agent for the U.S. Treasury
- Conduct domestic and foreign monetary operations through the New York Federal Reserve Bank as agent for the Federal Open Market Committee

BOARD OF GOVERNORS

Seven members appointed by the president and confirmed by the Senate. Terms are 14 years. The president names one member as chairman for a four-year term. The board is based in Washington, D.C.

What It Does

- Helps carry out policy for regulating the supply of money and credit by:
  –Setting reserve requirements for the depository institutions
  –Setting the discount rate on the Fed's loans to banks
- Makes margin rules for purchases of securities on credit
- Oversees major banks by regulating the nation's bank holding companies
- Inspects and regulates state-chartered banks that are members of the reserve system
- Monitors the economy
- Deals with international monetary problems
- Enforces consumer-credit laws
- Supervises Federal Reserve banks

FEDERAL OPEN MARKET COMMITTEE

Twelve members: The seven Federal Reserve governors and the president of the New York Federal Reserve Bank plus four of the presidents of the other eleven Federal Reserve banks on a rotating basis.

All twelve bank presidents attend the FOMC meetings, held every five to eight weeks.

What It Does

- Sets overall policy for regulating the supply of money and credit in the country
- Helps carry out that policy by directing the "trading desk" of the Federal Reserve Bank of New York to buy and sell government securities in the open market

FIGURE 14.3

The Long Reach of the Federal Reserve

Source: Copyright January 27, 1986, *U.S. News & World Report.*

rates to help keep inflation in check. Advocates of more rapid economic recovery openly criticized these decisions, for they feared that higher interest rates would slow down investment and perhaps stall economic growth.

The role of the Fed was no less controversial during the boom economy of the late 1990s. While the economy went through a transformation brought about by an expanding global economy and a revolution in information technology, the Fed remained vigilant against inflationary pressures. Led by its chair, Alan Greenspan, the governing board began raising interest rates whenever there were signs of inflation. Although some political leaders and economic analysts criticized these policies as too cautious, in 2000 President Clinton and the Congress rewarded Greenspan with his fourth four-year appointment as chair of that important policymaking body.

Starting in early 2001, an economic slowdown prompted Greenspan and the Fed to loosen the money supply by reducing interest rates to their lowest levels in decades. The events of September 11 proved to be a further shock to the economy, and the Fed maintained its lower-interest-rate policy into 2004. But in June of that year, the Fed began slowly raising interest rates by one-quarter percent each month as a hedge against the danger of inflation.

Greenspan was appointed to his fifth four-year term as chair of the Fed in 2004 by President George W. Bush, but retired early in 2006. He was replaced by economist Ben Bernanke, who had previously served as a member of the Fed's Board of Governors as well as chair of President Bush's Council of Economic Advisors. By all indications, Bernanke was likely to continue with the "measured" anti-inflation policies of his predecessor.

Fiscal Policy

Fiscal policy The management of government expenditures and tax rates as a means for conducting national economic policy. Policymakers raise or lower government spending and taxes to execute fiscal policy.

During the Depression, policymakers discovered that changes in how much the government spent and how much it collected in taxes could influence overall economic performance. The use of this **fiscal policy** became another way to manage the general performance of the economy. According to a widely accepted economic policy theory, the federal government can stimulate economic activity during sluggish periods through its purchases of goods and services. By reducing taxes, it can put money in the hands of consumers, who can further stimulate economic activity through their own increased purchases and investments. If, on the other hand, the economy is overheating, the government can cut spending and raise taxes, which takes money away from consumers and investors and thus reduces demand.

The Debate

The debate over how to manage the economy has raged for decades between those who believe that the government should be using monetary and fiscal tools to manage the overall direction of the economy and those who believe in a

Keynesians Followers of economist John Maynard Keynes. They advocate government spending when the economy is sluggish (even if a deficit results) in order to revive the economy.

Monetarists A group of economists who reject the argument that constant government intervention in the economy can bring either sustained prosperity or stability.

much more limited governmental role. The advocates of governmental activism include the **Keynesians** — the followers of John Maynard Keynes (pronounced "canes"), a British economist. His theory that government should engage in deficit spending during periods when the economy is sluggish provided the rationale for fiscal policies from the 1930s through the 1960s. The Keynesian approach is reflected in the *Employment Act of 1946*, which made national government officials responsible for ensuring maximum production, high employment, and increased purchasing power in the American economy. The sustained period of relative prosperity from the late 1940s until the late 1960s led many to assume that such government intervention had made the threat of economic stagnation, let alone major recessions, a thing of the past.[22]

The **monetarists**, a group of prominent economists led by Milton Friedman, reject the argument that constant government intervention in the economy can bring either constant prosperity or stability. They believe that the economy kept growing between 1946 and 1970 in spite of government fiscal and monetary policies, not because of them. Not only is government intervention in the economy not a solution, it has prevented even stronger economic growth. They argue that government intervention should be limited to maintaining a consistent growth in the nation's money supply in order to control inflation. During the 1970s and early 1980s, when the U.S. economy went through a period of both high inflation and rising unemployment, the country's economic policymakers gave greater attention to the monetarists' argument that government was doing too much through fiscal policies.[23]

By the late 1990s, many analysts had come to the conclusion that neither the Keynesians nor the monetarists had the definitive answer to how the economy should be managed. Some have argued that a "new economy" emerged in the last decade of the twentieth century, and that a new approach to managing the economy must be developed in order to deal with the changed conditions.[24] Such an approach has yet to emerge, but it is likely that the "necessary evil" myth will continue to play a critical role in shaping the policy choices of the future.

Deficits, Surpluses, and the National Debt

National debt The total amount of money the government owes as a result of spending more than it has taken in.
Budget surplus The result when budget revenues exceed expenditures.
Budget deficit The result when expenditures exceed revenues.

Two central issues in the ongoing debate over fiscal and monetary policies are the size of the federal deficit and what to do with any budget surpluses. The instrument for dealing with both questions is the national debt.[25] The **national debt** is the total amount of money the federal government owes as a result of having spent more funds than it has received in revenues. Each year the federal government accumulates either a **budget surplus** (when its revenues, or receipts, exceed spending, or expenditures) or a **budget deficit** (when expenditures exceed receipts). During most of the 1980s, the federal government recorded yearly deficits of between $73 billion and $221 billion. In 1992 the deficit reached a record level of $290 billion, though it declined to $255 billion the following year. After that, the annual deficit continued to decline. By the end of fiscal year 1996, it had decreased to $107 billion — less than half of its

1993 level. By 1998, the budget was generating a surplus ($69 billion that year and $124 billion in 1999), and it was projected at that time that surpluses would continue to grow through at least 2005. But the economic downturn of 2001 and the events of September 11 greatly altered that projection. When President George W. Bush issued his revised budget projection for fiscal year 2002, it contained a projected deficit of $165 billion. According to figures released in January 2006, the deficit for fiscal year 2005 would be $318 billion, and the projected deficit for fiscal year 2007 was estimated at $354 billion (see Figure 14.4). It was estimated that by July 2008 the national government's total outstanding debt would be more than $9.295 trillion.[26]

It is difficult to pinpoint the cause of this huge debt. Some of it has resulted from actions taken by the federal government during times of national emergency, such as a war or a major economic depression. When Franklin D. Roosevelt became president in 1933, he inherited a national debt of $22.5 billion. By the time the United States entered World War II, the debt had climbed to $48 billion. During that war, the federal government financed about 60 percent of its spending through borrowing. At the end of the war, the national debt stood at $280 billion. Another reason for the national debt is that we expect government to make large-scale capital investments that generate little or no return in the short term, or even in the long term. Unlike the situation in the private sector, where capital investments in buildings and equipment are expected to generate income and pay for themselves over time, the government's investments include highways, weapons systems, airports, and school buildings—all important **infrastructure projects** that are necessary for national economic health but that typically do not bring in sufficient revenues to offset their costs.

A third reason for government indebtedness is the growth of mandatory spending which comprises two-thirds of the budget. Mandatory spending includes both entitlement programs and government spending obligation. **Entitlement programs**, such as social security and unemployment benefits, commit the government to supplying funds or services to all citizens who meet specified eligibility requirements. Because the amount of money spent depends on the number of people who meet those standards, this spending is uncontrollable from year to year. For example, as more people reach retirement age or as more become unemployed during a recession, government spending increases without any congressional or executive action. The same is true for obligatory spending, such as interest payments on the national debt: The government has no choice but to spend the required amount. Figure 14.5 illustrates the past and projected trends in mandatory spending.

Still another significant reason for the growing national debt is that the American public sometimes demands more goods and services than it is willing to pay for through taxes or special fees. Politicians rarely advocate tax increases, and in recent years many elected officials have felt the impact of "taxpayer revolts" at the voting booths. Those same voters, however, are reluctant to support government officials who propose reductions in popular programs. The heads of families with college-age children, for instance, may lead the fight against a local property tax increase or a state sales tax measure while insisting that state colleges keep tuition costs low and guarantee admission to their sons and daughters.

Critical Thinking

Is government debt ever a good thing?

Infrastructure projects High-cost government capital investment projects such as highways and school buildings that are provided to support and enhance the economic health of the nation.

Entitlement programs Programs such as social security that commit the government to supply funds or services to all citizens who meet specified eligibility requirements.

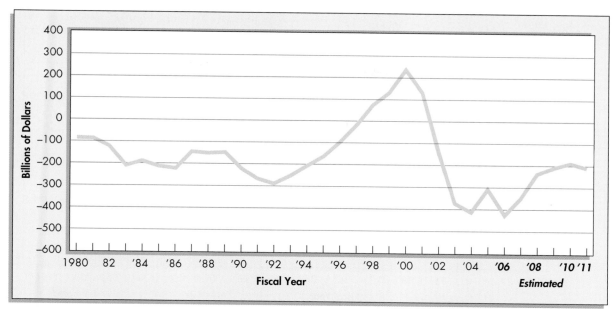

FIGURE 14.4

The Federal Budget Deficit/Surplus, 1980–2011 (est.)

After many years of federal deficits adding to the national debt, the U.S. government started generating annual budget surpluses in the mid-1990s. With the spending required by the war on terror and related programs (e.g., Homeland Security), the current and projected deficits are likely to continue for the foreseeable future.

Source: U.S. Office of Management and Budget, *Budget of the United States Government, Fiscal Year 2007*, Historical Tables.

Finally, government debt can increase when policymakers decide to fund current spending through borrowing rather than through taxes in order to sustain or stimulate economic activity. Helping the economy has been the primary reason used to justify the huge federal deficits that have been piling up in recent years. This is a strategy based on the Keynesian fiscal policy approach described earlier.

Regardless of what has caused the large U.S. national debt, its size is staggering to most people. During the 1990s, the debt became a major public policy issue. But it is not only its sheer size that worries many policymakers and analysts. Some believe that it is not fair to burden future generations with debt in order to finance our current consumption of public goods and services. Others see a large national debt as inflationary—that is, as causing higher prices for the private-sector goods and services we purchase today. Still others argue that financing the national debt is pushing all interest rates higher, thus making it more difficult for consumers and businesses to borrow money.[27]

Another school of analysts and policymakers argues that critics of the national debt are wrong. Relatively speaking, they point out, the public debt is not all that high. For example, while the federal government owed $4.7 trillion in 2005,

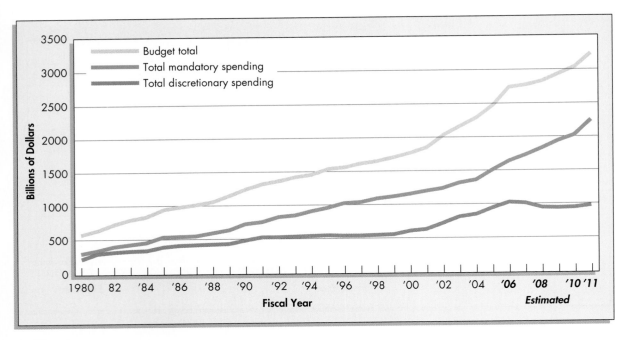

FIGURE 14.5

Mandatory and Discretionary Spending, 1980–2011 (est.)

Source: U.S. Office of Management and Budget, *Budget of the United States Government, Fiscal Year 2007*, Historical Tables.

American households owed $11.5 trillion and U.S. businesses owed another $8.3 trillion.[28] Nor is the national debt too large when it is measured against the country's assets or the annual gross national product. Some point out that while the national government's debt was growing for most of the post–Cold War period, state and local governments often ran budget surpluses each year that offset the national debt. Others stress the fact that most of the national debt is owed to ourselves—to the millions of Americans who directly or indirectly hold U.S. savings bonds, Treasury notes, and long-term Treasury bonds. And many of these analysts emphasize that the health of the American economy has frequently depended on the stimulus provided by government deficits.[29]

The concern with the growing national debt in the 1980s resulted in a number of efforts to reduce the annual deficits, and the national debt played a key role in recent presidential and congressional races. The economic boom of the late 1990s, however, radically altered the debate over government spending and deficits. With the federal budget generating annual surpluses starting in 1998, the question became how to spend the excess revenues. While some members of Congress favored tax cuts, others made paying down the accumulated debt a high priority. The question of what to do with the surplus became an issue in the 2000 presidential campaign, and one of the first acts of George W. Bush's administration was to push through a controversial tax cut that stretched out over a number of years. With the slowed economy and increased spending for national defense after 9/11 on the horizon, however, the surpluses upon which that cut was based may not materialize. Deficit spending and the growing national debt are likely to be at the center of debate for years to come.

Economic Development Policies

FOCUS QUESTION WHAT ARE THE ISSUES SURROUNDING THE FEDERAL GOVERNMENT'S EFFORTS TO ENHANCE OVERALL ECONOMIC GROWTH?

In addition to using monetary and fiscal policies to manage the economy and help stabilize it, policymakers have used **economic development policies** to help the economy grow. These policies have involved a range of approaches, from trade policies to industrial strategies.

Trade Policies and Globalization

For much of our history, our national economic development policies were closely associated with our **tariff** policies. In the 1800s, American business developed behind a wall of high protective tariffs on imported goods and services. From the turn of the century until 1929, tariffs continued to increase slowly. They took a big leap with the enactment of the Hawley-Smoot Tariff of 1929. Today Hawley-Smoot is often seen as a major cause of the Great Depression because of the turmoil it created in international markets. Consequently, Congress has been reluctant to pass protective tariff legislation for more than half a century. Most policymakers believe that **free trade** (the abolition of tariffs and other trade barriers) is the best policy to follow.[30]

The free trade policy raised little controversy from the 1940s through the 1970s. During those years the U.S. **balance of trade** — the net difference between the value of what Americans bought and what they sold overseas — ran a surplus, as Americans exported more goods and services than they imported. In 1975, for example, the United States exported $18 billion more in merchandise than it imported. By contrast, in 2005, Americans imported over $782 billion more in goods and services than they exported — the highest trade deficit in the nation's history. Furthermore, by 1985 the United States had become a debtor nation: The value of foreign investment in America exceeded U.S. overseas investment by more than $110 billion.

Responding to these conditions, some members of Congress advocated raising tariffs or taking other policy measures to protect U.S. industries and jobs from foreign competition. The administrations of Ronald Reagan, George H. W. Bush, and Bill Clinton, as well as other advocates of free trade, opposed such proposals, insisting that free and open international markets are the answer to trade deficits. The problem, they contended, was rooted in the barriers to free trade imposed by other countries, especially Japan. Instead of protective tariffs, they undertook diplomatic and other kinds of political pressures to persuade those nations to lower their barriers to the importation of U.S. goods and services.

The debate over free trade policies came to a head several times during the Clinton years. When he entered office, Clinton pushed for passage of the *North American Free Trade Agreement (NAFTA)*, which had been negotiated by President George H. W. Bush. The battle for ratification of the treaty was hard fought,

Economic development policies Policies intended to promote and protect businesses in order to enhance overall economic growth.

Tariffs Taxes on goods brought into the country from abroad; they are often intended to protect growing industries from foreign competition.
Free trade An international economic policy that calls for the abolition of tariffs and other barriers so that goods and services may be exchanged freely among nations.
Balance of trade The net difference between the value of what Americans buy and what they sell overseas.

pitting a coalition of labor, consumer, and farm groups against a coalition headed by some of the nation's top corporations. NAFTA was passed in 1993, but it remained a controversial policy for years, with opponents organizing to prevent its expansion.[31]

The issues raised by NAFTA and similar policies have become associated with a worldwide debate about **globalization**. Globalization is the idea that an increasing amount of human activity and social interrelations are being conducted on a global scale, rather than at the local, regional, or national levels that have been predominant for the past several centuries. The term actually implies at least four related trends.[32] First, it implies *internationalization* in the sense that a good deal more of our lives are linked to the world community, where national borders have less meaning. Second, globalization implies *economic liberalization*, in which national economic policies are seen as a barrier to economic well-being. Third, globalization is seen as *universalization*, implying a trend toward the emergence of a global culture and the eventual disappearance of cultural and national distinctions. Finally, globalization is perceived by some as a process of *modernization and westernization*, in which democracy and capitalism become the global standards. The debate has centered on whether or not these trends are desirable. If they are, then free trade policies such as NAFTA should be pursued vigorously; if they are not, then policies should be developed to counter these powerful trends.

The free trade and globalization issues again made headlines in December 1999, when the *World Trade Organization (WTO)* held a major meeting in Seattle, Washington. Formed in 1995 as an international organization designed to establish and enforce the rules of world trade, the WTO is a major facilitator of globalization, along with the *International Monetary Fund (IMF)* and the *World Bank*. The policies of all three have been regarded by some U.S. groups as a threat to American jobs, the environment, and the interests of many of the world's poorer nations. Protests by anti-WTO groups at the Seattle meeting turned violent and brought the issues of free trade back into focus for many Americans.[33] Similar protests have been organized wherever the WTO and related organizations have held their meetings, and the issues raised by globalization are likely to continue as the global economy expands.

Tax Incentives

The government can also use **tax incentives** to promote growth. Tax breaks can promote economic activity in certain industries. For example, the home-building industry has benefited greatly over the past several decades from a provision of the tax law that allows Americans to deduct their home mortgage interest costs from their personal income taxes. Another well-known but less popular tax break was an oil depletion allowance. Introduced during the 1920s, this tax break absolved owners of oil- or gas-producing properties from the need to pay taxes on more than a fourth of their income. Experts estimate that this tax break saved these property owners as much as $2.5 billion annually. The tax

Protesting Free Trade

A growing number of Americans expressed concern about free trade issues during the 1990s. In December 1999, thousands of protestors took to the streets of Seattle, the city where the controversial World Trade Organization was meeting.

Critical Thinking

Should Congress eliminate the tax deduction for interest paid on home mortgages?

break promoted oil and gas exploration, but many critics thought that its benefits were excessive and much too costly. It took more than fifty years, however, to get the tax break eliminated.

Industrial and Supply-Side Policies

Industrial policy A comprehensive strategy for using government policies to restructure the nation's economy.

During the 1980s, economic policy discussions often centered on a debate between two strategies. Some analysts argued that policymakers must develop a comprehensive economic development strategy for restructuring the economy. Under this approach, known as **industrial policy**, the United States would abandon certain industries in which labor costs were too high for successful competition with other nations. At the same time, it would rescue other industries and make them competitive in the world market. Most advocates of industrial policy also called for investments in new high-technology and service industries.

Supply-side economics An economic policy strategy popular during the Reagan administration that advocates increasing the production of goods by cutting taxes to help stimulate investment, lifting regulations in the marketplace, and eliminating other government restraints on private business initiatives.

By contrast, advocates of **supply-side economics** believed in putting more emphasis on policies that would promote increased production of goods by giving incentives to private producers. Thus, supply-siders supported cutting taxes to help stimulate investment, lifting regulations in the marketplace, and eliminating other government restraints on private business initiatives. Supply-siders claimed that in the past, government intervention in the economy had relied too much on consumer demand to stimulate economic growth and imposed too many obstacles to private investment. According to supply-side advocates, only through policies that increase suppliers' incentives can jobs be created and the economy grow.

Regulatory Policies

FOCUS QUESTION   HOW HAS THE FEDERAL GOVERNMENT USED REGULATORY POLICIES IN DEALING WITH ECONOMIC, SOCIAL, AND ENVIRONMENTAL PROBLEMS?

Another broad area of public policy involves the use of regulatory means to control and promote various types of behavior. Regulation involves the establishment and enforcement of a rule of behavior that is intended to achieve a policy objective; in the United States, it is most often associated with economic, environmental, and social policies.

Economic Regulation

Economic regulatory policies Economic policies through which the government monitors and controls critical industries and sectors of the economy.

Along with devising economic development policies, in the late 1800s Congress also expanded the scope of economic policy to include **economic regulatory policies**, through which the government monitors and controls critical industries and sectors of the economy. The Interstate Commerce Act of 1887 established the first regulatory commission, the *Interstate Commerce Commission (ICC)*, and authorized it to regulate prices and standards of service for interstate rail companies.[34]

During the next fifty years, Congress established other major economic regulatory agencies (see Chapter 12, on the bureaucracy). The *Food and Drug Administration (FDA)* came into being in 1906 to protect consumers from health-threatening products. The *Federal Trade Commission (FTC)* was formed in 1914 to provide safeguards against unfair methods of competition and deceptive practices in the marketplace. In the depths of the Great Depression, Congress created several other agencies. The *Federal Communications Commission (FCC)* was established to regulate the interstate telephone, telegraph, radio, and other telecommunications industries; the *Securities and Exchange Commission (SEC)* was established to oversee the activities of businesses in the securities and investment markets; and the Federal Power Commission (now called the *Federal Energy Regulatory Commission*, or *FERC*) was formed to regulate the interstate production and distribution of electric power and natural gas. Reacting to widely publicized violent confrontations between workers and their employers, Congress also established the *National Labor Relations Board (NLRB)* to regulate workplace relations between businesses and their employees who sought to unionize.

Congress also passed **antitrust laws** intended to promote greater economic competition through regulation. The *Sherman Antitrust Act of 1890* made it illegal for businesses to restrain trade or to monopolize a market for some product or service. The *Clayton Antitrust Act of 1914* outlawed business practices that might diminish competition or promote monopolies in a market. In 1936 the Clayton Act was amended to prevent corporate mergers that would reduce competition in a sector of the economy.

Antitrust laws Laws intended to promote greater economic competition. Among the major examples in U.S. history are the Sherman Antitrust Act of 1890 and the Clayton Antitrust Act of 1914.

The history of antitrust enforcement[35] began in the late 1890s and early 1900s. Among the most famous historical cases were the actions taken between 1905 and 1915 to break up DuPont, the American Tobacco trust, and the Standard Oil Company. More recently, antitrust actions resulted in the breakup of AT&T and the formation of the "Baby Bells" to provide phone service in various regions of the country. Cases brought against IBM, Xerox, and other major corporations have influenced the way companies do business. In perhaps the most watched case in recent years, the Department of Justice and a number of states took action against Microsoft Corporation in 1997. By 2002, Microsoft had reached an agreement with the federal regulators, but it was still entangled in antitrust lawsuits with several states.

Economic regulatory policy has been subject to a number of criticisms. As early as the 1950s, critics argued that the major economic regulatory agencies seemed to be serving the interests of those they regulated rather than the public interest.[36] In addition, studies conducted in the 1960s and 1970s showed that consumers often paid a higher price for goods and services produced by a regulated industry than they would have paid if the industry were unregulated. The call for economic **deregulation** that followed eventually led to legislation in 1978 that phased out the Civil Aeronautics Board.

Deregulation The reduction or elimination of government regulatory policies.

Under the Carter and Reagan administrations, Congress and the commissions lessened the restrictions on natural gas producers, banks, trucking companies, interstate buses, and railroads. The Securities and Exchange Commission deregulated stockbrokers' commissions. The Federal Communications Commission permitted local newspaper companies to own television and radio stations. The agencies charged with enforcing antitrust policies (the Federal Trade Commission and the Antitrust Division of the U.S. Department of Justice) relaxed their criteria for approving corporate mergers.[37]

By the early 1990s, some observers were arguing that economic deregulation had gone too far too fast. The elimination of airline and bus service to many communities, a wave of corporate buyouts and mergers, a stock market crash in 1987, the specter of a bailout for failing savings-and-loan institutions that would cost American taxpayers hundreds of billions of dollars, and other such events led some to call for re-regulation. Regulatory reform, they felt, had "turned out to be an exercise in national self-deception."[38]

For much of the 1990s, however, it remained difficult to overcome the myth of government as a necessary evil, and deregulation and antiregulatory policy efforts remained an important part of the U.S. public policy agenda. In 2002, however, a number of corporate management scandals led to stronger regulatory actions by the Securities and Exchange Commission as well as passage of a corporate anticorruption bill (Sarbanes-Oxley Act of 2002) that provided for tougher regulatory oversight of corporate accounting practices.

Environmental Regulation[39]

Regulation is also the primary approach that the government uses in its efforts to deal with environmental pollution. Pollution is not a new problem, but federal officials did not pay significant attention to it until the late 1960s. Most issues related to the environment were generally left to the states and localities where the problems existed or to the courts, where private individuals would seek solutions through litigation. The federal government did have a long history of conservation policies aimed at managing and preserving forests and other large tracts of land in the American West, but its pollution control activities were limited to prohibiting the dumping of waste or oil into harbors and coastal waters, which were part of Washington's jurisdiction under the Constitution. Water pollution control acts passed in the 1940s and 1950s did little more than declare that polluting was an illegal act; enforcement was left up to local officials.

Students of environmental policy cannot really pinpoint exactly what triggered the sudden explosion of concern over environmental pollution in the 1960s. Local controversies over power plant construction, the publication of books such as Rachel Carson's *Silent Spring*, media coverage of smog problems in cities from Los Angeles to Birmingham to New York—all these things seemed to come together in a political movement that Washington could not ignore. In 1969, Congress passed the *National Environmental Policy Act (NEPA)*, which, for the first time, explicitly identified environmental pollution as a national concern. This was followed in 1970 by President Nixon's creation (through an executive order) of an *Environmental Protection Agency (EPA)* comprising units and programs drawn from throughout the federal government. What followed was a series of congressional actions that established the regulatory programs that the EPA would enforce.

Environmental regulation covers a wide range of issues, but three major areas stand out: air pollution, water pollution, and earth pollution. The *Clean Air Act* was first passed in 1970 and gave the EPA jurisdiction over area, stationary, and mobile sources of air pollution. Area sources of air pollution include such things as pools of spilled solvents, smoke from leaf-burning fires or barbecue pits, gasoline storage tanks, and so on. Stationary air pollution sources are primarily industrial or residential smokestacks. Mobile sources include trucks, cars, buses, lawn mowers, and other vehicles. Under the Clean Air Act, the EPA was mandated to establish ambient air-quality standards for the country and to oversee efforts by both public and private entities to achieve the goals set under the standards.

The first major water pollution law was the *Federal Water Pollution Control Act Amendments of 1972*, which later became known as the Clean Water Act. The act prohibited the discharge of pollution into any navigable body of water from a specific "point" source (e.g., a factory) without a permit issued by the EPA. Using this regulatory authority, the EPA was able to require polluters to meet the clean water standards set by the law. In addition, the act provided federal funding for local sewage treatment and other wastewater facilities. Later amendments addressed issues of nonpoint sources, such as agricultural runoff and natural occurrences.

Earth pollution was initially addressed in the *Resource Conservation and Recovery Act of 1976*, which primarily focused on the disposal of hazardous wastes, but which also provided a framework that was later used by the EPA for regulating the disposal and recycling of nonhazardous waste. In 1980, Congress passed the *Comprehensive Environmental Response, Compensation, and Liability Act (Superfund)*, which provided for the cleanup of abandoned hazardous waste sites and catastrophic spills.

Federal environmental regulation has undergone a number of changes since 1970. Under pressure to deregulate during the Reagan administration, the EPA developed alternatives to strict regulatory control approaches, including providing economic incentives for operators of pollution sources to regulate themselves. Some of these have proved successful; others have not. All have emerged as "necessary" solutions to problems that the public believed only the federal government could deal with.

Social Regulation[40]

Protecting citizens from the major hazards associated with life in a highly industrialized economic system has also become a focus of regulatory policy.

The first federal **social regulation programs** emerged in the early 1900s in response to problems involving adulterated food and the deceptive advertising of drugs. Stirred to action by research conducted at the Department of Agriculture and investigations by muckraking journalists, Congress passed the *Pure Food and Drug Act of 1906* and the *Meat Inspection Act of 1907*. These and other **consumer protection policies** established federal agencies to deal with problems related to the safety and quality of food and drug products sold in the American marketplace. Over the years the laws have been modified to deal with new problems and demands. Other forms of social regulation have followed similar patterns.

Many of the economic regulatory agencies just mentioned continue to play a role in these policy areas. The Food and Drug Administration regulates a wide range of consumer products, including drugs, cosmetics, medical devices, and food (except for meat and poultry), to ensure their safety, purity, and effectiveness. For drugs and medical devices, FDA approval is needed before a product can be marketed. The FDA also investigates complaints about the safety or purity of food and cosmetics. If a product is found to be unsafe or adulterated, the FDA can order its removal from the marketplace. Overseeing the processing of meat and related products is the responsibility of the Food Safety and Inspection Service of the Department of Agriculture.

Critical Thinking

Almost all regulatory costs are ultimately passed on to the consumer. How much more are you willing to pay for goods and services as a result of government regulations that help maintain clean air and clean water?

Social regulation programs Programs aimed at protecting consumers from the hazards of life in a highly industrialized economic system.

Consumer protection policies Government laws and programs developed to deal with the safety and quality of consumer products and to protect consumers from deceptive business practices.

POLITICS & POPULAR CULTURE

The West Wing: Dramatizing the Public Policymaking Process

There are some types of governmental activity — for instance, law enforcement — that have been easily transformed into dramatic entertainment by the popular media. But until recently, no one in Hollywood was prepared to use the ongoing dramas of public policymaking as a basis for a movie or TV series. That changed in 1999, when NBC added *The West Wing* to its weekly TV fare.

The show, which aired its final episode in May 2006, starred Martin Sheen as President Josiah "Jed" Bartlet, a Ph.D. and Nobel laureate in economics from New Hampshire who won the 1998 presidential election (remember, this is fiction!) with 48 percent of the popular vote. Surrounding him in the first season was a cast of characters drawn from the personalities we often see in the national headlines, including a trusted chief of staff and his deputy; a director of communications (and his deputy), whose job it is to promote a positive image of the president and his administration; a political consultant; a press secretary (and her staff); the president's family (his physician wife and three daughters); a vice president who is regarded as a political threat to the president; members of the press corps; high-ranking military personnel; various members of Congress; lobbyists; diplomats; and an entourage who make up the White House staff closest to the president.

Like other popular TV series, *The West Wing* relied on the personal problems and interpersonal relationships of its characters to tie together the plots of various episodes. The chief of staff is an alcoholic with a past, the press secretary is "involved" with one of the White House reporters, and a key staffer has had a relationship with a call girl. But what was unique about the series during its first season (1999–2000) was how well it seemed to portray the dynamics of public policymaking on some very controversial issues.

In one episode, titled "Five Votes Down," the White House is engaged in frantic efforts to rally five votes to pass gun control legislation that the president favors. They have seventy-two hours before the vote. Part of the elaborate wheeling and dealing involves one member of Congress — the head of the Black Congressional Caucus — who is voting against the bill not because he opposes gun control, but because this legislation isn't strong enough. The White House chief of staff, Leo McGarry, meets privately with the congressman to plead his case, but Representative Richardson will have none of it. He criticizes the president's team for failing to back the stronger provisions he supports.

In the end, Richardson will not budge, and the White House turns for support to those favoring a watered-down version of the law. The legislation passes, but only after the staff reluctantly seeks help from the vice president, who will take credit for the bill's passage.

Much to the delight of many "political junkies" who grew attached to the show during its premier season, other episodes of *The West Wing* touched on real-world issues from the death penalty and campaign finance reform to the use of sampling in the national census and funding for public broadcasting.

The West Wing was, of course, fictional entertainment. Public policymaking is not always as dramatic as portrayed in the series. Many laws are passed and policies made without much controversy and without some of the trade-offs and compromises that many Americans dislike. Nevertheless, by focusing on the clash of power, priorities, and interests over the most visible issues, this unique show has helped establish a new and more refreshing image of the complex dynamics involved in passing laws and making policies.

Sources: Information on the show can be found at a number of websites. The official site was located at www.nbc.com/ The_West_Wing/.

Travelers and consumers have also been protected by government in the past. For many years, air, rail and bus passenger service was regulated by the Civil Aeronautics Board (CAB) and the Interstate Commerce Commission (ICC). The CAB was terminated in 1978, and the ICC in 1995, and those functions unrelated to passenger service (e.g., safety) were transferred to other agencies. Today, passenger service in all three areas is essentially unregulated. On the consumer side, the Federal Trade Commission (FTC) tries to keep businesses from using false advertising to deceive consumers. During Jimmy Carter's presidency, the FTC and related regulatory agencies increased their level of activity to keep businesses in line and protect the consumer. During Reagan's and George H. W. Bush's administrations, however, the activity at the FTC and other consumer protection agencies abated.[41] Under the Clinton administration, the FTC returned to a more activist role on certain issues, especially those related to tobacco and privacy on the Internet. In most areas, however, the FTC has become more reactive than proactive. In April 2006, for example, when gas prices rose dramatically across the United States, the FTC was urged by members of Congress to investigate. The agency responded that it would look into anticompetitive practices, but was not empowered to take action against the price increases themselves.

Through **worker protection programs**, the federal government has extended its reach into the workplace as well, especially in the areas of discrimination, workers' rights, and occupational safety and health. **Equal employment opportunity programs** prohibit discrimination in the workplace on the basis of race, sex, religion, national origin, or handicapped status. In addition, the federal government has required companies doing business with it to undertake affirmative action aimed at improving employment and promotion opportunities for minorities, women, the handicapped, and other groups that have traditionally suffered from workplace discrimination. Although these antidiscrimination programs have been in place for nearly two decades, they remain extremely controversial and are constantly being challenged in the courts (see Chapter 4, on the heritage of rights and liberties).

The best-known occupational safety and health program was established in 1970 under the Occupational Safety and Health Act. The primary goal of this legislation was "to assure so far as possible every working man and woman in the Nation safe and healthy work conditions." The act created the *Occupational Safety and Health Administration (OSHA)* to implement this policy through regulations and on-site inspections.

OSHA's regulations and enforcement programs have been controversial from the start. Many critics found its early regulations to be both trivial and costly. By 1986, however, OSHA had issued standards that would eliminate or minimize workers' exposure to a number of highly suspect materials, such as asbestos, vinyl chloride, arsenic, benzene, lead, ethylene oxide, and cotton dust. The agency also set workplace standards for construction sites, grain elevators, and chemical plants, where hazardous materials were handled. Although still subject to criticism, OSHA remains an important part of federal policies dealing with worker protection.

Worker protection programs Government programs that protect workers in the areas of discrimination, workers' rights, and occupational safety and health.

Equal employment opportunity Federal programs developed under civil rights legislation that prohibit workplace and other forms of discrimination on the basis of race, sex, religion, national origin, or handicapped status.

The Regulation of Worker Safety

The regulation of mine safety has been a job of the federal government for decades, but the effectiveness of these efforts come to public view only when tragedy strikes. Here black ribbons are tied to a fence at the Sago Mine in West Virginia where twelve miners died in an accident in January 2006.

In addition to OSHA, several other agencies are involved in workplace safety and health regulation. For example, agencies such as the *Mine Health and Safety Administration* and the *Nuclear Regulatory Commission* have jurisdiction over workplace conditions in specific industries. Overall, these agencies and programs represent a federal commitment to protecting workers from workplace hazards.

Social regulation policies have not been without their critics, who claim that their efforts are misdirected. Some of these critics accuse the government of interfering too much in the workings of the open marketplace through these regulations. They consider the laws of supply and demand to be the best means of protecting consumers and workers, and they worry about the costs of social regulatory policy.

Those who support social regulations, however, complain that the rules are still too few and that they are not enforced stringently enough. Consequently, consumer advocates such as Ralph Nader have been calling for a revival of the consumer protection movement that achieved so much in the 1960s and 1970s. On worker protection issues, some advocates of a comprehensive industrial policy for the United States have urged legislation that would establish a higher minimum wage, protect workers from sudden plant closings, and increase worker participation in corporate decisions.

Social Welfare Policies

FOCUS
QUESTION

**WHAT DOES THE FEDERAL GOVERNMENT DO TO ASSURE
THE ECONOMIC WELL-BEING OF INDIVIDUALS?**

Poor laws British laws enacted in the early 1600s that made local communities responsible for taking care of their own needy and sick. They were used as the basis for American social policies early in the nation's history.

Social welfare policies have deep roots in American history. America's earliest social policies were based on England's **poor laws** — enacted in the early 1600s — which made local communities responsible for taking care of their own needy and sick. Each town was to select an overseer for the poor, who was to dispense charity to the needy and to provide able-bodied men with work. State governments became involved in aiding the needy during the 1800s. Many states abolished local debtor's prisons, instituted child labor laws, mandated public education, and supported the creation of institutions to care for the orphaned, insane, blind and deaf, epileptic, or destitute, and for others who were in need. These state and local efforts continued to expand into the twentieth century.[42]

Except for a few small federal grant-in-aid programs to the states (described in Chapter 3, on federalism and intergovernmental relations), the national government did not become actively involved in social welfare policy until the Great Depression. The first national programs followed the same pattern as the traditional state and local efforts by attempting to meet the needs of the poor or to improve their circumstances. Beginning in the 1930s, national policies focused on promoting the general welfare through social programs for all Americans, regardless of their income level.[43] Thus, when we discuss welfare policy, we must address at least two types of government programs: those that provide benefits and services only to the poor and those that help meet the needs of the general public.[44]

Aiding the Poor

Federal policies aimed explicitly at helping those in need went through a major overhaul in 1996 with passage of the *Personal Responsibility and Work Opportunity Reconciliation Act.* To appreciate the significance of those changes, we must understand the welfare system that the 1996 act replaced.

Federal assistance programs Federal welfare programs that took three forms: *general assistance* in the form of cash and commodities; *work assistance* in the form of jobs and job training; and *categorical assistance* targeted at specific populations.

The Old Welfare System. Under the previous system for aiding the poor, federal welfare policies took three distinct forms:[45] **general assistance**, given in cash (such as emergency assistance) or in the form of food and other commodities or the means for buying them, such as food stamps, to those in need; **work assistance**, offering jobs or job-training programs; and **categorical assistance**, targeted at specific populations (for example, aid to families with dependent children and supplemental assistance to children with disabilities). Almost all the programs in these categories were intergovernmental programs, involving state and local funding and participation. (See Chapter 3, on federalism and intergovernmental relations.) The resulting welfare system was a complex arrangement of programs that drew criticism from all corners of the political arena. Among those criticisms, three stood out and helped shape the 1996 reforms.

First, the system was perceived as *too centralized and inflexible.* Many of the federal programs were designed to guarantee that people who needed help had roughly equivalent access to minimal welfare benefits, whether they resided in New York City or Jackson, Mississippi. This goal required that the national government establish basic program standards and ensure the implementation of minimal eligibility requirements throughout the country. It did so through specific provisions attached to the categorical grants it provided to the states to carry out the various programs. While the level of benefits for different federally funded programs might vary from state to state, program standards and a minimal level of benefits were set and enforced in Washington, D.C.

Initially, many Americans accepted this centralized system as necessary in order to guarantee some minimal assistance to the poor, no matter where they lived. By the 1980s, however, critics were successfully arguing that program centralization had gone too far and was hindering state and local efforts to deal with the special circumstances and needs of local residents. Attempts to modify or adapt federal programs to local circumstances through special waivers, which were allowed under existing law, were often rejected or severely limited. Starting in 1993, the Clinton administration invited and sanctioned a great many more such waivers, but the process was unwieldy and existing laws restricted allowable innovations.

The second criticism of the older welfare system was that it created *too much dependence* on government programs among the poor.[46] A growing chorus of critics from both the political left and right noted that existing welfare programs gave recipients little, if any, incentive to seek employment or job-related training. Instead, the system seemed to create a culture of poverty that increased the dependence of welfare recipients on government programs. Together with changing economic conditions, welfare programs were producing a social and economic underclass that had no incentive to break out of the cycle of impoverishment.

The large and growing costs of the existing welfare system gave rise to the third criticism. The system was proving *too expensive* for a nation that was increasingly concerned about the climbing national debt. Entitlement programs — programs in which all eligible individuals had a right to the program's benefits — dominated the welfare approach, requiring open-ended funding. In other words, no matter what federal, state, and local governments might budget for these programs in any given year, they were obligated to spend as much as was necessary to meet the needs of those who were entitled to the benefits. This obligation created uncertainty and anxiety about future expenditures — especially as projections indicated a steep rise in entitlement costs by 2000.

These and related criticisms of the welfare system helped to fuel reform efforts and eventually led to passage of the Personal Responsibility and Work Opportunity Reconciliation Act, which President Clinton signed into law on August 22, 1996. Another factor that spurred elected officials to action was the growing political popularity of reform. When he was running for the presidency in 1992, Clinton had promised to "end welfare as we know it." The Republican majority in the 104th Congress was also anxious to overhaul the welfare system before facing the voters in November 1996. These political pressures created the incentive for policymakers to make the most significant changes in American welfare policies in more than three decades.

The New Welfare System.[47] The 1996 welfare reform legislation addressed the three major criticisms of the previous system. It gave more power to the states, focused on the goal of reducing dependence on welfare, and placed limits on government spending for welfare programs.

Empowering the states.   The Personal Responsibility and Work Opportunity Reconciliation Act changed federalism as much as it changed the welfare system. To replace many of the highly centralized and inflexible categorical programs of the past, the 1996 reforms created a block grant titled *Temporary Assistance for Needy Families (TANF)*, funded by monies that had previously been allocated to Aid to Families with Dependent Children (AFDC), emergency assistance, and work assistance programs. TANF provided each state with resources to accomplish the legislation's four basic goals: (1) assisting needy families so that children could be cared for in their own homes or in the homes of relatives; (2) ending the dependence of needy parents on government benefits by promoting job preparation, work, and marriage; (3) reducing the incidence of out-of-wedlock pregnancies; and (4) encouraging the formation and maintenance of two-parent families.

Changing Welfare as We Knew It

In August 1996, President Clinton signed a welfare reform act that significantly changed assistance to the poor.

A New Beginning

While TANF gave the states considerably more power to shape their own welfare policies and programs, Congress did set some standards. To receive federal funding under TANF, states had to submit an acceptable welfare assistance plan to the national government by July 1, 1997. In that plan, each state had to demonstrate that its efforts would be equal to at least 80 percent of what it had spent on federally funded programs in fiscal year 1994. The plan also had to include provisions that would require most recipients to seek at least part-time employment after two years, as well as provisions that would end eligibility for TANF-funded programs for most recipients after five years. In addition, each state had to promise that it would hold the administrative costs of any programs funded under TANF to 15 percent or less of budget.

Critical Thinking

Can we trust the states to provide sufficient assistance for the needy, or must there be a national standard for welfare programs?

Ending dependence.   Instead of establishing a federal work assistance program, TANF requires the states to develop their own assistance programs offering welfare recipients incentives and opportunities to obtain employment and get off federally funded welfare. For example, the program was structured so that by 1999, in 90 percent of two-parent families who were still receiving TANF-related assistance, at least one adult would be gainfully employed or engaged in a job-training program.

The law also contained provisions allowing states to reduce or cut off assistance to a variety of groups. For example, the states can refuse support for teenage parents who do not participate in training or educational programs or who refuse to live in their parent's home. Anyone who refuses to help determine the paternity of children receiving aid can also lose some or all assistance. Furthermore, states could withhold additional support for children born to unwed mothers who are already on welfare. Persons convicted of drug-related felonies were not eligible for any federally funded cash or food stamp assistance under the new law, although states could aid their families if they so chose. These and other provisions of the 1996 act reflected the goal of ending welfare dependence.

Capping the costs of welfare.   In funding the TANF program, Congress limited federal spending to $16.4 billion through fiscal year 2002, thus stopping the open-ended funding of the past. In addition, the law expressly stated that the programs funded under TANF are not entitlements, and that both eligibility and benefits can be adjusted to keep the programs within spending limits. The law also included some additional funding provisions for states facing special circumstances, but even this amount was set at a specific level. Individual states could spend as much as they wished on other programs, but they would have to do so without federal financial assistance. Most analysts agreed that without the incentive of receiving help from Washington, most states were unlikely to provide a great deal of additional assistance to the poor. In short, the 1996 act was expected to rein in the growth of spending on welfare at all levels of government.

Other provisions.   While the 1996 act changed the structure of AFDC and other major entitlement programs, it did not make radical changes in some other

Social Programs

Head Start is one of the most successful federal social programs to emerge from President Lyndon Johnson's Great Society agenda.

parts of the welfare system. For example, *Supplemental Security Income (SSI)* was created in 1972 to provide direct monthly benefits from the federal government to the aged, blind, and disabled, regardless of the level of assistance they receive from other programs. Although the program was not eliminated in 1996, a major portion of it, affecting disabled children (and often used to supplement assistance to poor families), was modified to tighten eligibility requirements.

Another major entitlement program, *food stamps*, was also left mostly intact. Begun in 1961 as an experiment, the program slowly expanded until it became the primary source of food assistance for the poor. By 1994, more than 27 million people—about one-tenth of the U.S. population—were receiving some level of food-stamp support. Since eligibility for food stamps was often tied to AFDC and other programs replaced by TANF, some parts of the program were modified. For example, to receive food stamps, able-bodied recipients must fulfill work requirements. States were also permitted to simplify the operation of the food-stamp program and related programs.

In the case of both SSI and food stamps, the 1996 act initially made almost all noncitizens ineligible for either program. This particular provision of the act proved very controversial, especially in urban areas and populous states, where large numbers of political refugees and elderly legal immigrants resided. Without access to these and related federal entitlement programs, meeting the needs of poor noncitizens was likely to be a major burden for states and localities. By 1998, Congress and several states had passed legislation easing this limitation for many refugees and other legal immigrant groups.

In the area of health care, *Medicaid* remained the primary program for aiding the poor. Established in 1965 as part of the social security system (see later discussion), it was providing some form of assistance to more than 31 million Americans by 1994. Among those receiving Medicaid, about half were children and another 25 percent were elderly or disabled.

Although the 1996 act did not have a direct impact on Medicaid, its provisions significantly affected Medicaid eligibility, which had been automatically linked to eligibility for AFDC and other welfare programs. The 1996 act severed that automatic link, and eligibility for Medicaid was modified to maintain the entitlement based on mostly pre-TANF standards. The law also gave states the right to modify eligibility standards slightly and even to refuse Medicaid assistance to some who refused to find work. For the most part, however, Medicaid was left as a major entitlement program in America's welfare system.

Many other federally funded programs—including housing assistance, child nutrition, child care, and child support—were linked in some way to programs modified by the 1996 act, and each was affected in some way by the legislation. The true impact and long-term implications of welfare reform on these and other programs are becoming clear as the new act is implemented. The number of Americans on welfare rolls declined sharply over the first three years of the reform, and many of the former recipients have found employment. The overall number of Americans living at the official poverty level also declined. Nevertheless, even as the act came up for renewal in 2002, there were still many questions about how the poor would fare given the tighter economic conditions.[48]

Social Insurance

Although welfare programs for the poor have been a major part of America's social policies, many other policies have addressed the needs of all Americans, regardless of their level of income. Many people try to save for that rainy day when they cannot count on receiving a paycheck; few, however, actually set aside enough income to deal with such crises. **Social insurance programs** are intended to cover income losses caused by long-term illness, unemployment, retirement, and other interruptions to a person's working life. Funding for these benefits comes from "contributions" (actually involuntary taxes) that are levied on both employers and employees and placed in special trust funds. Once a person has made a minimum number of payments into a trust fund, he or she is entitled to participate in the program's benefits.

Among major industrialized nations, the United States was one of the last to adopt such a plan.[49] Unemployment insurance and retirement benefits were established by the Social Security Act of 1935. Under Social Security, employees and employers contribute a certain portion of employees' earnings to several trust funds administered by the *Social Security Administration (SSA)*. The SSA is supposed to use those funds to pay unemployment claims and to provide monthly pension checks when a worker retires. At the outset, the system assured

Social insurance programs Social policy programs administered by the Social Security Administration (SSA) that are intended to cover income losses due to long-term illnesses, unemployment, retirement, and other interruptions to a person's working life.

most American workers at least minimal coverage when they were temporarily unemployed or when they retired.

Over the years, social insurance programs have grown considerably. In addition to unemployment and old-age pension insurance, social security now applies to the disabled and to the survivors (widows, widowers, and children) of deceased contributors. The number of Americans covered by Social Security's general social insurance programs has expanded. In 1940, Social Security covered only 20 percent of the U.S. work force. By the late 1990s, the old-age, survivors', disability, and related federal programs covered 96 percent of the American labor force. A smaller portion, approximately 90 percent, was protected by unemployment insurance.

With the passage of *Medicare* in 1965, the federal government also began providing health insurance for the elderly and disabled. The basic Medicare program provided insurance for hospitalization, as well as extended care and home health services. It also contained a voluntary supplementary medical insurance program to help offset the costs of physicians' fees, lab tests, medical supplies and appliances, and related items. By 2001, 40 million elderly Americans were enrolled in the basic hospital insurance program, and most of those individuals paid an additional monthly premium to take part in the supplementary health insurance program. An additional 5.7 million were enrolled in an optional plan that helped them pay for their participation in private health-care plans.

Despite steady increases in the number of participants who contribute, the social insurance programs under Social Security—especially old-age pensions and Medicare—have faced short-term financial problems. For decades contributions to the SSA trust funds had typically equaled or exceeded the amount paid out in benefits, but by the early 1980s it was evident that significant problems were emerging. The American population was growing older, and policymakers had been expanding and increasing social security benefit levels for years. Critics warned of a pending crisis, but they were generally ignored until 1982, when the old-age and survivors' insurance trust fund—the largest of the SSA funds—had to borrow billions of dollars from other SSA trust funds (for instance, the disability and hospital trust funds) in order to maintain a minimal level of reserves for the future.

In 1983, a National Commission on Social Security Reform, chaired by Alan Greenspan (who would later serve as chair of the Federal Reserve System), issued a report with recommendations for dealing with the immediate problems. Congress responded by raising the retirement age for eligible beneficiaries from the then-current sixty-five to sixty-seven by the year 2027. Those who choose to retire before the age of sixty-five will have a cut of 20 to 30 percent in their benefits.[50] In addition, policymakers have been increasing the amount that each American contributes to Social Security insurance. The Social Security tax rate for all participating employees increased from 4.8 percent in 1970 to 6.13 percent in 1980, and then to 7.65 percent in 1990. Furthermore, in 1970 only the first $7,800 of income was taxed; by 2001 the maximum taxable earnings had increased to $80,400 for old-age, survivors', and disability insurance (OASDI), with additional taxes (1.45 percent for employees) applied on all income for Medicare insurance. Employers match those payments, and self-employed individuals pay the full amount (i.e., 12.4 percent for OASDI and 2.9 percent for Medicare). All this is being done in an attempt to keep the program solvent as far into the future as possible.

During the early 1990s, the long-term future of social security became a major issue as critics pointed out that some of the Social Security trust funds were projected to run out as early as 2011. The 1983 changes, they argued, were merely short-term patches, and a more significant overhaul of the system was required if the funds were to be saved from bankruptcy as the baby-boom generation began to reach retirement age. Led by the Concord Coalition, a group of influential citizens who had served in major government posts, the critics called for reforms that would reduce future financial obligations while expanding the options available to those who would otherwise rely on Social Security for support in their old age.[51] Defenders of the existing policies pointed out that forecasts of trust fund bankruptcies are based on the most pessimistic assumptions about the future of the American economy. For these opponents of radical change, the use of more realistic assumptions shows that most of the major trust funds in the Social Security system are likely to remain solvent until well beyond 2075.[52]

In early 2005, President Bush made the reform of Social Security a top priority for his second term in office. His proposal for "partial privatization" of the system generated considerable debate, but by May 2005 the initiative had lost the political energy it required to pass a congressional vote. Although Bush continued to promote Social Security reform into 2006, the likelihood of a major change in the program was not great.[53] Nevertheless, the issue of the future of Social Security will not disappear.[54]

Critical Thinking

Is it fair for government to support the elderly with money raised through payroll taxes on younger workers?

Conclusion: The Complexity of American Public Policy

We have touched on only a few of the major domestic policy arenas in which the federal government is involved today. The federal government has been extremely active in many other areas, including efforts to provide mass transit, construct new and safer highways, promote the conservation of our natural resources, and deal with energy shortages. Although each of those policy arenas has its own distinctive characteristics, each must contend with the popular myth of government as a necessary evil. That is, policymakers must design and implement policies in a way that will show an ever-suspicious public that the benefits gained from any given government program outweigh the perceived costs in terms of lost liberty, increased dependency, and increased inefficiencies.

This is no easy task, for the reality is that the world is more complex than the necessary evil myth implies. Public policies are responses to problems that we face as a society, and those problems do not *necessarily* require government's involvement. Rather, the decision to develop governmental solutions is often a choice that we make through the political process. As many economists will argue, there are various nongovernmental solutions to many of our collective problems. Do we really need *public* schools to educate our children? Must we rely on government alone to provide us with trash collection or to regulate radio and television broadcasting? Do we really need government to provide us with libraries and parks and roads and hospitals? Both logically and historically, the answer is no. These various policies and services can be provided privately, either by businesses or by charitable institutions. When we decide to have government address these needs, it is by political choice rather than out of necessity.

Nor is the public solution always evil. Governmental actions can enhance our ability to deal with poverty and inequality;[55] they can have a positive impact on our exercise of our liberties as well as threatening those liberties.[56] The freedom to act in the open marketplace is made possible by the existence of a legal infrastructure that helps to maintain the rules of exchange and punishes those who commit fraud or renege on their contractual obligations. Government is also capable of delivering public goods and services without relying on heavy-handed bureaucratic methods. By adopting innovative management practices, many federal agencies have demonstrated that they can conduct the public's business in an efficient and effective way.

Despite the complex reality that belies the myth of government as a necessary evil, there is some benefit to maintaining it as a limiting force in the American political system. If nothing else, it serves a useful function by keeping the public vigilant against possible abuses of governmental power while giving policymakers pause when they consider going "too far" in the design and implementation of public policies and programs.

Tying It Together

FOCUS QUESTIONS RECAP

* How is public policy made?
* What has been the federal government's role in dealing with issues related to education?
* How does the federal government attempt to manage the American economy?
* What are the issues surrounding the federal government's efforts to enhance overall economic growth?
* How has the federal government used regulatory policies in dealing with economic, social, and environmental problems?
* What does the federal government do to assure the economic well-being of individuals?

CHAPTER SUMMARY

1. The attitudes of Americans toward public policy have been influenced by the "government is a necessary evil" myth. This myth has deep roots in U.S. history and has helped shape what government does and how it does it.

2. The policymaking process in the United States is difficult to summarize because so many different policies emerge from so many different institutions. However, the overall process can be described in six stages: issue identification, agenda setting, policy formulation, policy adoption, policy implementation, and policy evaluation.

3. Within each stage, the method of decision making varies. Ideally, decisions would be made rationally, but in reality, decisions are often made incrementally — that is, through additions to and subtractions from current policies and programs. According to the elite model, decisions are made by a relatively small group of influential leaders who share a common perspective and common goals. Finally, many students of public policy have adopted a pluralist model, which holds that decisions are made as the result of pressures from a diverse population of interest groups.

4. Although education policy has traditionally been the concern of states and localities, the federal government has always played a role in dealing with issues of access, funding, and curriculum

content. Today, the stress is on issues of education quality and accountability.

5. The federal role in managing the economy has focused on monetary policy and fiscal policy approaches. In recent years, the issue of deficits and the national debt has become increasingly important.

6. Economic development policies of the federal government focus on issues of trade, tax incentives, industrial policy, and supply-side strategies.

7. Through rules made and enforced by various regulatory agencies, the federal government attempts to deal with economic, environmental, and social problems. In recent years there has been an effort to rely more on incentives and to move toward the "deregulation" of certain sectors of the economy.

8. Social welfare policies cover governmental actions to provide aid to low-income Americans and to promote the general welfare of all Americans.

9. No area of American domestic public policy escapes the pressures generated by the "necessary evil" myth. This is not necessarily bad, since policy debates and discussions invigorate the policymaking system. In addition, policies are often shaped and implemented in response to real or potential criticisms.

Key Terms

Public policies (405)
Issue identification (405)
Agenda setting (406)
Policy formulation (406)
Policy adoption (407)
Policy implementation (409)
Policy evaluation (409)
Rational model of decision making (410)
Incremental model of decision making (410)
Elite model of decision making (410)
Pluralist model of decision making (411)
Monetary policy (416)
Fiscal policy (418)
Keynesians (419)
Monetarists (419)

National debt (419)
Budget surplus (419)
Budget deficit (419)
Infrastructure projects (420)
Entitlement programs (420)
Economic development policies (423)
Tariffs (423)
Free trade (423)
Balance of trade (423)
Globalization (424)
Tax incentives (424)
Industrial policy (425)
Supply-side economics (426)
Economic regulatory policies (426)
Antitrust laws (427)

Net Work

Do you want to find out about the status of a particular piece of legislation that is in the news? Or how your state's U.S. senator or the U.S. representative from your district voted on a specific bill?

- When you want to research information on policymaking, the best place to start is the Library of Congress's "Thomas" site (**http://thomas.loc.gov**).

- Then, if you find yourself interested in a particular policy area, there are several other sites to explore. For example, you can learn about education policy by visiting the U.S. Department of Education website (**www.ed.gov**) or environmental programs by visiting the U.S. Environmental Protection Agency site (**www.epa.gov**).

- The news media are another important source of information on various policies and programs.

Some websites specialize in collecting links to other sites that deal with specific issues. A good example is found at **http://speakout.com**.

As an exercise, see what you can find out about the latest interest-rate policies of the Federal Reserve's Board of Governors. You can start by going to **www.economagic.com/fedbog.htm**, but you might also want to explore various news media, such as **www.cnnfn.com**, **http://cnbc.com**, or **www.bloomberg.com**. What was the Fed board's most recent decision concerning interest rates? What are the policy specialists saying about future policy directions? Will the Fed raise or lower interest rates over the next few months?

15

Foreign and Defense Policy

MYTH & REALITY

How vulnerable is the United States in the post–9/11 world, and what is America's vision of world order in these turbulent times?

FOCUS QUESTIONS

* What are the factors that are changing U.S. foreign and defense policies?

* What is the history of U.S. foreign and defense policy, and what does it tell us about America's role in the world today?

* Who is involved in the making of U.S. foreign and defense policies, and what roles do they play?

* What are the sources of diplomatic power available to those who conduct American foreign policy?

* What are the issues and choices facing those who make U.S. defense policies?

In post–9/11 America there is a growing concern with illegal immigration. According to some estimates, each year approximately 850,000 people enter the country without the necessary legal documents that are required under U.S. law. By some counts, there are nearly 12 million illegal immigrants already residing in the United States, a great many of whom entered through the U.S. border with Mexico. This has been occurring for quite some time, but what has officials most concerned is that the growing number of those entering at the Mexican border are not from Mexico. As one indicator of the problem, the *Denver Post* reported that, in 2005, 115,000 non-Mexicans were caught attempting to cross that border illegally. While in the past this number would have raised issues focused on the economic implications of this influx, today there are mounting concerns about security issues. According to one official, "[Agents] haven't encountered a terrorist crossing the southwest border at this point. But [the government is] concerned about the possibility."[1] It was in this atmosphere during the early part of 2006 that the U.S. Congress debated substantial revisions of the country's immigration laws — revisions that reflect major themes in today's U.S. foreign and defense policies.

One of these major themes, which we took note of in Chapter 1's discussion of September 11 and Hurricane Katrina, is the feeling of vulnerability that results when the country experiences tragic events. We also emphasized that this is not a new feeling for Americans, that it can be traced back to colonial times, and that there is no period in our country's history when the sense of vulnerability has really disappeared. In this chapter we will look more closely at this *myth of vulnerability,* and see the impact it has had on U.S. foreign and military policies for over two centuries. As we will see, this myth has substantial power because it seems to fit the realities that it describes. However, we will also see how it provides only partial insight into a complicated history, and how an accompanying myth, the *myth of the American project,* has provided an important sense of mission and purpose that complements the nation's need for security.

According to the myth of vulnerability, the United States must constantly guard against challenges to its territorial, political, and economic integrity. "We are and have always been a nation preoccupied with security," argue James Chace and Caleb Carr.[2] For at least the decades of the Cold War (generally dated from the end of World War II to the collapse of the Soviet Union in 1989), this preoccupation led to an urge to achieve "absolute security" in the face of immediate and potential challenges, both real and perceived. Many observers believed that after the fall of the Soviet Union, with America the one remaining superpower in the post–Cold War era, Americans would feel less vulnerable and more secure. But, as we shall see, that has not been the case. From the Persian Gulf War of 1991 to the war on terrorism initiated after the attacks on the World Trade Center and the Pentagon in 2001, Americans have retained their sense that the United States will never escape from the many threats emanating from a hostile world.

In its contemporary version, the myth of vulnerability has been accompanied by a belief that America's exposure to these threats cannot be addressed by withdrawing behind a "wall" of isolation. Rather, there is a strong commitment to

Attacks on America

The American myth of vulnerability is reinforced by the memory of two major attacks on U.S. territory: the Japanese attack on Pearl Harbor in 1941 and the attack on the World Trade Center and the Pentagon in 2001.

the idea that the country's vulnerability would increase if it ever decided to disengage from world affairs. As an example, they point to U.S. policies in the 1920s and 1930s. As discussed later in the chapter, between the two world wars, most Americans supported this nation's withdrawal from world affairs. The United States involved itself in only those events and crises that seemed to be in our narrowly defined national interest. Looking back on that policy, many analysts call American isolationism a major mistake and speculate as to whether a more actively engaged U.S. foreign policy might have prevented the rise of Hitler — and, in consequence, World War II.

There is a vocal minority who take an opposite stand, expressing a position of putting "America first" and calling for the United States to assume a perspective that would minimize its involvement and entanglements in world affairs. Led by national figures such as former third-party presidential candidates Patrick Buchanan[3] and Ross Perot, this group seeks a return to an earlier era when the myth of vulnerability was complemented by a strong belief in America's "virtuous isolation" from world affairs.[4] But as the American public's reaction to September 11 demonstrated, the once strong pull of isolationism has been replaced with a world view that accepts the inevitability of U.S. involvement in world affairs.

As a complement to the myth of vulnerability, the *myth of the American project* has taken several forms. According to Walter Russell Mead,[5] historically the United States has linked its interest in security to visions of world order that would make America less vulnerable. In one such vision, the American project — its mission or purpose — is a moral one in which the United States seeks to play a major role in establishing and defending a benign international legal order in which democracy and free markets can thrive in peace. Associated with President Woodrow Wilson's efforts to create the League of Nations after World War I, it is a vision that links American security to the support and success of bodies like the United Nations.

A second vision for the American project is to foster a world order that best serves the economic interests of the United States. As we see in the discussion that follows, this is closely associated with the views of Alexander Hamilton, the first secretary of the treasury, who was committed to doing whatever was necessary to give the new nation a stable economic standing in the world economic order of the day.

A third vision for the American project stresses the need for the United States to shape its foreign and defense policies to protect and sustain our country's democratic institutions. Linked historically to the views of Thomas Jefferson, this vision regards the United States as an exceptional political system and society that requires its leaders to be on guard against risky entanglements that might put the nation's unique political qualities at risk. The mission of the United States in world affairs is to stand out as an example for others to emulate, but to avoid getting involved in alliances or international arrangements that might sacrifice America's special "democratic experiment."

Finally, there is a fourth, more nationalistic vision of the American project, one that gives weight to national honor and the wisdom and judgment of the American public and its leaders at any particular time. This view is associated with the domestic populism of President Andrew Jackson, and in many respects shares the Jeffersonian vision of the United States as an exceptional country that should avoid foreign entanglements. But where the Jeffersonians are skeptical and weary about international affairs, Jacksonians are explicitly hostile to the idea of engaging in global politics on terms set by other nations. For Jacksonians, the special status of American democracy extends to how the United States conducts itself once it is drawn into world affairs. Jackson had little tolerance or respect for the niceties of diplomacy or international rules, and he felt the U.S. should follow its own code of behavior in its relations with other nations.

It is easy to see how each of these visions of the American project — and their associated views of America's mission in the world — would have a significant impact on the conduct of U.S. foreign and defense policies. Mead argues that these four visions of the American project (Wilsonian, Hamiltonian, Jeffersonian, and Jacksonian) have, in various forms and mixtures at various times in U.S. history, provided the logic for the country's foreign and defense policies. Indeed, when tied to the diverse feelings of national vulnerability over time, they offer us a means for understanding how these policies emerged and how they have changed over the years. For the Wilsonians, Americans will only be safe in a democratic world, and U.S. foreign policymakers should be guided by a sense of moral obligation to promote a world order reflecting democratic values. For the Hamiltonians, the greatest threats come from a world order that undermines the economic interests of the United States, and so American policymakers must see foreign affairs in terms of national economic self-interest. Jeffersonians, by contrast, regard the United States as an exemplar of modern democratic governance—a model to be nurtured and protected as much as possible from the corruption of international entanglements and intrigues. Finally, for Jacksonians it is the integrity and honor of the United States that is most vulnerable, and the country's foreign policymakers must be prepared to do whatever is necessary to defeat those who might threaten either.

It is within this context of these myth-driven feelings of vulnerability and mission that we take a closer look at America's foreign and defense policies.

Changing Parameters of Foreign and Defense Policies

FOCUS QUESTION   WHAT ARE THE FACTORS THAT ARE CHANGING U.S. FOREIGN AND DEFENSE POLICIES?

Americans tend to think of foreign and defense policies in relatively narrow terms. When they think about foreign policy, most Americans focus on the relations that the president and the U.S. State Department have with foreign nations. Foreign policy, from this perspective, is what happens when the president attends a summit meeting or the secretary of state attempts to resolve some dispute through "shuttle diplomacy." Such a view would also focus attention on the plan or military strategy our government has for achieving America's goals in the world community. These views are understandable, since these are the events and policies covered in the mass media and the ones that are described in history texts as our foreign and defense policies.

In today's "globalized" world (see Chapter 14, on domestic policy and policymaking), we need to take a broader perspective on U.S. foreign and defense policies. The United States doesn't have a single, overarching foreign policy, and its military policies are not limited to strategic plans for the defense of the country. Rather, our foreign and defense policies are as complex as the world they operate in. They involve a great many more actors than those in the White House, the State Department, and the Pentagon. On a practical level, America's **foreign and defense policies** cover all those governmental decisions and actions that are intended to deal with problems and issues in the international arena. Those policies are constantly being adapted to changes in both the types of issues and the actors who are found in that arena.

Foreign and defense policies Those governmental decisions and actions that are intended to deal with problems and issues in the international arena.

Changing Issues

In the past, those policies focused primarily on *territorial disputes* and *economic trade issues*. The early history of U.S. foreign policy is filled with examples of actions that were taken to secure or expand the country's borders, the most famous example being Thomas Jefferson's purchase of the Louisiana Territory from France in 1803. There is also a long history of negotiations and military actions to protect the young country's ability to trade in world markets. The first foreign mission conducted by the U.S. Marines, for example, was a deployment to Tripoli in 1804 to prevent pirates from operating from that port and other parts of the Barbary Coast.

Territorial and economic issues are still important today, but the U.S. government must also contend with more complex questions. *Social issues* are receiving more attention today than ever before, and the United States has responded in a number of ways, from sending relief to areas like Africa's Sahel desert region suffering from starvation as a result of drought, to assistance in the worldwide fight against the spread of HIV/AIDS. American policymakers have found themselves engaged in international efforts to contend with illiteracy, birth control, slavery, ethnic and gender discrimination, and a wide range of other humanitarian issues. *Environmental issues* such as global warming and the protection of endangered species have also become an important part of the American foreign policy agenda. And even the traditional economic problems of the past have become transformed by the growth of a globalized economy that is no longer contained by national borders.

New Actors

International organizations Bodies composed of member states that provide an institutional arena for today's world politics; an example is the United Nations.

Regional organizations International organizations composed of nations from a particular area of the world that perform defensive or economic functions.

Transnational organizations Large-scale nongovernmental organizations that perform relatively specialized functions across state borders; the Red Cross is an example.

Multinational corporations (MNCs) Large, private, for-profit organizations that operate transnationally; General Electric and IBM are examples.

The change in issues is also reflected in a fundamental change in the number of international actors that American foreign policymakers have to deal with. In the past, foreign policies were a matter of state-to-state, leader-to-leader negotiations. When the United States wanted to solve its territorial or trade problems, it would send delegations to London or Paris to speak with the foreign ministers of those countries. With the advent of **international organizations** such as the United Nations, the range of relevant actors was expanded, and in the latter part of the twentieth century the variety of important actors in the world arena was greatly expanded. Immediately after World War II, there were just over 50 member states in the newly formed UN; today there are 189. The number of international organizations has also proliferated, from the UN itself to more specialized agencies such as the International Monetary Fund, the World Bank, and the World Trade Organization (discussed later in the chapter). The United States is also involved with a growing number of **regional organizations**, such as the Organization of American States (OAS) and the North Atlantic Treaty Organization (NATO).

An even more significant development has been the growth in the number, types, and influence of transnational organizations. **Transnational organizations** are large-scale nongovernmental organizations that perform relatively specialized functions across international borders. Some have long histories of involvement in international affairs (for example, the Roman Catholic Church or the Red Cross), while others have come on the scene relatively recently (Médecins Sans Frontières, also known as Doctors Without Borders, was formed in 1971). Some are private, for-profit organizations, including **multinational corporations** such as General Electric and media giant VIACOM, while others are not-for-profit

Nongovernmental organizations (NGOs) Transnational, not-for-profit organizations that operate as advocacy groups in the international arena.

advocacy and service-oriented groups (usually called **nongovernmental organizations**, or NGOs) such as Greenpeace and the Salvation Army.

Today's international environment poses a challenge not only for U.S. policymakers, but also for the average American who is trying to comprehend the country's role in a globalized world. A first step is to understand the history of U.S. involvement in world affairs.

Vulnerability in Historical Perspective

FOCUS QUESTION   WHAT IS THE HISTORY OF U.S. FOREIGN AND DEFENSE POLICY, AND WHAT DOES IT TELL US ABOUT AMERICA'S ROLE IN THE WORLD TODAY?

There has always been some truth to the myth of a vulnerable America. Many historians contend that it was the country's vulnerability to an external attack that eventually convinced many otherwise reluctant leaders of the newly independent country to convene the 1787 Philadelphia Convention. That meeting ultimately produced a new constitution that strengthened the central government's capacity to deal with foreign affairs.[6] From the outset, however, the question "vulnerable to what?" was central to how the sense of vulnerability would shape American foreign and defense policies.

1789–1823: The Foundations of American Foreign Policy

When George Washington put together his first cabinet, he drew together the two individuals who would eventually lay the foundations for American foreign policies: Secretary of State Thomas Jefferson and Secretary of the Treasury Alexander Hamilton. As noted above, each took a distinct view as to what should constitute an appropriate approach to foreign affairs. Hamilton's primary goal was to make certain that the United States would become a viable economic entity, and to that end he sought good trade relations with Britain, which at that time had established itself as the world's leading economic power. This ran counter to Jefferson's admiration and support for the French, who were often engaged in conflicts with England. Jefferson also had concerns about Hamilton's designs for the country as a "commercial republic," and instead wanted to foster and protect an agrarian democracy that focused attention on the development and needs of local communities. Their fundamental difference in perspectives emerged from distinct views of the new nation's vulnerabilities, and each had an equally distinct vision for America's role in world affairs. As important, both men influenced the decisions of George Washington. This was most evident in Washington's often-cited **Farewell Address** published in 1796, which supported Hamilton's vision of a foreign policy that fostered commercial trade while taking up Jefferson's view of avoiding "entangling alliances" in European affairs.

Washington's Farewell Address A statement to the American public by George Washington that is regarded as the basic expression of the foundations of U.S. foreign policy.

The controversies and intrigues of this early period were complicated by the events in Europe, particularly the rise of French power (especially under Napoleon) and the British efforts to maintain their position as the dominant economic power. American presidents were pressured by both sides, and at times it looked as if the United States would join in the hostilities against one or the other. Both John Adams and Jefferson avoided going to war with either nation, although both were constantly engaged in diplomatic efforts to keep U.S. neutrality intact. Eventually, however, the United States went to war with Britain. The British attack on Washington, D.C., during the War of 1812 provided substantial support for the worst fears of the American public, for it demonstrated that the country was in fact vulnerable to direct attack.

Interestingly, the years following the War of 1812 witnessed an acceptance by Jefferson (by now a retired senior statesman) and his followers of the need for an alliance with Britain. In 1823, President James Monroe issued a policy statement that became the primary position of the United States for decades to come. "In the wars of the European powers in matters relating to themselves we have never taken any part," declares the **Monroe Doctrine**, "nor does it comport with our policy to do so." Nevertheless, he noted that the United States would regard any intrusion into the affairs of Latin America as an intrusion into the affairs of the United States. On the surface, this seemed like a bold assertion for a country that less than a decade earlier had suffered a foreign invasion. But in fact, the statement was issued with the implied blessing of Great Britain, which was happy to have the United States take on this role in the Western Hemisphere. The Americans were emerging as a pivotal actor in the complex world economic system that Britain had established.

Monroe Doctrine An American policy, established in 1823, that warned European nations not to interfere in Latin America while promising that the United States would not interfere in European affairs.

1823–1914: Isolationism, Unilateralism, and Expansionism

As part of the British-dominated world economic order of the nineteenth century, the United States was in a unique geographic position that permitted it to pursue the basic tenets of Washington's call for commercial relations without political entanglements. These views led to the adoption of policies that stressed isolationism and unilateralism. Combined with the myth of vulnerability, these approaches eventually created an atmosphere conducive to a policy of expansionism.

Isolationism meant that policymakers attempted to maintain American neutrality and to avoid any direct involvement in European affairs that might have dragged the new nation into commitments that would have made it politically or militarily vulnerable.

Isolationism characterized many American foreign and defense policies until World War I. But we should not conclude that the United States did not take part in world affairs at all during the 1800s. Our nation maintained an army and navy, engaged in diplomatic relations, and even took military actions to protect its neutrality and to assert its interests in the international arena. Policymakers were particularly concerned with protecting American interests in the Western Hemisphere.

Isolationism A basic tenet of American policy before World War I that advocated American neutrality and avoidance of direct involvement in European affairs.

Unilateralism The pre–World War I American policy of taking action independently in foreign affairs, avoiding political or military alliances.

Expansionism The pre–World War I American policy that led the United States to extend its boundaries to the Pacific while extending its influence in other areas of the world, for example, the Pacific islands, the Caribbean, and Asia.

What characterized these actions was the second tenet of U.S. foreign policy: **unilateralism**. Under unilateralism, Americans "went it alone" in world affairs and avoided political or military alliances. But acting unilaterally did not mean acting without consideration of what else was taking place in an international arena clearly dominated by British influence.

Expansionism emerged as the third major factor in American policies during the 1800s. The drive to expand U.S. boundaries from the Atlantic to the Pacific often influenced our conduct of foreign affairs. During that period, the United States purchased the Louisiana Territory from France, Alaska from Russia, and portions of the Southwest from Mexico. Territorial expansion also played a role in America's wars with Mexico (1846–1848), with a number of Native American tribes in the West, and with Spain (1898). The Spanish-American War turned out to be an important turning point, for as part of the conflict's settlement, Spain gave the United States its first colonial possessions: Puerto Rico, Cuba, Guam, and the Philippines. Earlier agreements and actions had extended U.S. control in Alaska, Hawaii, and the Sandwich Islands in the Pacific. Furthermore, during the 1890s and early 1900s, American presidents intervened politically and militarily in Nicaragua, Panama, the Dominican Republic, Haiti, and other Central American and Caribbean nations.

To some degree, U.S. expansionism in the nineteenth century was a response to Americans' sense of vulnerability. Efforts to extend American jurisdiction over the Great Plains and the southwestern and western territories were often justified in Jacksonian terms as a means of enhancing the security of U.S. borders and reducing the influence of European powers. American involvement in the Pacific and the Caribbean reflected a growing belief that without such holdings, the United States would remain both militarily and economically exposed to the imperial designs of Great Britain, Germany, Japan, and other world powers.[7] At the same time, America's actions on the world stage during the nineteenth century reflected a mixture of the Hamiltonian, Jeffersonian, and Jacksonian visions for the American project.

1914–1960: America Emerges as World Leader

Between 1914 and 1917, American policymakers faced growing pressures to enter World War I, but the isolationist pressure at home remained so strong that President Woodrow Wilson ran for reelection in 1916 using the popular slogan "He kept us out of war!" The neutrality of the United States, however, was rooted in the Jeffersonian-based belief that America should not get involved unless its own security was threatened. In 1917, publication of a secret German telegram proposing a military alliance with Mexico, combined with the sinking of ships carrying American passengers by German submarines, led President Wilson and others to conclude that the United States had to get involved in the conflict on the side of Great Britain and its allies.

When the war was over, Wilson believed that the United States could no longer barricade itself behind an isolationist strategy. He was also convinced that the United States would remain vulnerable as long as there were barriers to popular rule elsewhere in the world. Thus he played a major role in writing the treaty to end the war and helped design the League of Nations and the World Court. When Wilson returned home from Paris in 1919, however, he was criticized for his internationalist policies. Although he campaigned for ratification of the peace treaty throughout the United States, isolationist attitudes remained powerful and the Senate refused to ratify it.

Isolationism persisted through the 1920s and 1930s. Many Americans blamed the Great Depression on too much contact with Europe. They believed that increasing contact would only expose the United States to more economic turmoil. Even when the rise of militarism in Europe and the Pacific grew threatening, many Americans opposed involvement in another international war that did not seem to threaten them directly. It took the Japanese attack on the U.S. naval base at Hawaii's Pearl Harbor — for many, the ultimate proof of vulnerability — to launch the United States into that conflict.

World War II and its aftermath finally convinced many Americans that the United States had to adopt the Wilsonian vision of the American project and play a major role in world affairs. The United States emerged from that war as the world's industrial and military giant. As the world entered the nuclear age, however, Americans also began to realize just how vulnerable they were to events in the international arena.

Critical Thinking

Would greater U.S. involvement in world affairs after World War I have prevented World War II?

At the outset, America's leaders were hopeful about the prospects for an era of peace. The wartime alliance among the Big Three powers — the United States, Great Britain, and the Soviet Union — had been successful and seemed likely to last. The United States played a major role in creating the United Nations to promote world cooperation and peace. By 1946, however — only a year after the war had ended — the international scene had changed. The Soviet Union was tightening its political hold on Eastern Europe, North Korea, and other occupied areas. It was also challenging Britain's influence in Greece, Turkey, and the Middle East.

At first the United States tried to mediate between its two former allies, but before long it decided to openly support the British. Events came to a head in early 1947, when the British realized that they could no longer afford to meet their commitments to Greece or Turkey. Within a few weeks, President Harry S Truman had called for a policy that supported the efforts of "free peoples who are resisting attempted subjugations by armed minorities or by outside pressures." He advocated providing economic and financial aid to countries whose political and economic stability was threatened. This general policy marked the beginning of the Cold War.

Cold War The post–World War II period characterized by ideological and policy confrontations between the American-led West and the Soviet-led East.

The **Cold War** is a term applied to the international situation between 1947 and the late 1980s, characterized by hostile, yet for the most part not violent, relations between a Western alliance led by the United States and an Eastern alliance led by the Soviet Union. During most of the Cold War era, the American public and many policymakers tended to perceive the world as *bipolar*: They saw nations as being allied with one of the two "poles" represented by the United States and the Soviet Union.

For most Americans, Cold War battles raged primarily on the level of ideology: the "democracies" of the West against the "totalitarian regimes" of the East, the capitalism of the West against the communism of the East, and so on. Sometimes the Cold War became hot and bloody, but these conflicts were typically limited in scope. The Korean War (1950–1953), for example, pitted the United States and its allies against North Korean and Chinese troops (see the discussion later in this section). In addition, on several occasions the world held its breath as the two major powers confronted each other in crisis situations.

In 1948, for example, the United States and its allies challenged a ground-based blockade of Berlin by the Soviet Union by airlifting supplies into the city. The airlift was kept up until the Soviets eventually backed off eleven months later. In 1961, Soviet leaders demanded that the Allies negotiate their withdrawal from the city. President John F. Kennedy replied that the survival of West Berlin was not negotiable. The Soviets, in turn, responded by constructing a wall around the city that physically isolated it and would become a symbol of the Cold War until its destruction in 1989. Only a ground and air corridor through East Germany linked West Berlin to its base of support in West Germany. As in the case of the 1948 blockade, the Allies, led by the United States, held fast and demonstrated their resolve not to abandon their commitments to West Berlin.

Perhaps the "hottest" Cold War encounter between the United States and the Soviet Union came in October 1962, when Kennedy demanded that the Soviets dismantle the offensive missile sites they had placed in Cuba and halt the shipment of additional missiles to that Caribbean island. The world stood on the brink of nuclear war for thirteen days as Kennedy and Soviet Premier Nikita Khrushchev bargained back and forth in what became known as the *Cuban missile crisis.* Kennedy ordered a blockade of Cuba, and the U.S. Navy was told to make certain that no ships carrying additional missiles sailed into Cuban ports. One ship was boarded, and other Soviet vessels turned back rather than confront the blockade. In the meantime, the American and Soviet leaders exchanged heated messages. Finally, on October 28, 1962, the crisis ended when the Soviets agreed to dismantle the missile sites in return for assurances that the United States was in the process of removing some of its missiles from Turkey and Italy.[8]

While these specific confrontations played an important role in the Cold War, the United States followed a more general policy of containment during the period. According to proponents of **containment**, the Soviet Union was not seeking immediate victories. Instead, it was exercising patience, caution, and flexibility in pursuit of expansionist goals. Only through a policy of "long-term, patient, but firm and vigilant containment" would U.S. efforts succeed in countering the Soviet Union's unrelenting commitment to conquering the capitalist world.[9] In that sense, containment was a further extension of the American belief in the myth of vulnerability: Unless the Soviets were contained, they would soon extend their dominance throughout Europe, Asia, and the Americas.

Containment led to significant changes in American foreign policy. It resulted in greater U.S. expenditures for foreign aid to countries that were vulnerable to Soviet influence. It also caused a major shift in America's defense

Containment The foreign policy, pursued by the United States throughout the Cold War, that called for preventing the Soviet Union from making further expansionist moves in its effort to conquer the capitalist world.

policies. In 1949 President Truman signed a treaty establishing the *North Atlantic Treaty Organization (NATO)*. NATO was a response to the perceived threat of communist expansion in Europe. It closely tied American security to political conditions in Europe by guaranteeing the maintenance of Western European governments, and it committed the United States to ongoing military collaboration with the armed services of the other members of NATO. Most important, the establishment of NATO signified a break with policies of the past, formally ending the long-standing commitment of American policymakers to unilateralism during peacetime, and reflected American determination to halt communist expansion.[10] The policy of containment took on more obvious military dimensions in 1950, when President Truman ordered American forces to South Korea after that country was invaded by North Korean troops. More than 34,000 American lives were lost in that "police action," and another 103,000 U.S. personnel were wounded. Throughout the conflict, Truman maintained the limited objective of forcing the North Koreans and their Chinese allies back across the border between North and South Korea.

Under Truman's successor, Dwight D. Eisenhower, the United States avoided direct military actions while getting more involved in formal alliances with other nations. By 1960 it was committed to the defense of nations in almost every region of the world, especially those bordering on Soviet bloc states.

Eventually, however, the containment policy was tested when U.S. policymakers viewed the defense of South Vietnam as an opportunity to demonstrate America's commitments. A communist-led insurgency against an American-supported government in South Vietnam grew stronger in the late 1950s and early 1960s. Presidents Eisenhower, Kennedy, Lyndon B. Johnson, and Richard M. Nixon backed U.S. commitments with foreign aid, military assistance, and eventually American fighting forces. Between 1964 and 1973, nearly 3 million American military personnel served in Vietnam. At least 47,355 Americans died in the Vietnam conflict, and more than 300,000 were wounded. These costs proved too great for the American public, and the United States was forced to withdraw from Vietnam in 1975 as North Vietnamese troops entered South Vietnam's capital, Saigon (now called Ho Chi Minh City).[11]

Critical Thinking

Should the U.S. policy toward the Soviet Union and communism have been more aggressive in the early 1950s?

1960s–1980s: Containment in a Changing World

By the early 1960s, international conditions were changing rapidly. Third World nations emerged as important actors in world affairs. Poor, less-industrialized countries, such as India, Kenya, and Indonesia, sought aid from the industrialized world while avoiding excessive dependence on either the United States or the Soviet Union. Furthermore, both the American and the Soviet alliances experienced growing dissent. Within NATO, France developed a more independent foreign and defense policy. In the East, policy disagreements between the Soviet Union and the People's Republic of China weakened that fragile alliance, as did the desire of some Eastern European countries (for example, Albania, Yugoslavia, and Romania) to conduct their own foreign policies.

Détente The relaxation of tensions between nations. It became the name for President Nixon's policy of taking a more cooperative approach in dealing with Soviet bloc nations while enhancing U.S. security arrangements with its allies.

Balance of power strategy A "realist's" approach to foreign policy, based on the need to offset any imbalance in international relations that might lead to one nation becoming too powerful. Advocated by Henry Kissinger, it was the central premise of American foreign policy for most of the 1970s.

The seeming failure of the containment policy in Vietnam and the negative reaction of the American people to that war led to major changes in U.S. foreign policy—changes that shaped America's role in world affairs from 1975 until the late 1980s. Richard Nixon's administration established a policy of **détente**—or relaxation of tensions—reflecting a more cooperative approach to dealing with Soviet bloc nations, while enhancing U.S. security arrangements with its allies. It was a period of negotiations with the Soviets, bringing an end to direct American involvement in the Vietnam conflict, establishing diplomatic relations with the People's Republic of China, strengthening NATO and other alliances, and providing indirect assistance to nations threatened by communist takeovers.[12]

Behind these events was a new way of dealing with the sense of vulnerability and America's role in world affairs: the **balance of power strategy** advocated and implemented by Henry A. Kissinger, who served as Nixon's top adviser on foreign policy and eventually as his secretary of state. Kissinger believed that American foreign policy in the past had been too idealistic and not cold-blooded and calculating enough. Foreign policy, Kissinger argued, was not intended to promote idealistic causes, but rather to protect America's national interests (in the Hamiltonian sense), and that could be done only by focusing on maintaining an international balance of power. To accomplish this meant following one principle: "No nation could be permitted to be preeminent, however fleetingly, over the combination of forces that could be arrayed against it, for in the fleeting moment of neglect independence and identity could be irrevocably lost."[13]

The Period of Détente

President Richard Nixon used a policy of détente in his relations with the Soviet Union. Here he is pictured with Soviet Premier Leonid Brezhnev during one of several summit meetings.

POLITICS & POPULAR CULTURE

Americans at War—In the Movies

War has played a major role in the history of American film, and Hollywood has tended to show both the heroic and horrific sides of the ultimate form of human conflict. The first Academy Award for Best Picture went to the 1927 production of *Wings*, a silent film set in World War I that is best remembered for its aerial "dogfight" scenes and its glorification of war. Two years later, that prestigious award was given to *All Quiet on the Western Front*, a film that focused on the darker side of war and the sacrifices that soldiers make in the name of patriotism.

Contradictory views of war continued to emerge on movie theater screens throughout the decades that followed, but U.S. involvement in the Vietnam War had a decidedly negative impact on how war has been portrayed in American popular culture. In 1978, Jane Fonda and Jon Voight won Academy Awards for their portrayals of lovers whose lives were radically altered by the Vietnam War in *Coming Home*. That same year, Oscars for Best Picture and Best Director were given for *The Deer Hunter*, a movie that more explicitly confronted the brutality and personal traumas of war. In the years that followed, movies such as Francis Ford Coppola's 1979 film *Apocalypse Now*, Oliver Stone's *Platoon* (1986), and Stanley Kubrick's *Full Metal Jacket* (1987) continued to stress the personal horrors of war—and indirectly raised questions about the wisdom of policies that put American soldiers in harm's way.

While some of the best-known war movies of the 1970s and 1980s stressed the horrors of war, other popular films of the period focused attention on the traumas of those who returned from the war and the positive qualities of those in the fighting forces. In the first of several "Rambo" films

(*First Blood*, 1982), Sylvester Stallone portrays a disoriented Vietnam veteran who goes to war with local law enforcement after they imprison him for vagrancy. That same year, Richard Gere starred in *An Officer and a Gentleman*, a film that made almost no reference to war while stressing the character-building qualities of military service. Tom Cruise did get some action against enemy jets in the popular 1986 film *Top Gun*, but the focus again was on the character of those we might send off to war. In 1989, Cruise played the role of a wounded Vietnam veteran who returned from war feeling betrayed by his country in Oliver Stone's *Born on the Fourth of July*.

The horrors of active combat reemerged in the late 1990s with the release of *A Thin Red Line* (1998) and *Saving Private Ryan* (1999). Both films focused on bloody battles of World War II. In *A Thin Red Line* it is the battle for Guadalcanal, while *Saving Private Ryan* begins with scenes designed to replicate the sights, sounds, and feel of the D-Day invasion of Omaha Beach in 1944. But if anything is glorified in these movies, it is not the value of war against Japan or Germany. Rather, it is the character and personal sacrifice of those who put their lives on the line for their country.

More recent war movies include *Black Hawk Down* (2001) and *We Were Soldiers* (2002), both films that stressed heroics in the face of overwhelming odds, and *Jarhead*, a 2005 movie based on the experiences of a U.S. Marine as he goes from boot camp to Desert Storm, which received solid reviews for its realistic depiction of service in the Persian Gulf.

If there is a common thread emerging from these examples it is that "war is hell," but Americans cannot surrender nor turn their backs on those who are suffering injustices at the hands of their enemies. There is no glory in war, and the bloody and brutal nature of combat has been made increasingly visible on the cinematic screen for several decades. But there is also an emerging sense that there may be some things worth fighting for—including the lives and rights of total strangers.

For more information on the portrayal of war in movies, visit UC–Berkeley's "War and War-Era Movies" at www.lib.berkeley .edu/MRC/Warfilm.html./

Thus, Nixon and Kissinger believed that it was necessary to take unprecedented steps in order to counter the growing strength and influence of the Soviet Union. Those steps included supporting regimes and leaders whose behavior might otherwise be seen as deplorable by many Americans. Nixon and Kissinger opened diplomatic relations with mainland China, despite a long-standing commitment not to abandon the United States' anticommunist Chinese allies based in Taiwan. Reflecting on negotiations with communist China, Kissinger argued that the "many different strands that made up American thinking on foreign policy have so far proved inhospitable to an approach based on the calculation of the national interest and relationships of power. . . . We in the Nixon Administration felt that our challenge was to educate the American people in the requirements of the balance of power."[14]

Critical Thinking

The memory of Vietnam had a great influence on the attitudes of current leaders. Does it have the same effect on your generation?

Although the balance of power approach seemed to ease the sense of American vulnerability to the perils generated by the Soviet Union and China, it could not stop the anxiety caused by the Middle East and other parts of the oil-producing world. Under the banner of the *Organization of Petroleum Exporting Countries (OPEC)*, oil producers began raising the price and reducing the supply of crude oil during the early 1970s. By April 1973, the Nixon administration publicly declared that the United States had to take steps to reduce its vulnerability to the threat posed by the policies of OPEC and its member states. Then in October 1973, events in the Middle East elevated the situation to a foreign policy crisis. War had broken out between Israel and its Arab neighbors on October 6. In response to U.S. support for Israel, the Arab member states of OPEC unilaterally increased the price of crude oil dramatically, and on October 20 they declared an embargo on oil shipments to the West. Eventually the embargo ended, but by the end of 1973 it had significantly changed Americans' view of world affairs and U.S. foreign policy. The embargo marked the high point of an international energy crisis that brought home to Americans just how vulnerable the U.S. economy was to developments in the international arena.

The OPEC embargo was not the only embargo used in international affairs during this period. American policymakers also used that tactic when the Soviet Union invaded Afghanistan in 1979. At that time, President Jimmy Carter ended the era of détente by imposing a grain embargo. In addition, Carter canceled cultural exchange programs and withdrew U.S. teams from the 1980 Olympic Games, which were scheduled to take place in Moscow. Carter also pursued

Iran Hostage Crisis
In the late 1970s, international crises such as the seizure of U.S. embassy personnel in Tehran increased the feeling of vulnerability among Americans.

more formal relations with China, helped to negotiate a peace agreement between Israel and Egypt, concluded a treaty to give Panama control over the Panama Canal, and took other actions that helped adjust U.S. foreign and defense policies to the changing international scene of the 1970s. The continuing energy crisis and events in Iran, however, had the greatest impact on the Carter administration. In 1979, Iranian revolutionaries seized the U.S. embassy in Tehran and took more than a hundred Americans hostage. This and similar terrorist actions against American citizens added to the general public feeling that America was once again vulnerable. The Iranian hostage crisis preoccupied Americans during 1980, adding to the public's sense of vulnerability in an election year. The crisis lasted more than a year, ending on the day President Ronald Reagan was sworn into office in 1981.

At the outset, the Reagan administration stressed military superiority over the Soviet Union and the need to strengthen America's leadership in the Western world. Underlying the Reagan approach was the assumption that the United States must operate from a position of strength. Anything less, administration officials believed, would make the United States susceptible to the designs of Soviet leaders. Reagan supported stepped-up military spending and increased American involvement in the Middle East, Latin America, and other international "hot spots."[15] In many respects, his policies resembled the containment policies of the earlier Cold War period, but the changing realities of world affairs eventually posed major challenges to that approach.

At the center of those challenges were the changes that were taking place in the Soviet Union and Eastern Europe. The emergence of Mikhail Gorbachev as the leader of the Soviet Union in 1985 created a situation that even hard-line

The Wall Comes Tumbling Down

For many Americans, the tearing down of the Berlin Wall in November 1989 symbolized the end of the Cold War era and the beginning of a new period in U.S. foreign policy.

cold warriors in the Reagan administration could not ignore. The shift was dramatic, especially for President Reagan and the American public. In 1982, speaking before the British House of Commons, Reagan had called the Soviet Union an "evil empire." The American people seemed to support that belief; in 1983, nearly two-thirds of those polled regarded the Soviets as a real and immediate military threat to the United States. But by 1988, Reagan was walking through Moscow's Red Square with Gorbachev, waving and shaking hands with Soviet citizens; meanwhile, the number of Americans concerned about the Soviet military threat had decreased to less than one in three.[16] Even then, few observers predicted the coming end to the Cold War.

Policymakers in George H. W. Bush's administration were extremely pleased with the events that unfolded between 1988 and 1991. There were, of course, some setbacks and disappointments, such as the brutal suppression of China's student demonstrators in Beijing's Tiananmen Square in June 1989. Nevertheless, major changes were clearly in the wind. American-Soviet relations had been the pivotal feature shaping U.S. foreign policy since World War II; significant changes in those relations were bound to affect other foreign policy areas. America's NATO allies were especially eager to build on these improved relationships. This was particularly true of West Germany, where Gorbachev was popular and where there was considerable pressure for arms reduction and for reunification with East Germany. By May 1990, every Eastern European nation had new, more liberal leadership or policies. A more cooperative Soviet posture in Latin America, the Middle East, Africa, and other potential regional hot spots provided still more proof that real changes were taking place in the context in which U.S. foreign policy operated.

1990s: Rethinking Foreign and Defense Policies

Critical Thinking

To what extent can the policies of Ronald Reagan and George H. W. Bush be credited with bringing about the collapse of the Soviet Union? To what extent did the USSR collapse as a result of its own failings?

Shifting Contexts. The situation started to turn sour as early as August 1990. The new governments of Eastern Europe were beginning to face the hard realities of making the transition to democracy and free-market economies. In the Soviet Union, Gorbachev became anxious about the rapid pace of the changes he had initiated and began to turn his back on the reform movement. Equally ominous was the successful Iraqi invasion of Kuwait early that month. The outlook for the post–Cold War era suddenly seemed bleaker.

In 1991, however, hope returned in several arenas. The Persian Gulf War against Iraq, launched by a U.S.-led alliance, was quickly concluded, although the effort to remove Iraqi leader Saddam Hussein failed.[17] In August, several hard-liners in the Soviet regime staged an abortive coup against Gorbachev, and by the time the dust settled in December of that year, the Soviet Union was no more. In its place were the various republics that had once made up the USSR, each seeking to establish itself as an independent actor on the international stage. Foremost among these was Russia, which was still a powerful force to be reckoned with. There were other positive developments as well: In the Middle East, a U.S. initiative on peace talks began to take hold; in South Africa, progress was being made toward ending apartheid and establishing a majority-rule regime; and in Central America, peace talks in El Salvador were being brought to a successful conclusion. But this newly regained sense of hope was now tempered by the realization that the post–Cold War era was not without its uncertainties, despite the many changes that had occurred.

Post–Cold War Strategy. It was in this context that the administration of George H. W. Bush began to articulate a foreign and military strategy based on new assumptions.[18] Central to these assumptions was the sense that the United States, although the one remaining superpower, was still vulnerable to forces it could not control. Therefore, it needed to develop a strategy that would attempt to deter aggression and defend the nation's vital interests in an uncertain world.

Although not specific in content, the post–Cold War foreign policy strategy was based on four general principles. First, it assumed that American interests would be best served if the United States had a regional focus, as opposed to a more global perspective that ignored specific regional issues. Second, it stressed strong alliances within that regional framework rather than unilateral actions. Third, building on the model of the Persian Gulf War, the Bush administration would give preference to multinational joint operations when military action was required. Finally, the Bush strategy took into account the need to maintain the U.S. capability to act alone if necessary to protect the nation's vital interests. When presenting their revised strategic plans, Bush administration officials always emphasized the uncertainties facing the United States and its vulnerability to unexpected challenges.

The myth of vulnerability also remained active in the context of several key domestic issues that had important foreign policy implications. The administration declared a "War on Drugs" that included strategies to cut off the supply of cocaine and other drugs from Latin America. Environmental concerns also had international repercussions. Canada's leaders, for example, put considerable pressure on the United States to address the problems caused by the acid rain produced by U.S. industries. Global warming was by its very nature an international issue, as was popular concern about Brazil's destruction of the Amazon rain forests. In these and related cases, policymakers felt that their ability to deal effectively with problems was dependent on the actions of others — a situation that extended America's vulnerability in world affairs.

But it was in the area of economic policy that the greatest concerns emerged. During most of the Cold War, economics and national security were perceived as separate concerns, and when the two came into conflict, it was national defense that took priority.[19] However, in the early 1980s, economic concerns prompted President Reagan to appoint a National Commission on Industrial Competitiveness. In its 1985 report, the commission noted that the U.S. economy's "ability to compete internationally faces unprecedented challenge from abroad. Our world leadership is at stake, and so is our ability to provide for our people the standard of living and opportunity to which they aspire."[20] Although it did not receive a significant amount of public attention, the commission was expressing the theme of America's economic vulnerability, which would become increasingly important over the next decade.

Clinton Presidency. The 1992 election of Bill Clinton marked an important event in the history of American foreign and defense policies. Not only was he the first chief executive elected in the post–Cold War era, but his relative youth (he was forty-six when he was elected) meant that he had not personally experienced the threats posed by the Great Depression, Hitler, and Stalin. With a few notable exceptions, Clinton surrounded himself with advisers primarily drawn from his own generation — a generation that had formed its views of foreign and defense policies during the Vietnam War era, when most of its members opposed U.S. policies in Southeast Asia and elsewhere. And, like most of his advisers, Clinton regarded the domestic economy as the top priority for the new administration.[21] Thus, it was no surprise that the Clinton foreign policy team refocused the country's attention from issues of military vulnerability to those of economic security. The United States must remain an international leader, they argued, but not because of any military threat. "Today . . . the defense of the national interest requires a more subtle examination of the dangers and opportunities in a new world." To meet those new challenges, the Clinton administration adopted a Hamiltonian vision of the American project and gave top priority to integrating "a healthy American economy into a healthy global economy." In that context, the next foreign policy priority was "creating and expanding democratic governance and free markets overseas." By 1994, the more traditional Cold War objectives of national security "through skilled diplomacy and a strong, ready military" were relegated to being the third item on the administration's list of priorities.[22]

That emphasis on economic security was most evident in Clinton's first term. Trade policies, especially the implementation of the North American Free Trade

Agreement and the establishment of the World Trade Organization, took center stage. On a more general level, the Clinton administration developed policies that would help Americans compete in the emerging global economy, where physical boundaries and traditional national economic controls were becoming increasingly irrelevant. The trend toward globalization (see Chapter 14, on domestic policy and policymaking) presented American policymakers with a new set of challenges beyond those related to economics. The administration found itself dealing with a new set of "transnational" issues, including new forms of environmental degradation and organized criminal activity that knew no borders.[23]

Critical Thinking

In retrospect, did the Clinton administration put too much emphasis on the economic aspects of foreign policy?

This did not mean, however, that the Clinton administration could or would ignore the more traditional forms of military and national security vulnerability that remained even after the end of threats from the Soviets. The threat of nuclear war remained a real concern. The republics of Russia, Kazakhstan, Ukraine, and Belarus now owned the strategic nuclear weapons of the former Soviet Union, so that disarmament negotiations had to be conducted with several distinct states rather than with one. In addition, the potential for the spread of nuclear weapons increased when the centralized Soviet controls against proliferation disappeared. Fearing that Iraq, North Korea, and other "rogue" states might gain access to Soviet weaponry or develop their own nuclear capabilities, the United States was faced with unique diplomatic challenges. It was a situation that made old regional conflicts even more significant. There were potential nuclear flashpoints emerging all over the globe, especially in the Middle East, where Israel's capability to develop nuclear weapons was an open secret, and in South Asia, where both India and Pakistan demonstrated their nuclear prowess in 1998.

The Clinton administration also found itself confronted with humanitarian issues and strategic problems raised by a number of very bloody internal conflicts. American troops found themselves conducting special missions in Haiti, Suriname, Panama, Bosnia, Kosovo, northern Iraq, and many other places where civil strife was creating humanitarian crises. An ill-fated mission to Somalia resulted in the death of eighteen U.S. soldiers in 1993, reminding Americans of the risks associated with taking on these smaller missions around the world. And during his second term in office, Clinton seemed more directly engaged in diplomatic efforts, especially in the Middle East. His secretary of state during that period, Madeleine Albright, articulated a Wilsonian-like vision for U.S. foreign policy that stressed the creation of the new world order that President George H. W. Bush and others had talked about when the Berlin Wall fell.[24] Nevertheless, it was the economic dimensions of foreign affairs that formed the core of Clinton's policies.

2000s: Clashing Civilizations and the Response to September 11

During his last months in office, Clinton engaged in a number of diplomatic efforts designed to strengthen U.S. relations with its allies. He also attempted to have the Israelis and Palestinians come to an agreement, but that effort eventually failed. These efforts contrasted with the approach taken by the administration of George W. Bush during its first several months in office. By August 2001, analysts were characterizing Bush's foreign policy as more "unilateralist" than Clinton's. The United States withdrew from negotiations on global warming issues (the *Kyoto Protocol*), weapons proliferation, and efforts to verify compliance with biological and chemical weapons treaties. Instead, it signaled its willingness to "go it alone" on many issues, or to enter into limited bilateral agreements with countries that served America's interests. On military matters, attention was turned inward as the Pentagon continued to engage in its long-term program of modernization.

Whatever the future held for such approaches will never be known, for on September 11, 2001, the foreign and defense policies of the United States were radically altered by the attacks on the World Trade Center and the Pentagon. It was the ultimate confirmation that the United States, despite its status as the world's "sole superpower," was still extremely vulnerable. Declaring a "war on terrorism," the Bush administration focused its foreign policy and military resources on mobilizing the United States and its allies for that war effort. President Bush put the situation to the world community in blunt terms: "Every nation, in every region, now has a decision to make. Either you are with us, or you are with the terrorists."[25]

The potential for terrorist attacks on the United States was well known before September 11.[26] Prominent analysts had warned that the post–Cold War era would witness a "clash of civilizations" as "westernization" came into conflict with other strong cultures.[27] In addition, others had predicted that foreign policy decisions of the past would come back to haunt the United States.[28] Despite these warnings, the United States seemed to be taken by surprise by the events of September 11 and had difficulty dealing with some of the challenges associated with fighting a war on terrorism. At first, the focus was on Afghanistan, a country where the ruling Taliban regime was providing a haven for *al-Qaeda*, the terrorist network suspected of being behind the September 11 attacks. By December, the Taliban had been overthrown, and the United States began to focus on an international effort to find and eliminate the remaining vestiges of the worldwide terrorism networks.

By 2002, other issues were starting to reemerge on the foreign policy agenda. Relations between India and Pakistan became a central concern for the Bush administration given its reliance on the Pakistanis for support in Afghanistan. When the two nations threatened to go to war over a decades-old dispute about Kashmir, a province claimed by both countries, the United States found itself more involved than it might have been before September 11. The situation in Israel heated up as well and drew more attention from the Bush administration than it had earlier. While supportive of Israeli military actions in Palestinian areas taken as a result of a spate of suicide bombings, the United States, for the first time, endorsed the creation of a Palestinian state. Economic problems also began to loom large as several Latin American countries were faced with financial crises. In short, it was a period of continued crises throughout the world, and with each new problem came the sense of greater vulnerability.

Critical Thinking

Should U.S. foreign policymakers have been better prepared for terrorist attacks? If so, what should they have done to prevent the attacks?

But behind the scenes, planning for the next stage in the U.S. response to the attacks of September 11 was taking shape, and the focus was on Saddam Hussein's Iraq. With military planning for the invasion of Iraq well underway by the middle of 2002, key foreign policymakers in the Bush administration launched a campaign to convince the world (and the American public in particular) of the need to deal with Hussein's regime once and for all. After presenting their case before the UN Security Council, which asserted that Iraq posed a threat because it sought to develop and deploy **weapons of mass destruction (WMD)**, the United States and its allies launched their invasion of Iraq on March 20, 2003. On May 1, with Iraqi forces essentially defeated, President Bush declared victory. Weapons of mass destruction were never found, and the lack of planning for the postwar occupation and an insurgency plagued the U.S. effort to establish a viable regime in Iraq. By March 2006, on the third anniversary of the invasion, President Bush noted that progress was being made, but that the pullout of U.S. troops would be up to a future president.[29] By August 2006, sectarian violence between Iraq's Shi'a and Sunni populations had become serious enough that top U.S. military commanders were admitting that the situation in Iraq was deteriorating into a civil war.

Weapons of mass destruction (WMD) A term applied to nuclear, chemical, biological, and radiological weapons subject to indiscriminate use that are likely to cause casualties on a massive scale.

Making Foreign and Defense Policy

FOCUS QUESTION WHO IS INVOLVED IN THE MAKING OF U.S. FOREIGN AND DEFENSE POLICIES, AND WHAT ROLES DO THEY PLAY?

Foreign and defense policymaking has always been perceived as necessarily different from domestic policymaking in the United States. This is due in part to the constitutional premise that foreign policy is a responsibility of the national government that does not have to be shared with the states. Another factor has been the consensus that the president plays the central role in shaping and conducting foreign and defense policies. Nevertheless, foreign and defense policymaking is still subject to the same political pressures that shape domestic policymaking, including such widely held myths as the myth of American vulnerability.

Some observers note how much foreign and defense policy has changed in the post–Cold War era. During the Cold War there was a broad public consensus that the primary objective of American foreign policy was to protect our nation and its allies from the military threats posed by the Soviet Union and its allies. Thus, foreign policy was closely tied to military and defense policies — that is, **national security policy**. Under those conditions, efforts were made to keep foreign policy decision making relatively centralized and isolated from the hurly-burly of partisan and interest-group politics that characterizes domestic policymaking (see Chapter 14, on domestic policy and policymaking). It was an arena dominated by the president, his national security advisers, and military experts.[30]

National security policy A term used to focus on those policies, programs, and strategies related to the defense and safety of the country.

ASKED & ANSWERED

ASKED: Is the United States an empire?

ANSWERED: Americans do not take kindly to those commentators, foreign or domestic, who use the word *empire* to describe the current U.S. role in world affairs. We typically associate empires with the Dark Side (remember *Star Wars*?) and consider them evil (as when President Reagan referred to the Soviet Union as an "evil empire"). But in recent years a growing number of people have used the word *empire* to describe what the United States has become in the post–Cold War period. Does the label fit?

The answer depends on which image of *empire* you adopt. If you think of an empire in classical, military terms—as the direct rule of conquered foreign lands without the political involvement or endorsement of their inhabitants—then perhaps not. The United States has from time to time acted as an occupying force after winning a war, as it did in Japan and Germany after World War II, but those were regarded as periods of transition, after which rule was turned over to the citizens of the occupied nations.

But more contemporary views of *empire* regard it as the capacity of one nation to indirectly but effectively exercise power over the political, economic, and cultural aspects of another country. Under that view, one can argue that we are indeed operating as an American empire. There is no question that the United States is willing to use direct military intervention in its dealings with less powerful countries, but there is a sense that such actions should be limited and only when necessary. This has led some analysts to term the United States a "reluctant sheriff" or "reluctant imperialist."

British analyst Niall Ferguson points out that we often go out of our way to avoid calling the United States an empire. Instead, we rely on other terms, such as the world's "sole superpower" or "global power" exercising "primacy" in world affairs. Lawrence Summers, former treasury secre-

tary under President Clinton, likes to call the United States the world's first "nonimperialist superpower." Walter Russell Mead labels the present era "Pax Americana"—literally, "American Peace."

For many analysts, however, the most relevant word to apply to the United Sates is not empire but hegemon. The word *hegemon* was first applied to ancient Athens as it led and dominated the league of Greek city-states attempting to fend off the Persian Empire, and then to Sparta as its influence held sway during the Peloponnesian Wars. Today, "hegemony means more than mere leadership, but less than outright empire." A hegemon, rather than using conquest and coercion to assert its dominance in the world, emerges as the dominant actor through its possession of some critical resource and its capacity to form alliances with other major regional and local powers. As a hegemonic superpower, the United States has interests in every corner of the world, but in order to pursue those interests effectively, it must deal with regional powers. In dealing with the troubles in Bosnia and Kosovo during the 1990s, for example, the United States needed to work with Germany and its other European allies. In attempting to develop a diplomatic solution to the threats posed by North Korea, the United States finds itself relying increasingly on China and Japan. In planning its invasion of Iraq in 2003, the United States required the assistance of several countries in the Persian Gulf region. In other words, a hegemon may look like an empire, but it operates under severe limits.

For a discussion of the American empire, see Niall Ferguson, *Colossus: The Price of America's Empire* (New York: Penguin Press, 2004), especially pp. 3–13; the quote is from p. 9. See also Joseph Nye Jr., "The Changing Nature of World Power," *Political Science Quarterly*, 105, no. 2 (1990), 177–192; Lawrence Summers, "America: The First Nonimperialist Superpower," *New Perspectives Quarterly*, 15, no. 2 (1998), 34–35; and Walter Russell Mead, *Power, Terror, Peace, and War: America's Grand Strategy in a World at Risk* (New York: Vintage Books, 2005), chap. 3.

After the Cold War, the making of foreign policy took on some of the characteristics of domestic policymaking. Congress and a growing number of interest groups became increasingly involved, and American public opinion became more divided over specific foreign policy issues. Presidential leadership focused more on developing policies that satisfy a wide range of constituencies, and the State and Defense Departments worked more closely with other departments including Treasury, Commerce, and the Office of the U.S. Trade Representative.

The President and the White House

The president's role in foreign and military affairs is rooted in the constitutional provisions that give the president the power to make treaties, appoint ambassadors, receive diplomatic representatives from other nations, and serve as commander in chief of the armed forces (see the discussion of these roles in Chapter 11, on the presidency). Thus, although Congress shares some of the responsibility for shaping, funding, and implementing our foreign and defense policies, the lion's share of the power in these arenas traditionally and constitutionally belongs to the president of the United States.[31] Prior to the Cold War, there was not much question that U.S. foreign policymaking was conducted by the president and his secretary of state. Thus, although the Monroe Doctrine carries the name of the president at the time, historians note that it was a policy developed by his secretary of state, John Quincy Adams. Similarly, as secretary of state under Warren G. Harding, Charles Evans Hughes played the central role in several major U.S. foreign policy achievements during that period.

With the advent of the Cold War, however, formulating and implementing foreign and defense policies became a complex affair, and although the presidency remained the most important institution in these areas,[32] presidents found themselves relying more on special advisers. The *National Security Act of 1947* authorized the president to establish the **National Security Council (NSC)**, comprising the president, the vice president, the secretaries of defense and state, and other officials that the president wished to invite, such as the secretary of commerce, the director of the *Central Intelligence Agency (CIA)*, or the chair of the *Joint Chiefs of Staff* (see the discussion later in this chapter). The NSC's primary functions were to advise the president on national security issues and to coordinate the implementation of policy. It was not intended to be a decision-making body, but its members were called on for their opinions and advice during times of crisis.

The NSC staff also played an important role in shaping U.S. foreign and military policies. Typically, the staff consisted of experts who monitored the world situation for the White House, prepared analyses and policy options for the president's consideration, and oversaw the coordination of foreign and defense policies. This staff was headed by the special assistant to the president for national security affairs, often called the **national security adviser**. Under some presidents, the national security adviser strongly influenced foreign and defense policies. In the Nixon administration, for instance, Henry Kissinger played a

National Security Council (NSC) A council created by Congress in 1947 to advise the president on foreign policy and to coordinate its implementation.

National security adviser The head of the National Security Council staff, who may sometimes have a strong influence on foreign and defense policies.

central role in negotiating agreements with the Soviets, as well as in efforts to end the Vietnam War and to open relations with the People's Republic of China. Eventually, Nixon appointed Kissinger to serve simultaneously as both national security adviser and secretary of state. Zbigniew Brzezinski, a noted foreign policy expert, played an important role in shaping policy during the Carter presidency. During his two terms in office, Ronald Reagan appointed six national security advisers, including Colin Powell, who would go on to serve as chair of the Joint Chiefs of Staff (under George H. W. Bush and Bill Clinton) and later secretary of state (under George W. Bush).

Under President Clinton national security advisers were less well known to the general public. Anthony Lake, who served in the position during Clinton's first term, intentionally kept a low profile, knowing that some members of Congress distrusted him. His successor, Samuel Berger, came to the job almost completely unknown outside of Washington. George W. Bush appointed the relatively unknown Condoleezza Rice to the post when he entered office in 2001, and she has more recently gained prominence as the successor to Colin Powell as secretary of state. Stephen Hadley, longtime assistant to Rice, assumed the national security adviser's role in 2005.

In the post–Cold War period, the role of the president and his advisers remained central to the shaping of foreign policy, but on certain issues the White House found itself having to deal with a much more active Congress.[33] In matters of trade, for example, Congress was increasingly reluctant to give President Clinton the **"fast track" authority** enjoyed by his predecessors. Under "fast track" authority (also called "trade promotion authority"), the U.S. Trade Representative could negotiate an agreement on non-tariff barriers to trade with other nations that the president could then present to Congress for its approval without allowing changes. Once an agreement was submitted, it had to be voted on within ninety days under a rule that allowed no amendments. It was under "fast track" authority that some of the major trade agreements of the 1990s (e.g., NAFTA) were passed. But when that authority came up for renewal in 1998, Congress refused to extend it. After much debate and considerable lobbying by the George W. Bush White House, that authority was finally restored in August 2002.

But in matters that are regarded as highly volatile, the president is still given considerable discretion in the foreign and defense policy arenas. This was especially the case in the months following September 11.

"Fast track" authority Also called "trade promotion authority," it allows the U.S. Trade Representative to negotiate an agreement on non-tariff barriers to trade with other nations that the president can then present to Congress for its approval without allowing changes.

The Bureaucracies

During the Cold War, the president typically relied on several agencies outside the White House to help him formulate and implement foreign and defense policies — especially the Departments of State and Defense and the Central Intelligence Agency. The post–Cold War emphasis on economic security, however, has given a number of other bureaucracies important roles in the international relations arena.

The Bush Foreign Policy Team

Among the top members of a president's foreign policy team are the Secretary of State and the national security adviser. Here Secretary Condoleezza Rice and National Security Adviser Stephen Hadley speak to the press at a briefing on the Middle East in July 2006.

Department of State The cabinet department responsible for the day-to-day operation of embassies, the protection of U.S. interests abroad, formal negotiations between the United States and other nations, and the provision of advice and assistance to the president.

Foreign Service The core personnel system of the State Department, consisting of some 3,500 people with expertise and training in foreign policy.

Department of Defense The agency most closely linked with military policymaking. It includes the Departments of the Army, Navy, and Air Force.

The **Department of State** is the oldest agency associated with the conduct of foreign affairs. Its personnel manage the day-to-day operations of American foreign relations. They operate American embassies, look after U.S. interests abroad, conduct formal negotiations between the United States and other nations, and provide advice and assistance to the president and other foreign policymakers. At the heart of the State Department is the **Foreign Service**, consisting of approximately 3,500 people with expertise and training in diplomacy. Although secretaries of state now share their role as major foreign policy advisers to the president with others, the position remains an important and highly visible one. Colin Powell, who served as President George W. Bush's secretary of state during his first term, took the office after serving as both a national security adviser (under Ronald Reagan) and head of the Joint Chiefs of Staff (under both George H. W. Bush and Bill Clinton; see the discussion earlier in this chapter). Condoleezza Rice, who succeeded Powell as Secretary of State, had held the position of national security adviser during George W. Bush's first term.

The **Department of Defense** (also called the Pentagon, after its five-sided office complex) is the agency that is most closely linked to military policymaking. Actually, it comprises three subordinate agencies — the Departments of the Navy (which includes the U.S. Marine Corps), Army, and Air Force — that are responsible for managing their respective branches of the armed services. The civilian leaders of the Defense Department strive to integrate the policies and programs

Joint Chiefs of Staff (JCS) A group of high-ranking military officers who represent the army, navy, air force, and marines. They provide advice to the president and coordinate military actions undertaken by U.S. forces.

Intelligence-gathering agencies Organizations such as the Central Intelligence Agency (CIA) and the National Security Agency (NSA) that are responsible for gathering and analyzing information relevant to foreign and defense policymaking.

of the different military branches. In those tasks they are assisted by the **Joint Chiefs of Staff (JCS)**, a group of high-ranking military officers representing the navy, army, air force, and marines. The Joint Chiefs of Staff also advise the president and the National Security Council when requested, and in recent years, the chair of the JCS has played a key role in advising the president.[34]

No foreign or defense policymaking can take place without information provided through **intelligence-gathering agencies**. When policymakers need detailed or hard-to-get information, they often rely on the U.S. *Central Intelligence Agency (CIA)*. With a staff of 15,000 at the height of the Cold War, the CIA obtains much of its information from newspapers, magazines, public documents, and other openly available material, but it also has other resources for gathering needed intelligence, and it provides analyses of the data. It has also conducted covert, or secret, operations. In 1961, for example, the CIA trained and provided supplies for the anti-Castro troops who took part in the ill-fated invasion of Cuba. During the 1980s, CIA operatives helped pro-U.S. forces in Central America.

The CIA is not the only U.S. intelligence agency. In fact, it was estimated that in 1995 the CIA accounted for only 10 percent of U.S. expenditures for intelligence. The *National Security Agency (NSA)*, a highly secretive unit located just outside Washington, D.C., uses sophisticated technologies to obtain intelligence. The Defense Department operates the NSA as well as other intelligence-gathering units to collect needed information for military purposes.

The end of the Cold War led to much discussion about reorganizing, consolidating, and refocusing the intelligence-gathering functions. In its 1995 budget proposals, the Clinton administration noted that it wanted the size of the intelligence community reduced by 20 percent by 1999, and it gave priority to refocusing the attention of the various agencies on regional and economic security concerns as well as support for military operations.

The CIA and the NSA both came in for significant criticism in the post–September 11 period. The CIA was criticized for its inability to provide information that might have prevented the September 11 attacks, and in 2006 word was leaked to the press that the NSA, acting under presidential directive and without court-issued warrants, had been monitoring phone calls of U.S. citizens.[35] These and related problems have led to several changes in the intelligence bureaucracy, including a reorganization that establishes a director of national intelligence and the enhancement of congressional oversight of agency activities.

Other agencies that were important during the Cold War included the *Arms Control and Disarmament Agency*, which conducted negotiations on nuclear arms limitations with the Soviets and monitored compliance with existing agreements. The *United States Information Agency (USIA)* helped coordinate educational, cultural, and media programs to provide a positive image of the United States in foreign nations. Both independent agencies were integrated into the State Department in 1999. The *Agency for International Development (USAID)* helped organize economic aid programs to Third World nations and, in the post–Cold War era, to Eastern Europe and the republics that emerged from the breakup of the Soviet Union.

The end of the Cold War increased the importance of several agencies that had previously played a relatively small role in the foreign and defense policy arenas. The *Office of the U.S. Trade Representative* has taken on a pivotal role in U.S. trade policy.[36] Treated as a cabinet-level agency, the Office of the Trade Representative was at the center of efforts to promote free trade through negotiated treaties. Similarly, because of the increased emphasis on economic security, the Treasury Department and the Commerce Department emerged as major foreign policymaking agencies in the post–Cold War era. In recent years, top officials from both of these departments have spent as much time promoting U.S. trade interests overseas as they have dealing with domestic policy concerns.

The Congressional Role in Policymaking

Edward Corwin, one of this century's foremost authorities on the U.S. Constitution, described the provisions relating to foreign policy as "an invitation to struggle for the privilege of directing American foreign policy." While the Constitution does confer some foreign policy responsibilities on the presidency, it also gives the Senate and the House of Representatives roles to play as well. "[W]hich of these organs shall have the decisive and final voice in determining the course of the American nation is left for events to resolve."[37] Congress can rely on several mechanisms when it seeks to influence both foreign and defense policies.[38] The Senate can affect presidential policies through its *power to ratify treaties* negotiated by the White House. The ratification of NAFTA and the *General Agreement on Tariffs and Trade (GATT)* (ratified in 1994; now part of the World Trade Organization [WTO]) turned into national debates over free trade; both treaties did ultimately obtain the required sixty-seven votes, but the issue was highly divisive and eventually resulted in Congress refusing to renew "fast track" authority (see the previous discussion). In 1999, the Senate failed to ratify a comprehensive nuclear test ban treaty that had been signed by most of the world's powers, but that required U.S. participation in order to be truly effective. It was the first time a treaty had failed to pass the Senate since the end of World War I. The Senate can also express its displeasure with White House policies indirectly by delaying or denying the confirmation of a presidential appointment to a high-level post in the foreign or defense policy bureaucracy or to an ambassadorship.

Both the House and the Senate can influence foreign and defense policies through direct legislation. In 1973, for example, Congress approved the *War Powers Resolution*, limiting the president's power to commit U.S. troops overseas without congressional authorization (see Chapter 11, on the presidency). The act's provisions have been applied less strictly than intended, however, especially the requirement that Congress be consulted before U.S. forces are committed. More often, the White House adheres to the provision that requires that the president submit a "report" about each use of U.S. forces within a certain number of days. By 2001, ninety-six reports had been submitted to Congress since the act went into effect under President Gerald Ford.[39]

Congressional control of the nation's purse strings provides an additional source of influence over foreign and defense policies. In 1974, for example, Congress passed a budget authorization bill for military assistance that included a provision urging the president to substantially reduce assistance to any government that violated "internationally recognized human rights." Over the years, similar and often stronger provisions have been included in military aid and economic assistance budget authorizations, and in 1983 Congress denied a specific Reagan administration request for aid to Guatemala, citing the oppressive policies of that nation's leaders.[40]

When considering legislation or appropriations, members of Congress have an opportunity to question key foreign or defense policymakers. The secretaries of state and defense, the director of the CIA, and other agency chiefs or their assistants often appear before congressional committees and subcommittees to answer questions on a broad range of policy concerns. Congress also uses its investigative power to influence foreign and defense policies. Thus, in 1987 both houses of Congress established special committees to investigate the charges that members of Reagan's National Security Council staff had violated a 1985 congressional prohibition on the U.S. government's assisting rebel forces fighting the government of Nicaragua.[41] The right to conduct these and similar investigations gives Congress leverage in shaping U.S. foreign and defense policies.

In general, however, congressional involvement in foreign and defense policies was very limited during the Cold War period. Major policy decisions were rarely debated, and when they were, the result was typically overwhelming support for the president's position. In part, this was due to the constitutional preeminence of presidential power in foreign and defense matters; but it was also a result of the nature of the Cold War itself, where the "enemy" was clearly defined and there was widespread support for the objective of containment. But as noted previously, recent studies indicate that congressional involvement in foreign affairs is increasing.

The Mass Media and Attentive Publics

The media influence foreign and defense policymaking in several ways. In their search for stories that will stir the interest of their readers and listeners (see Chapter 9, on media and politics), news reporters constantly monitor American involvement in world affairs. News reports from Vietnam, for example, greatly affected public attitudes toward that war. The lessons of Vietnam have not been lost on foreign and defense policymakers. The White House is especially sensitive to the need to gain and hold the attention of the American public on important policy matters. "You don't let the press control the agenda," noted Dick Cheney when he served as secretary of defense in George H. W. Bush's administration. "They like to decide what's important. But if you let them do that, they're going to trash your presidency."[42]

The administration's task in the area of *media management* in foreign affairs has involved three major objectives: defining events, dominating the news, and silencing critics.[43] *Defining events* means being able to influence the way in which conditions or actions are depicted in the media. Several days prior to ordering an invasion of Haiti in 1994 to reinstate that country's deposed president, President Clinton called several news reporters into his office to show them gruesome pictures of murdered critics of Haiti's current leaders. As the time for decision neared, the media were briefed by other officials on the deteriorating conditions in that Caribbean nation. Although the invasion was eventually called off after an agreement was reached with Haiti's leaders, the effort to define the problem helped to justify the sending of troops to assist in implementing the accord.[44]

Similarly, the White House's ability to *dominate the news* is substantial. Through news conferences, speeches, staged events, and international trips, the president can provide a sense of leadership while drawing attention to the administration's foreign policy priorities. That helps to accomplish the third goal, which is to *silence critics* of the president's policies. In the foreign and defense policy arenas, critics of presidential policies have rarely gotten the attention accorded to the White House. The media's attention, in short, can be focused in a way that effectively keeps the voices of critics and doubters subdued.

Most students of American foreign policy point to the 1991 Persian Gulf War against Iraq as a classic case of media management by both the White House and the Defense Department. Press coverage of the military buildup and invasion was limited and at times tightly controlled in the name of security. After the conflict, the press learned just how much it had been misled, and it reacted bitterly to the way it had been manipulated. Policymakers had learned many lessons from their experience in Vietnam. As one veteran reporter wrote, "If Vietnam was in a sense the media's war, Iraq was the military's."[45]

The main audience for most media coverage of foreign and defense policies is not the mass public, but segments of the public that are normally more interested in and informed about relevant issues. Called **attentive publics**, these groups typically make up less than one-fifth of the American public, and yet they play an important role in the shaping of U.S. policies. Much of what the general public (see the discussion in the next section) knows and thinks about foreign and defense policies comes from contacts with these attentive publics.

An important characteristic of the attentive publics is that many of them join and support organizations and groups that have specific positions on U.S. foreign and defense policies. Although these interest groups do not play a formal role in deciding national security policy, they are often highly influential.

The activities of interest groups in the foreign and defense policy arenas have been extremely diverse. Groups such as the influential Council on Foreign Relations have worked to increase citizens' awareness of foreign and defense policy issues. Other groups have promoted a specific ideological perspective, such as defeating international communism or establishing a world government. Still others have advocated particular goals, such as support for the United Nations or promotion of human rights. Many more are devoted to advancing specific community or business interests. Greek American organizations, for example, have lobbied actively for U.S. policies that favor Greece and give less support to its

Attentive publics The segments of the population that are normally more interested in and better informed about relevant issues than the general public. These groups are the main audience for media coverage of foreign and defense policies.

Critical Thinking

Do you regard yourself as part of the attentive public? Who among your family and friends could be considered a member of the attentive public?

long-time foe, Turkey. Trade associations representing almost every sector of the U.S. economy—from farmers seeking international markets for their surplus crops and automobile manufacturers seeking protection from Japanese imports to defense contractors wanting Congress to fund a new weapons system—have also frequently become involved in the foreign policymaking process.

There are even lobbyists representing foreign governments that are seeking favorable policies from the White House and Congress.[46] Over the past three decades, one of the most influential interests in the foreign policy arena has been the pro-Israel lobby. Of particular significance have been the activities of the *American-Israel Public Affairs Committee (AIPAC)*, which has had a significant influence on U.S. policy in the Middle East. In the late 1970s, for example, efforts to shore up U.S. relations with Saudi Arabia by selling that nation armaments were subject to considerable debate in Congress because several members feared that the weapons would be used against Israel. AIPAC's access to members of Congress was enhanced by the substantial campaign contributions it had made over the years, as well as by its ability to mount major grassroots lobbying campaigns in key regions of the country. Although it was unable to halt the arms deal with the Saudis, through its lobbying AIPAC was able to have severe restrictions placed on the conditions of the sale. Such power did not go unnoticed, of course, and in the early 1980s the Arab American community formed a group to counter AIPAC's influence—the National Association of Arab Americans (NAAA).[47]

The Role of Public Opinion

Students of public opinion often note that the general American public does not show a deep or enduring interest in foreign and defense policies. For most Americans, domestic policy concerns and personal affairs overshadow world affairs. Most look to the president and other policymakers for leadership in foreign and defense matters. When it is aroused, the mass public's interest in foreign and defense policies usually focuses on some immediate threat or crisis.[48]

For example, until the Arab oil embargo of 1973, few Americans knew how heavily the United States relied on imported oil. Nor could most Americans point to Vietnam on a world map until thousands of American troops were sent there in the early 1960s. When the general public does pay attention to a national security issue, its responses are often highly volatile and based on scant information.

The volatility of public opinion poses a dilemma for policymakers. To gain public support in foreign and defense affairs, they must often oversell the challenges being faced or the need for the administration's programs. Examples abound. Presidential trips abroad and summit meetings with leaders of other nations become media events that dominate the news for weeks. Throughout the Cold War, the Pentagon issued annual reports showing the growing threat of Soviet military superiority. The dramatization of such events helps rouse the public out of its normal passivity in matters of foreign affairs and defense.[49]

Some analysts believe that the mass public's main influence on policy derives from its attitude, or "mood," regarding U.S. involvement in world affairs. According to this **mood theory**, the general public has very little direct impact on specific foreign and defense matters. But its perceived willingness to accept certain views, tactics, and programs carries considerable weight in policy decisions.[50]

Historically, the public's mood has fluctuated between a willingness to accept greater U.S. involvement in world affairs and a contrary urge to withdraw from the international scene. When the public mood favors involvement, policymakers find it easier to engage in diplomacy or military ventures. When the public mood favors withdrawal, policymakers are reluctant to sign treaties, increase foreign aid, or commit U.S. troops abroad. President Carter faced such a public mood during his term in office. After the Vietnam War, most Americans were leery of new diplomatic initiatives or military ventures on foreign soil. By 1986, however, President Reagan found the American public more willing to support increasing U.S. commitments abroad. The Reagan administration responded by calling for increased defense spending and a greater commitment in Central America.[51]

George H. W. Bush's administration faced still another challenge in the shifting public mood accompanying the end of the Cold War and the growing discomfort with the United States' deteriorating position as a world economic power. In early 1991, strong public support for his actions in the Persian Gulf War gave Bush the highest ratings in public opinion polls ever achieved by a sitting president. Less than a year later, however, Bush's popularity declined as the public turned its attention to domestic problems. During the presidential campaign of 1992, conservative columnist Patrick Buchanan ran against President Bush in several Republican primaries, stressing the need for an "America first" attitude in the White House. Buchanan was trying to tap the isolationist attitudes that had once been the dominant feature of the public mood. He attracted less than one-third of the votes in those primary contests, however. His overall lack of success in that campaign (as well as in 1996 and 2000) reflected the fact that during the Cold War, a constant majority of Americans had come to accept active U.S. involvement in world affairs — an acceptance that they have not relinquished since the Cold War ended (see Figure 15.1).

President Clinton's focus on domestic affairs during his first two years in office was, in part, a response to greater public concern about economic problems. As he reached the midpoint of his first term, however, Clinton began to pay greater attention to international affairs. Neither the devastating defeat suffered by the Democrats in the 1994 elections nor Clinton's own reelection in 1996 seemed to reflect any clear message from the voters regarding the administration's foreign and defense policies. Nor did public opinion polls during that same period provide clear signals about the public's mood. Yet it had become increasingly obvious to foreign and defense policymakers that mood and opinion would mean a great deal more in this post–Cold War period, in which there seemed to be no "common enemy" for the public to focus on.[52]

One of the consequences of September 11 and the "war on terrorism" that followed is that it has defined a new common enemy for the public to focus on.

FIGURE 15.1

Preferred U.S. Role in World Affairs

Americans have consistently favored an active role for the United States in world affairs since the end of World War II. This has remained true during the post-Vietnam and post–Cold War periods as well.

Source: Data from the *CCFR: American Public Opinion Report—2004*, by The Chicago Council on Foreign Relations.

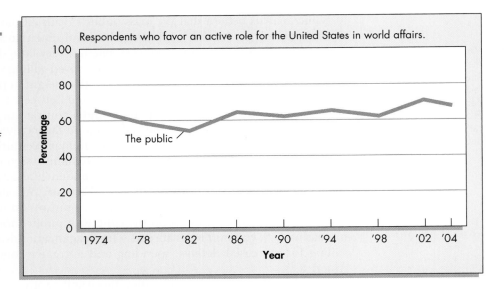

Respondents who favor an active role for the United States in world affairs.

The public

Wielding Diplomatic Power

FOCUS QUESTION   WHAT ARE THE SOURCES OF POWER AVAILABLE TO THOSE WHO USE DIPLOMACY TO CONDUCT AMERICAN FOREIGN POLICY?

But this enemy is more elusive than the Soviets, and the question remains whether the general public will be more attentive to world affairs in the long term as a result of those tragic events.

As with other areas of modern governance, power plays a key role in the conduct of foreign and defense policies. Joseph S. Nye, former dean of Harvard's Kennedy School of Government, posits that there are at least two types of power that a nation such as the United States can use in world affairs: *hard power* that relies on coercion, and *soft power* that relies on attraction.[53] Hard power, he argues, depends on military force (or the threat of its use) or on economic power in the form of payments or market incentives. In a related approach, Walter Russell Mead talks of two types of hard power: *sharp power*, which is found in the threatened use of military force, and *sticky power*, which is associated with commercial inducements and economic ties that, once developed, are difficult to break free of.[54]

Soft power attracts (like a magnet attracts) through exposure to cultural norms and values—to education and the exchange of ideas, to movies and music, to its promise of freedom and individual choice. Mead calls this *sweet power* because it relies on the desire of other nations and peoples to emulate what they see as attractive in the American model.

But as with all forms of potential power, the success of hard (sharp/sticky) or soft (attractive/sweet) power depends on how it is applied.

Diplomatic Tools

Like all nations, the United States uses several diplomatic tools in its relations with other countries (see the discussion in Chapter 11, on the presidency, of the president's role as chief diplomat). One of the most common tools is formal recognition of another nation. For the United States, **formal recognition** means that the president publicly accepts and acknowledges the sovereignty of another nation and receives its ambassador in Washington as that country's official representative. Granting or withdrawing formal recognition is a powerful tool of foreign policy. In 1948, President Truman formally recognized the State of Israel within hours of receiving word that the new nation had been formed. Because controversy and violence accompanied Israel's birth, diplomatic recognition by the United States was critically important and helped to establish a close relationship between the two countries. Similarly, as the Soviet Union collapsed in 1991, many of the emerging republics immediately sought recognition from the United States as a signal to the rest of the world of their legitimacy.

In contrast, when the United States fails to recognize a nation or breaks off formal diplomatic relations, it clearly signals its views on that country's leadership. American policymakers were often reluctant to extend recognition to communist countries even before the Cold War era. Although the Russian Revolution took place in 1917, the United States did not establish formal relations with the Soviet Union until 1933. Similarly, after a communist regime took over in China, nearly thirty years passed before the United States and the People's Republic of China agreed to exchange ambassadors.

Breaking off diplomatic relations is an extreme step in international affairs and is usually a response to some dramatic event. The United States ended its formal recognition of Cuba in 1961 when Fidel Castro seized American property without compensation and entered into a close relationship with the Soviet Union. In 1979, President Carter broke off formal ties with Iran after the American embassy was seized and its employees taken hostage.

In other cases, however, the United States has maintained formal relations with a country even if it objected to that country's policies. President Reagan, for example, did not sever American ties with the Nicaraguan government during the 1980s, even though his administration openly supported rebel groups (the *contras*) that were seeking to overthrow that nation's leadership. Reagan officials believed that by maintaining those relations, the United States would be able to provide more effective public support for the Nicaraguan opposition groups, who eventually won major elections in February 1990. Similarly, the United States maintained its relations with South Africa throughout the 1970s and

Formal recognition
The act whereby the president publicly accepts and acknowledges the sovereignty and government of another nation and receives its ambassador in Washington as that country's official representative.

1980s, despite widespread public condemnation of that country's apartheid policies. Many members of Congress and others urged the White House to sever diplomatic relations with China when its government violently crushed a student movement for democratic reforms in June 1989. President George H. W. Bush, who had once served as the American envoy to China, decided against taking such drastic measures.

Foreign aid is another major diplomatic tool. It usually takes the form of a grant of money or supplies to another nation, although it can also be a low-interest loan. The best-known example of foreign aid as a tool of U.S. foreign policy was the *Marshall Plan*. Proposed in 1947 by the then secretary of state George C. Marshall, the plan provided financial aid and low-cost loans to help the countries of Western Europe rebuild and strengthen their economies after World War II. The initiative for today's European Union can be traced to that effort.

As Third World nations emerged in the 1960s and 1970s, the United States provided an increasing amount of direct and indirect assistance for economic development. Foreign aid was also used to support and reward friendly governments that were threatened by internal rebellions or hostile neighbors. Most such aid was intended to strengthen the military capabilities of the recipient governments. President Reagan, for example, supported sending millions of dollars of military aid to El Salvador and other Central American nations as "security assistance" to help them withstand what the Reagan administration saw as the spread of Soviet influence in the region. Very little of that assistance was devoted to building schools and highways or promoting effective health-care and birth control programs.[55] The withholding of aid can also prove to be an effective tool. The Reagan administration showed its displeasure with the Nicaraguan government by halting U.S. aid to that nation. Many observers believe that this aid cutoff contributed to the economic problems that eventually led Nicaraguan voters to elect the opposition in 1990.

In the post–Cold War era, foreign aid has taken on new roles. Humanitarian aid was sent to the Kurdish people of Iraq after the Persian Gulf War and to the Ethiopian people, who suffered from both war and drought during the 1980s. George H. W. Bush's administration also provided some assistance to the republics emerging from the former Soviet Union as a means of supporting the move toward democracy and free-market economies in that region. When hundreds of thousands of Rwandans escaped to Zaire in 1994 following ethnic conflict that had resulted in the slaughter of thousands, the United States joined other nations in a major effort to provide shelter and clean water.

Treaties, a third major tool of diplomacy, are legally binding pacts by which two or more nations formalize an agreement reached through negotiation. Some treaties form the basis of international or regional organizations—for example, the United Nations Charter. Others establish standards of behavior among the nations that sign them—for example, treaties such as the NAFTA and GATT agreements discussed previously, which deal with trade issues, or, in the area of human rights, international agreements on the treatment of prisoners of war such as the Geneva Convention of 1949, or a treaty, which the United

Foreign aid Assistance provided by the United States to another country. This usually takes the form of a grant of money or supplies, but it can also be a low-interest loan.

Critical
Thinking

As the world's leading economic power, should we use foreign aid programs to enhance our influence or to help meet humanitarian needs in poorer nations?

Treaties Legally binding pacts by which two or more nations formalize an agreement reached through negotiation.

States signed in 1986, outlawing genocide (the mass murder of a specific group of people, such as occurred in Hitler's Germany during World War II). Other agreements address the treatment of prisoners of war and refugees. Treaties can also reflect solutions to disputes or problems arising between two or more nations. The United States and the Soviet Union signed a number of treaties after 1960 dealing with such issues as the proliferation of nuclear weapons, the use of nuclear weapons in outer space, the testing of nuclear weapons in the atmosphere, and arms limitations. The best-known use of treaties, however, relates to agreements about defense issues, such as NATO.

Covert actions — activities that are intentionally hidden from public view — can also have a considerable impact. Sometimes these actions are justified on the grounds that the operation could not be successfully conducted in full public view. At other times they are justified by the need to protect the lives of those involved. Nevertheless, the secrecy surrounding covert actions frequently raises questions about their legality. Covert actions range from gathering intelligence through bugging devices to paying an informant to planning the overthrow or assassination of another nation's leaders. The controversy that emerged in 2006 surrounding the news that the National Security Agency (NSA) had been monitoring U.S. domestic phones calls involving suspected terrorists was one of the rare instances when that top-secret agency's activities were scrutinized. The central issue was not the monitoring itself, but the fact that it involved domestic surveillance — something that is not permitted under normal circumstances. The involvement of the CIA in efforts to overthrow regimes is legendary, including the attempted 1961 invasion of Cuba; the training of 100,000 Laotian troops who fought in the Vietnam War; the funding of striking truckers in Chile to destabilize that country's government in the early 1970s; and the training and funding of Nicaraguan rebel forces through most of the 1980s.

In recent years there has been more attention paid to a tool called **public diplomacy**. A widely used definition of public diplomacy is "the government's process of communicating with foreign publics to create understanding of U.S. ideas and ideals, institutions and culture, and current goals and policies."[56] With its primary focus on the promotion of America's "soft power," public diplomacy is seen by its critics as a means to disseminate propaganda on behalf of U.S. policy. Others see it as a crucial part of American foreign policy in countries that get most of their impressions of the United States through U.S.-produced films and television shows that send mixed messages about American life.

Public diplomacy is associated with a variety of mechanisms such as libraries and book distribution; educational and cultural exchange programs; broadcasting programs such as Radio Liberty (targeted at Cuba), Radio Free Europe (which was broadcast into Eastern and Central Europe during the Cold War), and the Voice of America; and the production and dissemination of films and other media about the United States, its values, and policies. Prior to its integration into the State Department in the late 1990s, the United States Information Agency (USIA) was the major agency engaged in public diplomacy efforts, and its functions are now centered in the Office of the Under Secretary of State for

Covert actions Activities—ranging from gathering intelligence to assassinating foreign leaders—that are intentionally hidden from public view and may be of questionable legality.

Public diplomacy The officially sanctioned use of media and other information technology, cultural, and educational programs, and related means to promote the understanding and acceptance of a country's values and interests.

Public Diplomacy and Public Affairs. In the face of negative attitudes toward U.S. foreign policy, in 2005 the Bush administration appointed Karen Hughes, a close associate of President Bush, to head that post.

Military and Defense Strategies

FOCUS QUESTION WHAT ARE THE ISSUES AND CHOICES FACING THOSE WHO MAKE U.S. DEFENSE POLICIES?

During the Cold War era, American policymakers were convinced that the greatest threat posed by the Soviet Union and its allies was military in nature. They believed that communist influence could expand only through military conquest or through insurgent revolutions backed by the Soviet Union or China. It is little wonder, therefore, that so much of American foreign policymakers' attention was focused on military and defense strategies.

Two issues dominated the debate about America's military expenditures throughout the Cold War period and after. One was the amount of money spent on defense, which was at the heart of the "guns-or-butter" debate—a debate between those who believe that defense expenditures must take priority and those who think that additional funds should be spent on consumer goods and social services. The second issue was how to allocate the dollars being spent on defense.

Guns or Butter?

The key question in the guns-or-butter debate is how much of our nation's resources should go for defense. Before the Cold War, peacetime military spending in the United States remained relatively low compared with that in European nations. Our military expenditures consumed only a small portion of our economic resources—usually about 1 percent of the gross domestic product (GDP).

All that changed in the late 1940s. By 1950 the United States was a world power, and its leadership of the Western alliance made a large and costly military establishment necessary. That same year the Cold War became even more costly when the United States sent troops to help South Korea repel an attack by North Korea. The defense budget more than tripled, from $12.2 billion in 1950 to about $43 billion just five years later. During the 1960s, once the United States became actively involved in the Vietnam War, defense spending climbed to more than $80 billion and consumed nearly 9 percent of the nation's GDP (see Figure 15.2).

After American forces withdrew from Vietnam in the early 1970s, defense expenditures continued to grow, though at a slower rate. When Ronald Reagan took office in 1981, military spending had reached $157.5 billion (in real dollars), but that represented only 5.1 percent of the nation's GDP (see Figure 15.3). Within

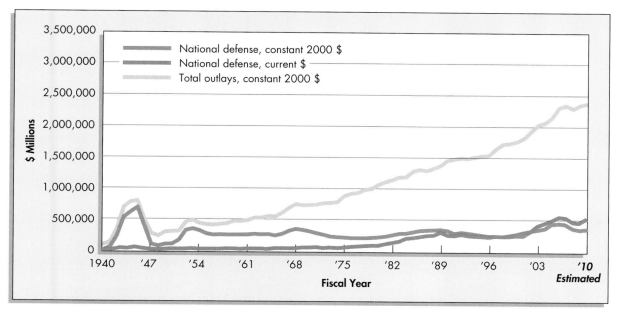

National defense, constant 2000 $
National defense, current $
Total outlays, constant 2000 $

$ Millions

3,500,000
3,000,000
2,500,000
2,000,000
1,500,000
1,000,000
500,000
0

1940   '47   '54   '61   '68   '75   '82   '89   '96   '03   '10

Fiscal Year   Estimated

FIGURE 15.2

Pre–September 11 Spending Patterns for National Defense

The amount of money spent on national defense seems much less when the value of the dollar is held constant (that is, when all dollars are adjusted to their fiscal year 2000 values). Using constant 2000 dollars, this figure shows that the overall growth of all federal government spending has increased regularly but the growth in military spending has remained relatively flat.

Source: Table 6.1, *Budget of the United States Government: Historical Tables, Fiscal Year 2007* (Washington, D.C.: GPO, 2006), pp. 118–125.

two years, however, Reagan administration policies had increased defense expenditures to nearly $209.9 billion, thus raising military expenditures to 6.1 percent of the nation's GDP. Only at the end of Reagan's term did the relative spending on defense begin to decline again.

Those who supported more spending for defense usually argued that the United States needed a strong military capability in the face of a constant Soviet military buildup. They pointed out that in 1982 the Soviet Union spent an estimated $952 per capita on its military, whereas the United States spent only $846 per capita. According to the U.S. Arms Control and Disarmament Agency, more than 15 percent of the Soviet Union's GDP was devoted to military expenditures — more than twice the figure for the United States. If we were to catch up with the Soviets on military spending, the argument ran, we must be willing to make as great an effort as they did.

During the late 1980s, Gorbachev's reforms in the Soviet Union undermined that justification, and the collapse of the Soviet regime in 1991 seemed to have eliminated that threat as a major factor in U.S. military policy. Nevertheless, advocates for maintaining high levels of U.S. defense spending pointed out that international threats remained — if not from the Soviets, then from the growing number of nuclear-armed Third World nations, international terrorists, and leaders such as Iraq's Saddam Hussein.[57] At the same time, a growing chorus of analysts and policymakers claimed that America neither needed nor could afford to spend more on defense. Even before the dramatic changes in the Soviet bloc, doubts had been raised about the need for such a large defense establishment. Opponents of defense spending pointed out that America's military strength was

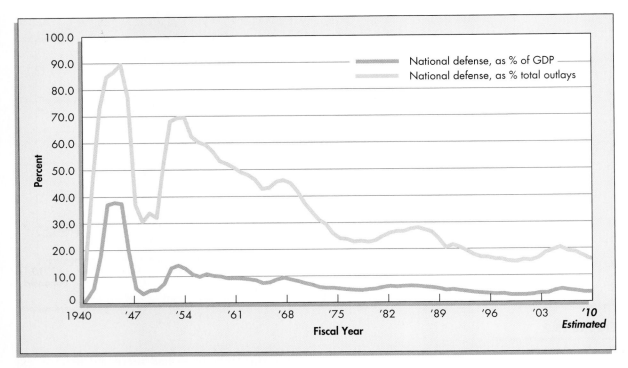

FIGURE 15.3

Relative Spending on National Defense Before September 11

The relative size of the national defense budget is also clear when seen as a percentage of the total budget (total outlays) or as a percentage of the economy (as measured by the gross domestic product).

Source: Table 6.1, *Budget of the United States Government: Historical Tables, Fiscal Year 2007* (Washington, D.C.: GPO, 2006), pp. 118–125.

already quite formidable, and that the economy could benefit from cutting back on defense expenditures.

The realization that the Cold War was over initially changed the nature of the guns-and-butter debate in two ways. First, there was general agreement that less would be spent on guns. A key question was, "How much less?" The Bush administration's plans called for a 25 percent reduction in military forces between 1992 and 1997. In its budget proposal for 1998, the Clinton administration called for spending levels at least $50 million lower than the amount spent on the military in 1989, the last year of the Cold War. Second, there was the question of what to do with the "*peace dividend*" generated by the projected decrease in defense spending. Should the government provide more butter — that is, should the savings on defense result in more spending on domestic programs — or should it use the dividend to reduce the deficit or federal taxes? By late 1994, however, policymakers realized that the hoped-for peace dividend was not going to materialize. That year alone, more than 110,000 troops were sent to various corners of the globe to deal with a wide range of post–Cold War missions. Rather than seek further reductions in defense spending, the Clinton administration announced that it would have to increase its projected budget requests for defense in the future, and by 2000, both the White House and Congress were advocating large increases in military expenditures. Citing personnel shortfalls and the need to spend more on maintenance and readiness, Clinton asked for the first major increase in military spending in more than a decade. Some members of Congress were advocating even greater increases, while experts in national security affairs argued that the Pentagon would require a major infusion of funds if it were to meet the challenges of the future.

The events of September 11, 2001, left no doubt about the need for more spending on the military. The fiscal year (FY) 2007 budget request for the Department of Defense was $439.3 billion — a 48 percent increase over the 2001 budget request. Another $42.7 billion was requested for the Department of Homeland Security—a 6 percent increase from the FY 2006 budget. All this meant, of course, that even less federal spending would be added to the "butter" side of the ledger.

Alternative Military Strategies

Throughout most of the Cold War era, the debate over how to allocate defense spending focused on what mix of nuclear and conventional forces would best meet the challenge posed by the Soviet Union. As difficult as that debate was, it relied on a consensus that the primary objective of military strategy was the containment of the Soviet threat. Today that consensus is gone, and the debate is more difficult.

The first and only use of nuclear weapons in time of war occurred in 1945, when the United States dropped atomic bombs on the Japanese cities of Hiroshima and Nagasaki. Nevertheless, the new weapon changed the nature of war and military strategy. A special report prepared in 1950 by the National Security Council staff underscored that change. It argued for a **deterrence strategy** based on the buildup of nuclear and conventional (nonnuclear) forces, so that any potential enemy would hesitate to attack the United States or its allies.

At first the council's appeal for a strategy based on both nuclear and conventional forces was ignored. During the 1950s, the principal defense strategy emphasized nuclear weapons. Called **massive retaliation**, this strategy entailed stockpiling nuclear weapons and warning the Soviet Union and its allies that any aggression against the United States or its allies could result in the destruction of Moscow and other major cities. However, the enormous buildup of the Soviet nuclear arsenal during the 1950s and 1960s focused attention on the dangers of massive retaliation as a policy. Given the development of intercontinental ballistic missiles (ICBMs), multiple independently targeted reentry vehicles (MIRVs), and other delivery technology, the Soviet Union could also devastate American cities. A new strategy emerged based on **mutual assured destruction (MAD)**: Each of the nuclear powers would hold the other in check by maintaining the ability to annihilate the other in any major confrontation.

Massive retaliation and its MAD variant were very risky and controversial strategies. In spending so much on nuclear weapons, the policymakers had let conventional forces deteriorate. By 1960, many felt that the United States had

Deterrence strategy The buildup and maintenance of nuclear and conventional forces and large stockpiles of weapons to discourage any potential enemy from attacking the United States or its allies.

Massive retaliation The military strategy favored by the United States during the 1950s, which involved warning the Soviet Union and its allies that any military confrontation could produce an annihilating nuclear attack on Moscow and other Soviet cities.

Mutual assured destruction (MAD) The strategy that evolved in the 1960s whereby each of the nuclear powers would hold the other in check by maintaining the ability to annihilate the other in any major nuclear confrontation.

Flexible response The
military strategy adopted
by the United States
during the 1960s that
shifted emphasis from
solely nuclear weapons
to increasing the United
States' ability to engage
in limited, conventional
wars in order to make
deterrence more credible.

lost its capacity to respond effectively to small, localized conflicts. Thus, during the 1960s, the emphasis shifted to a strategy of **flexible response**, which called for the buildup of America's nonnuclear, limited-war capabilities. Advocates of this strategy believed that strengthened conventional troops would make deterrence more credible, for the United States could counter enemy aggression with the right amount of force.

Throughout the 1970s, American policymakers stressed the need for keeping our nuclear weapons force at a level roughly equivalent to the Soviet force. In other words, nuclear equality, rather than nuclear superiority, would suffice. We would be safe — that is, invulnerable — if our enemies knew that we could retaliate effectively if we were attacked. As for nonnuclear forces, during the 1970s the U.S. defense strategy shifted to improving conventional weapons systems and training all-volunteer armed forces.

Two important developments during the Reagan–Bush years had a significant impact on U.S. defense policies: the development of a set of principles for the use of military force and a proposal for an elaborate missile defense system. Within the Pentagon, leadership passed to those who had served as field officers in Vietnam, and their views on the use of military force reflected the bitter lessons they had learned. Most of them were reluctant to have American forces engaged in any type of long-term, land-based operation that might lead to the kind of war fought in Vietnam.[58] The result was a policy statement articulated by Reagan's secretary of defense, Casper Weinberger, in 1984. Now called the **Weinberger Doctrine**, it laid out basic principles that effectively limited the use of U.S. military forces to situations "vital to our national interest or that of our allies" and where there was a willingness to commit the troops and other resources required to meet a clear and winnable objective.[59]

Weinberger Doctrine
A set of principles regarding the use of the U.S. military articulated by Reagan's secretary of defense. It became the basis for military strategy for the 1980s and most of the 1990s.

Although not always adhered to in practice during the Reagan–Bush years, those principles became the basis for discussions on the use of military force for the next decade and helped to determine how the United States fought the Persian Gulf War in 1991.[60]

On the nuclear side, President Reagan called for maintaining a weapons force to provide a margin of safety over the Soviets. The Reagan administration also sought more spending on new, more sophisticated nonnuclear weapons. But it was the **Strategic Defense Initiative (SDI)** that drew most of the attention during the latter part of the Reagan years. Often referred to as "Star Wars," it was a proposed $90 billion space-based weapons system that would render nuclear threats "impotent and obsolete."[61] It came the closest to reflecting the urge for absolute security embodied in the myth of vulnerability.

Strategic Defense Initiative (SDI) A plan endorsed by President Reagan that called for the development of a space-based defense shield against nuclear attack. Also referred to as "Star Wars."

In the post–Cold War era, attention focused on the development of a "balanced" approach that would allow the United States to deter aggression and protect the nation's "vital interests in an uncertain world." In 1997, the Clinton administration articulated an approach calling for a military capacity to deal with both peacetime operations and major military confrontations. On the one hand, the military must be ready to engage in a full range of small-scale unilateral and joint military operations, including "show-of-force operations, interventions, limited strikes, noncombatant evacuation operations, no-fly zone enforcement, peace enforcement, maritime sanctions enforcement, counter-terrorism operations, peacekeeping, humanitarian assistance, and disaster relief." On the other hand, it must maintain a capacity to fight and win "two nearly simultaneous major regional conflicts" anywhere in the world. There was no grand strategy involved in this approach, perhaps reflecting the absence of a clearly defined enemy or overarching military objective such as winning a war. The goal was to maintain the armed forces in a state of readiness just in case.[62]

On September 11, 2001, the Defense Department was in the process of completing its most recent comprehensive review of U.S. defense policies. The final report, issued a little over two weeks after the attack on the Pentagon, reflects an approach that was quickly adapted to the new realities of the war on terrorism. It called for shifting to a "capabilities-based model — one that focuses more on how an adversary might fight than who the adversary might be and where a war might occur." Such an approach "broadens the strategic perspective. It requires identifying capabilities that U.S. military forces will need to deter and defeat adversaries who will rely on surprise, deception, and asymmetric warfare to achieve their objectives."[63]

Equally significant, the report placed a high priority on providing defense for the territory of the United States. Although the word *defense* had often been used in discussions of U.S. military policy since World War II, little attention had been paid to actually developing defensive strategies for the United States, since an attack on American soil seemed unlikely. After September 11, however, defending the country became the Pentagon's top priority. The vulnerability was now real.

One consequence of this shift was a reorganization of the military's "joint command structure" that had been in place for two decades. Under the old structure, American forces were allocated to four major **Joint Commands**: US-PACOM, which had responsibility for military activities in the Pacific and most of Asia; USEUCOM, which covered Europe and most of Africa; USSOUTH-COM, which focused on South America and the Caribbean; and USCENTCOM, which covered most of the Middle East and Persian Gulf regions. Responsibility for the defense of North America was left to a Joint Forces Command that had general responsibility for projects and tasks that did not fall under the other four major Joint Commands. Following up on the recommendations made in the quadrennial report, in April 2002 the Pentagon announced the creation of a Northern Command — USNORTHCOM — that would have responsibility for coordinating the defense of the United States, Mexico, and Canada.

Joint Commands The basic command structures used by the U.S. military to coordinate operations in various regions of the world.

Conclusion: The Reshaping of Foreign and Defense Policy

American foreign and defense policies have undergone many periods of change, reflecting the many changes that have taken place in the world arena. The intrigues of European politics played a central role in shaping U.S. foreign and defense policies during the 1800s. Pressures created by European imperialism

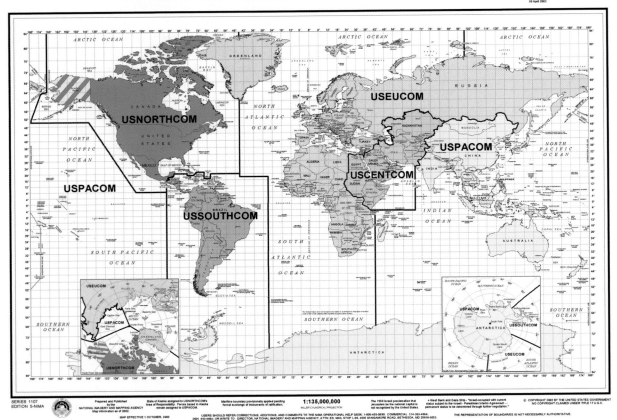

Restructuring U.S. Defenses

After the attacks of September 11, the U.S. military command structure was reorganized to include the U.S. Northern Command (USNORTHCOM), which would be responsible for defense of the North American continent.

and America's own urge to extend and protect its economic influence helped mold those policies at the turn of the past century. World wars and shifting international power helped define U.S. international activity until the middle of the twentieth century, and the mantle of international leadership passed to American presidents during the Cold War. Throughout the nation's history, however, there has been a constant urge to protect the country from the dangers of political, military, and economic vulnerability. Complementing those efforts to deal with perceived vulnerabilities have been at least four visions (Wilsonian, Hamiltonian, Jeffersonian, and Jacksonian) informing the U.S. role on the world stage. Faced with economic challenges in the form of energy shortages or competition from East Asia and Europe, U.S. foreign policymakers see their mission as the re-creation of a world order more favorable to American interests. In the wake of the collapse of the Soviet bloc and the rise of fundamentalist regimes, the United States engages in Wilsonian efforts to support emerging democracies. And there is no doubting the Jacksonian nature of the

Bush administration's initial reaction to the events of 9/11—an immediate declaration of an all-out war on terror reinforced by the president's announcement to the world that "Either you are with us, or you are with the terrorists."

The events of September 11, 2001, the war in Iraq, continued instability in the Middle East—these and other changes in the international arena are continuing to reshape U.S. foreign and defense policies. A great deal has already changed. Clearly, the myth of vulnerability remains a powerful factor guiding America's policymakers. The consequences of attachment to this myth can be both positive and negative. On the positive side, the myth creates a sense of caution that can result in more thoughtful decisions. On the negative side, there is always the danger that the urge for absolute security can distort the perspectives and choices of America's policymakers. Therefore, the central question remains concerning which of the American project visions—or which mixture of those visions—will emerge from the ongoing war on terrorism.

Tying It Together

FOCUS QUESTIONS RECAP

✳ What are the factors that are changing U.S. foreign and defense policies?

✳ What is the history of U.S. foreign and defense policy, and what does it tell us about America's role in the world today?

✳ Who is involved in the making of U.S. foreign and defense policies, and what roles do they play?

✳ What are the sources of diplomatic power available to those who conduct American foreign policy?

✳ What are the issues and choices facing those who make U.S. defense policies?

CHAPTER SUMMARY

1. American foreign and defense policies have been influenced by a myth of vulnerability and a resulting urge to minimize insecurity.

2. Initially, American policies were guided by the principles of isolationism and unilateralism established by George Washington and other early presidents. Combined with a sense of vulnerability, these principles led to American expansionist policies during the 1800s. Although U.S. involvement in world affairs increased significantly from the 1890s through the 1930s, not until World War II did American policymakers and the American people accept the nation's role as an international leader. After World War II, U.S. international involvement continued, but in response to the perceived threat of Soviet expansionism. That

involvement took the form of a policy of containment. The Cold War put an end to unilateralism, and the United States entered into formal alliances with the nations of Western Europe to form NATO. Other alliances followed.

In more recent years, the United States has adapted its foreign and defense policies to changes in world affairs. Among the most important of these changes have been the emergence of Third World nations and an end to the bipolar world situation as countries such as France and the People's Republic of China became more independent of their respective alliances.

The collapse of the Soviet Union has had a significant impact on the conduct of foreign policy. One major transformation during the Clinton years was the increased emphasis on economic security as a primary goal of U.S. foreign policy.

3. The making of U.S. foreign and defense policies involves a distinct set of policymaking institutions, although many factors help determine the decisions in each arena. During the Cold War era, the crucial decision makers in foreign and defense matters were part of an inner circle centered in the White House. However, the moods and attitudes of the general public also influenced the decisions made in both arenas. In the post–Cold War era, the nature of foreign and defense policymaking has been changing, with a greater role for both Congress and the public.

4. U.S. policymakers have a variety of foreign policy tools, or sources of power, at their disposal. These include formal recognition, foreign aid, treaties, and covert actions.

5. Two issues have marked American defense policies since the start of the Cold War: how much money to spend on defense and which defensive strategies to rely on. The end of the Cold War did not close that debate, but rather has changed the nature of the issues and questions being raised.

6. The events of September 11, 2001, have resulted in a sharp alteration of both foreign and defense policies, and the myth of vulnerability remains a powerful force shaping America's foreign and defense policies.

Key Terms

Foreign and defense policies (448)
International organizations (449)
Regional organizations (449)
Transnational organizations (449)
Multinational corporations (MNCs) (449)
Nongovernmental organizations (NGOs) (450)
Washington's Farewell Address (450)
Monroe Doctrine (451)
Isolationism (451)
Unilateralism (452)
Expansionism (452)
Cold War (453)
Containment (454)
Détente (456)
Balance of power strategy (456)
Weapons of mass destruction (WMD) (465)
National security policy (465)
National Security Council (NSC) (467)
National security adviser (467)
"Fast track" authority (468)

Department of State (469)
Foreign Service (469)
Department of Defense (469)
Joint Chiefs of Staff (JCS) (470)
Intelligence-gathering agencies (470)
Attentive publics (473)
Mood theory (475)
Formal recognition (477)
Foreign aid (478)
Treaties (478)
Covert actions (479)
Public diplomacy (479)
Deterrence strategy (483)
Massive retaliation (483)
Mutual assured destruction (MAD) (483)
Flexible response (484)
Weinberger Doctrine (484)
Strategic Defense Initiative (SDI) (484)
Joint Commands (485)

Net Work

Do you want to know more about a particular country, foreign policy issue, or military operation that you are curious about? Here are some potential starting points.

- If you are interested in a specific country, begin by visiting the Central Intelligence Agency's World Factbook website at **www.cia.gov/cia/publications/factbook/index.html**.

- If you want to find out about U.S. foreign policy topics, start at the U.S. State Department's policy website (**www.state.gov/www/policy.html**).

- Are you curious about the treaty obligations of the United States? Treaties and agreements currently in force can be accessed through the website of the Department of State's Office of Legal Counsel (**www.state.gov/www.global/legal_affairs/tifindex.html**). In 2006, there was considerable debate surrounding the legal obligations of the U.S. under the Geneva Conventions; these can be read at **www.genevaconventions.org**.

- U.S. military forces are stationed all over the world, and some of those forces have established websites to help families stay in touch and to provide information to anyone who might be curious about the mission or status of the operation. You can start your search for these websites at the U.S. Defense Department's information website, **www.defenselink.mil**.

As an exercise, use your Web-searching skills to find the sites with policy-relevant information, and as you do so, consider how the Internet has enhanced the general public's access to this material. For decades the public had to rely on the reporters who attended daily briefings at the State and Defense Departments for information about U.S. involvement in world affairs. Today, not only can anyone with access to the World Wide Web download material from those briefings, but they can also access an almost unlimited amount of additional online resources and perspectives.

Appendixes

The Declaration of Independence in Congress, July 4, 1776

The unanimous declaration of the thirteen United States of America

When, in the course of human events, it becomes necessary for one people to dissolve the political bands which have connected them with another, and to assume, among the powers of the earth, the separate and equal station to which the laws of nature and of nature's God entitle them, a decent respect to the opinions of mankind requires that they should declare the causes which impel them to the separation.

We hold these truths to be self-evident: That all men are created equal; that they are endowed by their Creator with certain unalienable rights; that among these are life, liberty, and the pursuit of happiness; that, to secure these rights, governments are instituted among men, deriving their just powers from the consent of the governed; that whenever any form of government becomes destructive of these ends, it is the right of the people to alter or to abolish it, and to institute new government, laying its foundation on such principles, and organizing its powers in such form, as to them shall seem most likely to effect their safety and happiness. Prudence, indeed, will dictate that governments long established should not be changed for light and transient causes; and accordingly all experience hath shown that mankind are more disposed to suffer, while evils are sufferable, than to right themselves by abolishing the forms to which they are accustomed. But when a long train of abuses and usurpations, pursuing invariably the same object, evinces a design to reduce them under absolute despotism, it is their right, it is their duty, to throw off such government, and to provide new guards for their future security. Such has been the patient sufferance of these colonies; and such is now the necessity which constrains them to alter their former systems of government. The history of the present King of Great Britain is a history of repeated injuries and usurpations, all having in direct object the establishment of an absolute tyranny over these states. To prove this, let facts be submitted to a candid world.

He has refused his assent to laws, the most wholesome and necessary for the public good.

He has forbidden his governors to pass laws of immediate and pressing importance, unless suspended in their operation till his assent should be obtained; and, when so suspended, he has utterly neglected to attend to them.

He has refused to pass other laws for the accommodation of large districts of people, unless those people would relinquish the right of representation in the legislature, a right inestimable to them, and formidable to tyrants only.

He has called together legislative bodies at places unusual, uncomfortable, and distant from the depository of their public records, for the sole purpose of fatiguing them into compliance with his measures.

He has dissolved representative houses repeatedly, for opposing, with manly firmness, his invasions on the rights of the people.

He has refused for a long time, after such dissolutions, to cause others to be elected; whereby the legislative powers, incapable of annihilation, have returned to the people at large for their exercise; the state remaining, in the mean time, exposed to all the dangers of invasions from without and convulsions within.

He has endeavored to prevent the population of these states; for that purpose obstructing the laws for naturalization of foreigners; refusing to pass others to encourage their migration hither, and raising the conditions of new appropriations of lands.

He has obstructed the administration of justice, by refusing his assent to laws for establishing judiciary powers.

He has made judges dependent on his will alone, for the tenure of their offices, and the amount and payment of their salaries.

He has erected a multitude of new offices, and sent hither swarms of officers to harass our people and eat out their substance.

He has kept among us, in times of peace, standing armies, without the consent of our legislatures.

He has affected to render the military independent of, and superior to, the civil power.

He has combined with others to subject us to a jurisdiction foreign to our constitution, and unacknowledged by our laws, giving his assent to their acts of pretended legislation:

For quartering large bodies of armed troops among us;

For protecting them, by a mock trial, from punishment for any murders which they should commit on the inhabitants of these states;

For cutting off our trade with all parts of the world;

For imposing taxes on us without our consent;

For depriving us, in many cases, of the benefits of trial by jury;

For transporting us beyond seas, to be tried for pretended offenses;

For abolishing the free system of English laws in a neighboring province, establishing therein an arbitrary government, and enlarging its boundaries, so as to render it at once an example and fit instrument for introducing the same absolute rule into these colonies;

For taking away our charters, abolishing our most valuable laws, and altering fundamentally the forms of our governments;

For suspending our own legislatures, and declaring themselves invested with power to legislate for us in all cases whatsoever.

He has abdicated government here, by declaring us out of his protection and waging war against us.

He has plundered our seas, ravaged our coasts, burned our towns, and destroyed the lives of our people.

He is at this time transporting large armies of foreign mercenaries to complete the works of death, desolation, and tyranny already begun with circumstances of cruelty and perfidy scarcely paralleled in the most barbarous ages, and totally unworthy the head of a civilized nation.

He has constrained our fellow-citizens, taken captive on the high seas, to bear arms against their country, to become the executioners of their friends and brethren, or to fall themselves by their hands.

He has excited domestic insurrections amongst us, and has endeavored to bring on the inhabitants of our frontiers the merciless Indian savages, whose known rule of warfare is an undistinguished destruction of all ages, sexes, and conditions.

In every stage of these oppressions we have petitioned for redress in the most humble terms; our repeated petitions have been answered only by repeated injury. A prince, whose character is thus marked by every act which may define a tyrant, is unfit to be the ruler of a free people.

Nor have we been wanting in our attentions to our British brethren. We have warned them, from time to time, of attempts by their legislature to extend an unwarrantable jurisdiction over us. We have reminded them of the circumstances of our emigration and settlement here. We have appealed to their native justice and magnanimity; and we have conjured them, by the ties of our common kindred, to disavow these usurpations, which would inevitably interrupt our connections and correspondence. They, too, have been deaf to the voice of justice and of consanguinity. We must, therefore, acquiesce in the necessity which denounces our separation, and hold them, as we hold the rest of mankind, enemies in war, in peace friends.

We, therefore, the representatives of the United States of America, in General Congress assembled, appealing to the Supreme Judge of the world for the rectitude of our intentions, do, in the name and by the authority of the good people of these colonies, solemnly publish and declare, that these United Colonies are, and of right ought to be, FREE AND INDEPENDENT STATES; that they are absolved from all allegiance to the British crown, and that all political connection between them and the state of Great Britain is, and ought to be, totally dissolved; and that, as free and independent states, they have full power to levy war, conclude peace, contract alliances, establish commerce, and do all other acts and things which independent states may of right do. And for the support of this declaration, with a firm reliance on the protection of Divine Providence, we mutually pledge to each other our lives, our fortunes, and our sacred honor.

JOHN HANCOCK
and fifty-five others

The Constitution of the United States of America*

PREAMBLE

We the people of the United States, in order to form a more perfect union, establish justice, insure domestic tranquility, provide for the common defense, promote the general welfare, and secure the blessings of liberty to ourselves and our posterity, do ordain and establish this Constitution for the United States of America.

ARTICLE I

Section 1 All legislative powers herein granted shall be vested in a Congress of the United States, which shall consist of a Senate and a House of Representatives.

*Passages no longer in effect are printed in italic type.

Section 2 The House of Representatives shall be composed of members chosen every second year by the people of the several States, and the electors in each State shall have the qualifications requisite for electors of the most numerous branch of the State Legislature.

No person shall be a Representative who shall not have attained to the age of twenty-five years, and been seven years a citizen of the United States, and who shall not, when elected, be an inhabitant of that State in which he shall be chosen.

Representatives and direct taxes shall be apportioned among the several States which may be included within this Union, according to their respective numbers, *which shall be determined by adding to the whole number of free persons, including those bound to service for a term of years and excluding Indians not taxed, three-fifths of all other persons.* The actual enumeration shall be made within three years after the first meeting of the Congress of the United States, and within every subsequent term of ten years, in such manner as they shall by law direct. The number of Representatives shall not exceed one for every thirty thousand, but each State shall have at least one Representative; *and until such enumeration shall be made, the State of New Hampshire shall be entitled to choose three, Massachusetts eight, Rhode Island and Providence Plantations one, Connecticut five, New York six, New Jersey four, Pennsylvania eight, Delaware one, Maryland six, Virginia ten, North Carolina five, South Carolina five, and Georgia three.*

When vacancies happen in the representation from any State, the Executive authority thereof shall issue writs of election to fill such vacancies.

The House of Representatives shall choose their Speaker and other officers; and shall have the sole power of impeachment.

Section 3 The Senate of the United States shall be composed of two Senators from each State, *chosen by the legislature thereof,* for six years; and each Senator shall have one vote.

Immediately after they shall be assembled in consequence of the first election, they shall be divided as equally as may be into three classes. The seats of the Senators of the first class shall be vacated at the expiration of the second year, of the second class at the expiration of the fourth year, and of the third class at the expiration of the sixth year, so that one-third may be chosen every second year; *and if vacancies happen by resignation or otherwise during the recess of the legislature of any State, the Executive thereof may make temporary appointments until the next meeting of the legislature, which shall then fill such vacancies.*

No person shall be a Senator who shall not have attained to the age of thirty years, and been nine years a citizen of the United States, and who shall not, when elected, be an inhabitant of that State for which he shall be chosen.

The Vice-President of the United States shall be President of the Senate, but shall have no vote, unless they be equally divided.

The Senate shall choose their other officers, and also a President *pro tempore*, in the absence of the Vice-President, or when he shall exercise the office of President of the United States.

The Senate shall have the sole power to try all impeachments. When sitting for that purpose, they shall be on oath or affirmation. When the President of the United States is tried, the Chief Justice shall preside: and no person shall be convicted without the concurrence of two-thirds of the members present.

Judgment in cases of impeachment shall not extend further than to removal from office, and disqualification to hold and enjoy any office of honor, trust or profit under the United States: but the party convicted shall nevertheless be liable and subject to indictment, trial, judgment and punishment, according to law.

Section 4 The times, places and manner of holding elections for Senators and Representatives shall be prescribed in each State by the legislature thereof; but the Congress may at any time by law make or alter such regulations, except as to the places of choosing Senators.

The Congress shall assemble at least once in every year, *and such meeting shall be on the first Monday in December, unless they shall by law appoint a different day.*

Section 5 Each house shall be the judge of the elections, returns and qualifications of its own members, and a majority of each shall constitute a quorum to do business; but a smaller number may adjourn from day to day, and may be authorized to compel the attendance of absent members, in such manner, and under such penalties, as each house may provide.

Each house may determine the rules of its proceedings, punish its members for disorderly behavior, and, with the concurrence of two-thirds, expel a member.

Each house shall keep a journal of its proceedings, and from time to time publish the same, excepting such parts as may in their judgment require secrecy; and the yeas and nays of the members of either house on any question shall, at the desire of one-fifth of those present, be entered on the journal.

Neither house, during the session of Congress, shall, without the consent of the other, adjourn for more than three days, nor to any other place than that in which the two houses shall be sitting.

Section 6 The Senators and Representatives shall receive a compensation for their services, to be ascertained by law and paid out of the treasury of the United States. They shall in all cases except treason, felony and breach of the peace, be privileged from arrest during their attendance at the session of their respective houses, and in going to and returning from the same; and for any speech or debate in either house, they shall not be questioned in any other place.

No Senator or Representative shall, during the time for which he was elected, be appointed to any civil office under the authority of the United States, which shall have been created, or the emoluments whereof shall have been increased, during such time; and no person holding any office under the United States shall be a member of either house during his continuance in office.

Section 7 All bills for raising revenue shall originate in the House of Representatives; but the Senate may propose or concur with amendments as on other bills.

Every bill which shall have passed the House of Representatives and the Senate, shall, before it become a law, be presented to the President of the United States; if he approve he shall sign it, but if not he shall return it with objections to that house in which it originated, who shall enter the objections at large on their journal, and proceed to reconsider it. If after such reconsideration two-thirds of that house shall agree to pass the bill, it shall be sent, together with the objections, to the other house, by which it shall likewise be reconsidered, and, if approved by two-thirds of that house, it shall become a law. But in all such cases the votes of both houses shall be determined by yeas and nays, and the names of the persons voting for and against the bill shall be entered on the journal of each house respectively. If any bill shall not be returned by the President within ten days (Sundays excepted) after it shall have been presented to him, the same shall be a law, in like manner as if he had signed it, unless the Congress by their adjournment prevents its return, in which case it shall not be a law.

Every order, resolution, or vote to which the concurrence of the Senate and House of Representatives may be necessary (except on a question of adjournment) shall be presented to the President of the United States; and before the same shall take effect, shall be approved by him, or being disapproved by him, shall be repassed by two-thirds of the Senate and House of Representatives, according to the rules and limitations prescribed in the case of a bill.

Section 8   The Congress shall have power

To lay and collect taxes, duties, imposts, and excises, to pay the debts and provide for the common defense and general welfare of the United States; but all duties, imposts, and excises shall be uniform throughout the United States;

To borrow money on the credit of the United States;

To regulate commerce with foreign nations, and among the several States, and with the Indian tribes;

To establish an uniform rule of naturalization, and uniform laws on the subject of bankruptcies throughout the United States;

To coin money, regulate the value thereof, and of foreign coin, and fix the standard of weights and measures;

To provide for the punishment of counterfeiting the securities and current coin of the United States;

To establish post offices and post roads;

To promote the progress of science and useful arts by securing for limited times to authors and inventors the exclusive right to their respective writings and discoveries;

To constitute tribunals inferior to the Supreme Court;

To define and punish piracies and felonies committed on the high seas and offenses against the law of nations;

To declare war, grant letters of marque and reprisal, and make rules concerning captures on land and water;

To raise and support armies, but no appropriation of money to that use shall be for a longer term than two years;

To provide and maintain a navy;

To make rules for the government and regulation of the land and naval forces;

To provide for calling forth the militia to execute the laws of the Union, suppress insurrections, and repel invasions;

To provide for organizing, arming, and disciplining the militia, and for governing such part of them as may be employed in the service of the United States, reserving to the States respectively the appointment of the officers, and the authority of training the militia according to the discipline prescribed by Congress;

To exercise exclusive legislation in all cases whatsoever, over such district (not exceeding ten miles square) as may, by cession of particular States, and the acceptance of Congress, become the seat of government of the United States, and to exercise like authority over all places purchased by the consent of the legislature of the State in which the same shall be, for erection of forts, magazines, arsenals, dockyards, and other needful buildings; and

To make all laws which shall be necessary and proper for carrying into execution the foregoing powers, and all other powers vested by this Constitution in the government of the United States, or in any department or officer thereof.

Section 9   *The migration or importation of such persons as any of the States now existing shall think proper to admit shall not be prohibited by the Congress prior to the year 1808; but a tax or duty may be imposed on such importation, not exceeding $10 for each person.*

The privilege of the writ of habeas corpus shall not be suspended, unless when in cases of rebellion or invasion the public safety may require it.

No bill of attainder or ex post facto law shall be passed.

No capitation, or other direct, tax shall be laid, unless in proportion to the census or enumeration herein before directed to be taken.

No tax or duty shall be laid on articles exported from any State.

No preference shall be given by any regulation of commerce or revenue to the ports of one State over those of another; nor shall vessels bound to, or from, one State, be obliged to enter, clear, or pay duties in another.

No money shall be drawn from the treasury, but in consequence of appropriations made by law; and a regular statement and account of the receipts and expenditures of all public money shall be published from time to time.

No title of nobility shall be granted by the United States: and no person holding any office of profit or trust under them, shall, without the consent of the Congress, accept of any present, emolument, office, or title, of any kind whatever, from any king, prince, or foreign state.

Section 10 No State shall enter into any treaty, alliance, or confederation; grant letters of marque and reprisal; coin money; emit bills of credit; make anything but gold and silver coin a tender in payment of debts; pass any bill of attainder, ex post facto law, or law impairing the obligation of contracts, or grant any title of nobility.

No State shall, without the consent of Congress, lay any imposts or duties on imports or exports, except what may be absolutely necessary for executing its inspection laws: and the net produce of all duties and imposts, laid by any State on imports or exports, shall be for the use of the treasury of the United States; and all such laws shall be subject to the revision and control of the Congress.

No State shall, without the consent of Congress, lay any duty of tonnage, keep troops or ships of war in time of peace, enter into any agreement or compact with another State, or with a foreign power, or engage in war, unless actually invaded, or in such imminent danger as will not admit of delay.

ARTICLE II

Section 1 The executive power shall be vested in a President of the United States of America. He shall hold his office during the term of four years, and, together with the Vice-President, chosen for the same term, be elected as follows:

Each State shall appoint, in such manner as the legislature thereof may direct, a number of electors, equal to the whole number of Senators and Representatives to which the State may be entitled in the Congress; but no Senator or Representative, or person holding an office of trust or profit under the United States, shall be appointed an elector.

The electors shall meet in their respective States, and vote by ballot for two persons, of whom one at least shall not be an inhabitant of the same State with themselves. And they shall make a list of all the persons voted for, and of the number of votes for each; which list they shall sign and certify, and transmit sealed to the seat of government of the United States, directed to the President of the Senate. The President of the Senate shall, in the presence of the Senate and House of Representatives, open all the certificates, and the votes shall then be counted. The person having the greatest number of votes shall be the President, if such number be a majority of the whole number of electors appointed; and if there be more than one who have such majority, and have an equal number of votes, then the House of Representatives shall immediately choose by ballot one of them for President; and if no person have a majority, then from the five highest on the list said house shall in like manner choose the President. But in choosing the President the votes shall be taken by States, the representation from each State having one vote; a quorum for this purpose shall consist of a member or members from two-thirds of the States, and a majority of all the States shall be necessary to a choice. In every case, after the choice of the President, the person having the greatest number of votes of the electors shall be the Vice-President. But if there should remain two or more who have equal votes, the Senate shall choose from them by ballot the Vice-President.

The Congress may determine the time of choosing the electors and the day on which they shall give their votes; which day shall be the same throughout the United States.

No person except a natural-born citizen, *or a citizen of the United States at the time of the adoption of this Constitution,* shall be eligible to the office of President; neither shall any person be eligible to that office who shall not have attained to the age of thirty-five years, and been fourteen years a resident within the United States.

In cases of the removal of the President from office or of his death, resignation, or inability to discharge the powers and duties of the said office, the same shall devolve on the Vice-President, and the Congress may by law provide for the case of removal, death, resignation, or inability, both of the President and Vice-President, declaring what officer shall then act as President, and such officer shall act accordingly, until the disability be removed, or a President shall be elected.

The President shall, at stated times, receive for his services a compensation, which shall neither be increased nor diminished during the period for which he shall have been elected, and he shall not receive within that period any other emolument from the United States, or any of them.

Before he enter on the execution of his office, he shall take the following oath or affirmation:

"I do solemnly swear (or affirm) that I will faithfully execute the office of the President of the United States, and will to the best of my ability preserve, protect and defend the Constitution of the United States."

Section 2 The President shall be commander in chief of the army and navy of the United States, and of the militia of the several States, when called into the actual service of the United States; he may require the opinion, in writing, of the principal officer in each of the executive departments, upon any subject relating to the duties of their respective offices, and he shall have power to grant reprieves and pardons for offenses against the United States, except in cases of impeachment.

He shall have power, by and with the advice and consent of the senate, to make treaties, provided two-thirds of the Senators present concur; and he shall nominate, and by and with the advice and consent of the Senate, shall appoint ambassadors, other public ministers and consuls, judges of the Supreme Court, and all other officers of the United States, whose appointments are not herein otherwise provided for, and which shall be established by law: but Congress may by law vest the appointment of such inferior officers, as they think proper, in the President alone, in the courts of law, or in the heads of departments.

The President shall have power to fill up all vacancies that may happen during the recess of the Senate, by granting commissions which shall expire at the end of their next session.

Section 3 He shall from time to time give to the Congress information of the state of the Union, and recommend to their consideration such measures as he shall judge necessary and expedient; he may, on extraordinary occasions, convene both houses, or ei-

ther of them, and in case of disagreement between them, with respect to the time of adjournment, he may adjourn them to such time as he shall think proper; he shall receive ambassadors and other public ministers; he shall take care that the laws be faithfully executed, and shall commission all the officers of the United States.

Section 4 The President, Vice-President and all civil officers of the United States shall be removed from office on impeachment for, and conviction of, treason, bribery, or other high crimes and misdemeanors.

ARTICLE III

Section 1 The judicial power of the United States shall be vested in one Supreme Court, and in such inferior courts as the Congress may from time to time ordain and establish. The judges, both of the Supreme and inferior courts, shall hold their offices during good behavior, and shall, at stated times, receive for their services a compensation which shall not be diminished during their continuance in office.

Section 2 The judicial power shall extend to all cases, in law and equity, arising under this Constitution, the laws of the United States, and treaties made, or which shall be made, under their authority; to all cases affecting ambassadors, other public ministers and consuls; to all cases of admiralty and maritime jurisdiction; to controversies to which the United States shall be a party; to controversies between two or more States; *between a State and citizens of another State*; between citizens of different States; between citizens of the same State claiming lands under grants of different States, and between a State, or the citizens thereof, and foreign states, citizens, or subjects.

In all cases affecting ambassadors, other public ministers and consuls, and those in which a State shall be party, the Supreme Court shall have original jurisdiction. In all the other cases before mentioned, the Supreme Court shall have appellate jurisdiction, both as to law and fact, with such exceptions, and under such regulations, as the Congress shall make.

The trial of all crimes, except in cases of impeachment, shall be by jury; and such trial shall be held in the state where said crimes shall have been committed; but when not committed within any State, the trial shall be at such place or places as the Congress may by law have directed.

Section 3 Treason against the United States shall consist only in levying war against them, or in adhering to their enemies, giving them aid and comfort. No person shall be convicted of treason unless on the testimony of two witnesses to the same overt act, or on confession in open court.

The Congress shall have power to declare the punishment of treason, but no attainder of treason shall work corruption of blood, or forfeiture except during the life of the person attained.

ARTICLE IV

Section 1 Full faith and credit shall be given in each State to the public acts, records, and judicial proceedings of every other State. And the Congress may by general laws prescribe the manner in which such acts, records, and proceedings shall be proved, and the effect thereof.

Section 2 The citizens of each State shall be entitled to all privileges and immunities of citizens in the several States.

A person charged in any State with treason, felony, or other crime, who shall flee from justice, and be found in another State, shall on demand of the executive authority of the State from which he fled, be delivered up, to be removed to the State having jurisdiction of the crime.

No person held to service or labor in one State, under the laws thereof, escaping into another, shall, in consequence of any law or regulation therein, be discharged from such service or labor, but shall be delivered up on claim of the party to whom such service or labor may be due.

Section 3 New States may be admitted by the Congress into this Union; but no new State shall be formed or erected within the jurisdiction of any other State; nor any State be formed by the junction of two or more States, or parts of States, without the consent of the legislatures of the States concerned as well as of the Congress.

The Congress shall have power to dispose of and make all needful rules and regulations respecting the territory or other property belonging to the United States; and nothing in this Constitution shall be so construed as to prejudice any claims of the United States, or of any particular State.

Section 4 The United States shall guarantee to every State in this Union a republican form of government, and shall protect each of them against invasion; and on application of the legislature, or of the executive (when the legislature cannot be convened), against domestic violence.

ARTICLE V

The Congress, whenever two-thirds of both houses shall deem it necessary, shall propose amendments to this Constitution, or, on the application of the legislatures of two-thirds of the several States, shall call a convention for proposing amendments, which, in either case, shall be valid to all intents and purposes, as part of this Constitution, when ratified by the legislatures of three-fourths of the several States, or by conventions in three-fourths thereof, as the one or the other mode of ratification may be proposed by the Congress; *provided that no amendments which may be made prior to the year one thousand eight hundred and eight shall in any manner affect the first and fourth clauses in the ninth section of the first article*; and that no State, without its consent, shall be deprived of its equal suffrage in the Senate.

ARTICLE VI

All debts contracted and engagements entered into, before the adoption of this Constitution, shall be as valid against the United States under this Constitution, as under the Confederation.

This Constitution, and the laws of the United States which shall be made in pursuance thereof; and all treaties made, or which shall be made, under the authority of the United States, shall be the supreme law of the land; and the judges in every State shall be bound thereby, anything in the Constitution or laws of any State to the contrary notwithstanding.

The Senators and Representatives before mentioned, and the members of the several State legislatures, and all executive and judicial officers, both of the United States and of the several States, shall be bound by oath or affirmation to support this Constitution; but no religious test shall ever be required as a qualification to any office or public trust under the United States.

ARTICLE VII

The ratification of the conventions of nine States shall be sufficient for the establishment of this Constitution between the States so ratifying the same.

Done in Convention by the unanimous consent of the States present, the seventeenth day of September in the year of our Lord one thousand seven hundred and eighty-seven and of the Independence of the United States of America the twelfth. In witness whereof we have hereunto subscribed our names.

GEORGE WASHINGTON
and thirty-eight others

Amendments to the Constitution*

AMENDMENT I

Congress shall make no law respecting an establishment of religion, or prohibiting the free exercise thereof; or abridging the freedom of speech, or of the press; or the right of the people peaceably to assemble, and to petition the government for a redress of grievances.

AMENDMENT II

A well-regulated militia being necessary to the security of a free State, the right of the people to keep and bear arms shall not be infringed.

AMENDMENT III

No soldier shall, in time of peace, be quartered in any house without the consent of the owner, nor in time of war, but in a manner to be prescribed by law.

*The first ten amendments (the Bill of Rights) were adopted in 1791.

AMENDMENT IV

The right of the people to be secure in their persons, houses, papers, and effects, against unreasonable searches and seizures, shall not be violated, and no warrants shall issue but upon probable cause, supported by oath or affirmation, and particularly describing the place to be searched, and the persons or things to be seized.

AMENDMENT V

No person shall be held to answer for a capital, or otherwise infamous crime, unless on a presentment or indictment of a grand jury, except in cases arising in the land or naval forces, or in the militia, when in actual service in time of war or public danger; nor shall any person be subject for the same offense to be twice put in jeopardy of life or limb; nor shall be compelled in any criminal case to be a witness against himself, nor be deprived of life, liberty, or property, without due process of law; nor shall private property be taken for public use without just compensation.

AMENDMENT VI

In all criminal prosecutions, the accused shall enjoy the right to a speedy and public trial, by an impartial jury of the State and district wherein the crime shall have been committed, which district shall have been previously ascertained by law, and to be informed of the nature and cause of the accusation; to be confronted with the witnesses against him; to have compulsory process for obtaining witnesses in his favor, and to have the assistance of counsel for his defense.

AMENDMENT VII

In suits at common law, where the value in controversy shall exceed twenty dollars, the right of trial by jury shall be preserved, and no fact tried by a jury shall be otherwise reexamined in any court of the United States, than according to the rules of the common law.

AMENDMENT VIII

Excessive bail shall not be required, nor excessive fines imposed, nor cruel and unusual punishments inflicted.

AMENDMENT IX

The enumeration in the Constitution, of certain rights, shall not be construed to deny or disparage others retained by the people.

AMENDMENT X

The powers not delegated to the United States by the Constitution, nor prohibited by it to the States, are reserved to the States respectively, or to the people.

AMENDMENT XI *[Adopted 1798]*

The judicial power of the United States shall not be construed to extend to any suit in law or equity, commenced or prosecuted against one of the United States by citizens of another State, or by citizens or subjects of any foreign State.

AMENDMENT XII *[Adopted 1804]*

The electors shall meet in their respective States, and vote by ballot for President and Vice-President, one of whom, at least, shall not be an inhabitant of the same State with themselves; they shall name in their ballots the person voted for as President, and in distinct ballots the person voted for as Vice-President, and they shall make distinct lists of all persons voted for as President, and of all persons voted for as Vice-President, and of the number of votes for each, which lists they shall sign and certify, and transmit sealed to the seat of government of the United States, directed to the President of the Senate; the President of the Senate shall, in the presence of the Senate and House of Representatives, open all the certificates and the votes shall then be counted; the person having the greatest number of votes for President shall be the President, if such number be a majority of the whole number of electors appointed; and if no per-

son have such majority, then from the persons having the highest numbers not exceeding three on the list of those voted for as President, the House of Representatives shall choose immediately, by ballot, the President. But in choosing the President, the votes shall be taken by States, the representation from each State having one vote; a quorum for this purpose shall consist of a member or members from two-thirds of the States, and a majority of all the states shall be necessary to a choice. And if the House of Representatives shall not choose a President whenever the right of choice shall devolve upon them, *before the fourth day of March next following,* then the Vice-President shall act as President, as in the case of the death or other constitutional disability of the President.

The person having the greatest number of votes as Vice-President shall be the Vice-President, if such number be a majority of the whole number of electors appointed; and if no person have a majority, then from the two highest numbers on the list the Senate shall choose the Vice-President; a quorum for the purpose shall consist of two-thirds of the whole number of Senators, and a majority of the whole number shall be necessary to a choice. But no person constitutionally ineligible to the office of President shall be eligible to that of Vice-President of the United States.

AMENDMENT XIII *[Adopted 1865]*

Section 1 Neither slavery nor involuntary servitude, except as a punishment for crime whereof the party shall have been duly convicted, shall exist within the United States, or any place subject to their jurisdiction.

Section 2 Congress shall have the power to enforce this article by appropriate legislation.

AMENDMENT XIV *[Adopted 1868]*

Section 1 All persons born or naturalized in the United States, and subject to the jurisdiction thereof, are citizens of the United States and of the State wherein they reside. No State shall make or enforce any law which shall abridge the privileges or immunities of citizens of the United States; nor shall any State deprive any person of life, liberty, or property, without due process of law; nor deny to any person within its jurisdiction the equal protection of the laws.

Section 2 Representatives shall be apportioned among the several States according to their respective numbers, counting the whole number of persons in each State, excluding Indians not taxed. But when the right to vote at any election for the choice of electors for President and Vice-President of the United States, Representatives in Congress, the executive and judicial officers of a State, or the members of the legislature thereof, is denied to any of the male inhabitants of such State, being twenty-one years of age and citizens of the United States, or in any way abridged, except for participation in rebellion, or other crime, the basis of representation therein shall be reduced in the proportion which the number of such *male* citizens shall bear to the whole number of *male* citizens *twenty-one* years of age in such State.

Section 3 No person shall be a Senator or Representative in Congress, or elector of President and Vice-President, or hold any office, civil or military, under the United States, or under any State, who, having previously taken an oath, as a member of Congress, or as an officer of the United States, or as a member of any State legislature, or as an executive or judicial officer of any State, to support the Constitution of the United States, shall have engaged in insurrection or rebellion against the same, or given aid or comfort to the enemies thereof. Congress may, by a vote of two-thirds of each house, remove such disability.

Section 4 The validity of the public debt of the United States, authorized by law, including debts incurred for payment of pensions and bounties for services in suppressing insurrection or rebellion, shall not be questioned. But neither the United States nor any State shall assume or pay any debt or obligation incurred in aid of insurrection or rebellion against the United States, or any claim for the loss of emancipation of any slave; but all such debts, obligations, and claims shall be held illegal and void.

Section 5 The Congress shall have power to enforce, by appropriate legislation, the provisions of this article.

AMENDMENT XV *[Adopted 1870]*

Section 1 The right of citizens of the United States to vote shall not be denied or abridged by the United States or by any State on account of race, color, or previous condition of servitude.

Section 2 The Congress shall have power to enforce this article by appropriate legislation.

AMENDMENT XVI *[Adopted 1913]*

The Congress shall have power to lay and collect taxes on incomes, from whatever source derived, without apportionment among the several States, and without regard to any census or enumeration.

AMENDMENT XVII *[Adopted 1913]*

Section 1 The Senate of the United States shall be composed of two Senators from each State, elected by the people thereof, for six years; and each Senator shall have one vote. The electors [voters] in each State shall have the qualifications requisite for electors of the most numerous branch of the State legislatures.

Section 2 When vacancies happen in the representation of any State in the Senate, the executive authority of such State shall issue writs of election to fill such vacancies: Provided, that the Legislature of any State may empower the executive thereof to make temporary appointments until the people fill the vacancies by election as the Legislature may direct.

Section 3 This amendment shall not be so construed as to affect the election or term of any Senator chosen before it becomes valid as part of the Constitution.

AMENDMENT XVIII
[Adopted 1919, repealed 1933]

Section 1 *After one year from the ratification of this article the manufacture, sale or transportation of intoxicating* liquors within, the importation thereof into, or the exportation thereof from the United States and all territory subject to the jurisdiction thereof, for beverage purposes, is hereby prohibited.

Section 2 *The Congress and the several States shall have concurrent power to enforce this article by appropriate legislation.*

Section 3 *This article shall be inoperative unless it shall have been ratified as an amendment to the Constitution by the legislatures of the several States, as provided by the Constitution, within seven years from the date of the submission thereof to the States by the Congress.*

AMENDMENT XIX *[Adopted 1920]*

Section 1 The right of citizens of the United States to vote shall not be denied or abridged by the United States or by any State on account of sex.

Section 2 The Congress shall have power to enforce this article by appropriate legislation.

AMENDMENT XX *[Adopted 1933]*

Section 1 The terms of the President and Vice-President shall end at noon on the 20th day of January, and the terms of Senators and Representatives at noon on the 3rd day of January, of the years in which such terms would have ended if this article had not been ratified; and the terms of their successors shall then begin.

Section 2 The Congress shall assemble at least once in every year, and such meetings shall begin at noon on the 3rd day of January, unless they shall by law appoint a different day.

Section 3 If, at the time fixed for the beginning of the term of the President, the President-elect shall have died, the Vice-President-elect shall become President. If a President shall not have been chosen before the time fixed for the beginning of his term, or if the President-elect shall have failed to qualify, then the Vice-President-elect shall act as President until a President shall have qualified; and the Congress may by law provide for the case wherein neither a President-elect nor a Vice-President-elect shall have

qualified, declaring who shall then act as President, or the manner in which one who is to act shall be selected, and such persons shall act accordingly until a President or Vice-President shall have qualified.

Section 4 The Congress may by law provide for the case of the death of any of the persons from whom the House of Representatives may choose a President whenever the right of choice shall have devolved upon them, and for the case of the death of any of the persons from whom the Senate may choose a Vice-President whenever the right of choice shall have devolved upon them.

Section 5 Sections 1 and 2 shall take effect on the 15th day of October following the ratification of this article.

Section 6 This article shall be inoperative unless it shall have been ratified as an amendment to the Constitution by the Legislatures of three-fourths of the several States within seven years from the date of its submission.

AMENDMENT XXI *[Adopted 1933]*

Section 1 The eighteenth article of amendment to the Constitution of the United States is hereby repealed.

Section 2 The transportation or importation into any State, Territory, or Possession of the United States for delivery or use therein of intoxicating liquors, in violation of the laws thereof, is hereby prohibited.

Section 3 This article shall be inoperative unless it shall have been ratified as an amendment to the Constitution by conventions in the several States, as provided in the Constitution, within seven years from the date of submission thereof to the States by the Congress.

AMENDMENT XXII *[Adopted 1951]*

Section 1 No person shall be elected to the office of President more than twice, and no person who has held the office of President, or acted as President, for more than two years of a term to which some other person was elected President shall be elected to the office of President more than once. But this article shall not apply to any person holding the office of President when this article was proposed by the Congress, and shall not prevent any person who may be holding the office of President, or acting as President, during the term within which this article becomes operative from holding the office of President or acting as President during the remainder of such term.

Section 2   This article shall be inoperative unless it shall have been ratified as an amendment to the Constitution by the legislatures of three-fourths of the several States within seven years from the date of its submission to the States by the Congress.

AMENDMENT XXIII   *[Adopted 1961]*

Section 1   The District constituting the seat of Government of the United States shall appoint in such manner as the Congress may direct:

A number of electors of President and Vice-President equal to the whole number of Senators and Representatives in Congress to which the District would be entitled if it were a State, but in no event more than the least populous State; they shall be in addition to those appointed by the States, but they shall be considered for the purposes of the election of President and Vice-President, to be electors appointed by a State; and they shall meet in the District and perform such duties as provided by the twelfth article of amendment.

Section 2   The Congress shall have the power to enforce this article by appropriate legislation.

AMENDMENT XXIV   *[Adopted 1964]*

Section 1   The right of citizens of the United States to vote in any primary or other election for President or Vice-President, for electors for President or Vice-President, or for Senator or Representative in Congress, shall not be denied or abridged by the United States or any State by reason of failure to pay any poll tax or other tax.

Section 2   The Congress shall have the power to enforce this article by appropriate legislation.

AMENDMENT XXV   *[Adopted 1967]*

Section 1   In case of the removal of the President from office or of his death or resignation, the Vice-President shall become President.

Section 2   Whenever there is a vacancy in the office of the Vice-President, the President shall nominate a Vice-President who shall take office upon confirmation by a majority vote of both Houses of Congress.

Section 3   Whenever the President transmits to the President *pro tempore* of the Senate and the Speaker of the House of Representatives his written declaration that he is unable to discharge the powers and duties of his office, and until he transmits to them a written declaration to the contrary, such powers and duties shall be discharged by the Vice-President as Acting President.

Section 4   Whenever the Vice-President and a majority of either the principal officers of the executive departments or of such other body as Congress may by law provide, transmit to the President *pro tempore* of the Senate and the Speaker of the House of Representatives their written declaration that the President is unable to discharge the powers and duties of his office, the Vice-President shall immediately assume the powers and duties of the office as Acting President.

Thereafter, when the President transmits to the President *pro tempore* of the Senate and the Speaker of the House of Representatives his written declaration that no inability exists, he shall resume the powers and duties of his office unless the Vice-President and a majority of either the principal officers of the executive department[s] or of such other body as Congress may by law provide, transmit within four days to the President *pro tempore* of the Senate and the Speaker of the House of Representatives their written declaration that the President is unable to discharge the powers and duties of his office. Thereupon Congress shall decide the issue, assembling within forty-eight hours for that purpose if not in session. If the Congress, within twenty-one days after receipt of the latter written declaration, or, if Congress is not in session, within twenty-one days after Congress is required to assemble, determines by two-thirds vote of both Houses that the President is unable to discharge the powers and duties of his office, the Vice-President shall continue to discharge the same as Acting President; otherwise, the President shall resume the powers and duties of his office.

AMENDMENT XXVI *[Adopted 1971]*

Section 1 The right of citizens of the United States, who are eighteen years of age or older, to vote shall not be denied or abridged by the United States or by any State on account of age.

Section 2 The Congress shall have power to enforce this article by appropriate legislation.

AMENDMENT XXVII *[Adopted 1992]*

No law, varying the compensation for the services of the senators and representatives shall take effect, until an election of representatives shall have intervened.

Federalist No. 10, 1787

To the People of the State of New York: Among the numerous advantages promised by a well-constructed union, none deserves to be more accurately developed than its tendency to break and control the violence of faction. The friend of popular governments, never finds himself so much alarmed for their character and fate, as when he contemplates their propensity to this dangerous vice. He will not fail, therefore, to set a due value on any plan which, without violating the principles to which he is attached, provides a proper cure for it. The instability, injustice, and confusion introduced into the public councils, have, in truth, been the mortal diseases under which popular governments have everywhere perished; as they continue to be the favourite and fruitful topics from which the adversaries to liberty derive their most specious declamations. The valuable improvements made by the American constitutions on the popular models, both ancient and modern, cannot certainly be too much admired; but it would be an unwarrantable partiality, to contend that they have as effectually obviated the danger on this side,

as was wished and expected. Complaints are everywhere heard from our most considerate and virtuous citizens, equally the friends of public and private faith, and of public and personal liberty, that our governments are too unstable; that the public good is disregarded in the conflicts of rival parties; and that measures are too often decided, not according to the rules of justice, and the rights of the minor party, but by the superior force of an interested and overbearing majority. However anxiously we may wish that these complaints had no foundation, the evidence of known facts will not permit us to deny that they are in some degree true. It will be found, indeed, on a candid review of our situation, that some of the distresses under which we labour have been erroneously charged on the operation of our governments; but it will be found, at the same time, that other causes will not alone account for many of our heaviest misfortunes; and, particularly, for that prevailing and increasing distrust of public engagements, and alarm for private rights, which are echoed from one end of the continent to the other. These must be chiefly, if not wholly, effects of the unsteadiness and injustice, with which a factious spirit has tainted our public administrations.

By a faction, I understand a number of citizens, whether amounting to a majority or minority of the whole, who are united and actuated by some common impulse of passion, or of interest, adverse to the rights of other citizens, or to the permanent and aggregate interests of the community.

There are two methods of curing the mischiefs of faction: The one, by removing its causes; the other, by controlling its effects.

There are again two methods of removing the causes of faction: The one, by destroying the liberty which is essential to its existence; the other, by giving to every citizen the same opinions, the same passions, and the same interests.

It could never be more truly said, than of the first remedy, that it was worse than the disease. Liberty is to faction what air is to fire, an aliment without which it instantly expires. But it could not be a less folly to abolish liberty, which is essential to political life, because it nourishes faction, than it would be to wish the annihilation of air, which is essential to animal life, because it imparts to fire its destructive agency.

The second expedient is as impracticable, as the first would be unwise. As long as the reason of man continues fallible, and he is at liberty to exercise it, different opinions will be formed. As long as the connection subsists between his reason and his self-love, his opinions and his passions will have a reciprocal influence on each other; and the former will be objects to which the latter will attach themselves. The diversity in the faculties of men, from which the rights of property originate, is not less an insuperable obstacle to an uniformity of interests. The protection of these faculties is the first object of government. From the protection of different and unequal faculties of acquiring property, the possession of different degrees and kinds of property immediately results; and from the influence of these on the sentiments and views of the respective proprietors, ensues a division of the society into different interests and parties.

The latent causes of faction are thus sown in the nature of man; and we see them everywhere brought into different degrees of activity, according to the different circumstances of civil society. A zeal for different opinions concerning religion, concerning government, and many other points, as well of speculation as of practice; an attachment to different leaders ambitiously contending for preeminence and power; or to persons of other descriptions whose fortunes have been interesting to the human passions, have, in turn, divided mankind into parties, inflamed them with mutual animosity, and rendered them much more disposed to vex and oppress each other, than to cooperate for their common good. So strong is this propensity of mankind, to fall into mutual animosities, that where no substantial occasion presents itself, the most frivolous and fanciful distinctions have been sufficient to kindle their unfriendly passions and excite their most violent conflicts. But the most common and durable source of factions, has been the various and unequal distribution of property. Those who hold, and those who are without property, have ever formed distinct interests in society. Those who are creditors, and those who are debtors, fall under a like discrimination. A landed interest, a manufacturing interest, a mercantile interest, a moneyed interest, with many lesser interests, grow up of necessity in civilized nations, and divide them into different classes, actuated by different sentiments and views. The regulation of these various and interfering interests forms the principal task of modern legislation, and involves the spirit of the party and faction in the necessary and ordinary operations of the government.

No man is allowed to be a judge in his own cause, because his interest will certainly bias his judgment, and, not improbably, corrupt his integrity. With equal, nay, with greater reason, a body of men are unfit to be both judges and parties at the same time; yet what are many of the most important acts of legislation, but so many judicial determinations, not indeed concerning the right of single persons, but concerning the rights of large bodies of citizens? And what are the different classes of legislators, but advocates and parties to the causes which they determine? Is a law proposed concerning private debts? It is a question to which the creditors are parties on one side, and the debtors on the other. Justice ought to hold the balance between them. Yet the parties are, and must be, themselves the judges; and the most numerous party, or, in other words, the most powerful faction, must be expected to prevail. Shall domestic manufactures be encouraged, and in what degree, by restrictions on foreign manufactures? Are questions which would be differently decided by the landed and the manufacturing classes; and probably by neither with a sole regard to justice and the public good. The apportionment of taxes, on the various descriptions of property, is an act which seems to require the most exact impartiality; yet there is, perhaps, no legislative act, in which greater opportunity and temptation are given to a predominant party to trample on the rules of justice. Every shilling, with which they overburden the inferior number, is a shilling saved to their own pockets.

It is in vain to say, that enlightened statesmen will be able to adjust these clashing interests, and render them all subservient to the public good. Enlightened statesmen will not always be at the helm: nor, in many cases, can such an adjustment be made at all, without taking into view indirect and remote considerations, which will rarely prevail over the immediate interest which one party may find in disregarding the rights of another, or the good of the whole.

The inference to which we are brought is, that the causes of faction cannot be removed; and that relief is only to be sought in the means of controlling its effects.

If a faction consists of less than a majority, relief is supplied by the republican principle, which enables the majority to defeat its sinister views, by regular vote. It may clog the administration, it may convulse the society; but it will be unable to execute and mask its violence under the forms of the constitution. When a majority is included in a faction, the form of popular government, on the other hand, enables it to sacrifice to its ruling passion or interest, both the public good and the rights of other citizens. To secure the public good, and private rights, against the danger of such a faction, and at the same time to preserve the spirit and the form of popular government, is then the great object to which our inquiries are directed. Let me add, that it is the great desideratum, by which alone this form of government can be rescued from the opprobrium under which it has so long laboured, and be recommended to the esteem and adoption of mankind.

By what means is this object attainable? Evidently by one of two only. Either the existence of the same passion or interest in a majority, at the same time, must be prevented; or the majority, having such coexistent passion or interest, must be rendered, by their number and local situation, unable to concert and carry into effect schemes of oppression. If the impulse and the opportunity be suffered to coincide, we well know that neither moral nor religious motives can be relied on as an adequate control. They are not found to be such on the injustice and violence of individuals, and lose their efficacy in proportion to the number combined together; that is, in proportion as their efficacy becomes needful.

From this view of the subject, it may be concluded, that a pure democracy, by which I mean a society consisting of a small number of citizens, who assemble and administer the government in person, can admit of no cure for the mischiefs of faction. A common passion or interest will, in almost every case, be felt by a majority of the whole; a communication and concert, results from the form of government itself; and there is nothing to check the inducements to sacrifice the weaker party, or an obnoxious individual. Hence, it is, that such democracies have ever been spectacles of turbulence and contention; have ever been found incompatible with personal security, or the rights of property; and have in general been as short in their lives, as they have

been violent in their deaths. Theoretic politicians, who have patronized this species of government, have erroneously supposed, that by reducing mankind to a perfect equality in their political rights, they would, at the same time, be perfectly equalized and assimilated in their possessions, their opinions, and their passions.

A republic, by which I mean a government in which the scheme of representation takes place, opens a different prospect, and promises the cure for which we are seeking. Let us examine the points in which it varies from pure democracy, and we shall comprehend both the nature of the cure and the efficacy which it must derive from the union.

The two great points of difference, between a democracy and a republic, are, first, the delegation of the government, in the latter, to a small number of citizens, elected by the rest; secondly, the greatest number of citizens, and greater sphere of country, over which the latter may be extended.

The effect of the first difference is, on the one hand, to refine and enlarge the public views, by passing them through the medium of a chosen body of citizens, whose wisdom may best discern the true interest of their country, and whose patriotism and love of justice, will be least likely to sacrifice it to temporary or partial considerations. Under such a regulation, it may well happen, that the public voice, pronounced by the representatives of the people, will be more consonant to the public good, than if pronounced by the people themselves, convened for the purpose. On the other hand the effect may be inverted. Men of factious tempers, of local prejudices, or of sinister designs, may by intrigue, by corruption, or by other means, first obtain the suffrages, and then betray the interest of the people. The question resulting is, whether small or extensive republics are most favourable to the election of proper guardians of the public weal; and it is clearly decided in favour of the latter by two obvious considerations.

In the first place, it is to be remarked that, however small the republic may be, the representatives must be raised to a certain number, in order to guard against the cabals of a few; and that however large it may be, they must be limited to a certain number, in order to guard against the confusion of a multitude. Hence, the number of representatives in the two cases not being in proportion to that of the constituents, and being proportionally greatest in the small republic, it follows, that if the proportion of fit characters be not less in the large than in the small republic, the former will present a greater option, and consequently a greater probability of a fit choice.

In the next place, as each representative will be chosen by a greater number of citizens in the large than in the small republic, it will be more difficult for unworthy candidates to practise with success the vicious arts, by which elections are too often carried; and the suffrages of the people being more free, will be more likely to centre in men who possess the most attractive merit, and the most diffusive and established characters.

It must be confessed, that in this, as in most other cases, there is a mean, on both sides of which inconveniences will be found to lie. By enlarging too much the number of electors, you render the representative too little acquainted with all their local circumstances and lesser interests; as by reducing it too much, you render him unduly attached to these, and too little fit to comprehend and pursue great and national objects. The federal constitution forms a happy combination in this respect; the great and aggregate interests being referred to the national, the local and particular to the state legislatures.

The other point of difference is, the greater number of citizens, and extent of territory, which may be brought within the compass of republican, than of democratic government; and it is this circumstance principally which renders factious combinations less to be dreaded in the former, than in the latter. The smaller the society, the fewer probably will be the distinct parties and interests composing it; the fewer the distinct parties and interests, the more frequently will a majority be found of the same party; and the smaller the number of individuals composing a majority, and the smaller the compass within which they are placed, the more easily will they concert and execute their plans of oppression. Extend the sphere, and you take in a greater variety of parties and interests; you make it less probable that a majority of the whole will have a common motive to invade the rights of other citizens; or if such a common motive exists, it will be more difficult for all who feel it to discover their own strength, and to act in unison with each other. Besides other impediments, it may be re-

marked, that where there is a consciousness of unjust or dishonourable purposes, communication is always checked by distrust, in proportion to the number whose concurrence is necessary.

Hence, it clearly appears, that the same advantage, which a republic has over a democracy, in controlling the effects of faction, is enjoyed by a large over a small republic,—is enjoyed by the union over the states composing it. Does this advantage consist in the substitution of representatives, whose enlightened views and virtuous sentiments render them superior to local prejudices, and to schemes of injustice? It will not be denied that the representation of the union will be most likely to possess these requisite endowments. Does it consist in the greater security afforded by a greater variety of parties, against the event of any one party being able to outnumber and oppress the rest? In an equal degree does the increased variety of parties, comprised within the union, increase the security? Does it, in fine, consist in the greater obstacles opposed to the concert and accomplishment of the secret wishes of an unjust and interested majority? Here, again, the extent of the union gives it the most palpable advantage.

The influence of factious leaders may kindle a flame within their particular states, but will be unable to spread a general conflagration through the other states; a religious sect may degenerate into a political faction in a part of the confederacy; but the variety of sects dispersed over the entire face of it, must secure the national councils against any danger from that source: a rage for paper money, for an abolition of debts, for an equal division of property, or for any other improper or wicked project, will be less apt to pervade the whole body of the union than a particular member of it; in the same proportion as such a malady is more likely to taint a particular county or district, than an entire state.

In the extent and proper structure of the union, therefore, we behold a republican remedy for the diseases most incident to republican government. And according to the degree of pleasure and pride we feel in being republicans, ought to be our zeal in cherishing the spirit, and supporting the character of federalists.

JAMES MADISON

Federalist No. 51, 1788

To the People of the State of New York: To what expedient then shall we finally resort for maintaining in practice the necessary partition of power among the several departments, as laid down in the constitution? The only answer that can be given is, that as all these exterior provisions are found to be inadequate, the defect must be supplied, by so contriving the interior structure of the government, as that its several constituent parts may, by their mutual relations, be the means of keeping each other in their proper places. Without presuming to undertake a full development of this important idea, I will hazard a few general observations, which may perhaps place it in a clearer light, and enable us to form a more correct judgment of the principles and structure of the government planned by the convention.

In order to lay a due foundation for that separate and distinct exercise of the different powers of government, which to a certain extent, is admitted on all hands to be essential to the preservation of liberty, it is evident that each department should have a will of its own; and consequently should be so constituted, that the members of each should have as little agency as possible in the appointment of the members of the others. Were this principle rigorously adhered to, it would require that all the appointments for the supreme executive, legislative, and judiciary magistracies, should be drawn from the same fountain of authority, the people, through channels, having no communication whatever with one another. Perhaps such a plan of constructing the several departments would be less difficult in practice than it may in contemplation appear. Some difficulties however, and some additional expense, would attend the execution of it. Some deviations therefore from the principle must be admitted. In the constitution of the judiciary department in particular, it might be inexpedient to insist rigorously on the principle; first, because peculiar qualifications being essential in the members, the primary consideration ought to be to select that mode of choice, which best secures these qualifications; secondly, because the permanent tenure by which the appointments are held in that department, must soon destroy all sense of dependence on the authority conferring them.

It is equally evident that the members of each department should be as little dependent as possible on those of the others, for the emoluments annexed to their offices. Were the executive magistrate, or the judges, not independent of the legislature in this particular, their independence in every other would be merely nominal.

But the great security against a gradual concentration of the several powers in the same department, consists in giving to those who administer each department, the necessary constitutional means, and personal motives, to resist encroachments of the others. The provision for defense must in this, as in all other cases, be made commensurate to the danger of attack. Ambition must be made to counteract ambition. The interest of the man must be connected with the constitutional rights of the place. It may be a reflection on human nature, that such devices should be necessary to control the abuses of government. But what is government itself but the greatest of all reflections on human nature? If men were angels, no government would be necessary. If angels were to govern men, neither external nor internal controls on government would be necessary. In framing a government which is to be administered by men over men, the great difficulty lies in this: You must first enable the government to control the governed; and in the next place, oblige it to control itself. A dependence on the people is no doubt the primary control on the government; but experience has taught mankind the necessity of auxiliary precautions.

This policy of supplying by opposite and rival interests, the defect of better motives, might be traced through the whole system of human affairs, private as well as public. We see it particularly displayed in all the subordinate distributions of power; where the constant aim is to divide and arrange the several offices in such a manner as that each may be a check on the other; that the private interest of every individual, may be a sentinel over the public rights. These inventions of prudence cannot be less requisite in the distribution of the supreme powers of the state.

But it is not possible to give to each department an equal power of self defense. In republican government the legislative authority, necessarily, predominates. The remedy for this inconveniency is, to divide the legislature into different branches; and to render them by different modes of election, and different principles of action, as little connected with each other, as the nature of their common functions, and their common dependence on the society, will admit. It may even be necessary to guard against dangerous encroachments by still further precautions. As the weight of the legislative authority requires that it should be thus divided, the weakness of the executive may require, on the other hand, that it should be fortified. An absolute negative, on the legislature, appears at first view to be the natural defense with which the executive magistrate should be armed. But perhaps it would be neither altogether safe, nor alone sufficient. On ordinary occasions, it might not be exerted with the requisite firmness; and on extraordinary occasions, it might be perfidiously abused. May not this defect of an absolute negative be supplied, by some qualified connection between this weaker department, and the weaker branch of the stronger department, by which the latter may be led to support the constitutional rights of the former, without being too much detached from the rights of its own department?

If the principles on which these observations are founded be just, as I persuade myself they are, and they be applied as a criterion, to the several state constitutions, and to the federal constitution, it will be found, that if the latter does not perfectly correspond with them, the former are infinitely less able to bear such a test.

There are moreover two considerations particularly applicable to the federal system of America, which place that system in a very interesting point of view.

First. In a single republic, all the power surrendered by the people, is submitted to the administration of a single government; and usurpations are guarded against by a division of the government into distinct and separate departments. In the compound republic of America, the power surrendered by the people, is first divided between two distinct governments, and then the portion allotted to each, subdivided among distinct and separate departments. Hence a double security arises to the rights of the people. The different governments will control each other; at the same time that each will be controlled by itself.

Second. It is of great importance in a republic, not only to guard the society against the oppression of its rulers; but to guard one part of the society against the injustice of the other part. Different interests necessarily exist in different classes of citizens. If a majority be united by a common interest, the rights of the minority will be insecure. There are but two methods of providing against this evil: The one by creating a will in the community independent of the majority, that is, of the society itself; the other by comprehending in the society so many separate descriptions of citizens, as will render an unjust combination of a majority of the whole, very improbable, if not impracticable. The first method prevails in all governments possessing an hereditary or self appointed authority. This at best is but a precarious security; because a power independent of the society may as well espouse the unjust views of the major, as the rightful interests, of the minor party, and may possibly be turned against both parties. The second method will be exemplified in the federal republic of the United States. While all authority in it will be derived from and dependent on the society, the society itself will be broken into so many parts, interests and classes of citizens, that the rights of individuals or of the minority, will be in little danger from interested combinations of the majority. In a free government, the security for civil rights must be the same as for religious rights. It consists in the one case in the multiplicity of interests, and in the other in the multiplicity of sects. The degree of security in both cases will depend on the number of interests and sects; and this may be presumed to depend on the extent of country and number of people comprehended under the same government. This view of the subject must particularly recommend a proper federal system to all the sincere and considerate friends of republican government: Since it shows that in exact proportion as the territory of the union may be formed into more circumscribed confederacies or states, oppressive combinations of a majority will be facilitated; the best security under the republican form, for the rights of every class of citizens, will be diminished; and consequently, the stability and independence of some member of the government, the only other security, must be proportionally increased. Justice is the end of government. It is the end of civil society. It ever has been, and ever will be pursued, until it be obtained, or until liberty be lost in the pursuit. In a society under the forms of which the stronger faction can readily unite and oppress the weaker, anarchy may as truly be said to reign, as in a state of nature where the weaker individual is not secured against the violence of the stronger: And as in the latter state even the stronger individuals are prompted by the uncertainty of their condition, to submit to a government which may protect the weak as well as themselves: So in the former state, will the more powerful factions or parties be gradually induced by a like motive, to wish for a government which will protect all parties, the weaker as well as the more powerful. It can be little doubted, that if the state of Rhode Island was separated from the confederacy, and left to itself, the insecurity of rights under the popular form of government within such narrow limits, would be displayed by such reiterated oppressions of factious majorities, that some power altogether independent of the people would soon be called for by the voice of the very factions whose misrule had proved the necessity of it. In the extended republic of the United States, and among the great variety of interests, parties and sects which it embraces, a coalition of a majority of the whole society could seldom take place on any other principles than those of justice and the general good; and there being thus less danger to a minor from the will of the major party, there must be less pretext also, to provide for the security of the former, by introducing into the government a will not dependent on the latter; or in other words, a will independent of the society itself. It is no less certain that it is important, notwithstanding the contrary opinions which have been entertained, that the larger the society, provided it lie within a practicable sphere, the more duly capable it will be of self government. And happily for the republican cause, the practicable sphere may be carried to a very great extent, by a judicious modification and mixture of the federal principle.

JAMES MADISON

References

Chapter 1

Myth and Reality in American Politics, pp. 1–22

1. For perspectives on the events of September 11, 2001, see Allan J. Cigler, *Perspectives on Terrorism: How 9/11 Changed U.S. Politics* (Boston: Houghton Mifflin, 2002). On the events and reactions related to Hurricane Katrina, see Douglas Brinkley, *The Great Deluge: Hurricane Katrina, New Orleans, and the Mississippi Gulf Coast* (New York: Morrow, 2006).
2. Paul J. Lim et al., "A Plan for All Seasons; After September 11, Americans Are Taking Care of Family Financial Needs; Chicago; Boston," *U.S. News & World Report*, December 10, 2001.
3. Jill Lepore, *The Name of War: King Philip's War and the Origins of American Identity* (New York: Knopf, 1998).
4. Jack P. Greene, *The Intellectual Construction of America: Exceptionalism and Identity from 1492 to 1800* (Chapel Hill: University of North Carolina Press, 1993).
5. Frederick Jackson Turner, "The Significance of the Frontier in American History," in *History, Frontier, and Section: Three Essays*, ed. Martin Ridge (Albuquerque: University of New Mexico Press, 1993).
6. Richard Hofstadter, *The Paranoid Style in American Politics and Other Essays* (New York: Vintage Books, 1967).
7. See William W. Boyer, "Political Science and the 21st Century: From Government to Governance," *PS: Political Science & Politics*, 23, no. 1 (1990); also Richard Rose, "Models of Governing," *Comparative Politics* 5, no. 4 (1973), and Richard Rose, *What Is Governing? Purpose and Policy in Washington* (Englewood Cliffs, N.J.: Prentice-Hall, 1978).
8. See the discussion in Peter Heehs, "Myth, History, and Theory," *History and Theory* 33, no. 1 (1994).
9. Karl Raimund Popper, *Conjectures and Refutations: The Growth of Scientific Knowledge*, 5th ed. (London and New York: Routledge, 1989).
10. For a general overview of the study of myths, see William G. Doty, *Mythography: The Study of Myths and Rituals*, 2nd ed. (Tuscaloosa: University of Alabama Press, 2000).
11. For example, see Joseph Campbell, *The Masks of Gods* (New York: Arkana, 1991).
12. This famous myth was originally found in Mason L. Weems, *The Life of Washington* (1800; reprint, Cambridge, Mass.: Belknap Press of Harvard University Press, 1962).
13. These and similar stories are so popular that they have been a standard feature on nightly news broadcasts for years; for example, *NBC Nightly News* has a regular feature called "The Fleecing of America" that often focuses on government programs.
14. See Geoffrey A. Hosking and George Schöpflin, eds., *Myths and Nationhood* (New York: Routledge in association with the School of Slavonic and East European Studies, University of London, 1997); also Richard Slotkin, *Regeneration Through Violence: The Mythology of the American Frontier, 1600–1860* (Norman: University of Oklahoma Press, 2000).
15. See Murray Edelman, *Politics as Symbolic Action: Mass Arousal and Quiescence* (Chicago: Markham Publishing, 1971); and Murray J. Edelman, *Constructing the Political Spectacle* (Chicago: University of Chicago Press, 1988).
16. Two popular examples of such stories are Clyde V. Prestowitz Jr., *Trading Places: How We Are Giving Our Future to Japan and How to Reclaim It* (New York: Basic Books, 1988); and Pat Choate, *Agents of Influence* (New York: Touchstone, 1990).
17. See Robert B. Reich, *The Work of Nations: Preparing Ourselves for 21st-Century Capitalism* (New York: Vintage Books, 1992).
18. According to H. Mark Roelofs, myths offer us a "nationally shared framework of political consciousness" by which we become aware of ourselves as "a people, as having an identity in history," and by which we are "prepared to recognize some governing regime . . . as legitimate." See H. Mark Roelofs, *Ideology and Myth in American Politics: A Critique of a National Political Mind* (Boston: Little, Brown, 1976), p. 4. Also see Christopher Flood, *Political Myth: A Theoretical Introduction* (New York: Routledge, 1996); and Andrew Delbanco, *The Real American Dream: A Meditation on Hope* (Cambridge, Mass.: Harvard University Press, 1999).
19. Robert C. Tucker, *Political Culture and Leadership in Soviet Russia: From Lenin to Gorbachev* (New York: Norton, 1987), pp. 22–23.
20. James Oliver Robertson, *American Myth, American Reality* (New York: Hill and Wang, 1980), p. 17.
21. See Tucker, *Political Culture and Leadership in Soviet Russia: From Lenin to Gorbachev.*
22. Murray Edelman, *The Symbolic Uses of Politics* (Urbana: University of Illinois Press, 1964), pp. 2–3.
23. See Walter Russell Mead, *Special Providence: American Foreign Policy and How It Changed the World* (New York: Knopf, 2001).

24. Christopher Lasch, *The True and Only Heaven: Progress and Its Critics* (New York: Norton, 1991), p. 93.

25. Quoted from Frances FitzGerald, *Fire in the Lake,* in Robertson, p. 5.

26. See Lawrence L. LeShan, *The Psychology of War: Comprehending Its Mystique and Its Madness,* expanded ed. (New York: Helios Press, 2002) for a discussion of how people characterize their enemies in wartime.

27. Bob Woodward, *The Commanders* (New York: Simon & Schuster, 1991), pp. 306–307; also James Kitfield, *Prodigal Soldiers: How the Generation of Officers Born of Vietnam Revolutionized the American Style of War* (Washington, D.C.: Brassey's, 1995).

28. Arthur M. Schlesinger Jr., *The Cycles of American History* (Boston: Houghton Mifflin, 1986), p. 219.

29. See Stuart Bruchey, *The Roots of American Economic Growth, 1607–1861: An Essay in Social Causation* (New York: Harper Torchbooks, 1968); Stuart Bruchey, *The Wealth of the Nation: An Economic History of the United States* (New York: Harper & Row, 1988); also Frank Bourgin, *The Great Challenge: The Myth of Laissez-Faire in the Early Republic* (New York: George Braziller, 1989).

30. See Theda Skocpol, *Protecting Soldiers and Mothers: The Political Origins of Social Policy in the United States* (Cambridge, Mass.: Belknap Press, 1992); also Michael B. Katz, *The Price of Citizenship: Redefining America's Welfare State* (New York: Metropolitan Books, 2001).

31. See Richard N. L. Andrews, *Managing the Environment, Managing Ourselves: A History of American Environmental Policy* (New Haven, Conn.: Yale University Press, 1999).

32. For an in-depth discussion of authority, see Richard Sennett, *Authority* (New York: Vintage Books, 1980).

33. For an extended analysis of power, see Dennis H. Wrong, *Power: Its Forms, Bases, and Uses* (New York: Harper & Row, 1979).

34. On the relationship between myths and ideologies, see Flood; also Roelofs, p. 4. On the concept of ideology, see David E. Apter, *Introduction to Political Analysis* (Cambridge, Mass.: Winthrop, 1977), chap. 8.

35. See Tucker; see also Zbigniew Brzezinski and Samuel P. Huntington, *Political Power: USA/USSR* (New York: Viking, 1964), pp. 45ff.

36. See Joel D. Aberbach, Robert D. Putnam, and Bert A. Rockman, *Bureaucrats and Politicians in 36 Western Democracies* (Cambridge, Mass.: Harvard University Press, 1981), chap. 5.

Chapter 2

Constitutional Foundations, pp. 23–65

1. The events surrounding the drafting and passage of the new Iraqi constitution were extensively covered by the U.S. media. For general coverage and analysis, see National Public Radio's website at www.npr.org/templates/story/story.php?storyId=4818908.

2. From a speech before the annual convention of the Veterans of Foreign Wars, August 22, 2005, in Salt Lake City. See www.whitehouse.gov/news/releases/2005/08/20050822-1.html.

3. *McCulloch v. Maryland,* 4 Wheat 316, 415.

4. Quoted in Charles A. Beard, *The Republic: Conversations on Fundamentals* (New York: Viking Compass Books, 1943), p. 77.

5. See Charles Crowe, "The Emergence of Progressive History," *Journal of the History of Ideas,* 27, no. 1 (1966). Charles A. Beard was among the most influential and articulate advocates of this view; see Charles Austin Beard and Mary Ritter Beard, *The Rise of American Civilization,* one-volume ed. (New York: Macmillan, 1933); as well as Beard, *The Republic: Conversations on Fundamentals.*

6. See Herman Belz, "Changing Conceptions of Constitutionalism in the Era of World War II and the Cold War," *Journal of American History,* 59, no. 3 (1972). Also G. Edward White, "The 'Constitutional Revolution' as a Crisis in Adaptivity," *Hastings Law Journal,* 48 (1997).

7. Robert G. Ferris and James H. Charleton, *The Signers of the Constitution* (Flagstaff, Ariz.: Interpretive Publications, 1986), pp. 14–15. For a thorough and groundbreaking treatment of the politics and ideas that led to the convention, see Gordon S. Wood, *The Creation of the American Republic, 1776–1787* (New York: Norton, 1972).

8. Shays led 1,000 ragtag insurgents against the arsenal, but the defeat of the uprising was made possible only after local merchants and bankers financed a defense of the weapons storehouse. The congress could not afford to do more than provide a few guards for the arsenal. See Wood, p. 19.

9. Martin Diamond, *The Founding of the Democratic Republic* (Itasca, Ill.: F. E. Peacock Publishers, 1981), p. 15. For an authoritative general overview of the convention, see Max Farrand, *The Framing of the Constitution of the United States* (New Haven, Conn.: Yale University Press, 1913). See also Ferris and Charleton, pp. 35–36; and Catherine Drinker Bowen, *Miracle at Philadelphia: The Story of the Constitutional Convention, May to September 1787* (Boston: Atlantic–Little, Brown, 1966).

10. The quoted characterizations were communicated to the French foreign ministry by the French ambassador to the United States in 1788. See Saul K. Padover, *The Living U.S. Constitution* (New York: Mentor Books, 1953), pp. 51ff. For more general biographies of the delegates, see M. E. Bradford, *Founding Fathers: Brief Lives of the Framers of the United States Constitution,* 2nd ed. (Lawrence: University Press of Kansas, 1994); also Ferris and Charleton, part 2.

11. See Richard Brookhiser, *Founding Father: Rediscovering George Washington* (New York: Free Press, 1996).

12. See H. W. Brands, *The First American: The Life and Times of Benjamin Franklin* (New York: Doubleday, 2000).

13. "Speech in the Convention at the Conclusion of Its Deliberations," in *Benjamin Franklin: Writings,* ed. J. A. Leo Lemay (New York: Literary Classics of the United States, 1987), pp. 1139–1141. On Franklin's health, see Ferris and

Charleton, p. 35. For other supportive comments attributed to Franklin at the convention, see Farrand, p. 194.

14. For an in-depth analysis of the roots of the Constitution, see Donald S. Lutz, *The Origins of American Constitutionalism* (Baton Rouge: Louisiana State University Press, 1988). Also see Jack P. Greene, *The Intellectual Heritage of the Constitutional Era: The Delegate's Library* (Philadelphia: The Library Company of Philadelphia, 1986).

15. Charles Howard McIlwain, *The American Revolution: A Constitutional Interpretation* (Ithaca, N.Y.: Cornell University Press, 1958), p. 5.

16. It would be an error, however, to think of the American system as a mere variation on the modern British system. See Bruce A. Ackerman, *We the People*, vol. 1, *Foundations* (Cambridge, Mass.: Belknap/Harvard University Press, 1991), especially his "dualist model" versus "monist model" argument in chap. 1.

17. A classic exposition of the development of the British constitutional system is found in Walter Bagehot, *The English Constitution* (London: Oxford University Press, 1928/ 1963). His views on the use of charters are presented on pp. 247–249. On the Magna Carta, see James Clarke Holt, *Magna Carta*, 2nd ed. (Cambridge, U.K., and New York: Cambridge University Press, 1992).

18. Later in the 1600s, as the Stuarts attempted to reassert royal authority, Parliament joined the courts in elevating common law to "higher-law" status; see Greene, chap. 4.

19. See Ackerman; see also Sanford Levinson, *Constitutional Faith* (Princeton, N.J.: Princeton University Press, 1988).

20. See the reference to Bonham's Case and common-law tradition in Charles Rembar, *The Law of the Land: The Evolution of Our Legal System* (New York: Simon & Schuster, 1980), pp. 43–47, 286–287.

21. For an excellent introduction to life and culture in the British colonies, see David Hackett Fischer, *Albion's Seed: Four British Folkways in America* (New York: Oxford University Press, 1989).

22. Lutz contends that this situation came about because for most of the seventeenth century the British were preoccupied with trying to settle their own constitutional problems. See Lutz, p. 63.

23. See Lawrence J. R. Herson, *The Politics of Ideas: Political Theory and American Public Policy* (Homewood, Ill.: Dorsey Press, 1984), pp. 28–29.

24. For example, see David Thomas Konig, "Constitutional Contexts: The Theory of History and the Process of Constitutional Change in Revolutionary America," in *Constitutionalism and American Culture: Writing the New Constitutional History*, ed. Sandra F. VanBurkleo, Kermit Hall, and Robert J. Kaczorowski (Lawrence: University Press of Kansas, 2002).

25. See Robert N. Bellah, *The Broken Covenant: American Civil Religion in Time of Trial*, 2nd ed. (Chicago: University of Chicago Press, 1992). Also see Isaac Kramnick and R. Laurence Moore, *The Godless Constitution: The Case Against Religious Correctness* (New York: Norton, 1997).

26. See Daniel Walker Howe, "Why the Scottish Enlightenment Was Useful to the Framers of the American Constitution," *Comparative Studies in Society and History*, 31, no. 3 (1989).

27. Vincent Ostrom, "The American Contribution to a Theory of Constitutional Choice," *Journal of Politics*, 38, no. 3 (1976). Also Walter Berns, "The New Pursuit of Happiness," *The Public Interest*, no. 86 (1986), pp. 68–69.

28. See Greene, chap. 2. Also see Joshua Foa Dienstag, "Between History and Nature: Social Contract Theory in Locke and the Founders," *Journal of Politics*, 58, no. 4 (1996).

29. In fact, of all the philosophers and authors cited by those who debated the Constitution, Montesquieu was mentioned most often. See Greene, pp. 43–44; also Lutz, pp. 139–147.

30. See Diamond, pp. 3–6. For a controversial interpretation of the Declaration, see Garry Wills, *Inventing America: Jefferson's Declaration of Independence* (New York: Vintage Books, 1978).

31. For an interesting analysis of the Constitution based on a perspective that gives special standing to the constitutional mechanisms that support the legitimacy of "We the People," see Ackerman. Also see Beard, *The Republic: Conversations on Fundamentals*, chap. 1.

32. See Preston King, *Federalism and Federation* (Baltimore: Johns Hopkins University Press, 1982). Also see Ronald L. Watts, "Federalism, Federal Political Systems, and Federations," *Annual Review of Political Science*, 1, no. 1 (1998).

33. See Paul Schumaker and Burdett A. Loomis, eds., *Choosing a President: The Electoral College and Beyond* (New York: Chatham House, 2002).

34. The controversy over a national bank has a long history. For more details, see Bray Hammond, "The Bank Cases," in *Quarrels That Have Shaped the Constitution*, ed. John Arthur Garraty (New York: Perennial Library, 1987). See also William Greider, *Secrets of the Temple: How the Federal Reserve Runs the Country* (New York: Simon & Schuster, 1987), chaps. 8–9.

35. James Madison, "Federalist No. 39," in *The Federalist*, ed. Jacob E. Cooke (Middletown, Conn.: Wesleyan University Press, 1961).

36. The privilege was suspended most recently in the then-territory of Hawaii when it was placed under martial law immediately after the bombing of Pearl Harbor. The state of martial law lasted nearly three years and was eventually lifted and later declared unconstitutional. See Harry N. Scheiber and Jane L. Scheiber, "Bayonets in Paradise: A Half-Century Retrospect on Martial Law in Hawaii, 1941–1946," *University of Hawaii Law Review*, 19 (1997).

37. See Michael Allen Gillespie and Michael Lienesch, eds., *Ratifying the Constitution* (Lawrence: University Press of Kansas, 1989).

38. The most articulate advocate of this approach over the past century was Rexford Tugwell, a well-known member of Roosevelt's New Deal administration; see Rexford G.

Tugwell, *The Compromising of the Constitution* (Early Departures) (Notre Dame, Ind.: University of Notre Dame Press, 1976).

39. For a history of the amending process, see Richard B. Bernstein and Jerome Agel, *Amending America: If We Love the Constitution So Much, Why Do We Keep Trying to Change It?* (New York: Times Books, 1993).

40. See Stephen M. Griffin, *American Constitutionalism: From Theory to Politics* (Princeton, N.J.: Princeton University Press, 1996).

41. Daniel N. Hoffman, *Our Elusive Constitution: Silences, Paradoxes, Priorities* (Albany: State University of New York Press, 1997).

42. See Hamilton's "Federalist No. 11," in *The Federalist*, ed. Jacob E. Cooke.

43. See Keith E. Whittington, *Constitutional Construction: Divided Powers and Constitutional Meaning* (Cambridge, Mass.: Harvard University Press, 1999); and Keith E. Whittington, *Constitutional Interpretation: Textual Meaning, Original Intent, and Judicial Review* (Lawrence: University Press of Kansas, 1999).

44. From transcription of remarks, *A Call for Reckoning: Religion and the Death Penalty (January 25) — Session Three: Religion, Politics, and the Death Penalty*, E. J. Dionne Jr., Moderator (Pew Forum on Religion and Public Life, University of Chicago, 2002, accessed July 10, 2002); available from http://pewforum.org/deathpenalty/resources/transcript3.php3.

45. Political scientist Robert A. Dahl, for example, contends that the American Constitution is rather behind the times when compared with the constitutions of other advanced industrialized nations. When it comes to "protection of fundamental rights, fair representation," and the reliance on democratic consensus in making key policy decisions, Dahl believes the United States compares rather unfavorably to the world's other major democracies. He places a good deal of the blame for this on the flaws in the American constitutional system, which he believes can be traced to institutional features that have not changed over the decades. See Robert Alan Dahl, *How Democratic Is the American Constitution?* (New Haven, Conn.: Yale University Press, 2001).

46. Bruce A. Ackerman, *We the People*, vol. 2, *Transformations* (Cambridge, Mass.: Belknap Press of Harvard University Press, 1998).

47. Kermit L. Hall, *The Magic Mirror: Law in American History* (New York: Oxford University Press, 1989), p. 6; also see Cass R. Sunstein, *The Partial Constitution* (Cambridge, Mass.: Harvard University Press, 1993).

48. Sunstein, pp. 32–37.

49. For an excellent introduction to how the rule of law affects public officials, see David H. Rosenbloom, James D. Carroll, and Jonathan D. Carroll, *Constitutional Competence for Public Managers: Cases and Commentary* (Itasca, Ill.: F. E. Peacock Publishers, 2000).

50. Jack N. Rakove, *The Beginnings of National Politics: An Interpretive History of the Continental Congress* (Baltimore: Johns Hopkins University Press, 1979), pp. 394–395.

51. Fortas would later resign his associate justice position after questions were raised about his personal finances that reflected badly on his role as a justice.

52. During the Cold War, several sitting members of Congress retained their high-ranking positions in the military reserve forces — a seeming violation of the prohibition against holding positions in more than one branch of the national government because the military is part of the executive branch.

53. John Tyler, Andrew Johnson, Grover Cleveland, Herbert Hoover, Harry S Truman, Richard M. Nixon, Ronald Reagan, George H. W. Bush, and Bill Clinton.

54. A move to impeach a member of the Senate was dismissed in 1797 when the Senate determined that the process did not apply to members of Congress. Two other cases against judges ended with resignations before trials could take place, and the impeachment of a cabinet member resulted in an acquittal.

55. In the case of President Richard Nixon, he resigned after the House Judiciary Committee had voted to send articles of impeachment to the full chamber, but before the House could consider those charges.

56. See "Federalist No. 44" in *The Federalist*, ed. Jacob E. Cooke.

57. Breyer expressed these views in lectures given at Harvard University in November 2004; they can be found at www.supremecourtus.gov/publicinfo/speeches/sp_11-17-04.html. These remarks are also published in Stephen G. Breyer, *Active Liberty: Interpreting Our Democratic Constitution* (New York: Knopf, 2005).

58. Samuel P. Huntington, *American Politics: The Promise of Disharmony* (Cambridge, Mass.: Belknap/Harvard University Press, 1981), p. 30.

59. In a September 1987 Gallup Poll, 44 percent stated that the Constitution needed to be updated; in a July 2000 Rasmussen Research poll, 37 percent expressed a similar opinion.

60. The research was conducted by the Rasmussen Research group as part of its "Portrait of America" project; see www.portraitofamerica.com.

61. Kammen, p. 3.

62. Levinson, p. 4.

Chapter 3

Federalism and Intergovernmental Relations, pp. 66–94

1. The formal approval of the site selection triggered additional steps, including a DOE application (in ninety days) to the Nuclear Regulatory Commission (NRC) for a license to construct and operate a nuclear facility. The NRC is required to make its decision within three years, and at that point the approval process for construction is regarded as complete.

2. Howard Kunreuther, William H. Desvousges, and Paul Slovic, "Nevada's Predicament," *Environment*, October 1988, p. 16.

3. For a general overview of the early history of federalism, see Forrest McDonald, *States' Rights and the Union: Imperium in Imperio, 1776–1876 American Political Thought* (Lawrence: University Press of Kansas, 2000).

4. For a detailed survey of the concept of federalism, see S. Rufus Davis, *The Federal Principle: A Journey Through Time in Quest of Meaning* (Berkeley: University of California Press, 1978).

5. For a general overview of the conflicting theories of federalism, see Richard H. Leach, *American Federalism* (New York: Norton, 1970), chap. 1. See also William H. Riker, *Federalism: Origin, Operation, Significance* (Boston: Little, Brown, 1964).

6. This view had its most direct expression in the Virginia and Kentucky resolutions of 1798. Written by Jefferson and Madison, the resolutions called for the "nullification" of the unpopular Alien and Sedition Acts — laws that had led to the conviction of several newspaper editors critical of American foreign policy decisions. The resolutions circulated among the states, but the election of Jefferson as president in 1800 seemed to end the controversy —since the new president was a leading advocate of this view.

7. The quote is from Justice Barbour's decision in *Miln v. New York* (1837); quoted in W. Brooke Graves, *American Intergovernmental Relations: Their Origin, Historical Development, and Current Status* (New York: Charles Scribner's Sons, 1964), pp. 319–320.

8. Charles Sumner of Massachusetts was severely beaten on the floor of the U.S. Senate by Representative Preston Brooks, a member of the House from South Carolina who took exception to remarks made by the senator. Sumner did not return to the Senate chamber for three years and never really recovered from the attack. Brooks resigned from the House but was reelected by his constituents, who regarded him as a hero.

9. From the Supreme Court decision in Tarbel's Case, quoted in Deil S. Wright, *Understanding Intergovernmental Relations*, 3rd ed. (Pacific Grove, Calif.: Brooks/Cole, 1988), p. 41. For a more general discussion, see Graves, pp. 321–324.

10. *Hammer v. Dagenhart* (1918).

11. McDonald, pp. 24–25.

12. The federal government had provided special funding for canals and similar projects earlier in the century, and the states had received parts of a national budget surplus into the 1830s. However, the first formal grant-in-aid program was the Morrill Act. See Graves, chap. 14.

13. See David B. Walker, *The Rebirth of Federalism: Slouching Toward Washington* (Chatham, N.J.: Chatham House, 1995), pp. 82–83.

14. U.S. Bureau of the Census, *Historical Statistics of the United States, Colonial Times to 1970* (Washington, D.C.: U.S. Government Printing Office, 1975), Table Y638, p. 1125.

15. Walker, chap. 4; also Wright, pp. 71–72.

16. Roscoe C. Martin, *The Cities and the Federal System* (New York: Atherton Press, 1965), chaps. 4 and 5.

17. See Kenneth T. Palmer, "The Evolution of Grant Policies," in *The Changing Politics of Federal Grants*, ed. Lawrence D. Brown, James W. Fossett, and Kenneth T. Palmer (Washington, D.C.: The Brookings Institution, 1984).

18. For a general overview of how the national government used this strategy, see Advisory Commission on Intergovernmental Relations (ACIR), *Regulatory Federalism: Policy, Process, Impact and Reform: A Commission Report* (Washington, D.C.: ACIR, 1984).

19. For the story of how these cuts were accomplished, see David A. Stockman, *The Triumph of Politics: How the Reagan Revolution Failed* (New York: Harper & Row, 1986).

20. See George E. Peterson, "Federalism and the States: An Experiment in Decentralization," in *The Reagan Experiment: An Examination of Economic and Social Policies Under the Reagan Administration*, ed. John L. Palmer and Isabel V. Sawhill (Washington, D.C.: Urban Institute Press, 1982), p. 228.

21. Historical and up-to-date figures on federal grants to states and localities are included in the annual federal budget submitted by the president. This can be found at http://w3.access.gpo.gov/usbudget/.

22. Thomas R. Swartz and John E. Peck, "The Changing Face of Fiscal Federalism," *Challenge*, November/December 1990, pp. 41–46.

23. Clinton was prominently featured in one book that addressed the strengths of state governments in the 1980s; see David Osborne, *Laboratories of Democracy* (Boston: Harvard Business School Press, 1988).

24. Ruben Barrales, "Federalism in the Bush Administration," *Spectrum: Journal of State Government*, Summer 2001, pp. 5–6.

25. For background on this approach, see E. J. Dionne and John J. DiIulio, eds., *What's God Got to Do with the American Experiment?* (Washington, D.C.: Brookings Institution Press, 2000).

26. *Federal Maritime Commission v. South Carolina State Ports Authority*, 122 S. Ct. 1864 (2002).

27. In *Baker v. Carr* (1962), for instance, the Court forced the states to reapportion their legislative seats to guarantee equal representation for all their citizens. In *Roe v. Wade* (1973), the Court limited the authority states have to regulate abortion (see Chapter 4). Finally, in *Garcia v. San Antonio Metropolitan Transit Authority* (1985), the Court held that federal wage and hour laws apply to state and local governments.

28. Morris P. Fiorina, *Congress: Keystone of the Washington Establishment* (New Haven, Conn.: Yale University Press, 1977), p. 48.

29. David E. Satterfield III, representative from Richmond, Virginia, quoted in Rochelle L. Stanfield, "Federal Aid — Taking the Good with the Bad," *National Journal*, July 8, 1978, p. 1076.

30. See David B. Walker, "The Advent of an Ambiguous Federalism and the Emergence of New Federalism, III," *Public Administration Review*, 56, no. 3 (1996), 271.

31. See Advisory Commission on Intergovernmental Relations (ACIR), *State Laws Governing Local Government Structure and Administration* (Washington, D.C.: ACIR, 1993).

32. Ann O'M. Bowman and Richard C. Kearney, *The Resurgence of the States* (Englewood Cliffs, N.J.: Prentice-Hall, 1986), p. 136.

33. See Osborne; also Bowman and Kearney, pp. 25–27. Each year, *Governing* magazine publishes numerous state and local "government success stories" that rarely make headlines elsewhere. Visit http://governing.com/.

34. Luther Gulick, quoted in Terry Sanford, *Storm over the States* (New York: McGraw-Hill, 1967), p. 21.

35. See John D. Donahue, *Disunited States* (New York: Basic Books, 1997) for a critical perspective; in contrast, see Bowman and Kearney.

36. See Richard L. Cole and John Kincaid, "Public Opinion and American Federalism: Perspectives on Taxes, Spending and Trust," *Spectrum: Journal of State Government*, Summer 2001, pp. 14–18.

37. For an interesting perspective on how Americans have viewed their local governments, see Anwar Hussain Syed, *The Political Theory of American Local Government* (New York: Random House, 1966).

38. The U.S. Census Bureau conducts its Census of Government every five years. For the latest figures, visit http://www.census.gov/govs/www/.

39. Robert Pear, "Saying Medicaid Experiments Cut Services to Poor, Clinics Sue," *New York Times*, June 12, 1994, p. A30.

40. On the growth of public-sector interest groups, see Donald H. Haider, *When Governments Come to Washington: Governors, Mayors, and Intergovernmental Lobbying* (New York: Free Press, 1974). See also Alan Ehrenhalt, "As Interest in Its Agenda Wanes, a Shrinking Urban Bloc in Congress Plays Defense," *Governing*, 2, no. 10 (July 1989), 21–25; and Jonathan Walters, "Lobbying for the Good Old Days," *Governing*, 4, no. 9 (June 1991), 32–37.

41. Parris Glendening, "Pragmatic Federalism and State-Federal Partnerships," *Spectrum: Journal of State Government*, Summer 2001, pp. 7–8.

Chapter 4

The Heritage of Rights and Liberties, pp. 95–131

1. Quoted in Mary Ann Glendon, *Rights Talk: The Impoverishment of Political Discourse* (New York: Free Press, 1991), p. 8.

2. *Barron v. Baltimore*, 32 U.S. (7 Pet.) 243 (1833).

3. See Justice Black's concurring opinion in *Adamson v. California*, 332 U.S. 67 (1947).

4. *Palko v. Connecticut*, 302 U.S. 319 (1937).

5. *Milk Wagon Drivers Union v. Meadowmoor Dairies*, 312 U.S. 287 (1941).

6. *Schenck v. United States*, 249 U.S. 47 (1919).

7. *Gitlow v. New York*, 268 U.S. 652 (1925).

8. *Texas v. Johnson*, 491 U.S. 397 (1989).

9. *United States v. Eichman*, 496 U.S. 310 (1990).

10. *Madsen v. Women's Health Center Inc.*, 512 U.S. 753 (1994).

11. *Hill v. Colorado,*120 S. Ct. 2480 (2000).

12. *West Virginia State Board of Education v. Barnette*, 319 U.S. 624 (1943).

13. *Near v. Minnesota*, 283 U.S. 697 (1931).

14. *New York Times v. United States*, 403 U.S. 713 (1971).

15. *New York Times v. Sullivan*, 376 U.S. 254 (1964).

16. *Time, Inc. v. Firestone*, 424 U.S. 96 (1976).

17. *Flynt v. Falwell*, 485 U.S. 46 (1988).

18. *Roth v. United States*, 354 U.S. 476 (1957).

19. *Memoirs of a Woman of Pleasure v. Massachusetts*, 382 U.S. 975 (1966).

20. *Miller v. California*, 413 U.S. 15 (1973).

21. C. Herman Pritchett, *Constitutional Civil Liberties* (Englewood Cliffs, N.J.: Prentice-Hall, 1984), pp. 132–133.

22. *Everson v. Board of Education*, 330 U.S. 1 (1947).

23. *Lemon v. Kurtzman*, 403 U.S. 602 (1971).

24. *Zelman v. Simmons-Harris*, 122 S. Ct. 2460 (2002).

25. *Engel v. Vitale*, 370 U.S. 421 (1962).

26. *School District of Abington Township v. Schempp*, 374 U.S. 203 (1963).

27. *Santa Fe Independent School District v. Doe*, 168 F. 3d 806 (2000).

28. *Marsh v. Chambers*, 463 U.S. 783 (1983).

29. *Allegheny County v. American Civil Liberties Union*, 492 U.S. 573 (1989).

30. *Reynolds v. United States*, 98 U.S. 145 (1879).

31. *Braunfeld v. Brown*, 366 U.S. 599 (1961).

32. *Jacobson v. Massachusetts*, 197 U.S. 11 (1905).

33. *Wisconsin v. Yoder*, 406 U.S. 215 (1972).

34. *Employment Division, Dept. of Human Resources of Oregon v. Smith*, 494 U.S. 872 (1990).

35. *City of Boerne v. Flores*, 521 U.S. 507 (1997).

36. *Powell v. Alabama*, 287 U.S. 45 (1932).

37. *Gideon v. Wainwright*, 372 U.S. 335 (1963).

38. *Argersinger v. Hamlin*, 407 U.S. 25 (1972).

39. *Escobedo v. Illinois*, 378 U.S. 478 (1964).

40. *Miranda v. Arizona*, 384 U.S. 436 (1966).

41. *Duckworth v. Eagan*, 492 U.S. 195 (1989).

42. *New York v. Quarles*, 467 U.S. 649 (1984).

43. *Arizona v. Fuliminante*, 111 S. Ct. 1246 (1991).

44. *Dickerson v. United States*, 166 F. 3d 667 (2000).

45. *Schneckloth v. Bustamonte*, 412 U.S. 218 (1973).

46. *Mapp v. Ohio*, 367 U.S. 643 (1961).

47. *Nix v. Williams*, 476 U.S. 431 (1984).

48. *United States v. Leon*, 468 U.S. 897 (1984).

49. *Robinson v. California*, 370 U.S. 660 (1962).

50. *Hammelin v. Michigan*, 111 S. Ct. 2680 (1991).

51. *Furman v. Georgia*, 408 U.S. 238 (1972).

52. *Woodson v. North Carolina*, 428 U.S. 280 (1976).

53. *Atkins v. Virginia*, 122 S. Ct. 2242 (2002).

54. *Ring v. Arizona*, 122 S. Ct. 2428 (2002).

55. Charles Warren and Louis Brandeis, "The Right of Privacy," *Harvard Law Review*, 4 p. 1937 (1890), 193.

56. *Griswold v. Connecticut*, 381 U.S. 479 (1965).

57. *Roe v. Wade*, 410 U.S. 113 (1973).

58. *Webster v. Reproductive Health Services*, 492 U.S. 490 (1989).

59. *Planned Parenthood of Southeastern Pennsylvania v. Casey*, 505 U.S. 833 (1992).

60. *Washington v. Glucksberg*, 117 S. Ct. 2258 (1997). The limits to state power were further defined by the Court in *Stenberg v. Carhart*, 530 U.S. 914 (2000) when the Court, by a 5–4 vote, overturned Nebraska's ban on what is often called the partial-birth abortion procedure. In outlawing such procedures, Nebraska had, according to Justice Stephen Breyer, written so broadly that it prohibited other types of previability procedures, not just partial-birth abortions. The statute's breadth thus constituted an undue burden on a woman's right to an abortion. Although the Court may in the future uphold bans on partial-birth abortions, it has made it clear that such bans would have to be narrowly tailored to prohibit only a specific procedure.

61. *Vacco v. Quill*, 521 U.S. 793 (1997).

62. C. Vann Woodward, *The Strange Career of Jim Crow* (New York: Oxford University Press, 1966).

63. *Plessy v. Ferguson*, 163 U.S. 537 (1896).

64. Paul Oberst, "The Strange Career of *Plessy v. Ferguson*," *Arizona Law Review*, 15 (1973).

65. *Cumming v. Richmond County Board of Education*, 175 U.S. 528 (1899).

66. *Missouri ex rel. Gaines v. Canada*, 305 U.S. 337 (1938).

67. *Sweatt v. Painter*, 339 U.S. 629 (1950).

68. *Brown v. Board of Education of Topeka*, 347 U.S. 483 (1954).

69. *Brown v. Board of Education II*, 349 U.S. 294 (1955).

70. *Alexander v. Holmes County Board of Education*, 396 U.S. 19 (1969).

71. *Milliken v. Bradley*, 418 U.S. 717 (1974).

72. See Pritchett, p. 345.

73. *Chisom v. Roemer*, 501 U.S. 380 (1991) and *Houston Lawyers' Association v. Attorney General of Texas*, 501 U.S. 419 (1991).

74. *Goesaert v. Cleary*, 335 U.S. 464 (1948).

75. *Hoyt v. Florida*, 368 U.S. 62 (1961).

76. *J. E. B. v. Alabama ex rel.*, 511 U.S. 127 (1994).

77. *Craig v. Boren*, 429 U.S. 190 (1976).

78. *Kahn v. Shevin*, 416 U.S. 351 (1974).

79. *United States v. Virginia*, 518 U.S. 515 (1996).

80. Quoted in Susan Gluck Mezey, *In Pursuit of Equality: Women, Public Policy, and the Federal Courts* (New York: St. Martin's, 1991), p. 97.

81. *General Electric Co. v. Gilbert*, 429 U.S. 125 (1976).

82. *Williams v. Saxbe*, 413 F. Supp. 654 (D.D.C. 1976).

83. *Meritor Savings Bank v. Vinson*, 477 U.S. 57 (1986).

84. *Harris v. Forklift*, 570 U.S. 17 (1993).

85. *Bowers v. Hardwick*, 478 U.S. 186 (1986).

86. *Romer v. Evans*, 517 U.S. 620 (1996).

87. *Lawrence v. Texas*, 539 U.S. 123 (2003).

88. *Plyler v. Doe*, 457 U.S. 202 (1982).

89. *Regents of the University of California v. Bakke*, 438 U.S. 265 (1978).

90. *Gratz v. Bollinger*, 539 U.S. 244 (2003).

Chapter 5

Public Opinion and Political Participation, pp. 132–158

1. Survey by the Gallup Organization, February 19–21, 2001.

2. Gallup Poll News Service, July 18, 2005.

3. W. H. Hartley and W. S. Vincent, *American Civics*, 4th ed. (New York: Harcourt Brace Jovanovich, 1983), p. 221.

4. V. O. Key Jr., *Public Opinion and American Democracy* (New York: Knopf, 1961).

5. *Public Perspective*, November/December 1993, p. 75.

6. Gallup Poll News Service, December 8, 2005.

7. Max J. Skidmore, *Ideologies: Politics in Action* (New York: Harcourt Brace Jovanovich, 1989), p. 7.

8. M. Margaret Conway, *Political Participation in the United States*, 3rd ed. (Washington, D.C.: Congressional Quarterly Press, 2000), pp. 25–29; Bernard Hennessy, *Public Opinion*, 5th ed. (Monterey, Calif.: Brooks/Cole, 1985), p. 200.

9. The Kaiser Family Foundation survey, 1999.

10. Harold W. Stanley and Richard G. Niemi, *Vital Statistics on American Politics 2005–2006* (Washington, D.C.: Congressional Quarterly Press, 2006), p. 194.

11. See Daniel Elazar, *American Federalism: A View from the States*, 2nd ed. (New York: Crowell, 1972), and Robert S. Erikson, Gerald C. Wright, and John P. McIver, *Statehouse Democracy* (New York: Cambridge University Press, 1993), for two excellent discussions of political culture, subculture, and public opinion.

12. For a systematic and readable review of polling and the measurement of public opinion, see Herbert Asher, *Polling and the Public*, 6th ed. (Washington, D.C.: Congressional Quarterly Press, 2004).

13. National Election Study, Center for Political Studies, University of Michigan, Ann Arbor, 2000.

14. Richard Morin, "The Public May Not Know Much, But It Knows What It Doesn't Like," *Washington Post National Weekly Edition*, January 23–29, 1989, p. 37.

15. National Opinion Research Center of International Studies, Princeton University, Princeton, N.J., March 1960.

16. CNN/USA Today/Gallup poll, June 2005.

17. Adam Clymer, "U.S. Attitudes Altered Little by September 11," *New York Times*, May 20, 2002.

18. National Election Studies, available at www.umich.edu/~nes.

19. Stanley and Niemi, p. 143.

20. Gary Langer, www.ABC.com, March 11, 2002.

21. *America Unplugged: Citizens and Their Government*, Council for Excellence in Government, 1999.

22. John H. Pryor, Sylvia Hurtado, Victor B. Saenz, Jennifer A. Lindholm, William S. Korn, and Kathryn M. Mahoney, *The American Freshman: National Norms for Fall 2005* (Los Angeles: Higher Education Research Institute, Graduate School of Education, UCLA, 2005).

23. Ibid., pp. 24, 33.

24. Ibid., see pp. 32, 52, and 72 for a more detailed breakdown.

25. "The Black and White of Public Opinion," Pew Research Center for the People and the Press, October 31, 2005. For

additional polling on racial attitudes among Americans, see also "Racial and Ethnic Harmony Detected in New Ratings," Gallup Poll News Service, July 8, 2004.

26. *Newsweek* poll, as reported by MSNBC, September 10, 2005.

27. "The Black and White of Public Opinion."

28. Stanley and Niemi, p. 119.

29. CNN exit polls, November 2004.

30. Robert Suro, Richard Fry, and Jeffrey Passel, "Hispanics and the 2004 Election: Population, Electorate and Voters," Pew Hispanic Center, June 27, 2005.

31. Juan Andrade and Andrew Hernandez, *The Almanac of Latino Politics 2000* (Chicago: United States Hispanic Leadership Institute, 1999), p. 9.

32. Patrick Reddy, "Up the Ladder from Down the Ballot," *Public Perspective*, June/July 1999, p. 7.

33. See David C. Leege and Lyman A. Kellstadt, eds., *Rediscovering the Religious Factor in American Politics* (Armonk, N.Y.: M. E. Sharpe, 1993).

34. The latter part of the definition of participation, given in quotes, comes from Conway, pp. 3–4.

35. Quote from Everett Carll Ladd, *Public Perspective*, March/April 1994, based on a study by Sidney Verba, Kay L. Schlozman, Henry R. Brady, and Norman H. Nie, "The Citizen Participation Project: Summary Findings," a project supported by the National Science Foundation and the Spencer, Ford, and Hewlett Foundations, with survey work done in 1990 by the National Opinion Research Center.

36. National Election Studies, available at www.umich.edu/~nes.

37. Hart and Teeter polling, 1999, conducted for the Council for Excellence in Government.

38. Sidney Verba and Norman H. Nie, *Participation in America: Political Democracy and Social Equality* (New York: Harper & Row, 1972), pp. 95–101.

39. National Election Studies, available at www.umich.edu/~nes.

40. Adam Claymer, "College Students Not Drawn to Voting or Politics, Poll Shows," *New York Times*, January 12, 2000, p. A14; Pryor et al., pp. 24–25.

41. The International Social Justice Project, 1991.

42. Reported in *Public Perspective*, March/April 1994, pp. 16–18, 34.

43. Stanley and Niemi, p. 16.

44. Center for the American Woman and Politics (CAWP), Eagleton Institute of Politics, Rutgers University, New Brunswick, N.J., 2005.

45. Ibid.

46. *New York Times*, July 5, 2005, p.18.

47. U.S. Census Bureau, 2005.

48. Stanley and Niemi, pp. 60, 62.

49. Reddy, p. 7; see also www.congressonalblackcaucus.net.

50. Stanley and Niemi, pp. 284–285.

51. Suro et al.

52. Stanley and Niemi, pp. 284–285.

53. *Los Angeles Times*, March 4, 1997; U.S. Census Bureau, February 27, 2002.

54. "The Asian American Vote: A Report on the AALDEF Multilingual Exit Poll in the 2004 Presidential Election," Asian American Legal Defense and Education Fund, 2005, p. 1.

55. "Asian American Access to Democracy in the 2004 Elections," Asian American Legal Defense and Education Fund, August 2005, p. 3.

56. Stanley and Niemi, pp. 283–284.

Chapter 6

Political Parties, pp. 159–183

1. Gallup Poll News Service, "Public's Ratings of Parties Low in Historical Perspective," September 29, 2005.

2. Survey by the Media Studies Center/Roper Center, February 1996.

3. Gallup Poll News Service, "Public's Ratings," September 29, 2005.

4. William J. Keefe, *Parties, Politics, and Public Policy in America*, 8th ed. (Washington, D.C.: Congressional Quarterly Press, 1998), p. 11.

5. Alan R. Gitelson, M. Margaret Conway, and Frank B. Feigert, *American Political Parties: Stability and Change* (Boston: Houghton Mifflin, 1984), p. 4.

6. For a brief comparative overview of select party systems around the world, see Mark Kesselman, Joel Krieger, and William A. Joseph, eds., *Introduction to Comparative Politics*, 3rd ed. (Boston: Houghton Mifflin, 2004). See also Kay Lawson, *Cleavages, Parties, and Voters: Studies from Bulgaria, the Czech Republic, Hungary, Poland, and Romania* (Westport, Conn.: Greenwood, 1999); and Kay Lawson and Thomas Poguntke, *How Political Parties Respond: Interest Aggregation Revisited* (New York: Routledge, 2004).

7. Reference to this term can be found in Paul Allen Beck and Frank J. Sorauf, *Party Politics in America*, 7th ed. (Glenview, Ill.: HarperCollins, 1992); and Marjorie Randon Hershey, *Party Politics in America*, 12th ed. (New York: Pearson Longman, 2007).

8. Survey by the Gallup Organization, August 2005.

9. Jeffrey M. Jones, "GOP Image Taking a Hit," Gallup News Service, November 7, 2005.

10. See Gallup Poll News Service, "Public's Rating of Parties" for a discussion of historically low public opinion of political parties. See www.poll.gallup.com for public polling on the Iraq War. For a discussion on the decline of parties from the early 1950s to the mid-1990s, see Martin P. Wattenberg, *The Decline of American Political Parties: 1952–1996* (Cambridge, Mass.: Harvard University Press, 1998). For a discussion on the decline or resurgence of parties, see Jeffrey E. Cohen, Richard Fleisher, and Paul Kantor, eds., *American Political Parties: Decline or Resurgence?* (Washington, D.C.: Congressional Quarterly Press, 2001).

11. See Alan R. Gitelson and Patricia Bayer Richard, "Ticket-Splitting: Aggregate Measures v. Actual Ballots," *Western Political Quarterly*, 36 (September 1983), 410–419; and Frank

B. Feigert, "Illusions of Ticket-Splitting," *American Politics Quarterly*, 7 (October 1979), 470–488.

12. Pew Research Center, May 21, 2002. For an in-depth discussion of the voting patterns and beliefs of self-declared independents, see Bruce E. Keith, David B. Magleby, Candice J. Nelson, Elizabeth Orr, Mark C. Westlye, and Raymond E. Wolfinger, *The Myth of the Independent Voter* (Berkeley: University of California Press, 1992).

13. Gitelson, Conway, and Feigert, p. 131; Harold W. Stanley and Richard G. Niemi, *Vital Statistics on American Politics* (Washington, D.C.: Congressional Quarterly Press, 2006), p. 116.

14. For one of the classic defenses of the role of parties, see E. E. Schattschneider, *Party Government* (New York: Rinehart, 1942). For an equally compelling argument in support of parties by a leading proponent of the view that parties are in decline, see Walter Dean Burnham, "The Changing Shape of the American Political Universe," in *Controversies in American Voting Behavior*, ed. Richard G. Niemi and Herbert F. Weisberg (San Francisco: Freeman, 1976), pp. 451–483.

15. Allan D. Monroe, "American Party Platforms and Public Opinion," *American Journal of Political Science*, 27 (February 1983), 27–42; and Gerald M. Pomper, with Susan S. Lederman, *Elections in America: Control and Influences in Democratic Politics*, 2nd ed. (New York: Longman, 1980).

16. Pomper, with Lederman, pp. 173–174.

17. John P. Frendreis and Alan R. Gitelson, "Local Political Parties in an Age of Change," *The American Review of Politics*, 14 (Winter 1993), 533–548; and John Frendreis and Alan R. Gitelson, "Local Parties in the 1990s: Spokes in a Candidate-Centered Wheel," in *The State of the Parties*, 3rd ed., ed. John C. Green and Daniel M. Shea (Lanham, Md.: Rowman & Littlefield, 1999), pp. 135–153.

18. Stanley and Niemi, pp. 218–219.

19. Woodrow Wilson, *Constitutional Government in the United States* (New York: Columbia University Press, 1961), pp. 206, 217.

20. For the most comprehensive discussion of the realignment process, see V. O. Key Jr., "A Theory of Critical Elections," *Journal of Politics*, 17 (February 1955), 3–18; Walter Dean Burnham, *Critical Elections and the Mainspring of American Politics* (New York: Norton, 1970); and James L. Sundquist, *Dynamics of the Party System: Alignment and Realignment of Political Parties in the United States*, rev. ed. (Washington, D.C.: The Brookings Institution, 1983).

21. See, for example, Paul Allen Beck, "The Dealignment Era in America," in *Electoral Change in Advanced Industrial Democracies: Realignment or Dealignment?* ed. Russell J. Dalton, Scott C. Flanagan, and Paul Allen Beck (Princeton, N.J.: Princeton University Press, 1984), pp. 240–266.

22. For a review of the several theories that we discuss in this section, see Hershey, pp. 29–33.

23. Two proponents of the institutionalist explanation for the two-party system are Schattschneider; and Maurice Duverger, *Political Parties* (New York: Wiley, 1954).

24. V. O. Key Jr., *Politics, Parties, and Pressure Groups*, 5th ed. (New York: Crowell, 1964); and Louis Hartz, *The Liberal Tradition in America* (New York: Harcourt, Brace and World, 1955).

25. For a discussion of reform club activities in the United States and their impact on the electoral system, see Alan R. Gitelson, "Reform Clubs," in *Political Parties & Elections in the United States: An Encyclopedia*, ed. L. Sandy Maisel (New York: Garland, 1991), II, pp. 926–931.

26. See John Frendreis, Alan R. Gitelson, Gregory Flemming, and Anne Layzell, "Local Political Parties and the 1992 Campaign for the State Legislature," paper presented at the annual meeting of the American Political Science Association, Washington, D.C., September 2–5, 1993; John P. Frendreis and Alan R. Gitelson, "Local Political Parties in an Age of Change," *American Review of Politics*, 14 (Winter 1993), 533–548.

27. See John F. Bibby, *Politics, Parties, and Elections in America* (Belmont, Calif.: Thomson/Wadsworth, 2003), pp. 124–134.

28. For comprehensive reviews of party reform during the past two decades, see Robert L. Dudley and Alan R. Gitelson, *American Elections: The Rules Matter* (New York: Longman, 2002), pp. 38–42; William Crotty, *Political Reform and the American Experiment* (New York: Crowell, 1977); William Crotty, *Party Reform* (New York: Longman, 1983).

29. See Burnham; William Crotty, *American Parties in Decline* (Boston: Little, Brown, 1984); and Wattenberg; Walter Dean Burnham, "The Changing Shape of the American Political Universe," in *Controversies in American Voting Behavior*, ed. Richard G. Niemi and Herbert F. Weisberg (San Francisco: Freeman, 1976), pp. 451–483; Walter Dean Burnham, *Critical Elections and the Mainspring of American Politics* (New York: Norton, 1970).

30. See Gitelson, Conway, and Feigert, chap. 15, for a discussion of the transformation of political parties. See also Hershey, chap. 16.

Chapter 7

Campaigns and Elections, pp. 184–218

1. Stephen A. Salmore and Barbara G. Salmore, *Candidates, Parties, and Campaigns: Electoral Politics in America* (Washington, D.C.: Congressional Quarterly Press, 1985), p. 28. See also Wayne C. Williams, *William Jennings Bryan* (New York: Putnam, 1936), p. 162.

2. Francis T. Russell, *The Shadow of Blooming Grove* (New York: McGraw-Hill, 1968), p. 125. See also Salmore and Salmore, p. 29.

3. Salmore and Salmore, p. 29.

4. For a comprehensive overview of the nomination process and the impact of election rules and laws on the campaign process, see Robert L. Dudley and Alan R. Gitelson, *American Elections: The Rules Matter* (New York: Longman, 2002).

5. For an excellent discussion of the 2004 elections and voter turnout, see Paul R. Abramson, John H. Aldrich, and David W. Rohde, *Change and Continuity in the 2004 Elections* (Washington, D.C.: Congressional Quarterly Press, 2006), chap. 4.

6. Harold W. Stanley and Richard G. Niemi, *Vital Statistics on American Politics 2005–2006* (Washington, D.C.: Congressional Quarterly Press, 2006), p. 143. See also G. Calvin Markenzie and Judith M. Labiner, "Opportunity Lost: The Rise and Fall of Trust and Confidence After September 11," Center for Public Service, The Brookings Institution, May 30, 2002, p. 8.

7. Federal Election Commission, February 3 and 18, 2005.

8. Michael J. Malbin, "1994 Vote: The Money Story," in *America at the Polls 1994*, ed. Everett Carll Ladd (Storrs, Conn.: The Roper Center for Public Opinion Research, 1995), p. 128.

9. See Joseph A. Schlesinger, *Ambition and Politics: Political Careers in the United States* (Chicago: Rand McNally, 1966), pp. 16–20; Gordon Black, "A Theory of Political Ambition: Career Choices and the Role of Structural Incentives," *American Political Science Review*, 66 (March 1972), 144–159. For an excellent study on political ambition that points out the limitations of Schlesinger's opportunity structure theory, see Linda L. Fowler and Robert D. McClure, *Political Ambition: Who Decides to Run for Congress* (New Haven, Conn.: Yale University Press, 1989).

10. M. I. Ostrogorski, *Democracy and the Organization of Political Parties* (New York: Macmillan, 1902), XI, p. 4.

11. 2000 U.S. Lexis 4303.

12. Federal Election Commission, February 3, 2005.

13. For a concise discussion of the presidential nomination process, see William Crotty and John S. Jackson III, *The Politics of Presidential Selection*, 2nd ed. (New York: Longman, 2001).

14. Barbara Farah, "Delegate Polls: 1944–1984," *Public Opinion*, August/September 1984, p. 44.

15. PoliticsNow Classroom website, March 11, 1997.

16. George Thayer, *Who Shakes the Money Tree?* (New York: Simon & Schuster, 1973), p. 150.

17. Federal Election Commission, February 3, 2005.

18. Federal Election Commission, July 21, 2005.

19. Government Accountability Office as reported in AdAge .com, online edition of *Advertising Age*, February 13, 2006.

20. Federal Election Commission, news release, November 4, 1994.

21. Trevor Potter and Kirk L. Jowers, "Summary Analysis of Bipartisan Campaign Finance Reform Act Passed by House and Senate and Sent to President," The Brookings Institution, March 2002; *New York Times*, February 15, 2002, p. A18.

22. "New Study Finds That State Parties Are Soft Money Conduits," Campaign and Media Legal Center press release, June 25, 2002.

23. Richard A. Oppell, quoting Charles Lewis, "State Parties Adept at Raising Soft Money, Report Shows," *New York Times*, June 26, 2002, p. A19.

24. www.opensecrets.org/527s.

25. For a discussion of the impact of spending by challengers in congressional races, see Paul R. Abramson, John H. Aldrich, and David W. Rohde, *Change and Continuity in the 2004 Elections* (Washington, D.C.: Congressional Quarterly Press, 2006), pp. 227–231.

26. Gary C. Jacobson, "Money in the 1980 and 1982 Congressional Elections," in *Money and Politics in the United States: Financing Elections in the 1980s*, ed. Michael J. Malbin (Chatham, N.J.: Chatham House, 1984), p. 65.

27. Alan R. Gitelson, M. Margaret Conway, and Frank B. Feigert, *American Political Parties: Stability and Change* (Boston: Houghton Mifflin, 1984), p. 242; for a contemporary examination of polling, see Herbert Asher, *Polling and the Public: What Every Citizen Should Know*, 6th ed. (Washington, D.C.: Congressional Quarterly Press, 2004).

28. For a comprehensive study of campaign consultants, see James A. Thurber and Candice J. Nelson, *Campaign Warriors: Political Consultants in Elections* (Washington, D.C.: The Brookings Institution, 2000).

29. Todd Blair and Garrett Biggs, "Cable Advertising: An Underrated Medium for Local Elections," *Campaigns & Elections* (September 2005), pp. 40–41.

30. Marchette Chute, *The First Liberty: A History of the Right to Vote in America, 1619–1850* (New York: Dutton, 1969), p. 223; for a brief but concise review of the early development of the electorate, see Bruce Campbell, *The American Electorate: Attitudes and Action* (New York: Holt, Rinehart and Winston, 1979), chap. 2.

31. Campbell, pp. 12–13.

32. See Raymond E. Wolfinger and Steven J. Rosenstone, *Who Votes?* (New Haven, Conn.: Yale University Press, 1980).

33. Ibid., p. 18.

34. Paul R. Abramson and John H. Aldrich, "The Decline of Electoral Participation in America," *American Political Science Review*, 76 (September 1982), 502–521; and Richard A. Brody, "The Puzzle of Participation in America," in *The New American Political System*, ed. Anthony King (Washington, D.C.: American Enterprise Institute, 1978).

35. Abramson, Aldrich, and Rohde, chap. 6.

36. Ibid., pp. 140–143.

37. For the most comprehensive discussion of retrospective voting, see Morris P. Fiorina, *Retrospective Voting in American National Elections* (New Haven, Conn.: Yale University Press, 1999).

38. Abramson, Aldrich, and Rohde, p. 181.

39. Ibid., pp. 109–110.

40. For a discussion on the electoral college and alternative plans for electing the president, see Dudley and Gitelson, chap. 6.

41. See Gerald M. Pomper, with Susan S. Lederman, *Elections in America: Control and Influence in Democratic Politics*, 2nd ed. (New York: Longman, 1980).

42. See data from a project by Terry Royed and Steven Borrelli, "Party Pledges and Policy Change in the UK and US, 1970s–1990s," funded by National Science Foundation grant #SBR-9730785.

43. Ibid.

Chapter 8

Interest Groups, pp. 219–243

1. Jonathan Weisman and Charles R. Babcock, "K Street's New Ways Spawn More Pork," *Washington Post,* January 27, 2006, p. A1.
2. The actual number of individuals who lobby in Washington is unknown since the rules governing registration are ambiguous and penalties for not registering are slight. See Todd S. Purdum, "Go Ahead, Try and Stop K Street," *New York Times,* January 8, 2006, Section 4, p. 1.
3. Adam Nagourney and Janet Elder, "New Poll Finds Mixed Support for Wiretaps," *New York Times,* January 27, 2006, p. 1.
4. See Jeffrey M. Berry, *The Interest Group Society,* 3rd ed. (New York: Longman, 1997); Kay Lehman Schlozman and John T. Tierney, *Organized Interests and American Democracy* (New York: Harper & Row, 1986); and Allan J. Cigler and Burdett A. Loomis, *Interest Group Politics,* 5th ed. (Washington, D.C.: Congressional Quarterly Press, 1998).
5. Alan R. Gitelson, M. Margaret Conway, and Frank B. Feigert, *American Political Parties: Stability and Change* (Boston: Houghton Mifflin, 1984), pp. 333–335.
6. Schlozman and Tierney, p. 50.
7. Steven Greenhouse, "Membership in Unions Drops Again," *New York Times,* January 28, 2005, p. A14. In recent years, the AFL-CIO has been challenged from within its ranks and several large unions have broken off from the federation.
8. For an excellent discussion of public interest groups, see Jeffrey Barry, *The Interest Group Society,* 4th ed. (New York: Addison Wesley, 2001); and Jeffrey M. Berry, *Lobbying for the People* (Princeton, N.J.: Princeton University Press, 1977).
9. These categories are drawn, in part, from Schlozman and Tierney's excellent study on interest-group politics, pp. 45–49.
10. Ibid., pp. 45–46.
11. Berry, *The Interest Group Society,* pp. 139–161.
12. Federal Election Commission press release, February 23, 2006.
13. www.opensecrets.org/527s.
14. See Mancur Olson, *The Logic of Collective Action* (Cambridge, Mass.: Harvard University Press, 1965).
15. Ibid. See also E. E. Schattschneider, *The Semisovereign People* (New York: Holt, Rinehart and Winston, 1960).
16. Schlozman and Tierney, pp. 103–106.
17. Ibid., p. 106.
18. Berry, *The Interest Group Society,* p. 114.
19. Schlozman and Tierney, pp. 150–151.
20. *Current American Government: Fall 1991 Guide* (Washington, D.C.: Congressional Quarterly Press, 1991), p. 150.
21. Ronald Hrebenar, *Interest Group Politics in America,* 3rd ed. (Armonk, N.Y.: M. E. Sharpe, 1997), pp. 279–281.
22. *Guide to Current American Government, Spring 1983* (Washington, D.C.: Congressional Quarterly Press, 1983), p. 48.
23. Schlozman and Tierney, p. 104.
24. Ibid., p. 150.
25. Jeffrey Taylor, "Accountants' Campaign Contributions Are About to Pay Off in Legislation on Lawsuit Protection," *Wall Street Journal,* March 8, 1995, p. 1; see also Berry, *The Interest Group Society,* pp. 154–160.
26. Trevor Potter and Kirk L. Jowers, "Recent Developments in Campaign Finance Reform," The Brookings Institution, June 2002.
27. Harold W. Stanley and Richard G. Niemi, *Vital Statistics on American Politics 2005–2006* (Washington, D.C.: Congressional Quarterly Press, 2006), pp. 74–75.
28. Gitelson, Conway, and Feigert, p. 339.
29. Berry, *The Interest Group Society,* p. 131. See also John W. Kingdon, *Congressmen's Voting Decisions,* 2nd ed. (New York: Harper & Row, 1981).
30. Quoted in David S. Broder, "News of the Weak," *Washington Post* National Weekly Edition, January 13–19, 1997, p. 21.
31. See Haynes Johnson and David S. Broder, *The System* (Boston: Little, Brown, 1996), p. 215.
32. Karen O'Connor, *Women's Organizations' Use of the Courts* (Lexington, Mass.: Lexington Books, 1980), p. 118.

Chapter 9

Media and Politics, pp. 244–265

1. The Pew Research Center for the People and the Press, "Perceptions of Partisan Bias Seen as Growing — Especially by Democrats," January 11, 2003, www.people-press.org.
2. Roan Conrad, "TV News and the 1976 Election: A Dialogue," *The Wilson Quarterly,* 1 (Spring 1977), 84.
3. Ronald Berkman and Laura W. Kitch, *Politics in the Media Age* (New York: McGraw-Hill, 1986), p. 21.
4. Phillip Knightley, *The First Casualty* (New York: Harcourt Brace Jovanovich, 1975), p. 56.
5. Quoted in Berkman and Kitch, p. 25.
6. Stephen Ansolabehere, Roy Behr, and Shanto Iyengar, *The Media Game: American Politics in the Television Age* (New York: Macmillan, 1993), p. 44.
7. Doris A. Graber, *Mass Media and American Politics,* 3rd ed. (Washington, D.C.: Congressional Quarterly Press, 1989), p. 45.
8. Kathleen Hall Jamieson and Karlyn Kohrs Campbell, *The Interplay of Influence* (Belmont, Calif.: Wadsworth, 1983), p. 10.
9. George F. Gilder, *Life After Television* (New York: Norton, 1994).
10. Quoted in Robert W. McChesney, *Rich Media, Poor Democracy* (Urbana: University of Illinois Press, 1999), p. 120.
11. Jamieson and Campbell, p. 16.
12. Graber, pp. 84–86.
13. Herbert J. Gans, *Deciding What's News: A Study of CBS Evening News, NBC Nightly News, Newsweek and Time* (New York: Vintage, 1980), p. 9.
14. John Fiske, *Television Culture* (New York: Routledge, 1995), p. 281.

15. Quoted in Leonard Downie Jr. and Robert C. Kaiser, *The News About the News* (New York: Knopf, 2002), p. 117.

16. Quoted in Bill Kovach and Tom Rosenstiel, *Warp Speed: America in the Age of Mixed Media* (New York: Century Foundation Press, 1999), p. 71.

17. Paul Lazarfeld, Bernard Berelson, and H. Gaudet, *The People's Choice* (New York: Columbia University Press, 1948).

18. Thomas E. Patterson, *The Mass Media Election: How Americans Choose Their President* (New York: Praeger, 1980), pp. 86–91.

19. Benjamin I. Page, Robert Y. Shapiro, and Glenn R. Dempsey, "What Moves Public Opinion," *American Political Science Review*, 81 (March 1987), 23–43.

20. Shanto Iyengar, *Is Anyone Responsible? How Television Frames Political Issues* (Chicago: University of Chicago Press, 1991).

21. Austin Ranney, *Channels of Power: The Impact of Television on American Politics* (New York: Basic Books, 1983), p. 17.

22. Shanto Iyengar, Mark D. Peters, and Donald R. Kinder, "Experimental Demonstrations of the 'Not-so-Minimal' Consequences of Television News Programs," *American Political Science Review*, 76 (December 1982), 848–858.

23. Ansolabehere, Behr, and Iyengar, p. 148.

24. The Center for Media and Public Affairs, "Journalists Monopolize TV Election News," October 30, 2000, www.cmpa.com.

25. Stephen Hess, "President Clinton and the White House Press Corps — Year One," *Media Studies Journal*, 8 (Spring 1994), 4.

26. Dayton Duncan, *Press, Polls, and the 1988 Campaign: An Insider's Critique* (Cambridge, Mass.: Joan Shorenstein Barone Center for the Press and Public Policy, John F. Kennedy School of Government, Harvard University, April 1989), pp. 3, 5.

27. Quoted in Graber, p. 235.

28. Fred Smoller, "The Six O'Clock Presidency: Patterns of Network News Coverage of the President," *Presidential Studies Quarterly*, 16 (Winter 1986), 31–49.

29. David Wise, *The Politics of Lying: Government Deception, Secrecy, and Power* (New York: Vintage, 1973), p. 460.

30. Michael Baruch Grossman and Martha Joynt Kumar, *Portraying the President: The White House and the Media* (Baltimore: Johns Hopkins University Press, 1981), p. 116.

31. Quoted in Charles Peters, "Why the White House Press Didn't Get the Watergate Story," *Washington Monthly*, 4 (July/August 1973), 6.

32. Quoted in Joseph C. Spear, *Presidents and the Press: The Nixon Legacy* (Cambridge, Mass.: MIT Press, 1984), pp. 10–11.

33. For a complete discussion of "going public," see Samuel Kernell, *Going Public: New Strategies of Presidential Leadership*, 3rd ed. (Washington, D.C.: Congressional Quarterly Press, 1997).

34. Stephen Hess, *The Washington Reporters* (Washington, D.C.: The Brookings Institution, 1981), pp. 98–99.

35. Quoted in David M. O'Brien, *Storm Center: The Supreme Court in American Politics* (New York: Norton, 1986), p. 281.

Chapter 10

Congress, pp. 266–295

1. Albert D. Cover, "One Good Term Deserves Another: The Advantage of Incumbency in Congressional Elections," *American Journal of Political Science*, 21 (August 1977), 523–541.

2. *Wesberry v. Sanders*, 376 U.S. 1 (1964).

3. Gary C. Jacobson, *The Politics of Congressional Elections*, 2nd ed. (Boston: Little, Brown, 1987), p. 13.

4. Morris Fiorina, *Congress: Keystone of the Washington Establishment* (New Haven, Conn.: Yale University Press, 1977), pp. 17–19.

5. Jim Wright, *You and Your Congressman* (New York: Coward, McMann and Geoghegan, 1972), p. 22.

6. David R. Mayhew, *Congress: The Electoral Connection* (New Haven, Conn.: Yale University Press, 1974), p. 37.

7. Ibid., p. 61.

8. Richard F. Fenno Jr., *Home Style: House Members in Their Districts* (Boston: Little, Brown, 1978), p. 61.

9. Jacobson, p. 50.

10. *McCulloch v. Maryland*, 17 U.S. (4 Wheat.) 316 (1819).

11. For a detailed account of the budget process, see Allen Schick, *Congress and Money* (Washington, D.C.: The Urban Institute, 1980). See also James P. Pfiffner, *The President, the Budget, and Congress: Impoundment and the 1974 Budget Act* (Boulder, Colo.: Westview Press, 1979).

12. Richard Doyle and Jerry McCaffery, "The Budget Enforcement Act of 1990: The Path to No Fault Budgeting," *Public Budgeting and Finance*, 11 (Spring 1991), 29.

13. Richard Shapiro, *Frontline Management: A Guide for Congressional District/State Offices* (Washington, D.C.: Congressional Management Foundation, 1989), pp. 1–7.

14. Morris P. Fiorina, "The Case of the Vanishing Marginals: The Bureaucracy Did It," *American Political Science Review*, 71 (March 1977), 180.

15. Fenno, *Home Style*, p. 240.

16. See Mathew McCubbins and Thomas Schwartz, "Congressional Oversight Overlooked: Police Patrols Versus Fire Alarms," *American Journal of Political Science*, 28 (February 1984), 165–179.

17. Quoted in Barbara Hinckley, *Stability and Change in Congress* (New York: Harper & Row, 1983), p. 243.

18. *Immigration and Naturalization Service v. Chadha*, 103 S.Ct. 2764 (1983).

19. For a general discussion of the legislative veto and its alternatives, see Joseph Cooper, "The Legislative Veto in the 1980s," in *Congress Reconsidered*, ed. Lawrence C. Dodd and Bruce I. Oppenheimer, 3rd ed. (Washington, D.C.: Congressional Quarterly Press, 1985), pp. 364–389.

20. Hinckley, p. 16.

21. Paul Boller, *Presidential Anecdotes* (New York: Penguin, 1981), p. 18.

22. See Steven S. Smith and Christopher J. Deering, *Committees in Congress*, 2nd ed. (Washington, D.C.: Congressional Quarterly Press, 1990).

23. Richard Fenno Jr., *Congressmen in Committees* (Boston: Little, Brown, 1973).

24. Norman J. Ornstein, Thomas E. Mann, and Michael J. Malbin, *Vital Statistics on Congress: 1989–1990* (Washington, D.C.: Congressional Quarterly Press, 1990).

25. Quoted in Hedrick Smith, *The Power Game: How Washington Works* (New York: Ballantine, 1989), p. 287.

26. Ibid., p. 266.

27. Quoted in *Origins and Development of Congress*, p. 122.

28. For an excellent discussion of House and Senate rules, see Walter J. Oleszek, *Congressional Procedures and the Policy Process* (Washington, D.C.: Congressional Quarterly Press, 1978).

29. Quoted in William J. Keefe and Morris S. Ogul, *The American Legislative Process: Congress and the States* (Englewood Cliffs, N.J.: Prentice-Hall, 1981), pp. 259–260.

30. David R. Mayhew, *America's Congress: Actions in the Public Sphere, James Madison Through Newt Gingrich* (New Haven, Conn.: Yale University Press, 2000).

31. Quoted in Helen Dewar, "On Capitol Hill, Symbols Triumph," *Washington Post*, November 26, 1991, p. A4.

32. Woodrow Wilson, *Congressional Government*, rev. ed. (New York: Meridian Books, 1956), p. 210.

Chapter 11

The Presidency, pp. 296–328

1. Thomas E. Cronin, *The State of the Presidency* (Boston: Little, Brown, 1980).

2. Louis W. Koenig, *The Chief Executive*, 3rd ed. (New York: Harcourt Brace Jovanovich, 1975).

3. Michael Nelson, "Evaluating the Presidency," in *The Presidency and the Political System*, ed. Michael Nelson (Washington, D.C.: Congressional Quarterly Press, 1984), pp. 5–28.

4. Quoted in Koenig, p. 8.

5. Quoted in Edward S. Corwin, *The President: Office and Powers* (New York: New York University Press, 1957), p. 22.

6. Paul F. Boller Jr., *Presidential Anecdotes* (New York: Penguin, 1981), p. 86.

7. Nelson, pp. 5–28.

8. Marcus Cunliffe, "A Defective Institution?" *Commentary* (February 1968), 28.

9. Arthur M. Schlesinger Jr., *The Imperial Presidency* (Boston: Houghton Mifflin, 1973).

10. Thomas Franck, ed., *The Tethered Presidency* (New York: New York University Press, 1981).

11. Charles Funderburk, *Presidents and Politics: The Limits of Power* (Monterey, Calif.: Brooks/Cole, 1982), p. 7.

12. Michael Novak, *Choosing Our King* (New York: Macmillan, 1974).

13. Mary Klein, ed., *Viewpoints on the Presidency: The Power and the Glory* (Minneapolis: Winston Press, 1974), pp. 18–19.

14. *Humphrey's Executor v. United States*, 295 U.S. 602 (1935).

15. 418 U.S. 683.

16. See *Clinton v. Jones*, 520 U.S. 681 (1997).

17. See *In Re Sealed Case (Espy)*, 121 F.3d 729 (1997) and *In Re Lindsey*, 158 F.3d 1263 (1998).

18. See *In Re Sealed Case (Secret Service)*, 148 F.3d 1073 (1998).

19. Quoted in Louis Fisher, *The Politics of Shared Power: Congress and the Executive* (Washington, D.C.: Congressional Quarterly Press, 1981), p. 9.

20. Richard M. Pious, *The American Presidency* (New York: Basic Books, 1979), p. 340.

21. Corwin, p. 189.

22. Quoted in Pious, p. 395.

23. For an excellent discussion of the Gulf War and the War Powers Resolution, see Marcia Lynn Whicker, Raymond A. Moore, and James P. Pfiffner, *The Presidency and the Persian Gulf War* (Lexington: University of Kentucky Press, 1996).

24. Richard Neustadt, "The Presidency and Legislation: Planning the President's Program," *American Political Science Review*, 49 (1955), 1015.

25. Quoted in Michael L. Mezey, *Congress, the President, and Public Policy* (Boulder, Colo.: Westview Press, 1989), p. 10.

26. Clinton Rossiter, *The American Presidency* (New York: Harcourt, Brace, 1960).

27. For a complete account of the growth of presidential staffing, see Stephen Hess, *Organizing the Presidency* (Washington, D.C.: The Brookings Institution, 1976).

28. Cronin, pp. 276–278.

29. For a history of such clearance procedures, see Richard E. Neustadt, "Presidency and Legislation: The Growth of Central Clearance," *American Political Science Review*, 48 (1954), 150–158.

30. George Edwards and Stephen Wayne, *Presidential Leadership: Politics and Policy Making* (New York: St. Martin's, 1985), p. 189.

31. Barbara Hinckley, *Problems of the Presidency: A Text with Readings* (Glenview, Ill.: Scott, Foresman, 1985), p. 101.

32. Quoted in ibid., p. 105.

33. Quoted in Richard E. Neustadt, *Presidential Power: The Politics of Leadership from FDR to Carter* (New York: Wiley, 1980), p. 9.

34. Ibid., chap. 3.

35. Quoted in Doris Kearns, *Lyndon Johnson and the American Dream* (New York: Harper & Row, 1976), p. 226.

36. Quoted in Pious, p. 189.

37. George Edwards, *Presidential Influence in Congress* (San Francisco: Freeman, 1980), p. 89.

38. Douglas Rivers and Nancy L. Rose, "Passing the President's Program: Public Opinion and Presidential Influence in Congress," *American Journal of Political Science*, 29 (1985), 187.

39. Paul C. Light, *The President's Agenda: Domestic Policy Choice from Kennedy to Carter* (Baltimore: Johns Hopkins University Press, 1983), pp. 36–37.

40. Paul Brace and Barbara Hinckley, *Follow the Leader* (New York: Basic Books, 1994), p. 161.

Chapter 12

Bureaucracy, pp. 329–370

1. Daniel Franklin, "The FEMA Phoenix: How One Federal Agency Rose from the Ashes to Become a Symbol of What Government Can Do." *Washington Monthly*, 27 (July 8, 1995), p. 38.
2. See the transcript of Michael Brown's interview with Fox News on March 6, 2006, at www.foxnews.com/printer _friendly_story10,3566,186860,00.html.
3. See Al Gore, "Common Sense Government Works Better and Costs Less — Third Report of the National Performance Review" (Washington, D.C.: National Performance Review, 1995), p. 12.
4. www.pbs.org/wgbh/pages/frontline/storm/interviews/witt .html.
5. See National Election Studies, Center for Political Studies, University of Michigan, "The NES Guide to Public Opinion and Electoral Behavior: Do People in Government Waste Tax Money, 1958–2004," www.umich.edu/~nes/nes guide/toptable/tab5a_3.htm.
6. Peter D. Hart and Robert Teeter, "America Unplugged: Citizens and Their Government," www.excelgov.org/ publication/excel/usunplugged.htm.
7. For these and related survey results, see National Election Studies, Center for Political Studies, University of Michigan, "The NES Guide to Public Opinion and Electoral Behavior," www.umich.edu/~nes/nesguide/nesguide.htm (Ann Arbor: University of Michigan Center for Political Studies [producer and distributor], 1995–2004).
8. The figures for 2005 government employment are from tables found in Section 17 of "Historical Tables of the Fiscal Year 2007 U.S. Budget"; see www.gpoaccess.gov/usbudget/ fy07/hist.html.
9. The rest are employed in the legislative (approximately 39,000) and judicial (28,000) branches. Civilian employment does not include figures from the Central Intelligence Agency and other intelligence-gathering organizations. These and other detailed statistics are gathered and issued on a regular basis by the U.S. Office of Personnel Management (OPM). See www.opm.gov/feddata/index.htm.
10. For 2004 and 2005 figures, see the data and profiles from OPM, posted at www.opm.gov/feddata/. The site contains the annual Fact Book on federal government personnel, as well as FedScope, an elaborate interactive databank that contains the most up-to-date information available.
11. Data on presidential appointees are posted by OPM on a regular basis; for access, see www.opm.gov/feddata/. The Plum Book is found at www.gpoaccess.gov/plumbook/ index.html.
12. See Matthew A. Crenson, *The Federal Machine: Beginnings of Bureaucracy in Jacksonian America* (Baltimore: Johns Hopkins University Press, 1975).
13. For more information on the SES, visit its website at www .opm.gov/ses/index.htm.
14. For a historical perspective on federal agencies, see George Thomas Kurian, ed., *A Historical Guide to the U.S. Government* (New York: Oxford University Press, 1998).
15. Donald D. Kettl, *Government by Proxy: (Mis?) Managing Federal Programs* (Washington, D.C.: Congressional Quarterly Press, 1988).
16. The data on the top 200 federal government contractors are published in the August issue each year by *Government Executive* magazine; for 2004 data, see www.govexec.com/ features/0805-15/0805-15s2s1.htm.
17. Richard Joseph Stillman, *The American Bureaucracy: The Core of the Modern Government* (Belmont, Calif.: Wadsworth/ Thomson Learning, 2004), pp. 180–188.
18. Information on the various offices in the EOP can be found at the EOP White House website, www.whitehouse .gov/government/eop.html.
19. Technically, some of these more specialized policy units are located within the White House Office.
20. See Theodore Draper, *A Very Thin Line: The Iran-Contra Affair* (New York: Touchstone, 1991).
21. Documents related to the proposal were posted at www .whitehouse.gov/deptofhomeland/.
22. See Max J. Skidmore, *Social Security and Its Enemies: The Case for America's Most Efficient Insurance Program* (Boulder, Colo.: Westview Press, 1999); also Paul Light, *Artful Work: The Politics of Social Security Reform* (New York: Random House, 1985).
23. See Cornelius M. Kerwin, *Rulemaking: How Government Agencies Write Law and Make Policy* (Washington, D.C.: Congressional Quarterly Press, 1994).
24. Leonard D. White, *The Federalists* (New York: Macmillan, 1948); Leonard D. White, *The Jacksonians: A Study in Administrative History, 1829–1861* (New York: Macmillan, 1954); Leonard D. White, *The Jeffersonians* (New York: Macmillan, 1951).
25. Leonard D. White, *The Republican Era, 1869–1901: A Study in Administrative History* (New York: Macmillan, 1958).
26. Data on government employment are drawn from federal census and budgetary data posted at www.census.gov/ and http://gpo.gov/usbudget/.
27. Herbert Kaufman, *Red Tape: Its Origins, Uses, and Abuses* (Washington, D.C.: The Brookings Institution, 1977).
28. David A. Stockman, *The Triumph of Politics: How the Reagan Revolution Failed* (New York: Harper & Row, 1986).
29. For example, see R. Douglas Arnold, *Congress and the Bureaucracy: A Theory of Influence* (New Haven, Conn.: Yale University Press, 1979).
30. Norton E. Long, "Power and Administration," *Public Administration Review*, 9 (Autumn 1949), 257–264.
31. See Francis E. Rourke, *Bureaucracy, Politics, and Public Policy*, 3rd ed. (Boston: Little, Brown, 1984).
32. See Arnold.
33. A. Lee Fritschler and James M. Hoefler, *Smoking and Politics: Policy Making and the Federal Bureaucracy*, 5th ed. (Upper Saddle River, N.J.: Prentice-Hall, 1996); Richard

Kluger, *Ashes to Ashes: America's Hundred-Year Cigarette War, the Public Health, and the Unabashed Triumph of Philip Morris* (New York: Vintage Books, 1997).

34. On the recent efforts, see David A. Kessler, *A Question of Intent: A Great American Battle with a Deadly Industry* (New York: Public Affairs, 2001).

35. The concept of issue networks was first described in detail in Hugh Heclo, "Issue Networks and the Executive Establishment," in *The New American Political System*, ed. Anthony King (Washington, D.C.: American Enterprise Institute, 1978).

36. See Norman J. Vig and Michael E. Kraft, eds., *Environmental Policy in the 1980s: Reagan's New Agenda* (Washington, D.C.: Congressional Quarterly Press, 1984).

37. Stockman, pp. 278, 296–297.

38. Richard P. Nathan, *The Administrative Presidency* (New York: Wiley, 1983).

39. See Joel D. Aberbach, "The President and the Executive Branch," in *The Bush Presidency: First Appraisals*, ed. Colin Campbell and Bert A. Rockman (Chatham, N.J.: Chatham House, 1991), especially pp. 232–235.

40. Regarding presidential control of the bureaucracy, see the website of the Office of Management and Budget at www.whitehouse.gov/omb/.

41. Quoted in James L. Sundquist, *The Decline and Resurgence of Congress* (Washington, D.C.: The Brookings Institution, 1981), p. 320.

42. Alfred A. Marcus, *Promise and Performance: Choosing and Implementing an Environmental Policy* (Westport, Conn.: Greenwood Press, 1980).

43. See Joel D. Aberbach, *Keeping a Watchful Eye: The Politics of Congressional Oversight* (Washington, D.C.: The Brookings Institution, 1990).

44. For a study of how Congress has responded to the emergence of the administrative state, see David H. Rosenbloom, *Building a Legislative-Centered Public Administration: Congress and the Administrative State, 1946–1999* (Tuscaloosa: University of Alabama Press, 2000).

45. For information on the 1998 legislation and IRS efforts to meet congressional demands, visit the IRS website at www.irs.gov/.

46. See David H. Rosenbloom, *Public Administration and Law: Bench v. Bureau in the United States* (New York: Marcel Dekker, 1983); also David H. Rosenbloom, James D. Carroll, and Jonathan D. Carroll, *Constitutional Competence for Public Managers: Cases and Commentary* (Itasca, Ill.: F. E. Peacock, 2000).

47. See Louis Fisher, "The Administrative World of Chadha and Bowsher," *Public Administration Review*, 47, no. 3 (May/June 1987), 213–219.

48. For more information on whistle-blowing, see the website of the National Whistleblower Center at www.whistleblowers.org/.

49. See Paul C. Light, *Monitoring Government: Inspectors General and the Search for Accountability* (Washington, D.C.: The Brookings Institution, 1993).

50. Charles T. Goodsell, *The Case for Bureaucracy: A Public Administration Polemic*, 3rd ed. (Chatham, N.J.: Chatham House, 1994).

51. See Gerald E. Caiden, "What Is Maladministration?" *Public Administration Review*, 51, no. 6 (November/December 1991), 486–493. See also William T. Gormley, *Taming the Bureaucracy: Muscles, Prayers, and Other Strategies* (Princeton, N.J.: Princeton University Press, 1989).

52. James Q. Wilson, *Bureaucracy: What Government Agencies Do and Why They Do It* (New York: Basic Books, 1989), pp. 326–331.

53. Frederic A. Bergerson, *The Army Gets an Air Force: Tactics of Insurgent Bureaucratic Politics* (Baltimore: Johns Hopkins University Press, 1980).

54. E. S. Savas, *Privatization: The Key to Better Government* (Chatham, N.J.: Chatham House, 1987); John D. Donahue, *The Privatization Decision: Public Ends, Private Means* (New York: Basic Books, 1989) provides a more critical perspective. For an overview of worldwide privatization efforts, see Graeme A. Hodge, *Privatization: An International Review of Performance, Theoretical Lenses on Public Policy* (Boulder, Colo.: Westview Press, 1999).

55. On the logic behind this general perspective, see Ronald J. Oakerson, *Governing Local Public Economies: Creating the Civic Metropolis* (Oakland, Calif.: ICS Press, 1999). On education, see John E. Chubb and Terry M. Moe, *Politics, Markets, and America's Schools* (Washington, D.C.: The Brookings Institution, 1990).

56. See, for example, Paul A. Volcker, Chairman, *Leadership for America: Rebuilding the Public Service: The Report of the National Commission on the Public Service* (Washington, D.C.: The National Commission on the Public Service, 1989).

57. David Osborne and Ted Gaebler, *Reinventing Government: How the Entrepreneurial Spirit Is Transforming the Public Sector* (Reading, Mass.: Addison-Wesley, 1992).

58. For information on PART, visit www.whitehouse.gov/omb/part/.

59. See Melvin J. Dubnick and Barbara S. Romzek, *American Public Administration: Politics and the Management of Expectations* (New York: Macmillan, 1991), especially chap. 3; Barbara S. Romzek and Melvin J. Dubnick, "Accountability," in *Defining Public Administration: Selections from the International Encyclopedia of Public Policy and Administration*, ed. Jay M. Shafritz (Boulder, Colo.: Westview Press, 2000); Melvin J. Dubnick and Barbara S. Romzek, "Accountability and the Centrality of Expectations in American Public Administration," in *Research in Public Administration*, ed. James L. Perry (Greenwich, Conn.: JAI Press, 1993).

Chapter 13

Courts, Judges, and the Law, pp. 371–401

1. Richard J. Richardson and Kenneth N. Vines, *The Politics of Federal Courts: Lower Courts in the United States* (Boston: Little, Brown, 1970).

2. For a comprehensive discussion of the uses of diversity jurisdiction, see Victor E. Flango, "Attorney's Perspectives on Choice of Forum in Diversity Cases," *Akron Law Review*, 25 (Summer 1991), 1–82.

3. "CQ Law/Judiciary," *Congressional Quarterly Weekly Report*, November 26, 1988, p. 3393.

4. Quoted in Howard Ball, *Courts and Politics: The Federal Judicial System* (Englewood Cliffs, N.J.: Prentice-Hall, 1980), p. 176.

5. "CQ on the Floor," *Congressional Quarterly Weekly Report*, March 20, 1970, p. 776.

6. See Laurence H. Tribe, *God Save This Honorable Court: How the Choice of Supreme Court Justices Shapes Our History* (New York: Random House, 1985).

7. Quoted in Stephen Wasby, *The Supreme Court in the Federal System*, 2nd ed. (New York: Holt, Rinehart and Winston, 1984), p. 89.

8. *The Supreme Court: Justice and the Law* (Washington, D.C.: Congressional Quarterly Press, 1981), p. 163.

9. John Schmidauser, *Judges and Justices: The Federal Appellate Judiciary* (Boston: Little, Brown, 1979), p. 96.

10. Sheldon Goldman and Thomas P. Jahnige, *The Federal Courts as a Political System* (New York: Harper & Row, 1985), p. 250.

11. See Stephen Wasby, *The Supreme Court in the Federal System*, 3rd ed. (New York: Holt, Rinehart and Winston, 1984), pp. 91–97.

12. Quoted in Henry J. Abraham, *The Judicial Process* (New York: Oxford University Press, 1980), p. 203.

13. *Webster v. Reproductive Health Services*, 492 U.S. 490 (1989).

14. Doris Marie Provine, *Case Selection in the United States Supreme Court* (Chicago: University of Chicago Press, 1980).

15. Quoted in David M. O'Brien, *Storm Center: The Supreme Court in American Politics*, 2nd ed. (New York: Norton, 1990), p. 283.

16. Quoted in Bob Woodward and Scott Armstrong, *The Brethren: Inside the Supreme Court* (New York: Avon Books, 1979), p. 490.

17. *Brown v. Board of Education II*, 349 U.S. 294 (1955).

18. William J. Brennan, "Inside View of the High Court," *New York Times Magazine*, October 6, 1963, p. 22.

19. *Marbury v. Madison*, 5 U.S. (1 Cranch) 137 (1803).

20. For a complete discussion of the *Marbury* decision, see Craig R. Ducat, *Modes of Constitutional Interpretation* (St. Paul, Minn.: West, 1978), pp. 1–41.

21. See in particular Nathan Glazer, "Toward an Imperial Judiciary," *The Public Interest*, 47 (Fall 1975), 104–123; and Raoul Berger, *Government by the Judiciary: The Transformation of the Fourteenth Amendment* (Cambridge, Mass.: Harvard University Press, 1977).

22. Tribe, p. 42.

23. For a conservative critique of the original intent approach, see Richard A. Posner, "What Am I? A Potted Plant?", *New Republic*, September 28, 1987, pp. 23–25.

24. *Furman v. Georgia*, 408 U.S. 238 (1972).

25. See Jack Peltason, *Fifty-eight Lonely Men: Southern Federal Judges and School Desegregation* (Urbana: University of Illinois Press, 1971).

26. *Oregon v. Mitchell*, 400 U.S. 112 (1970).

27. Cited in O'Brien, p. 361.

28. Quoted in Richard Kluger, *Simple Justice: The History of Brown v. Board of Education and Black America's Struggle for Equality* (New York: Knopf, 1976), p. 753.

Chapter 14

Domestic Policy and Policymaking, pp. 402–443

1. For an exceptionally well-written history and assessment of the 1994 debate over health-care reform, see Theda Skocpol, *Boomerang: Health Care Reform and the Turn Against Government* (New York: Norton, 1997), especially chap. 5.

2. For a classic statement of this position, see Arthur M. Okun, *Equality and Efficiency: The Big Tradeoff* (Washington, D.C.: The Brookings Institution, 1975). Ironically, Okun's purpose was to present a realistic justification for government intervention in the economy under some circumstances.

3. Garry Wills, *A Necessary Evil: A History of American Distrust of Government* (New York: Simon & Schuster, 1999), p. 17.

4. See Herbert Stein, *Presidential Economics: The Making of Economic Policy from Roosevelt to Reagan and Beyond*, rev. ed. (New York: Touchstone, 1985).

5. For example, see George Gilder, *Wealth and Poverty* (New York: Basic Books, 1981); also Charles Murray, *Losing Ground: American Social Policy, 1950–1980* (New York: Basic Books, 1984).

6. For example, in May 1992, pollsters asked Americans whether the government was spending too much, too little, or the right amount on "assistance to the poor." In response, 64 percent said "too little," while only 13 percent said "too much," and 16 percent said "the right amount." Responses were quite different when the word "welfare" was substituted for "assistance to the poor." In that case, only 23 percent said "too little" was being spent, while 27 and 44 percent, respectively, said "the right amount" and "too much." Similarly, while 62 percent of those surveyed in 1993 believed that it was government's responsibility to "take care of people who can't take care of themselves," a full 80 percent agreed with the contention that "poor people have become too dependent on government assistance." The 1993 survey of 1,507 Americans was conducted by the Times Mirror Center for the People and the Press (now called the Pew Research Center for the People and the Press). There was nothing unique about those results, however, as comparisons of polls before and since have reflected the fact that the way an issue is phrased makes a great deal of difference in the response received. See Chapter 5, on public opinion and political participation.

7. See James E. Anderson, *Public Policymaking: An Introduction*, 6th ed. (Boston: Houghton Mifflin, 2006).

8. Considerable controversy and drama accompanied the "discovery" of AIDS; it is chronicled in Randy Shilts, *And the Band Played On: Politics, People, and the AIDS Epidemic* (New York: Penguin Books, 1988).

9. Matthew A. Crenson, *The Un-Politics of Air Pollution: A Study of Non-Decision-making in the Cities* (Baltimore: Johns Hopkins University Press, 1971), pp. 1–2.

10. On the 1988 reforms, see Julie Rovner, "Welfare Reform: The Issue That Bubbled Up from the States to Capitol Hill," *Governing*, 2, no. 2 (December 1988), 17–21. For an overview of the history behind the 1996 reforms, see the timeline provided by the American Public Human Services Association at www.aphsa.org/Policy/HistoryWelfare.asp.

11. See Theda Skocpol, *Boomerang: Health Care Reform and the Turn Against Government* (New York: Norton, 1997).

12. Jeffrey H. Birnbaum and Alan S. Murray, *Showdown at Gucci Gulch: Lawmakers, Lobbyists, and the Unlikely Triumph of Tax Reform* (New York: Vintage, 1987).

13. Paul C. Light, *Forging Legislation* (New York: Norton, 1992).

14. The Court's decision-making process remains one of the mysteries of Washington. Whatever insights we have into the process come from the recollections of law clerks and others who served the justices. One popular effort to understand what takes place inside the Court is found in Bob Woodward and Scott Armstrong, *The Brethren: Inside the Supreme Court* (New York: Simon & Schuster, 1979).

15. John M. Logsdon, *The Decision to Go to the Moon: Project Apollo and the National Interest* (Chicago: University of Chicago Press, 1970).

16. See Paul A. Sabatier, *Theories of the Policy Process, Theoretical Lenses on Public Policy* (Boulder, Colo.: Westview Press, 1999).

17. You can access a copy of the Northwest Ordinance at www.yale.edu/lawweb/avalon/nworder.htm.

18. On the work of the Office of Civil Rights, see www.ed.gov/offices/OCR/docs/ensure99.html.

19. You can read a summary of the major provision of the NDEA at http://ishi.lib.berkeley.edu/cshe/ndea/ndea.html.

20. For more on the early history of economic policy in the United States, see Carl Bridenbaugh, *Cities in the Wilderness: The First Century of Urban Life in America, 1625–1742*, 2nd ed. (New York: Knopf, 1955); Gerald D. Nash, *State Government and Economic Development: A History of Administrative Policies in California, 1849–1933* (Berkeley, Calif.: Institute of Governmental Studies/University of California, 1964), pp. 10–26; and Stuart Bruchey, *The Roots of American Economic Growth, 1607–1861: An Essay in Social Causation* (New York: Harper Torchbooks, 1968). For an interesting study of Jefferson's views, see Frank Bourgin, *The Great Challenge: The Myth of Laissez-Faire in the Early Republic* (New York: George Braziller, 1989), chaps. 7 and 8.

21. For insight into the importance of the policymaking process at the Fed, see William Greider, *Secrets of the Temple: How the Federal Reserve Runs the Country* (New York: Simon & Schuster, 1987).

22. Arthur M. Okun, *The Political Economy of Prosperity* (New York: Norton, 1970); Herbert Stein, *The Fiscal Revolution in America* (Chicago: University of Chicago Press, 1969).

23. See Alan S. Blinder, *Economic Policy and the Great Stagflation*, student ed. (New York: Academic Press, 1981).

24. The idea of an emerging "new economy" is most often attributed to management theorist Peter F. Drucker. See his *The New Realities: In Government and Politics/In Economics and Business/In Society and World View* (New York: Harper & Row, 1989) and *Management Challenges for the 21st Century* (New York: HarperBusiness, 1999).

25. For a readable and stimulating overview of the national debt issue, see Donald F. Kettl, *Deficit Politics: Public Budgeting in Its Institutional and Historical Context* (New York: Macmillan, 1992); see also David P. Calleo, *The Bankrupting of America: How the Federal Budget Is Impoverishing America* (New York: William Morrow, 1992).

26. All these figures rely on the most current U.S. budget as well as historical data. To get the exact amount of the national debt "to the penny" on any given day, see www.publicdebt.treas.gov/opd/opdpenny.htm.

27. See Calleo.

28. Data on outstanding sectoral debt are issued by the Federal Reserve System in its "Flow of Funds Accounts of the United States," issued annually. These can be found at www.federalreserve.gov/RELEASES/Z1/.

29. A growing number of analysts contend that although there is nothing inherently wrong with a national debt, it should be tolerated only if the indebtedness is targeted toward socially and economically beneficial "investments." See Benjamin M. Friedman, *Day of Reckoning: The Consequences of American Economic Policy Under Reagan and After* (New York: Random House, 1988). For a recent critical assessment of the problems posed by the growing debt and other factors, see Kevin P. Phillips, *American Theocracy: The Peril and Politics of Radical Religion, Oil, and Borrowed Money in the 21st Century* (New York: Viking, 2006).

30. I. M. Destler, *American Trade Politics: System Under Stress* (Washington, D.C.: Institute for International Economics, 1986).

31. One of the vigilant opponents was Ralph Nader's Public Citizen group, which continues to monitor the treaty's implementation and impact. See the group's website at www.citizen.org/trade/.

32. Based on discussion in Jan Aart Scholte, "Global Capitalism and the State," *International Affairs*, 73, no. 3 (1997).

33. For information on the World Trade Organization, visit its website at www.wto.org/wto/.

34. The act also provided for regulation of grain elevators. Later, the Interstate Commerce Commission was given jurisdiction over other forms of interstate transport, such as trucks, water carriers, and buses.

35. For information on antitrust activity, visit the websites of the two federal agencies that do most of the enforcement in this area: the Federal Trade Commission (at www.ftc.gov/ftc/antitrust .htm) and the Antitrust Division of the Department of Justice (at www.usdoj.gov/atr/overview.html).

36. See Louis M. Kohlmeier Jr., *The Regulators: Watchdog Agencies and the Public Interest* (New York: Harper & Row, 1969).

37. Larry N. Gerston, Cynthia Fraleigh, and Robert Schwab, *The Deregulated Society* (Pacific Grove, Calif.: Brooks/Cole, 1988); see also George C. Eads and Michael Fix, *Relief or Reform? Reagan's Regulatory Dilemma* (Washington, D.C.: Urban Institute, 1984); and Roger G. Noll and Bruce M. Owen, *The Political Economy of Deregulation: Interest Groups in*

the Regulatory Process (Washington, D.C.: American Enterprise Institute, 1983).

38. Susan J. Tolchin and Martin Tolchin, *Dismantling America: The Rush to Deregulate* (Boston: Houghton Mifflin, 1983).

39. For details on environmental legislation, visit the EPA website at www.epa.gov/epahome/laws.htm. Also see Richard N. L. Andrews, *Managing the Environment, Managing Ourselves: A History of American Environmental Policy* (New Haven, Conn.: Yale University Press, 1999); Cynthia H. Enloe, *The Politics of Pollution in a Comparative Perspective: Ecology and Power in Four Nations* (New York: David McKay, 1975); and Lettie McSpadden Wenner, *One Environment Under Law: A Public-Policy Dilemma* (Pacific Palisades, Calif.: Goodyear Publishing, 1976).

40. Much of the discussion in this section relies on Kenneth J. Meier, E. Thomas Garman, and Lael R. Keiser, *Regulation and Consumer Protection: Politics, Bureaucracy & Economics,* 3rd ed. (Houston: Dame Publications, 1998).

41. See Richard A. Harris and Sidney M. Milkis, *The Politics of Regulatory Change: A Tale of Two Agencies* (New York: Oxford University Press, 1989).

42. See Theda Skocpol, *Protecting Soldiers and Mothers: The Political Origins of Social Policy in the United States* (Cambridge, Mass.: Belknap/Harvard, 1992). See also Sidney Fine, *Laissez Faire and the General Welfare State: A Study in Conflict in American Thought, 1865–1901* (Ann Arbor, Mich.: Ann Arbor Paperbacks, 1969), pp. 22–23, 360–361; Clarke A. Chambers, *Seedtime of Reform: American Social Service and Social Action, 1918–1933* (Ann Arbor, Mich.: Ann Arbor Paperbacks, 1963); and Robert Morris, *Social Policy of the American Welfare State: An Introduction to Policy Analysis,* 2nd ed. (New York: Longman, 1985).

43. For a general discussion of contemporary social welfare policy, see Theodore R. Marmor, Jerry L. Mashaw, and Philip L. Harvey, *America's Misunderstood Welfare State: Persistent Myths, Enduring Realities* (New York: Basic Books, 1990).

44. In recent years, growing attention has been given to what some analysts term "corporate welfare" programs. These are programs that subsidize the activities of America's large corporations and that can be associated with the industrial policies discussed in the section on economic development policies. The issue of corporate welfare made it onto the national agenda in late 1994 when then Secretary of Labor Robert Reich gave a speech focusing attention on such programs. The Clinton White House quickly distanced itself from such talk. In 1997, however, a bipartisan and ideologically diverse coalition — including Ralph Nader and the National Taxpayers Union — joined forces with members of Congress to pursue an end to "corporate welfare." The Nader group, Public Citizen, maintains a website monitoring corporate welfare at www.citizen.org/congress/welfare/index.cfm. The Cato Institute, a libertarian-oriented think tank, has also adopted corporate welfare as an issue; see the www.cato.org/fiscal/corporate-welfare.html.

45. For an overview of the "old" welfare system, see Thomas E. Patterson, *America's Struggle Against Poverty, 1900–1980* (Cambridge, Mass.: Harvard University Press, 1981); U.S. House of Representatives, Committee on Ways and Means, *Overview of Entitlement Programs: 1994 Green Book* (Washington, D.C.: U.S. Government Printing Office, July 15, 1994).

46. See Charles Murray, *Losing Ground: American Social Policy* (New York: Basic Books, 1984). See also Nathan Glazer, *The Limits of Social Policy* (Cambridge, Mass.: Harvard University Press, 1988). For a counterargument, refer to John E. Schwarz, *America's Hidden Success: A Reassessment of Twenty Years of Public Policy* (New York: Norton, 1983). See also William Julius Wilson, *The Truly Disadvantaged: The Inner City, the Underclass, and Public Policy* (Chicago: University of Chicago Press, 1987).

47. For a comparison of the old and new welfare policies, go to http://aspe.os.dhhs.gov/hsp/isp/reform.htm. The U.S. Department of Health and Human Services (HHS) intermittently issues updates on the Personal Responsibility and Work Opportunity Reconciliation Act of 1996; see www.hhs.gov/news/press/2002pres/welfare.html for the 2002 "fact sheet." The National Conference of State Legislatures also provides constant updates at its website; see www.ncsl.org/statefed/WELFARE/welfare.htm.

48. The Urban Institute conducted an ongoing assessment of the 1996 act as it was being implemented. See www.urban.org/Content/Research/NewFederalism/AboutANF/AboutANF.htm.

49. For a general survey of social insurance programs, see Arnold J. Heidenheimer, Hugh Heclo, and Carolyn Teich Adams, *Comparative Public Policy: The Politics of Social Choice in Europe and America,* 3rd ed. (New York: St. Martin's, 1990), chap. 7. Also see the SSA publication "Social Security Programs Throughout the World," which can be found at www.ssa.gov/statistics/ssptw/1999/English/index.html.

50. On the politics of dealing with that crisis, see Paul Light, *Artful Work: The Politics of Social Security Reform* (New York: Random House, 1985).

51. The Concord Coalition has posted its assessments of social security, as well as its proposals for reform, at www.concordcoalition.org/issues/socsec/index.html#ss-reform-series.

52. See Max J. Skidmore, *Social Security and Its Enemies: The Case for America's Most Efficient Insurance Program* (Boulder, Colo.: Westview Press, 1999). For the latest projections of trust fund solvency, see the annual Trustees Report, posted at www.ssa.gov/OACT/TR/.

53. See the Bush White House website on Social Security reform at www.whitehouse.gov/infocus/social-security/.

54. For an analysis of the proposals for reform by the Government Accountability Office, see www.gao.gov/new.items/d05193sp.pdf.

55. Benjamin I. Page and James Roy Simmons, *What Government Can Do: Dealing with Poverty and Inequality, American Politics and Political Economy* (Chicago: University of Chicago Press, 2000).

56. For a discussion of the view that government may be a necessary good, see Wills, chap. 24.

Chapter 15

Foreign and Defense Policy, pp. 444–490

1. Dean Boyd, spokesperson for U.S. Immigration and Customs Enforcement, as quoted in Bruce Finley, "Mexico Is Global Turnstile to U.S.: More Non-Mexicans Are Crossing Border," DenverPost.com, March 26, 2006.

2. James Chace and Caleb Carr, *America Invulnerable: The Quest for Absolute Security from 1812 to Star Wars* (New York: Summit Books, 1988), p. 12.

3. See Patrick J. Buchanan, *A Republic, Not an Empire: Reclaiming America's Destiny* (Washington, D.C.: Regnery Publishers, 1999).

4. Walter Russell Mead, *Special Providence: American Foreign Policy and How It Changed the World* (New York: Knopf, 2001), pp. 57–66.

5. The concept of "the American project" developed here draws heavily from Walter Russell Mead, *Special Providence: American Foreign Policy and How It Changed the World* (New York: Knopf, 2001). See also Walter Russell Mead, *Power, Terror, Peace, and War: America's Grand Strategy in a World at Risk* (New York: Vintage, 2005).

6. See William H. Riker, *Federalism: Origin, Operation, Significance* (Boston: Little, Brown, 1964); Chace and Carr, chaps. 2–4.

7. This particular crisis has been studied in great depth, but the best-known study is the "insiders'" view provided in Robert F. Kennedy, *Thirteen Days: A Memoir of the Cuban Missile Crisis* (New York: Norton, 1971).

8. The policy of containment is most closely associated with George F. Kennan, an American diplomat and scholar who was very influential in shaping U.S. strategies during the Cold War. See his *American Diplomacy, 1900–1950* (New York: Mentor Books, 1951).

9. See Stephen E. Ambrose, *Rise to Globalism: American Foreign Policy Since 1938* (Baltimore: Penguin Books, 1971), pp. 174–175.

10. For a history of the Vietnam conflict, see Stanley Karnow, *Vietnam: A History* (New York: Penguin Books, 1983).

11. Henry Kissinger, *Years of Upheaval* (Boston: Little, Brown, 1982), pp. 235–246, 339.

12. Ibid., p. 50.

13. Ibid.

14. See Congressional Quarterly, *U.S. Foreign Policy: The Reagan Imprint* (Washington, D.C.: Congressional Quarterly Press, 1986).

15. See R. W. Apple Jr., "Poll Finds That Gorbachev's Rule Eases American Minds on Soviets," *New York Times*, May 16, 1989, pp. A1, A10.

16. For a detailed and critical analysis of the Gulf War, see Michael R. Gordon and Bernard E. Trainor, *The Generals' War: The Inside Story of the Conflict in the Gulf* (Boston: Little, Brown, 1995).

17. This summary of the strategy of George H. W. Bush's administration was drawn primarily from public presentations and related documents given by the Department of Defense during March 1992.

18. M. Destler, "Foreign Policy Making with Economy at Center Stage," in *Beyond the Beltway: Engaging the Public in U.S. Foreign Policy*, ed. Daniel Yankelovich and I. M. Destler (New York: Norton, 1994), pp. 26–42.

19. President's Commission on Industrial Competitiveness, *Global Competition: The New Reality* (Washington, D.C.: U.S. Government Printing Office, 1985), p. 1.

20. For an assessment of the factors that made the Clinton presidency different, see Donald M. Snow and Eugene Brown, *United States Foreign Policy: Politics Beyond the Water's Edge* (Boston: Bedford/St. Martin's, 2000), pp. 124–130.

21. Executive Office of the President, Office of Management and Budget, *Budget of the United States Government, Fiscal Year 1995* (Washington, D.C.: U.S. Government Printing Office, 1994), pp. 213–217.

22. See Maryann K. Cusimano, ed., *Beyond Sovereignty: Readings for a Global Agenda* (New York: Worth, 1998).

23. Madeleine K. Albright, "The Testing of American Foreign Policy," *Foreign Affairs*, 77, no. 6 (November/December 1998), 50–64.

24. From Bush's "Address to a Joint Session of Congress and the American People," delivered on September 20, 2001; see www.whitehouse.gov/news/releases/2001/09/20010920-8 .html.

25. For a surprisingly prescient analysis of the national security threats facing the United States, see the work of the U.S. Commission on National Security at www.nssg.gov/index .html.

26. Samuel P. Huntington, *The Clash of Civilization and the Remaking of World Order* (London: Touchstone/ Simon & Schuster, 1996).

27. Chalmers A. Johnson, *Blowback: The Costs and Consequences of American Empire* (New York: Metropolitan Books, 2000).

28. For an initial assessment of the changes taking place in U.S. foreign policymaking, see Arnold Kanter, "Adapting the Executive Branch to the Post–Cold War World," in *Beyond the Beltway: Engaging the Public in U.S. Foreign Policy*, ed. Daniel Yankelovich and I. M. Destler (New York: Norton, 1994).

29. On the planning for the Iraq invasion, see Michael R. Gordon and Bernard E. Trainor, *COBRA 2: The Inside Story of the Invasion and Occupation of Iraq* (New York: Pantheon Books, 2006); and Bob Woodward, *Plan of Attack* (New York: Simon & Schuster, 2004).

30. See Edward S. Corwin, *The President: Office and Powers, 1787–1857* (New York: New York University Press, 1957), chap. 5.

31. See Aaron Wildavsky, "The Two Presidencies [Reprint]," *Society*, 35, no. 2 (1996).

32. See James M. Scott, "In the Loop: Congressional Influence in American Foreign Policy," *Journal of Political and Military Sociology*, 25, no. 1 (1997); Richard Fleisher et al., "The Demise of the Two Presidencies," *American Politics Quarterly*, 28, no. 1 (2000); also Scot Schraufnagel and Stephen M. Shellman, "The Two Presidencies, 1984–98: A Replication and Extension," *Presidential Studies Quarterly*, 31, no. 4 (2001).

33. For an interesting and readable introduction to the operations of the defense bureaucracy under the George H. W. Bush administration, see Bob Woodward, *The Commanders* (New York: Simon & Schuster, 1991). Also see Gordon and Trainor. You can gain some insight into the operations of the Defense Department by visiting its public website, www.defenselink.mil.

34. See Steve Dryden, *Trade Warriors: USTR and the American Crusade for Free Trade* (New York: Oxford University Press, 1995).

35. See Thomas H. Kean and Lee Hamilton, *The 9/11 Commission Report: Final Report of the National Commission on Terrorist Attacks Upon the United States.* (Washington, D.C.: National Commission on Terrorist Attacks Upon the United States. U.S. Government Printing Office, 2004). See also James Risen, *State of War: The Secret History of the CIA and the Bush Administration* (New York: Free Press, 2006).

36. Edward S. Corwin, *The President: Office and Powers, 1787–1957: History and Analysis of Practice and Opinion*, 4th rev. ed. (New York: New York University Press, 1957), p. 171.

37. Corwin, p. 171.

38. See Norman J. Ornstein, "The Constitution and the Sharing of Foreign Policy Responsibility," in *The President, the Congress, and Foreign Policy*, ed. Edmund S. Muskie, Kenneth Rush, and Kenneth W. Thompson (Lanham, Md.: University Press of America, 1986), pp. 35–66.

39. These included four by Gerald Ford; one by Jimmy Carter; fourteen from Ronald Reagan; seven from George H. W. Bush; fifty-eight from Bill Clinton; and six from George W. Bush as of November 20, 2001. These figures are issued intermittently by the Congressional Research Service.

40. G. Calvin Mackenzie, "Resolving Policy Differences: Foreign Aid and Human Rights," in *Who Makes Public Policy? The Struggle for Control Between Congress and the Executive*, ed. Robert S. Gilmour and Alexis A. Halley (Chatham, N.J.: Chatham House, 1994), pp. 261–288.

41. See Theodore Draper, *A Very Thin Line: The Iran-Contra Affairs* (New York: Simon & Schuster, 1991).

42. Quoted in James A. Nathan and James K. Oliver, *Foreign Policy Making and the American Political System*, 3rd ed. (Baltimore: Johns Hopkins University Press, 1994), p. 174.

43. See Stephen Ansolabehere, Roy Behr, and Shanto Iyengar, *The Media Game: American Politics in the Television Age* (New York: Macmillan, 1993), pp. 195–202.

44. The media strategy used by Clinton was very similar to that used by Reagan to set the stage for his invasion of Grenada in 1983.

45. Stephen Rosenfeld, quoted in Nathan and Oliver, p. 186.

46. Pat Choate, *Agents of Influence* (New York: Touchstone/Simon & Schuster, 1990).

47. See Harold H. Saunders, "The Middle East, 1973–84: Hidden Agendas," in *The President, the Congress, and Foreign Policy*, ed. Muskie et al., chap. 7. Also see Nathan and Oliver, pp. 199–204.

48. See Gabriel A. Almond, *The American People and Foreign Policy* (New York: Praeger, 1960). Many advocates of the "mood theory" approach tend to regard the American public's opinions as "fickle and undependable." For a contrasting view, see Benjamin I. Page and Robert Y. Shapiro, *The Rational Public: Fifty Years of Trends in Americans' Policy Preferences* (Chicago: University of Chicago Press, 1992), chap. 5.

49. See Theodore J. Lowi, *The Personal President: Power Invested, Promise Unfulfilled* (Ithaca, N.Y.: Cornell University Press, 1985), pp. 170–173.

50. The mood theory concept was originally articulated by Frank L. Klingberg. See Jack E. Holmes, *The Mood/Interest Theory of American Foreign Policy* (Lexington: University Press of Kentucky, 1985).

51. Bruce Russett and Donald R. DeLuca, "'Don't Tread on Me,' Public Opinion and Foreign Policy in the Eighties," *Political Science Quarterly*, 96, no. 3 (Fall 1981), 381–387; also Congressional Quarterly, *U.S. Foreign Policy: The Reagan Imprint.*

52. See Daniel Yankelovich and John Immerwahr, "The Rules of Public Engagement," in *Beyond the Beltway*, pp. 43–77. Every other year the Chicago Council on Foreign Relations issues a report on American public opinion regarding foreign affairs and foreign policy issues. The most recent report can be found at www.ccfr.org/publications/opinion/opinion.html.

53. Joseph S. Nye, *Soft Power: The Means to Success in World Politics* (New York: Public Affairs, 2004).

54. Mead, *Power, Terror, Peace.*

55. In his 1985 State of the Union address, Reagan equated this aid with defense rather than diplomacy. He argued that "dollar for dollar, our security assistance contributes as much to global security as our own defense budget." See Congressional Quarterly, *U.S. Foreign Policy: The Reagan Imprint.*

56. Hans N. Tuch, "Improving Public Diplomacy: Setting More Modest Goals for USIA," *Foreign Service Journal*, 67 (1990), 14–18.

57. See Gerald F. Seib, "Prodded by Quayle and Cheney, Bush Becomes Fervent Supporter of Strategic Defense Initiative," *Wall Street Journal*, February 23, 1990, p. A12.

58. See James Kitfield, *Prodigal Soldiers: How the Generation of Officers Born of Vietnam Revolutionized the American Style of War* (Washington, D.C.: Brassey's, 1995).

59. Weinberger presented these points at a speech before the National Press Club on November 28, 1984; they are posted at www.pbs.org/wgbh/pages/frontline/shows/military/force/weinberger.html. Today, these principles are often referred to as the Weinberger-Powell Doctrine to reflect Colin Powell's role in developing them as an adviser to Weinberger, as well as his commitment to them when he served as chair of the Joint Chiefs of Staff.

60. Gordon and Trainor.

61. See Frances FitzGerald, *Way Out There in the Blue: Reagan, Star Wars, and the End of the Cold War* (New York: Simon & Schuster, 2000).

62. This summarizes the strategies articulated in the 1997 Report of the Quadrennial Defense Review.

63. The 2001 Quadrennial Defense Review Report can be found at www.defenselink.mil/pubs/qdr2001.pdf. The quote is from p. 13 of the report.

Credits

Illustration Credits

Chapter 1: p. 2, AP–Wide World Photos; p. 3, © Robert Galbraith/Reuters/Corbis; p. 7, Grant Wood, *Parson Weem's Fable*, 1939, oil on canvas, 1970, Amon Carter Museum, Ft. Worth, Texas; p. 13, Joe Marquette/AP–Wide World Photos; p. 18, Elise Amendola/AP–Wide World Photos.

Chapter 2: p. 27, © Bettmann/Corbis; p. 43, AP–Wide World Photos; p. 51, AP–Wide World Photos; p. 60, Getty Images.

Chapter 3: p. 67, AP–Wide World Photos; p. 72, Print Collection, Miriam and Ira D. Wallach Division of Art, Prints and Photographs, The New York Public Library, Astor, Lenox and Tilden Foundations; p. 77, AP–Wide World Photos; p. 90, Photo courtesy of the Big Dig.

Chapter 4: p. 99, Eric Gay/AP–Wide World Photos; p. 100, Dennis Brack/Black Star; p. 111, © Bettmann/Corbis; p. 119, © Bettmann/Corbis; p. 127, Larry Kolvoord/The Image Works.

Chapter 5: p. 134, David Bacon/The Image Works; p. 137, Bob Daemmrich/The Image Works; p. 143, Chip Somodevilla/Getty Images; p. 153, Ken Lambert/AP–Wide World Photos.

Chapter 6: p. 160, Jean-Marc Giboux; p. 173, Justin Sullivan/Getty Images; p. 176, H. Rumph, Jr./AP–Wide World Photos; p. 178, © Tribune Media Service, Inc. All Rights Reserved. Reprinted with permission.

Chapter 7: p. 186, Library of Congress; p. 189, © Tribune Media Service, Inc. All Rights Reserved. Reprinted with permission; p. 192, Lauren McFalls/AP–Wide World Photos; p. 203 (top), Alex Wong/Getty Images; p. 203 (bottom), Jason Connel/Getty Images.

Chapter 8: p. 221, Dennis Brack/Black Star; p. 224, Bob Daemmrich/The Image Works; p. 229, photo by Irene Schwoeffermann/photo courtesy of the U.S. Student Association, www.usstudents.org; p. 234, © Gary Markstein/Copley News Service; p. 239, AP–Wide World Photos.

Chapter 9: p. 247, Library of Congress; p. 250, TOLES © 2000 The Washington Post. Reprinted with permission of Universal Press Syndicate. All Rights Reserved; p. 255, Luke Frazza/Getty Images; p. 258, Stephen Chernin/Getty Images; p. 263, © Matthew Cavanaugh/epa/Corbis.

Chapter 10: p. 269, Steve Warmowski/The Image Works; p. 278, Win McNamee/Getty Images; p. 282, AP–Wide World Photos; p. 285, AP–Wide World Photos.

Chapter 11: Doug Mills/AP–Wide World Photos; p. 306, © Larry Downing/Reuters/Corbis; p. 310, Eric Draper, White House via Getty Images; p. 315, © Win McNamee/Reuters/Corbis; p. 321, AP–Wide World Photos.

Chapter 12: p. 331, Jocelyn Augustino/FEMA; p. 340, Eric Sander/Getty Images; p. 349, AP–Wide World Photos; p. 356, AP–Wide World Photos.

Chapter 13: p. 374, Vince Bucci/Getty Images; p. 377, © Matthew Cavanaugh/epa/Corbis; p. 386, AP–Wide World Photos; p. 390, AP–Wide World Photos.

Chapter 14: p. 415, © North American Syndicate; p. 425, AP–Wide World Photos; p. 432, © Jason Cohn/Reuters/Corbis; p. 435, © Richard Ellis/Corbis Sygma; p. 437, Marty Heitner/The Image Works.

Chapter 15: p. 446, AP–Wide World Photos; p. 446, Richard Drew/AP–Wide World Photos, p. 456, © JP Laffont/Corbis; p. 459, © Alain Mingam/Gamma Press, Ltd.; p. 460, Stephen Ferry/Getty Images; p. 469, © Jason Reed/Reuters/Corbis.

Text Credits

Chapter 1: p. 20, Adapted from William S. Maddox and Stuart A. Lilie, *Beyond Liberal and Conservative: Reassessing the Political Spectrum* (Washington, D.C.: The Cato Institute, 1984).

Chapter 3: p. 86, "Sweet Home Alabama," by Lynyrd Skynyrd, copyright © 1974, MCA Records.

Chapter 6: p. 164, © 2006 by the Pew Research Center. Reprinted with permission; p. 165, © 2006 by the Pew Research Center. Reprinted with permission; p. 168, © 2004 by *San Francisco Chronicle*. Reproduced with permission of the *San Francisco Chronicle*.

Chapter 7: p. 213, Robert L. Dudley and Alan R. Gitelson, *American Elections*, © 2002. Reprinted by permission of Pearson Education, Inc.; p. 214, U.S. National Archives and Records Administration, Washington, D.C.

Chapter 12: p. 347, courtesy of Dr. Jay Jakub.

Chapter 13: p. 376, Baum, Lawrence, *American Courts: Process and Policy*, Second Edition. Copyright © 1998 by Houghton Mifflin Company. Reprinted with permission.

Chapter 14: p. 417, Copyright U.S. News & World Report, L.P. Reprinted with permission.

Index